A
Harmony
of the
Four Gospels
in
Delaware

The translation by
Ira D. Blanchard and James Conner (1837-1839)

Volume I

Edited and Translated by
Ives Goddard

Mundart Press

2021

Copyright © 2021 by Joshua Jacob Snider
Mundart Press, 807 Howard Street, Petoskey MI 49770

All rights reserved. No part of this book may be reproduced or
transmitted in any form or by any means, electronic or mechanical,
including photocopying, recording, or by any information storage
and retrieval system, without permission in writing from the publisher.

The publisher hereby grants such permission to the Delaware Tribe of
Indians and the Delaware Nation of Western Oklahoma for any tribal
educational or cultural purpose.

A publication of the Recovering Voices Program of the Smithsonian
Institution, supported in part by a gift from the Shoniya Fund.

Publisher's Cataloguing-in-Publication Data

Names: Blanchard, Ira D., 1808-1872, translator. | Conner, James, 1817-1872, translator. |
    Goddard, Ives, 1941- editor, translator.
Title: A harmony of the four Gospels in Delaware : the translation by Ira D. Blanchard and
    James Conner / edited and translated by Ives Goddard.
Other titles: Bible. Gospels. Delaware.
Description: Petoskey, MI : Mundart Press, 2021. | Includes bibliographical references.
Identifiers: ISBN: 978-0-9903344-4-6 (v.1) | 978-0-9903344-5-3 (v.2) | LCCN: 2021902981
Subjects: LCSH: Bible. Gospels--Harmonies. | Delaware language--Texts. | Delaware Tribe
    of Indians--Missions. | Delaware Nation, Oklahoma--Missions.
Classification: LCC: BS345.D4 2021 | DDC: 226.1/0597345--dc23

Table of Contents

Introduction.	v
Bibliography.	ix
Abbreviations, Punctuation, and Bracketing.	xii
Abbreviations.	xii
Abbreviations for Person Marking.	xiii
Punctuation and Bracketing.	xiii
Text, Transcription, and Translation	1-789

Introduction

This is an edition of the Delaware translation of a Harmony of the four Gospels of the New Testament that was done by the Baptist missionary Ira D. Blanchard aided by a young interpreter named James Conner and very likely one or more others. Blanchard's title was, in shortened form: *The history of our Lord and Saviour Jesus Christ*. The book translates an English rendition of a German Harmony by Samuel Lieberkühn. Although the date "1837" appears on the title page, the printing, in what was then Indian Territory but is now Kansas, took most of three years to complete, and the translation must have proceeded apace. The language is specifically what was historically the Southern Unami dialect of Delaware and is now also called Lenape (ISO code unm). It was originally spoken in southern New Jersey, a corner of eastern Pennsylvania, and part of Delaware. It is the heritage language of the Delaware Tribe of Indians (Bartlesville, Okla.) and the Delaware Nation of Western Oklahoma (Anadarko). The last two speakers died in 2000 and 2002.

Ira D. Blanchard and his Publications

Blanchard arrived at Shawanoe Baptist Mission in what was then Indian Territory in September of 1831. Apparently self-motivated and self-funded, he went to live among the Delawares, most of whom had recently resettled north of the Kansas River, in order to learn their language and "mak[e] himself useful." The mission (also then called the Shawnee Baptist Mission) was south of the Kansas River, about a mile southeast of where the city of Merriam now is in Johnson County, Kansas (Dan Cole, personal communication 2016). By February of 1833 Blanchard was reported to have "pretty thoroughly acquired" the Delaware language, and later that year, after being baptized, he was formally sponsored by the Baptists to be a teacher at their new mission on the Delaware Reservation (Hancks 2007:109-118). It was later the same year that the printer Jotham Meeker arrived at Shawanoe, and in January he finished setting up the secondhand press he had had shipped from Cincinnati. In Michigan Meeker had learned some Potawatomi and had later become apparently even more proficient in Ottawa, and he formed a plan to devise orthographies for Indian languages using the letters of the English alphabet in partly arbitrary values. The alphabet Blanchard used to write Delaware was of this type, which was referred to as the "new system" (McCoy 1835:26, 1836:28, 29, 1838:65; McMurtrie and Allen 1930:16-30, 47).

Blanchard's first Delaware book was a 24-page primer that was printed by Meeker on March 21, 1834, the first book of any kind printed in the Indian Territory (Blanchard 1834a). At the end of October an expanded, 48-page Delaware primer came off Meeker's press (Blanchard 1834b). The fact that he later called his 1842 primer "The Delaware First Book .. Second Edition" (Blanchard 1842) suggests that he regarded the first 1834 primer as a draft attempt.

Blanchard was away from the mission for several months in 1835, returning with a new bride. He soon turned himself to writing hymns, and in June of 1836 Blanchard's 24-page Delaware hymnbook was printed. (No copy of this has been located, but reprints survive.)

In 1837 the printing of Blanchard's *Harmony* began, the first two forms being completed by Meeker in February and May (with signatures A and B, pp. 1-32). At this point John G. Pratt took over the printing duties at the mission, and he completed four forms the same year (signatures C-F, pp. 33-96). Pratt printed two more forms by December, 1838 (signatures G and H, pp. 97-128), an additional three by the end of March, 1839 (signatures I-K, pp. 129-176), and the last three forms (signatures L-N, pp. 177-221) by the time he left in the fall of that year (McMurtrie and Allen 1930:152-154).

The fact that the book was not completed until two and a half years after the printing of the title pages and the first 28 pages of text in 1837 helps explain the improvement in the quality of the translation and transcription that is evident over the course of the work. This fact also complicates the question of who helped Blanchard with his translation. The name of his assistant is given on the Delaware title page as "NHIME" (i.e., [nčimi·]), a spelling of "Jimmy," but as the title pages were set in type with the first pages of the text, other Delaware speakers could have assisted Blanchard later (and some of the spelling variation in the text suggests that this was the case). Jimmy can be identified as James Conner, who was being paid as the official "Interpreter" for the Delawares already by January 1835 (McCoy 1835:26) and must have been the interpreter named Conner that Meeker mentions as assisting Blanchard in reading proofs in 1836 and 1837 (McMurtrie and Allen 1930:76, 81). Conner was born in 1817, being listed on the 1862 tribal roll as 45-years old (James Rementer, personal communication 2016). His father was William Conner, a White fur trader and interpreter, and his mother, Elizabeth Conner, was a daughter of William Anderson, a Delaware chief. She was known by her Delaware name məkə́nč·e·s, the nickname for the youngest child of a family. (The Wikipedia article about his mother "Mekinges" gives his dates as 1817-1872, citing an unpublished legal document.)

In the revision of his primer issued in 1842, Blanchard lists as his co-author "HALUS" (presumably čá·ləs), a spelling of "Charles." (Again the collaborator is only named on the Delaware title page.) This must have been Charles Journeycake (b. 1817, d. 1894), a literate bilingual who became a Baptist minister and a tribal chief, and if that was the case, it is obviously quite possible that Journeycake also helped translate part of the *Harmony*. When Journeycake was baptized in 1833, his mother, Sally Williams Journeycake, the daughter of a White captive and wife of a Delaware chief, was serving as an interpreter at the mission (Hancks 2007:119), and in 1859 she provided ethnographic information to Lewis Henry Morgan (Morgan 1959:52). Clearly she could also have been someone who helped Blanchard.

Blanchard's translation was based on a harmony of the gospels that was originally written by Samuel Lieberkühn (1769) using the German translation of the Bible by Martin Luther and was printed for the Moravian Church (the United Brethren) in Barby, Saxony. (A few verses from the Acts of the Apostles and other New Testament books are included towards the end.) In the English translation of this, printed in London in 1771, the text of the King James Bible (the Authorized Version) was substituted by an anonymous editor, who stated that "only a few words are occasionally inserted for the sake of connection, or by way of illustration" (Lieberkühn 1771). This English version was re-issued as a "second edition revised" (Lieberkühn 1823), but although the texts have not been closely compared it appears that any changes were slight.

The Moravian missionary Johannes Roth translated the final part (sections 86-139) of Lieberkühn's German text into the Northern Unami dialect spoken in the missions during the years 1770-1772 (Roth and Whritenour 2015). David Zeisberger, another Moravian, later translated the entire book; his preface is dated 1806, two years before his death (Zeisberger 1821). Zeisberger quotes from the title page of the English edition, but a close examination would be necessary to determine what text he worked from. Later, the Moravians worked on revising and retranslating Zeisberger's translation (Luckenbach 2018, Zeisberger and Denke 2019a and 2019b).

Blanchard obviously used the printed English text of the *Harmony*, but there are occasional differences. He numbered his chapters (headed "Rlathemwif" [ēlātčīmwing] /e·la·č·i·mwink/ 'account, relation') starting at the beginning, while Lieberkühn began numbering his sections after the "Introduction" from John 1.1-18. This makes the numbering out of phase, a situation that recurs several times. Blanchard reverses the order of Lieberkühn's sections 7 and 8 and occasionally divides a section or puts two together. Most of the original content is translated, but Blanchard clearly did not believe that he had to follow his exemplar word-for-word, as it is often recast idiomatically. In some places long sentences are rearranged and redundancies are removed. Some of Lieberkühn's added words are omitted, as well as a few other brief segments. In many places it is clear that Blanchard worked with the English Bible in front of him and selected different or additional wording from a parallel text.

Confusion has been caused by Blanchard's long subtitle describing Lieberkühn's compilation as "Translated into the Delaware language, in 1806, by Rev. David Zeisberger, missionary of the United Brethren. Re-translated, so as to conform to the present idiom of the language, by I.D. Blanchard." These are accurate statements, and the word "re-translated" explicitly indicates that Blanchard has redone the translation entirely in putting it into the distinct modern form of the language, which descends from the Southern Unami dialect of southern New Jersey and nearby areas. But even while the new translation was still coming off the press, the influential Baptist missionary Isaac McCoy (1838:65) referred to what Blanchard was doing as "revising," and all subsequent bibliographers and cataloguers have fallen into this error, listing Zeisberger as a co-author (Pilling 1891:547; OCLC [WorldCat] online). He was not. We can only speculate about why Blanchard thought it appropriate to mention Zeisberger, whether it could be, for example, simply an explanation for why he used a Moravian-derived English text as exemplar.

Goddard (2019) is an appreciation of some of the linguistic contributions of Blanchard in his work on the Delaware language.

The Edition

In this edition each of Blanchard's chapters has a heading that gives the number of the chapter, the number of the corresponding section in Lieberkühn, and a specification of the corresponding verses in the King James Bible. The Bible verses are also specified in the left margin, along with the page numbers in Blanchard's book, which are placed under the designation of the first verse that begins on each page. In cases where the original verses were identical or nearly identical in more that one gospel, or where wording from different gospels has been combined, specifying the original verses may be complicated or difficult. In some cases the verses listed as the source by Lieberkühn have been given, although these are often overly inclusive and may simply specify parallel passages in the synoptic gospels. More complicated cases, as where Blanchard has used additional or different source texts, are noted to the extent possible. Where Blanchard has rearranged the components of the text, the orginal order in Lieberkühn's text is indicated by parenthesized numerals. In all of these matters an attempt has been made to provide information that might be useful to the student of the Delaware text, but this is not an essay of biblical exegesis or an analysis of Lieberkühn's work.

For each verse (or shorter segment) line (/b), given first, has Blanchard's text. Next, on line (/p), is a transcription of this text in a phonemic spelling of the Southern Unami language (also called Oklahoma Delaware or Lenape). Line (/t) has the translation of the text on line (/p). And below this is the original English text that Blanchard translated. This is usually ultimately from the King James Bible (Authorized Version; KJV) and hence labeled (/k), but it is sometimes the variant text given by Lieberkühn's Harmony (/l), or the same text given in both sources if this happened to be noted (/kl). In a few cases translations from the Revised Standard Version (RSV) are given where these might be helpful, and parallel verses in other gospels are included where it appears that they may have been additional sources for the translation.

The aim has been to transcribe Blanchard's text exactly, and to note emendations separately at the right or just below. These notes often include the number of times different variants are found (a number plus "x"), or the range of pages where they occur. For example, the notation "⟨rlkeqc⟩ 3x for ⟨rlkeqi⟩ 73x" means that first spelling (the one in the text) is found in two other places, and the second variant is found 73 times. This information can make it possible to infer which variant Blanchard eventually settled on as correct, as in this example. More information on textual questions is often to be found in the *Glossary*.

The variety of Delaware Blanchard learned and used in Kansas was the immediate precursor of what was spoken until recently by the Delaware groups in Oklahoma and continued dialects spoken earlier in southern New Jersey and nearby areas. The phonemic transcription used here is linguistically precise, writing explicitly all of the meaningful (contrastive) speech sounds of the language. In particular, it differs from some other transcriptions in consistently distinguishing short and long consonants and vowels and single and double consonants. Words that could not be phonemicized are preceded by the symbol †; these are almost all names, and their phonemic transcription is highly conjectural. In a few cases a part of a word with an uncertain pronunciation is enclosed in brackets.

The sources of words and grammatical features that are referred in the *Glossary* and the *Grammar* are given by a reference to the original book, chapter, and verse of Bible. These references should take the reader to the correct passage in Blanchard, although where the text is a synthesis of different verses they may not specify the original source. The list of *Locations* appended to the *Glossary* gives the page in Blanchard for the Bible verses; these are the page numbers given at the left side of the page in the text of the *Harmony* in the format "(p. 5)".

Bibliography

Blanchard, Ira D., 1834a. *Linapi'e Lrkvekun.* ['Delaware book'; a primer; 24 pages.] (McMurtrie and Allen 1930:129, no. 4.)

Blanchard, Ira D., 1834b. *Linapie Lrkvekun, Ave Apwatuk.* ['Delaware book that is very easy'; a primer; 48 pages.] (McMurtrie and Allen 1930:134, no. 18a.)

Blanchard, Ira D., [and James Conner]. 1836. [Delaware Hymns. 24 pages.] (No copy located.) (McMurtrie and Allen 1930:147, no. 45.) (Reprinted as Hymns in the Delaware Language: [1] Herald Steam Printing House, Wyandott, Kansas, 1875; [2] Journal Steam Printing House, Coffeyville, Kansas, 1894.)

Blanchard, Ira D., [and James Conner]. 1837 [completed in 1839]. *The history of our Lord and Saviour Jesus Christ; comprehending all that the four evangelists have recorded concerning him; all their relations being brought together in one narrative, so that no circumstance is omitted, but that inestimable history is continued in one series, in the very words of Scripture, by the Rev. Samuel Lieberkuhn, M.A.* Translated into the Delaware language, in 1806, by Rev. David Zeisberger, missionary of the United Brethren. Re-translated, so as to conform to the present idiom of the language, by I.D. Blanchard. J. Meeker, Printer, Shawanoe Baptist Mission [Indian Territory]. [A harmony of the Gospels; 221 pages.] (McMurtrie and Allen 1930:151-154, no. 57.) [Notes: Signatures C-N were printed by John G, Pratt. The text was transcribed from a copy in the Bartlesville Public Library; this has the signature of the former owner, Nellie V Johnstone Cannon, and annotations identifying sources and marking some misprints. A scan of a clean copy has been posted online by the Kansas Historical Society: http://www.kansasmemory.org/item/211693/page/4.] (Reprinted in 1906; see below.)

Blanchard, Ira D., [and Charles Journeycake]. 1842. *The Delaware First Book.* Second Edition. Shawanoe Baptist Mission Press: J. G. Pratt. [A primer; 24 pages.] (McMurtrie and Allen 1930:163, no. 72.)

Blanchard, Ira D., [and James Conner]. 1906. *The history of our Lord and Savior Jesus Christ; comprehending all that the four evangelists have recorded concerning him[;] all their relations being brought together in one narrative, so that no circumstance is omitted, but that inestimable history is continued in one series, in the very words of scripture[,] by the Rev. Samuel Lieberkuhn, M.A.* Translated into the Delaware language in 1806 by Rev. David Zeisberger, missionary of the United Brethren. Re-translated, so as to conform to the present idiom of the language, by I.D. Blanchard. J. Meeker, Printer, Shawanoe Baptist Mission, 1837. Re-printed from the original by the Bartlesville Daily Enterprise. Bartlesville, I.T. [Note: pp. [i]-[ii], 1-221; reduced font size on pp. 197-221.]

Denke, Christian Frederick. 2014. *The Gospel of John in Delaware.* Edited by Raymond Whritenour. Butler, N.J.: Lenape Texts and Studies.

Goddard, Ives. 2019. The Kansas Unami writings of Ira D. Blanchard, Pioneering Algonquian Linguist. *Papers of the Forty-Eighth Algonquian Conference*, ed. by Monica Macaulay and Margaret Noodin, pp. 87-106. East Lansing: Michigan State University Press.

Halfmoon, Charles. 1874. *A Collection of Hymns in Muncey and English.* Toronto: The Wesleyan Missionary Society.

Hancks, Larry K. 1998. The Emigrant Tribes, Wyandot, Delaware & Shawnee, A Chronology (online; preface dated June 2007).

Hancks, Larry K. 2005. The Delaware Indians in Kansas. John G. Pratt and the Delaware Baptist Mission (online: lenapedelawarehistory.net).

Heckewelder, John. 1819. An Account of the History, Manners, and Customs of the Indian Nations, Who Once Inhabited Pennsylvania and the Neighbouring States. *Transactions of the Historical & Literary Committee of the American Philosophical Society* 1:1-348.

Hewson, John. 1993. *A Computer-Generated Dictionary of Proto-Algonquian.* Hull, Que.: Canadian Museum of Civilization.

Lieberkühn, Samuel. 1769. *Die Geschichte unsers Herrn und Heilandes Jesu Christi aus den vier Evangelisten zusammengezogen.* Barby: Heinrich Detlef Ebers. [Re-issued 1770.]

Lieberkühn, Samuel. 1771. *The Acts of the Days of the Son of Man, or the History of Our Lord and Saviour Jesus Christ.* London: M. Lewis.

Lieberkühn, Samuel. 1823. *A Harmony of the Four Gospels, or the History of Our Lord and Saviour Jesus Christ.* Second edition revised. London: W. M'Dowall.

Luckenbach, Abraham. 2018. *The Gospel in Mission Delaware. The History of Our Lord and Savior Jesus Christ.* (A Harmony of the Four Gospels.) Vol. 1. Butler, N.J.: Lenape Texts & Studies.

McCoy, Isaac. 1835. *Annual Register of Indian Affairs within the Indian (or Western) Territory.* [No. 1.] Shawanoe Mission.

McCoy, Isaac. 1836. *Annual Register of Indian Affairs within the Indian (or Western) Territory.* [No. 2.] Shawanoe Mission.

McCoy, Isaac. 1838. *Annual Register of Indian Affairs within the Indian Territory.* [No. 4.] Washington.

McMurtrie, Douglas C., and Albert H. Allen. 1930. *Jotham Meeker, Pioneer Printer of Kansas.* With a bibliography of the known issues of the Baptist Mission Press at Shawanoe, Stockbridge, and Ottawa, 1834-1854. Chicago: Eyncourt Press.

Morgan, Lewis Henry. 1959. *The Indian Journals, 1859-62.* Edited by Leslie A. White. Ann Arbor: The University of Michigan Press.

O'Meara, John. 1996. *Delaware-English / English-Delaware Dictionary.* Toronto: University of Toronto Press.

Pilling, James C. 1891. *Bibliography of the Algonquian Languages.* Bureau of American Ethnology Bulletin 13. Washington: G.P.O.

Roth, Johannes, and Raymond Whritenour. 2015. *A Northern Unami Canon.* Part 5 of Lieberkuhn's Harmony of the Four Gospels. Vol. 2: Text. Butler, N.J.: Lenape Texts & Studies.

Wampum, John B., and H.C. Hogg. [1886.] *Morning and Evening Prayer, the Administration of the Sacraments, and Certain Other Rites and Ceremonies of the Church of England; Together with Hymns:* [Munsee and English]. London: Society for Promoting Christian Knowledge.

Wolley, Charles. 1902. *A Two Years' Journal in New York (1701).* Cleveland: The Burrows Brothers Company.

Zeisberger, David. 1821. *The history of Our Lord and Saviour Jesus Christ: comprehending all that the four evangelists have recorded concerning him: all their relations being brought together in one narration, so that no circumstance is omitted, but that inestimable history is continued in one series, in the very words of Scripture by the Rev. Samuel Lieberkuhn;* translated into the Delaware Indian language by the Rev. David Zeisberger, missionary of the United Brethren. New-York: Daniel Fanshaw.

Zeisberger, David, and Christian Frederick Denke. 2019a. *The Gospel in Mission Delaware. The History of Our Lord and Savior Jesus Christ.* (A Harmony of the Four Gospels.) Vol. 2. Edited by Raymond Whritenour. Butler, N.J.: Lenape Texts & Studies.

Zeisberger, David, and Christian Frederick Denke. 2019b. *The Gospel in Mission Delaware. The History of Our Lord and Savior Jesus Christ.* (A Harmony of the Four Gospels.) Vol. 3. Edited by Raymond Whritenour. Butler, N.J.: Lenape Texts & Studies.

Abbreviations, Punctuation, and Bracketing

Abbreviations

Acts	Acts of the Apostles
anim.	animate
/b	Blanchard text
B.	Blanchard
BPL	Bartlesville Public Library
cf.	compare
Cor	Corinthians
/cp	Anglican *Book of Common Prayer* (1662)
disc.	discourse
/e	emended text
em.	emended, emendation, to be emended
exc.	exclusive
fut.	future
Heb	Hebrews
i.e.	that is
inan.	inanimate
inc.	inclusive
Jn	John
/k	King James text (Authorized Version)
K, KJV	King James Bible
/kl	King James and Lieberkühn texts
L.	Lieberkühn
L.1	Lieberkühn (1771)
L.2	Lieberkühn (1823)
/l	Lieberkühn text (1823)
lit.	literally
Lk	Luke
Mk	Mark
Mt	Matthew
ms.	manuscript
neg.	negative
NSOED	*New Shorter Oxford English Dictionary* (1993)
obj.	object
obv.	obviative
om.	omitted
p. (pp.)	page (pages)
/p	phonemic interpretation

pl.	plural
ppl.	participle
prox.	proximate
PV	preverb
/r, RSV	Revised Standard Version
s.b.	should be
sect.	section
sg.	singular
subj.	subject
/t	translation of line "/p"
x	[number]x = [so many] times

Abbreviations for Person Marking

1s	first person singular
2s	second person singular
2p	second person plural
3s	third person singular
3p	third person plural
2s–3	second person singular acting on third person
2p–3	second person plural acting on third person

Punctuation and Bracketing

†	phonemic shape conjectured
/	(1) in line /b on p. [3], separates the printed lines
	(2) in lines /p and /t, separates segments of text that do not cohere idiomatically
|	marks a line break in Blanchard's text
‖	marks a page break in Blanchard's text
/../	enclose a phonemic transcription
[..]	(in lines /k, /kl, or /l) enclose words that were not translated
⟨..⟩	enclose the exact spelling of the source
-	(1) separates the parts of a compound stem, or flags parts that are not contiguous
	(2) indicates omitted letters at the beginning or end of text cited in ⟨..⟩; not a hyphen
=	marks the following word as an enclitic
ẋ	(any underdotted letter in /b) uncertain (because of imperfect type)

Text, Transcription, and Translation

(p. [3]; Delaware Title Page.)

/b	Rlathemwakunek / wtclawswakun / Nrvlalkwf Krthwvalkwf /	
/p	e·la·č·i·məwá·k·ani·k wtəla·wsəwá·k·an nehəlá·lkɔnkw, ke·č·o·ha·lkɔnkw,	
/t	History of the life of Our Lord, Our Savior,	

/b	Nhesus Klyst;	
/p	nčí·sas kəláist.	
/t	Jesus Christ.	

/b	Cntu / Jijwanukif wuntunasw /	[⟨k⟩ for ⟨q⟩]
/p	énta-šəšəwánahkwink wəntəná·s·u,	
/t	It was taken from English,	

/b	cntu / Linexsif tclextwnrw / Mplcnhes /	
/p	énta-ləní·xsink təli·xto·né·ɔ mpəlénči·s,	[/nč/ or /nč·/]
/t	and it was set into Delaware by Blanchard	

/b	Nhime tcli wehwmat. /	
/p	nčími tə́li-wí·č·əma·t.	[crossing wí·č·əma·t and tə́li-wí·č·əma·n]
/t	and Jimmy, who helped him.	

/b	Jawanouf, / tali kejetwn. / 1837.
/p	†ša·wanó·unk táli-ki·š·í·to·n, 1837.
/t	It was made at Shawanoe, 1837.

Chapter 1 (pp. 5-6). [L. Introduction, pp. 1-2.] (John 1.1-18)

Jn 1.1	/b	Aptwnakun vetamexunwp, wethrvkwnrp nc Aptwnakun Kejrlumwrt,
(p. 5)	/p	a·pto·ná·k·an hitamí·x·əno·p, wwi·č·e·ykó·ne·p nə́ a·pto·ná·k·an ki·š·e·ləmúwe·t,
	/t	The word was the first thing, and the word was with God.
	/k	In the beginning was the Word, and the Word was with God,

/b	Kejrlumwkwfwp nc Aptwnakun.
/p	ki·š·e·ləmuk·ónko·p nə́ a·pto·ná·k·an.
/t	The word was God.
/k	and the Word was God.

1

Jn 1.2 /b Nunu ncki wnutavpenrp Kejrlumwrt.
/p ná ná-néke wənutahpí·ne·p ki·š·e·ləmúwe·t.
/t At that time then God had existed from the beginning.
/k The same was in the beginning with God.

Jn 1.3 /b Wrmi krkw nani wunhi manetaswp.
/p wé·mi kéku náni wə́nči-manni·tá·s·o·p.
/t Everything was made by him.
/k All things were made by him;

/b Cntxi kejrlintasekwp krkw tcli kejrlintuminrp.
/p éntxi-ki·š·e·lənta·s·í·k·əp kéku tə́li-ki·š·e·ləntamə́ne·p.
/t All the things that were created, he was the one to create.
/k and without him was not any thing made that was made.

Jn 1.4 /b Vokif vatrp lrlrxrokun;
/p hɔ́k·enk hát·e·p lehəle·x·e·ɔ́·k·an.
/t Life was in him.
/k In him was life;

/b wlrlrxrokun woxwrkamakwnrop b cntu lawsethek.
/p wəlehəle·x·e·ɔ́·k·an wɔ·x·e·kama·k·o·né·ɔ·p yú entala·wsí·č·i·k.
/t And his life shone a light for mankind.
/k and the life was the light of men.

Jn 1.5 /b Nani oxrrk, woxrkamun cntu peskrk
/p ná=ní ɔ·x·é·e·k wɔ·x·é·kamən énta-pí·ske·k,
/t That was the light that lit up the darkness,
/k And the light shineth in darkness;

/b jwk bni peskrk mutu woxrkakwnrp.
/p šúkw yó·ni pí·ske·k máta wɔ·x·e·ka·k·ó·wɔne·p.
/t but this darkness did not give light to them.
/k and the darkness comprehended it not.   [RSV: "has not overcome it"]

Jn 1.6 /b Kejrlumwrtif wcntalokalqwswp lino lwcnswp Nhan.
/p ki·š·e·ləməwé·t·ink wəntalo·ka·lkwə́s·o·p lə́nu, luwénso·p nčá·n.
/t A man was sent from God named John.
/k There was a man sent from God, whose name was John.

Jn 1.7 /b Wunhi panrp, mrothemwet tclih athemwen nc oxrrk;
/p wwə́nči-pá·ne·p, me·a·ɔ·č·í·mwi·t, tə́li=č -a·č·í·mwi·n nə́ ɔ·x·é·e·k.
/t Why he came was as a witness, to tell about that light,
/k The same came for a witness, to bear witness of the Light,

	/b	wunhih wrmi awrn vokyelet khwvalkwk.
	/p	wə́nči-=č wé·mi awé·n hɔk·aí·li·t -kčo·há·lkuk.
	/t	so that everyone would be ransomed by his life.
	/k	that all men through him might believe.

Jn 1.8 /b Mutu xun tu nrku, nini oxrrk; jwk tclih myathemwen nini oxrrk.
                                                        [⟨mya⟩ for /maya·ɔ·/; cf. Jn 1.15]
/p máta=xán=tá né·k·a nə́ni ɔ·x·é·e·k, šúkw tə́li-=č -maya·ɔ·č·í·mwi·n nə́ni ɔ·x·é·e·k.
/t He was not that light himself, however, but he was to testify about that light.
/k He was not that Light, but was sent to bear witness of that Light.

Jn 1.9 /b Nul nuni mrai oxrrk, oxrkumaot cntxi b tclawselethi.
/p nál nə́ni me·á·i-ɔ·x·é·e·k, ɔ·x·e·kamáɔ·t éntxi- yú -tala·wsi·lí·č·i.
/t That was the true light, which shines a light for all mankind.
/k That was the true Light, which lighteth every man that cometh into the world.

Jn 1.10 /b Topenrp xqetakumeqc, ok nrku tcli kejrlintuminrp,
/p tɔp·í·ne·p xkwi·thakamí·k·we, ɔ́·k né·k·a tə́li-ki·š·e·ləntamə́ne·p,
/t He was on earth, and he himself was the one who had created it,
/k He was in the world, and the world was made by him,

      /b jwk takw wnunakwnrp.   [⟨kwn⟩ for /k·ó·wən/]
/p šúkw takó· wənəna·k·ó·wəne·p.
/t but it did not recognize him.
/k and the world knew him not.

Jn 1.11 /b Cntu nevlatuf pounrp, jwk nc ncvlatuf jifybkwn,   [⟨ou⟩ for ⟨o⟩; ⟨ji-⟩ for /wši-/]
/p énta-nihəlá·t·ank pó·ne·p, šúkw nə́ nehəlá·t·ank wšinkayó·k·o·n.
/t He came to what was his, but what was his was unwilling to receive him.
/k He came unto his own, and his own received him not.

Jn 1.12 /b jwk cntxi wifybkki, mwelapani
/p šúkw éntxi-winkayó·kwki mwi·lá·p·ani
/t But to all who were willing to receive him he gave
/k But as many as received him, to them gave he

      /b wnhi kuski qesumwkvetet Kejrlumwkwfwi,
/p wə́nči-káski-kkwi·s·əmukhwíti·t ki·š·e·ləmuk·ónkwi
/t (something) by which they were able to be sons of God (*lit.*, our creator),
/k power to become the sons of God,

      /b eli nrlel cntxi wlamvetakwk;
/p ílli né·li·l éntxi-wəla·mhitá·k·uk.
/t even to all those that believe in him.   [ílli for KJV "even" (omitted in RSV)]
/k even to them that believe on his name:

Jn 1.13	/b	cntxi mutu mvwkwf jita wewsif, jita awrn rletrvat wunhi kejekethek,
	/p	éntxi- máta mhúkunk ší=tá wió·s·ink ší=tá awé·n e·li·t·é·ha·t -wə́nči-ki·š·i·k·í·č·i·k,
	/t	as many as were born not of blood, or of flesh, or of anyone's thought,
	/k	Which were born, not of blood, nor of the will of the flesh, nor of the will of man,
	/b	jwk Kejrlumwkwf.
	/p	šúkw ki·š·e·ləmúk·ɔnkw.
	/t	but of God.
	/k	but of God.
Jn 1.14	/b	Wewswp nu Aptwnakun, ok qetavpemkwnrnap, [⟨-swp⟩ for /-s·ó·o·p/]
	/p	wio·s·ó·o·p nə́ a·pto·ná·k·an, ɔ́·k kəwitahpi·mko·né·na·p.
	/t	The word became flesh, and it lived with us.
	/k	And the Word was made flesh, and dwelt among us,
	/b	ok kunrmunrnap wlenakswakun jekunj wcnhekif oxwf,
	/p	ɔ́·k kəne·məné·na·p o·li·na·kwsəwá·k·an, ší·kanč wenčí·k·ink ó·x·unk.
	/t	And we saw his glorious appearance, which comes entirely from his father.
	/k	(and we beheld his glory, the glory as of the only begotten of the Father,)
	/b	ave wletrvrw ok owlamwrw. ‖
	/p	áhi-wəli·t·é·he·w ɔ́·k ɔwəlá·məwe·w.
	/t	He was very good-hearted and always told the truth.
	/k	full of grace and truth.
Jn 1.15	/b	Nhan myothemapani amufexswp rlwrtc. [⟨myoth-⟩ for ⟨myaoth-⟩ (Jn 8.46);
(p. 6)	/p	nčá·n mɔya·ɔ·č·i·má·p·ani, amankí·xso·p, e·ləwé·t·e, ⟨my-⟩ for /mɔy-/]
	/t	John testified about him, and he shouted when he said,
	/k	John bare witness of him, and cried, saying,
	/b	Nul ta wuni rkunemukup, rlwranc
	/p	"nál=tá wáni e·k·əni·mák·əp, e·ləwe·á·ne,
	/t	"This is who I was talking about when I said,
	/k	This was he of whom I spake,
	/b	wrtrkyet rlwrlumwksw rli nenwtavpetup. [first ⟨rl-⟩ for ⟨al-⟩]
	/p	we·t·é·kai·t aləwe·ləmúkwsu, é·li·ni·nutahpí·t·əp.
	/t	'The one who comes after me is thought the most of, since he existed from the beginning.
	/k	He that cometh after me is preferred before me: for he was before me.
Jn 1.16	/b	Ok wtrpswakun kwrmi mjekakwnrn lalupi wletrvrokun.
	/p	ɔ́·k wte·psəwá·k·an kəwé·mi·məši·ka·k·ó·ne·n, lahəlápi o·li·t·e·he·ɔ́·k·an.
	/t	And his abundance came over all of us, and again and again his good-heartedness.
	/k	And of his fulness have all we received, and grace for grace.

Jn 1.17 /b Mwjij qwlintvekrnrp qetulitwakun;
/p mó·šəš kwələnthiké·ne·p khwitələt·əwá·k·an,
/t Moses gave people the law to have,
/k For the law was given by Moses,

/b kahi Nhesus Klyst, wletrvrokun, ok wlamwrokun.
/p káč·i nčí·sas kəláist, wəli·t·e·he·ó·k·an ó·k wəla·məwe·ó·k·an.
/t but Jesus Christ (gave people) good-heartedness and truth.
/k but grace and truth came by Jesus Christ.

Jn 1.18 /b Takw vuji awrn wnroeul Kejrlumwrthi
/p takó· háši awé·n wəne·ɔ·í·ɔl ki·š·e·ləməwé·č·i.
/t No one has ever seen God.
/k No man hath seen God at any time;

/b nu jekunj tcli mawsen wrqesif, wtwlvyelet oxul tupen
/p nə́ ší·kanč tə́li-má·wsi·n we·k·wí·s·ink, wto·lhaí·li·t ó·x·ɔl tóp·i·n,
/t The only one is the Son, being in his father's breast,
/k the only begotten Son, which is in the bosom of the Father,

/b tcli watulwkwnrnap.   [⟨t-⟩ for /kt-/]
/p ktə́li-wwa·təluk·o·né·na·p.
/t and being the one who made him known to us.
/k he hath declared him.

Chapter 2 (pp. 6-7). [L. section 1.] (Luke 1.5-25)

Lk 1.5 /b Ncki lrkveqc sakematc Vclut Nhwteuf tali,
/p néke ləkhíkwi sa·k·i·má·t·e †hélat †nčo·tí·yunk táli,
/t At the time when Herod was king in Judaea
/k There was in the days of Herod, the king of Judaea,

/b wrvevwfrt lwcnswp Sakulyus
/p wehi·húnke·t luwénso·p †sa·kaláyas.
/t there was a priest named Zacharias.
/k a certain priest named Zacharias,

/b Rpyu rlvakret wunheywp tclenawaqwswakun;
/p †é·paya e·lhaké·i·t wənčí·ayo·p, təlinnuwahkəs·əwá·k·an;
/t He was from the Abia division (of the priesthood), as his official function.
/k of the course of Abia: [*lit.* 'tribe'; RSV "division," *i.e.*, a division of the priests]

	/b	wekemathi lwcnswp Elisuput, Rlunif wunheywp.
	/p	wi·k·i·má·č·i luwénso·p †i·lísapat, †é·lanink wənčí·ayo·p.
	/t	His wife was named Elisabeth, and she came from Aaron's (family).
	/k	and his wife was of the daughters of Aaron, and her name was Elisabeth.

Lk 1.6 /b Jaxakaprwpanek rlifwrxif Kejrlumwkwf,
        /p šaxahka·p·e·yó·p·ani·k e·linkwé·x·ink ki·š·e·ləmúk·ɔnkw,
        /t They were righteous people before God,
        /k And they were both righteous before God,

        /b rli na nani lrlrxrtetup wrmi toptwnakun Nrvlalqetet.
        /p é·li- ná ná=ní -lehəle·x·ehtí·t·əp wé·mi tɔ·pto·ná·k·an nehəla·lkwíhti·t.   [ná=ní(?)]
        /t as they then lived by the whole of the word of their Lord.
        /k walking in all the commandments and ordinances of the Lord blameless.

Lk 1.7 /b Takw tomeminsumeeuk, rli takw wewunethanetwp, ok rle kikywpanek.
        /p takó· tɔmi·mənsəmi·í·ɔk, é·li- takó· -wi·wəni·č·a·ní·t·əp, ɔ́·k ellí·i khikayó·p·ani·k.
        /t They had no children, as she had never had a child, and they were both old.
        /k And they had no child, because that Elisabeth was barren, and they both were now well stricken in years.

Lk 1.8 /b Nrli mekintumaotup Kejrlumwkwf rlifwcxif nc tali xifwekaonif,
        /p né·li-mi·kəntamaɔ́·t·əp ki·š·e·ləmúk·ɔnkw e·linkwé·x·ink nə́ táli xinkwi·k·á·ɔnink,
        /t While he was working for God before him in the house of worship,
        /k And it came to pass, that while he executed the priest's office before God

        /b lenuwavqwswakun rlexif.
        /p linnuwahkəs·əwá·k·an e·lí·x·ink,
        /t the way the official duty was set,   ['in accordance with how official duty was set']
        /k in the order of his course,   [RSV: "when his [priestly] division was on duty"]

Lk 1.9 /b Rli lexumwkset tclih nrkuma wivifemakwiksimən,
        /p é·li-li·x·əmúkwsi·t tə́li-=č né·k·əma -wihinki·ma·khwiksə́ma·n,
        /t according to his appointment that *he* was to be the one to burn incense,
        /k According to the custom of the priest's office, his lot was to burn incense

        /b tumekrtc Nrvlalkwfe wekwavmif.   [⟨wfe⟩ for /ɔnkwí·i/]
        /p təmi·k·é·t·e nehəla·lkɔnkwí·i-wi·k·əwáhəmink,
        /t when he entered the Lord's house,
        /k when he went into the temple of the Lord.

Lk 1.10 /b Xrli kwhumif tali patamapanek,
        /p xé·li kɔ́čəmink táli-pa·tamá·p·ani·k,
        /t there were many outside praying
        /k And the whole multitude of the people were praying without

	/b	srki wekwavmif tali wifemakvwiksimuf.
	/p	sé·ki- wi·k·əwáhəmink -táli-winki·ma·khwiksə́mank.
	/t	while the incense was burned in the building.
	/k	at the time of incense.

Lk 1.11
	/b	Nunc tuntu wncntulwkwn voky, Nrvlalkwfe Rvalokalint,
	/p	ná=nə tə́nta- wənentəlúk·o·n hɔ́k·ay nehəla·lkɔnkwí·i-ehalo·ká·lənt.
		[tə́nta- wənentəlúk·o·n is presumably an incorrect revision of tə́nta-nentəlúk·o·n]
	/t	And there an angel of the Lord appeared (*lit.*, showed himself) to him,
	/k	And there appeared unto him an angel of the Lord

	/b	wtcnavanif wuntaqc wnepyenrp cntu wifemakvwiksasek.
		[⟨-navan-⟩ for ⟨-navaon-⟩ 12x]
	/p	wtənna·há·ɔnink wə́ntahkwi wəni·p·aí·ne·p énta-winki·ma·khwiksá·s·i·k.
	/t	and stood on the right side of the incense altar (lit, where incense was burned).
	/k	standing on the right side of the altar of incense.

Lk 1.12
	/b	Sakulyus nrotc, salavkevulrp ok wejavlrp.
	/p	†sa·kaláyas ne·ɔ́·t·e, salaxkíhəle·p, wi·š·áhəle·p.
	/t	When Zacharias saw him, he was agitated and got scared.
	/k	And when Zacharias saw him, he was troubled, and fear fell upon him.

Lk 1.13
	/b	Jwk rvalokalint tclapani, kahi ta wejasevun Sakulyus,
	/p	šúkw ehalo·ká·lənt təlá·p·ani, "káči=tá wi·š·a·s·í·han, †sa·kaláyas,
	/t	But the angel said to him, "Don't be afraid, Zacharias,
	/k	But the angel said unto him, Fear not, Zacharias:

	/b	rli puntasw ta kupatamwrokun,
	/p	é·li pəntá·s·u=tá kpa·tamwe·ɔ́·k·an.
	/t	for your prayer has been heard.
	/k	for thy prayer is heard;

	/b	wekemut ‖ kejeketaqh wrqeseun,
	/p	wi·k·í·mat kki·š·i·k·í·ta·kw=č we·k·wí·s·ian.
	/t	Your wife will bear you a son.
	/k	and thy wife Elisabeth shall bear thee a son,

(p. 7)
	/b	ktclwevaluh Nhan.
	/p	ktələwíhəla=č 'nčá·n'.
	/t	You shall call him 'John'.
	/k	and thou shalt call his name John.

Lk 1.14
	/b	Kwlrlintumh kejeketc, okh xrli awrn,
	/p	"ko·le·ló́ntam=č ki·š·i·k·í·t·e, ɔ́·k=č xé·li awé·n.
	/t	"You will be glad when he is born, and so will many people.
	/k	And thou shalt have joy and gladness; and many shall rejoice at his birth.

Lk 1.15 /b rli xifwrlumwkswh rlifwrxif Nrvlalkwf;
        /p é·li xinkwe·ləmúkwsu=č e·linkwé·x·ink nehəlá·lkɔnkw.
        /t For he will be well thought of in the eyes of our Lord.
        /k For he shall be great in the sight of the Lord,

        /b wyn, ok krkw avwf, mutuh memunri,
        /p wáin ɔ́·k kéku áhɔnk, máta=č mi·məné·i.
        /t Wine and anything strong he will never drink,
        /k and shall drink neither wine nor strong drink;

        /b rli somi pelseleth wthehufumul ncki kejeketc wunhi.
        /p é·li-sɔ́·mi-pi·lsí·li·t=č wči·čánkəmal néke ki·š·i·k·í·t·e wə́nči.
        /t as his spirit will be too holy from the time he is born.
        /k and he shall be filled with the Holy Ghost, even from his mother's womb.

Lk 1.16 /b Xrlih Islul tomemisumul, qwlpunkw   [⟨mis⟩ for /məns/]
        /p xé·li=č †ísələl tɔmi·mə́nsəmal kkwəlpə́nk·u
        /t He will turn many of Israel's children
        /k And many of the children of Israel shall he turn

        /b li Nrvlalwrtif Kejrlumwkvwetethif,
        /p lí nehəla·ləwé·t·ink, ki·š·e·ləmukhwití·č·ink.
        /t to the Lord, their God (*lit.*, their creator),
        /k to the Lord their God.

Lk 1.17 /b ok avhifvalethi prjwaunh jaxakawselethek wlipwrokunwauf,   [/pw-/ ⟨p-⟩;
                                                                        ⟨-aunh⟩ for ⟨-anh⟩; -lí·č·i·k: s.b. -lí·č·i]
        /p ɔ́·k ahčinkxa·lí·č·i pwé·š·əwa·n=č šaxahka·wsi·lí·č·i·k wələp·we·ɔ·k·anəwá·unk,
        /t and the disobedient he will then bring to the wisdom of the righteous,
        /k and the disobedient to the wisdom of the just;

        /b wcnhih kejrnakswkrtwnt awrni Nrvlalwrt,   [⟨jrn⟩ for /š·əıı/]
        /p wénči-=č -ki·š·əna·kwso·ké·tunt awé·ni nehəlá·ləwe·t.
        /t so that people will be made ready for the Lord.
        /k to make ready a people prepared for the Lord.

        /b rli wnekanetamawlh, Elyus tclswakunif.
        /p é·li wəni·k·a·ni·tamá·ɔl=č †i·láyas təlsəwá·k·anink."
        /t as he will go before him acting for ('in the power of') Elias."
        /k And he shall go before him in the spirit and power of Elias, [to turn the hearts of the fathers to the children, and the disobedient to the wisdom of the just; to make ready a people prepared for the Lord.]

Lk 1.18 /b Sakulyus tclapani rlokalinhi; tuh vuh nc nwnhi watwn?
        /p †sa·kaláyas təlá·p·ani e·lo·ka·lə́nči, "tá=č=háč nə̄ núnči-wwá·to·n?

/t Zacharias said to the angel, "What's the reason I will know that?
/k And Zacharias said unto the angel, Whereby shall I know this?

/b somi mrhi ntavi kvekwwsi, ok wehrok mrhi kveky.
/p sɔ́·mi mé·či ntáhi-khikəwə́s·i, ɔ́·k wi·č·é·ɔk mé·či khík·ay."
/t I'm now much too old, and my wife is already an old woman."
/k for I am an old man, and my wife well stricken in years.

Lk 1.19 /b Rvalokalint tclapani; Frplil nvaky,
/p ehalo·ká·lənt təlá·p·ani, "†nké·pələl nhák·ay.
/t The angel said to him, "I am Gabriel.
/k And the angel answering said unto him, I am Gabriel,

/b Kejrlumwkwf rlifwcxif nepy.
/p ki·š·e·ləmúk·ɔnkw e·linkwé·x·ink nní·p·ai.
/t I stand before God.
/k that stand in the presence of God;

/b Mprtalokalkc, wcnhi wlaptwnalun;
/p mpe·t·alo·ká·lke wénči-wəla·pto·nállan.
/t I was sent here in order that I tell you good news.
/k and am sent to speak unto thee, and to shew thee these glad tidings.

Lk 1.20 /b bqc punu kwptwnuh wunhih mutu kuski krkw lwreun
/p yúkwe pənáh, kkəptó·na=č, wə́nči-=č máta -káski- kéku -luwé·ɔn,   [-ɔn: or -an]
/t Now, you will be mute, such that you will not be able to speak,
/k And, behold, thou shalt be dumb, and not able to speak,

/b kxuntki pchi nuni kejqek cntuh wrmi bni keji lrk,
/p kxántki péči nə́ni kí·škwi·k énta-=č wé·mi yó·ni -kíši-lé·k,
/t until the day when all this shall have happened,
/k until the day that these things shall be performed,

/b rli klwvwetamun rlwru,
/p é·li-kəlo·hítaman e·ləwé·a,
/t since you don't believe what I said,
/k because thou believest not my words,

/b rli somi mutu nkukulwnri.
/p é·li sɔ́·mi máta nkak·əlo·né·i.
/t as I absolutely do not lie."
/k which shall be fulfilled in their season."

Lk 1.21	/b	Xrlwpanek prvathek Sakulyusul,	
	/p	xe·ló·p·ani·k pe·há·č·i·k †sa·kalayás·al.	
	/t	There were many who waited for Zacharias.	
	/k	And the people waited for Zacharias,	

/b wlrlumrlintumwpanek, rli qwnakrt li wekwavmif.
/p wəle·ləme·ləntamó·p·ani·k, é·li-kwəná·ke·t lí wi·k·əwáhəmink.
/t They were astonished, because he was gone a long time in the building.
/k and marvelled that he tarried so long in the temple.

Lk 1.22 /b Kchetc mutu kuski krkw lwkwewau, [⟨kuski⟩ for /kóski-/]
/p ke·č·í·t·e, máta kóski- kéku -luk·o·wiwwá·ɔ.
/t When he came out, he was unable to speak to them.
/k And when he came out, he could not speak unto them:

/b tclrlumawaul awrn ct wnraol
/p təle·ləmawwá·ɔl, "awé·ni=ét wəne·ɔ́·ɔl," [awe·ni: ⟨awrn⟩]
/t They thought he must have seen some being,
/k and they perceived that he had seen a vision in the temple:

/b wcnhi hetqwset, jwk wtitpetaqaw. [⟨q⟩ for /k·əw/]
/p wénči-či·tkwəs·i·t, šúkw wtətpi·ta·k·əwá·ɔ.
/t which was why he remained silent and just made signs to them.
/k for he beckoned unto them, and remained speechless.

Lk 1.23 /b Lwilrkc nrl kejqekc srki wevwfrt nu mothenrp,
/p ló·wi-lé·k·e né·l ki·škwí·k·i sé·ki-wi·húnke·t, ná mɔ·č·í·ne·p.
/t When the days when he was a priest were past, he went home.
/k And it came to pass, that, as soon as the days of his ministration were accomplished, he departed to his own house.

Lk 1.24 /b wekemathi Elisuputul alumi powp,
/p wi·k·i·má·č·i †i·lisapát·al áləmi-pó·o·p.
/t And his wife Elisabeth became pregnant.
/k And after those days his wife Elisabeth conceived,

/b Palrnax txi jejoxwf svake kuntavpwp; laptonrp, [⟨jejoxwf⟩ for ⟨kejoxwf⟩]
/p palé·naxk txí-ki·š·ó·x·unk sháki-kántahpo·p, la·ptó·ne·p.
/t She stayed in hiding for five months, and she said,
/k and hid herself five months, saying,

Lk 1.25 /b nani ntclevkwn Nrvlalet, nani kejqek prnyetc,
/p "ná=ní ntəlíhko·n nehəlá·li·t, nəni kí·škwi·k pe·naí·t·e,
/t "That's what my Lord made happen to me, that day when he looked at me
/k Thus hath the Lord dealt with me in the days wherein he looked on me,

/b palernifc rlavtrlumif, b cntu lawsethek.
/p palí·i ennínke e·lahté·ləmink yú entala·wsí·č·i·k.
/t and removed the disapproval of me from mankind." ['how I am looked down on']
/k to take away my reproach among men.

Chapter 3 (pp. 7-8). [L. section 2.] (Luke 1.26-38)

Lk 1.26 /b Ny wunhi kwtaj kejoxif Kejrlumwrt, pehi qwnhinawul lupi rvalokalint Frplilul,
/p ná=yú wənči kwət·a·š ki·š·ó·x·ink ki·š·e·ləmúwe·t péči kwənččəná·ɔl lápi ehalo·ká·lənt †nke·pəlɔ́lal, [⟨Ny⟩ for later ⟨Ny b⟩]
/t Six months from then God again sent the angel Gabriel here,
/k And in the sixth month the angel Gabriel was sent from God

/b li Fcluleuf, ‖ wtrnif rlwcnsek Ncsulut,
/p lí †nkelalí·yunk, o·t·é·nink e·ləwénsi·k †nésəlat,
/t to Galilee and a town named Nazareth,
/k unto a city of Galilee, named Nazareth,

Lk 1.27 /b kekxqru nuvkwntuwuk linoul lwcnsw Nhosi,
(p. 8) /p ki·kxkwé·ɔ; naxkúntəwak lónəwal, luwénsu '†nčɔ́·si',
/t to a virgin; she was engaged to a man named Josey,
/k To a virgin espoused to a man whose name was Joseph,

/b Ntrpit myai rlafqomatpani,
/p †nté·pit mayá·i e·lanko·ma·tpáni.
/t a direct descendant (*lit.*, "true relative") of David.
/k of the house of David;

/b nuni skexqc lwcnswp Mrli.
/p náni skí·xkwe luwénso·p mé·li.
/t That young woman was named Mary.
/k and the virgin's name was Mary.

Lk 1.28 /b Rvalokalint mwtumekamapani, tclapani; tcliofoman
/p ehalo·ká·lənt mwət·əmi·k·amá·p·ani, təlá·p·ani, tɔ́li-ɔnkó·ma·n,
/t The angel came in to where she was and said to her, by way of greeting her,
/k And the angel came in unto her, and said, Hail,

/b mruxifwrlumwkset; Nrvlalwrt ktupetaq, [⟨mrux-⟩ for ⟨mrx-⟩]
/p "me·x·inkwe·ləmúkwsi·t, nehəlá·ləwe·t ktap·í·ta·kw,
/t "Highly esteemed one, the Lord abides in you,
/k thou that art highly favoured, the Lord is with thee:

	/b	rlwapcnseun wrmi rxqreun.
	/p	e·ləwa·p·énsian wé·mi e·xkwé·ian."
	/t	you who are the most blessed of all you women."
	/k	blessed art thou among women.

Lk 1.29 /b Nrotc wejaswp;
/p ne·ó·t·e, wi·š·á·s·o·p.
/t When she saw him, she was frightened.
/k And when she saw him, she was troubled at his saying,

/b letrvrp, tu tu puna nc rlenakw ofomqwswakun?
/p li·t·é·he·p, "tá=tá pənáh nə́ e·li·ná·k·ɔ ɔnko·mkwəs·əwá·k·an?"
/t She thought, "Well now, what kind of a greeting is that?"
/k and cast in her mind what manner of salutation this should be.

Lk 1.30 /b Rvalokalint tclapani, kahi wejasevun Mrli; ktukawsetumwk Kejrlumwkwf.—
/p ehalo·ká·lənt təlá·p·ani, "káči wi·š·a·s·í·han, mé·li; ktək·awsí·tamukw ki·š·e·ləmúk·ɔnkw.
/t The angel said to her, "Don't be afraid, Mary; God regards you favorably.
/k And the angel said unto her, Fear not, Mary: for thou hast found favour with God.

Lk 1.31 /b Klistyel: kpoeth, kejekwh pelaihih;
/p kələstái·l: kpó·i=č; ki·š·í·k·u=č pi·laéčəč.
/t Listen to me: you will be pregnant, and a boy will be born.
/k And, behold, thou shalt conceive in thy womb, and bring forth a son,

/b ktclwivuluh NHESUS:
/p ktələwíhəla=č nčí·sas.
/t You shall name him Jesus.
/k and shalt call his name JESUS.

Lk 1.32 /b xifwrlumwkswh, ok lwevulauh Rlwrlumwkset qesul, [⟨-lauh⟩ for ⟨-lah⟩]
/p xinkwe·ləmúkwsu=č, ɔ́·k luwíhəla·=č e·ləwe·ləmúkwsi·t kkwí·s·al.
/t He shall be regarded highly and called the son of the one most highly regarded.
/k He shall be great, and shall be called the Son of the Highest:

/b ok Nrvlalwrt Kejrlumwrt mwelanh lrvlumutupelet oxufu Ntrpitul ;
/p ɔ́·k nehəlá·ləwe·t ki·š·e·ləmúwe·t mwí·la·n=č lehələmatahpí·li·t o·x·únka †nte·pít·al.
/t And the Lord, God, shall give him the throne (*lit.*, seat) of his (ancestral) father David.
/k and the Lord God shall give unto him the throne of his father David:

Lk 1.33 /b okh osakemaimwkul Islulul rvalumakamek,
/p ɔ́·k=č o·s·a·k·i·ma·yəmúk·o·l †isələ́lal ehaləmá·kami·k.

/t And he shall be the king of Israel forever.
[*lit.*, 'Israel (obv.) will have him as king']
/k And he shall reign over the house of Jacob for ever;

/b okh wsakemaokun mutu weeqri.
/p ó·k=č wsa·k·i·ma·ó·k·an máta wi·i·kwé·i."
/t and his kingdom shall never end."
/k and of his kingdom there shall be no end.

Lk 1.34 /b Mrli tclapani: tuh vuh wunhi kuski nc lrw?
/p mé·li təlá·p·ani, "tá=č=háč wənči-káski- nə́ -lé·w?
/t Mary said to him, "How will that be possible?
/k Then said Mary unto the angel, How shall this be,

/b rli mutu nwavai lino.
/p é·li máta no·wa·há·i lə́nu."
/t For I know no man."
/k seeing I know not a man?

Lk 1.35 /b Rvalokalint tclapani, Pelvik Hehufwakun kwtvwkh,
/p ehalo·ká·lənt təlá·p·ani, "pí·lhik či·čankəwá·k·an kó·txukw=č,
/t The angel said to her, "A holy spirit shall visit you,
/k And the angel answered and said unto her, The Holy Ghost shall come upon thee,

/b ok Rlwrlumwkset tolweliswakun qewunekakwnh;
/p ó·k e·ləwe·ləmúkwsi·t tɔləwí·i-ləs·əwá·k·an kəwi·wəni·ká·k·o·n=č.
/t and the power of the one who is most highly regarded shall envelop you.
/k and the power of the Highest shall overshadow thee:

/b nani wunhi pelseth, kvakif kejeket;
/p ná=ní wə́nči-pí·lsi·t=č khák·enk ki·š·í·k·i·t.
/t That's why what will be born of you will be holy.   [*lit.*, 'in you']
/k therefore also that holy thing which shall be born of thee

/b ktclwevuluh Kejrlumwrt Qesul.
/p ktələwíhəla=č ki·š·e·ləmúwe·t kkwí·s·al.
/t You shall call him God's son.
/k shall be called the Son of God.

Lk 1.36 /b "Ok rlafomut Elisuput mrhi pow, pelyhihul, mrhi kvekyetc,
/p "ó·k e·lankó·mat ǂi·lísapat mé·či pɔ́·u, pi·laečə́č·al, mé·či khikaí·t·e.
/t And your relative Elisabeth is now pregnant, with a boy, when she is already old.
/k And, behold, thy cousin Elisabeth, she hath also conceived a son in her old age:

	/b	bqc mrhi kwtaj kejoxif;
	/p	yúkwe mé·či kwət·a·š ki·š·ó·x·ink,
	/t	It has now already been six months,
	/k	and this is the sixth month with her, who was called barren.

Lk 1.37 /b rli Kejrlumwrt mutu poi krkw liset.
         /p é·li- ki·š·e·ləmúwe·t máta -pó·i- kéku -ləs·i·t."
         /t since nothing is impossible for God to do."
         /k For with God nothing shall be impossible.

Lk 1.38 /b Nu Mrli tclapani; punaw, wrtalokakwnumkwk Nrvlalwrlethi.
         /p ná mé·li təlá·p·ani, "pənáw we·t·alo·ka·k·anəmkuk nehəla·ləwe·lí·č·i.
         /t And then Mary said to him, "Regard one who is the Lord's servant.
         /k And Mary said, Behold the handmaid of the Lord;

         /b Lrwh nvakif rlwranup.
         /p lé·w=č nhák·enk e·ləwé·anəp.
         /t It shall happen in me as you have said.
         /k be it unto me according to thy word.

         /b Nu Rvalokilint wnukalanrp.   [⟨Rvalokilint⟩: for ⟨Rvalokalint⟩]
         /p ná ehalo·ká·lənt wənək·alá·ne·p.
         /t Then the angel left her.
         /k And the angel departed from her.

Chapter 4 (pp. 8-9). [L. section 3.] (Matthew 1.18-24)

Mt 1.18 /b Nrlumu Mrli ok Nhosi wethaoteepanek, jwk keji naxkwntwpanek,
         /p né·ləma mé·li ó·k †nčó·si wi·č·e·wti·í·p·ani·k, šúkw kíši-naxkuntó·p·ani·k,
         /t Mary and Josey were not yet married, but they were already engaged,
         /k When as his mother Mary was espoused to Joseph, before they came together,
         /l Now as Mary, the mother of Christ was espoused to Joseph, before they came together,

         /b wrovwntc Mrli tcli poen wunhi Pelset Hehuf. ‖   [⟨-vwntc⟩: /-hə́nte/]
         /p we·ɔ·hə́nte mé·li tə́li-pó·i·n wə́nči pí·lsi·t čí·čankw.
         /t when it became known that Mary was pregnant by the Holy Spirit.
         /k she was found with child of the Holy Ghost.

Mt 1.19 /b Wekemathi Nhoseul rli wliliseletup takw kutu mexanalaeul,   [⟨kut-⟩ for /kót·/]
(p. 9)   /p wi·k·i·má·č·i †nčó·sial, é·li·wə́li-ləs·i·lí·t·əp, takó· kót·a-mi·x·ana·la·í·ɔl.
         /t Her husband, Josey, as he was a kind man, did not want to be ashamed of her.
         /k Then Joseph her husband, being a just man, and not willing to make her a publick example,

	/b	letrvrp kemeh mpwneva.
	/p	li·t·é·he·p, "ki·mí·i=č mpo·ní·ha."
	/t	He thought, "I shall leave her alone in secret."
	/k	was minded to put her away privily.

Mt 1.20
- /b Nu lupi Nrvulalwrt valokalathi wtxwkwn cntukaet. [⟨val-⟩: for ⟨rval-⟩]
- /p ná lápi nehəlá·ləwe·t ehalo·ka·lá·č·i o·txúk·o·n énta-kaí·t.
- /t Then again an angel of the Lord came to him when he was asleep.
- /k But while he thought on these things, behold, the angel of the Lord appeared unto him in a dream,

- /b Tclapani Nhosi Ntrpitu qesul,
- /p təlá·p·ani, "†nčó·si, †nte·pít·a kkwí·s·al,
- /t He said to him, "Josey, son of David,
- /k saying, Joseph, thou son of David,

- /b kahi hanrlintufvun, ktcli wrtunan wekeman Mrli rli poet;
- /p káči čane·ləntánkhan ktəli-wé·t·əna·n, -wi·k·í·ma·n mé·li é·li-pó·i·t.
- /t do not be reluctant to take Mary to be your wife because she is pregnant.
- /k fear not to take unto thee Mary thy wife:

- /b Pelset ta Hehwfwf wcnheyw, [⟨Hehwfwf⟩ for ⟨Hehufwf⟩]
- /p pí·lsi·t=tá či·čánkunk wənčí·ayu.
- /t It is from the Holy Spirit.
- /k for that which is conceived in her is of the Holy Ghost.

Mt 1.21
- /b kejekwvrh pelyhihu; [⟨pely|hihu⟩]
- /p ki·š·i·k·ó·he·=č pi·laečə́č·a.
- /t She will give birth to a boy.
- /k And she shall bring forth a son,

- /b ktclwevuluh Nhesus, rlih krthwvrt wtunaprmul mutawswakunwauf wunhi.
- /p ktələwíhəla=č nčí·sas, é·li=č ke·č·ó·he·t wtənna·p·é·yəmal mət·a·wsəwa·k·anəwá·unk wə́nči.
- /t You shall name him Jesus, as he is one who will rescue his people from their sins.
- /k and thou shalt call his name Jesus: for he shall save his people from their sins.

Mt 1.22
- /b Wrmi bni lrwp, wunhi pavkunhi lrk, Nrvlalwrt rlwrtup
- /p wé·mi yó·ni lé·p, wə́nči-pahkánči-lé·k nehəlá·ləwe·t e·ləwé·t·əp,
- /t All of this happened so that it would happen exactly as the Lord said,
- /k Now all this was done, that it might be fulfilled

- /b aptwnrtwvtetup nrnekaniwrwsetpanifu rlwrtc; [⟨-ani⟩ for /-a·ní·i/]
- /p a·pto·ne·tuhtí·t·əp nehəni·k·a·ní·i-we·wsi·tpanínka. e·ləwé·t·e,
- /t which was reported by the prophets, when he said,
- /k which was spoken of the Lord by the prophet, saying,

Mt 1.23 /b Punw, kekxqr powh pelyhih kejekw,
/p "pənó· kí·kxkwe. pɔ́·u=č, pi·laéčəč ki·š·í·k·u.
/t "Regard the virgin. She will be pregnant, and a boy will be born.
/k Behold, a virgin shall be with child, and shall bring forth a son,

/b tclwevulawuh Imrnbul, (lwrn cntu anvwkathemwif,) Kejrlumwrt qetavpemkwnu.
/p tələwihəlawwá·ɔ=č †ime·niyó·wəl, lúwe·n énta-a·nhukɔ·č·í·mwink 'ki·š·e·ləmúwe·t kəwitahpi·mkó·na'."
/t They shall name him Emmanuel, meaning, when interpreted, 'God is with us'."
/k and they shall call his name Emmanuel, which being interpreted is, God with us.

Mt 1.24 /b Nhosi twkevlatc nani tclsenrp,
/p †nčɔ́·si to·kihəlá·t·e, ná=ní təlsí·ne·p,
/t When Josey woke up, that is what he did,
/k Then Joseph being raised from sleep did

/b Nrvlalwrt rvalokalathi cntxi latup,
/p nehəlá·ləwe·t ehalo·ka·lá·č·i éntxi-lá·t·əp.
/t everything the angel of the Lord had told him to.
/k as the angel of the Lord had bidden him,

/b natunapani wekemathi.
/p nɔ·t·əná·p·ani wi·k·i·má·č·i.
/t He accepted his wife.
/k and took unto him his wife:

Mt 1.25 /b Jwk wrnehaneletc pchi mutu wavawun.
/p šúkw we·ni·č·a·ni·lí·t·e péči máta o·wa·há·wən.
/t But until she had her child he did not know her.
/k And knew her not till she had brought forth her firstborn son:

Chapter 5 (pp. 9-10). [L. section 4.] (Luke 1.39-56)

Lk 1.39 /b Nunu ncki pusqen Mrli eku tonrp ohwf rtrk Nhwtue wtrny,
/p ná ná-néke pɔ́skwi·n mé·li, íka tɔ́·ne·p ɔhčúnk, é·te·k †nčo·taí·i-o·t·é·nay.
/t At that time then Mary got up and went to the hills where a town of Juda was.
/k And Mary arose in those days, and went into the hill country with haste, into a city of Juda;

Lk 1.40 /b wtumekamapani Sakulyusul tuntu ofomanrp Elisuputul.
/p wtəmi·k·amá·p·ani †sa·kalayás·al, tə́nta-ɔnko·má·ne·p †i·lisapát·al.
/t She went into Zacharias's house and greeted Elisabeth there.
/k And entered into the house of Zacharias, and saluted Elisabeth.

Text, Transcription, and Translation

Lk 1.41
/b Mrhi Elisuput puntufc wafwnswakun,
/p mé·či †i·lísapat pəntánke wɔnkunsəwá·k·an,
/t When Elisabeth heard her greeting,
/k And it came to pass, that, when Elisabeth heard the salutation of Mary,

/b nunu memintitul lamavtc mwtrxenulen.
/p nána mi·məntət·al lá·mahte mɔt·e·x·í·nəli·n.
/t the baby then kicked in the womb.
/k the babe leaped in her womb;

/b Nunu wexkawhi Pelset Hehuf vokif motrxenulen Elisuputul,
/p nána wi·xkaɔ́či pí·lsi·t čí·čankw hɔ́k·enk mɔt·e·x·í·nəli·n †i·lisapát·al.
/t Then suddenly Elisabeth landed in the holy spirit's body. [See *Glossary*.]
/k and Elisabeth was filled with the Holy Ghost:

Lk 1.42
/b amufexswp rlwrtc.
/p amankí·xso·p e·ləwé·t·e,
/t She spoke with a loud voice when she said,
/k And she spake out with a loud voice, and said,

/b Ktalwapcnsenuk kihi xqreuk, ok rlapcnsw lamatc wunheyekh, [⟨rl-⟩ for ⟨wl-⟩]
/p "ktaləwa·p·ensí·nak kíči-xkwé·ɔk, ɔ́·k wəla·p·ensɔ́·u lá·mahte wənčí·ai·k=č.
/t "You are more blessed than the other women, and what shall come from the womb is blessed.
/k Blessed art thou among women, and blessed is the fruit of thy womb.

Lk 1.43
/b Ta vuh ct lrw wunhi Nrvlalet kovrsw toxet. [⟨kovrsw⟩: for ⟨kovrsu⟩]
/p tá=háč=ét lé·w wənči- nehəlá·ləwe·t kɔhé·s·a -tɔ́x·i·t.
/t What could have happened to be the reason the Lord's mother is visiting me?
/k And whence is this to me, that the mother of my Lord should come to me?

Lk 1.44
/b Puna prtrvulakc nvetaokif ofomqwswakwn,
/p pənáh, pe·t·ehəlá·k·e nhitaɔ́k·ink ɔnko·mkwəs·əwá·k·an,
/t See, when the sound of the greeting reached my ears,
/k For, lo, as soon as the voice of thy salutation sounded in mine ears,

/b nu jai lamavtif motrxenun memintit, rli wlrlintuf,
/p ná šá·e llá·mahtenk mɔt·e·x·í·nən mi·mɔ́ntət, é·li-wəle·lɔ́ntank.
/t the baby immediately kicked in my womb, because he was happy.
/k the babe leaped in my womb for joy.

Lk 1.45
/b lapcnsw xqr wrlamvetuf; [⟨l-⟩ for ⟨wl-⟩, /wəl-/]
/p wəla·p·énsu xkwé· we·la·mhítank.
/t Blessed is the woman who believed.
/k And blessed is she that believed:

	/b	cntxi latup Nrvlalwrt; pavkunhih lrw.
	/p	éntxi-lá·t·əp nehəlá·ləwe·t pahkánči-=č -lé·w."
	/t	All that the Lord told her shall come true."
	/k	for there shall be a performance of those things which were told her from the Lord.

Lk 1.46
	/b	Nu Mrli tclwrnrp; nhehufum muxifavkunema ‖ Nrvlalwrlethi [⟨mu-⟩ for /mɔ-/]
	/p	ná mé·li tələwé·ne·p, "nči·čánkəm mɔx·inkɔhkəní·ma nehəla·ləwe·lí·č·i.
	/t	And then Mary said, "My soul praises the Lord.
	/k	And Mary said, My soul doth magnify the Lord,

Lk 1.47
(p. 10)
	/b	nwlelyvkwp ntrvif, Kejrlumwrt krthwvalet
	/p	no·li·laéhko·p nté·hink ki·š·e·ləmúwe·t ke·č·o·há·li·t,
	/t	God, my savior, has made me feel good in my heart,
	/k	And my spirit hath rejoiced in God my Saviour.

Lk 1.48
	/b	rli avrlumat nwntyrlselet tolokakunu. [⟨nwntyrlselet⟩ for ⟨nwnty rlselet⟩]
	/p	é·li-ahé·ləma·t nuntá·i e·lsí·li·t tɔlo·ká·k·ana.
	/t	by having a high regard for his lowly servant.
	/k	For he hath regarded the low estate of his handmaiden:

	/b	Bqi puna wrmi rkvokret ntclwevulwkh wrlapcnset,
	/p	"yúkwe pənáh wé·mi e·khɔké·i·t ntələwíhəlukw=č 'we·la·p·énsi·t',
	/t	"Now, all nations will call me 'blessed,'
	/k	for, behold, from henceforth all generations shall call me blessed.

Lk 1.49
	/b	rli mrxifwiliset kanjilevet,
	/p	é·li- me·x·ínkwi-ləs·i·t -kánši-lí·hi·t.
	/t	for the mighty one has done a great thing to me.
	/k	For he that is mighty hath done to me great things;

	/b	lwcnsw Wrli pelset
	/p	luwénsu wé·li-pí·lsi·t.
	/t	His name is 'the holy one'.
	/k	and holy is his name.

Lk 1.50
	/b	Pwnwntulan cntxakrlehi anvwqwi kejekelethi qwtumakrlintoakun;
	/p	pwənúntəla·n entxa·ke·i·lí·č·i, a·nhúkwi ki·š·i·k·i·lí·č·i, kwət·əma·k·e·ləntəwá·k·an,
	/t	He shows his mercy to all nations, to the succeeding generations,
	/k	And his mercy is on them that fear him from generation to generation.

	/b	wrmi cntxi wlamvetufek,
	/p	wé·mi éntxi-wəla·mhitánki·k.
	/t	as many as believe.
	/k	—

Lk 1.51
- /b wnaxkif wunhi pwnwntvekrn wthetaniswakun;
- /p wənáxkink wə́nči pwənunthíke·n wči·t·anəs·əwá·k·an.
- /t He showed strength with his arm.
- /k He hath shewed strength with his arm;

- /b tusrskaol rvrlinselethi, nrli punyrlintumevtet wtrwaif tali,
- /p tɔs·e·skaɔ́·ɔl ehe·lənsi·lí·č·i né·li-pəna·eləntamíhti·t wtehəwá·ink táli.
- /t He scattered the proud ones as they reflected in their hearts.
- /k he hath scattered the proud in the imagination of their hearts.

Lk 1.52
- /b ok vupi mrxifwiliselet lrvlumutupelet wunhi vakif valawul;
- /p ɔ́·k hápi me·x·ínkwi-ləs·í·li·t lehələmatahpí·li·t wwə́nči- hákink -halá·ɔl.
- /t And he put down the mighty from their accustomed seats (thrones?) as well.
- /k He hath put down the mighty from their seats,

- /b nuntyrlselethi ajiti tospunaol;
- /p nuntá·i e·lsi·lí·č·i a·šíte tɔspəná·ɔl.
- /t On the other hand, he raised up the lowly.
- /k and exalted them of low degree.

Lk 1.53
- /b qespwlan wrlvik krtopwelethi;
- /p kwi·spó·la·n wé·lhik ke·t·o·p·wi·lí·č·i.
- /t He filled the hungry with what is good.
- /k He hath filled the hungry with good things;

- /b ajiti rvoprelethi tolxi paleliskaol.
- /p a·šíte ehɔ·p·e·i·lí·č·i tólxi- palí·i -ləskaɔ́·ɔl.
- /t On the other hand he sent the rich away empty.
- /k and the rich he hath sent empty away.

Lk 1.54
- /b Wehumapanel talokakunul Islilul, mijatufc qwtumakrlintwakun,   [⟨tal-⟩ for /tɔl-/]
- /p "wwi·č·əmá·p·ani·l tɔlo·ká·k·anal †isəlǝ́lal, məša·t·ánke kwət·əma·k·e·ləntəwá·k·an,
- /t "He helped his servant Israel, when he remembered his mercy,
- /k He hath holpen his servant Israel, in remembrance of his mercy;

Lk 1.55
- /b rlatup kumuxomsnanifu Rplivemul;   [⟨-vemul⟩ for ⟨-vcmul⟩]
- /p e·lá·t·əp kəmux·o·msəna·nínka †e·pəlihémal,
- /t as he had said to our ancestor ('grandfather (abs.)') Abraham,
- /k As he spake to our fathers, to Abraham,

- /b ok anvoqi vokif wcnhekelethi rvalumakumek.
- /p ɔ́·k a·nhúkwi hɔ́k·enk wenči·k·i·lí·č·i ehaləmá·kami·k."
- /t and those descended from him forever." [*lit.*, 'those born from him in succession']
- /k and to his seed for ever.

Lk 1.56 /b Nuxa kejoxif avpami soki wetyrmapani, nu kcnh mothenrp.
/p naxá ki·š·ó·x·ink ahpá·mi só·ki-wi·t·ae·má·p·ani, ná kə́nč mɔ·č·í·ne·p.
/t She stayed with her for about three months and only then went home.
/k And Mary abode with her about three months, and returned to her own house.

Chapter 6 (pp. 10-12). [L. section 5.] (Luke 1.57-80)

Lk 1.57 /b Nu wtupsqevlatanrp Elisuput wtclih nwnjrn. Qesul kejekelenrp. [⟨vlat⟩ for ⟨lavt⟩]
/p ná wtəpskwilahtá·ne·p †i·lísapat, wtə́li-=č -núnše·n, kkwí·s·al -ki·š·i·k·i·lí·ne·p.
/t Then Elisabeth's time had come, for her to give birth and for her son to be born.
/k Now Elisabeth's full time came that she should be delivered; and she brought forth a son.

Lk 1.58 /b Pcxohekalkwki, ok rlafomathi puntamevtetc
/p pe·x·o·č·i·k·a·lkúk·i ó·k e·lanko·má·č·i pəntamihtí·t·e
/t When her neighbors and relatives heard
/k And her neighbours and her cousins heard

/b Nrvlalwrt rlkeqi pwnwntulat qwtumakrlintwakun,   [⟨pwnwn⟩ for ⟨punwn⟩]
/p nehəlá·ləwe·t e·lkí·kwi-pənúntəla·t kwət·əma·k·e·ləntəwá·k·an,
/t how much the Lord had showed her his mercy,
/k how the Lord had shewed great mercy upon her;

/b wrmi wihi wlrlintumwpanek.
/p wé·mi wíči-wəle·ləntamó·p·ani·k.
/t they were all happy along with her.
/k and they rejoiced with her.

Lk 1.59 /b Mrhi xaj cntxi kejqekc, myrxrpanek moi okajawaul memintitul.   [⟨x⟩ for /x·w/]
/p mé·či xá·š éntxi-ki·škwí·k·e, ma·e·x·wé·p·ani·k, mói-ɔ·ka·š·awwá·ɔl mi·məntət·al.
/t Eight days later, they gathered, going to circumcise the baby.
/k And it came to pass, that on the eighth day they came to circumcise the child;

/b Tclwevulaowapani Sakulyus, rlwcnseletup oxul.
/p tələwihəlawwá·p·ani '†sa·kaláyas', e·ləwensi·lí·t·əp ó·x·ɔl.
/t They named him 'Zacharias', his father's name.
/k and they called him Zacharias, after the name of his father.

Lk 1.60 /b Jwk kovrsul lwrp mutaa; wlava lwcnsw Nhan.
/p šúkw kɔhé·s·al lúwe·p, "máta=á·. wə́lah=á· luwénsu 'nčá·n'."
/t But his mother said, "It shouldn't be so. His name should rather be 'John'."
/k And his mother answered and said, Not so; but he shall be called John.

Lk 1.61 /b Tclwapani, takw avpee rlafomuthek nuni rlwcnset.   [⟨Tclwa⟩ for ⟨Tclawa⟩]
/p təlawwá·p·ani, "takó· ahpí·i e·lanko·máč·i·k nə́ni e·ləwénsi·t."

| | /t | They said to her, "There is no one of your relatives with that name." |
| | /k | And they said unto her, There is none of thy kindred that is called by this name. |

Lk 1.62
/b Nu wtutpetawunru nrl wrqeselethi, krkwh vuh ktclwihulu.
/p ná wtətpi·ta·o·né·ɔ né·l we·k·wi·s·i·lí·č·i, "kéku=č=háč ktələwíhəla?"
/t Then they made signs to the boy's father, "What will you name him?"
/k And they made signs to his father, how he would have him called.

Lk 1.63
/b Wtutpetakw rli kutatuf cntu lrkvekrt, ‖
/p wtətpi·tá·k·u é·li-kahtá·t·ank énta-le·khí·k·e·t.   [or énta-=á·(?)]
/t He signed to them that he wanted a place to write.   ['them': *lit.*, 'him']
/k And he asked for a writing table,

(p. 11)
/b nu wtclrkvamun, lwcnswh Nhan;
/p ná wtəle·khámən, "luwénsu=č 'nčá·n'."
/t Then he wrote, "His name shall be 'John'."
/k and wrote, saying, His name is John.

/b nu kanjrlintumwpanek.
/p ná kanše·ləntamó·p·ani·k.
/t And they were amazed.
/k And they marvelled all.

Lk 1.64
/b Nu jai wtwftwnrnrp ok welano luxuqevulrp,
/p ná šá·e wtunkto·né·ne·p, ó·k wí·lanu laxak·wíhəle·p.
/t Then immediately his mouth opened, and his tongue loosened,
/k And his mouth was opened immediately, and his tongue loosed,

/b nu toptwnrn; muxifakunemaul Kejrlumwrthi.
/p ná tɔ·ptó·ne·n, mɔx·inkɔhkəni·má·ɔl ki·š·e·ləməwé·č·i.
/t And then he spoke, and he praised God.
/k and he spake, and praised God.

Lk 1.65
/b Alumwpanek okai prmekrthek,
/p a·ləmó·p·ani·k ɔ·ká·i pe·mi·k·é·č·i·k,
/t The people living all around became afraid,
/k And fear came on all that dwelt round about them:

/b wrmi rlrk pwntakvokc rlekvatif hwrwf Nhwteuf,
/p wé·mi é·le·k pənta·khóke e·li·khátink čuwé·yunk †nčo·tí·yunk.
/t when everything that happend was heard about in the hill country of Judaea.
/k and all these sayings were noised abroad throughout all the hill country of Judaea.

Lk 1.66 /b wrmi puntufek wlvatwnrwp wtrwaif;
/p wé·mi pəntánki·k o·lhato·né·ɔ·p wtehəwá·ink.
/t All who heard it put it away in their hearts.
/k And all they that heard them laid them up in their hearts, .

/b lwruk ta vuh wtclsenh nu memintit?
/p luwé·ɔk, "tá=háč wtə́lsi·n=č ná mi·məntət?"
/t They said, "What is it that that child will do?"
/k saying, What manner of child shall this be!

/b Rli wnaxkif Nrvlalwrt wunhi kulinunt.
/p é·li- wənáxkink nehəlá·ləwe·t -wə́nči-kələ́nənt.
/t For he was held by the hand of the Lord.
/k And the hand of the Lord was with him.

Lk 1.67 /b Nu oxul Sakulyusul wtrpsenrpani Pelselet Hehuful
/p ná ó·x·ɔl †sa·kalayás·al wte·psi·né·p·ani pi·lsí·li·t či·čánkɔl
/t Then his father Zacharias was full of the Holy Spirit
/k And his father Zacharias was filled with the Holy Ghost,

/b laptwnrp rlwrtc;
/p la·ptó·ne·p, e·ləwé·t·e:
/t and said words, when he said:
/k and prophesied, saying,

Lk 1.68 /b Muxifakunemqwsetch Nrvlalwrt Kejrlumwkki Islul,
/p "maxinkɔhkəni·mkwəs·í·t·eč nehəlá·ləwe·t ki·š·e·ləmúkwki †ísələl,
/t "May the Lord, the God of Israel, be praised,
/k Blessed be the Lord God of Israel;

/b rli punaotup ok nevelatamwrtup wtunaprmul,   [⟨mwrt⟩ for ⟨mwrwvrt⟩]
/p é·li-pənaó·t·əp ó·k -nihəla·t·amwe·whé·təp wtənna·p·é·yəmal,
/t for he has seen and redeemed (lit., set free) his people,
/k for he hath visited and redeemed his people,

Lk 1.69 /b rli mrhi kejekunif wrlawswvalkwfh, nani wekwavumif wtalokakunifu Ntrpitul;
/p é·li- mé·či -ki·š·í·k·ənink we·la·wso·há·lkɔnkw=č nə́ni wi·k·əwáhəmink
    wtalo·ka·k·anínka †nte·pít·al.
/t as he has now raised what will be our salvation in the house of his servant David.
/k And hath raised up an horn of salvation for us in the house of his servant David;

Lk 1.70 /b nenwhi rlaptonrtup
/p ni·núči e·la·pto·né·t·əp
/t as he said in the beginning
/k As he spake

/b wnhi wtwnuwaif wrmi pelset nrnekanewrwsetpanifu,
/p wə́nči wto·nəwá·ink wé·mi pí·lsi·t nehəni·k·a·ní·i-we·wsi·tpanínka,
/t by the mouths of every holy one of the prophets,
/k by the mouth of his holy prophets,

/b cntxethek avpwpanek ncki krkw kejrlintasekc bqc pchi,
/p entxí·č·i·k ahpó·p·ani·k néke kéku ki·š·e·lənta·sí·k·e yúkwe péči,
/t as many as there were at the time when things were created and until now,
/k which have been since the world began:

Lk 1.71
/b ktclih kthwvalkrnrn wunhi jifalkreuf, ok wunhi prlekofwek,
/p ktə́li-=č -kčo·ha·lké·ne·n wə́nči šinka·lké·ankw, ó·k wə́nči pe·lihkónkwi·k.
/t that we would be saved from our enemy and from those that destroy us,
/k That we should be saved from our enemies, and from the hand of all that hate us;

Lk 1.72
/b wtclih punwntvekrn qwtumakrlintwakun, rlatup kumaxomsunanifu,
/p wtə́li-=č -pənunthíke·n kwət·əma·k·e·ləntəwá·k·an, e·lá·t·əp kəmux·o·msəna·nínka,
/t that he would show his mercy, as he told our ancestors,
/k To perform the mercy promised to our fathers, and to remember his holy covenant;

Lk 1.73
/b qetaptonakun hetani rlatup kumuxomsunanu Rplivcmul;
/p kwi·ta·pto·ná·k·an čí·t·ani e·lá·t·əp kəmux·o·msəná·na †e·pəlihémal,
/t his assurance, as he firmly told our ancestor Abraham,
/k The oath which he sware to our father Abraham,

Lk 1.74
/b wcnhih kuski ktheuf wunhi jifalkreuf,
/p wénči-=č -káski-kčíankw wə́nči šinka·lké·ankw,
/t so that we would be able to escape from our enemy,
/k That he would grant unto us, that we being delivered out of the hand of our enemies

/b wunhih mutu kxoreuf kpatumanrn,   [⟨-reuf⟩: -é·ɔnkw or -é·ankw]
/p wə́nči-=č máta -kxuwé·ɔnkw kpa·tamá·ne·n,
/t so that we would not fear to pray,
/k might serve him without fear,

Lk 1.75
/b pelawswakunif, ok jaxakaprokunif rlifwrxif tali srki lrlrxreuf.
/p pi·la·wsəwá·k·anink ó·k šaxahka·p·e·ó·k·anink e·linkwé·x·ink táli sé·ki-lehəle·x·é·ankw.
/t in holiness and in righteousness before him as long as we live.
/k In holiness and righteousness before him, all the days of our life.

24   Blanchard's Harmony of the Gospels

Lk 1.76 /b   Ok ke memintet, ktclwivlkch nrnekanewrwsetumal Mrxifwiliset,   [⟨n-⟩ for ⟨wn-⟩]
           /p   "ɔ·k kí·, mi·móntət, ktələwílke=č wənehəni·k·a·ní·i-we·wsí·t·əmal
                me·x·ínkwi-lə́s·i·t,
           /t   "And *you*, child, will be called the prophet of the mighty one,
           /k   And thou, child, shalt be called the prophet of the Highest:

           /b   rli knekanetamunh Nrvlalwrt, ktclih wletaon mwtumakun,   [⟨-nh⟩ for ⟨-h⟩]
           /p   é·li kəni·k·a·ní·tama=č nehəlá·ləwe·t, ktə́li-=č -wəlí·taɔ·n mwət·əmá·k·an,
           /t   for you will go before the Lord to prepare his way for him,
           /k   for thou shalt go before the face of the Lord to prepare his ways;

Lk 1.77 /b   okh kwatulalen wtunaprmul wlawswakun,
           /p   ɔ́·k=č ko·wa·təlá·li·n wtənna·p·é·yəmal wəla·wsəwá·k·an,
           /t   and you will let his people know about salvation
           /k   To give knowledge of salvation unto his people

           /b   paketatamawtwakun wcnhi mutawswakunwu,   [⟨wcnhi⟩ for /wə́nči/]
           /p   pahki·t·a·t·ama·ɔhtəwá·k·an wə́nči mɔt·a·wsəwa·k·anúwa,
           /t   by the forgiveness of their sins,
           /k   by the remission of their sins,

Lk 1.78 /b   wcnhi avoltwek qwtumakrlintwakun Kejrlumwkwf,
           /p   wə́nči ahɔ·ltó·wi·k kwət·əma·k·e·ləntəwá·k·an ki·š·e·ləmúk·ɔnkw,
           /t   by the loving mercy of God (*lit.*, our creator),
           /k   Through the tender mercy of our God;

           /b   wcnhi prtapuf vwqruf wunhi toxkwf,
           /p   wénči- pe·t·á·p·ank hukwé·yunk wə́nči -tɔ́xkɔnkw,
           /t   by which the dawn from up above visited us,
           /k   whereby the dayspring from on high hath visited us,

Lk 1.79 /b   wcnhi oxrkumaot lrmutupelethi cntu peskrk,   [⟨mutup⟩ for /mahtap·/]
           /p   wénči-ɔ·x·e·kamáɔ·t le·mahtap·i·lí·č·i énta-pí·ske·k,
           /t   by which he gave light to those sitting in the dark,
           /k   To give light to them that sit in darkness

           /b   ok nrk trvaqvekamaqvetet ufulwakun,   [⟨ufulwa-‖kun⟩]
           /p   ɔ́·k né·k te·ha·khwikama·khwíti·t ankələwá·k·an.
           /t   and when death cast a shadow over them.
           /k   and in the shadow of death,

(p. 12)   /b   ok myaextakwnrn nsetunanul li wlufwntwakunif.
           /p   ɔ́·k kəmaya·i·xta·k·ó·ne·n nsi·t·əná·nal lí wəlankuntəwá·k·anink."   [/kə-/ missing]
           /t   And it guides our feet to peace."   [/n-/ exc. wrongly for /k-/ inc.]
           /k   to guide our feet into the way of peace.

Lk 1.80 /b Pumekwp nu memins, ok alumi hetanekelwpani wthehufumul.
/p pəmíkʼoʼp ná mímə́ns, ɔ́k áləmi-čiʼtʼani-kʼiʼlóʼpʼani wčiʼčánkəmal.
/t The child grew, and his spirit became strong.
/k And the child grew, and waxed strong in spirit,

/b Aphi trkunu pumenwp, kxuntkc, kejqek prnwntulatc Islilul voky.
/p áʼpči téʼkəna pəmínnoʼp, kxántki kíʼškwiʼk peʼnuntəláʼte †isəlɔ́lal hɔ́kʼay.
/t He always stayed in the wilderness, until the day he showed himself to Israel.
/k and was in the deserts till the day of his shewing unto Israel.

Chapter 7 (pp. 12-13). [L. section 6.] (Luke 2.1-21; end of 2.21 om.)

Lk 2.1 /b Ncki lukveqi Akustus Sesul ktakematc, [⟨kt-⟩ for ⟨krt-⟩]
/p néke ləkhíkwi †akástəs †síʼsal keʼtaʼkʼiʼmáʼtʼe,
/t At the time when Augustus Caesar was emperor,
/k [See below.]

/b wtaptonakun alumivulrp wcnhih lrkvwnt wrmi cntxakrt, [⟨-rt⟩ for /-éʼiʼt/]
/p wtaʼptoʼnáʼkʼan aləmíhəleʼp wénči-=č -léʼkhunt wéʼmi entxaʼkéʼiʼt.
/t his order ('word') went forth, by which all nations were to be enrolled.
/k And it came to pass in those days, that there went out a decree from Caesar Augustus, that all the world should be taxed.

Lk 2.2 /b Sylenus kupunuletc Siliu tali, nwhi nc lrp.
/p †sailíʼnas †kapənalíʼtʼe †sília táli, núči nɔ́ léʼp.
/t When Cyrenius was governor in Syria that began to be done.
/k (And this taxing was first made when Cyrenius was governor of Syria.)

Lk 2.3 /b Wrmi cntxakrt nevluhi wtwtrnif rrp lih lrkvwn. [⟨-rt⟩ for /-éʼiʼt/; ⟨rrp⟩ for ⟨rp⟩]
/p wéʼmi entxaʼkéʼiʼt nihəláči wtoʼtʼéʼnink éʼp líʼ=č -léʼkhɔn.
/t Every nation (tribe) went to their own city to be enrolled.
/k And all went to be taxed, every one into his own city.

Lk 2.4 /b Nu Nhosi, Fcluleuf Nasulute wtrnif wunhi eku rp Nhwteu vakif Ntrpitu wtwtrnif lwcnswp Mpctlevcm: rli lafomatup Ntrpitifu,
/p ná †nčɔ́ʼsi †nkelalíʼyunk †nasəlatʼíʼiʼoʼtʼéʼnink wánči íka éʼp †nčoʼtíʼa hákʼink, †nteʼpítʼa wtoʼtʼéʼnink, luwénsoʼp †mpetəlíhem, éʼli-lankoʼmáʼtʼəp †nteʼpitʼínka,
/t Then Josey went from Galilee, the city of Nazareth, to the land of Judaea, to the city of David called Bethlehem, as he was related to David.
/k And Joseph also went up from Galilee, out of the city of Nazareth, into Judaea, unto the city of David, which is called Bethlehem; (because he was of the house and lineage of David:)

Lk 2.5 /b nale Mrle ncxkwntetet, ave mu poep.
      /p nahəlíˑi méˑli neˑxkuntíhtiˑt; áhi-=máh -pɔ́ˑiˑp.
      /t along with Mary, who was engaged to him; she was far along in her pregnancy.
      /k To be taxed with Mary his espoused wife, being great with child.

Lk 2.6 /b Nrlavpetup tpisqelavtap wtclih nwnjrn,
      /p neˑlahpíˑtˑəp, tpəskwílahtaˑp wtə́li-=č -núnšeˑn,
      /t And while she was there, the time was completed for her to give birth,
      /k And so it was, that, while they were there, the days were accomplished that she should be delivered.

Lk 2.7 /b wnetamwnjakunu,
      /p wənitamunšáˑkˑana.
      /t to her firstborn child.
      /k And she brought forth her firstborn son,

      /b ktumakenavkatwp cntu wexqrxumunt   [⟨-navkat-⟩ for ⟨-nakavt-⟩ or ⟨-nakovt-⟩]
      /p ktəmaˑkˑiˑnákɔhtoˑp énta-wiˑxkwéˑxˑəmənt.
      /t It looked pitiful where he was wrapped up.
      /k and wrapped him in swaddling clothes,

      /b jifexumanro cntu nrvnafrsuk xamunt,   [⟨jif-⟩ for ⟨wjcf-⟩; ⟨naf⟩ for /naɔnk/]
      /p wšenkiˑxˑəmaˑnéˑɔ énta- nehənaɔnkéˑsˑak -xámənt,
      /t They laid him in a manger (lit., where horses were fed),
      /k and laid him in a manger;

      /b rli qelu myekrvtetup myekrekanif.
      /p éˑli-kwíˑla-maiˑkˑehtíˑtˑəp maiˑkˑeˑiˑkˑáˑɔnink.
      /t because they had not been able to spend the night in an inn.
      /k because there was no room for them in the inn.

Lk 2.8 /b Avpwpanek nwtumathek mrkesu peskrwune cntu mukukrk.
      /p ahpóˑpˑaniˑk noˑtˑəmáˑčˑiˑk mekíˑsˑa piˑskeˑwəníˑi énta-məkɔ̀kˑeˑk.
      /t There were (shepherds) watching sheep at night in the open country.
      /k And there were in the same country shepherds abiding in the field, keeping watch over their flock by night.

Lk 2.9 /b Nu punu, Nrvlalwrt rvalokalathi tuxkwnrw,
      /p ná pənáh, nehəláˑləweˑt ehaloˑkaˑláˑčˑi [pwéči-]tɔxkoˑnéˑɔ.
      /t Then here an angel sent by the Lord came to them.
      /k And, lo, the angel of the Lord came upon them,

      /b oxrkamun Nrvulalwrt okai ncni rpevtet,   [⟨oxr-⟩ for ⟨woxr-⟩]
      /p wɔˑxˑéˑkamən nehəláˑləweˑt ɔˑkáˑi nəni eˑpˑíhtiˑt.
      /t The Lord lit up the area around where they were.
      /k and the glory of the Lord shone round about them:

	/b	ave wejaswpanek.
	/p	áhi-wi·š·a·s·ó·p·ani·k.
	/t	They were very afraid.
	/k	and they were sore afraid.

Lk 2.10 /b Rvalokalint tclapani kahi wejasevrq,
/p ehalo·ká·lənt təlá·p·ani, "káči wi·š·a·s·í·he·kw,
/t The angel said to them, "Don't be afraid,
/k And the angel said unto them, Fear not:

/b rli kprtwlvwmwp wlathemwakun wcnhih wlrlintuf wrmi awrn.
/p é·li kpe·t·o·lhúmɔ·p wəla·č·i·məwá·k·an, wénči-=č -wəle·lə́ntank wé·mi awé·n.
/t for I have brought you good news because of which everyone will be glad.
/k for, behold, I bring you good tidings of great joy, which shall be to all people.

Lk 2.11 /b Rli bqc mrhi kejekw krthwvalwrt, nc tali wtwtrnif Ntrpitu;
/p é·li yúkwe mé·či ki·š·í·k·u ke·č·o·há·ləwe·t, nə́ táli wto·t·é·nink †nte·pí·ta.
/t For now a savior of people has been born, in the city of David.
/k For unto you is born this day in the city of David a Saviour,

/b nul nuni Klyst Nrvlalwrt.
/p nál náni kəláist, nehəlá·ləwe·t.
/t He is Christ, the Lord.
/k which is Christ the Lord.

Lk 2.12 /b Kekenwlawakun bqc b; kumuxkaoh nu memintit
/p khiki·no·ləwá·k·an yúkwe yú: kəmáxkaɔ=č ná mi·mə́ntət,
/t This will be a sign: You will find the baby,
/k And this shall be a sign unto you; Ye shall find the babe

/b tumakenaqwt wexqrxumunt   [⟨t-⟩ for ⟨kt-⟩ (Lk 2.7)]
/p ktəma·k·i·ná·k·ɔt wi·xkwe·x·əmənt,
/t and it will look pitiful where he is wrapped up,
/k wrapped in swaddling clothes,

/b wjifexenun cntu nrvnafcsuk xamunt.   [⟨naf⟩ for /naɔnk/]
/p wšenki·x·í·nən énta- nehənaɔnké·s·ak -xámənt."
/t and he will be lying in a manger (lit., where horses were fed)."
/k lying in a manger.

Lk 2.13 /b Nu wexkawhi rvalokalintif tcli nroawl xrli osavkumi wunheyethek;   [⟨os-‖avk⟩]
/p ná wi·xkaɔ́či ehalo·ka·lə́ntink təli-ne·ɔwwá·ɔl xé·li ɔ·s·áhkame wənči·aí·č·i·k.
/t Then suddenly they saw by the angel many who came from heaven.
/k And suddenly there was with the angel a multitude of the heavenly host

(p. 13) /b muxifwrlumwukunemawapani Kejrlumwrlethi: Lwrpanek
/p mɔx·inkwe·ləməwahkəni·mawwá·p·ani ki·š·e·ləməwe·lí·č·i; luwé·p·ani·k,
/t They praised God; they said,
/k praising God, and saying,

Lk 2.14 /b muxrlumwkswakunekch Kejrlumwrt li vwqruf,
/p "maxe·ləmukwsəwa·k·aní·k·eč ki·š·e·ləmúwe·t lí hukwé·yunk,
/t "Let there be glory (or honor) to God on high,
/k Glory to God in the highest,

/b ok wlufuntwakunekch vakif li, ok wlrlumwksetch b cntu lawset.
/p ó·k wəlankuntəwa·k·aní·k·eč hák·ink lí, ó·k wəle·ləmukwsí·t·eč yú entalá·wsi·t."
/t and let there be peace on earth, and let mankind be well regarded."
/k and on earth peace, good will toward men.

Lk 2.15 /b Mrhi mahetetc rvalwkalinthek li osavkumi nwtumathek litwpanek,
/p mé·či ma·č·ihtí·t·e ehalo·ka·lǝ́nči·k lí ɔ·s·áhkame, no·t·əmá·č·i·k lət·ó·p·ani·k,
/t After the angels went home to heaven, the shepherds said to each other,
/k And it came to pass, as the angels were gone away from them into heaven, the shepherds said one to another,

/b bv ta eku atumwk Mpctlevcmif,
/p "yúh=tá íka á·t·amo·kw †mpetəlihémink.
/t "Alright, let's all go to Bethlehem.
/k Let us now go even unto Bethlehem,

/b my lenamwtumwk rlrk, cntxi Nrvlalwrt watulwkwf;
/p mái·li·namó·t·amo·kw é·le·k, éntxi- nehəlá·ləwe·t -wwa·təlúk·ɔnkw."
/t Let us go and see what has happened, everything the Lord made known to us."
/k and see this thing which is come to pass, which the Lord hath made known unto us.

Lk 2.16 /b eku pravtetc muxkaoapanek Nhoseul ok Mrleul navle memintitul jifɛxenru cntu xamunt nrvnafcsu.   [⟨panek⟩ for ⟨pani⟩; tǝli- missing]
/p íka pe·ahtí·t·e, mɔxkaɔwwá·p·ani †nčó·sial ó·k †mé·lial, nahəlí·i mi·məntə́t·al [tǝli-]šenki·x·i·nəné·ɔ énta-xámənt nehənaɔnké·s·a.
/t When they got there, they found Josey and Mary, as well as the baby, lying in a manger.
/k And they came with haste, and found Mary, and Joseph, and the babe lying in a manger.

Lk 2.17 /b Mrhi nrovtetc;
/p mé·či ne·ɔhtí·t·e,
/t After they had seen him (or them),
/k And when they had seen it,

/b nu talumi wutvekrnru rlqevtet rvalokalinhi, wunhi nrl memintitul.
   [⟨wut-⟩ for ⟨wat-⟩]
/p ná tólǝmi-wwa·thike·né·ɔ e·lkwíhti·t ehalo·ka·lә́nči wә́nči né·l mi·mǝntә́t·al.
/t then they began making known what the angel had told them about the baby.
/k they made known abroad the saying which was told them concerning this child.

(Lk 2.18. [omitted])

Lk 2.19 /b Mrli qwlrlintumun cntxi puntufup.
         /p mé·li kwǝle·lә́ntamǝn éntxi-pǝntánkǝp.
         /t Mary reflected on everything she had heard.
         /k But Mary kept all these things, and pondered them in her heart.

Lk 2.20 /b Nunu qwtkenro nrvnwtumathek, tolumi avrlumwukunemawau Kejrlumwrthi,
         /p nána kkwǝtki·né·ɔ nehǝno·t·ǝmá·č·i·k, tólǝmi-ahe·lǝmuwahkǝni·mawwá·ɔ ki·š·e·lǝmǝwé·č·i,
         /t Then the shepherds returned, and they began praising God,
         /k And the shepherds returned, glorifying and praising God

         /b rli lenamevtetup, ok puntamevtetup cntxi lintup.
         /p é·li-li·namihtí·t·ǝp ó·k -pǝntamihtí·t·ǝp éntxi-lә́ntǝp.
         /t because of what they had seen and everything they heard that they had been told.
         /k for all the things that they had heard and seen, as it was told unto them.

Lk 2.21 /b Mrhi xaj cntxoqwnakvakc nu okajanrp nu memintit.
         /p mé·či xá·š entxo·k·wǝnakháke, ná ɔ·ka·š·á·ne·p ná mi·mә́ntǝt.
         /t After it had been eight days, then the baby was circumcised.
         /k And when eight days were accomplished for the circumcising of the child, ...

Chapter 8 (pp. 13-14). [L. section 8.] (Luke 2.22-39.)

Lk 2.22 /b Mrhi tpisqevulakc tclih pelevan vokyu Mrli,
         /p mé·či tpǝskwihǝlá·k·e tóli-=č -pi·lí·ha·n hókaya mé·li,
         /t After the time had come for Mary to purify herself,
         /k And when the days of her purification .. were accomplished,

         /b rlextakup Mojiju,
         /p e·li·xtá·k·ǝp †mo·šә́š·a,
         /t as had been laid down in law by Moses,
         /k .. according to the law of Moses ..

	/b	prjwuwapani Nhelwsulumif, wunhih nepalat Nrvlalwrt rlifwcxif, [⟨p-⟩ for ⟨pw-⟩]
	/p	pwe·š·əwawwá·p·ani †nči·lo·sələmink, wə́nči-=č -ní·p·ala·t nehəlá·ləwe·t e·linkwé·x·ink.
	/t	they brought him to Jerusalem to make him stand before the Lord.
	/k	they brought him to Jerusalem, to present him to the Lord;

Lk 2.23 /b rli lwrt Nrvlalwrt toptwnakunif; cntxet pelyhihet nrtami kejeket lrlumwkswh pelset Nrvlawrt rlifwcxif,
/p (é·li-lúwe·t nehəlá·ləwe·t tɔ·pto·ná·k·anink, "éntxi·t pi·laečə́č·i·t né·tami-ki·š·í·k·i·t le·ləmúkwsu=č pí·lsi·t nehəlá·ləwe·t e·linkwé·x·ink")
/t (Because the Lord says in his law (*lit.*, word), "Every boy who is a first-born shall be honored as holy before the Lord"),
/k (As it is written in the law of the Lord, Every male that openeth the womb shall be called holy to the Lord;)

Lk 2.24 /b krkwh awrn melawl Nrvlalwrlet, lwrp aptwnakunif tali   [⟨m-⟩ for ⟨mw-⟩]
/p "kéku=č awé·n mwi·lá·ɔl nehəla·ləwé·li·t," lúwe·p a·pto·ná·k·anink táli.
/t "A person shall give something to the Lord," he said in the law (*lit.*, word).
/k And to offer a sacrifice according to that which is said in the law of the Lord,

/b nejuh mamrtvakrmwwk, ji tu neju amemetituk.   [⟨-mwwk⟩ for ⟨-mwuk⟩]
/p "ní·š·a=č ma·me·thake·mó·wak, ší=tá ní·š·a ami·mi·t·ə́t·ak."
/t "It shall be two (mourning) doves, or two young (passenger) pigeons."
/k A pair of turtledoves, or two young pigeons.

Lk 2.25 /b Avpwp lino Nhelwsulumif lwncswp Simeun,   [⟨lwncswp⟩ for ⟨lwcnswp⟩]
/p ahpó·p lə́nu †nči·lo·sələmink, luwénso·p †símian.
/t There was a man in Jerusalem whose name was Simeon.
/k And, behold, there was a man in Jerusalem, whose name was Simeon;

/b wliliswp ok jaxaxkawswp nvakrlintamwakun Islilul.
/p wə́li-lə́s·o·p ɔ́·k šaxahká·wso·p, [..] nhake·e·ləntaməwá·k·an †isələ́lal.   [word lost]
/t He was a good person and lived an upright life, [awaiting] the hope (of?) Israel.
/k and the same man was just and devout, waiting for the consolation of Israel:

/b Pelselet Hehufum topetakwpani. ‖   [⟨Hehufum⟩ for ⟨Hehufw⟩]
/p pi·lsí·li·t či·čánkɔ tɔp·i·ta·k·ó·p·ani.
/t The holy spirit was with him.
/k and the Holy Ghost was upon him.

Lk 2.26 /b Rli Pelselet Hehufw watulwkwn
(p. 14) /p é·li pi·lsí·li·t či·čánkɔ o·wa·təlúk·o·n,
/t For the holy spirit made it known to him
/k And it was revealed unto him by the Holy Ghost,

	/b	tclih mutu eufulwun, kcnjh nrotc Nrvlalwrt Klystumul,	[⟨Kl-⟩ for /kwəl-/]
	/p	táli-=č máta -i·ankəló·wən, kə́nč=č ne·ó·t·e nehəlá·ləwe·t kwəláistəmal.	
	/t	that he would never die until he saw the Lord's Christ.	
	/k	that he should not see death, before he had seen the Lord's Christ.	

Lk 2.27
/b nunu Hehuf patamwrekanif tclelyrmapani.
/p ná ná čí·čankw pa·tamwe·i·k·á·ɔnink təli·lae·má·p·ani
/t And then the spirit persuaded him to (go to) the temple.
/k And he came by the Spirit into the temple:

/b Kekyuk prjwavtetc memintitul Nhesusul patamwrekanif,
/p khíkayak pe·š·əwahtí·t·e mi·məntə́t·al nči·sás·al pa·tamwe·i·k·á·ɔnink,
/t And when the parents brought the child Jesus to the temple,
/k and when the parents brought in the child Jesus,

/b moi levanro rlwif aptonakunif tali,   [⟨rlwif⟩ for ⟨rlwcf⟩]
/p mói-li·ha·né·ɔ é·ləwenk a·pto·ná·k·anink táli.
/t they went to do for him what is said in the law (*lit.*, word).
/k to do for him after the custom of the law,

Lk 2.28
/b nu wrtunan qunapani, mxifovkuneman Kejrlumwrthi, laptonrp   [⟨mx-⟩ for /mɔx·-/]
/p ná wwé·t·əna·n, kwənná·p·ani, mɔx·inkɔhkəní·ma·n ki·š·e·ləməwé·č·i, la·ptó·ne·p,
/t Then he took him, and held him, and praised God, and he declared,
/k Then took he him up in his arms, and blessed God, and said,

Lk 2.29
/b Nrvlaliun bqc lrlumel nalai ufulin rlaptwnaleanup,
/p "nehəlá·lian, yúkwe lé·ləmi·l nnálai-ánkələn, e·la·pto·na·liánəp,
/t "My Lord, now let me die peacefully, in accordance with what you told me,
/k Lord, now lettest thou thy servant depart in peace, according to thy word:

Lk 2.30
/b rli nrmu kthwvaltwakun,
/p é·li-né·ma kčo·ha·ltəwá·k·an,   [or emend to: kkəč·o·ha·ltəwá·k·an 'your salvation']
/t for I have seen the salvation,
/k For mine eyes have seen thy salvation,

Lk 2.31
/b ktcli kejextaon rlifwcxif wrmi rkvokret;
/p któli-ki·š·i·xtáɔ·n e·linkwé·x·ink wé·mi e·khɔké·i·t
/t and that you prepare before all nations
/k Which thou hast prepared before the face of all people;

Lk 2.32
/b kejvaqtrk oxrkaokh ovolumekrthek, ok Islulul wluvkunemqwswakunwu.
/p ki·šhákwte·k; ɔ·x·e·kaɔ́·ɔk=č ɔhəlɔmi·k·é·č·i·k; ɔ́·k isəlɔ́lal, o·lahkəni·mkwəs·əwa·k·anúwa."
/t a light; those living far away will be given light; and for those of Israel, their praise."
/k A light to lighten the Gentiles, and the glory of thy people Israel.

Lk 2.33　/b　Nhosi ok wethrothi wlrlumrlintumwpanek puntaotetc rlwrlet.
　　　　/p　†nčɔ́·si ɔ́·k wi·č·e·ɔ́·č·i wəle·ləme·ləntamó·p·ani·k pəntaɔhtí·t·e e·ləwé·li·t.
　　　　/t　Josey and his wife were astonished when they heard what he said.
　　　　/k　And Joseph and his mother marvelled at those things which were spoken of him.

Lk 2.34　/b　Nu Simeun wlafomanrp, tclapani wrnehanelethi Mrleul;
　　　　/p　ná †símian o·lanko·má·ne·p, təlá·p·ani we·ni·č·a·ni·lí·č·i †mé·lial,
　　　　/t　Then Simeon greeted them kindly, and he said to Mary, his mother,
　　　　/k　And Simeon blessed them, and said unto Mary his mother,

　　　　/b　puna wuni memintit tclexenun, tclih punancven, ok amwekunan xrli awrni Islulif;
　　　　/p　"pənáh, wáni mi·mə́ntət təli·x·í·nən, təli·=č -pənaníhi·n, ɔ́·k -a·mwí·kəna·n xé·li awé·ni †isəlólink.
　　　　/t　"Now, this baby is destined to throw down and raise up many people in Israel.
　　　　/k　Behold, this child is set for the fall and rising again of many in Israel;

　　　　/b　ok tclexenun voky wunhi hehanenevwten
　　　　/p　ɔ́·k təli·x·í·nən hɔ́k·ay wə́nči čəčani·nehó·t·i·n,
　　　　/t　and he is destined for there to be disputes about him,
　　　　/k　and for a sign which shall be spoken against;

Lk 2.35　/b　wcnhih wavkw xrli awrn rletrvat;
　　　　/p　wénči-=č -wwáhkɔ xé·li awé·n e·li·t·é·ha·t.
　　　　/t　so that the thoughts of many people will be known.
　　　　/k　(2) that the thoughts of many hearts may be revealed.　　　[numbers = order in KJV]

　　　　/b　kovan, ok tufamekun ktrvif li kuntavulc.
　　　　/p　(kɔhán, ɔ́·k tankamí·k·an kté·hink lí-kəntáhəle·.)"
　　　　/t　(Indeed, and a sword (will) pierce your heart.)"
　　　　/k　(1) (Yea, a sword shall pierce through thy own soul also,)

Lk 2.36　/b　　Ok mu nrnekanewrwset xqr avpwp lwcnswp Ani, Prnwcl tonul, Ajul rlvakretup,
　　　　/p　　ɔ́·k=máh nehəni·k·a·ní i·wé·wsi·t xkwé· ahpó·p, luwénso·p †ani, †pé·nəwel tó·nal, †á·šəl e·lhake·í·t·əp.
　　　　/t　　And there was a woman who was a prophet, named Anna, the daughter of Phanuel, who had been of the Aser tribe.
　　　　/k　　And there was one Anna, a prophetess, the daughter of Phanuel, of the tribe of Aser:

　　　　/b　ave kvekywp, nejaj txi kavtenri wekefrp,
　　　　/p　áhi-khíkayo·p, ní·š·a·š txí-kahtəné·i wi·k·ínke·p,
　　　　/t　She was very old; she had been married for seven years,
　　　　/k　she was of a great age, and had lived with an husband seven years from her virginity;

Text, Transcription, and Translation

Lk 2.37 /b xajtxenxki ok nrwa kavtinamwp, aphi patamwrekanif avpwp,
/p xá·š txí·nxke ó·k né·wa kahtənámo·p, á·pči pa·tamwe·i·k·á·ɔnink ahpó·p.
/t and she was eighty-four years old and was always in the temple.
/k And she was a widow of about fourscore and four years, which departed not from the temple,

/b qwnikejwk, ok qwnitpwk mekintamaopani Kejrlumwkwfwi;   [⟨me-⟩ for ⟨mwe-⟩]
/p kwə́ni-kí·š·ukw ó·k kwə́ni-tpó·kw mwi·kəntamaó·p·ani ki·š·e·ləmuk·ónkwi.
/t Day and night she served God (*lit.*, our creator).
/k but served God with fastings and prayers night and day.

Lk 2.38 /b nwv tumekrnrp,
/p ná wtəmi·k·é·ne·p,
/t She came in then,
/k And she coming in

/b qrnamapani, Nrvlalwrlethi tukunwtumaonrp nrl memintitul
/p kwe·na·má·p·ani nehəla·ləwe·lí·č·i, tɔk·əno·t·əmaó·ne·p né·l mi·məntə́t·al,
/t and she gave thanks to the Lord, and spoke about the baby to them,
/k that instant gave thanks likewise unto the Lord, and spake of him

/b nrk prtwvtet levelatamwrokun rpethek Nhelwsulumif.   [⟨levela⟩: for ⟨nev(e)la⟩]
/p né·k pe·túhti·t nihəla·t·amwe·ó·k·an e·p·í·č·i·k †nči·lo·səlómink.
/t and about the freedom that those in Jerusalem were waiting for.   [recast]
/k to all them that looked for redemption in Jerusalem.

Lk 2.39 /b Prkunji lisetc wrmi cntxi lwrtup; Nrvlalwrt wtaptwnakunif tali
/p pe·k·ánči-ləs·í·t·e wé·mi entxi-luwé·t·əp nehəlá·ləwe·t wta·pto·ná·k·anink táli,
/t When he completed everything as the Lord had said in his law (*lit.*, word),
/k And when they had performed all things according to the law of the Lord,

/b lupi mahepanek Fclulewf, wwtrnawawf Nasulut.   [⟨nawa⟩: for ⟨nywa⟩ 2x]
/p lápi ma·č·í·p·ani·k †nkelalí·yunk, wo·t·e·nayəwá·unk †násəlat.
/t they returned home to Galilee, to their city of Nazareth.
/k they returned into Galilee, to their own city Nazareth.

Chapter 9 (pp. 14-16). [L. section 7.] (Matthew 2.1-23)

Mt 2.1 /b Mrhi Nhesus kejeketc Mpctlevcmif Nhwteu vakif,
/p mé·či nčí·sas ki·š·i·k·í·t·e †mpetəlihémink †nčo·tí·a hák·ink,
/t After Jesus was born in Bethlehem in the land of Judaea,
/k Now when Jesus was born in Bethlehem of Judaea

/b ncki lrkveqc Vclut sakematc.
/p néke ləkhíkwi †hélat sa·k·i·má·t·e,
/t at the time when Herod was king,
/k in the days of Herod the king,

/b Nhelwsrlumif prpanek lipwrenouk, wcnhi kthifwcvulak wcnheyethek;   [⟨Nhelwsrlu-‖mif⟩]
/p †nči·lo·séləmink pé·p·ani·k ləpwe·innúwak wénči-kčinkwéhəla·k wenči·aí·č·i·k.
/t there came to Jerusalem some wise men who were from the east.
/k behold, there came wise men from the east to Jerusalem,

Mt 2.2   /b lwrpanek, ta vuh topen Nhwe sakema wrski kejeket?
(p. 15) /p luwé·p·ani·k, "tá=háč tóp·i·n nčo·wí·i-sa·k·í·ma wé·ski-ki·š·í·k·i·t?
         /t They said, "Where is the new-born Jewish king?
         /k Saying, Where is he that is born King of the Jews?

/b Rli nrowunu talufumul wcnhi kthifwcvulak tali.
/p "é·li nne·ó·wəna tɔlánkəmal wénči-kčinkwéhəla·k táli.
/t "For we saw his star in the east.
/k for we have seen his star in the east,

/b Wunhi panrn numy xifakunemawunu.   [⟨Wunhi⟩ for ⟨Nwnhi⟩ /núnči-/]
/p "núnči-pá·ne·n, nəmái-xinkɔhkəni·má·wəna."
/t "We come to worship him."
/k and are come to worship him.

Mt 2.3   /b Sakemu Vclut mrhi puntafc, salavkevulrp,
         /p sa·k·í·ma †hélat mé·či pəntánke, salaxkíhəle·p,
         /t After the king Herod heard about it, he became agitated,
         /k When Herod the king had heard these things, he was troubled,

/b ok wrmi Nhelwsulumif rpethek.
/p ó·k wé·mi †nči·lo·səlómink e·p·í·č·i·k.
/t and also all who were in Jerusalem.
/k and all Jerusalem with him.

Mt 2.4   /b Mrhi marmatc rlrkvekrthek ok lrpothek,
         /p mé·či ma·e·má·t·e / ehəle·khi·k·é·č·i·k ó·k le·p·ó·č·i·k, [proximates for obviatives]
         /t After he called together / the scribes and the learned (lit., wise) ones,
         /k And when he had gathered all the chief priests and scribes of the people together,

/b nutwvtawn cntu kejekeleth Klystul.
/p nɔt·o·xtáɔ·n énta-ki·š·i·k·í·li·t=č kəláistal.
/t he asked them where Christ would be born.
/k he demanded of them where Christ should be born.

Mt 2.5 /b Tclapani, Mpctlivcmif Nhwteu vakif
        /p təláˑpˑani, "†mpetəlihémink †nčoˑtíˑa hákˑink,
        /t They told him, "In Bethlehem in the land of Judaea,
        /k And they said unto him, In Bethlehem of Judaea:

        /b rli nuni lrkvekrtetup nrnekanewrwsetpanifu;
        /p éˑli- nə́ni -leˑkhiˑkˑehtíˑtˑəp nehəniˑkˑaˑníˑi-weˑwsiˑtpanínka:
        /t as that is what the prophets of old wrote:
        /k for thus it is written by the prophet,

Mt 2.6 /b Ke Mpctlivcm, takw ktuftetei sakemaokunif,
        /p 'kíˑ †mpetəlíhem, takóˑ ktanktiˑtˑíˑi saˑkˑiˑmaˑɔ́ˑkˑanink,
        /t 'O (lit., you) Bethlehem, you are not the smallest (lit., small) in the kingdom,
        /k And thou Bethlehem, in the land of Juda, art not the least among the princes of Juda:

        /b rli kvakif wunheyet sakemunh wrsakemaimiteth ntunaprmuk Isliluk.
        /p éˑli- khákˑenk -wənčíˑaiˑt saˑkˑíˑma=č, weˑsˑaˑkˑiˑmaˑyəmíhtiˑt=č ntənnaˑpˑéˑyəmak †isəlɔ́lak.' "   [⟨-nh⟩ for ⟨-h⟩]
        /t for out of you will come a king, who will be the king of my people, the Israelites.' "   [lit., 'who my people will have as king']
        /k for out of thee shall come a Governor, that shall rule my people Israel.

Mt 2.7 /b Nu Vclut keme wcnhemanrp nrlel lipwrenoul;
        /p ná †hélat kiˑmíˑi wwenčiˑmáˑneˑp néˑliˑl ləpweˑinnúwal.
        /t Then Herod secretly summoned the wise men.
        /k Then Herod, when he had privily called the wise men,

        /b wli ntotumapanel mya rlkeqi nrxqusetup nu alafq;   [⟨map⟩ for ⟨maop⟩]
        /p óˑli-ntoˑtˑəmaɔ́ˑpˑaniˑl, mayáˑi eˑlkíˑkwi-neˑykwəsˑíˑtˑəp ná alánkw.
        /t He carefully asked them the exact time when the star had appeared.
        /k enquired of them diligently what time the star appeared.

Mt 2.8 /b nu telanrp Mpctlivcmif aq, wli ntwnw nu memintit,
        /p ná təláˑneˑp, "†mpetəlihémink áˑkw; wə́li-ntóˑnoˑ ná miˑmə́ntət.
        /t Then he said to them, "Go to Bethlehem, and search carefully for the baby.
        /k And he sent them to Bethlehem, and said, Go and search diligently for the young child;

        /b muxkarqch pchi watulemoi wcnhih nrpi, moxifakunemuk.
        /p maxkaéˑkˑwe=č, péči-wwaˑtəliˑmɔ́ˑe, wénči-=č néˑpe -maxinkɔhkəníˑmak."
        /t When you find him, come and let me know, so that I, too, can worship him."
        /k and when ye have found him, bring me word again, that I may come and worship him also.

Mt 2.9
/b Mrhi puntaotetc nrl sakemaul, nu tolumskanrop;
/p mé·či pəntaohtí·t·e né·l sa·k·i·má·ɔl, ná tɔləmska·né·ɔ·p.
/t After they heard the king, they left.
/k When they had heard the king, they departed;

/b krkw van wu lupi alufq, cntu kthifwcvulak nwhi nrovtetup; nekanetaqaul,
/p kéku=xán wá lápi alánkw énta-kčinkwéhəla·k núči ne·ohtí·t·əp
    wəni·k·a·ni·ta·k·əwá·ɔl.   [⟨n-⟩ for /wən-/]
/t But here again was the star they had seen before in the east going ahead of them,
/k and, lo, the star, which they saw in the east, went before them,

/b eku pchi tpisqi vwqrwf rvpetup memintit,   [⟨rvp⟩ for ⟨rp⟩]
/p íka péči tpə́skwi hukwé·yunk e·p·í·t·əp mi·mə́ntət.
/t coming to (stand) right above the place where the baby was.
/k till it came and stood over where the young child was.

Mt 2.10
/b nrovtetc tcli navkoxwrlen, ave wlrlintamwpanek.
/p ne·ohtí·t·e tə́li-nahko·x·wé·li·n, áhi-wəle·ləntamó·p·ani·k.
/t When they saw it stop, they were very glad.
/k When they saw the star, they rejoiced with exceeding great joy.

Mt 2.11
/b Trmekrtetc wnroapanel nrl memintitul qwnwkwpani kovrsul,
/p te·mi·k·ehtí·t·e, wəne·ɔwwá·p·ani·l né·l mi·məntə́t·al, kwənnuk·ó·p·ani kɔhé·s·al,
/t When they came in, they saw the baby being held by his mother,
/k And when they were come into the house, they saw the young child with Mary his mother,

/b vakif tclanevenrop vokywu qrnamawapani,
/p hákink təlanihi·né·ɔ·p hɔk·ayúwa, kwe·na·mawwá·p·ani.
/t and they fell down and worshipped him.   [lit., 'threw themselves']
/k and fell down, and worshipped him:

/b lrxwrnimevtetc wtclathrswakunwal   [⟨lrxwrn-⟩: correct word ⟨lrxun-⟩]
/p le·x·ənəmihtí·t·e wtəlač·e·s·əwa·k·anəwá·ɔl,   [B. has 'scatter' for 'unwrap']
/t When they unwrapped their goods,
/k and when they had opened their treasures,

/b mwelawapani fwl, ok wefemakvwk krkw.   [⟨-kvwk⟩ for ⟨-kvwki⟩]
/p mwi·lawwá·p·ani nkó·l ó·k winki·ma·khɔ́ki kéku.
/t they gave him gold and sweet-smelling things.
/k they presented unto him gifts; gold, and frankincense, and myrrh.

Mt 2.12
/b Qetulapani Kejrlumwrt cntu kaelet, tclih mutu Vclutif awunru,
/p kkwi·təlá·p·ani ki·š·e·ləmúwe·t énta-kaí·li·t, təli-=č máta †helát·ink -a·wəné·ɔ.
/t God warned them as they slept not to go to Herod.
/k And being warned of God in a dream that they should not return to Herod,

	/b	nu pale pumskanrop mavhevtetc.
	/p	ná palí·i pwəmska·né·ɔ·p ma·č·ihtí·t·e.
	/t	Then they went a different way when they went home.
	/k	they departed into their own country another way.

Mt 2.13
- /b Mrhi rlumskavtetc, nu otxwkw nrli kaet, rvalokalinthi Nhosi. ‖
- /p mé·či e·ləmskahtí·t·e, ná o·txúk·u né·li-kaí·t ehalo·ka·lə́nči †nčɔ́·si.
- /t After they left, then an angel came to Josey as he slept.
- /k And when they were departed, behold, the angel of the Lord appeareth to Joseph in a dream,

(p. 16)
- /b Tclapani, amwel; alumoxul nu memintit navle kovrsul,
- /p təlá·p·ani, "á·mwi·l; alǝmó·x·ɔl ná mi·mə́ntǝt nahǝlí·i kɔhé·s·al;
- /t He said to him, "Get up, and take the baby along with his mother;
- /k saying, Arise, and take the young child and his mother,

- /b Ehipt lijemweq.
- /p †í·čipt ləš·í·mwi·kw.
- /t flee to Egypt, all of you.
- /k and flee into Egypt,

- /b Nuh nc ksakavpen, kenjh lupi puntyeunc;
- /p ná=č nǝ́ ksá·kahpi·n, kǝ́nč=č lápi pǝntaiáne,
- /t That's where you must stay until you hear from me again,
- /k and be thou there until I bring thee word:

- /b rli ntonaoth Vclut bl memintitul, kutwnalath.
- /p é·li-ntó·naɔ·t=č †hélat yó·l mi·mǝntǝ́t·al, -kahtó·nala·t=č."
- /t for Herod will look for this baby and will seek to kill him."
- /k for Herod will seek the young child to destroy him.

Mt 2.14
- /b Amwetc, wrtanapani memintitul, ok kovrselet,
- /p a·mwí·t·e, wwe·t·əná·p·ani mi·məntə́t·al, ɔ́·k kɔhe·s·í·li·t,
- /t When he got up, he took the baby and his mother,
- /k When he arose, he took the young child and his mother

- /b peskrwune alumskrpanek li Ehipt.
- /p pi·ske·wəní·i aləmské·p·ani·k lí †í·čipt.
- /t and they departed by night to Egypt.
- /k by night, and departed into Egypt:

[Mt 2.15: part after v. 20.]

Mt 2.16	/b	Vclut mrhi wrotaqc, tcli kealokwl nrli lipwrenoul ave manwfswp;
	/p	†hélat mé·či we·ɔ·tá·k·we tɔ́li-ki·ɔlúk·o·n né·li ləpwe·innúwal áhi-manúnkso·p.
	/t	When Herod knew that he was fooled by the wise men, he was very angry.
	/k	Then Herod, when he saw that he was mocked of the wise men, was exceeding wroth,

	/b	talokrmwenrp li nvelan wrmi meminsul avpami Mpctlivcmif,
	/p	tɔlo·ke·mwí·ne·p lí-nhíla·n wé·mi mi·mə́nsal ahpá·mi †mpetəlihémink,
	/t	And he sent orders for all children in and around Bethlehem to be killed,
	/k	and sent forth, and slew all the children that were in Bethlehem, and in all the coasts thereof,

	/b	svaki neju kavtinumethek,	[⟨neju⟩ ní·š·a is not idiomatic; em. to /níši-/]
	/p	sháki níši-kahtənamí·č·i·k,	
	/t	up to the age of two,	
	/k	from two years old and under,	

	/b	rlkeqc wli totumaotup nrl lipwrenwul.
	/p	e·lkí·kwi-wə́li-nto·t·əmaɔ́·t·əp né·l ləpwe·innúwal.
	/t	the time he had carefully asked of the wise men.
	/k	according to the time which he had diligently enquired of the wise men.

Mt 2.17	/b	Nu nani tali pavkanhi lrp nrnekaniwrwsetpanu Nhclemyu rlwrtup.
	/p	ná ná=ní táli-pahkánči-lé·p nehəni·k·a·ní·i-we·wsi·tpána †nčeli·máya e·ləwé·t·əp:
	/t	Then that was where what the prophet Jeremiah had said came true:
	/k	Then was fulfilled that which was spoken by Jeremy the prophet, saying,

Mt 2.18	/b	Ohwf prmekvatif li puntavkavtwp	[⟨tavk⟩ for ⟨tak⟩]
	/p	"ɔhčúnk pe·mi·khátink lí-pəntákɔhto·p	
	/t	"In the hill country was heard	
	/k	In Rama was there a voice heard,	

	/b	kanjalamwakun, salamwakun, mawuntwakun ok jerlintamwakun:
	/p	kanšala·məwá·k·an, sala·məwá·k·an, mawəntəwá·k·an, ɔ́·k ši·e·ləntaməwá·k·an.
	/t	screaming, weeping, mourning, and sorrow.
	/k	lamentation, and weeping, and great mourning,

	/b	Lrhil moemaul wnehanul, ok mutu kuske leelymaep; rli mutu avpelet.
	/p	†lé·čəl mɔi·má·ɔl wəni·č·á·nal, ɔ́·k máta káski-li·i·lae·má·i·p, é·li- máta -ahpí·li·t."
	/t	Rachel weeps for her children, and she could not be comforted, as they are gone."
	/k	Rachel weeping for her children, and would not be comforted, because they are not.

Mt 2.19	/b	Mrhi ufulukc Vclut;
	/p	mé·či ankələ́k·e †hélat,

Text, Transcription, and Translation

/t After Herod died,
/k But when Herod was dead,

/b lupi Nrvlalwrt rvalokalathi wnintulan voky cntu kaelet Nhoseul Ehiptif;
/p lápi nehəláləweˑt ehaloˑkaˑláˑčˑi wənéntəlaˑn hɔ́kˑay énta-kaíˑliˑt †nčɔ́ˑsial †iˑčíptink.
/t an angel of the Lord again appeared to Josey as he slept in Egypt.
/k behold, an angel of the Lord appeareth in a dream to Joseph in Egypt,

Mt 2.20
/b tclapani, amwel wrtun nu memintit navle kovrsul,
/p təláˑpˑani, "áˑmwiˑl, wéˑtˑən ná miˑmə́ntət, nahəlíˑi kɔhéˑsˑal,
/t He said to him, "Get up, and take the baby along with his mother,
/k Saying, Arise, and take the young child and his mother,

/b kutvakrl li Islile vakif,
/p katháke·l lí †isələlíˑi-hákˑink,
/t and move (your residence, your family) to the land of Israel,
/k and go into the land of Israel:

/b rli wfulwfu krtwnalatpanek nrl memintitu,   [⟨wfulwfu⟩ for ⟨ufulwfu⟩]
/p éˑli ankəlúnka keˑtˑoˑnalaˑtpániˑk néˑl miˑməntə́tˑa."
/t for those that wanted to kill the baby are dead."
/k for they are dead which sought the young child's life.

Mt 2.15.
/b Nu pavkunji lrp nrvnekaniwrwsetpanifu rlwcvtetup,
/p ná pahkánči-léˑp nehəniˑkˑaˑníˑi-weˑwsiˑtpanínka eˑləwehtíˑtˑəp:
/t Then what the prophets had said came true:
/k ... that it might be fulfilled which was spoken of the Lord by the prophet, saying,

/b Ehiptif ntcli wcnhemap Nqes.
/p "†iˑčíptink ntə́li-wenčíˑmaˑp nkwíˑs."
/t "I have called my son out of Egypt."
/k Out of Egypt have I called my son.

Mt 2.21
/b Amwetc, wrtanapani memintitul ok kovrselet,
/p aˑmwíˑtˑe, wweˑtˑənáˑpˑani miˑməntə́tˑal ɔ́k kɔheˑsˑíˑliˑt,
/t When he got up, he took the baby and his mother,
/k And he arose, and took the young child and his mother,

/b tonrap Islil cntu ncvlatuf;
/p tɔˑnéˑɔˑp †ísələl énta-nihəláˑtˑank.
/t and they went to the country of Israel.   [*lit.*, 'the place Israel owned']
/k and came into the land of Israel.

Mt 2.22 /b jwk puntufc tcli, Ahelrus sakeman Nhwteu tali,
/p šúkw pəntánke táli- †a·či·lé·yas -sa·k·í·ma·n †nčo·tí·a táli,
/t But when he heard that Archelaus was king in Judaea,
/k But when he heard that Archelaus did reign in Judaea

/b rli lupavpet oxufu Vclutifu,
/p é·li-lápahpi·t o·x·únka †helat·ínka,
/t taking the place of his late father Herod,
/k in the room of his father Herod,

/b qetaminrp eku ton; ok Kejrlumwrt wuntamanrp cntu kaelet, [⟨man⟩ for ⟨maon⟩]
/p kkwi·tamə́ne·p íka tó·n, ó·k ki·š·e·ləmúwe·t wwəntamaó·ne·p énta-kaí·li·t.
/t he was afraid to go there, and also God informed him about it as he slept.
/k he was afraid to go thither: notwithstanding, being warned of God in a dream,

/b nu wcnhi Fcluleuf li kutvakrn, [⟨wcnhi⟩ for /wwə́nči/]
/p nə́ wwə́nči- †nkelalí·yunk -lí-katháke·n.
/t For that reason he took his family to Galilee.
/k he turned aside into the parts of Galilee:

Mt 2.23 /b nu eku ponrp wtwtrnif, Ncsulut rlwcntasek. Na nani pumenenrp,
/p ná íka pó·ne·p wto·t·é·nink, †nesəlat e·ləwentá·s·i·k. ná ná=ní pwəminní·ne·p,
/t Then he came to his city, which was called Nazareth. Then that is where he stayed,
/k And he came and dwelt in a city called Nazareth:

/b Wwnhi pavkunhih lrk rlwrtetup nrnekanewawsetpanifu.
       [⟨Wwnhi⟩ for ⟨Wunhi⟩; ⟨waw⟩ for ⟨wrw⟩]
/p wə́nči-pahkánči-=č -lé·k e·ləwehtí·t·əp nehəni·k·a·ní·i-we·wsi·tpanínka:
/t so that what the prophets of old had said would come true:
/k that it might be fulfilled which was spoken by the prophets,

/b Lwcnswh Ncsulutee. ‖ [⟨-ee⟩ for /-i·i/]
/p "luwénsu=č †nesəlat·í·i."
/t "He shall be named 'of Nazareth'."
/k He shall be called a Nazarene.

Chapter 10 (p. 17). [L. section 9.] (Luke 2.41-52)

Lk 2.41 /b Aphi cntxun kavtif qekybbmu eku rpanek Nhelwsulum;
(p. 17) /p á·pči éntxən-kahtínk kwi·kayó·yəma íka é·p·ani·k †nči·ló·sələm,
/t Every year his parents went to Jerusalem,
/k Now his parents went to Jerusalem every year

/b muxifwi kejqek lwcntaswp lwif.—
/p maxínkwi-kí·škwi·k, luwentá·s·o·p 'ló·wink'.
/t for a holiday (*lit.*, great day) called the Passover.
/k at the feast of the passover.

Lk 2.42
/b Tclin ok neju krtinumetc, lupi eku rpanek wunhi rli xifwi metsavtif.
/p télən ó·k ní·š·a ke·t·ənamí·t·e, lápi íka é·p·ani·k wə́nči é·li-xínkwi-mi·tsáhtink.
/t When he was twelve years old, they again went there because of the feast.
/k And when he was twelve years old, they went up to Jerusalem after the custom of the feast.

Lk 2.43
/b Mrhi lwclrkc lupi mathepanek,
/p mé·či ló·wi-lé·k·e lápi ma·č·í·p·ani·k,
/t After it was over, they went home again,
/k And when they had fulfilled the days, as they returned,

/b jwk Nhesustit peevulrp eku Nhelwsulumif;
/p šúkw nči·sástət pi·íhəle·p íka †nči·lo·sələmink.
/t but the young Jesus stayed behind in Jerusalem.
/k the child Jesus tarried behind in Jerusalem;

/b kovrsul navle Nhosi, mutu wavkwepani;
/p kɔhé·s·al nahəlí·i †nčɔ́·si máta o·wahko·wí·p·ani.
/t Neither his mother nor Josey knew about him.
/k and Joseph and his mother knew not of it.

Lk 2.44
/b letrvrpanik, nekani ct li wetrw.
/p li·t·e·hé·p·ani·k, "ni·k·á·ni=ét lí-wí·t·e·w."
/t They thought, "He must be going on ahead with others."
/k But they, supposing him to have been in the company,

/b Nqwti kejqc srki pavtet. Soki ntwnaonrwp li cntu lafwntuf, ok wrowkwkpani.
/p nkwə́ti-kí·škwe sé·ki-páhti·t sɔ́·ki-nto·naɔ·né·ɔ·p lí énta-lankúntank ɔ́·k we·ɔhkukpáni.
/t All day long as they went they looked for him among his relatives and acquainances.
/k went a day's journey; and they sought him among their kinsfolk and acquaintance.

Lk 2.45
/b Qelawtetc, qwtukepanek li Nhelusulumif, wnatonawaul;   [⟨lus⟩ for ⟨lws⟩]
/p kwi·laɔhtí·t·e, kwtək·í·p·ani·k lí †nči·lo·sələmink, wənat·o·naɔwwá·ɔl.
/t When they could not find him, they turned back to Jerusalem and looked for him.
/k And when they found him not, they turned back again to Jerusalem, seeking him.

Lk 2.46 /b neji kejqekc kenh muxkawapani patamwrekanif lrmutuvpet, ok
             wnunatwvtumakwpani: [⟨kenh⟩ for ⟨kcnh⟩]
         /p níši-ki·škwí·k·e kə́nč mɔxkaɔwwá·p·ani pa·tamwe·i·k·á·ɔnink le·mátahpi·t, ɔ́·k
             wənana·t·o·xtama·k·ó·p·ani.
         /t Finally, after two days they found him sitting in the temple, and the others were
             asking him questions.
         /k And it came to pass, that after three days they found him in the temple, sitting in
             the midst of the doctors, both hearing them, and asking them questions.

Lk 2.47 /b Wrmi cntxi puntakwk kanjrlintamwpanek, rli naxkwtif, ok rli puntamat.
         /p wé·mi éntxi-pəntá·k·uk kanše·ləntamó·p·ani·k, é·li-naxkó·t·ink
             ɔ́·k é·li-pə́ntama·t.
         /t All that heard him were astonished at how he answered and how he understood.
         /k And all that heard him were astonished at his understanding and answers.

Lk 2.48 /b   Nrovtetc kanjrlintumwpanek,
         /p   ne·ɔhtí·t·e, kanše·ləntamó·p·ani·k.
         /t   When they saw him, they were astonished.
         /k   And when they saw him, they were amazed:

         /b tclkw kovrsu, Fwes krkw vuh wunhi nc liviif?
         /p tə́lku kɔhé·s·a, "nkwí·s, kéku=háč wə́nči- nə́ -lí·hienk?
         /t His mother said to him, "My son, why did you do that to us?
         /k and his mother said unto him, Son, why hast thou thus dealt with us?

         /b punaw kwx ok nrpc nenwhi jerlintumwi ntwnwlvwmunu.   [⟨-wi⟩ for /-əwí·i/]
         /p pənáw kó·x, ɔ́·k né·pe; nni·núči-ši·e·ləntaməwí·i-nto·no·lhúməna."
         /t Look at your father, and me also; we've been sorrowfully looking for you
             forever."
         /k behold, thy father and I have sought thee sorrowing.

Lk 2.49 /b Tclapani, Ta vuh lrw wunhi ntwnaerq?
         /p təlá·p·ani, "tá=háč lé·w wə́nči-nto·naie·kw'?
         /t He said to them, "How was it that you looked for me?
         /k And he said unto them, How is it that ye sought me?

         /b muta ksi kwatwunru ntclih Nwx mekintumaon?
         /p máta=ksí ko·wa·to·wəné·ɔ ntə́li-=č nó·x -mi·kəntamáɔ·n?"
         /t Ought you not to know that I would be serving (lit., working for) my father?"
         /k wist ye not that I must be about my Father's business?

Lk 2.50 /b jwk mutu puntumwnru wunhi nc lwqvetet,   [⟨punt-⟩ for /pwənt-/]
         /p šúkw máta pwəntamo·wəné·ɔ wə́nči- nə́ -lukhwíti·t.
         /t But they did not understand why he told them that.
         /k And they understood not the saying which he spake unto them.

Lk 2.51 /b wehropani li Nasulutif, ok wowlamvetaopani.
/p wwi·č·e·ɔ́·p·ani lí †nasəlát·ink, ɔ́·k wɔwəla·mhitaɔ́·p·ani.
/t He went with them to Nazareth and was obedient to them.
/k And he went down with them, and came to Nazareth, and was subject unto them:

/b Jwk kovrsul qwlrlintuminrp wrmi rlwrf.
/p šúkw kɔhé·s·al kwəle·ləntamə́ne·p wé·mi é·ləwenk.
/t But his mother reflected on everything that was said.
/k but his mother kept all these sayings in her heart.

Lk 2.52 /b Evekalihi lukviqi lipwrp Nhesus, ok lukel,
/p ihikalíči ləkhíkwi-ləpwé·p nčí·sas, ɔ́·k -lə́k·i·l,
/t Jesus gradually became wiser and taller,
/k And Jesus increased in wisdom and stature,

/b ok ekalihi tclrlumwkw Kejrlumwkwfwi, ok b cntu lawselethi.
/p ɔ́·k ikalíči təlé·ləmukw ki·š·e·ləmuk·ɔ́nkwi ɔ́·k yú entala·wsi·lí·č·i.
/t and he became better thought of by God and mankind.
/k and in favour with God and man.

Chapter 11 (pp. 17-19). [L. section 10.] (Luke 3.1-6, 10-18; Matthew 3.2, 4-10; Mark 1.1-2)

Lk 3.1 /b Mrhi tclin ok palrnax txi kavtinri sakematc Typelus; Pylut krkyimvrtc Nhuteiftali, ok Vclut Krkyimvrtc tali Faluleuf, wemavtul Pilupsul Krkyimvrtc Ytwliif tali, ok avpami Tlrkanitusif, ok Lisanius, Krkyimvrtc Apyliuif,
[⟨Apyliuif⟩ for ⟨Apylinif⟩]
/p mé·či télən ɔ́·k palé·naxk txí-kahtəné·i sa·k·i·má·t·e †taipí·las, †páilat ke·kayəmhé·t·e †nčo·tí·ink táli, ɔ́·k hélat ke·kayəmhé·t·e táli †nka·lalí·yunk, wí·mahtal †pilápsal ke·kayəmhé·t·e †aitó·liink táli ɔ́·k ahpá·mi †təle·kanitás·ink, ɔ́·k †lisánias ke·kayəmhé·t·e †a·pailə́nink,
/t When Tiberius had been emperor for fifteen years, and Pilate was the ruler in Judaea, and Herod was the ruler in Galilee and his brother Philip the ruler in Ituraea and around Trachonitis, and Lysanias the ruler in Abilene,
/k Now in the fifteenth year of the reign of Tiberius Caesar, Pontius Pilate being governor of Judaea, and Herod being tetrarch of Galilee, and his brother Philip tetrarch of Ituraea and of the region of Trachonitis, and Lysanias the tetrarch of Abilene,

Lk 3.2 /b weevufrtpanek Anus ok Krupus. ‖ [⟨weevuf-⟩ for ⟨wcvevuf-⟩]
/p wehi·hunke·tpáni·k †á·nas ɔ́·k †ke·ápas.
/t the priests were Annas and Caiaphas.
/k Annas and Caiaphas being the high priests,

(p. 18)	/b	Kejrlwmwkwf toptwnakun otxwkwnrp Nhan Sakulyus qesul, trkunu tali.
	/p	ki·š·e·ləmúk·ɔnkw tɔ·pto·ná·k·an o·txuk·ó·ne·p nčá·n, †sa·kaláyas kkwí·s·al, té·kəna táli.
	/t	The word of God came to John, the son of Zacharias, in the wilderness.
	/k	the word of God came unto John the son of Zacharias in the wilderness.

Lk 3.3 /b Eku prp Nhutune sepwf prmekvatif, pwpamtwnvatuminrp, hvopunintwakun,
/p íka pé·p †nčataní·i-sí·p·unk pe·mi·khátink, pup·a·mto·nha·t·amə́ne·p čhɔ·pwənəntəwá·k·an,
/t He came to the country along the Jordan River and preached about the baptism,
/k And he came into all the country about Jordan, preaching the baptism

/b wunhih awrn jerlintuf qwlupetc, jerlintumoetrvat
/p wə́nči-=č awé·n ši·e·ló́ntank, kwələp·í·t·e, -ši·e·ləntaməwi·t·é·ha·t,
/t by which anyone who is sorry, if they are converted, will have a repentant heart,
/k of repentance

/b wunhi puketatumwnt mutawswakun.
/p wə́nči-pahki·t·á·t·amunt mɔt·a·wsəwá·k·an.
/t whereby their sins are forgiven.
/k for the remission of sins;

Mt 3.2 /b Lwr, Qwlwpel rli prxothevulak osavkumre sakemaokun.
/p lúwe·, "kwələp·i·l, é·li-pe·x·o·č·íhəla·k ɔ·s·ahkame·í·i-sa·k·i·ma·ó·k·an."
/t He said, "Repent, for the kingdom of heaven comes near."
/k And saying, Repent ye: for the kingdom of heaven is at hand.

Mk 1.1 /b Bqc bni puntakovtwp rlaptwnif wunhi Nhesns Klyst Kejrlumwrt qesul,
/p yúkwe yó·ni pəntákɔhto·p e·la·ptó·nenk wə́nči nčí·sas kəláist, ki·š·e·ləmúwe·t kkwí·s·al,
/t This was heard that was told about Jesus Christ, the son of God,
/k The beginning of the gospel of Jesus Christ, the Son of God;

Mk 1.2 /b rlwrvtetup nrnekanewrwsetpanifu.
/p e·ləwehtí·t·əp nehəni·k·a·ní·i-we·wsi·tpanínka.
/t as the prophets of old said:
/k As it is written in the prophets,

/b Puna ntalokaluh awrn knekanetamwkwn rlifwrxenun;
/p "pənáh, ntalo·ká·la=č awé·n, kəni·k·a·ni·tamúk·o·n e·linkwe·x·í·nan.
/t "Now, I shall send a messenger to go ahead of you, in front of you.
/k Behold, I send my messenger before thy face,

/b nanih wletwn tumakun ranh.
/p náni=č o·lí·to·n təmá·k·an e·á·an=č."

| | /t | He will make the path where you will go." |
| | /k | which shall prepare thy way before thee. |

Mt 3.3 /b Rli nunul ta wuni rlwrtup nrnekanewrwsetpanu Esrusu, rlwrtc;
/p é·li nánal=tá wáni e·ləwé·t·əp nehəni·k·aní·i-we·wsi·tpána †i·se·yə́s·a, e·ləwé·t·e:
/t For this is the one the prophet Esaias said it of, when he said:
/k For this is he that was spoken of by the prophet Esaias, saying,

/b Puntaqwt aptwnakun trkunu tali, lwrtaqwt,
/p "pəntá·k·ɔt a·pto·ná·k·an té·kəna táli, luwe·tá·k·ɔt:
/t "A voice is heard in the wilderness, saying:
/k The voice of one crying in the wilderness,

/b Kejextwk rath Nrvlalwrt, jaxaketwl mwtumakun.
/p 'ki·š·í·xto·kw é·a·t=č nehəlá·ləwe·t; šaxahkí·to·l mwət·əmá·k·an.'
/t 'Prepare the way that the Lord will go; make his path straight.'   [you pl.; you sg.]
/k Prepare ye the way of the Lord, make his paths straight.

Lk 3.5 /b Wrmi cntxi pasyrk hovatasekch; ok wrmi ovhwul vakifh tclanivenrw,
/p wé·mi éntxi-pahsá·e·k čuhɔta·s·í·k·eč, ó·k wé·mi ɔhčúwal hákink=č təlanihi·né·ɔ,
/t Let every valley be filled, and all hills they shall throw down,
/k Every valley shall be filled, and every mountain and hill shall be brought low;

/b okh cntu okhakrxif wrmih jaxakunasw, okh cntu amutsisek wletasw;
/p ó·k=č énta-ɔ·khaké·x·ink, wé·mi=č šaxahkəná·s·u, ó·k=č énta-amatsə́s·i·k wəli·tá·s·u,
/t and crooked roads shall all be made straight, and rough ground shall be made nice,
/k and the crooked shall be made straight, and the rough ways shall be made smooth;

Lk 3.6 /b wunhih wrmi awrn nrf qwthwvaltwakun.
/p wə́nči-=č wé·mi awé·n -nénk kwəč·o·ha·ltəwá·k·an."
/t so that everyone shall see their salvation."
/k And all flesh shall see the salvation of God.

Mt 3.4 /b Nul wuni Nhan wjakvwqeunwp kamile mexrkunu, helwkrs kulumumpeswp;
/p nál wáni nčá·n wša·khuk·wí·ɔno·p †kaməlí·i-mi·x·é·k·əna, či·ló·k·e·s kəlamampí·s·o·p.
/t That same John wore a coat of camel hair, and he wore a leather strap as a belt.
/k And the same John had his raiment of camel's hair, and a leathern girdle about his loins;

/b pakufr, ok amwre jwkul methwakunwp.   [⟨-kufr,⟩ for ⟨-kufro⟩; ⟨me-⟩ for ⟨mwe-⟩]
/p pa·kanké·ɔ ó·k a·məwe·í·i-šó·k·əl mwi·č·əwá·k·ano·p.
/t Locusts and honey (*lit.*, bee sugar) was his food.
/k and his meat was locusts and wild honey.

Mt 3.5 /b Moi toxwpanel Nhelwsulum wunheyethek, [⟨toxw-⟩ for ⟨toxkw-⟩]
 /p mói-tɔxkó·p·ani·l †nči·ló·sələm wənči·aí·č·i·k,
 /t People from Jerusalem went to visit him,
 /k Then went out to him Jerusalem,

 /b ok Nhwteethek, ok wrmi avpami Nhutune sepwf
 /p ó·k †nčo·ti·í·č·i·k, ó·k wé·mi ahpá·mi †nčataní·i-sí·p·unk.
 /t and Judaeans, and [people from] all around the Jordan River.
 /k and all Judaea, and all the region round about Jordan,

Mt 3.6 /b hvopunwkwapani Nhutunif tali, quthelatwnrw mutawswakunwu.
 [⟨hvop-⟩ for /wčɔhɔ·p-/]
 /p wčɔhɔ·pwənuk·əwá·p·ani †nčátanink táli, kwəč·ilahto·né·ɔ mɔt·a·wsəwa·k·anúwa.
 /t They were baptized by him in the Jordan and confessed their sins.
 /k And were baptized of him in Jordan, confessing their sins.

Mt 3.7 /b Nrotc xrli Paluseu, ok Satuseu [..] toxkwn cntu hvopunwrt, [word lost]
 /p ne·ó·t·e xé·li †pa·ləsi·í·ɔ ó·k †sa·tasí·ɔ [táli-]tóxko·n énta-čhɔ·pwənúwe·t,
 /t When he saw many Pharisees and Sadducees come to where he was baptizing people,
 /k But when he saw many of the Pharisees and Sadducees come to his baptism,

 /b wtclapanel;
 /p wtəlá·p·ani·l,
 /t he said to them,
 /k he said unto them,

 /b Kelwu wrnehanumwqrq qejkumwruk,
 /p "ki·ló·wa we·ni·č·a·nəmúk·we·kw kwi·škaməwé·ɔk,
 /t "You offspring of copperheads,
 /k O generation of vipers,

 /b awrn vuh tclkwnru wjintamwq prtwxrekh manwfswakun? [⟨t-⟩ for ⟨kt ⟩]
 /p awé·n=háč ktəlko·né·ɔ, 'wšántamo·kw pe·t·o·x·wé·i·k=č manunksəwá·k·an?'
 /t who told you, 'Flee from the anger that will come'?
 /k who hath warned you to flee from the wrath to come?

Mt 3.8 /b Ktcnamwq krkw tcpi wunhi nrvqwtuk ktcli jerlintumunru. [⟨nam⟩ for /nəm/]
 /p ktənamo·kw kéku tépi wənči-ne·ykót·ək ktáli-ši·e·ləntaməné·ɔ.
 /t Bring out things that are enough for it to be seen from them that you are sorry.
 /k Bring forth therefore fruits meet for repentance:
   [RSV: "Bear fruit that befits repentance."]

Mt 3.9 /b Kahi letrvavrq, ok kahi lwrvrq, Rpulivam ta notoxumawunu. [⟨Rpu-‖livam⟩]
 /p káči li·t·e·há·he·kw, ó·k káči luwé·he·kw, '†e·pəlíham=tá no·t·o·x·əmá·wəna.'

/t   Do not think, and do not say, 'We have Abraham as our father.'
/k   And think not to say within yourselves, We have Abraham to our father:

(p. 19)   /b   Ktclwvumw, Kejrlumwrt wtcpi a bl asinul, wunhi kejevaul meminsu
/p   ktəllúhəmɔ, 'ki·š·e·ləmúwe·t wtépi-=á· yó·l ahsə́nal -wə́nči-ki·š·i·há·ɔl mi·mə́nsa,
/t   I tell you, 'God would be able to make children from these stones,
/k   for I say unto you, that God is able of these stones to raise up children

/b   Rpulivamu wrnehanet.
/p   †e·pəliháma we·ni·č·á·ni·t.
/t   with Abraham (abs.) being their father.
/k   unto Abraham.

Mt 3.10   /b   Mrhi tamrvekun vetkwf hwpvikif nepavtr,
/p   mé·či təmahí·k·an hítkunk čəphíkink nípahte·,
/t   An axe now stands next to the trees at the roots,
/k   And now also the axe is laid unto the root of the trees: (also Lk 3.9)

/b   wunhi cntxi vetkwf mutu wclvik wcnhekunwk, keskvoh,
        [⟨vetkwf⟩ (repeated from the preceeding line as if hítkunk) written for hít·ukw]
/p   wə́nči éntxi [hít·ukw] máta wé·lhik wenčí·k·əno·kw kí·skhɔ·=č,
/t   by which every tree from which good (fruit) does not come shall be cut down
/k   therefore every tree which bringeth not forth good fruit is hewn down,

/b   okh tuntrwf laniven.
/p   ɔ́·k=č tənté·yunk laníhi·n."
/t   and thrown into the fire."
/k   and cast into the fire.

Lk 3.10   /b   Lwruk nrk mrxrlkek, Krkwh ksi ntclsevunu?
/p   luwé·ɔk né·k me·x·é·lki·k, "kéku=č=ksí ntəlsíhəna?"
/t   The crowd said, "What, then, shall we do?"
/k   And the people asked him, saying, What shall we do then?

Lk 3.11   /b   Tclapani, Awrn nejefih jakvoqeunu, kwtih mwelau awrni mutu wrlvatwleq,
/p   təlá·p·ani, "awé·n, ni·š·ínki=č ša·khuk·wí·ɔna, kwə́t·i=č mwi·lá·ɔ awé·ni máta
        we·lhatɔ́·li·kw,   [presumably read: ni·š·ínke=č šɔ·khuk·wí·ɔna]
/t   He said to them, "If someone has two coats he shall give one to someone who has
        none,   [emended meaning (*lit.*): 'if his coats are two']
/k   He answereth and saith unto them, He that hath two coats, let him impart to him
        that hath none;

/b   okh awrn mwethwakunetc, nani tclsen.
/p   ɔ́·k=č awé·n mwi·č·əwa·k·aní·t·e, ná=ní tə́lsi·n.
/t   and if someone has food, they will do the same.
/k   and he that hath meat, let him do likewise.

Lk 3.12 /b Mcrmyrnifek mwni, nc ponrw my hvopwnauk; [⟨Mcrm-⟩ for ⟨Mcvm-⟩]
 /p mehəma·e·nínki·k móni nə́ po·né·o, mái-čho·pwəná·ok.
 /t Tax (*lit.*, money) collectors came there, coming to be baptized.
 /k Then came also publicans to be baptized,

 /b tcalwapani, Rvakrkifrt; krkwh vah ntclsevnu? [⟨tcalwapani⟩ for ⟨tclawapani⟩]
 /p təlawwá·p·ani, "ehahke·kínke·t, kéku=č=háč ntəlsíhəna?"
 /t They said to him, "Teacher, what shall we do?"
 /k and said unto him, Master, what shall we do?

Lk 3.13 /b tclapanel, Kahi ekalisi katatufvrq, jwk entxi lextakrrq.
 /p təlá·p·ani·l, "káči ikalísi kahta·t·ánkhe·kw, šúkw éntxi-li·xta·k·é·e·kw."
 /t He said to them, "Do not desire more than the amount set for you."
 /k And he said unto them, Exact no more than that which is appointed you.

Lk 3.14 /b Sohulu tclkwpani; Krkwh vuh nrpunu ntclsevnu?
 /p só·čəla təlkó·p·ani, "kéku=č=háč né·pəna ntəlsíhəna?"
 /t Soldiers said to him, "And us, what shall we do?"
 /k And the soldiers likewise demanded of him, saying, And what shall we do?

 /b Tclapani, Kahi awrn mavhevavrq, jitu kahi nwhiqc kulwvwetawerkrq awrn,
 /p təlá·p·ani, "káči awé·n mahči·há·he·kw, ší·tá káči nó·čkwe kəlo·hitawié·k·ač
   awé·n." [⟨kulwvwet⟩ for /kəlo·hit-/]
 /t He said to them, "Don't treat anyone badly, or don't frivolously disbelieve them."
 /k And he said unto them, Do violence to no man, neither accuse any falsely;

 /b ok tcprlintamwq rlrnvakrrq.
 /p ó·k te·p·e·ləntamo·kw e·le·nha·k·é·e·kw."
 /t and be satisfied with what you are paid."
 /k and be content with your wages.

Lk 3.15 /h Xrlwpanek prvwrthek
 /p xe·ló·p·ani·k pehəwé·č·i·k.
 /t There were many who were waiting.
 /k And as the people were in expectation,

 /b pwnyrlumwapani Nhanul wtrwaif; [⟨mwap⟩ for ⟨mawap⟩]
 /p pwənae·ləmawwá·p·ani nčá·nal wtehəwá·ink,
 /t They thought about John in their hearts,
 /k and all men mused in their hearts of John,

 /b tclrlumawapani, nul ct wu Klyst.
 /p təle·ləmawwá·p·ani, "nál=ét wá kəláist?"
 /t wondering if he could be Christ.
 /k whether he were the Christ, or not;

Lk 3.16 /b Nhan lwrp, Kehe mpif ktcli hvopunul.
/p nčá·n lúwe·p, "khičí·i mpínk ktə́li-čhɔ́·pwənəl.
/t John said, "I do indeed baptize you (sg.) in water.
/k John answered, saying unto them all, I indeed baptize you with water;

/b Jwk wrtrkyet alwelisw, eli muthepavko nontyilinsen luxunimawn.

[⟨tyil-⟩ for ⟨tyrl-⟩]

/p šúkw we·t·é·kai·t aləwí·i-lə́s·u; ílli mɔč·ípahkɔ nnuntae·lə́nsi·n llax·ənəmáɔ·n.
/t But one coming after me is greater; I feel unworthy even to untie his shoes.
/k but one mightier than I cometh, the latchet of whose shoes I am not worthy to unloose:

/b Khovopwnwkh Pelselet Hehufwf, ok tuntrwf,
/p kčɔhɔ́·pwənukw=č pi·lsí·li·t či·čánkunk ɔ́·k tənté·yunk.
/t He will baptize you (sg.) in the holy spirit and in fire.
/k he shall baptize you with the Holy Ghost, and with fire:

Lk 3.17 /b qwnimun pawulrtekun;
/p kwənnə́mən paɔle·tí·k·an,
/t He holds the winnowing basket in his hand.
/k Whose fan is in his hand,

/b wlih peletwn cntu paetrvuf;
/p ɔ́·li-=č -pi·lí·to·n énta-pai·téhank,
/t He will thoroughly clean the place where he threshes it;
/k and he will throughly purge his floor,

/b wlih paolrtamun, mocvumunh vwet li rvatrk,
/p ɔ́·li-=č -paɔlé·tamən, mɔ·éhəmən=č hwí·t lí ehháte·k,
/t he will thoroughly winnow the wheat and will gather it into the granary.
/k and will gather the wheat into his garner;

/b jwk nc olrq, wlwsumunh nuni tuntrwf muta eatifprq;
/p šúkw nɔ́ ɔlé·kw wəlɔ́·s·əmən=č nə́ni tənté·yunk máta i·a·ténkpe·kw."
/t But the chaff he will burn in the fire that is never extinguished."
/k but the chaff he will burn with fire unquenchable.

Lk 3.18 /b xrlrnaovki, ok peli krkw tclavkrkemapani.
/p xe·lennáɔhki ɔ́·k pí·li kéku təlahke·ki·má·p·ani.
/t Many kinds of different things he taught them.
/k And many other things in his exhortation preached he unto the people.

Chapter 12 (pp. 19-20). [L. section 11.] (Matthew 3.13-17; Luke 3.23.)

Lk 3.21 /b Mrhi xrli awrn hvopwnuntc,
/p mé·či xé·li awé·n čhɔ·pwənə́nte,
/t After many people had been baptized,
/l It came to pass in those days, when all the people were baptized,
/k Now when all the people were baptized,

Mt 3.13 /b nu ponrp Nhesus, Fcluleuf wunhi, Nasulute wtrnif Nhutunif,   [word missing]
/p ná pó·ne·p nčí·sas †nkelalí·yunk wə́nči, †nasəlat·í·i-o·t·é·nink, [lí] †nčátanink
/t Then Jesus came from Galilee, the city of Nazareth, to the Jordan,
/k Then cometh Jesus from Galilee to Jordan unto John,

/b tcli a hovopunwkwn Nhanul.   [⟨hovop⟩ for ⟨hvop⟩]
/p tə́li-=á· -čhɔ·pwənúk·o·n nčá·nal.
/t to be baptized by John.
/k to be baptized of him.

Mt 3.14 /b Jwk Nhan topihi lawl, ‖ tclawl; ke a wlava khvopwni,   [⟨khvop⟩ for ⟨khovop⟩]
/p šúkw nčá·n tɔpíči-lá·ɔl, təlá·ɔl, "kí·=á· wəláha kčɔhó·pwəni.   [tɔpíči: uncertain]
/t But John put him off, telling him, "*You* should rather baptize *me*.
/k But John forbad him, saying, I have need to be baptized of thee,

(p. 20) /b quh vuh nvakaliun?
/p kwáč=háč nhaká·lian?"
/t Why do you rely on me?"
/k and comest thou to me?

Mt 3.15 /b Jwk Nhesus tclapani, Konu bqc nani lrkch;
/p šúkw nčí·sas təlá·p·ani, "kóna yúkwe nə́ni lé·k·eč,
/t But Jesus said to him, "Let that be done now,
/k And Jesus answering said unto him, Suffer it to be so now:

/b rli nani lexenufq ktclih pavkunhi lisenrn wrmi jaxakawswakun.
/p é·li- ná=ní -li·x·í·nankw, ktə́li-=č -pahkánči-lərs·í·ne·n wé·mi šaxahka·wsəwá·k·an."
/t for that is what is set for us, to make all righteousness complete."
/k for thus it becometh us to fulfil all righteousness.

/b Nu qwlsitaon.
/p ná kwəlsə́t·aɔ·n.
/t Then he did what he asked.
/k Then he suffered him.

Mt 3.16 /b Nhesus keji hvopunwntc, nu kopanrp,
/p nčí·sas kíši-čhɔ·pwənə́nte, ná kɔp·á·ne·p.

/t   After Jesus was baptized, he went out of the water.
/k   And Jesus, when he was baptized, went up straightway out of the water:

/b   ok nrli patumatup, vokwf taoluvkunumawn,
/p   ɔ́·k né·li-pa·tamá·t·əp, hɔ́kunk taɔ·lahkənəmáɔ·n.
/t   And then while he was praying, a hole in heaven was opened to him.
/k   and, lo, the heavens were opened unto him,

/b   nu wnronrp Kejrlumwrlethi Hehuful tcli vokif prthevlalen, tclenaqsen mrmrtvakrmwf,
/p   ná wəne·ɔ́·ne·p ki·š·e·ləməwe·lí·č·i či·čánkɔl, tə́li- hɔ́k·enk -pe·č·ihəlá·li·n, təli·ná·kwsi·n me·me·thaké·munk.
/t   Then he saw God the spirit coming to him, looking like a dove.
/k   and he saw the Spirit of God descending like a dove, and lighting upon him:

Mt 3.17 /b   nu aptonakun prthevulrp osavkumc wunhi, lwrw,   [⟨-rw⟩ for ⟨-rww⟩]
/p   ná a·pto·ná·k·an pe·č·íhəle·p ɔ·s·áhkame wə́nči, luwe·yó·u,
/t   Then a voice came from heaven, saying,
/k   And lo a voice from heaven, saying,

/b   Nul ta wuni rvoluk Fwes, vokif nwnhi wlrlintum.
/p   "nál=tá wáni ehɔ́·lak nkwí·s; hɔ́k·enk núnči-wəle·ləntam.
/t   "This is my son that I love; I am pleased because of him."
/k   This is my beloved Son, in whom I am well pleased.

Lk 3.23 /b   Mrhi Nhesus ncki lukveqc alumi avpami xentxki txi kavtinamwp.
/p   mé·či nčí·sas néke ləkhíkwi áləmi- ahpá·mi xí·nxke -txí-kahtə́namo·p.
/t   At that time Jesus had begun to be about thirty years old.
/k   And Jesus himself began to be about thirty years of age, ...

Chapter 13 (pp. 20-21). [L. section 12.] (Luke 4.1-2, 6-7, 13; Matthew 4.1, 3-8, 10; Mark 1.13.)

Lk 4.1 /b   Nhesus mrhi wlavulatc Pelselet Hehufu, qtwkep wunhi Nhutun,
/p   nčí·sas mé·či wəlahəlá·t·e pi·lsí·li·t či·čánkɔ, kwtə́k·i·p wə́nči †nčátan.
/t   After Jesus had the holy spirit, he went back from the Jordan.
/k   And Jesus being full of the Holy Ghost returned from Jordan,

/b   tolomoxulaul nani Hehuf trkunu li,
/p   tɔləmo·x·ɔlá·ɔl náni či·čankw té·kəna lí,
/t   The spirit led him into the wilderness,
/k   and was led by the Spirit into the wilderness,

Mt 4.1 /b rlih avqrhevkwk mavtuntwul.
/p é·li-=č -ahkwe·č·íhkuk mahtant·ó·wal.
/t for the devil to tempt him.
/k ... to be tempted of the devil.

Mk 1.13 /b Nrenxkc txoqwnc wethropani yrsisu,
/p ne·í·nxke txó·k·wəni wwi·č·e·ó·p·ani aesə́s·a.
/t He was with the wild animals for forty days.
/k And he was there in the wilderness forty days, [tempted of Satan;] and was with the wild beasts; ...

/b nancsoki mavtuntwul avqrvhevkwn,   [⟨qrvhevk⟩ for ⟨qrhevk⟩]
/p ná=nə só·ki- mahtant·ó·wal -ahkwe·č·íhko·n.
/t For that long the devil tempted him.
/k ... tempted of Satan; ...

Lk 4.2 /b ok nanu soki mutu metsewnrp; nu kunh kotopwenrp.
/p ó·k ná=nə só·ki- máta -mi·tsí·wəne·p; ná kə́nč kot·o·p·wí·ne·p.
/t And for that long he did not eat; only then was he hungry.
/k [Being forty days tempted of the devil.] And in those days he did eat nothing: and when they were ended, he afterward hungered.

Mt 4.3 /b Praletc qrqrthekwki, tclkwl,
/p pe·a·lí·t·e kwe·k·we·č·ihkúk·i, tə́lko·l,
/t When the one who tempted him came, he said to him,
/k And when the tempter came to him, he said,

/b Kehi Qesumwkwnc Kejrlumwrt, lwrl avponekch bl asinul.
/p "khičí·i kkwi·s·əmúk·ɔne ki·š·e·ləmúwe·t, lúwe·l, 'ahpɔ·ní·k·eč yó·l ahsə́nal.' "
/t "If you are truly the son of God, say, 'Let these stones be bread.' "
/k If thou be the Son of God, command that these stones be made bread.

Mt 4.4 /b Jwk tclawl lrkvasw ta tclih mutu awrn avpon jwk wunhi lrlrxrwun, wlava wtoptonakun cntxaptwnrt nani Kejrlumwrt.
/p šúkw təlá·ɔl, "le·khá·s·u=tá, tə́li-=č máta awé·n ahpɔ́·n šúkw -wə́nči-lehəle·x·é·wən, wəláha wtɔ·pto·ná·k·an entxa·ptó·ne·t náni ki·š·e·ləmúwe·t."
/t But he said to him, "It is written that no one shall live by bread alone, rather (by) every word that God utters."
/k But he answered and said, It is written, Man shall not live by bread alone, but by every word that proceedeth out of the mouth of God.

Mt 4.5 /b Nunu mavtuntw tolomoxalanrp, li pelvik wtrnif,
/p ná ná mahtánt·u tɔləmo·x·ɔlá·ne·p lí pí·lhik o·t·é·nink,
/t Then the devil took him to the holy city,
/k Then the devil taketh him up into the holy city,

	/b	wnepalan patamwrekanif xqetakc.
	/p	wəní·p·ala·n pa·tamwe·i·k·á·ɔnink xkwi·t·á·k·e.
	/t	and stood him on the roof of the temple.
	/k	and setteth him on a pinnacle of the temple,

Mt 4.6 /b Nu tclan, Kehe Qesumwkwnc Kejrlumwrt; punakhcvuli b wunhi,
/p ná tə́la·n, "khičí·i kkwi·s·əmúk·ɔne ki·š·e·ləmúwe·t, pəna·kčéhəli yú wə́nči.
/t Then he said to him, "If you are truly the son of God, jump down from here.
/k And saith unto him, If thou be the Son of God, cast thyself down:

/b rli lrkvasw, Rvalokalathih qrnavkevqwh wnaxkwaifh wunhi uspunwkw,
/p é·li le·khá·s·u, 'ehalo·ka·lá·č·i=č kwe·nahkíhku=č, wənaxkəwá·ink=č wwə́nči-aspənúk·u,
/t For it is written, 'His angels shall take care of him and lift him up in their hands,
/k for it is written, He shall give his angels charge concerning thee: and in their hands they shall bear thee up,

/b wunhi mutu kjetrxif ksetul avsinif.
/p wə́nči- máta -kši·té·x·ink ksí·t·al ahsə́nink."
/t so that your feet are not hurt on a stone."
/k lest at any time thou dash thy foot against a stone.

Mt 4.7 /b Nhesus tclawl, Ok lupi lrkvasw; Kahi avqrheverkuh Nrvlalkwn Kejrlumwkwn.
/p nčí·sas təlá·ɔl, "ó·k lápi le·khá·s·u, 'káči ahkwe·č·i·hié·k·ač nehəlá·lkɔn, ki·š·e·ləmúk·ɔn.' "
/t Jesus said to him, "And again it is written,'Do not tempt your Lord, your God (*lit.*, creator).' "
/k Jesus said unto him, It is written again, Thou shalt not tempt the Lord thy God.

Mt 4.8 /b Nu ajiti xqetavtinc tcloxulaul cntu mxutif,   [⟨mx-⟩ for /max-/; ⟨mx-‖utif⟩]
/p ná a·šíte xkwitahtə́ne təlo·x·ɔlá·ɔl énta-maxát·ink.
/t Then instead he took him to the top of a high mountain.
/k Again, the devil taketh him up into an exceeding high mountain,

Lk 4.5   /b pwnuntulanrp wrmi sakemaokun bv prmvakumekrk,
(p. 21) /p pwənuntəlá·ne·p wé·mi sa·k·i·ma·ɔ́·k·an yúh pe·mhakamí·k·e·k,
/t And he showed him all the kingdoms of the world
/k ... shewed unto him all the kingdoms of the world

/b qwti spufwruliokunc lukviqi;   [⟨spufwruliokunc⟩ for ⟨spufwrvlrokunc⟩]
/p kwə́t·i spankwehəle·ɔ́·k·ane ləkhíkwi.
/t in one instant of time.
/k in a moment of time.

Lk 4.6 /b wtclapani nu mavtuntw, Wrmih b liswakun kumelun,
/p wtəlá·p·ani ná mahtánt·u, "wé·mi=č yú ləs·əwá·k·an kəmíllən,
/t The devil said to him, "All this power I shall give you,
/k And the devil said unto him, All this power will I give thee,

/b ok nc muxifwrlumwkswakun,   [⟨mux-⟩ for ⟨mox-⟩]
/p ó·k nə́ mɔx·inkwe·ləmukwsəwá·k·an,
/t and their glory,   ['their': representative singular, construed as anim.]
/k and the glory of them:

/b rli nevelatumun ntcli a awvrn melan.
/p é·li-nihəlá·t·aman ntə́li-=á· awé·n -mí·la·n.
/t for I have control over possibly giving it to anyone.
/k for that is delivered unto me; and to whomsoever I will I give it.

Lk 4.7 /b Bqc a wlukunemeanc, wrmih knevlatumun.
/p yúkwe=á· wəlak·əni·miáne, wé·mi=č kənihəlá·t·amən."
/t If you would worship me now, all of it will be yours."
/k If thou therefore wilt worship me, all shall be thine.

Mt 4.10 /b Jwk Nhesus tclapani, Pali al mavtuntw,
/p šúkw nčí·sas təlá·p·ani, "palí á·l, mahtánt·u,
/t But Jesus said to him, "Get away, devil,
/k Then saith Jesus unto him, Get thee hence, Satan:

/b rli lrkvasw, kmuxifovkunemuh Nrvlalkwn Kejrlumwkwn.
/p é·li le·khá·s·u, 'kəmax·inkɔhkəní·ma=č nehəlá·lkɔn, ki·š·e·ləmúk·ɔn.'
/t for it is written, 'You shall worship your Lord, your God.'"
/k for it is written, Thou shalt worship the Lord thy God, ...

Lk 4.13 /b Nu mavtuntw keji avqrhevatc, paletonrp luvupu.
/p ná mahtánt·u kíši-ahkwe·č·i·há·t·e, palí·i tó·ne·p lahápa.
/t Then after the devil finished tempting him, he departed for a while.
/k And when the devil had ended all the temptation, he departed from him for a season.

Mt 4.11 /b Nu nrl rvalokalinhi otxwkwnrp my evalokalauk.
/p ná né·l ehalo·ka·lə́nči o·txuk·ó·ne·p, mái-ihalo·ka·lá·ɔk.
/t Then the angels went to him to be servants.   [*lit.*, 'they went to be given tasks']
/k ... and, behold, angels came and ministered unto him.

Chapter 14 (p. 21). [L. section 13.] (John 1.19-28.)

Jn 1.19 /b Nhelwsulumeuk alokalrpanek, wrvevwfrlethi, ok Lepyeuk,
/p †nči·lo·sələmí·ɔk alo·ka·lé·p·ani·k wehi·hunke·lí·č·i, ó·k †li·paí·ɔk;

Text, Transcription, and Translation

/t The people of Jerusalem sent priests, and Levites;
/kl ... the Jews sent priests and Levites from Jerusalem

/b moi lawaul Nhanul, Awrn vuh kvaky?
/p mói-lawwá·ɔl nčá·nal, "awé·n=háč khák·ay?"
/t they went and asked (*lit.*, said to) John, "Who are you?"
/kl to ask him, Who art thou?

Jn 1.20
/b Jr b rlatup, jaxakathemwp mutu paswrep, tcli mutu Flystewun. [⟨Fl-⟩ for ⟨Kl-⟩]
/p šé· yú e·lá·t·ǝp: šaxahka·č·í·mo·p, máta pahsǝwé·i·p, tǝ́li- máta -kǝlaistí·wǝn.
/t This is what he said: he told the truth and did not deny that he was not Christ.
/k And he confessed, and denied not; but confessed, I am not the Christ.

Jn 1.21
/b Lupi tclawaul, Awrn kselav? Elyus vuh kvaky?
/p lápi tǝlawwá·ɔl, "awé·n=ksí=láh? †i·láyas=háč khák·ay?"
/t Again they said to him, "Who, then? Are you Elias?"
/k And they asked him, What then? Art thou Elias?

/b tclaul, Takw ta.
/p tǝlá·ɔl, "takó·=tá."
/t He said to them, "No."
/k And he saith, I am not.

/b Mutu vuh ke, nani nrnekanewrwset?
/p máta=háč kí· náni nehǝni·k·a·ní·i-wé·wsi·t?"
/t "Are *you* not that prophet?"
/k Art thou that prophet?

/b tclaul, Takw.
/p tǝlá·ɔl, "takó·."
/t He said to them, "No."
/k And he answered, No.

Jn 1.22
/b Nu lapi tclawpani, Awrn vuh kvaky kehe? [⟨tclawpani⟩ for ⟨tclawapani⟩]
/p ná lápi tǝlawwá·p·ani, "awé·n=háč khák·ay khičí·i?"
/t Then they again said to him, "Who are you really?"
/k Then said they unto him, Who art thou?

/b rli kavtav athemwlxcf prtalokalqifek.
/p é·li-káhta-a·č·i·mó·lxenk pe·t·alo·ka·lkwénki·k.
/t For we want to report to those that sent us.
/k that we may give an answer to them that sent us.

           /b   Krkw vuh ktclakunemu kvaky.
           /p   kéku=háč ktəlahkəní·ma khák·ay?"
           /t   What do you say about yourself?"
           /k   What sayest thou of thyself?

Jn 1.23   /b   Lwrp, Ne ta puntakvwk kanjalamwif, trkunu tali,
           /p   lúwe·p, "ní·=tá pəntá·khɔk kanšalá·mwink té·kəna táli.
           /t   He said, "I am the sound of screaming heard in the wilderness.
           /k   He said, I am the voice of one crying in the wilderness,

           /b   wcnhavkinumu rath Nrvlalwrt, rlwrtup nrnekanewrwsetpanu Esrusu.
           /p   'wenčahkə́nəmaw é·a·t=č nehəlá·ləwe·t,' e·ləwé·t·əp nehəni·k·a·ní·i-we·wsi·tpána
                 †i·se·yə́s·a.
           /t   'Make ready the way that the Lord will go,' as the prophet Esaias said."
           /k   Make straight the way of the Lord, as said the prophet Esaias.

Jn 1.24   /b   Nrk rlokalintpanek, Palusee lakrwpanek.
           /p   né·k e·lo·ka·ləntpáni·k †pa·ləsi·í·i-la·ke·yó·p·ani·k.
           /t   Those that were sent were of the sect (*lit.*, tribe) of the Pharisees.
           /k   And they which were sent were of the Pharisees.

Jn 1.25   /b   Tclawapani Koh vuh hvopunwrun,
           /p   təlawwá·p·ani, "kɔ́č=háč čhɔ·pwənəwé·an,
           /t   They said to him, "Why do you baptize people,
           /k   And they asked him, and said unto him, Why baptizest thou then,

           /b   mutu xa Klysteonc, ok mutu Elyuseonc, ok nuni nrnekanewrwseteonc?
           /p   máta=x=á· kəlaistí·ɔne, ɔ́·k máta i·layas·í·ɔne,
                 ɔ́·k náni nehəni·k·a·ní·i-we·wsi·t·í·ɔne?"
           /t   if in fact you are not Christ, and not Elias, and not that prophet?"
           /k   if thou be not that Christ, nor Elias, neither that prophet?

Jn 1.26   /b   Nhan nuxkwmapani, tclapani, Mpif ntevili hvopunwc,
           /p   nčá·n nɔxko·má·p·ani, təlá·p·ani, "mpínk ntíhəli-čhɔ·pwənúwe,
           /t   John answered them, saying to them, "I baptize people in water,
           /k   John answered them, saying, I baptize with water:

           /b   jwk kwethekrmkwu awrn, mutu wrovarq,
           /p   šúkw kəwi·č·i·k·e·mkúwa awé·n máta we·ɔ·há·e·kw.
           /t   but there is a neighbor of yours that you do not know.
           /k   but there standeth one among you, whom ye know not;

Jn 1.27   /b   nrku ta wrtrkaet, ntalovekaoq,   [⟨kaoq⟩ for ⟨kaq⟩]
           /p   né·k·a=tá we·t·é·kai·t ntaluhíka·kw.
           /t   He who comes after me is greater than me.
           /k   He it is, who coming after me is preferred before me,

/b mothepavkul nontyrlinsen luxunimun.
/p mɔč·ípahkɔl nnuntae·lə́nsi·n llax·ənə́mən."
/t I do not feel worthy to untie his shoes."
/k whose shoe's latchet I am not worthy to unloose.

Jn 1.28 /b Bqc bv rlrk, Pctuprli tali lrp tupisqi kamif Nhutun Nhan cntu hvopunwrtup. ‖
/p yúkwe yúh é·le·k, †petapé·li táli-lé·p, tpə́skwi ká·mink †nčátan, nčá·n énta-čhɔ·pwənəwé·t·əp.
/t This thing that happened happened in Bethabara, on the opposite side of the Jordan from where John baptized people.
/k These things were done in Bethabara beyond Jordan, where John was baptizing.

Chapter 15 (pp. 22-23). [L. section 14.] (John 1.29-51.)

Jn 1.29 /b Lupi opufc Nhan wnropani Nhesusul prat,
(p. 22) /p lápi ɔ·p·ánke nčá·n wəne·ɔ́·p·ani nči·sás·al pé·a·t.
/t The next day John saw Jesus coming.
/k The next day John seeth Jesus coming unto him,

/b nu tclwrn, Pwnw, Kejrlumwrt mrketit, palerloxataq motawswakunelet b cntu lawselethi,
/p ná tə́ləwe·n, "pənó· ki·š·e·ləmúwe·t mekí·t·ət, palí·i e·lúxɔhta·kw mot·a·wsəwa·k·aní·li·t yú entala·wsi·lí·č·i.
/t And then he said, "Regard God the lamb, who takes away the sins of mankind.
/kl and saith, Behold the Lamb of God, which taketh away the sin of the world.

Jn 1.30 /b nul ta wuni rlwranup nwtrkaoq, ntalovekaoq, rli nekanetametup.
[⟨kaoq⟩ for ⟨kaq⟩ 2x]
/p nál=tá wáni e·ləwe·á·nəp, 'no·t·é·ka·kw, ntaluhíka·kw, é·li-ni·k·a·ni·tamí·t·əp.
/t This is the one of whom I said, 'He comes after me and is over me, as he was before me.
/kl This is he of whom I said, After me cometh a man which is preferred before me: for he was before me.

Jn 1.31 /b Mpav hvopunwrn li mpif, wunhi mpwnwntulan Isliluk.   [garbled]
/p mpá čhɔ·pwənúwe·n lí mpínk, wə́nči mpənúntəla·n †isəlɔ́lak.
[mpá, núnči-čhɔ·pwənúwe·n lí mpínk, lí-pənúntəla·n †isəlɔ́lak.   (emended)]
/t I came, and I baptized people in water so that he will be shown to the Israelites.
/kl [And I knew him not: but] that he should be made manifest to Israel, therefore am I come baptizing with water.

Jn 1.32 /b Nhan qetathemwlxapani, Nrop Hehufq prthevlat wunhi vokwf,
/p nčá·n kwi·ta·č·i·mo·lxá·p·ani, "nné·ɔ·p čí·čankw pe·č·íhəla·t wə́nči hɔ́kunk
/t John testified to them, "I saw the spirit that came from up above.
/k And John bare record, saying, I saw the Spirit descending from heaven

/b   mrmrtvakrmwf lenaksw, vokif li naovlrp.
/p   me·me·thaké·munk li·ná·kwsu; hók·enk lí-naóhəle·p.
/t   It looked like a dove, and it landed on him.
/k   like a dove, and it abode upon him.

Jn 1.33
/b   Mutu nunawep,
/p   máta nnənaó·i·p.
/t   I did not know who he was.
/k   And I knew him not:

/b   jwk prtalwkaletup ntclih mpif hvopunwrn, nul nuni ntclkwp,
/p   šúkw pe·t·alo·ka·lí·t·əp ntəli-=č mpínk -čhɔ·pwənúwe·n, nál náni ntəlko·p,
/t   But the one who sent me to baptize people in water was the one that told me,
/k   but he that sent me to baptize with water, the same said unto me,

/b   vokifh awrn, nrotc tcli prthevlalen Hehufu, ok tcli nani avpelen,
/p   "hók·enk=č awé·n ne·ót·e təli-pe·č·ihəlá·li·n či·čánkɔ, ó·k təli- nəni -ahpí·li·n,
/t   "If you see the spirit land on someone's body and stay there,
/k   Upon whom thou shalt see the Spirit descending, and remaining on him,

/b   nulh nuni hvopunwrt Pelset Hehufwf.
/p   nál=č náni čhɔ·pwənúwe·t pí·lsi·t či·čánkunk.'
/t   that is the one who baptizes people in the holy spirit.'
/k   the same is he which baptizeth with the Holy Ghost.

Jn 1.34
/b   Nrop, fetathemwi nul ta wuni kehe Kejrlumwrt Qesul.
/p   nné·ɔ·p, nki·ta·č·í·mwi, nál=tá wáni khičí·i ki·š·e·ləmúwe·t kkwí·s·al."
/t   I saw it, and I testify; he is truly the son of God."
/k   And I saw, and bare record that this is the Son of God.

Jn 1.35
/b   Lupi rlavpyrkc nepwp Nhan, ok neju rkrkematpani,
/p   lápi e·lahpa·é·k·e ní·p·o·p nčá·n, ó·k ní·š·a e·k·e·ki·ma·tpáni.
/t   The next morning John was standing, along with two of his disciples.
/k   Again the next day after John stood, and two of his disciples;

Jn 1.36
/b   nrotc Nhesus prmskalet, lwrp, Punw, Kejrlumwrt mrketit.   [s.b. ⟨Nhesusul⟩,
/p   ne·ó·t·e nčí·sas pe·mská·li·t, lúwe·p, "pənó· ki·š·e·ləmúwe·t mekí·t·ət."   nči·sás·al]
/t   When he saw Jesus walking, he said, "Regard God the lamb."
/k   And looking upon Jesus as he walked, he saith, Behold the Lamb of God!

Jn 1.37
/b   Nrk neju rkrkematpani pwntawaul rlwrlet, wtrkawapani Nhesusul.
/p   né·k ní·š·a e·k·e·ki·ma·tpáni pwəntaɔwwá·ɔl e·ləwé·li·t, o·t·e·kaɔwwá·p·ani
     nči·sás·al.   [obv. ppl. construed as prox.]
/t   Those two disciples of his heard what he said, and they followed Jesus.
/k   And the two disciples heard him speak, and they followed Jesus.

Jn 1.38
/b Nhesus qrtkwqrtc wnropani tcli wtrkakwn;
/p nčí·sas kwe·tko·kwé·t·e, wəne·ɔ́·p·ani o·t·e·ká·k·o·n,
/t When Jesus turned his head, he saw them following him,
/k Then Jesus turned, and saw them following,

/b tclapani, Krkw knatwnumwvwmw?
/p təlá·p·ani, "kéku kənat·o·namúhəmɔ?"
/t and he said to them, "What are you seeking?"
/k and saith unto them, What seek ye?

/b tclawapani, Rkrkemqif ta vuh kweken?
/p təlawwá·p·ani, "e·k·e·kí·mkwenk, tá=háč kəwí·k·i·n?"
/t They said to him, "Teacher (*lit.*, he who teaches us), where do you live?"
/k They said unto him, Rabbi, (which is to say, being interpreted, Master,) where dwellest thou?

Jn 1.39
/b Wehreq knrmunruh.
/p "wi·č·é·i·kw; kəne·məné·ɔ=č."
/t "Come with me; you will see it."
/k [He saith unto them,] Come and see.

/b Eku prpanek wnrmunrop wekelet.
/p íka pé·p·ani·k, wəne·məné·ɔ·p wi·k·í·li·t.
/t They came there, and they saw the house where he lived.
/k They came and saw where he dwelt,

/b Nuni kejqek wtupetawapani, rli mrhi kexki loqekup.
/p náni kí·škwi·k wtap·i·taɔwwá·p·ani, é·li- mé·či kí·xki -lɔ·k·wí·k·əp.
/t That day they stayed with him, as it was already nearly evening.
/k and abode with him that day: for it was about the tenth hour.

Jn 1.40
/b Mawsw nrk puntaotup Nhanul ok wethropani, lwcnswp Antlw, Symun Petul wemavtul.
/p má·wsu né·k pəntaɔ́·t·əp nčá·nal ɔ́·k wwi·č·e·ɔ́·p·ani, luwénso·p †ántəlu, †sáiman-pí·təl wí·mahtal.
/t One of those, who heard John and he followed him, was named Andrew, Simon Peter's brother.
/k One of the two which heard John speak, and followed him, was Andrew, Simon Peter's brother.

Jn 1.41
/b Nuni vetami muxkaopanel nrl wemavtul Symunul.
/p náni hítami mɔxkaɔ́·p·ani·l né·l wí·mahtal †sáimanal.
/t *He* first found his brother Simon.
/k He first findeth his own brother Simon,

/b Telapani numuxkaonu Misyu; mulaji lwrn Klyst,
/p təláˑpˑani, "nəmaxkaóˑwəna †misáya, málahši lúweˑn 'kəláist'."
/t And he said to him, "We have found the Messiah, as if to say 'Christ'."
/k and saith unto him, We have found the Messias, which is, being interpreted, the Christ.

Jn 1.42 /b pwrjwapani Nhesusif.
/p pweˑšˑəwáˑpˑani nčiˑsásˑink.
/t And he brought him to Jesus.
/k And he brought him to Jesus.

/b Nhesus nrotc tclapani, Symun Nhonus qesul kvaky,
/p nčíˑsas neˑóˑtˑe, təláˑpˑani, "†sáiman, †nčóˑnas kkwíˑsˑal khákˑay.
/t When Jesus saw him he said to him, "You are Simon, the son of Jona.
/k And when Jesus beheld him, he said, Thou art Simon the son of Jona:

/b ktclwilkch Avsin. ‖
/p ktələwílke=č 'ahsə́n'.
/t You shall be named 'Stone'.
/k thou shalt be called Cephas, which is by interpretation, A stone.

Jn 1.43 /b Rlavpyrkc Nhesus, Faluleuf kavtu rp,
(p. 23) /p eˑlahpaˑéˑkˑe nčíˑsas †nkaˑlalíˑyunk káhta-éˑp,
/t The next morning Jesus had a desire to go to Galilee.
/k The day following Jesus would go forth into Galilee,

/b muxkaopani Pilupsul, tclapani wehrel.
/p mɔxkaóˑpˑani †pilápsal, təláˑpˑani, "wiˑčˑéˑiˑl."
/t He found Philip and said to him, "Come with me."
/k and findeth Philip, and saith unto him, Follow me.

Jn 1.44 /b Wu Pilups Petsritrif wunheywp wtwtrnif Antlw, ok Petul.
/p wá †pílaps †piˑtseˑitéˑink wənčíˑayoˑp, wtoˑtˑéˑnink †ántəlu óˑk †píˑtəl.
/t This Philip was from Bethsaida, the city of Andrew and Peter.
/k Now Philip was of Bethsaida, the city of Andrew and Peter.

Jn 1.45 /b Pilups muxkaopani Nrtanilu; tclapani,
/p †pílaps mɔxkaóˑpˑani †neˑtáˑnəla, təláˑpˑani,
/t Philip found Nathaniel and said to him,
/k Philip findeth Nathanael, and saith unto him,

/b numuxkawunu nani, Mojiju, ok nrnekanewrwsetpanifu rlrkvotetup;
/p "nəmaxkaóˑwəna náni †moˑšə́šˑa óˑk nehəniˑkˑaˑníˑi-weˑwsiˑtpanínka eˑleˑkhɔhtíˑtˑəp,
/t "We found the one that Moses and the prophets wrote about:
/k We have found him, of whom Moses in the law, and the prophets, did write,

/b Nhesus, Nasulutif wunheyet, Nhosi qesul.
/p nčí·sas, †nasəlát·ink wənčí·ai·t, †nčó·si kkwí·s·al."
/t Jesus, who comes from Nazareth, the son of Josey."
/k Jesus of Nazareth, the son of Joseph.

Jn 1.46 /b Nrtanil tclapani, Kuski vuh a krkw wrlvik wunheyw Nasulutif?
/p †ne·tá·nəl təlá·p·ani, "káski-=háč=á· kéku wé·lhik -wənčí·ayu †nasəlát·ink?"
/t Nathaniel said to him, "Can anything good come from Nazareth?"
/k And Nathanael said unto him, Can there any good thing come out of Nazareth?

/b Pilups tclapani Wuntax al punaw.
/p †pílaps təlá·p·ani, "wə́ntax á·l; pənáw."
/t Philip said to him, "Come and see him."   [*lit.*, 'come here; look at him']
/k Philip saith unto him, Come and see.

Jn 1.47 /b Nhesus wnropani Nrtanilu pralet; tclapani,
/p nčí·sas wəne·ó·p·ani †ne·tá·nəla pe·á·li·t, təlá·p·ani,
/t Jesus saw Nathaniel coming and said to him,
/k Jesus saw Nathanael coming to him, and saith of him,

/b Pcnw, Islilet kehe mutu eavkevokrt.
/p "pənó· †isələli·t khičí·i máta i·ahki·hóke·t."
/t "Regard an Israelite who truly never cheats."
/k Behold an Israelite indeed, in whom is no guile!

Jn 1.48 /b Nrtanil tclapani; Ta vuh kwnhi waven?
/p †ne·tá·nəl təlá·p·ani, "tá=háč kúnči-wwá·hi·n?"
/t Nathaniel said to him, "How come you know me?"
/k Nathanael saith unto him, Whence knowest thou me?

/b Nhesus tclapani,
/p nčí·sas təlá·p·ani,
/t Jesus said to him,
/k Jesus answered and said unto him,

/b Nrlumu Pilups wcnhemkwunc vetkwf, lrmutupeunc knrwlwvwmp.
/p "né·ləma †pílaps wenči·mkó·wane, hítkunk le·mahtap·iáne, kəne·wəlúhump."
/t "Before Philip called you, when you were sitting under a tree, I saw you."
/k Before that Philip called thee, when thou wast under the fig tree, I saw thee.

Jn 1.49 /b Nrtanil tclapani, Rkrkemeif, ke ta Kejrlumwrt Qesul,
/p †ne·tá·nəl təlá·p·ani, "e·k·e·kí·mienk, kí·=tá ki·š·e·ləmúwe·t kkwí·s·al;
/t Nathaniel said to him, "Teacher, *you* are the son of God;
/k Nathanael answered and saith unto him, Rabbi, thou art the Son of God;

	/b	ke ta Islile sakema.
	/p	kíˑ=tá †isələ́líˑi-saˑkˑíˑma.
	/t	*you* are the king of Israel."
	/k	thou art the King of Israel.

Jn 1.50 /b Nhesus tclapani; Rli lilun knrwl li vetkwf, kwnhivuh wlamvetamun?
/p nčíˑsas təláˑpˑani, "éˑli-lə́lan, 'kənéˑwəl lí hítkunk,' kúnči-=háč -wəlaˑmhítamən?"
/t Jesus said to him, "Do you believe because I told you I saw you under a tree?"
/k Jesus answered and said unto him, Because I said unto thee, I saw thee under the fig tree, believest thou?

/b ekalisih ktclenam bqc rlrk.
/p ikalísi=č ktəlíˑnam yúkwe éˑleˑk."
/t You shall see things greater than what happened this time."
/k thou shalt see greater things than these.

Jn 1.51 /b Tclapani, Kukihe ktclwvumw, ktclenumunruh li taolavkut li vokwf
/p təláˑpˑani, "kəkhičíˑi ktəllúhəmɔ, ktəliˑnaməné·ɔ lí-taɔ́·lahkat lí hókunk,
/t And he said to them, "I tell you very truly, you shall see a hole open in heaven,
/k And he saith unto him, Verily, verily, I say unto you, Hereafter ye shall see heaven open,

/b Kejrlumwrt rvalokalathi, pwrthevlanro lino Wrnehanif, ok vokif wunhi.
/p kiˑšˑeˑləmúweˑt ehaloˑkaˑláˑčˑi pweˑčˑihəlaˑné·ɔ / lə́nu weˑniˑčˑáˑnink, ɔ́ˑk hɔ́kˑenk wə́nči. [prox. for obv.]
/t and God's angels coming to the man who is the Son, and from him.
/k and the angels of God ascending and descending upon the Son of man.

Chapter 16 (pp. 23-24). [L. section 15.] (John 2.1-11.)

Jn 2.1 /b Nrxokwnakvakc takwpwvaltenrp, tali Krnrif Faluleuf,
/p neˑxˑoˑkˑwənakháke tahkɔpˑoˑhaˑltíˑneˑp táli †keˑnéˑink, †nkaˑlalíˑyunk.
/t Three days later there was a wedding in Cana, in Galilee.
/k And the third day there was a marriage in Cana of Galilee;

/b eku avpwp Nhesus kovrsu.
/p íka ahpóˑp nčíˑsas kɔhéˑsˑa.
/t Jesus's mother was there.
/k and the mother of Jesus was there:

Jn 2.2 /b Wcnhemapanek Nhesus ok rkrkematpani, cntu takwpwvaltif.
/p wenčiˑmáˑpˑaniˑk nčíˑsas ɔ́ˑk eˑkˑeˑkiˑmaˑtpáni énta-tahkɔpˑoˑháˑltink.
/t Jesus and his disciples were invited to the wedding.
/k And both Jesus was called, and his disciples, to the marriage.

Jn 2.3	/b	Nwntcvlatc wyn, wrnehanul Nhesusul telaul, Wyn mutu wlatweuk.
		[⟨wrnehanul⟩ s.b. ⟨wrnehanet⟩]
	/p	nuntehəláˑtˑe wáin weˑniˑčˑáˑniˑt nčiˑsásˑal, təláˑɔl, "wáin máta wəlaˑtoˑwíˑɔk."
	/t	When there was no wine for Jesus's mother, she told him, "They have no wine."
	/k	And when they wanted wine, the mother of Jesus saith unto him, They have no wine.
Jn 2.4	/b	Nhesus tclaul, Krkw ksi wunhi nahevkun?
	/p	nčíˑsas təláˑɔl, "kéku=ksí wə́nči-naˑčíhkɔn?
	/t	Jesus said to her, "Why does it concern you?
	/k	Jesus saith unto her, Woman, what have I to do with thee?
	/b	Nrlumu tu ntupsqelatac.
	/p	néˑləma=tá ntəpskwilahtáˑi.
	/t	It is not yet time for me."
	/k	mine hour is not yet come.
Jn 2.5	/b	Wrnehanet tclaul nrl alokakunu, Krkwh lwkwrqc nani lisemoi. [⟨lw-‖kwrqc⟩]
	/p	weˑniˑčˑáˑniˑt təláˑɔl néˑl aloˑkáˑkˑana, "kéku=č lukˑwéˑkˑwe, ná=ní ləsˑiˑmɔ́ˑe.
	/t	His mother said to the servants, "If he tells you to do something, do it."
	/k	His mother saith unto the servants, Whatsoever he saith unto you, do it.
Jn 2.6	/b	Nani topenro kwtaj seskwu vwsuk mpi rvatrk,
(p. 24)	/p	náˑní tɔpˑiˑnéˑɔ kwə́tˑaˑš siˑskəwahóˑsˑak, mpí ehhátˑeˑk,
	/t	Six clay vessels for holding water were there,
	/k	And there were set there six waterpots of stone,
	/b	rvcntu pelyvosetet rvrlinumevtetup Nhwuk;
	/p	ehə́nta-piˑlaehɔˑsˑíhtiˑt ehələnəmihtíˑtˑəp nčóˑwak.
	/t	where they performed acts of purification the way the Jews used to do.
	/k	after the manner of the purifying of the Jews,
	/b	neju, jitu nuxa kcluntif trpvatr.
	/p	níˑšˑa ší=tá naxá kelántink teˑphátˑeˑ.
	/t	Two or three gallons could be held (in each).
	/k	containing two or three firkins apiece.
Jn 2.7	/b	Nhesus tclapani, Hovalw bk vwsuk mpi.
	/p	nčíˑsas təláˑpˑani, "čuhɔ́loˑ yóˑk hóˑsˑak mpí."
	/t	Jesus said to them, "Fill these vessels with water."
	/k	Jesus saith unto them, Fill the waterpots with water.
	/b	Nu ovhovprnru. [⟨ovh-⟩ for /ɔwč-/]
	/p	ná ɔwčuwpeˑnéˑɔ.
	/t	Then they were filled to the brim.
	/k	And they filled them up to the brim.

Jn 2.8	/b	Tclapani, Bqc ansvamwq,
	/p	təlá·p·ani, "yúkwe anshámo·kw,
	/t	He told them, "Now dip some up
	/k	And he saith unto them, Draw out now,

/b ok loxatwq krkyimvrtif cntu metsavtif; [⟨loxat⟩ for /lúxɔht-/]
/p ɔ́·k lúxɔhto·kw ke·kayəmhé·t·ink énta-mi·tsáhtink."
/t and take it to the "governor" of the feast.
/k and bear unto the governor of the feast.

/b nu eku tloxavtonro. [⟨tloxavt⟩ for /təluxɔht-/]
/p ná íka təluxɔhto·né·ɔ.
/t Then they took it to him.
/k And they bare it.

Jn 2.9	/b	Nekanexif mrhi qrtantufc b wyn mpif wcnhi manetwf,
	/p	ni·k·a·ní·x·ink mé·či kwe·t·antánke yú wáin mpínk wénči-manní·tunk,
	/t	When the "leader" tasted the wine that had been made from water,
	/k	When the ruler of the feast had tasted the water that was made wine,

/b mutu watwn wcnheyek,
/p máta o·wa·tó·wən wenčí·ai·k.
/t he did not know where it came from.
/k and knew not whence it was:

/b alokakunuk unsvumevtetup, jwk watwnro;
/p alo·ká·k·anak anshamihtí·t·əp šúkw o·wa·to·né·ɔ.
/t Only the servants that had dipped it up knew.
/k (but the servants which drew the water knew;)

/b nekanexif cntu metsavtif wcnhemapanc trkovpwvalinthi linou. [⟨-nc⟩ for ⟨-ni⟩]
/p ni·k·a·ní·x·ink énta-mi·tsáhtink wwenči·má·p·ani tekɔhpo·ha·lə́nči lə́nəwa.
/t The "leader" of the feast called over the man being married.
/k the governor of the feast called the bridegroom,

Jn 2.10	/b	Tclawl, Awrn vufq vetami mrq, wrlvik wyn,
	/p	təlá·ɔl, "awé·n=hánkw hítami mé·kw wé·lhik wáin.
	/t	He said to him, "Usually someone first gives out good wine.
	/k	And saith unto him, Every man at the beginning doth set forth good wine;

/b trprlintumevtetc, nu kcnh nwnty rlrk.
/p te·p·e·ləntamihtí·t·e, ná kə́nč nuntá·i é·le·k.
/t And after they have had enough, then the inferior sort.
/k and when men have well drunk, then that which is worse:

| | /b | Ke xun kwlvatwn wrlvik wyn bqc svaki.
| | /p | kí·=xán ko·lháto·n wé·lhik wáin yúkwe sháki."
| | /t | But *you* kept the good wine until now."
| | /k | but thou hast kept the good wine until now.

Jn 2.11 /b Wnetami konji krkw lyvosenrp, tali Krnr Faluleuf,   [⟨konji⟩ for ⟨kanji⟩]
         /p wəní·tami- kánši-kéku -laehɔ·s·í·ne·p táli †ké·ne· †nka·lalí·yunk,
         /t He performed his first miracle in Cana, in Galilee,
         /k This beginning of miracles did Jesus in Cana of Galilee,

         /b prnwntvekrtc wtaloeliswakun, rkrkemathi wlsitakwpani.
         /p pe·nunthiké·t·e wtaləwí·i-ləs·əwák·an; e·k·e·ki·má·č·i o·lsət·a·k·ó·p·ani.
         /t when he showed his power; and his disciples believed him.
         /k and manifested forth his glory; and his disciples believed on him.

Chapter 17 (pp. 24-25). [L. section 16.] (John 2.12-25.)

Jn 2.12 /b Lwev lrkc, nu Kupunium rp,
         /p ló·wi-lé·k·e, ná †kapə́niam é·p,
         /t After it was over, he went to Capernaum,
         /k After this he went down to Capernaum,

         /b nrku ok kovrsu ok wxesmusu, navle rkrkemathi;   [⟨wx-⟩ for /xw-/]
         /p né·k·a ɔ́·k kɔhé·s·a ɔ́·k xwi·s·əmə́s·a, nahəlí·i e·k·e·ki·má·č·i;
         /t he and his mother, and his younger brothers, as well as his disciples.
         /k he, and his mother, and his brethren, and his disciples:

         /b mutu vwosku xrlwquni avpeepanek.
         /p máta hwə́ska xe·ló·k·wəni ahpi·í·p·ani·k.
         /t They did not stay for very many days.
         /k and they continued there not many days.

Jn 2.13 /b Nhwe xifwi metsavtif pcxwthevlrp; lwcnswp Lwif.
         /p nčo·wí·i-xínkwi-mi·tsáhtink pe·x·o·č·íhəle·p, luwénso·p 'ló·wink',
         /t The time was near for the great Jewish feast called 'Passover',
         /k And the Jews' passover was at hand,

         /b Wunhi Nhesus eku anrp Nhelwsulumif.
         /p wwə́nči- nčí·sas íka -á·ne·p †nči·lo·sələ́mink.
         /t and because of it Jesus went to Jerusalem.
         /k and Jesus went up to Jerusalem,

Jn 2.14 /b Patamwrekanif muxkaopani, mumvalumwnhi aksunul, ok mrkesul, ok mrmrtvakrmwul,
/p pa·tamwe·i·k·á·ɔnink mɔxkaɔ́·p·ani memhalamúnči a·ksə́nal, ɔ́·k mekí·s·al, ɔ́·k me·me·thake·mó·wal,
/t In the temple he found the sellers of oxen, sheep, and doves,
/k And found in the temple those that sold oxen and sheep and doves,

/b ok rvajwntrnifek mwni lrmutupethek.
/p ɔ́·k eha·š·unte·nínki·k mɔ́ni le·mahtap·í·č·i·k.
/t and the changers (*lit.*, traders) of money sitting.
/k and the changers of money sitting:

Jn 2.15 /b Kejetwp seaq, helwkrse tupunasw;
/p ki·š·í·to·p sía·kw, či·lo·k·e·s·í·i, təp·əná·s·u.
/t He made a whip, of leather strips and twisted together.
/k And when he had made a scourge of small cords,

/b qwtskaopani wunhi patamwrekanif, ok mrkesu, ok aksunu,
/p kwətskaɔ́·p·ani pa·tamwe·i·k·á·ɔnink, ɔ́·k mekí·s·a ɔ́·k a·ksə́na.
/t He drove them out of the temple, and the oxen and the sheep.
/k he drove them all out of the temple, and the sheep, and the oxen;

/b ok swkvamun rvajuntrnumulethi mwnemwu.   [⟨s-⟩ for /ws-/]
/p ɔ́·k wso·khámən eha·š·unte·nəməlí·č·i mmɔni·yəmúwa.
/t And he spilled the changers' (*lit.*, traders') money.
/k and poured out the changers' money, and overthrew the tables;

Jn 2.16 /b Tclapanel nrlel mumvalumwnhi mrmrtvakrmwul, Palelwvatwl;
                                    [⟨lwvatwl⟩ for /lúxɔhto·l/]
/p təlá·p·ani·l né·li·l memhalamúnči me·me·thake·mó·wal, "palí·i lúxɔhto·l.
/t He said to those selling doves, "Take it elsewhere.
/k And said unto them that sold doves, Take these things hence;

/b kahi letrvavrq mumvalumuntekaon Nox weket;
/p káči li·t·e·há·he·kw memhalamunti·k·á·ɔn nó·x wí·k·i·t."
/t Don't treat (*lit.*, think of) my father's house as a merchant's store (you pl.)."
/k make not my Father's house an house of merchandise.

Jn 2.17 /b Rkrkemathel mijatumin, ‖ tcli nwhi lrkvaswp,
                     [⟨mij-⟩ for /mwəš·-/; ⟨tcli⟩ for ⟨li⟩, with ms. note "li nenwhi"]
/p e·k·e·ki·má·č·i·l mwəš·á·t·amən, lí·núči·le·khá·s·o·p,   [agreement as prox. sg.]
/t His disciples remembered that it had been written before,
/k And his disciples remembered that it was written,

(p. 25) /b Patamwrekane wejwkswakun nmovwkwn.   [⟨kan⟩ for ⟨kaon⟩]
/p "pa·tamwe·i·k·a·ɔní·i-wi·šəksəwá·k·an nəmuhó·k·o·n."

/t   "The zeal of the temple consumed (*lit.*, ate) me."
/k   The zeal of thine house hath eaten me up.

Jn 2.18 /b   Nhwuk tclawapani, Tavuh lexun kekenwlwakun prnwntuleif,
/p   nčó·wak təlá·p·ani, "tá=háč lí·x·ən khiki·no·ləwá·k·an pe·nuntəlíenk,
/t   The Jews said to him, "What sign is there that you show us,
/k   Then answered the Jews and said unto him, What sign shewest thou unto us,

/b   rli bni lyvoseun?
/p   é·li- yó·ni -laehó·s·ian?"
/t   as you do this?"
/k   seeing that thou doest these things?

Jn 2.19 /b   Nhesus tclapani, Paletwq bni patamwrekaon,
/p   nčí·sas təlá·p·ani, "palí·to·kw yó·ni pa·tamwe·i·k·á·ɔn.
/t   Jesus said to them, "Destroy this temple.
/k   Jesus answered and said unto them, Destroy this temple,

/b   muxoqunakvakch lupi ntuspetwn.   [⟨mux-⟩ for ⟨nux-⟩]
/p   naxo·k·wənakháke=č lápi ntaspí·to·n."
/t   In three days I will raise it up again."
/k   and in three days I will raise it up.

Jn 2.20 /b   Nu tclwrnrop, nrentxki ok qwtaj kavtinri manetaswp patamwrekaon;
/p   ná tələwe·né·ɔ·p, "ne·í·nxke ó·k kwə́t·a·š kahtəné·i manni·tá·s·o·p
     pa·tamwe·i·k·á·ɔn.
/t   They they said, "The temple was built in forty-six years.
/k   Then said the Jews, Forty and six years was this temple in building,

/b   keh vuh nuxi kejqekc, tuspakunimun?   [⟨t-⟩ for ⟨kt-⟩]
/p   kí·=č=háč náxi-ki·škwí·k·e ktaspa·k·ənə́mən?"
/t   Will you raise it up in three days?"
/k   and wilt thou rear it up in three days?

Jn 2.21 /b   Jwk rlwrtrli vokyet patamwrekaon.
/p   šúkw é·ləwe·t é·li-hók·ai·t pa·tamwe·i·k·á·ɔn.
/t   But what he meant was how his body was a temple.
/k   But he spake of the temple of his body.

Jn 2.22 /b   Mrhi amwetc wunhi ufulwakunif rkrkematpani mijatumunrop,   [⟨mi-⟩: /mwə-/]
/p   mé·či a·mwí·t·e wə́nči ankələwá·k·anink, e·k·e·ki·ma·tpáni mwəš·a·t·aməné·ɔ·p,
/t   After he rose from the dead, his disciples remembered
/k   When therefore he was risen from the dead, his disciples remembered

	/b	tcli nuni lwkwnrop,
	/p	tə́li- nə́ni -luk·o·né·ɔ·p.
	/t	that he had said that to them.
	/k	that he had said this unto them;

	/b	ok wlamvetawapani nrl lrkvekunul, ok rlwrtup Nhesus.
	/p	ɔ́·k o·la·mhitaɔwwá·p·ani né·l le·khí·k·anal, ɔ́·k e·ləwé·t·əp nčí·sas.
	/t	And they believed the book and what Jesus had said.
	/k	and they believed the scripture, and the word which Jesus had said.

Jn 2.23	/b	Srki avpetup Nhelwsulumif wunhi Lwif nani xifwi metsavtif kejqek;
	/p	sé·ki-ahpí·t·əp †nči·lo·sələmink wə́nči ló·wink, nə́ni xínkwi-mi·tsáhtink kí·škwi·k,
	/t	While he was in Jerusalem for Passover, the day of the great feast,
	/k	Now when he was in Jerusalem at the passover, in the feast day,

	/b	krxwuk wrlamvetufek wtclswakun
	/p	ké·x·əwak we·la·mhitánki·k wtəlsəwá·k·an,
	/t	there were several who believed his powers
	/k	many believed in his name,

	/b	nrmvetetc rlkeqi avkanjyvosetup.
	/p	ne·mhití·t·e e·lkí·kwi-ahkanšaehɔ·s·í·t·əp.
	/t	when they saw how great were the miracles he performed.
	/k	when they saw the miracles which he did.

Jn 2.24	/b	Nhesus mutu eku totwun voky, rli wavaul wrmi awrn, [⟨awrn⟩ for ⟨awrni⟩]
	/p	nčí·sas máta íka tɔ·tó·wən hók·ay, é·li o·wa·há·ɔl wé·mi awé·ni.
	/t	Jesus did not put himself forth (*lit.*, there), as he knew about everyone.
	/k	But Jesus did not commit himself unto them, because he knew all men, [RSV: "did not trust himself to them"]

Jn 2.25	/b	mutu kotatumwnrp tclkwn awrn rletvat bv cutu lawset; [prox. for obv. 2x]
	/p	máta kɔt·a·t·amó·wəne·p tə́lko·n awé·n e·li·t·é·ha·t yú entalá·wsi·t,
	/t	He did not desire any person to tell him what people thought,
	/k	And needed not that any should testify of man:

	/b	rli wli wavat rlselet.
	/p	é·li-wə́li-wwá·ha·t e·lsí·li·t.
	/t	as he well knew their nature and actions.
	/k	for he knew what was in man.

Chapter 18 (pp. 25-27). [L. section 17.] (John 3.1-21.)

Jn 3.1	/b	Avpwp nu Palusee lino, lwcnswp Nikotemus Krkyimvrt Nhwif tali.
	/p	ahpó·p ná †pa·ləsi·í·i-lə́nu, luwénso·p †nikotí·mas, ke·kayə́mhe·t nčó·wink táli.

/t   There was a Pharisee man named Nicodemus, a ruler among the Jews.
/k   There was a man of the Pharisees, named Nicodemus, a ruler of the Jews:

Jn 3.2   /b   Nul nuni Nhesusif prp peskrwune, tclapani;
/p   nál náni nči·sás·ink pé·p pi·ske·wəní·i, təlá·p·ani,
/t   He it was who came to Jesus at night, and said to him,
/k   The same came to Jesus by night, and said unto him,

/b   Rvakrkifrs nwatwnrn ktcli evavkrkifrn wunhi Kejrlumwrtif,
/p   ehahke·kínke·s, no·wa·tó·ne·n któli-ihahke·kínke·n wə́nči ki·š·e·ləməwé·t·ink.
/t   "Teacher, we know that you are a teacher from God.
/k   Rabbi, we know that thou art a teacher come from God:

/b   mutu awrn a kuski lyvoset kwnjyvoswakun, mutu Kejrlumwrlethi wehrvkwqc.
                                  [⟨lyvoset⟩ for ⟨lyvosei⟩; ⟨kwnj-⟩ for ⟨kanj-⟩]
/p   máta awé·n=á· káski-laehɔ·s·í·i kanšaehɔ·s·əwá·k·an, máta ki·š·e·ləməwe·lí·č·i wi·č·e·ykó·k·we."
/t   No one would be able to perform miracles if God was not with him."
/k   for no man can do these miracles that thou doest, except God be with him.

Jn 3.3   /b   Nhesus tclapani; Kehe kehe ktclun, awrn mutu lupi wuski kejeketc
/p   nčí·sas təlá·p·ani, "khičí·i, khičí·i ktə́llən, awé·n máta lápi wə́ski-ki·š·i·k·í·t·e,
/t   Jesus said to him, "Truly, truly I tell you, if someone is not born again anew,
/k   Jesus answered and said unto him, Verily, verily, I say unto thee, Except a man be born again,

/b   ta koski nrmwun Kejrlumwrt wsakemaokun.
/p   tá=á· kɔ́ski-ne·mó·wən ki·š·e·ləmúwe·t wsa·k·i·ma·ɔ́·k·an."
/t   he will not be able to see the kingdom of God."
/k   he cannot see the kingdom of God.

Jn 3.4   /b   Nikutemus tclapani; Ta vuh a wunhi kuski awrn kejeken mrhi kekyetc?
/p   †nikɔtí·mas təlá·p·ani, "tá=háč=á· wwə́nči-káski- awé·n -ki·š·í·k·i·n mé·či khikaí·t·e?
/t   Nicodemus said to him, "How would anyone be able to be born if they are already old?
/k   Nicodemus saith unto him, How can a man be born when he is old?

/b   kuski vuh a lupi lamatc kovrsif avpw, wunhi a kejeket? ‖
/p   káski-=háč=á· lápi lá·mahte kɔhé·s·ink -ahpú, wə́nči-=á· -ki·š·í·k·i·t?"
/t   Could he be in his mother's womb again, from which he would be born?"
/k   can he enter the second time into his mother's womb, and be born?

Jn 3.5   /b   Nhesus tclapani. Kehe heke ktclun,
(p. 26)   /p   nčí·sas təlá·p·ani, "khičí·i, khičí·i ktə́llən,
          /t   Jesus said to him, "Truly, truly I tell you,
          /k   Jesus answered, Verily, verily, I say unto thee,

          /b   Mutu kejekeqc mpif wunhi ok hehwfwf,
          /p   máta ki·š·i·k·í·k·we mpínk wə́nči ó·k či·čánkunk,
          /t   if he is not born from water and the spirit,
          /k   Except a man be born of water and of the Spirit,

          /b   muta tumekrun Kejrlumwrt wsakemaokun.   [⟨t-⟩ for ⟨wt-⟩ (ms. note adds ⟨w⟩)]
          /p   máta=á· wtəmi·k·é·wən ki·š·e·ləmúwe·t wsa·k·i·ma·ó·k·an."
          /t   he will not enter the kingdom of God.
          /k   he cannot enter into the kingdom of God.

Jn 3.6   /b   Wavtwvrpif, wcnhekif wavtwvrpiw vufq,
          /p   "wahtuhé·p·ink wenčí·k·ink wahtuhe·p·í·yu=hánkw,
          /t   "What is born from flesh (lit., body) is flesh,
          /k   That which is born of the flesh is flesh;

          /b   ok awrn hehufwakunif wcnhekif hehufw vufq.
          /p   ó·k awé·n či·čankəwá·k·anink wenčí·k·ink či·čánku=hánkw.   [awé·n is spurious]
          /t   and what is born from spirit is spirit.
          /k   and that which is born of the Spirit is spirit.

Jn 3.7   /b   Kahi kanjalintufvun rli lilun, ktcli a lupi kejeken.   [⟨kanjal-⟩ for ⟨kanjrl-⟩]
          /p   káči kanše·ləntánkhan é·li-lə́lan, ktə́li-=á· lápi -ki·š·í·k·i·n.
          /t   Don't be amazed that I tell you that you should be born again.'
          /k   Marvel not that I said unto thee, Ye must be born again.

Jn 3.8   /b   Krjxif vufq nevlatamwrw; piji kpuntamun prmvetaku;
                    [⟨-rw⟩ for /-e·yó·u/: BPL copy has a caret below (cf. ⟨-rbw⟩ in Jn 4.37)]
          /p   ké·šxink=hánkw nihəla·t·amwe·yó·u; píši kpə́ntamən pe·mhitá·k·ɔ,
          /t   The wind blows freely (lit., is free, autonomous); you do hear its sound,
          /k   The wind bloweth where it listeth, and thou hearest the sound thereof,

          /b   jwk mutu kuski watwun tutu wcnhivulak, jita rlivulak.
          /p   šúkw máta kkáski-wwa·tó·wən wenčíhəla·k, ší=tá e·líhəla·k.
          /t   but you cannot tell where it comes from or where it goes.
          /k   but canst not tell whence it cometh, and whither it goeth:

          /b   Jr nuni tclsen awrn cntxi kejeket hehufuwakunif wunhi.
          /p   šé· nə́ni tə́lsi·n éntxi-ki·š·í·k·i·t či·čankəwá·k·anink wə́nči."
          /t   This is how it is with everyone who is born from the spirit."
          /k   so is every one that is born of the Spirit.

Text, Transcription, and Translation

Jn 3.9 /b Nikutemus tclapani, Tani vam ct wunhi kuski nc lrw?
                [ms. note in BPL copy changes ⟨Tani⟩ to ⟨Tane⟩ (intending /=néh/)]
    /p †nikɔtí·mas təlá·p·ani, "tá=néh=á·m=ét wə́nči-káski- nə́ -lé·w?"
    /t Nicodemus said to him, "How could that posssibly be so?"
    /k Nicodemus answered and said unto him, How can these things be?

Jn 3.10 /b Nhesus tclapani Islilif krkyimvrt vuh ke kvaky,
    /p nčí·sas təlá·p·ani, "†isələ́link ke·kayə́mhe·t=háč kí· khák·ay,
    /t Jesus said to him, "Are you a ruler in Israel,
    /k Jesus answered and said unto him, Art thou a master of Israel,

    /b ok mutu kwatwun bni rlrk?
    /p ɔ́·k máta ko·wa·tó·wən yó·ni é·le·k?
    /t and you do not know these things (*lit.*, this) that happened?
    /k and knowest not these things?

Jn 3.11 /b Kehe kehe ktclun;
    /p khičí·i, khičí·i ktə́llən,
    /t Truly, truly, I tell you,
    /k Verily, verily, I say unto thee,

    /b nelwnu ntclaptwncvinu krkw wrotyif, ok mpunwntvekrnrn krkw nrmif
    /p ni·ló·na ntəla·pto·néhəna kéku we·ɔ́·taenk, ɔ́·k mpənunthiké·ne·n kéku né·menk,
    /t we report things we know about and testify to (*lit.*, show) things we have seen,
    /k We speak that we do know, and testify that we have seen;

    /b jwk mutu kwrtunimwnru mpunwntvekrokuninu.
    /p šúkw máta kəwe·t·ənəmo·wəné·ɔ mpənunthike·ɔ·k·anə́na.
    /t but you (pl.) do not accept our testimony.
    /k and ye receive not our witness.

Jn 3.12 /b Eli a lilrqc, bni rlrk xqetvakumeqc, mutu a kwlamvetyvwmo,
    /p ílli=á· ləlé·k·we yó·ni é·le·k xkwi·thakamí·k·we, máta=á· ko·la·mhitai·húmɔ.
    /t You won't believe me even if I tell you what happens here on earth.
    /k If I have told you earthly things, and ye believe not,

    /b ta vuh a kwnhi wlamvetaminru lilrqc rlrk osavkamc?
    /p tá=háč=á· kúnči-wəla·mhitaməné·ɔ ləlé·k·we é·le·k ɔ·s·áhkame?
    /t How would you believe it if I tell you what happens in heaven?
    /k how shall ye believe, if I tell you of heavenly things?

Jn 3.13 /b Takw awrn avpe osavkamc pcvpat;
    /p takó· awé·n ahpí·i ɔ·s·áhkame péhpa·t,
    /t There is no one who has ever been to heaven,
    /k And no man hath ascended up to heaven,

	/b	jwk nuni wifwp lino Wrqesumwkwk osavkumc rpelethi.
	/p	šúkw nə́ni wénkəp lə́nu, we·k·wi·s·əmúk·wək ɔ·s·áhkame e·p·i·lí·č·i.
	/t	except the man who came from there, the son of the one who is in heaven.
	/k	but he that came down from heaven, even the Son of man which is in heaven.

Jn 3.14 /b Mulaji Mwjiju uspunaotup uxkwkul trkunu tali,   [ms. caret below ⟨o⟩ of ⟨nao⟩
                                                            and slanting line below ⟨u⟩ of ⟨uxk⟩, presumably to delete them]
    /p málahši mo·šə́š·a aspəná·t·əp xkó·k·al té·kəna táli.
    /t Like Moses, who lifted up the snake in the wilderness,
    /k And as Moses lifted up the serpent in the wilderness,

    /b nuh ok nc lino Wrqesumwkwk li uspunaon   [ms. caret below ⟨o⟩ of ⟨nao⟩,
                                                            presumably to delete it]
    /p ná=č ɔ́·k nə́ lə́nu we·k·wi·s·əmúk·wək lí-áspəna·n,
    /t that is also how the man who is the son of him shall be lifted up,
    /k even so must the Son of man be lifted up:

Jn 3.15 /b wcnhih cntxi wlamvetufek mutu tafulevtet,   [⟨taf⟩ for ⟨taof⟩: ms. caret below ⟨af⟩]
    /p wénči-=č éntxi-wəla·mhitánki·k máta -taɔnkəlíhti·t,
    /t so that all those that believe will not be lost,
    /k That whosoever believeth in him should not perish,

    /b jwk nuxpawsevtet rvalumwqwnaku pumawswakun.
    /p šúkw -naxpa·wsíhti·t ehaləmo·k·wənák·a pəma·wsəwá·k·an.
    /t but have (*lit.*, live having) life forever.
    /k but have eternal life.

Jn 3.16 /b Kejrlumwrt tulvkeqc avolan bni cntu lawselethek,   [⟨qc⟩: ms. caret under ⟨c⟩]
    /p ki·š·e·ləmúwe·t təlkí·kwi-ahɔ́·la·n yó·ni entala·wsi·lí·č·i·k,   [-lí·č·i·k: s.b. -lí·č·i]
    /t God loved mankind so much
    /k For God so loved the world,

    /b wcnhi mrkun mawselethi Qesul;   [⟨wcnhi⟩ for /wwə́nči/]
    /p wwə́nči-mé·k·ən ma·wsi·lí·č·i kkwí·s·al,
    /t that he gave his only son,
    /k that he gave his only begotten Son,

    /b wunhih wrmi cntxi wlamvetufek mutu tafulevtet   [BPL copy has a slanting line
                                                            below the ⟨f⟩ in ⟨taf-⟩]
    /p wə́nči-=č wé·mi éntxi-wəla·mhitánki·k máta -taɔnkəlíhti·t,
    /t so that all who believe would not be lost,
    /k that whosoever believeth in him should not perish,

    /b jwk nuxpawsevtet rvalumwqwnaku pumawswakun.
    /p šúkw -naxpa·wsíhti·t ehaləmo·k·wənák·a pəma·wsəwá·k·an.

/t   but have life forever.
/k   but have everlasting life.

Jn 3.17
/b   Kejrlumwrt mutu wunhi prtalokalawun Qesul cntu lawsif
/p   ki·š·e·ləmúwe·t máta wwə́nči-pe·t·alo·ka·lá·wən kkwí·s·al entalá·wsink
/t   God did not send his son into the world
/k   For God sent not his Son into the world

/b   tcli a ktumakevan nuni cntu lawselethi,
/p   táli-=á· -ktəma·k·í·ha·n nə́ni entala·wsi·lí·č·i,
/t   to condemn those that live there,
/k   to condemn the world;

/b   jwk vokif wunhi kthwvalau b cntu lawselethi.   [⟨-lau⟩ for ⟨-lan⟩]
/p   šúkw hɔ́k·enk wwə́nči-kčo·há·la·n yú entala·wsi·lí·č·i.
/t   but to save mankind by means of himself.
/k   but that the world through him might be saved.

Jn 3.18
/b   Awrnh wlamvetaotc mutu a qwtumakevkwun;   [⟨qwtumakevkw-‖un⟩]
/p   awé·n=č wəla·mhitaɔ́·t·e, máta=á· kwət·əma·k·ihkó·wən,
/t   If someone shall believe in him, he would not be condemned by it,
/k   He that believeth on him is not condemned:

(p. 27)
/b   jwk krvkulwvetuf qwtumakevkwn mrhi,
/p   šúkw kehkəlo·hítank kwət·əma·k·íhko·n mé·či,
/t   but the unbeliever is already condemned by it,
/k   but he that believeth not is condemned already,

/b   rli mutu wlamvetuf tclwcnswakun Kejrlumwrt mawselet Qesul.
/p   é·li- máta -wəla·mhítank tələwensəwá·k·an ki·š·e·ləmúwe·t ma·wsí·li·t kkwí·s·al.
/t   as he does not believe in the name of God's only son.
/k   because he hath not believed in the name of the only begotten Son of God.

Jn 3.19
/b   Nul nuni qtumakswakun; oxrrk wtxwkwn bni cntu lawset,
/p   nál nə́ni ktəma·ksəwá·k·an: ɔ·x·é·e·k o·txúk·o·n yó·ni entalá·wsi·t,
/t   This is the pitiful thing: light came to mankind,
/k   And this is the condemnation, that light is come into the world,

/b   tolowrlintumun peskrk, nontyi oxrrk, rli mrtvik mekintumevtet.
/p   tələwe·lə́ntamən pí·ske·k nuntá·i ɔ·x·é·e·k, é·li- mé·thik -mi·kəntamíhti·t.
/t   and they preferred darkness more than light, because they do evil.
/k   and men loved darkness rather than light, because their deeds were evil.

Jn 3.20 /b Awrn mrtvik mekintufc wjifatumun oxrrk,
         /p awé·n mé·thik mi·kəntánke, wšinká·t·amən ɔ·x·é·e·k.
         /t If anyone does evil, he hates the light.
         /k For every one that doeth evil hateth the light,

         /b takw kotu pawun cntu oxrrk rli a wuntamwnt rlset.
         /p takó· kɔ́t·a-pá·wən énta-ɔ·x·é·e·k, é·li-=á· -wə́ntamunt é·lsi·t.
         /t He does not want to come into the light, as he would be shown what he did.
         /k neither cometh to the light, lest his deeds should be reproved.

Jn 3.21 /b Awrn wlamwrokunif lisetc, wifoxrw cntu oxrrk,
         /p awé·n wəla·məwe·ɔ́·k·anink ləs·í·t·e, winkó·x·we·w énta-ɔ·x·é·e·k,
         /t If someone acts in truth, he likes to go into the light,   ['in the way of truth'?]
         /k But he that doeth truth cometh to the light,

         /b wcnhih nrxkutuk rlyvoset tcli Kejrlumwrt rlwrt lyvosen.   [⟨nrx|kutuk⟩]
         /p wénči-=č -ne·ykɔ́t·ək e·laehɔ́·s·i·t, tə́li- ki·š·e·ləmúwe·t é·ləwe·t -laehɔ́·s·i·n."
         /t so that what he does would be seen to be doing what God says."
         /k that his deeds may be made manifest, that they are wrought in God.

Chapter 19 (pp. 27-28). [L. section 18.] (John 3.22-36.)

Jn 3.22 /b   Nhesus ok rkrkemathel Nhwtee vakif pumenenrop,
         /p   nčí·sas ɔ́·k e·k·e·ki·má·č·i·l †nčo·ti·í·i-hák·ink pəminni·né·ɔ·p,
         /t   Jesus and his disciples stayed in the land of Judaea
         /kl After these things came Jesus and his disciples into the land of Judaea;

         /b   ok hhvopunwrpanek.   [⟨hh-⟩ 1x for ⟨hih-⟩ 4x]
         /p   ɔ́·k čičhɔ·pwənəwé·p·ani·k.
         /t   and baptized people.
         /kl and there he tarried with them, and baptized [L. note: By his disciples].

Jn 3.23 /b   Ok Nhan Enanif tuntu hvopunwrnrp, kexki Srlum, rli xrlit nu tali mpi;
         /p   ɔ́·k nčá·n †í·nanink tə́nta-čhɔ·pwənəwé·ne·p, kí·xki †sé·ləm, é·li xé·lət nə́ táli mpí.
         /t   And John baptized people in Enon, near Salim, as there was much water there.
         /k   And John also was baptizing in Aenon (L. Enon) near to Salim, because there was much water there:

         /b   eku prpanek nu tuntu hvopunan,
         /p   íka pé·p·ani·k, nə́ tə́nta-čhɔ́·pwəna·n.
         /t   They came there, and there he baptized them.
         /k   and they came, and were baptized.

Jn 3.24 /b   rli nrlumu Nhan kpavaseq.
         /p   é·li- né·ləma nčá·n -kpahá·s·i·kw.

/t For John had not yet been imprisoned.
/k For John was not yet cast into prison.

Jn 3.25 /b Ncki lrkreqc alintc Nhan rkrkemathel, ok Nhwuk, ⟨lrkreqc⟩ for ⟨lrkveqc⟩]
/p néke ləkhíkwi a·lə́nte nčá·n e·k·e·ki·má·č·i·l ɔ́·k nčó·wak
/t At that time some of John's disciples and the Jews
/k Then there arose a question between some of John's disciples and the Jews

/b tolumi akunwtumunru pelyvoswakun;
/p tɔ́ləmi-ahkəno·t·əməné·ɔ pi·laehɔ·s·əwá·k·an.
/t began discussing purification.
/k about purifying.

Jn 3.26 /b eku prpanek Nhanif tclapani;
/p íka pé·p·ani·k nčá·nink, təlá·p·ani,
/t They came to John and said to him,
/k And they came unto John, and said unto him,

/b Rkrkemulun wehrvkonrp li Nhutunif kamif; mrothemwlxatup,
[⟨-konrp⟩ 1x for ⟨-konup⟩ 1x; ⟨mroth-⟩ for ⟨mraoth-⟩]
/p "e·k·e·kí·məlan, wi·č·e·ykɔ́nəp lí †nčátanink ká·mink, me·a·ɔ·č·i·mo·lxát·əp,
/t "Student (lit., you who I teach[!; error for 'you who teach me; Teacher']), the one who was with you on the other side of the Jordan, the one you bore witness for,
/k Rabbi, he that was with thee beyond Jordan, to whom thou barest witness,

/b nul wuni hvopwnan, wrmi awrn wtxwkwl.
/p nál wáni čhɔ́·pwəna·n wé·mi awé·n o·txúk·o·l." [garbled]
/t he is the one / is baptized / everyone (prox.) / they (obv.) come to him."
/e nál wáni čhɔ́·pwəna·[t] wé·mi awé·ni, o·txúk·o·l." [possible emendation]
/t he is the one that baptizes everyone, and they come to him."
/k behold, the same baptizeth, and all men come to him.

Jn 3.27 /b Nhan tclapani b cntu lawsethek mutu kuski wrtunumwi krkw; [pl. + sg. verb]
/p nčá·n təlá·p·ani, "yú entala·wsí·č·i·k máta káski-we·t·ənəmó·wi kéku,
/t John said to them, "Mankind cannot receive anything
/k John answered and said, A man can receive nothing,

/b kcnjh osavkumc wunhi melintc;
/p kɔ́nč=č ɔ·s·áhkame wə́nči-mi·lə́nte.
/t except if it is given to them from heaven. [lit., until it shall be]
/k except it be given him from heaven.

Jn 3.28 /b Kelwu kumy athemwlxevunu ne rlwranup. [⟨kumy athem⟩ for ⟨kumyaothem⟩]
/p ki·ló·wa kəmaya·ɔ·č·i·mo·lxíhəna ní· e·ləwe·á·nəp,
/t You yourselves were witnesses for us about what I said,
/k Ye yourselves bear me witness, that I said,

/b Mutu Flyste, jwk nekanalokalqwsi.
/p 'máta nkəlaistí·i, šúkw nni·k·a·nalo·ka·lkwə́s·i.'
/t 'I am not Christ but was sent ahead.
/k I am not the Christ, but that I am sent before him.

Jn 3.29
/b Awrn nrxkwmkwkc kekvqrul nulh wuni trkavpwvalinth.
/p awé·n ne·xko·mkúk·e ki·kxkwé·ɔl, nál=č wáni tekɔhpo·há·lənt=č.
/t When someone has the consent of an unmarried girl, he will be the one who will be married.
/k He that hath the bride is the bridegroom:

/b Wetesul nuni trkavpwvalinth, kexki nepw, punawaul,   [⟨pun-⟩ for /pwənt-/]
/p wi·t·í·s·al náni tekɔhpo·há·lənt=č kí·xki ní·p·o·, pwəntaɔwwá·ɔl.
/t The friend of that one who will be married stands near; they listen to him.
/k but the friend of the bridegroom, which standeth and heareth him,

/b ave wlrlintum rli puntaot, trkavpwvalinth rlwrt.
/p áhi-wəle·lə́ntam é·li-pə́ntaɔ·t tekɔhpo·há·lənt=č é·ləwe·t.
/t He is very glad when he hears what the one who is to be married says.
/k rejoiceth greatly because of the bridegroom's voice:

/b Nul bni nwlrlintumwakun mrhi pavkunhi lro.
/p nál yó·ni no·le·ləntaməwá·k·an; mé·či pahkánči-lé·w.
/t This is my joy; it has now been fulfilled.
/k this my joy therefore is fulfilled.

Jn 3.30
/b Evekalisih txwuk nrkumu;
/p ihikalísi=č txúwak né·k·əma;
/t He and his shall be more and more;
/k He must increase,

/b ne, nwntyih ntuntxixunu. ‖
/p ní·, nuntá·i=č ntəntxíhəna.
/t I and mine shall be less.
/k but I must decrease.

Jn 3.31
(p. 28)
/b Voqruf wunheyet alowelisw;
/p "hukwé·yunk wənčí·ai·t aləwí·i-lə́s·u.
/t "The one who comes from above is greater.
/k He that cometh from above is above all:

/b vakif wunheyet, vakew, tokunwtumun vuf bv vakif rlrk,
/p hák·ink wənčí·ai·t hakí·yu, tɔk·ənó·t·əmən=hánkw yú hák·ink é·le·k.
/t The one who comes from the earth is of earth and speaks of what happens here on earth.
/k he that is of the earth is earthly, and speaketh of the earth:

/b osavkumc wunheyet ave aloe lisw.
/p ɔ·s·áhkame wənčí·ai·t áhi-aləwí·i-lə́s·u.
/t He that comes from heaven is very much greater.
/k he that cometh from heaven is above all.

Jn 3.32
/b Cntxi krkw nrfup, ok puntufup, nani tuntxi myothemwen.   [⟨yo⟩ for /aya·ɔ·/]
/p "éntxi- kéku -nénkəp ɔ́·k -pəntánkəp, ná=ní tə́ntxi-maya·ɔ·č·í·mwi·n,
/t "As many things as he has seen and heard, that is how much he testifies to,
/k And what he hath seen and heard, that he testifieth;

/b Mutu awrni wrtunumakwun rlathemwet.
/p máta awé·ni wwe·t·ənəma·k·ó·wən e·la·č·í·mwi·t.
/t and no one accepts his testimony.
/k and no man receiveth his testimony.

Jn 3.33
/b Awrn wrtunifc rlathemwet whetanexun, tcli wlamwrn Kejrlumwrt,
                                                              [⟨-xun⟩ for ⟨-xtwn⟩]
/p awé·n we·t·anínke e·la·č·í·mwi·t wči·t·aní·xto·n tə́li-wəlá·məwe·n ki·š·e·ləmúwe·t.
/t If someone accepts his testimony, he makes it firm that God tells the truth.
/k He that hath received his testimony hath set to his seal that God is true.

Jn 3.34
/b rli Kejrlumwrt prtalokalat; aptwnatuf Kejrlumwrt toptonakun,
/p é·li- ki·š·e·ləmúwe·t pe·t·alo·ká·la·t -a·pto·ná·t·ank ki·š·e·ləmúwe·t tɔ·pto·ná·k·an,
/t For the one that God sent speaks God's word,
/k For he whom God hath sent speaketh the words of God:

/b rli mutu Kejrlumwrt kekvataq melatc hehufu.
/p é·li- máta ki·š·e·ləmúwe·t †-khikháta·kw mi·lá·t·e či·čánkɔ.   [see *Glossary*]
/t as God does not measure it out (stintingly)(?) when he gives him the spirit.
/k for God giveth not the Spirit by measure unto him.

Jn 3.35
/b Wrtoxumwnt tovolawl Qesul, wrmi krkw mwelan wnaxkif.
/p "we·t·ó·x·əmənt tɔhɔ·lá·ɔl kkwí·s·al; wé·mi kéku mwí·la·n wənáxkink.
/t "The father loves his son, and he gives everything into his hands.
/k The Father loveth the Son, and hath given all things into his hand.

Jn 3.36
/b Awrn wrlamvetaot Wrqesifi rvalumwqunaku pumawswakun wnuxpawsenh.
/p awé·n we·la·mhítaɔ·t we·k·wi·s·ínki ehaləmo·k·wənák·a pəma·wsəwá·k·an wənaxpá·wsi·n=č.
/t Anyone who believes in the son will have (*lit.*, live with) life forever.
/k He that believeth on the Son hath everlasting life:

/b okh awrn mutu wlamvetaotc Wrqesifi mutuh pumawswakun nrmwi,
/p ɔ·k=č awé·n máta wəla·mhitaɔ́·t·e we·k·wi·s·ínki máta=č pəma·wsəwá·k·an ne·mó·wi,
/t And anyone who does not believe in the son will not see life,
/k and he that believeth not the Son shall not see life;

/b jwk Kejrlumwrt wjifaltwakun mwjekakwn.
/p šúkw ki·š·e·ləmúwe·t wšinka·ltəwá·k·an mwəshiká·k·o·n."
/t but God's hatred comes upon them."
/k but the wrath of God abideth on him.

Chapter 20 (pp. 28-31). [L. section 19.] (John 4.1-42.)

Jn 4.1 /b Wrotaqc Nrvlalwrt, tcli puntumanrop Palrseuk,
/p we·ɔ·tá·k·we nehəlá·ləwe·t, tɔ́li-pəntaməné·ɔ·p †pa·ləsi·í·ɔk,
/t When the Lord knew that the Pharisees had heard
/k When therefore the Lord knew how the Pharisees had heard

/b tcli Nhesus alwe txelen rkrkemathel, hvopunathel, nani Nhan
/p tɔ́li- nčí·sas -aləwí·i-txí·li·n e·k·e·ki·má·č·i·l čhɔ·pwəná·č·i·l, náni nčá·n,
/t that there were more of Jesus's disciples that he baptized than of John's,
/k that Jesus made and baptized more disciples than John,

Jn 4.3 /b wnuvkuvtuminrp Nhwteuf, lupi rp Faluleuf.   [⟨wnuvkuvt-⟩ for ⟨wnukuvt-⟩]
/p wənəkahtəməne·p †nčo·tí·yunk, lápi é·p †nka·lalí·yunk.
/t he left Judaea and went again to Galilee.
/k He left Judaea, and departed again into Galilee.

Jn 4.2 /b Nhesus alwt mutu hvopwnwrep; rkrkemathel jwk.
/p (nčí·sas alót máta čhɔ·pwənəwé·i·p, e·k·e·ki·má·č·i·l šúkw.)
/t (Actually, Jesus had not baptized people, only his disciples.)
/k (Though Jesus himself baptized not, but his disciples,)

Jn 4.4 /b Uskc nc tclwxrn Sumrleif.
/p áski nə təló·x·we·n †same·lí·ink.
/t And he had to go through Samaria.
/k And he must needs go through Samaria.

Jn 4.5 /b Eku ponrp Sumrlie wtrnif lwcntaswp Sykul;
/p íka pó·ne·p †same·líí·i-o·t·é·nink, luwentá·s·o·p †sáikəl,
/t And he came to a city of Samaria named Sychar,
/k Then cometh he to a city of Samaria, which is called Sychar,

/b kexki rtrkup nuni vaki Nhrkupu melatup qesul Nhosiu.
/p kí·xki e·té·k·əp nəni hák·i †nče·kə́pa mi·lá·t·əp kkwí·s·al †nčó·sia.

Text, Transcription, and Translation 79

/t which was near the land that Jacob had given to his son Josey.
/k near to the parcel of ground that Jacob gave to his son Joseph.

Jn 4.6 /b Nhrkupu walprkum vatr.
/p †nče·kə́pa wɔ·lpé·k·əm hát·e·.
/t Jacob's well was there.
/k Now Jacob's well was there.

/b Nhesus rli metoxrp weqevulc, nu walprkwf wlumutupen,   [⟨mutup⟩ for /mahtáp·/]
/p nčí·sas é·li mhitó·x·we·p wi·kwíhəle·; ná ɔ·lpé·k·unk wələmahtáp·i·n.
/t Jesus, as he had been walking, was tired, and he sat on the well.
/k Jesus therefore, being wearied with his journey, sat thus on the well:

/b mrhi alumi paxaqc.   [⟨x⟩ for /xh/]
/p mé·či áləmi-pa·xhákwe·.
/t It was already toward noon.
/k and it was about the sixth hour.

Jn 4.7 /b Sumrlie uxqr pwchi mpi natumun.
/p †same·liáxkwe pwéči- mpí -ná·t·əmən.
/t And there was a Samaritan woman who came to get water.
/k There cometh a woman of Samaria to draw water:

/b Nhesus tclapani munivel.
/p nčí·sas təlá·p·ani, "məníhi·l."
/t Jesus said to her, "Give me a drink."
/k Jesus saith unto her, Give me to drink.

Jn 4.8 /b Rkrkemathel rpanek, my mvalumwk methwakun.
/p (e·k·e·ki·má·č·i·l é·p·ani·k, mái-mhálamo·k mi·č·əwá·k·an.)
/t (His disciples had gone to buy food.)
/k (For his disciples were gone away unto the city to buy meat.)

Jn 4.9 /b Sumrlie uxqr, tclapani;
/p †same·liáxkwe təlá·p·ani,
/t The Samaritan woman said to him,
/k Then saith the woman of Samaria unto him,

/b Ta vuh lrw wunhi leun munivel. Nhw vun kvaky; ‖ kahe ne Sumrlie uxqr;
/p "tá=háč lé·w wə́nči-lían, 'məníhi·l'? nčó·=xán khák·ay, káč·i ní· †same·liáxkwe.
/t "How is it that you ask me for a drink? Even though you are a Jew, but I am a Samaritan woman.
/k How is it that thou, being a Jew, askest drink of me, which am a woman of Samaria?

(p. 29) /b rli Nhwuk ok Sumrliethek mutu wifrlumaeuk.
/p é·li nčó·wak ó·k †same·lií·č·i·k máta winke·ləma·í·ɔk."
/t For Jews and Samaritans are not accepted on friendly terms.
/k for the Jews have no dealings with the Samaritans.

Jn 4.10 /b Nhesus tclapani, Kwatwn vun Kejrlumwrt nuxpufuntwakunw,   [garbled]
/p nčí·sas təlá·p·ani, "ko·wá·to·n=xán ki·š·e·ləmúwe·t naxpankuntəwá·k·anu,
/t Jesus said to her, "You know, however, / God / it is a gift,
/k Jesus answered and said unto her, If thou knewest the gift of God,

/b ok awrn rlkon munivel;
/p ó·k awé·n é·lkɔn, 'məníhi·l,'
/t and who said to you, 'Give me a drink.'
/k and who it is that saith to thee, Give me to drink;

/b kwenwumvkwn a, kumelkwn pumawswek mpi.   [garbled]
/p kəwi·nəwámko·n=á·, kəmí·lkɔn pəma·wsó·wi·k mpí."
/t He would ask you for it (!; for 'you would ask him for it'), (and) he (would have) given you the living water."
/k thou wouldest have asked of him, and he would have given thee living water.

Jn 4.11 /b Xqr tclapani, Takw krkw kinumwi unsekreun;   [⟨reun⟩: /-é·an/]
/p xkwé· təlá·p·ani, "takó· kéku kkənnəmó·wi anshi·k·é·an,
/t The woman said to him. "You don't have anything to scoop up water with.
/k The woman saith unto him, Sir, thou hast nothing to draw with,

/b qwnaluvkwt olprq;   [⟨-aluvkwt⟩ for ⟨-aluvkut⟩]
/p kwəná·lahkat ó·lpe·kw.
/t The well is deep.
/k and the well is deep:

/b ta vuh kwntcn nc pumawswek mpi?
/p tá=háč kúntən nɔ́ pəma·wsó·wi·k mpí?
/t From where do you get that living water?
/k from whence then hast thou that living water?

Jn 4.12 /b Ktalwe ksi lisen noxunanu Nhrkupu melkonup bni wolprq?
/p ktaləwí·i-=ksí -lə́s·i·n no·x·əná·na †nče·kə́pa, mi·lkɔ́·nəp yó·ni ó·lpe·kw?
/t Are you greater than our ancient father Jacob, who gave me this well?
/k Art thou greater than our father Jacob, which gave us the well,

/b nrkumu wcvcnhi munrnrp, ok tomeminsumul ok tolumwnsul.
/p né·k·əma wwihə́nči-məné·ne·p, ó·k tɔmi·mə́nsəmal ó·k tɔləmúnsal."
/t He himself used to drink from it, and his children and his animals."
/k and drank thereof himself, and his children, and his cattle?

Jn 4.13
/b Nhesus tclapani, awrn munrtc bni mpi, lupi vuf kuvtwsumw.
/p nčí·sas tǝlá·p·ani, "awé·n mǝné·t·e yó·ni mpí, lápi=hánkw kahtó·s·ǝmu.
/t Jesus said to her, "If anyone drinks this water they'll be thirsty again.
/k Jesus answered and said unto her, Whosoever drinketh of this water shall thirst again:

Jn 4.14
/b Jwk awrn munrtc mpi ne meluk ta vuji lupi kuvtwsumwe.
/p šúkw awé·n mǝné·t·e mpí ní· mí·lak, tá=á· háši lápi kahto·s·ǝmwí·i.
/t But if anyone drinks the water that *I* give them, they would never again be thirsty.
/k But whosoever drinketh of the water that I shall give him shall never thirst;

/b Wlava nuni mpi ne meluk rvlelamufh vokif
/p wǝláha nǝ́ni mpí ní· mí·lak, ehǝlí·lamank=č hɔ́k·enk,
/t Rather, that water that *I* give them, which will be a source of water in their body,
/k but the water that I shall give him shall be in him a well of water

/b kjwpcvulrw rvalumakumek pumawswakunif.
/p kšǝp·éhǝle·w ehalǝmá·kami·k pǝma·wsǝwá·k·anink.
/t will flow in eternal life.
/k springing up into everlasting life.

Jn 4.15
/b Xqr tclapani, Munivel nuni mpi
/p xkwé· tǝlá·p·ani, "mǝníhi·l nǝ́ni mpí,
/t The woman said to him, "Give me that water to drink,
/k The woman saith unto him, Sir, give me this water,

/b wunhi a mutu katwsumweu ok mutu pepchi mpi natumwu.   [⟨-eu⟩: /-í·ɔ/ or /-ía/]
/p wǝ́nči-=á· máta -kahto·s·ǝmwí·ɔ, ɔ́·k máta -pi·p·éči- mpí -na·t·ǝmó·wa."
/t so that I would not be thirsty and would never come here to get water."
/k that I thirst not, neither come hither to draw.

Jn 4.16
/b Nhesus tclapani, My wcnhem wekemut, wuntaxatch.
/p nčí·sas tǝlá·p·ani, "mái-wénči·m wi·k·í·mat; wǝ́ntax á·t·eč."
/t Jesus said to her, "Go call your husband; let him come here."
/k Jesus saith unto her, Go, call thy husband, and come hither.

Jn 4.17
/b Xqr lwr takw nwekifri.
/p xkwé· lúwe·, "takó· nǝwi·k·inké·i."
/t The woman said, "I am not married."
/k The woman answered and said, I have no husband.

/b Nhesus tclapani, Kwlamwr rlwrun mutu nwekifri;
/p nčí·sas tǝlá·p·ani, "ko·lá·mǝwe e·lǝwé·an, 'máta nǝwi·k·inké·i.'
/t Jesus said to her, "You tell the truth in saying you are not married.
/k Jesus said unto her, Thou hast well said, I have no husband:

Jn 4.18 /b rli palrnax txwpani wekematpanek, [⟨txwpani⟩ s.b. ⟨txwpanek⟩]
/p é·li palé·naxk txó·p·ani·k wi·k·i·matpáni·k.
/t For there have been five that have been your husbands,
/k For thou hast had five husbands;

/b ok wuni wekemut bqc wekemut, takw kehe kwekemai;
/p ó·k wáni wi·k·í·mat yúkwe wi·k·í·mat, takó· khičí·i kəwi·k·i·má·i.
/t and this husband of yours you're now married to, you're not really married to.
/k and he whom thou now hast is not thy husband:

/b nani rlwrun kwlamwc.
/p nə́ni e·ləwé·an ko·lá·məwe.
/t You told the truth in what you said.
/k in that saidst thou truly.

Jn 4.19 /b Xqr tclapani Mrhi nrmun nrnekaniwrwset kvaky.
/p xkwé· təlá·p·ani, "mé·či nné·mən nehəni·k·a·ní·i-wé·wsi·t khák·ay.
/t The woman said to him, "I now see that you are a prophet.
/k The woman saith unto him, Sir, I perceive that thou art a prophet.

Jn 4.20 /b Noxunanifu bni ovhwf tuntu patumanrop;
/p no·x·əna·nínka yó·ni ɔhčúnk tə́nta-pa·tama·né·ɔ·p.
/t Our forefathers prayed on this mountain.
/k Our fathers worshipped in this mountain;

/b ajiti kelwu ktclwcvumu, Nhelwsulumif tuntu a patumanru.
/p a·šíte ki·ló·wa ktələwéhəmɔ, †nči·lo·sələ́mink tə́nta-=á· -pa·tama·né·ɔ."
/t You (pl.) on the other hand say that they should have prayed in Jerusalem."
/k and ye say, that in Jerusalem is the place where men ought to worship.

Jn 4.21 /b Nhesus tclapani, Xqr wlamvetyel;
/p nčí·sas təlá·p·ani, "xkwé·, wəla·mhítai·l.
/t Jesus said to her, "Woman, believe me.
/k Jesus saith unto her, Woman, believe me,

/b Pcxotyeli bni ovhwf, ok Nhelwsulumif mutu patamaorq Koxunu. [⟨ye⟩ for ⟨y e⟩]
/p pé·x·o·t=á· ílli yó·ni ɔhčúnk ó·k †nči·lo·sələ́mink máta pa·tamaɔ́·e·kw kó·x·əna.
/t Soon you will not pray to our father even on this mountain and in Jerusalem.
/k the hour cometh, when ye shall neither in this mountain, nor yet at Jerusalem, worship the Father.

Jn 4.22 /b Takw kwavai awrn patamaot, nelwnu patumaif nwavawunu;
/p takó· ko·wa·há·i awé·n pa·tamáɔt; ni·ló·na pa·tamáenk no·wa·há·wəna,
/t You (sg.) do not know who you pray to; who *we* pray to we know,
/k Ye worship ye know not what: we know what we worship:

	/b	rli kthwvaltwakun Nhwif wunheyek.
	/p	é·li- kčo·ha·ltəwá·k·an nčó·wink -wənčí·ai·k,
	/t	for salvation comes from the Jews.
	/k	for salvation is of the Jews.

Jn 4.23	/b	Prthivulch lukveqc, ok mrhi bqc lro, wlamwri ‖ patamaothek,
	/p	pe·č·íhəle·=č ləkhíkwi, ó·k mé·či yúkwe lé·w, wəla·məwé·i-pa·tamaó·č·i·k,
	/t	The time will come and is already happening now, for ones who pray to him truly,
	/k	But the hour cometh, and now is, when the true worshippers

(p. 30)	/b	tclih patumanru Wrtoxumwnhi hehufwf, ok wlamwrokunif. [⟨man⟩ for ⟨maon⟩]
	/p	tə́li·=č -pa·tamaɔ·né·ɔ we·t·o·x·əmə́nči či·čánkunk ó·k wəla·məwe·ó·k·anink,
	/t	that they will pray to the father in spirit and in truth,
	/k	shall worship the Father in spirit and in truth:

	/b	Rli Wrtoxumunt nunuli nrl ntonaot patumakwkh.
	/p	é·li- we·t·ó·x·əmənt nanáli né·l -ntó·naɔ·t pa·tamá·k·uk=č.
	/t	for the father seeks the one who will pray to him.
	/k	for the Father seeketh such to worship him.

Jn 4.24	/b	Kejrlumwrt hehufw,
	/p	ki·š·e·ləmúwe·t či·čánku.
	/t	God is a spirit.
	/k	God is a Spirit:

	/b	cntxi patumathek potumawauh wcnhi hehwf, ok wlamwrokun. [⟨mat⟩ for ⟨maot⟩]
	/p	éntxi-pa·tamaó·č·i·k pɔ·tamaɔwwá·ɔ=č wə́nči čí·čankw ó·k wəla·məwe·ó·k·an."
	/t	All who pray to him must pray to him by spirit and truth."
	/k	and they that worship him must worship him in spirit and in truth.

Jn 4.25	/b	Xqr tclapani, Nwatwn tclih pan Misyus, rlwcnset Klyst.
	/p	xkwé· təlá·p·ani, "no·wá·to·n tə́li·=č -pá·n †misáyas, e·ləwénsi·t kəláist.
	/t	The woman said to him, "I know that the Messiah will come, who is called Christ.
	/k	The woman saith unto him, I know that Messias cometh, which is called Christ:

	/b	Patch nwntumakwnrnh wrmi krkw.
	/p	pá·t·e=č, nuntama·k·ó·ne·n=č wé·mi kéku."
	/t	When he comes, he will tell us about everything."
	/k	when he is come, he will tell us all things.

Jn 4.26	/b	Nhesus tclapani, Bqc avaptwnalkwn, nul nuni.
	/p	nčí·sas təlá·p·ani, "yúkwe aha·pto·ná·lkɔn, nál náni."
	/t	Jesus said to her, "The one speaking to you now is that one."
	/k	Jesus saith unto her, I that speak unto thee am he.

Jn 4.27 /b Rkrkemathel, wexkawhih pruk,   [⟨-hih⟩ for ⟨-hi⟩]
         /p e·k·e·ki·má·č·i·l wi·xkaóči pé·ɔk,
         /t His disciples suddenly arrived,
         /k And upon this came his disciples,

         /b wlrlumrlintumwpanek rli wiftwnvalat nrl xqrul;
         /p wəle·ləme·ləntamóp·ani·k é·li-winkto·nhá·la·t né·l xkwé·ɔl.
         /t and they were astonished at how he was having a conversation with the woman.
         /k and marvelled that he talked with the woman:

         /b alwt mutu awrn lwrep, krkw vuh knatwnum, jitu quh vuh wiftwnvalut?
         /p aló·t máta awé·n luwé·i·p, "kéku=háč kənat·ó·nam?" ší=tá, "kwáč=háč winkto·nhá·lat?"
         /t Yet no one said, "What are you looking for?" or "Why are you having a conversation with her?"
         /k yet no man said, What seekest thou? or, Why talkest thou with her?

Jn 4.28 /b Nu jai xqr wnukulan twvwsu, wtrnif tujevulan,
         /p ná šá·e xkwé· wənək·ala·n tɔhó·s·a, o·t·é·nink təš·íhəla·n.
         /t The woman then abruptly left her pot and ran into the city.
         /k The woman then left her waterpot, and went her way into the city,

         /b tclapani wrmi rpelethi,
         /p təlá·p·ani wé·mi e·p·i·lí·č·i,
         /t She told everyone there,
         /k and saith to the men,

Jn 4.29 /b Wuntaxaq, punw lino rlet wrmi krkw rlseu.
         /p "wə́ntax á·kw, pənó· lə́nu é·li·t wé·mi kéku e·lsía.
         /t "Come and see the man who told me everything I have done.
         /k Come, see a man, which told me all things that ever I did:

         /b Mutu vuh nuni Klyst?
         /p máta=háč náni kəláist?"
         /t Is he not Christ?"
         /k is not this the Christ?

Jn 4.30 /b Nu wrtotrnyethek, eku ruk.
         /p ná we·t·o·t·e·naí·č·i·k íka é·ɔk.
         /t Then the townspeople went there.
         /k Then they went out of the city, and came unto him.

Jn 4.31 /b Srkvakrt tclapani rkrkemathel, Mametseq Rkrkemulrq.
         /p se·kháke·t, təlá·p·ani e·k·e·ki·má·č·i·l, "ma·mí·tsi·kw, e·k·e·kí·məle·kw.

/t   While she was gone, he said to his disciples, "Have something to eat, my disciples." [meaning reversed]
/k   In the mean while his disciples prayed him, saying, Master, eat.

Jn 4.32 /b   Jwk tclapani, Vatr ta numethwakun, mutu wrotwrq.
/p   šúkw təlá·p·ani, "hát·e·=tá nəmi·č·əwá·k·an, máta we·ɔ·tó·we·kw.
/t   But he only said to them, "There is food of mine that you do not know about."
/k   But he said unto them, I have meat to eat that ye know not of.

Jn 4.33 /b   Rkrkemathi litwpanek,
/p   e·k·e·ki·má·č·i lət·ó·p·ani·k,
/t   His disciples said to each other,
/k   Therefore said the disciples one to another,

/b   Pwrtwn vuh ct awrn, krkw methet?
/p   "pwé·t·o·n=háč·ét awé·n kéku mí·č·i·t?"
/t   "Has anyone perhaps brought something for him to eat?"
/k   Hath any man brought him ought to eat?

Jn 4.34 /b   Nhesus tclapani, Numethwakun; prtalokaletup mwekintamin,
/p   nčí·sas təlá·p·ani, "nəmi·č·əwá·k·an pe·t·alo·ka·lí·t·əp mwi·kə́ntamən,
/t   Jesus said to them, "My food is the work of the one who has sent me here,
/k   Jesus saith unto them, My meat is to do the will of him that sent me,

/b   ntclih kejalokasen wmekumoswakun.   [⟨wm-⟩ for ⟨mw-⟩]
/p   ntə́li-=č -ki·š·alo·ká·s·i·n mwi·kəmo·s·əwá·k·an.
/t   for me to finish his work.
/k   and to finish his work.

Jn 4.35 /b   "Mutu vuh aphi nrwu kejoxif nuh vwet tumjasw?
/p   "máta=háč á·pči né·wa ki·š·ó·x·ink, ná=č hwí·t təmšá·s·u.
/t   "Are there not still four months before the wheat will be harvested?
/k   Say not ye, There are yet four months, and then cometh harvest?

/b   Ktclwvumw apvwqrq, lifwrxenwk vakevakunekri.
/p   ktəllúhəmɔ, 'a·phúkwe·kw, linkwe·x·í·no·kw haki·ha·k·ani·ké·i.'
/t   I say to you, 'Lift your gaze and look towards the fields.'
/k   behold, I say unto you, Lift up your eyes, and look on the fields;

/b   Mrhi rlumi opevulrw; tcpi a tumjasw.   [⟨rlumi⟩ for ⟨alumi⟩]
/p   mé·či áləmi-ɔ·p·ihəlé·ɔ; tépi-=á· -təmšá·s·u.
/t   They have already turned white; it would be ready to harvest.
/k   for they are white already to harvest.

Jn 4.36 /b Nrk tumjifek vwet ernvaok;　　　　　　[⟨tumj-⟩ for ⟨trmj-⟩; ⟨ernv-⟩ 1x for ⟨evrnv-⟩ 2x]
　　　　 /p né·k te·mšínki·k hwí·t ihe·nhaɔ́·ɔk.
　　　　 /t Those who reap the wheat get paid.
　　　　 /k And he that reapeth receiveth wages,

　　　　 /b mocvumun vufq kejekif rvalumwqunakue pumawswakunif tali,
　　　　 /p mɔ·éhəmən=hánkw ki·š·í·k·ink ehaləmo·k·wənak·aí·i-pəma·wsəwá·k·anink táli,
　　　　 /t He gathers the crop in eternal life,
　　　　 /k and gathereth fruit unto life eternal:

　　　　 /b wcnhi srnrvethek navle trmjefek tavqe wlrlintumivtet.　　　　[⟨srnrv-⟩ for ⟨srnev-⟩]
　　　　 /p wénči- se·nihí·č·i·k nahəlí·i te·mšínki·k tahkwí·i -wəle·ləntamíhti·t.
　　　　 /t so that those that sow it and also those that reap it rejoice together.
　　　　 /k that both he that soweth and he that reapeth may rejoice together.

Jn 4.37 /b Puna wlamwrbw bni lwrokun.
　　　　 /p pənáh, wəla·məwe·yó·u yó·ni luwe·ɔ́·k·an:
　　　　 /t Now, this saying is true:
　　　　 /k And herein is that saying true,

　　　　 /b Mawsw srnevet, ok takok tumjimun.　　　　　　　　　　　　[⟨t-⟩ for /wt-/]
　　　　 /p má·wsu se·níhi·t, ɔ́·k tákɔ·k wtəmšə́mən.
　　　　 /t There is one who sows it, and another reaps it.
　　　　 /k One soweth, and another reapeth.

Jn 4.38 /b Ktolokalwvwmwp, kumy tumjiminro vwet, jwk mutu kmekintumwnrop;
　　　　 /p ktalo·kallúhəmɔ·p, kəmái-təmšəməné·ɔ hwí·t, šúkw máta
　　　　 　　kəmi·kəntamo·wəné·ɔ·p.
　　　　 /t I sent you, and you went to reap the wheat, but you did no work on it.
　　　　 /k I sent you to reap that whereon ye bestowed no labour:

　　　　 /b peli awrnek mekumwswpanek; ajiti kelwu kpanru wmekumoswakunwaif. ‖
　　　　 /p pí·li awé·ni·k mi·kəmɔ·s·ó·p·ani·k, a·šíte ki·ló·wa kpa·né·ɔ
　　　　 　　mwi·kəmɔ·s·əwa·k·anəwá·ink."　　　　　　　　　[⟨wm-⟩ for /mw-/]
　　　　 /t Other people worked, and *you*, on the other hand, came into their work."
　　　　 /k other men laboured, and ye are entered into their labours.

Jn 4.39 /b Xrli wlistumwk, Sumrleuk, wunheyethek nuni wtrnif,　　[Sumrleuk: cf. Jn 4.40]
(p. 31) /p xé·li wləstámo·k †same·líí·ɔk wənči·aí·č·i·k nɔ́ni o·t·é·nink,
　　　　 /t Many Samaritans from that city believed,
　　　　 /k And many of the Samaritans of that city believed on him

　　　　 /b rli lwrtup nuni xqr, prnwntvekrt tclkwn wrmi krkw rlset.
　　　　 /p é·li-luwé·t·əp náni xkwé· pe·nunthíke·t, tə́lko·n wé·mi kéku é·lsi·t,
　　　　 /t for that woman that testified had said he told her everything she had done.
　　　　 /k for the saying of the woman, which testified, He told me all that ever I did.

Jn 4.40 /b Mrhi wrtxwkkc Sumrlieuk, tove laol myekrl; [⟨laol⟩ s.b. ⟨lawaol⟩]
/p mé·či we·txúkwke †same·líí·ɔk, tóhi-lá·ɔl, "maí·k·e·l." [prox. for obv.]
/t When the Samaritans came to him, they implored him to stay with them.
/k So when the Samaritans were come unto him, they besought him that he would tarry with them:

/b nc mu topenrp nejoqwnc,
/p nə́=máh tɔp·í·ne·p ni·š·ó·k·wəni.
/t He stayed there for two days.
/k and he abode there two days.

Jn 4.41 /b puntawtetc lupi xrli wlamvetakw,
/p pəntaɔhtí·t·e, lápi xé·li o·la·mhitá·k·u.
/t When they heard him, he was believed by many more (*lit.*, again).
/k And many more believed because of his own word;

Jn 4.42 /b tclawapani nuni xqr; Bqc mrhi nwlamvetamwvunu,
/p təlawwá·p·ani / náni xkwé·, "yúkwe mé·či no·la·mhitamúhəna. [prox. for obv.!]
/t They said to her / that woman, "Now we believe.
/k And said unto the woman, Now we believe,

/b mutu xun ta wunhi rlwranup rli puntyeif wunhi; [⟨puntyeif⟩ for /pə́ntaenk/]
/p máta=xán=tá wə́nči e·ləwé·anəp; é·li-pə́ntaenk wə́nči.
/t Although it is not because of what you said; because we heard him.
/k not because of thy saying: for we have heard him ourselves,

/b nwatwnrn wuni kehe Klyst krthwvalat bni cntu lawsethek.
/p no·wa·tó·ne·n wáni khičí·i kəláist, ke·č·o·há·la·t / yó·ni entala·wsí·č·i·k.
[prox. for obv.!]
/t We know that this is truly Christ, the savior of / mankind.
/k and know that this is indeed the Christ, the Saviour of the world.

Chapter 21 (pp. 31-32). [L. section 20.] (John 4.43-54.)

Jn 4.43 /b Mrhi nejoqwnakvakc, nu tolumskanrp li Faluleuf,
/p mé·či ni·š·o·k·wənakháke ná tɔləmská·ne·p lí †nka·lalí·yunk,
/t After two days he departed to Galilee.
/k Now after two days he departed thence, and went into Galilee.

Jn 4.44 /b rli Nhesus pwnwntvekrnrp
/p é·li nčí·sas pwənunthiké·ne·p
/t For Jesus testified
/k For Jesus himself testified,

88 Blanchard's Harmony of the Gospels

/b tcli, nrnekanewrwset mutuh axrlumwksewun, cntu kejekwvifup. [⟨ax-⟩ for ⟨av-⟩]
/p tə́li- nehəni·k·aní·i-wé·wsi·t máta=č -ahe·ləmukwsí·wən énta-ki·š·i·k·o·hénkəp.
/t that a prophet would not be honored in the place where he had been raised.
/k that a prophet hath no honour in his own country.

Jn 4.45
/b Mrhi eku pratc Faluleuf, Falulethek wetwtrnyrvrmau, [⟨-mau⟩ s.b. ⟨-mawau⟩]
/p mé·či íka pe·á·t·e †nka·lalí·yunk, †nka·lalí·č·i·k wwi·t·o·t·e·nayahe·má·ɔ,
/t After he arrived in Galilee, the Galileans treated him as a fellow townsman,
/k Then when he was come into Galilee, the Galilaeans received him,

/b rli nrmvetetup wrmi krkw cntxi lyvosetup Nhelwsulumif, cntu xifwi metsavtifup,
/p é·li-ne·mhití·t·əp wé·mi kéku éntxi-laehɔ·s·í·t·əp †nči·lo·sələmink,
   énta-xínkwi-mi·tsahtínkəp,
/t as they had seen all the things he had done in Jerusalem at the great feast,
/k having seen all the things that he did at Jerusalem at the feast:

/b rli nrkumau eku rpanek.
/p é·li ne·k·əmá·ɔ íka é·p·ani·k.
/t as they had gone there, themselves.
/k for they also went unto the feast.

Jn 4.46
/b Nhesus lupi rp li Krni Faluleuf,
/p nčí·sas lápi é·p lí †ké·ni †nka·lalí·yunk.
/t Jesus again went to Cana in Galilee.
/k So Jesus came again into Cana of Galilee,

/b mpif wunhi manetwnrp wyn. Nuni tali
/p mpínk wwə́nči-manni·tó·ne·p wáin nə́ni táli. [nə́ni táli: as in Jn 5.13]
/t He had made the wine from water there.
/k where he made the water wine.

/b xifwrlumwkset lino avpw,
/p xinkwe·ləmúkwsi·t lə́nu ahpú,
/t There was a highly regarded man,
/k And there was a certain nobleman,

/b palselwul qesul Kupuniumif tali.
/p pa·lsí·ləwal kkwí·s·al †kapəniámink táli.
/t and his son was sick in Capernaum.
/k whose son was sick at Capernaum.

Jn 4.47
/b Puntufc tcli Nhesus Nhwteuf mun, ok Faluleuf prw, nu eku ton.
/p pəntánke tə́li- nčí·sas †nčo·tí·yunk -mmə́n, ɔ́·k †nka·lalí·yunk pé·w, ná íka tɔ́·n.
/t When he heard that Jesus came from Judaea and came to Galilee, he went there.
/k When he heard that Jesus was come out of Judaea into Galilee, he went unto him,

/b Tave lawl tclih eku pan, my kekrvan qesul; [⟨tave⟩ for /tɔhi/]
/p tɔ́hi-lá·ɔl, tǝli-=č íka -pá·n, -mái-ki·k·é·ha·n kkwí·s·al,
/t He implored him to come there, going to cure his son,
/k and besought him that he would come down, and heal his son:

/b rli kavti uful.
/p é·li káhti-ánkǝl.
/t as he was almost dead.
/k for he was at the point of death.

Jn 4.48
/b Nhesus tclapani, Mutu knrmwun, fanjyvoswakun, muta kwlamvetyei.
/p nčí·sas tǝlá·p·ani, "máta kǝne·mó·wǝn nkanšaehɔ·s·ǝwá·k·an, máta=á· ko·la·mhitaí·i." ['if' omitted]
/t Jesus said to him, "You did not see my miracles; you would not believe me."
/k Then said Jesus unto him, Except ye see signs and wonders, ye will not believe.

Jn 4.49
/b Wuni xifwrlumwkset tclawl, eku paul, nrlumu ufulwi nehan.
/p wáni xinkwe·lǝmúkwsi·t tǝlá·ɔl, "íka pá·l; né·lǝma ankǝló·wi nní·č·a·n."
/t The highly regarded one said to him, "Come there; my child is not yet dead."
/k The nobleman saith unto him, Sir, come down ere my child die.

Jn 4.50
/b Nhesus tclapani, Eku aul mrhi lrlrxrlwul qesul. [⟨aul⟩ for ⟨al⟩]
/p nčí·sas tǝlá·p·ani, "íka á·l"; mé·či lehǝle·x·é·lǝwal kkwí·s·al.
/t Jesus told him to go there; that his son was now living. [direct and indirect disc.]
/k Jesus saith unto him, Go thy way; thy son liveth.

/b Wlamvetamun Nhesus toptonakun, nu tolumskan.
/p o·la·mhítamǝn nčí·sas tɔ·pto·ná·k·an, ná tɔlǝmska·n.
/t He believed Jesus's word, and then he departed.
/k And the man believed the word that Jesus had spoken unto him, and he went his way.

Jn 4.51
/b Rlumi mahetc wnukeskaul tolokakunu.
/p é·lǝmi-ma·č·í·t·e, wǝnak·i·skaó·ɔl tɔlo·ká·k·ana.
/t After he started home, he met his servant. [or 'servants', but sg. below]
/k And as he was now going down, his servants met him,

/b Tclkwpani, Lrlrxr qes.
/p tǝlkó·p·ani, "lehǝlé·x·e· kkwí·s."
/t He told him, "Your son lives."
/k and told him, saying, Thy son liveth.

Jn 4.52
/b Nu notwtumaun ‖ rlkeqc alumi wlumalset. [⟨rlkeqc⟩ 3x for ⟨rlkeqi⟩ 73x]
/p ná nɔt·o·t·ǝmáɔ·n, e·lkí·kwi-álǝmi-wǝlamálsi·t.
/t Then he asked him, when he began to get better.
/k Then enquired he of them the hour when he began to amend.

(p. 32)   /b   Tclapani, Loqc alwehi paxaqr, wnukalwkwn polswakun.   [⟨q⟩ for /k·əw/]
          /p   təlá·p·ani, "ló·k·əwe aləwíči pa·xhákwe·, wənək·alúk·o·n pə·lsəwá·k·an.
          /t   And he said to him, "It was yesterday a little past noon that his illness left him."
          /k   And they said unto him, Yesterday at the seventh hour the fever left him.

Jn 4.53   /b   Nu oxul wavkwn, tcli nul nuni rlkeqc Nhesus rlwrtup, Lrlrxrlwul qesul.
          /p   ná ó·x·ɔl o·wáhko·n, táli nál nəni e·lkí·kwi- nčí·sas e·ləwé·t·əp, "lehəle·x·é·ləwal kkwí·s·al."   [/e·lkí·kwi- .. e·ləwé·t·əp/ s.b. /e·lkí·kwi- .. -ləwé·t·əp/]
          /t   Then his father knew that that was the same time when Jesus had said, "His son lives."
          /k   So the father knew that it was at the same hour, in the which Jesus said unto him, Thy son liveth:

          /b   Nunu myae wlamvetamun, cntxetet rpethek lamekwavumc.
          /p   nána mayá·i o·la·mhítamən, entxíhti·t e·p·í·č·i·k la·mi·k·əwáhəme.
          /t   Then he truly believed, and everyone that was inside the house.
          /k   and himself believed, and his whole house.

Jn 4.54   /b   Mrhi bqc li nejun konjyvosen Nhesus, ncki patc Nhwteuf li Faluleuf.
          /p   mé·či yúkwe lí ní·š·ən kənšaehó·s·i·n nčí·sas, néke pá·t·e [wə́nči] †nčo·tí·yunk, lí †nka·lalí·yunk.   [first /lí/ (printed above the other one) is spurious; word missing]
          /t   Now Jesus had done two miracles when he came [from] Judaea, to Galilee.
          /k   This is again the second miracle that Jesus did, when he was come out of Judaea into Galilee.

Chapter 22 (pp. 32-35). [L. section 21.] (John 5.1-47.)

Jn 5.1   /b   Lupi xrfwi metsavtwuk Nhwuk, ok Nhesus eku rp Nhelwsulumif.
          /p   lápi xínkwi-mi·tsahtúwak nčó·wak, ó·k nčí·sas íka é·p †nči·lo·səlómink.
          /t   The Jews had another great feast, and Jesus went to Jerusalem.
          /k   After this there was a feast of the Jews; and Jesus went up to Jerusalem.

Jn 5.2   /b   Vatrw munoprqtut Nhelwsulumif, kexkt tuntu ajwntrnan mrkesu,
                                              [⟨kexkt⟩: ⟨t⟩ perhaps broken, but not ⟨i⟩]
          /p   hát·e·w mənəp·é·kwtət †nči·lo·səlómink, kí·xki tónta-a·š·unté·na·n mekí·s·a.
          /t   There was a pool in Jerusalem, and he traded sheep near there.
          /k   Now there is at Jerusalem by the sheep market a pool,

          /b   lwcntaswp Pctsrtr Vepulwe lwentasw, palrnax txinw eakanu okai;
          /p   luwentá·s·o·p †petsé·te·, †hi·pəlo·wí·i-luwentá·s·u, palé·naxk txə́nu ya·k·á·ɔna ɔ·ká·i.
          /t   It was called Bethesda, being named in Hebrew 'there are five arbors around it'.
          /k   which is called in the Hebrew tongue Bethesda, having five porches.

Jn 5.3	/b	xrli wjifexenunrw palsethek. krkrpifothek, ovomvqekethek, swnswksethek,
	/p	xé·li wšenki·x·i·néné·ɔ pa·lsí·č·i·k, ke·k·e·p·inkɔ́·č·i·k, †ɔhɔ·m(x)kwi·k·í·č·i·k, sunso·ksí·č·i·k,
	/t	Many unhealthy people lay there, who were blind, lame(?), and "withered."
	/k	In these lay a great multitude of impotent folk, of blind, halt, withered,

/b nrk pwrtwnrw qwhwkprkevlr nc mpi.
/p né·k pwe·to·né·ɔ kwčukwpe·k·íhəle· nə́ mpí.
/t They waited for the water to tremble.
/k waiting for the moving of the water.

Jn 5.4 /b Rli tamsi rvrlukveqc prthevuli munoprkwf rvalokalint;   [⟨-evuli⟩ for ⟨-evulat li⟩]
/p é·li tá·mse ehələkhíkwi-pe·č·íhəla·t lí mənəp·é·k·unk ehalo·ká·lənt,
/t For at certain times when an angel flew down to the pool
/k For an angel went down at a certain season into the pool,

/b my qhuk welavtwn nc mpi.   [⟨qh-|uk welavtwn⟩ for ⟨qhukwelavtwn⟩]
/p mɔ́i-kwčuk·wílahto·n nə́ mpí.
/t he made the water move.
/k and troubled the water:

/b Mrhi qhwkwelukc mpi;
/p mé·či kwčuk·wihəlá·k·e mpí,
/t After the water moved,
/k whosoever then first after the troubling of the water

/b awrn nrtami ekupat nu, qekrn krkw rlufulwkwp.
/p awé·n né·tami- íka -pá·t, ná kwí·k·e·n kéku e·lankələ́k·əp.
/t whoever went there first was then cured of whatever their ailment had been.
/k stepped in was made whole of whatsoever disease he had.

Jn 5.5 /b Mawsw line avpwp xintxki ok xaj txi kavtinri nwhi palsw.   [⟨line⟩ for ⟨lino⟩]
/p má·wsu lə́nu ahpó·p, xí·nxke ɔ́·k xá·š txí-kahtəné·i núči-pá·lsu.
/t There was a certain man there, and he had had an ailment for thirty-eight years.
/k And a certain man was there, which had an infirmity thirty and eight years.

Jn 5.6 /b Nhesus unrol tcli jifexenulen, ok waval tcli qen mrhi palselen.   [⟨un-⟩ for ⟨wn-⟩]
/p nčí·sas wəne·ɔ́·ɔl tə́li-šenki·x·í·nəli·n, ɔ́·k o·wa·há·ɔl tə́li- kwí·n mé·či -pa·lsí·li·n.
/t Jesus saw him lying there, and he knew that he had had an ailment for a long time.
/k When Jesus saw him lie, and knew that he had been now a long time in that case,

/b Tclaol, Kutatumun vuh kekrn?
/p təlá·ɔl, "kkat·á·t·amən=háč kkí·k·e·n?"
/t He said to him, "Do you want to be cured?"
/k he saith unto him, Wilt thou be made whole?

Jn 5.7 /b Palset tclaol;
/p pá·lsi·t təlá·ɔl,
/t The sick one said to him,
/k The impotent man answered him,

/b Nrvlaleun, mutu awrn avpe wehumet, qhukwevlakc mpi,
/p "nehəlá·lian, máta awé·n ahpí·i wí·č·əmi·t, kwčuk·wihəlá·k·e mpí,
/t "My lord, there is no one to help me, when the water moves,
/k Sir, I have no man, when the water is troubled,

/b wunhi a eku lwxulif.
/p wənči-=á· íka -ló·x·ɔlink.
/t so that I would be taken there.
/k to put me into the pool:

/b Mrhi eku paunc, krkw van vufq bv mrhi naomukc.   [⟨van⟩ for /=xán/]
/p mé·či íka pa·á·ne, kéku=xán=hánkw yúh mé·či nnaɔmə́k·e." [naɔm-: see *Glossary*]
/t By the time I get there, why, already I am beaten to it."
/k but while I am coming, another steppeth down before me.

Jn 5.8 /b Nhesus tclaol, Paswqel wrtuni topeny, ok pumwskal.
/p nčí·sas təlá·ɔl, "pahsúk·wi·l, wé·t·əni tɔp·í·nay, ɔ́·k pəmə́ska·l."
/t Jesus said to him, "Get up, pick up his[!; error for 'your'] bed, and walk."
/k Jesus saith unto him, Rise, take up thy bed, and walk.

Jn 5.9 /b Nu jai nu lino wlumalsen wrtunimun nc topeny nu tcli alumskan.
/p ná šá·e ná lə́nu o·lamálsi·n; wwe·t·ənə́mən nə́ tɔp·í·nay, ná tə́li-alə́mska·n.
/t And immediately then the man was well; he picked up his bed and so departed.
/k And immediately the man was made whole, and took up his bed, and walked:

/b *N*ani kejqek, alaxemwi kejkw.—   [⟨-wi⟩ for /-əwí·i/]
/p nə́ni kí·škwi·k ala·x·i·məwí·i-kí·šku.
/t That day was the day of rest.
/k and on the same day was the sabbath.

Jn 5.10 /b *N*awuk tclaol kekrvunt; Alaxemwi ta bqc kejkw;   [⟨*N*ạwuk⟩: for ⟨Nhwuk⟩ 34x]
/p nčó·wak / təlá·ɔl / ki·k·é·hənt, "ala·x·i·məwí·i=tá yúkwe kí·šku.
              [3s for 3p; prox. ppl. for obv. (as if 'the one cured said to them']
/t The Jews / he said to him, them / the one that was cured, "Today is the day of rest.
/k The Jews therefore said unto him that was cured, It is the sabbath day:

/b takw wlexnw ktcli kulinumun ktupeny. ‖   [⟨-nw⟩ for /-nó·u/]
/p takó· wəli·x·ənó·u ktə́li-kələ́nəmən ktap·í·nay."   [/-ó·u/ for older /-ó·i/]
/t It is not right for you to carry your bed."
/k it is not lawful for thee to carry thy bed.

Jn 5.11	/b	Tclaol, Kekrvetup ntclkwn, Wrtuni ktupeny ok pumiskal.
(p. 33)	/p	təláˑɔl, "kiˑkˑeˑhíˑtˑəp ntə́lkoˑn, 'wéˑtˑəni ktapˑíˑnay, ɔ́ˑk pəmə́skaˑl.' "
	/t	He said to them, "The one that cured me told me, 'Pick up your bed and walk.' "
	/k	He answered them, He that made me whole, the same said unto me, Take up thy bed, and walk.

Jn 5.12	/b	Nu notoxtaon, Awrn vuh rlwrt wrtuni ktupeny, ok pumiskal?
	/p	ná nɔtˑoˑxtáɔˑn, "awéˑn=háč éˑləweˑt, 'wéˑtˑəni ktapˑíˑnay, ɔ́ˑk pəmə́skaˑl.' "
	/t	Then he asked him. "Who's the one that said, 'Pick up your bed and walk.' "
	/k	Then asked they him, What man is that which said unto thee, Take up thy bed, and walk?

Jn 5.13	/b	Jwk kekrvunt mutu wavaeul,
	/p	šúkw kiˑkˑéˑhənt máta oˑwaˑhaˑíˑɔl,
	/t	But the one that was cured did not know who he was,
	/k	And he that was healed wist not who it was:

	/b	rli Nhesus pale ru somi xrlin nuni tali.	[⟨ru⟩: for ⟨rw⟩ 2x]
	/p	éˑli nčíˑsas palíˑi éˑw; sɔ́ˑmi-xéˑlən nə́ni táli.	
	/t	as Jesus went away; the crowd was too great there.	
	/k	for Jesus had conveyed himself away, a multitude being in that place.	

Jn 5.14	/b	Nakyrkc Nhesus wnroul patamwrekaonif;
	/p	naˑkˑaˑéˑkˑe nčíˑsas wəneˑɔ́ˑɔl paˑtamweˑiˑkˑáˑɔnink,
	/t	After a while Jesus saw him in the temple
	/k	Afterward Jesus findeth him in the temple,

	/b	tclaol, Jrlav, mrhi kekc.	
	/p	təláˑɔl, "šé=láh, méˑči kkíˑkˑe.	
	/t	and said to him, "Here now, you are cured.	[or 'Look at you!']
	/k	and said unto him, Behold, thou art made whole:	

	/b	Kahi heh mutawsevun wunhih mutu heh ekalisi muhamalseun.	
	/p	káči číˑč mahtaˑwsíˑhan, wə́nči-=č máta číˑč ikalísi -mahčamalsíˑɔn."	[or -ían]
	/t	Don't sin again, so as to not once more have an even worse condition."	
	/k	sin no more, lest a worse thing come unto thee.	

Jn 5.15	/b	Nu lino alumskrw tclaol Nhwu, Nhesus ta ntcli kekckwn.
	/p	ná lə́nu alə́mskeˑw, təláˑɔl nčóˑwa, "nčíˑsas=tá ntə́li-kiˑkˑéhkoˑn."
	/t	The man left and told the Jews, "It was Jesus that cured me."
	/k	The man departed, and told the Jews that it was Jesus, which had made him whole.

Jn 5.16 /b Nanu Nhwuk wntrlumanru Nhesusu, ok kotwnulawau,   [⟨wnt-⟩ for ⟨wunt⟩]
         /p ná=nə nčó·wak wwənte·ləma·né·ɔ nči·sás·a, ɔ́·k kɔt·o·nalawwá·ɔ,
         /t Because of that the Jews were concerned about Jesus and wanted to kill him,
         /k And therefore did the Jews persecute Jesus, and sought to slay him,

         /b rli nuni lisetup alaxmwce kejqek.
         /p é·li- nə́ni -ləs·í·t·əp ala·x·i·məwe·í·i-kí·škwi·k.
         /t for he had done that on the day of rest.
         /k because he had done these things on the sabbath day.

Jn 5.17 /b Jwk Nhesus tclaol, Nox mekintufup bqc pchi, ok nrpc nmekintumun.
         /p šúkw nčí·sas təlá·ɔl, "nó·x mi·kəntánkəp yúkwe péči ɔ́·k né·pe nəmi·kə́ntamən."
         /t But Jesus said to them, "What my father has done until now I do also."
         /k But Jesus answered them, My Father worketh hitherto, and I work.

Jn 5.18 /b Nani wunhi Nhwuk aloe katwnalanru,
         /p nə́ni wwə́nči- nčó·wak aləwí·i -kahto·nala·né·ɔ,
         /t Because of that the Jews wanted to kill him even more,
         /k Therefore the Jews sought the more to kill him,

         /b rli mutu jwk pwqelavtwq alaxemwce kejqek,
         /p é·li- máta šúkw -po·kwílahto·kw ala·x·i·məwe·í·i-kí·škwi·k,
         /t since he not only broke the day of rest,
         /k because he not only had broken the sabbath,

         /b jwk ok lwrt Kejrlumwrt nwtwxumu, nevelahi tupsqrlinsen Kejrlumwrtif.
         /p šúkw ɔ́·k -lúwe·t, "ki·š·e·ləmúwe·t no·t·ó·x·əma," nihəláči wtəpskwe·lə́nsi·n
             ki·š·e·ləməwé·t·ink.
         /t but he also said, "God is my father," thinking of himself as equal to God.
         /k but said also that God was his Father, making himself equal with God.

Jn 5.19 /b Nhesus tclapani, kehe kehe ktclun,
         /p nčí·sas təlá·p·ani, "khiči·i, khiči·i, ktə́llən.
         /t Jesus said to him (or them), "Truly, truly, I tell you (sg.).
         /k Then answered Jesus and said unto them, Verily, verily, I say unto you,

         /b Wrqesif takw nevlahi krkw lisee, jwk krkw rlenaot Wxul rvuliselet,
         /p we·k·wí·s·ink takó· nihəláči kéku ləs·í·i, šúkw kéku e·lí·naɔ·t ó·x·ɔl ehələs·í·li·t,
         /t The son does nothing on his own, but only the things he sees his father do,
         /k The Son can do nothing of himself, but what he seeth the Father do:

         /b rli nrkuma rlalokaset, nu ok Wrqesif tpisqi wtclsen.
         /p é·li né·k·əma e·lalo·ká·s·i·t, ná ɔ́·k we·k·wí·s·ink tpə́skwi wtə́lsi·n.
         /t For the things *he* does, then the son also does equally.
         /k for what things soever he doeth, these also doeth the Son likewise.

Jn 5.20
/b Wrtwxif tovolau Qesul, ok wrmi pwnwntulan nevlahi rlalokaset,
/p we·t·ó·x·ink tɔhɔ·lá·ɔ kkwí·s·al, ɔ́·k wé·mi pwənúntəla·n nihəláči e·lalo·ká·s·i·t.
/t The father loves his son, and he shows him everything he himself has done.
/k For the Father loveth the Son, and sheweth him all things that himself doeth:

/b okh aloe pwnwntulan mrxifwenako lyvoswakun,
/p ɔ́·k=č aləwí·i pwənúntəla·n me·x·inkwi·ná·k·ɔ laehɔ·s·əwá·k·an,
/t And he will show him deeds of an even greater kind,
/k and he will shew him greater works than these,

/b   wunhih kanjrlintamunru;
/p wwə́nči-=č -kanše·ləntaməné·ɔ.
/t so that they will be astonished.
/k that ye may marvel.

Jn 5.21
/b rli Wrtwxif amwekunat rfulilethi, ok lrlrxrmvalat,
/p é·li- we·t·ó·x·ink -a·mwí·kəna·t e·nkələlí·č·i, ɔ́·k -lehəle·x·e·mhá·la·t,
/t As the father raises the dead and brings them back to life,
/k For as the Father raiseth up the dead, and quickeneth them;

/b ok wtclkqi Wrqesif lrlrxrmvalan awrni letrvatc.   [⟨wtclkqi⟩ for ⟨wtclkeqi⟩]
/p ɔ́·k wtəlkí·kwi- we·k·wí·s·ink -lehəle·x·e·mhá·la·n awé·ni, li·t·e·há·t·e.
/t the son likewise also brings people back to life, if he wants to.
/k even so the Son quickeneth whom he will.

Jn 5.22
/b Wrtwxumunt takw avkrkvwri
/p we·t·ó·x·əmənt takó· ahke·khəwé·i,
/t The father does not judge,
/k For the Father judgeth no man, [but hath committed all judgment unto the Son:]

Jn 5.23
/b wunhih wrmi awrn xifwrlumat Qesu rlkeqi xifwrlumunt Wrtwxumunt.
/p wə́nči-=č wé·mi awé·n -xinkwé·ləma·t kkwí·s·a, e·lkí·kwi-xinkwé·ləmənt we·t·ó·x·əmənt.
/t so that everyone will honor his son to the same degree that the father is honored.
/k That all men should honour the Son, even as they honour the Father.

/b Awrn xifwrlwmatc Wrqesifi, ok nc xifwrluma Wrtwxumwnt prtalokalat.
/p awé·n xinkwe·ləmá·t·e we·k·wi·s·ínki, ɔ́·k ná xinkwé·ləma· we·t·ó·x·əmənt pe·t·alo·ká·la·t.   [⟨nc⟩ for /ná/; cf. next line]
/t If someone honors the son, the father that sent him is also honored.
/k [He that honoureth not the Son honoureth not the Father] which hath sent him.

/b Awrn mutu xifwrlumatc Wrqesifi, ok nu mutu Wrtwxumunt. ‖
/p awé·n máta xinkwe·lǝmá·t·e we·k·wi·s·ínki, ɔ́·k ná máta we·t·ó·x·əmənt.
/t If someone does not honor the son, they also do not (honor) the father.
/k He that honoureth not the Son honoureth not the Father [which hath sent him.]

Jn 5.24	/b	Kehe kehe kclwvumw,	[⟨kclwvumw⟩ for ⟨ktclwvumw⟩ 7x]
(p. 34)	/p	"khičí·i, khičí·i, ktəllúhəmɔ,	
	/t	"Truly, truly, I tell you (pl.),	
	/k	Verily, verily, I say unto you,	

/b   Awrn puntufc ntaptwnakun, ok wlamvetaotc prtalokalethi
                                                    [⟨prtalokalethi⟩ for ⟨prtalwkalele(t)hi⟩ 5x]
/p   awé·n pəntánke nta·pto·ná·k·an, ɔ́·k wəla·mhitaɔ́·t·e pe·t·alo·ka·[li·]lí·č·i,
/t   if someone hears my words, and if he believes in the one that sent me,
/k   He that heareth my word, and believeth on him that sent me,

/b   rvalumakumekh pwmawswakun nuxpawsw,   [⟨pwm-⟩ for /pəm-/]
/p   ehaləmá·kami·k=č pəma·wsəwá·k·an naxpá·wsu.
/t   he shall possess (*lit.*, live with) eternal life.
/k   hath everlasting life,

/b   ta vuji eku pri kuntrlumwkswakunif
/p   tá=á· háši íka pé·i kənte·ləmukwsəwá·k·anink,
/t   He will never come to damnation,
/k   and shall not come into condemnation;

/b   rli ufulwakunif mrhi lwet pumawswakunif tcli pan.
/p   é·li- ankələwá·k·anink mé·či -ló·wi·t, pəma·wsəwá·k·anink təli-pá·n.
/t   as he has already passed over death to come to life.
/k   but is passed from death unto life.

Jn 5.25	/b	Kehe kehe ktclwvumw, Tpisqevlrh; ok mrhi lr,
	/p	"khičí·i, khičí·i, ktəllúhəmɔ, tpəskwíhələ=č, ɔ́·k mé·či lé·,
	/t	"Truly, truly, I say to you (pl.), the time will come, and it has already happened,
	/k	Verily, verily, I say unto you, The hour is coming, and now is,

/b   tcli rfulukek puntamunro Kejrlumwrt Qesul toptwnakun.
/p   təli- enkəlák·i·k -pəntaməné·ɔ ki·š·e·ləmúwe·t kkwí·s·al tɔ·pto·ná·k·an,
/t   for the dead to hear the words of the son of God.
/k   when the dead shall hear the voice of the Son of God: ...

Jn 5.26	/b	Rlkeqi Wrtwxif nevlahi lrlrxrt,	
	/p	e·lkí·kwi- we·t·ó·x·ink nihəláči -lehəléx·e·t,	
	/t	As much life as the father has himself,	[*lit.*, 'the extent to which he lives']
	/k	For as the Father hath life in himself;	

/b   ok tpisqi mwelapani Wrqesif, wtclkeqi nevlahi lrlrxrn,
/p   ɔ́·k tpəskwi mwi·lá·p·ani we·k·wí·s·ink, wtəlkí·kwi- nihəláči -lehəléx·e·n.
/t   he gave equally also to the son, for him to have as much life himself.
/k   so hath he given to the Son to have life in himself;

Jn 5.27
/b ok mwelapani alweliswakun,
/p ɔ́·k mwi·lá·p·ani aləwí·i-ləs·əwá·k·an,
/t And he gave him power;
/k And hath given him authority

/b nuni wunhi kuski mekintamun jaxakawswakun,
/p nə́ni wwə́nči-káski-mi·kə́ntamən šaxahka·wsəwá·k·an,
/t that is how he can perform righteous acts,
/k to execute judgment also,

/b ok xun bni cntu lawset Qesu.
/p ɔ́·k=xán yó·ni entalá·wsi·t kkwí·s·a.
/t although also the son of mankind. [See *Glossary* under kkwi·s·i·-.]
/k because he is the Son of man.

Jn 5.28
/b Kahi kanjrlintamwvrq, rli tpisqevlrh,
/p káči kanše·ləntamó·he·kw, é·li tpəskwíhəle·=č,
/t Do not be astonished, for the time will come
/k Marvel not at this: for the hour is coming,

/b wrmi rpethek mahekamekqekri puntamunroh rlwrtaqset,
/p wé·mi e·p·í·č·i·k mahči·k·ami·k·wi·ké·i pwəntaməné·ɔ=č e·ləwe·tá·kwsi·t.
/t for all those in graves to hear his voice.
/k in the which all that are in the graves shall hear his voice,

Jn 5.29
/b ok ktheukh, nrk wrlawsetpanek, amweokh li pumawswakanif,
/p ɔ́·k kčí·ɔk=č; né·k we·la·wsi·tpáni·k, a·mwí·ɔk=č lí pəma·wsəwá·k·anink,
/t And they shall emerge; those that led good lives shall rise to life,
/k And shall come forth; they that have done good, unto the resurrection of life;

/b ok nrk mrtawsetpanek amweokh li kuntrlumwkswakunif.
/p ɔ́·k né·k me·t·a·wsi·tpáni·k, a·mwí·ɔk=č lí kənte·ləmukwsəwá·k·anink.
/t and those that led bad lives shall rise to damnation.
/k and they that have done evil, unto the resurrection of damnation.

Jn 5.30
/b Mutua kuski krkw nevlahi lisee; [⟨kuski⟩ s.b. ⟨fuski⟩]
/p "máta=á· nkáski- kéku nihəláči -ləs·í·i. [nkáski- 1s: em. from kkáski- 2s]
/t "I would not be able to do anything by myself.
/k I can of mine own self do nothing:

/b krkw mpuntamun, nu, avkrkvamu: ok xun, wlexun ntavkrkvamwrokun,
 [A preverb is missing; /nkát·a/ is conjectured.]
/p kéku mpə́ntamən, ná *nkát·a*-ahke·kháma; ɔ́·k=xán wəlí·x·ən ntak·e·khamwe·ɔ́·k·an.
/t Let me hear something, and I [want to (?)] judge; and yet my judgment is right.
/k as I hear, I judge: and my judgment is just;

	/b	rli mutu ntwnamwu rletrvau, jwk Nwx prtalokaletup rletrvat.
	/p	é·li- máta -nto·namó·wa e·li·t·e·há·a, šúkw nó·x pe·t·alo·ka·lí·t·əp e·li·t·é·ha·t.
	/t	For I do not seek my will, but the will of my father who has sent me here.
	/k	because I seek not mine own will, but the will of the Father which hath sent me.

Jn 5.31 /b Ne a nevlahi punwntvekranc nvaky ta wlamwrenavkovtwi. [⟨avkovt⟩ for ⟨akovt⟩]
       /p "ní·=á· nihəláči pənunthike·á·ne nhák·ay, tá=á· wəla·məwe·i·nakɔhtó·wi.
       /t "If *I* were to testify about *myself*, it would not be seen to be true.
       /k If I bear witness of myself, my witness is not true.

Jn 5.32 /b Jwk peli awrn avpw
       /p šúkw pí·li awé·n ahpú,
       /t But someone else exists
       /k There is another

       /b wunhi punwntvekrn
       /p wwə́nči-pənunthíke·n;
       /t and gives testimony about me,   [*lit.*, 'it'; 'me' = nhák·ay (in Jn 5.31)]
       /k that beareth witness of me;

       /b wlamwrenakot.
       /p wəla·məwe·i·ná·k·ɔt.
       /t and it is seen to be true.
       /k and I know that the witness which he witnesseth of me is true.

Jn 5.33 /b Ktclalokalanrop Nhanif, nrkuma wlamwrokun qwlintvekrnrp;
       /p ktəlalo·ka·la·né·ɔ·p nčá·nink; né·k·əma wəla·məwe·ó·k·an kwələnthiké·ne·p.
       /t You sent (someone) to John; and *he* gave people the truth for them to have.
       /k Ye sent unto John, and he bare witness unto the truth.

Jn 5.34 /b jwk mutu fkutatumwun bni cntu lawset pwnwntvekrn nvaky;
       /p šúkw máta nkat·a·t·amó·wən, yó·ni entalá·wsi·t pwənunthíke·n nhák·ay.
       /t But I do not desire that the world testify about me.
       /k But I receive not testimony from man:

       /b jwk ntaptwnc wenhih kuski kthwvalkrrq.   [⟨wenhi⟩ for ⟨wcnhi⟩]
       /p šúkw nta·ptó·ne, wénči-=č -káski-kčo·ha·lké·e·kw.
       /t I only speak so that you will be able to be saved.
       /k but these things I say, that ye might be saved.

Jn 5.35 /b Nhan kejvaqtrp osulrnekun.
       /p nčá·n ki·šhákwte·p, ɔ·s·əle·ní·k·an.
       /t John was a light and a lantern.
       /k He was a burning and a shining light:

Text, Transcription, and Translation

/b Jwk kelwu takiti kutu wlrlintamwvmw cntu oxrkamaqrq wunhi.
/p šúkw ki·ló·wa thakíti kkát·a-wəle·ləntamúhəmɔ énta-ɔ·x·e·kamá·k·we·kw wə́nči.
/t But you for a little while wanted to rejoice in the light he cast on you.
/k and ye were willing for a season to rejoice in his light.

Jn 5.36
/b Jwk ne vatr aloe xifwi punwntvekrokun Nhan punwntvekrtup;
/p šúkw ní· hát·e· aləwí·i pənunthike·ɔ́·k·an, nčá·n pənunthiké·t·əp,
/t But *I* have a greater witness than the testimony of John,
/k But I have greater witness than that of John:

/b rli lyvoswakun Nwx meletup ntclih kejalokasen,
/p é·li- laehɔ·s·əwá·k·an nó·x -mi·lí·t·əp, ntə́li-=č -ki·š·alo·ká·s·i·n.
/t for my father has given me deeds for me to complete.
/k for the works which the Father hath given me to finish,

/b nul nuni ntclyvoswakun ‖ mpunwntvekrn, ntcli Nwx prtalokalkwnrp;
/p nál nə́ni ntəlaehɔ·s·əwá·k·an mpənunthíke·n, ntə́li- nó·x -pe·t·alo·ka·lkó·ne·p.
/t By those very deeds of mine I give evidence that my father sent me here.
/k the same works that I do, bear witness of me, that the Father hath sent me.

Jn 5.37
(p. 35)
/b ok Nwx prtalokaletup, pwnwntvekrnrp wunhi nvaky.
/p ɔ́·k nó·x pe·t·alo·ka·lí·t·əp pwənunthiké·ne·p wə́nči nhák·ay.
/t And my father, who has sent me here, has given testimony about me.
/k And the Father himself, which hath sent me, hath borne witness of me.

/b Takw vuji kupuntaoewu, ok takw vuji kunroewu rlenaqset,
/p takó· háši kpəntaɔ·íwwa, ɔ́·k takó· háši kəne·ɔ·íwwa e·li·ná·kwsi·t.
/t You never hear him, and you never see what he looks like.
/k Ye have neither heard his voice at any time, nor seen his shape.

Jn 5.38
/b ok toptwnakun mutu ktupetakwnru, rli mutu kwlsitaoewu prtalokalahi.
/p ɔ́·k tɔ·pto·ná·k·an máta ktap·i·ta·k·o·wəné·ɔ, é·li máta ko·lsət·aɔ·íwwa pe·t·alo·ka·lá·č·i.
/t And his word is not in you, as you do not believe the one he sent here.
/k And ye have not his word abiding in you: for whom he hath sent, him ye believe not.

Jn 5.39
/b Lrkvekunif ntwnamwq,
/p le·khí·k·anink ntó·namo·kw,
/t Search in the scriptures,
/k Search the scriptures;

/b rli ketrvavumw rlumwqunaku pumawswakun tali maxkasek,
/p é·li-, kti·t·e·háhəmɔ, e·ləmo·k·wənák·a pəma·wsəwá·k·an -táli-maxká·s·i·k,
/t for (you think) eternal life is found there,
/k for in them ye think ye have eternal life:

	/b	ok nuni ntuntu akunemkrn,
	/p	ó·k ná=ní ntə́nta-ahkəní·mke·n.
	/t	and that is where I am talked about.
	/k	and they are they which testify of me.

Jn 5.40 /b jwk kjefi wuntaxavamw wunhi a pumawswakun mijinamrq.
/p šúkw kšínki- wə́ntax -áhəmɔ, wə́nči-=á· pəma·wsəwá·k·an -məšə́nəme·kw.
/t But you are unwilling to come here so that you would obtain life.
/k And ye will not come to me, that ye might have life.

Jn 5.41 /b Takw nwrtunimwun xifwrlumwkswakun bni wunheyek.
/p takó· nəwe·t·ənəmó·wən xinkwe·ləmukwsəwá·k·an yó·ni wənčí·ai·k.
/t I do not receive honor from here.
/k I receive not honour from men.

Jn 5.42 /b Jwk kehe kwalwvwmw ktcli mutu Kejrlumwrt avolaonru.
/p šúkw khičí·i ko·wahəlúhəmɔ, ktə́li- máta ki·š·e·ləmúwe·t -ahɔ·la·wəné·ɔ.
/t But for sure I know that you do not love God.
/k But I know you, that ye have not the love of God in you.

Jn 5.43 /b Nwx tclswakun mpchi nuxpwxrn; jwk mutu kwifywevwmw;
/p nó·x təlsəwá·k·an mpéči-naxpó·x·we·n, šúkw máta kəwinkayəwi·húmɔ.
/t I come with my father's power, but you are not willing to receive me.
/k I am come in my Father's name, and ye receive me not:

/b peli awrn, nevlahi patc, nani a kwifywawu.
/p pí·li awé·n nihəláči pá·t·e, náni=á· kəwinkayəwáwwa.
/t If someone else comes on his own, you would be willing to receive *him*.
/k If another shall come in his own name, him ye will receive.

Jn 5.44 /b Ta vuh kwnhi wlamvetamunru?
/p tá=háč kúnči-wəla·mhitaməné·ɔ,
/t How can you believe,
/k How can ye believe,

/b Kelwu nrtwnamrq xifwrlinswakun ajwntri kvakywaif wunhi,
/p ki·ló·wa ne·t·ó·name·kw xinkwe·lənsəwá·k·an a·š·unté·i khak·ayəwá·ink wə́nči?
/t you who seek honor from each other?
/k which receive honour one of another,

/b jwk Kejrlumwrtif wunheyw xifwrlumwkswakun mutu kutatumwnru.
/p šúkw ki·š·e·ləməwé·t·ink wənčí·ayu xinkwe·ləmukwsəwá·k·an, máta kkat·a·t·amo·wəné·ɔ.
/t But honor comes from God, and you do not want it.
/k and seek not the honour that cometh from God only?

Jn 5.45
- /b Kahi letrvavrq ktcli a avkunwtumwlinru Nwxif tali.
- /p káči li·t·e·há·he·kw, ktə́li-=á· -ahkəno·t·əmo·ləné·ɔ nó·x·ink táli.
- /t Do not think that I would accuse you before my father.   [*lit.*, 'at my father's']
- /k Do not think that I will accuse you to the Father:

- /b Avpw rkunemqrq, nrku Mwjiju nunvakalrkup.   [⟨nun-⟩ for ⟨ncn-⟩]
- /p ahpú e·k·əní·mkwe·kw, né·k·a mo·šə́š·a nenhaka·lé·k·əp.
- /t There is someone who accuses you, Moses himself, who you rely on.
- /k there is one that accuseth you, even Moses, in whom ye trust.

Jn 5.46
- /b Mwjiju a wlistyrkpanc, ok a ne kwlamvetyevwmwp,
- /p mo·šə́š·a=á· wələstae·kpáne, ó·k=á· ní· ko·la·mhitaíhəmɔ·p,
- /t If you had listened to Moses, you would also have believed *me,*
- /k For had ye believed Moses, ye would have believed me:

- /b rli wunhi nvakif rlrk lrkvekrtup,
- /p é·li- wə́nči nhák·enk é·le·k -le·khi·k·é·t·əp.
- /t as he wrote of what happens concerning me.
- /k for he wrote of me.

Jn 5.47
- /b jwk mutu wlamvetamwrqc rlrkvekrtup;
- /p šúkw máta wəla·mhitamo·wé·k·we e·le·khi·k·é·t·əp,
- /t But if you do not believe what he wrote,
- /k But if ye believe not his writings,

- /b ta vuh a kwnhi wlamvetamunru ntaptwnakun?
- /p tá=háč=á· kúnči-wəla·mhitaməné·ɔ nta·pto·ná·k·an?
- /t how would you believe my words?
- /k how shall ye believe my words?

Chapter 23 (pp. 35-37). [L. section 22.] (Luke 3.19-20, 4.14-32, Matthew 4.12, 14-17.)

Lk 3.19-20
- /b Nanc lukveqi sakema Vclut kwpvopani Nhanul;
- /p ná=nə ləkhíkwi sa·k·í·ma †hélat kwphó·p·ani nčá·nal,
- /t At that time, king Herod put John in prison,
- /l (1) [*About this time*] Herod the tetrarch   [numbers = sequence in L.]
  (5) [that he] shut up John in prison.
- /k But Herod the tetrarch, being reproved by him for Herodias his brother Philip's wife, and for all the evils which Herod had done, / 3.20 Added yet this above all, that he shut up John in prison.

/b rli qetulatup, rli wematu Pilupsu wekemathi wekematup Vclotiusu. Wunhi
/p é·li-khwitəlá·t·əp, é·li- wí·mahta †pilápsa wi·k·i·má·č·i -wi·k·i·má·t·əp, †helɔ·tiás·a, wə́nči,   [⟨Wunhi⟩ /wə́nči/ goes with the /é·li/ clause that precedes; cf. next]
/t because he had admonished him, for having married the wife of his brother Philip, Herodias,
/l (2) being reproved by him for Herodias his brother Philip's wife,

/b wrmi rli mutyvosetup wunhi anvwqi nc lro.
/p wé·mi é·li-mahtaehɔ·s·í·t·əp wə́nči; a·nhúkwi nə́ lé·w.   [/wə́nči/ with /é·li/ clause]
/t and for all the evil he had done; that was done in addition.
/l (3) and for all the evils which Herod had done, (4) added yet this above all, ...

Mt 4.12
/b Nhesus mrhi puntufic tcli Nhan kpavasen, lupi qwtukep Faluleuf li,
                                                        [⟨-fic⟩ for ⟨-fc⟩]
/p nčí·sas mə́·či pəntánke, tə́li- nčá·n -kpahá·s·i·n, lápi kwtə́k·i·p †nka·lalí·yunk lí,
/t When Jesus heard that John was put in prison, he returned again to Galilee,
/k Now when Jesus had heard that John was cast into prison, he departed into Galilee;

Lk 4.14
/b rli wejwkswek muntwakun;
/p é·li-wi·šəksó·wi·k mɔnt·uwwá·k·an.
/t as his spiritual power was strong.
/k [And Jesus returned] in the power of the Spirit [into Galilee:]

/b nu jac puntavkovtwp voky wrmi rlwtrnyek;
/p ná šá·e pəntákɔhtɔ·p hɔ́k·ay wé·mi e·lo·t·é·nai·k.
/t Then immediately a report was heard of him through all the towns.
/k and there went out a fame of him through all the region round about.

Lk 4.15
/b ok ‖ pumitwnvrp cntu mycvuluf,
/p ɔ́·k pəmɔt·ó·nhe·p énta-ma·éhəlank,
/t And he preached in the synagogues,
/k And he taught in their synagogues,

/b rli wlrlumwkwpani wrmi awrni.
/p é·li o·le·ləmuk·ó·p·ani wé·mi awé·ni.
/t for he was well liked by everyone.
/k being glorified of all.

Lk 4.16
(p. 36)
/b Nu kunh eku ponrp cntu kejekwvifup Nasulutif[.]
/p ná kə́nč íka pó·ne·p énta-ki·š·i·k·o·hénkəp †nasəlát·ink
/t And then he came to Nazareth, where he had been raised.
/k And he came to Nazareth, where he had been brought up:

/b Alaxemwce kejqekc nu eku tonru patamwrekanif,
/p ala·x·i·məwe·í·i-ki·škwí·k·e, ná íka tɔ·né·ɔ pa·tamwe·i·k·á·ɔnink.

/t On the day of rest, they then went to the temple.
/k and, as his custom was, he went into the synagogue on the sabbath day,

/b paswkwep rli kutu avkemat lrkvekunu,
/p pahsúk·wi·p, é·li-káhta-ahkí·ma·t le·khí·k·ana.
/t And he stood up, as he wanted to read scriptures.
/k and stood up for to read.

Lk 4.17 /b nu melanrp lrkvekunu, nrnekanewrwsetpanu Esrusu rlrkvotpani.
/p ná mi·lá·ne·p le·khí·k·ana, nehəni·k·a·ní·i-we·wsi·tpána †i·se·yə́s·a e·le·khɔ·tpáni.
/t Then he was given the book that the prophet Esaias had written.
/k And there was delivered unto him the book of the prophet Esaias.

/b Mrhi apkunatc lrkvekunu moxkaminrp cntu lrkvasek,
/p mé·či a·pkəná·t·e le·khí·k·ana, mɔxkamə́ne·p entale·khá·s·i·k,
/t After he had opened the book, he found the place where it was written,
/k And when he had opened the book, he found the place where it was written,

Lk 4.18 /b Nrvlakwf muntwakun ntupetakwn, [⟨Nrvlakwf⟩ for ⟨Nrvlalkwf⟩ 3x]
/p "nehəlá·lkɔnkw mɔnt·uwwá·k·an ntap·i·tá·k·o·n,
/t "The spiritual power of our Lord is in me,
/k The Spirit of the Lord is upon me,

/b rli ntukrkvwq
/p é·li ntak·e·kho·kw,
/t as he selected me
/k because he hath anointed me

/b ntclih pumitwnvatumaon wrlvik aptwnakun katumakset;   [⟨katum-⟩ for ⟨krtum-⟩]
/p ntə́li-=č -pəmət·o·nha·t·amáɔ·n wé·lhik a·pto·ná·k·an ke·t·əmá·ksi·t.
/t to preach the gospel (lit., good word) to the poor.
/k to preach the gospel to the poor;

/b mprtalokalkwn ntcli kekrvan palsclethi-wtrvwaul,
/p mpe·t·alo·ká·lko·n, ntə́li-ki·k·é·ha·n pa·lsi·lí·č·i wtehəwá·ɔl,
/t And he sent me to heal their sick hearts,
/k he hath sent me to heal the brokenhearted,

/b ok ntclih pumitwnvalan trvwnunthek wunhih nevlavtumavtet,
/p ɔ́·k ntə́li-=č -pəmət·o·nhá·la·n tehwənə́nči·k, wə́nči-=č -nihəla·t·amáhti·t,
/t and to preach to the captives, so that they would be free,
/k to preach deliverance to the captives,

	/b	ok wunhih krpifothek lupi nrmvetet,
	/p	ó·k wənči-=č ke·p·inkó·č·i·k lápi -ne·máhti·t, [-ne·máhti·t: emending -ne·mhíti·t]
	/t	and in order that the blind would see again,
	/k	and recovering of sight to the blind,

	/b	ok tclih nevelatamunru tumakevunhek
	/p	ó·k tə́li-=č -nihəla·t·ama·né·ɔ ktəma·k·i·hə́nči·k, [⟨tum-⟩ for /ktəm-/]
	/t	and for the persecuted to be free,
	/kl	to set at liberty them that are bruised,

Lk 4.19	/b	ok ntcli rli nalwxif wunhi Nrvlalkwf. [word missing]
	/p	ó·k ntə́li-[pəmət·ó·nhe·n] é·li-naló·x·ink wə́nči nehəlá·lkɔnkw."
	/t	and for me to [preach about] how it is the time for our Lord."
	/kl	to preach the acceptable year of the Lord. [RSV "proclaim"]

Lk 4.20	/b	Nu pwpxkawunanrp lrkvekunu lupi mwelan alokakunu, nu mwjvakrn.
	/p	ná pupxkawəná·ne·p le·khí·k·ana, lápi mwí·la·n alo·ká·k·ana, ná mwəšháke·n.
	/t	Then he closed (*lit.*, folded) the book, gave it back to the servant, and sat down.
	/k	And he closed the book, and he gave it again to the minister, and sat down.

	/b	Wrmi rpethek patamwrekaonif tove xavifomawau.
	/p	wé·mi e·p·í·č·i·k pa·tamwe·i·k·á·ɔnink tóhi-xahinkɔ·mawwá·ɔ.
	/t	Everyone in the temple had their eyes fixed firmly on him.
	/k	And the eyes of all them that were in the synagogue were fastened on him.

Lk 4.21	/b	Nu tolumi lan. Bqc kejqek mrhi pavkunhi lro nuni rlrkvasek.
	/p	ná tóləmi-lá·n, "yúkwe kí·škwi·k mé·či pahkánči-lé·w nə́ni e·le·khá·s·i·k.
	/t	And then he began to say to them, "Today that scripture has come true."
	/k	And he began to say unto them, This day is this scripture fulfilled in your ears.

Lk 4.22	/b	Wrmi wlamvetamunro
	/p	wé·mi o·la·mhitaməné·ɔ.
	/t	They all believed it.
	/k	And all bare him witness,

	/b	ok wlrlumrlintamwpanek rli wlaptwnrt wtwnif wunhi.
	/p	ó·k wəle·ləme·ləntamó·p·ani·k é·li-wəla·ptó·ne·t wtó·nink wə́nči.
	/t	And they had been astonished at the good words he spoke from his mouth.
	/k	and wondered at the gracious words which proceeded out of his mouth.

	/b	Lwrpanek, Mutu vuh wu Nhosi qesul?
	/p	luwé·p·ani·k, "máta=háč wá †nčɔ́·si kkwí·s·al?"
	/t	They had said, "Isn't he Josey's son?"
	/k	And they said, Is not this Joseph's son?

Lk 4.23	/b	Nn tclan nrl, Krvlu kehe ktclkwnru bni lwrokun;	[⟨Nn⟩ for ⟨Nu⟩]
	/p	ná tə́la·n né·l, "kéhəla khičí·i ktəlko·né·ɔ yó·ni luwe·ɔ́·k·an:	
	/t	And then he said to them, "Really he truly tells you (pl.) this saying:	[reversed]
	/k	And he said unto them, Ye will surely say unto me this proverb,	

/b Ntaktul kekrvaw kvaky:
/p 'ntá·ktəl, ki·k·é·haw khák·ay,'
/t 'Doctor, cure yourself.'
/k Physician, heal thyself:

/b krkw rli puntamufq Kupunium, nu ok nc lrkch ktakenanif.
/p kéku é·li-pə́ntamankw †kapə́niam, ná ɔ́·k nə lé·k·eč kta·ki·yəná·nink.
/t What we (inc.) heard to be in Capernaum, may that also be done in our land.
/k whatsoever we have heard done in Capernaum, do also here in thy country.

Lk 4.24 /b Jwk ktclwvmw kehe,
/p šúkw ktəllúhəmɔ khičí·i,
/t But I say to you truly,
/k And he said, Verily I say unto you,

/b nrnekanewrwset mutu xifwrlumwqwsei cntu kejeket.
/p 'nehəni·k·a·ní·i-wé·wsi·t máta xinkwe·ləmukwsí·i énta-ki·š·í·k·i·t.'
/t 'A prophet is not regarded highly where he is born and raised.'
/k No prophet is accepted in his own country.

Lk 4.25 /b Ok ktclwvumw, krxu kotvwethek avpwpanek Islilif ncki lukveqi lrlrxrtc Elyusu
/p ɔ́·k ktəllúhəmɔ, ké·x·a kɔ·tho·wí·č·i·k ahpó·p·ani·k †isələ́link néke ləkhíkwi lehəle·x·é·t·e †i·layás·a.
/t And I tell you, there were some widows in Israel at the time when Elias lived.
/k But I tell you of a truth, many widows were in Israel in the days of Elias,

/b mutu seswkulanwep nuxi kavtinri ok kwtaj kejwxif,
/p máta si·s·o·k·əla·nó·wi·p náxi-kahtəné·i ɔ́·k kwə́t·a·š ki·š·ó·x·ink,
/t It never rained for three years and six months,
/k when the heaven was shut up three years and six months,

/b ok ave katwpvotenrp wrmi b tali.
/p ɔ́·k áhi-kahto·phɔtí·ne·p wé·mi yú táli.
/t and there was great famine everywhere here.
/k when great famine was throughout all the land;

Lk 4.26 /b Elyus rlalokalintup takw krxu awrnek; jwk kwti
/p †i·láyas e·lalo·ka·lə́ntəp, takó· ké·x·a awé·ni·k, šúkw kwə́t·i,
/t Where Elias was sent, it was not several people but only one,
/k But unto none of them was Elias sent,

	/b	Suluptre wtrnif Sytunif kotvwxqrwf:
	/p	†salapte·í·i-o·t·é·nink †sáitanink, kɔ·tho·xkwé·yunk.
	/t	in the city of Sarepta in Sidon, to a widow.
	/k	save unto Sarepta, a city of Sidon, unto a woman that was a widow.
Lk 4.27	/b	ok krxu neskufulukek tali Islilif Elyusu rpetc, ⟨ne-‖skufulukek⟩]
	/p	ɔ́·k ké·x·a ni·skankəlǝ́k·i·k táli †isǝlǝ́link †i·layás·a e·p·í·t·e,
	/t	And there were some with the nasty disease in Israel when Elias was around,
	/k	And many lepers were in Israel in the time of Eliseus the prophet;
(p. 37)	/b	jwk mutu nuxpuni kwti awrn pelseep Islilif, jwk Silie lino lwenswp Nrmun xovu.
	/p	šúkw máta náxpəne kwǝ́t·i awé·n pi·lsí·i·p †isǝlǝ́link, šúkw †silí·i-lǝ́nu †né·man xó·ha."
	/t	but not even one person was cleansed in Israel, except for a lone Syrian man named Naaman."
	/k	and none of them was cleansed, saving Naaman the Syrian.
Lk 4.28	/b	Mrhi puntumetetc,
	/p	mé·či pəntamihtí·t·e,
	/t	After they heard it,
	/k	And all they in the synagogue, when they heard these things,
	/b	nu wrmi rpethek patamwrekaonif, ave manwfswuk,
	/p	ná wé·mi e·p·í·č·i·k pa·tamwe·i·k·á·ɔnink áhi-manunksúwak.
	/t	everyone in the temple was very angry.
	/k	were filled with wrath,
Lk 4.29	/b	nu pusqenro ktamruxenwk wunhi wtrnif, [⟨mru-|x⟩ for /me·x/; also Lk 1.28]
	/p	ná pɔskwi·né·ɔ, kta·me·x·í·no·k wǝ́nči o·t·é·nink,
	/t	Then they stood up, and they streamed out of the city,
	/k	And rose up, and thrust him out of the city,
	/b	kwkcnshinawau li apetaufwc, tcli a ahehkolanevenro.
	/p	kuk·ənččənawwá·ɔ lí a·phita·ɔ́nkwe, tǝ́li-=á· -ahči·čkɔlanihi·né·ɔ.
	/t	driving him to below the top of the hill, in order to throw him down head-first.
	/k	and led him unto the brow of the hill [whereon their city was built,] that they might cast him down headlong.
Lk 4.30	/b	Jwk wexkawhi nu tolomi hwpwen, tutu krtu at nuni ton.
	/p	šúkw wi·xkaɔ́či ná tɔ́ləmi-čǝ́p·wi·n, tǝtá ké·t·a-á·t ná=ní tɔ́·n.
	/t	But suddenly then he disappeared off into the crowd and went wherever he wanted to go.
	/k	But he passing through the midst of them went his way,
Lk 4.31	/b	Eku prp Kupuniumif, Falule vakif,
	/p	íka pé·p †kapəniámink, †nka·lalí·i-hák·ink,

| | /t | He came to Capernaum, in the land of Galilee, |
| | /k | And came down to Capernaum, a city of Galilee, |

	/b	alaxemwie kejqekc pumtwnvalapani.
	/p	ala·x·i·məwe·í·i-ki·škwí·k·e pwəmto·nha·lá·p·ani.
	/t	and preached to them on the day of rest.
	/k	and taught them on the sabbath days.

Lk 4.32 /b Wrmi ave kanjrluntamwpanek, rli toptwnakun hetani lrk.
/p wé·mi áhi-kanše·ləntamó·p·ani·k, é·li- tɔ·pto·ná·k·an -čí·t·ani-lé·k.
/t They were all astonished, as his words had power.
/k And they were astonished at his doctrine: for his word was with power.

Mt 4.14 /b Wunhi pavkunhi lrp rlaptwnrtup nrnekanewrwsetpanu Esrisu, rlwrtc,
/p wə́nči-pahkánči-le·p e·la·pto·né·t·əp nehəni·k·a·ní·i-we·wsi·tpána †i·se·yə́s·a, e·ləwé·t·e,
/t Whereby it came true what the prophet Esaias had told about, when he said,
/k That it might be fulfilled which was spoken by Esaias the prophet, saying,

Mt 4.15 /b vake Scpulun, ok vake Naptulwm rlamrk munwprq Nhutunif kamif, ok nrlwawsethek rpethek Faluleuf;
/p "hák·i †sépələn ɔ́·k hák·i †na·ptálǝm e·lá·me·k mǝnǝ́p·e·kw †nčátanink ká·mink ɔ́·k ne·lo·wa·wsí·č·i·k e·p·í·č·i·k †nka·lalí·yunk,
/t "The land of Zabulon and the land of Nephthalim, along the sea, on the other side of the Jordan, the heathen who are in Galilee—
/k The land of Zabulon, and the land of Nephthalim, by the way of the sea, beyond Jordan, Galilee of the Gentiles;

Mt 4.16 /b nrk peskrkif rpethek nrmunro xifwi oxrrk,   [⟨nrm-⟩ for ⟨wnrm-⟩]
/p né·k pi·ské·k·ink e·p·í·č·i·k wǝne·mǝné·ɔ xínkwi-ɔ·x·é·e·k,
/t those who were in darkness saw a great light,
/k The people which sat in darkness saw great light;

/b ok nrk lrmutupethek cntu tavako ufulwakun oxrrk prtapunwp,
/p ɔ́·k né·k le·mahtap·í·č·i·k énta-thá·kɔ ankǝlǝwá·k·an, ɔ·x·é·e·k pe·t·á·p·ano·p."
/t and for those sitting in the shadow of death, a light dawned."
/k and to them which sat in the region and shadow of death light is sprung up.

Mt 4.23 /b rli Nhesus msi rp.   [repeated below]
/p é·li nčí·sas mə́si-é·p.
/t For Jesus went all over.
/k And Jesus went about all Galilee,

Mt 4.17 /b Nu nckc wnwhi Nhesus pwmitwnvrnrp.
/p ná-néke wənúči- nčí·sas -pəmət·o·nhé·ne·p,
/t And beginning then Jesus preached,
/k From that time Jesus began to preach,

/b Lwrp, Qwlwpeq, wcnhi rli sakemaokun osavkamre pcxothevulak.
/p lúwe·p, "kwələp·i·kw, wə́nči é·li- sa·k·i·ma·ɔ́·k·an ɔ·s·ahkame·í·i -pe·x·o·č·íhəla·k."
/t saying, "Repent, because the kingdom of heaven approaches."
/k and to say, Repent: for the kingdom of heaven is at hand.

Chapter 24 (pp. 37-38). [L. section 23.] (Matthew 4.18-22; Mark 1.16-20; Luke 5.1-11)

Mt 4.18 /b Prmskatc Nhesus Falule munwprkwf, wnropani Symun, ok Antlw wemavtul,
/p pe·mská·t·e nčí·sas †nka·lalí·i-mənəp·é·k·unk, wəne·ɔ́·p·ani †sáiman ɔ́·k †ántəlu wí·mahtal, [two proximate names for obviatives]
/t When Jesus walked by the sea of Galilee, he saw Simon and his brother Andrew,
/kl And Jesus, walking by the sea of Galilee, saw two brethren, Simon called Peter, and Andrew his brother,

/b pravkonathek namrsu;
/p pé·-ahkɔ·ná·č·i·k namé·s·a.
/t who were fishing with a net.
/kl casting a net into the sea: for they were fishers.

Mt 4.21 /b ok ekalihi pravtetc wnroaul lupi neju wremavtintehek Nhim ok Nhan, ok wxwau,
/p ɔ́·k ikalíči pe·ahtí·t·e, wəne·ɔwwá·ɔl lápi ní·š·a we·i·mahtəntí·č·i·k, nčím ɔ́·k nčá·n, ɔ́·k o·x·əwá·ɔ, [Object noun phrase has three proximates for obviatives.]
/t And when they went on further, they saw two more brothers, Jim and John, and their father.
/l (1) And when he had gone a little further thence, he saw other two brethren, James [the son of Zebedee], and John [his brother], (3) with [Zebedee] their father,
/k And going on from thence, he saw other two brethren, James the son of Zebedee, and John his brother,

/b moxolif avpwpanek tonhetwnro avkonekun.
/p mux·ó·link ahpó·p·ani·k, tɔnči·to·né·ɔ ahkɔ·ní·k·an.
/t They were in a boat, mending the net.
/l (2) who also were in a ship (4) mending their nets.
/k in a ship with Zebedee their father, mending their nets; ...

Lk 5.1 /b Mrxrlkek kotu puntamunru Kejrlumwrt toptwnakun:
/p me·x·é·lki·k kót·a-pəntaməné·ɔ ki·š·e·ləmúwe·t tɔ·pto·ná·k·an.
/t A large crowd desired to hear the word of God.
/l And as the people [pressed upon him] to hear the word of God,

```
         /b  rli tavhekaotet,
         /p  é·li-tahči·ka ́hti·t,
         /t  And because they crowded up against him,
         /l  ... pressed upon him ...
```

Lk 5.3
```
         /b  nu Nhesus moxwlif tcli pwsen Symun tumxwlif.
         /p  ná nčí·sas mux·ó·link tə́li-pó·s·i·n, †sáiman tɔmxó·link.
         /t  then Jesus got into a boat, Simon's boat.
         /l  he entered into one of the ships, which was Simon's,
```

```
         /b  Nu tclan, Kunjhakvo krxiti wunhi eapri;
         /p  ná tə́la·n, "kənččá·khɔ ke·xíti wə́nči ya·p·é·i."
         /t  Then he said to him, "Push it off a little way from the shore."      [i.e., with a pole]
         /kl and prayed him that he would thrust out a little from the land.
```

```
         /b  nu Nhesus wlumuvtupen, nu tolomi pumitwnvalan nc wunhi moxwlif.
         /p  ná nčí·sas wələmahtáp·i·n; ná tólǝmi-pəmət·o·nhá·la·n nə́ wə́nči mux·ó·link.
         /t  Then Jesus sat down; and then he began preaching to them from the boat.
         /kl And he sat down, and taught the people out of the ship.
```

Lk 5.4
```
         /b  Mrhi ala ‖ pumitwnvrtc, tclau Symunu alumelavtal li cntu xetqrk,
         /p  mé·či ála-pəmət·o·nhé·t·e, təlá·ɔ †sáimana, "alǝmílahta·l lí énta-xítkwe·k,
         /t  After he had stopped preaching, he said to Simon, "Move the boat out to where it is deep,
         /k  Now when he had left speaking, he said unto Simon, Launch out into the deep,
```

(p. 38)
```
         /b  ok khvoponevenh ktakonekun.                                            [⟨khvo-⟩ for ⟨khovo-⟩]
         /p  ɔ́·k kčɔhɔ·poníhi·n=č ktak·o·ní·k·an."
         /t  and you must throw in your net."
         /k  and let down your nets for a draught.
```

Lk 5.5
```
         /b  Symun tclapani, Rkrkemiun qwnitupwq numekumusevunu
         /p  †sáiman təlá·p·ani, "e·k·e·kí·mian, kwə́ni-tpó·kw nəmi·kəmɔ·s·íhəna.
         /t  Simon said to him, "My teacher, we worked all night long.
         /k  And Simon answering said unto him, Master, we have toiled all the night,
```

```
         /b  takw krkw mputamwvwmnu,
         /p  takó· kéku mpəthamo·húməna.
         /t  We caught nothing.
         /k  and have taken nothing:
```

```
         /b  jwk nc rlaptwnaleun, nanc ntclsen, nhovoponeven ntukonekun.
         /p  šúkw e·la·pto·ná·lian, ná=nə ntə́lsi·n, nčɔhɔ·poníhi·n ntak·o·ní·k·an."   [no fut.]
         /t  But as you tell me to, I'll do that and throw in my net."
         /k  nevertheless at thy word I will let down the net.
```

Lk 5.6	/b	Mrhi nanc lisetc xavrli ptavwr namrsu,
	/p	mé·či ná=nə ləs·í·t·e, xahé·li ptáhwe· namé·s·a;
	/t	After he had done that, he caught a great many fish.
	/k	And when they had this done, they inclosed a great multitude of fishes:

	/b	nanc wunhi pwqevulr tokonekun.
	/p	ná=nə wə́nči-po·kwíhəle· tɔk·ɔ·ní·k·an. \
	/t	And because of that his net broke.
	/k	and their net brake.

Lk 5.7	/b	Nu wtitpetaonru weteswau li peli moxwif [⟨moxwif⟩ for ⟨moxwlif⟩]
	/p	ná wtətpi·taɔ·né·ɔ wi·t·i·s·əwá·ɔ lí pí·li mux·ó·link,
	/t	Then they made signs to their friends in another boat
	/k	And they beckoned unto their partners, which were in the other ship,

	/b	tcli a my wehumwkwnru.
	/p	tə́li-=á· -mái-wi·č·əmuk·o·né·ɔ.
	/t	to come and help them.
	/k	that they should come and help them.

	/b	Mrhi prthevulakc moxwl, rlee hovotru, kati qwtawvetcvunw.
	/p	mé·či pe·č·ihəlá·k·e múx·o·l, ellí·i čuhɔté·ɔ, káhti-kwtawhité·x·ənu.
	/t	After the boat came, both were filled, and they almost sank from it.
	/k	And they came, and filled both the ships, so that they began to sink.

Lk 5.8	/b	Symun Petul nc rlenufc, wnejetqetao Nhesusu, laptwnrp,
	/p	†sáiman-pí·təl nə́ e·li·nánke, wəni·š·i·tkwi·taɔ́·ɔ nči·sás·a, la·ptó·ne·p,
	/t	When Simon Peter saw that, he knelt down to Jesus, and he said,
	/k	When Simon Peter saw it, he fell down at Jesus' knees, saying,

	/b	Nivlaliun, pali al wuhi nvakif rli mrtawset nvaky.
	/p	"nehəlá·lian, palí·i á·l wə́nči nhák·enk, é·li me·t·á·wsi·t nhák·ay."
	/t	"My lord, go away from me, as I am a sinner."
	/k	Depart from me; for I am a sinful man, O Lord.

Lk 5.9	/b	Rli ave kanjrlintaf wejaswakun toxkwp ok wrmi wethrvkwki,
	/p	é·li-áhi-kanše·ləntank, wi·š·a·s·əwá·k·an tóxko·p, ɔ́·k wé·mi wi·č·e·ykúk·i,
	/t	As he was greatly astonished, fear came over him, and all who were with him,
	/k	For he was astonished, and all that were with him,

	/b	rli somi xrli namrsu twnavtet.
	/p	é·li- sɔ́·mi xé·li namé·s·a -thwənáhti·t.
	/t	as they had caught very many fish.
	/k	at the draught of the fishes which they had taken:

Lk 5.10 /b   Nhesus tclapani Symunul, Kahi wejasevun,
         /p   nčí·sas təlá·p·ani sáimanal, "káči wi·š·a·s·í·han;
         /t   Jesus said to Simon, "Do not be afraid;
         /k   ... And Jesus said unto Simon, Fear not;

         /b   bqch wunhi linoh ktetvwnu,
         /p   yúkwe=č wə́nči lə́nu=č ktithwə́na."
         /t   from now on you will be catching men."
         /kl from henceforth thou shalt catch men.

Mt 4.18-19, 21
         /b   nu nrku ok Antlws tclapani wtrkyeq;
         /p   ná né·k·a ó·k †ántəlo·s, təlá·p·ani, "wté·kai·kw."   [two prox. topics for obviatives]
         /t   Then as for him and Andrew, he said to them, "Follow me."
         /l   And he said to him and Andrew, Follow me, ...

         /b   na ok wcnhemanrp Nhimu ok Nhanu.
         /p   ná ó·k wwenči·má·ne·p nčíma ó·k nčá·na.
         /t   And then also he invited Jim and John.
         /l   He also called James and John.

Lk 5.11 /b   Mrhi eku prtwvtetc tomxwlwau eapri,
         /p   mé·či íka pe·t·uhtí·t·e tɔmxo·ləwá·ɔ ya·p·é·i,
         /t   After they brought their boats to the shore,
         /k   And when they had brought their ships to land,

         /b   nu wrmi krkw wnukavtimunrop, tolomi wtrkawpani.
                                [⟨wtrka-|wpani⟩ for ⟨wtrkawapani⟩ or ⟨wtrkaowapani⟩]
         /p   ná wé·mi kéku wənəkahtəməné·ɔ·p, tólǝmi-wte·kaɔwwá·p·ani.
         /t   they then left everything behind and began following him.
         /k   they forsook all, and followed him.   [B. omits L. addition from Mark 1.20.]

Chapter 25 (pp. 38-39). [L. section 24.] (Matthew 4.23-25; Mark 3.7 [part], 3.8 [end], 9-12.)

Mt 4.23 /b   Nhesus msi rp avpami Faluleuf, avkrkifrp tali cntu mycvaluf,
         /p   nčí·sas mə́si-é·p ahpá·mi †nka·lalí·yunk, ahke·kínke·p táli énta-ma·éhəlank.
         /t   Jesus went all over around Galilee, teaching in synagogues.
         /k   And Jesus went about all Galilee, teaching in their synagogues,

         /b   pumtwnvatuminrp wrlvik aptwnakun sakemaokune
         /p   pwəmto·nha·t·amə́ne·p wé·lhik a·pto·ná·k·an sa·k·i·ma·ɔ·k·aní·i.
         /t   He preached the gospel (*lit.*, good word) of the kingdom.
         /k   and preaching the gospel of the kingdom,

/b wrmi qekrvapani palselethi, tuk tu krkw rlufulilet.
/p wé·mi kwi·k·e·há·p·ani pa·lsi·lí·č·i, tákta kéku e·lankəláli·t.
/t He cured all the sick of any diseases and conditions they had.
/k and healing all manner of sickness and all manner of disease among the people.

Mt 4.24 /b Wrmi loxrwp wlrlumwkswakun avpami Silieuf, [⟨rwp⟩ for /-e·yó·o·p/]
/p wé·mi lo·x·we·yó·o·p o·le·ləmukwsəwá·k·an ahpá·mi †silií·yunk.
/t And his good reputation went all around Syria.
/k And his fame went throughout all Syria:

/b prtaonu palselethi wrmi cntxrnaoki lufulilethi, ok wesavkamalselethi,
/p pe·t·aɔ́·na pa·lsi·lí·č·i wé·mi entxennáɔhki-lankəlálí·č·i, ɔ́·k wisahkamalsi·lí·č·i,
/t And there were brought to him sick people with all kinds of afflictions and ones in pain,
/k and they brought unto him all sick people that were taken with divers diseases and torments,

/b ok bk wrvokyethek mavtuntwu, ok wrwhepesethek, ok hepyufulukek,
/p ɔ́·k yó·k we·hɔk·aí·č·i·k mahtant·ó·wa, ɔ́·k wewči·p·i·s·í·č·i·k, ɔ́·k či·p·ayankələk·i·k.
/t and those possessed by devils, and that had fits, and that had "palsy."
/k and those which were possessed with devils, and those which were lunatick, and those that had the palsy;

/b wrmi ‖ qekrvao.
/p wé·mi kwi·k·e·há·ɔ.
/t He cured them all.
/k and he healed them.

Mk 3.7 /b Jwk Nhesus munwprkwf rp, ok rkrkemathi wehrvkwpani, [⟨rkrk|emathi⟩]
(p. 39) /p šúkw nčí·sas mənəp·é·k·unk é·p, ɔ́·k e·k·e·ki·má·č·i wwi·č·e·ykó·p·ani.
/t But Jesus went to the sea, and his disciples went with him.
/k But Jesus withdrew himself with his disciples to the sea: ...

Mt 4.25 /b ok xrli wrtrkaotpanek wunhi Faluleuf, ok wunhi Tclin-wtrnif, ok wunhi Nhwteuf, ok wunhi Nhelwsulumif, ok Nhutunif kamif wunheyethek,
/p ɔ́·k xé·li we·t·e·kaɔ·tpáni·k wənči †nka·lalí·yunk, ɔ́·k wənči télən-o·t·é·nink, ɔ́·k wənči †nčó·tí·yunk, ɔ́·k wənči †nči·lo·sələmink, ɔ́·k †nčátanink ká·mink wənči·aí·č·i·k,
/t And there were many who followed him from Galilee, and from Ten-City, and from Judaea, and from Jerusalem, and ones who came from across the Jordan,
/k And there followed him great multitudes of people from Galilee, and from Decapolis, and from Jerusalem, and from Judaea, and from beyond Jordan.

Mk 3.8 /b ok Tyul ok Sytun okai rpethek,
/p ɔ́·k †táyal ɔ́·k †sáitan ɔ·ká·i e·p·í·č·i·k.

/t and ones who lived around Tyre and Sidon.
/k ... and they about Tyre and Sidon,

/b vwsku ave xrlwk mri toxathek puntamevtetc konjyvoswakun.
/p hwə́ska áhi-xéˑloˑk méˑi-tɔxˑáˑčˑiˑk, pəntamihtíˑtˑe kɔnšaehɔˑsˑəwáˑkˑan.
/t There were a great many who came to him after they heard about his miracles.
/k a great multitude, when they had heard what great things he did, came unto him.

Mk 3.9 /b Tclaol rkrkemathel, Wlexun a wlataufwc moxwltit
/p təláˑɔl eˑkˑeˑkiˑmáˑčˑiˑl, "wəlíˑxˑən=áˑ wəlaˑtaɔ́nkwe muxˑóˑltət,"
/t He said to his disciples, "It would be good if we had a small boat,"
/k And he spake to his disciples, that a small ship should wait on him

/b wunhi a mutu somi tavhekakwk,
/p wə́nči-=áˑ máta sɔ́ˑmi -tahčiˑkáˑkˑuk.
/t so that they would not crowd up against him too much.
/k because of the multitude, lest they should throng him.

Mk 3.10 /b rli mrhi kekrvat xrli, wunhi palselethi tavhekakwn.
/p éˑliˑ méˑči -kikˑéˑhaˑt xéˑli, wwə́nči- paˑlsiˑlíˑčˑi -tahčiˑkáˑkˑoˑn.
/t Because he had healed many, and therefore the sick crowded up to him.
/k For he had healed many; insomuch that they pressed upon him for to touch him, as many as had plagues.

Lk 5.17 /b Rli wtclswakun vokif wunhevulrp wunhi wrmi kekrvatup.
/p éˑli wtəlsəwáˑkˑan hɔ́kˑenk wənčíhəleˑp, wə́nči- wéˑmi -kikˑeˑháˑtˑəp.
/t Because his power came from him (his body), by which he cured them all.
/k and the power of the Lord was present to heal them.

Mk 1.32 /b Qekrvapani wrvokyelet mavtuntwu.
/p kwiˑkˑeˑháˑpˑani weˑhɔkˑaíˑliˑt mahtantˑóˑwa.
/t And he cured ones possessed by devils.
/k ... them that were possessed with devils.

Mk 3.11 /b Ok neski manitwethek nrovtetc tclanevenrwp vakywu rlifwcxenulet,
/p ɔ́ˑk níˑski-manətˑoˑwíˑčˑiˑk neˑɔhtíˑtˑe, təlanihiˑnéˑɔˑp hɔkˑayúwa eˑlinkweˑxˑíˑnəliˑt,
/t And when those with unclean spirits saw him, they threw themselves down before him.
/k And unclean spirits, when they saw him, fell down before him,

/b kanjalamwpanek, lwrpanek, Krtanetwet Qesu kvaky.
/p kanšalaˑmóˑpˑaniˑk, luwéˑpˑaniˑk, "keˑtanətˑóˑwiˑt kkwíˑsˑa khákˑay."
/t They shouted, saying, "You are God's son."
/k and cried, saying, Thou art the Son of God.

Mk 3.12 /b Jwk qetulapani, wunhi a mutu kthevlalwkwq.
/p šúkw kkwi·təlá·p·ani, wə́nči-=á· máta -kčihəlalúk·o·kw.
/t But he admonished them so that they would not expose him.
/k And he straitly charged them that they should not make him known.

Chapter 26 (pp. 39-49). [L. section 25.] (Matthew 5.1-48, 6.1-33, 7.1, 6-29; Mark 3.13-19; Luke 6.12-17, 20-49 [Luke 6.41-42 = Matthew 7.3-5])

Mt 5.1 /b Jwk nrovtetc mrxrlulethi, cntu muxutif pr   [⟨pr⟩ presumably for ⟨rp⟩]
/p šúkw ne·ɔhtí·t·e me·x·e·ləlí·č·i, énta-maxát·ink é·p.
/t But when he saw the crowds, he went to a high mountain.
/kl And seeing the multitudes, he went up into a mountain: ...

Lk 6.12 /b my patam, qwnitpwq potumao Kejrlumwkwfwi.
/p mái-pá·tam, kwə́ni-tpó·kw pɔ·tamaɔ́·ɔ ki·š·e·ləmuk·ónkwi.
/t He went to pray, and he prayed all night to God.
/kl ... he went [out into a mountain] to pray, and continued all night in prayer to God.

Lk 6.13 /b Mrhi opufc wcnhemapani rkrkemathi,
/p mé·či ɔ·p·ánke, wenči·má·p·ani e·k·e·ki·má·č·i.
/t The next day, he called for his disciples to come.
/k And when it was day, he called unto him his disciples:

/b tclin ok neju tokrkvoo, nrlel wtclwevulau rvalokalinhek;
/p télən ó·k ní·š·a tɔk·e·khɔ́·ɔ, né·li·l wtələwihəlá·ɔ 'ehalo·ka·lónči·k':
/t He selected twelve, and those he named 'apostles (*lit.*, messengers)':
/k and of them he chose twelve, whom also he named apostles;

Lk 6.14 /b Symun Petul, ok Antlw wemavtul, Nhim ok Nhan, Pilups ok Patalumws,
/p †sáiman-pí·təl, ó·k †ántəlu, wí·mahtal, nčím ó·k nčá·n, †pílapɔ ó·k †pa·tá·lamo·ɜ,
/t Simon Peter and Andrew his brother, Jim and John, Philip and Bartholomew,
/k Simon, (whom he also named Peter,) and Andrew his brother, James and John, Philip and Bartholomew,
/l (For Lk 6.14-16 L. has a list with additional information.)

Lk 6.15 /b Matws ok Tumus Nhim, nani qesu Alpius, ok Symun Selotw,
/p †má·to·ɜ ó·k †támas, nčím, náni kkwí·s·a †a·lpías, ó·k †sáiman †si·ló·tu,
/t Matthew and Thomas, James the son of Alphaeus, and Simon Zelotes,
/k Matthew and Thomas, James the son of Alphaeus, and Simon called Zelotes,

Lk 6.16 /b ok Nhwtus Nhim wemavtul, ok Nhwtus Iskaliut krthevulalwqki.
/p ó·k †nčó·tas, nčím wí·mahtal, ó·k †nčó·tas †iská·liat, ke·č·ihəlalúkwki.
/t And Judas, James's brother, and Judas Iscariot, who betrayed ('exposed') him.
/k And Judas the brother of James, and Judas Iscariot, which also was the traitor.

Lk 6.17 /b Nu eku wunhi punusenru rkrkemathi cntu pukvakrrk ruk.
/p ná íka wwə́nči-pənas·i·né·ɔ e·k·e·ki·má·č·i, énta-pakhaké·e·k é·ɔk.
/t Then he and his disciples came down from there, going to the plain (*lit.*, flat land).
/k And he came down with them, and stood in the plain,

/b Rkrkemathi xrli, ok xrlwk navkoi awrnek, wrtxwkki mri klistakwk,
/p e·k·e·ki·má·č·i xé·li, ɔ́·k xé·lo·k nahkɔ́·i awé·ni·k we·txúkwki mé·i-kələstá·k·uk,
/t Many were his disciples, and there were many ordinary people who came to the one they went to hear,
/k and the company of his disciples, and a great multitude of people which came to hear him,

/b ok krtu kekrvunhek wrmi krkw rli palsevtet.
/p ɔ́·k ké·t·a-ki·k·e·hə́nči·k wé·mi kéku é·li-pa·lsíhti·t.
/t and ones who wanted to be cured of everything that ailed them.
/k and to be healed of their diseases;

Mt 5.1 /b Mrhi lrmutupetc,
/p mé·či le·mahtap·í·t·e,
/t After he had sat down,
/kl and when he was set, [his disciples came unto him:]

Lk 6.20 /b apvwqr rkrkemathi punao;
/p a·phúkwe·, e·k·e·ki·má·č·i pwənaɔ́·ɔ.
/t he lifted his gaze and looked at his disciples.
/kl [And] he lifted up his eyes on his disciples, ... [L. "lift"]

Mt 5.2 /b nu tolomi pumitwnvrn, lwrp,
/p ná tóləmi-pəmət·ó·nhe·n, lúwe·p,
/t And then he began to preach, and he said,
/k And he opened his mouth, and taught them, saying,

Mt 5.3 /b Wlapcnswuk ktumakrlinsethek, rli wnevlatumunrw osavkamc sakemaokun. ‖
/p "wəla·p·énsəwak ktəma·k·e·lənsí·č·i·k, é·li wənihəla·t·aməné·ɔ ɔ·s·áhkame sa·k·i·ma·ɔ́·k·an.
/t "Blessed are the humble, for the kingdom of heaven is theirs.
/k Blessed are the poor in spirit: for theirs is the kingdom of heaven.

Mt 5.4 /b Wlapcnswuk jerlintufek, rli wlatrnumwukh.
(p. 40) /p "wəla·p·énsəwak ši·e·ləntánki·k, é·li wəla·te·namúwak=č.
/t "Blessed are those that grieve, for they shall be in good spirits.
/k Blessed are they that mourn: for they shall be comforted.

Mt 5.5 /b Wlapcnswuk tufrlinsethek, rlih nevlavtumevtet prmvakamekrk. [⟨lavt⟩ for ⟨lat⟩]
/p "wəla·p·énsəwak tanke·lənsí·č·i·k, é·li-=č -nihəla·t·amíhti·t pe·mhakamí·k·e·k.
/t "Blessed are those that think little of themselves, as they shall own the world.
/k Blessed are the meek: for they shall inherit the earth.

Mt 5.6 /b Wlapcnswuk krtopwethek, ok krtwsumwethek wunhi jaxakawswakun,
/p "wəla·p·énsəwak ke·t·o·p·wí·č·i·k ó·k ke·t·o·s·əmwí·č·i·k wə́nči šaxahka·wsəwá·k·an,
/t "Blessed are those that are hungry and thirsty for righteousness,
/k Blessed are they which do hunger and thirst after righteousness:

/b rlih kespwlin. [⟨-in⟩ for ⟨-int⟩]
/p é·li-=č -ki·spó·lənt.
/t for their hunger shall be satisfied.
/k for they shall be filled.

Mt 5.7 /b Wlapcnswuk trtavpalwrthek, rlih tavpalint.
/p "wəla·p·énsəwak tetahpa·ləwé·č·i·k, é·li-=č -tahpá·lənt.
/t "Blessed are those that are merciful to people, for people will be merciful to them.
/k Blessed are the merciful: for they shall obtain mercy.

Mt 5.8 /b Wlapcnswuk peletrvathek, rlih nrovtet Kejrlumwrlethi.
/p "wəla·p·énsəwak pi·li·t·e·há·č·i·k, é·li-=č -ne·óhti·t ki·š·e·ləməwe·lí·č·i.
/t "Blessed are those with pure hearts, for they shall see God.
/k Blessed are the pure in heart: for they shall see God.

Mt 5.9 /b Wlapcnswuk wcvwlufwnswvalwrthek, rlih lwivlunt Kejrlumwrt tomeminsumul.
/p "wəla·p·énsəwak wehwəlankunso·ha·ləwé·č·i·k, é·li-=č -luwíhələnt ki·š·e·ləmúwe·t tɔmi·mə́nsəmal,
/t "Blessed are those that make people be friends, for they shall be called God's children.
/k Blessed are the peacemakers: for they shall be called the children of God.

Mt 5.10 /b Wlapcnswuk krtumakevcnhek wunhi jaxakawswakun,
/p "wəla·p·énsəwak ke·t·əma·k·i·hə́nči·k wə́nči šaxahka·wsəwá·k·an,
/t "Blessed are those that are persecuted because of righteousness,
/k Blessed are they which are persecuted for righteousness sake:

/b rli wnevlatumunru osavkamc sakemaokun.
/p é·li wənihəla·t·aməné·ɔ ɔ·s·áhkame sa·k·i·ma·ó·k·an.
/t for they own the kingdom of heaven.
/k for theirs is the kingdom of heaven.

Lk 6.22 /b Kwlapcnsevumw, bni cntu lawset jifenavqrqc, ok hprlumwkqrqc,
/p "ko·la·p·ensíhəmɔ, yó·ni entalá·wsi·t šinki·na·k·wé·k·we, ó·k čpe·ləmuk·wé·k·we,

| | /t | "Blessed are you if people (*lit.*, mankind) hate you and exclude you, |
| | /kl | Blessed are ye, when men shall hate you, and when they shall separate you from their company, |

/b amahi lwkqrqc, amuthwelqrqc, mutakunemqeqc wunhi lino Wrqesif; jwk rli kulwncvtet.
/p amáči-luk·wé·k·we, amač·əwilkwé·k·we, mahtak·əni·mkwé·k·we wə́nči lə́nu we·k·wí·s·ink, šúkw é·li-kəlo·néhti·t.
/t if they say bad things to you, call you bad names, and defame you because of the man who is the Son, but they are lying.

Lk 6.22 /kl and shall reproach you, and cast out your name as evil, for the Son of man's sake.
Mt 5.11 /kl when men shall revile you, and persecute you, and shall say all manner of evil against you falsely, for my sake.

Mt 5.12 /b Wlrlintamwq nvakrilintamwq, rli xifwi rnvaotwakunw tali osavkumc;
/p "wəle·lə́ntamo·kw, nhake·e·lə́ntamo·kw, é·li xínkwi-e·nha·ɔhtəwá·k·anu táli ɔ·s·áhkame,
/t "Be glad and be hopeful, for there is a great reward in heaven,
/k Rejoice, and be exceeding glad: for great is your reward in heaven: (L. adds.)

/b rli nanc tclkeqi katwnalanrop nrnekanewrwseletpanifu nrtami avpetpanek.
/p é·li ná=nə təlkí·kwi-kahto·nala·né·ɔ·p nehəni·k·a·ní·i-we·wsi·li·tpanínka, né·tami-ahpi·tpáni·k.
/t for that is how much they persecuted the prophets, the ones that were first.
/k for so persecuted they the prophets which were before you. (L. adds.)

Lk 6.24 /b Bqc ajitc kelwu avoprerq, avotukh,
/p "yúkwe a·šíte ki·ló·wa ahɔ·p·é·ie·kw, áhɔhtək=č,
/t "For you who are rich now, on the other hand, it will be trouble,
/k But woe unto you that are rich!

/b rli mrhi mrjinifek kwlelyuntwakunwu.
/p é·li mé·či me·š·ənínki·k ko·li·laentəwa·k·anúwa.
/t as being ones who have already received your comfort.
/k for ye have received your consolation.

Lk 6.25 /b Ok kelwu wrmi krkw weukserq, avotukh, rli katopwevmwh.
/p ɔ́·k ki·ló·wa wé·mi kéku wiaksíe·kw, áhɔhtək=č, é·li kkat·o·p·wíhəmɔ=č.
/t And for you who have plenty of everything, it will be trouble, for you will be hungry.
/k Woe unto you that are full! for ye shall hunger.

/b   Ok kelwu bni tali kuluksavterq, avotukh, rli ksalamwevumwh ok klupavkwvwmwh.
/p   ɔ́·k ki·ló·wa yó·ni táli kǝlǝksahtíe·kw, áhɔhtǝk=č, é·li ksala·mwíhǝmɔ=č ɔ́·k kǝlǝpahkúhǝmɔ=č.
/t   And for you who laugh here, it will be trouble, for you shall cry out and weep.
/k   Woe unto you that laugh now! for ye shall mourn and weep.

Lk 6.26   /b   Avoth, rlkeqi wrmi awrn wlukunemqrq,
/p   áhɔt=č, e·lkí·kwi- wé·mi awé·n -wǝlak·ǝní·mkwe·kw;
/t   It will be difficult for you who are so well spoken of by everyone;
/k   Woe unto you, when all men shall speak well of you!

/b   nani wxwaufu tpisq wtclevanrop krkulwnrthek mrmrmunsethek.
/p   ná=ní o·x·ǝwa·únka tpǝ́skwi wtǝli·ha·né·ɔ·p ke·k·ǝlo·né·č·i·k me·me·mantsí·č·i·k.
/t   that is how their fathers likewise treated the soothsayers that lied.
/k   for so did their fathers to the false prophets.

Mt 5.13   /b   Ksekyevmw tali cntu lawsif;
/p   "ksi·khaíhǝmɔ táli entalá·wsink,
/t   "You are salt in the world.
/k   Ye are the salt of the earth:

/b   jwk afvetyrqc sekvrokun, ta vuh a wunhi lupi sekrww?
/p   šúkw ankhitaé·k·we si·khe·ɔ́·k·an, tá=háč=á· wǝ́nči- lápi -si·khe·yó·u?
/t   But if you lose saltiness, what would make it be salty again?
/k   but if the salt have lost his savour, wherewith shall it be salted?

/b   takw heh krkw laprmkwtwi,
/p   takó· čí·č kéku la·p·e·mkɔt·ó·wi,
/t   It is not good for anything anymore.
/k   it is thenceforth good for nothing,

/b   jwkh kwthumif laniven cntuh uvupekasek.
/p   šúkw=č kɔ́čǝmink laníhi·n énta-=č -ahhaphiká·s·i·k.
/t   It will just be thrown outside, where it will be trampled on.
/k   but to be cast out, and to be trodden under foot of men.

Mt 5.14   /b   Kelwu oxrkamrq cntu lawsif.
/p   ki·ló·wa ɔ·x·é·kame·kw entalá·wsink.
/t   You are what lights up the world.
/k   Ye are the light of the world.

/b   Wtrny ovhwf, ta kuski kuntvatwun.
/p   o·t·é·nay ɔhčúnk tá=á· káski-kantható·wǝn.
/t   A city on a hill cannot be hidden.
/k   A city that is set on an hill cannot be hid.

Mt 5.15 /b Awrn naxqsatc ‖ osulrnekunu ta lamwfwc, vwsif tovulyeu;
/p awé·n naxkwsá·t·e ɔ·s·əle·ní·k·ana, tá=á· la·múnkwe hó·s·ink tɔhəla·í·ɔ,
/t If someone lights a candle, they would not put it under a pot,
/k Neither do men light a candle, and put it under a bushel,

(p. 41) /b jwk kta nrnepyet, wunhi wrmi wli osulrk li wekwavmif.
/p šúkw=ktá nehəní·p·ai·t, wənči- wé·mi -wə́li-ɔ́·s·əle·k lí wi·k·əwáhəmink.
/t but rather indeed on a candlestick, so that it gives a nice light in the whole house.
/k but on a candlestick; and it giveth light unto all that are in the house.

Mt 5.16 /b Letwk nenwhi kosulrnekunwu, kejvaqtrkch wrmi awrn rlifwrxif,
/p lí·to·kw ni·núči kɔ·s·əle·ni·k·anúwa; ki·šhakwté·k·eč wé·mi awé·n e·linkwé·x·ink,
/t Let your light be before: let it shine in front of everyone, [*before* misunderstood]
/k Let your light so shine before men,

/b wunhih nrmvetet kwlalokaswakunwu,
/p wənči-=č -ne·mhíti·t ko·lalo·ka·s·əwa·k·anúwa,
/t so that they will see your good deeds
/k that they may see your good works,

/b ok xifwrlumukvwtet Kwxwau rpet osavkamc. [⟨kvw⟩ for ⟨kvwe⟩]
/p ɔ́·k -xinkwe·ləmukhwíti·t ko·x·əwá·ɔ é·p·i·t ɔ·s·áhkame.
/t and be regarded highly by your father who is in heaven. [subj. and obj. reversed]
/k and glorify your Father which is in heaven.

Mt 5.17 /b Kahi letrvavrq,
/p "káči li·t·e·há·he·kw,
/t "Do not think
/k Think not

/b ntcli wunhi pan, kavtu lokunimun bl xowi aptonakunul,
/p ntə́li-wənči-pá·n, -káhta-lo·kənə́mən yó·l xúwi-a·pto·ná·k·anal,
/t that I come because I want to destroy these ancient laws
/k that I am come to destroy the law,

/b jita nrnekanewrwsetpanifu rlaptwnctetup;
/p ší=tá nehəni·k·a·ní·i-we·wsi·tpanínka e·la·pto·nehtí·t·əp.
/t or what the prophets have said.
/k or the prophets:

/b takw nuni nwunhi pawun ntcli a lokunimun; jwk ntcli a pavkunhextwn.
  [⟨nwunhi⟩ for ⟨nwnhi⟩]
/p takó· nəni núnči-pá·wən ntə́li-=á· -lo·kənə́mən, šúkw ntə́li-=á· -pahkančí·xto·n.
/t I did not come to destroy that, but to fulfill it.
/k I am not come to destroy, but to fulfil.

Mt 5.18 /b Rli kehe ktclwvwmw, Pchi alu vatrkc osavkamc, ok bni vake,
/p é·li khičí·i ktəllúhəmɔ, péči ála-hat·é·k·e ɔ·s·áhkame ɔ́·k yó·ni hák·i,
/t For I tell you truly, until heaven and this earth no longer exist,
/k For verily I say unto you, Till heaven and earth pass,

/b takw nuxpunc kotc bl xowi aptwnakwnul, mutu lri; kxuntkih pavkunhi lrw.
/p takó· náxpəne kwə́t·i yó·l xúwi-a·pto·ná·k·anal máta lé·i, kxántki=č pahkánči-lé·w.
/t not even one of these old words (will) not be so, until it comes true.
/k one jot or one tittle shall in no wise pass from the law, till all be fulfilled.

Mt 5.19 /b Nani wunhi awrn lokunifc, ok nanc lukrkifrtc nuxpuni tufrtek bl aptwnakunul,
/p nə́ni wə́nči awé·n lo·k·ənínke, ɔ́·k ná=nə lak·e·kinké·t·e, náxpəne tanké·t·i·k yó·l a·pto·ná·k·anal,
/t Therefore, if anyone breaks even the least of these laws, and teaches that way,
/k Whosoever therefore shall break one of these least commandments, and shall teach men so,

/b lwevulauh ave tuftetw tali osavkamc sakemaokunif: [⟨-auh⟩ for ⟨-ah⟩]
/p luwíhəla·=č, áhi-tanktí·t·u táli ɔ·s·áhkame sa·k·i·ma·ɔ́·k·anink.
/t he will be called: He is the least (*lit.*, very small) in the kingdom of heaven.
/k he shall be called the least in the kingdom of heaven:

/b jwk awrn lisetc, ok nanc lukrkifrtc,
/p šúkw awé·n ləs·í·t·e, ɔ́·k ná=nə lak·e·kinké·t·e,
/t But if anyone does so and teaches that way,
/k but whosoever shall do and teach them,

/b nulh nuni moxkelun osavkamc sakemaokunif.
/p nál=č náni mɔxkí·lən ɔ·s·áhkame sa·k·i·ma·ɔ́·k·anink.
/t *he* shall be great in the kingdom of heaven.
/k the same shall be called great in the kingdom of heaven.

Mt 5.20 /b Kehe ktclwvmw, mutu aloe lrkc kjaxakawswakunwu,
/p "khičí·i ktəllúhəmɔ, máta aləwí·i-lé·k·e kšaxahka·wsəwa·k·anúwa
/t "I tell you truly, if your righteousness is not more
/k For I say unto you, That except your righteousness shall exceed

/b rlkeqi nrk rvrlrkekrthek, ok nrk Paluseuk,
/p e·lkí·kwi né·k ehəle·khi·k·é·č·i·k ɔ́·k né·k †pa·ləsi·í·ɔk,
/t than that of the scribes and the Pharisees,
/k the righteousness of the scribes and Pharisees,

/b ta tcxi tumekrwunro osavkamc sakemaokun.   [⟨t-⟩ for ⟨kt-⟩]
/p tá=á· téxi ktəmi·k·e·wəné·ɔ ɔ·s·áhkame sa·k·i·ma·ɔ́·k·an.
/t you will not at all enter the kingdom of heaven.
/k ye shall in no case enter into the kingdom of heaven.

Mt 5.21
/b Kpuntamovmw lomwc rlqevtetup; Kahi nvelwrvan;
/p kpəntamúhəmɔ lɔ́·məwe e·lkwihtí·t·əp: káči nhiləwé·han;
/t You have heard what they (obv.) said to them long ago: Do not murder anyone;
/k Ye have heard that it was said by them of old time, Thou shalt not kill;

/b ok awrn nvelwrtc, potatwnh xifwi ntwtwmaotwakun.
/p ɔ́·k awé·n nhiləwé·t·e, pɔ·tá·to·n=č xínkwi-nto·t·əma·ɔhtəwá·k·an.
/t and if anyone murders anyone, he shall earn himself a great judgment.
/k and whosoever shall kill shall be in danger of the judgment:

Mt 5.22
/b Jwk ktclwvwmw,
/p šúkw ktəllúhəmɔ,
/t But I say to you,
/k But I say unto you,

/b awrn manwfsetaotc wemavtu nwhqc, potatwnh li athemwlsen,
/p awé·n manunksi·taɔ́·t·e wí·mahta nó·čkwe, pɔ·tá·to·n=č lí-a·č·i·mó·lsi·n,
/t if anyone is angry at his brother for no reason, he will earn a council being held,
/k That whosoever is angry with his brother without a cause shall be in danger of the judgment:

/b ok awrn wemavtul latc mrtseset potatwnh wunhih xifwi athemwlsif.
/p ɔ́·k awé·n wí·mahtal lá·t·e me·tsí·si·t, pɔ·tá·to·n=č wə́nči-=č -xínkwi-a·č·i·mó·lsi·n.
/t And if anyone calls his brother a bad one, he will earn there being a great council because of it.
/k and whosoever shall say to his brother, Raca, shall be in danger of the council:

/b Jwk awrn late, Krphat kvaky, potatwnh mrxrk-tunty.
/p šúkw awé·n lá·t·e, "ké·pča·t khák·ay," pɔ·tá·to·n=č mé·x·e·k tə́ntay.
/t But if anyone says to him, "You're an idiot," he will earn the great fire.
/k but whosoever shall say, Thou fool, shall be in danger of hell fire.

Mt 5.23
/b Nuni wunhi, prtaonc kmeltwakun cntu wevwfif,
/p nə́ni wə́nči, pe·t·aɔ́ne kəmi·ltəwá·k·an énta-wi·húnkenk,
/t Therefore, if you bring your gift to the altar,
/k Therefore if thou bring thy gift to the altar,

/b ok nc tali mijatumanc kemut ktcli mutu wifrlumwkwun;
/p ɔ́·k nə́ táli-məša·t·amáne kí·mat ktə́li- máta -winke·ləmuk·ó·wən,
/t and remember there that your brother is not on friendly terms with you,
/k and there rememberest that thy brother hath ought against thee;

Mt 5.24 /b vatwl kmeltwakun cntu wevwfif,
         /p hát·o·l kəmi·ltəwá·k·an énta-wi·húnkenk,
         /t set down your gift at the altar,
         /k Leave there thy gift before the altar,

         /b vetami al my ifrlum kemut,   [⟨ifrlum⟩ for ⟨wifrlum⟩]
         /p hítami á·l, mái-winké·ləm kí·mat,
         /t and first go and get on good terms with your brother,
         /k and go thy way; first be reconciled to thy brother,

         /b nu kcnh pal ok wevwfrl kmeltwakun.
         /p ná kə́nč pá·l ó·k wi·húnke·l kəmi·ltəwá·k·an.
         /t and only then come back and offer your gift.
         /k and then come and offer thy gift.

Mt 5.25 /b Jai ‖ lafom jifalkon, srki wetawswmut,
         /p šá·e lánko·m šinká·lkɔn, sé·ki-wi·t·a·wsó·mat,
         /t Quickly agree with your adversary, while you are with him,
         /k Agree with thine adversary quickly, whiles thou art in the way with him;

(p. 42) /b rlih ta tamsc jifalkon eku loxolwkon cntu avkrkwtif,   [⟨ta tamsc⟩ for ⟨tatamsc⟩]
         /p é·li-=č ta·tá·mse šinká·lkɔn íka -lo·x·ɔlúk·ɔn énta-ahke·khó·t·ink,
         /t for sometimes your adversary will take you to court,
         /k lest at any time the adversary deliver thee to the judge,

         /b ok ajitc avkrkvwnt konu lenow tctvwnwrs ktalumoxulwkwn, kwpvwkwn.
         /p ó·k a·šíte -ahké·khunt "kə́na lí·naw," tethwə́nəwe·s ktaləmo·x·ɔlúk·o·n,
             kkəphó·k·o·n.
         /t and be instead judged innocent (lit., "let him go!"), and the policeman takes you
             away and puts you in prison.
         /k and the judge deliver thee to the officer, and thou be cast into prison.

Mt 5.26 /b Kehe ktclil mutu a kwnhi kthewun. kcnh pavkuntrnvreunc.   [⟨reu⟩ for /é·a/]
         /p khičí·i ktə́ləl, máta=á· kúnči-kčí·wən kə́nč pahkante·nhé·ane.
         /t Truly I say to you, you would not come out until you paid completely.
         /k Verily I say unto thee, Thou shalt by no means come out thence, till thou hast paid
             the uttermost farthing.

Mt 5.27 /b Kpuntamwlvwmw lomwc rlaptwnrfup;   [⟨-amwlvwmw⟩ for ⟨-amwvwmw⟩]
         /p kpəntamúhəmɔ ló·məwe e·la·pto·nénkəp:
         /t You have heard what was said long ago:
         /k Ye have heard that it was said by them of old time,

         /b Kahi pwqwnifvan wekifrokun.
         /p káči po·kwənínkhan wi·k·inke·ó·k·an.

| | /t | Do not commit adultery (*lit.*, break apart a marriage). |
| | /k | Thou shalt not commit adultery: |

Mt 5.28
- /b Jwk ne ktclwvumw, Tuk ta awrn punaotc xqru rli katalat,
- /p šúkw ní· ktəllúhəmɔ, tákta awé·n pənaɔ́·t·e xkwé·ɔ é·li-kahtá·la·t,
- /t But *I* say to you, if anyone whoever looks at a woman in a way to desire her,
- /k But I say unto you, That whosoever looketh on a woman to lust after her

- /b nul nuni wtrif tuntu pwqwnimun nuni aptwnakun. [⟨wtrif⟩ for ⟨wtrvif⟩]
- /p nál náni wté·hink tə́nta-po·kwənəmən nə́ni a·pto·ná·k·an.
- /t he is one who has broken that vow (*lit.*, word) in his heart,
- /k hath committed adultery with her already in his heart.

Mt 5.29
- /b Hanelyrkonc kijkifq, kutanevenh, kpuketwnh.
- /p čani·laehkɔ́ne kə́škinkw, kkət·aníhi·n=č, kpak·í·t·o·n=č.
- /t If your eye offends (*lit.*, mistreats) you, you must tear it out and throw it away.
- /k And if thy right eye offend thee, pluck it out, and cast it from thee:

- /b Aloeh kwlapcntumun kwti pvakr afvetaonc
- /p aləwí·i=č ko·la·p·éntamən, kwə́t·i pháke ankhitaɔ́ne,
- /t You will benefit more from it, if you lose one part
- /k for it is profitable for thee that one of thy members should perish,

- /b wunhih mutu msithri kvaky mavtuntwf lanivif.
- /p wə́nči-=č máta məsəč·é·i khák·ay mahtánt·unk -laníhink.
- /t so that your whole body will not be thrown into Hell.
- /k and not that thy whole body should be cast into hell.

Mt 5.30
- /b Hanelyrkonc ktanrvaon, ktumjimunh kpuketwnh, [⟨ktan-⟩ for ⟨ktun-⟩]
- /p "čani·laehkɔ́ne ktənne·há·ɔn, ktəmšə́mən=č, kpak·í·t·o·n=č.
- /t "If your right hand offends you, you must cut it off and throw it away.
- /k And if thy right hand offend thee, cut if off, and cast it from thee:

- /b rli aloeh kwlapcntamun kwti pvakr mutu vatrkc,
- /p é·li aləwí·i=č ko·la·p·éntamən, kwə́t·i pháke máta hat·é·k·e,
- /t For you will benefit more from it, if one part is missing,
- /k for it is profitable for thee that one of thy members should perish,

- /b wunhih mutu msithri kvaky mavtuntwif lanivif.
- /p wə́nči-=č máta məsəč·é·i khák·ay mahtánt·unk -laníhink.
- /t so that your whole body will not be thrown into Hell.
- /k and not that thy whole body should be cast into hell.

Mt 5.31 /b Ok laptwnakutwp, Awrn kavta falatc wehrohi,
/p "ɔ·k la·pto·nahkát·o·p, awé·n káhta-nkalá·t·e wi·č·e·ɔ́·č·i,
/t "And it has been said, if someone wants to divorce (*lit.*, leave) his wife,
/k It hath been said, Whosoever shall put away his wife,

/b melah lrkvekunu wunhi falat.
/p mí·la·=č le·khí·k·ana wə́nči-nkála·t.
/t she must be given a written document by which he divorces her.
/k let him give her a writing of divorcement:

Mt 5.32 /b Jwk ne ktclwvmw: Awrn falatc wehrohi,
/p šúkw ní· ktəllúhəmɔ, awé·n nkalá·t·e wi·č·e·ɔ́·č·i,
/t But *I* say to you, if anyone divorces his wife,
/k But I say unto you, That whosoever shall put away his wife,

/b keme weprfrokun jwk wunhi, pwqnimun wekifrokun;
/p ki·mí·i-wi·penke·ɔ́·k·an šúkw wə́nči, ppo·kwənə́mən wi·k·inke·ɔ́·k·an.
/t except because of unfaithfulness (*lit.*, secretly sleeping with someone), he commits adultery (*lit.*, breaks the marriage),
/k saving for the cause of fornication, causeth her to commit adultery:

/b ok awrni wehratc nu xqr nrkanr pwqunimun wekifrokun.
/p ɔ́·k awé·ni wi·č·e·ɔ́·t·e ná xkwé·, né·k·a né· ppo·kwənə́mən wi·k·inke·ɔ́·k·an.
/t and if that woman marries anyone, he too commits adultery.
/k and whosoever shall marry her that is divorced committeth adultery.

Mt 5.33 /b Ekalisi kpuntamwvwmw, lomwc lwrnrp;
/p "ikalísi kpəntamúhəmɔ, lɔ́·məwe luwé·ne·p:
/t "Furthermore, you have heard that it was said long ago: ['you (pl.)']
/k Again, ye have heard that it hath been said by them of old time,

/b Kahi nwhqc ketaptwnrvan;
/p káči nó·čkwe khita·pto·né·han;
/t do not swear for no reason. ['you (sg.)']
/k Thou shalt not forswear thyself,

/b Krtanitwet ketaptwnalatc, ok nani tupisqi lisel.
/p ke·tanət·ó·wi·t khita·pto·na·lát·e, ɔ́·k ná=ní tpə́skwi lə́s·i·l. ['you (sg.)']
/t If you swear an oath to God, likewise do that also.
/k but shalt perform unto the Lord thine oaths:

Mt 5.34 /b Jwk ne ktclwvwmw ktclih mutu tcxi ketaptwnrwnru.
/p šúkw ní· ktəllúhəmɔ, ktə́li-=č máta téxi -khita·pto·ne·wəné·ɔ. ['you (pl.)' 2x]
/t But *I* tell you, not to swear at all.
/k But I say unto you, Swear not at all;

/b Kahi ketaptwnrvun li mrtvikif wunhi osavkamc, rli Kejrlumwrt wlrlumutupifum.
/p káči khita·pto·né·han lí me·thíkink wənči ɔ·s·áhkame, é·li ki·š·e·ləmúwe·t wəlehələmatahpínkəm,
/t Do not swear to evil by heaven, for it is God's throne (*lit.*, customary seat).
/k neither by heaven; for it is God's throne:

Mt 5.35
/b Ok kahi wunhi vaki, rli nuni nrku alekrt.
/p ɔ́·k káči wənči hák·i, é·li- nə́ni né·k·a -alí·ke·t.
/t And not by the earth, as he himself steps on it.
/k Nor by the earth; for it is his footstool:

/b Ok kahi wunhi Nhelwsulum, rli nuni xifwi sakemu wtwtrny.
/p "ɔ́·k káči wənči †nči·ló·sələm, é·li ná=ní xínkwi-sa·k·í·ma wto·t·é·nay.
/t "And not by Jerusalem, as that is the great king's city.
/k neither by Jerusalem; for it is the city of the great King.

Mt 5.36
/b Ok kahi wunhi ketapwnrvun kelif,
/p ɔ́·k káči wənči-khita·pto·né·han kí·link,
/t And also do not swear by your head,
/k Neither shalt thou swear by thy head,

/b rli muta kuski naxpuni kwti meluxk opetwun jitu suketwun.
/p é·li- máta=á· -káski- náxpəne kwə́t·i mí·laxk -ɔ·p·i·tó·wan, ší·tá -sək·i·tó·wan.
/t as you would not be able to make even one hair white or black.
/k because thou canst not make one hair white or black.

Mt 5.37
/b Lexifch ktclwrokun, kovun, ‖ kovun, takw, takw,
/p li·x·ínkeč ktələwe·ɔ́·k·an, 'kɔhán, kɔhán; takó·, takó·.'
/t Let your (sg.) word be: 'It is so! It is not so!'
/k But let your communication be, Yea, yea; Nay, nay:

(p. 43)
/b aloeh lwrqe mrtvikif wunheyw.   [⟨lwrqe⟩ for ⟨lwrrqe⟩]
/p aləwí·i=č luwe·é·k·we, me·thíkink wənčí·ayu.
/t If you (pl.) say more, it comes from evil.
/k for whatsoever is more than these cometh of evil.

Mt 5.38
/b Kpuntamwvvwmw rlaptwnifup, Wijkifq wunhi wijkifq, wepet wunhi wepet.
/p kpəntamúhəmɔ e·la·pto·nénkəp: wə́škinkw wənči wə́škinkw, wí·p·i·t wənči wí·p·i·t.
/t You have heard what has been said: An eye for an eye, a tooth for a tooth.
/k Ye have heard that it hath been said, An eye for an eye, and a tooth for a tooth:

Mt 5.39
/b Jwkne ktclwvvmw, Kahi alwtavrq.   [⟨Jwkne⟩ for ⟨Jwk ne⟩]
/p šúkw ní· ktəllúhəmɔ: káči alo·t·á·he·kw.
/t But *I* say to you: Do not fight back.
/k But I say unto you, That ye resist not evil:

	/b	Ta tamsc awrn kwnunwf pavkumkonc lupi takok eku lelavtwmc.
	/p	ta·tá·mse awé·n kɔnánunk pahkamkɔ́ne, lápi tákɔ·k íka lilahtó·me.
	/t	If sometime someone hits you on your cheek, turn the other one to him also.
		[*lit.*, 'again direct the other to him']
	/k	but whosoever shall smite thee on thy right cheek, turn to him the other also.

Mt 5.40 /b Ok tamsc awrn swmkonc wrtunumakonc kjakvoqeun melwmc,
/p ɔ́·k tá·mse awé·n so·mkɔ́ne, we·t·ənəmá·k·ɔne kša·khuk·wí·ɔn, mi·ló·me,
/t And if sometime someone sues you and takes your coat, give it to him,
/k And if any man will sue thee at the law, and take away thy coat,

/b ok nc kmuxifokvwkqeun.
/p ɔ́·k nə́ kəmax·inkɔ·khuk·wí·ɔn,
/t and also your greatcoat.
/k let him have thy cloke also.

Mt 5.41 /b Ok awrn amunhemkonc ktcli a wethron kwti mylif svaki, wethrwmc savkc neju.
[⟨savkc⟩ for ⟨svaki⟩ 15x]
/p ɔ́·k awé·n amənči·mkɔ́ne ktə́li-=á· -wi·č·é·ɔ·n kwə́t·i máilink sháki, wi·č·e·yó·me sháki ní·š·a.
/t And if someone coerces you to go with him for a mile, go with him for two.
/k And whosoever shall compel thee to go a mile, go with him twain.

Mt 5.42 /b Melwmc wenwumvkon.
/p mi·ló·me wi·nəwámkɔn.
/t Give to the one that asks you.
/k Give to him that asketh thee,

/b Ok awrn kavtu kekyetc, kahi muvtrlumerkuh.
/p ɔ́·k awé·n káhta-ki·kaí·t·e, káči mahte·ləmié·k·ač.
/t And if someone wants to borrow, do not scorn him.
/k and from him that would borrow of thee turn not thou away.

Mt 5.43 /b Kpuntamwvwmw rlaptonifup, Ktavoluh rlafomut, ok kjifaluh jifalkon.
/p kpəntamúhəmɔ e·la·pto·nénkəp: ktahɔ́·la=č e·lankó·mat, ɔ́·k kšinká·la=č šinká·lkɔn.
/t You (pl.) have heard what has been said: You (sg.) must love your (sg.) relative and hate your (sg.) enemy.
/k Ye have heard that it hath been said, Thou shalt love thy neighbour, and hate thine enemy.

Mt 5.44 /b Jwk ne ktclwvwmw; Avolwmoc jifalqrq,
/p šúkw ní· ktəllúhəmɔ: ahɔ·lo·mó·e šinká·lkwe·kw,
/t But *I* say you (pl.): Love your (pl.) enemy (*lit.*, the one that hates you pl.),
/k But I say unto you, Love your enemies,

	/b	wlaptwnal amutaptwnalkon, wlevwmc jifalkon,
	/p	wəla·ptó·na·l amat·a·pto·ná·lkɔn, wəli·hó·me šinká·lkɔn,
	/t	say good things about the one that says bad things about you (sg.), do good for your enemy (*lit.*, the one that hates you sg.),
	/k	bless them that curse you, do good to them that hate you,

	/b	ok patamwrlxwmc muvtuhavkon, ok krtwnalwkon;
	/p	ɔ́·k pa·tamwe·lxó·me mahtač·áhkɔn ɔ́·k ke·t·o·nalúk·ɔn,
	/t	and pray for the one that treats you (sg.) badly and persecutes you (sg.),
	/k	and pray for them which despitefully use you, and persecute you;

Mt 5.45 /b ktcli a tomeminsumwkwn Kwx osavkamc rpet.
/p ktə́li-=á· -tɔmi·mənsəmúk·o·n kó·x ɔ·s·áhkame é·p·i·t.
/t so that you (sg.) may be the child of your father who is in heaven.
/k That ye may be the children of your Father which is in heaven:

/b Rli nrkuma levat wunhi kthifwcvulat qejoxumu cntu mutawsif, ok cntu wlawsif;
/p é·li- né·k·əma -lí·ha·t wənči-kčinkwéhəla·t kwi·š·ó·x·əma énta-mahtá·wsink ɔ́·k énta-wəlá·wsink.
/t For *he* makes it so that his sun rises where the evil are and where the good are,
/k for he maketh his sun to rise on the evil and on the good,

/b ok swkulanvr cntu jaxakawsif ok cntu mutu jaxakawsif.
/p ɔ́·k so·k·əlá·nhe· énta-šaxahká·wsink ɔ́·k énta- máta -šaxahká·wsink.
/t and he makes rain where the righteous are and where the unrighteous are.
/k and sendeth rain on the just and on the unjust.

Mt 5.46 /b Jwk avolutc rvolkon, krkwh vuh li rnvaotwakunw
/p šúkw ahɔ·lát·e ehɔ́·lkɔn, kéku=č=háč lí-e·nha·ɔhtəwá·k·anu?
/t If you (sg.) only love one who loves you, what will be the reward?
/k For if ye love them which love you, what reward have ye?

/b mutu vuh a nanc ktupisqi lisewun mrtawsetif? [⟨ktupisqi⟩ for ⟨ktupsqi⟩]
/p máta=háč=á· ná=nə ktə́pskwi-ləs·í·wən me·t·a·wsí·t·ink?
/t Would you not be doing exactly the same as a sinner?
/k do not even the publicans the same?

Lk 6.32 /b rli mrtawsethik avolavtet rvolqetethi.
/p é·li- me·t·a·wsí·č·i·k -ahɔ·láhti·t ehɔ·lkwihtí·č·i.
/t For sinners love those that love them.
/k ... for sinners also love those that love them.

Mt 5.47 /b Jwk kematuk wlufwmutc, krkw vuh li aloe lrw?
/p šúkw kí·mahtak wəlanko·mát·e, kéku=háč lí aləwí·i-lé·w?
/t If you are only on good terms with your brothers, in what way is it exceptional?
/k And if ye salute your brethren only, what do ye more than others?

	/b	mutu vuh a ok nanc ktclsewun mrtawsetif?
	/p	máta=háč=á· ɔ́·k ná=nə ktəlsí·wən me·t·a·wsí·t·ink?
	/t	Would you not also be doing the same as a sinner?
	/k	do not even the publicans so?

Lk 6.34 /b Kekyivutc nrk rletrvan, lupih nmujinimun, krkw vuh nc lrw?   [⟨-van⟩ for ⟨-vaun⟩]
     /p ki·kai·hát·e né·k e·li·t·e·há·an, 'lápi=č nəməš·ənə́mən,' kéku=háč nə́ lé·w?]
     /t If you lend to those of whom you think, 'I'll get it back again,' what is that?
     /k And if ye lend to them of whom ye hope to receive, what thank have ye?

     /b Mrtawselethi keyevatc nu mrtawset, tcli a lupi nani txi mijinamun.
                                                                              [⟨keyevatc⟩ for ⟨kekyevatc⟩]
     /p me·t·a·wsi·lí·č·i ki·kai·hát·e ná me·t·á·wsi·t, tə́li-=á· ná=ní txí -məšə́nəmən.
     /t If the sinner lends to sinners to get the same amount.   ["If" is a misunderstanding.]
     /k for sinners also lend to sinners, to receive as much again.

Lk 6.35 /b Avolw jifalqrqek; wlevw, ok kekyevw nwhi.
     /p ahɔ́·lo· šinka·lkwé·k·wi·k; wəlí·ho· ɔ́·k ki·kaí·ho· nó·čkwe.   ['you (pl.)']
     /t Love those that hate you; treat them well and lend to them for nothing.
     /k But love ye your enemies, and do good, and lend, hoping for nothing again;

     /b Nuh xifwi ktrnvaotwakun, ok kwtameminsumwqh Rlwrlumwqset;
     /p ná=č xinkwi kte·nha·ohtəwá·k·an, ɔ́·k ko·t·ami·mə́nsəmukw=č e·ləwe·ləmúkwsi·t.
     /t Then your reward shall be great, and you will be the child of the most highly esteemed one.   ['your (sg.)'; 'you (sg.)']
     /k and your reward shall be great, and ye shall be the children of the Highest:

     /b rli nrkuma ktumakrlumat, mutu wewlrlintumulethi, ok mrhi liselethi.
     /p é·li- né·k·əma -ktəma·k·é·ləma·t máta wi·wəle·ləntaməlí·č·i ɔ́·k méči-ləs·i·lí·č·i.
     /t For *he* takes pity on those who are never glad and those who do wrong.
     /k for he is kind unto the unthankful and to the evil.

Mt 5.48 /b Pavkunhi liseq, ‖ rlkeqi pavkunhi liset Kwxwu nu osavkamc.
     /p pahkánči-ləs·i·kw, e·lkí·kwi-ləs·i·t kó·x·əwa ná ɔ·s·áhkame.
     /t Be perfect to the same degree that your father who is in heaven is.   ['you (pl.)']
     /k Be ye therefore perfect, even as your Father which is in heaven is perfect.

Mt 6.1 /b Katu awrn naxpufwmatc, kahi lisevun ktcli a awrn nrvkwn.   [⟨Katu⟩ for ⟨Kavtu⟩]
(p. 44) /p káhta- awé·n -naxpanko·mát·e, káči ləs·í·han któli-=á· awé·n -né·yko·n.
     /t If you (sg.) want to give a present to someone, don't do so to be seen by people.
     /k Take heed that ye do not your alms before men, to be seen of them:

     /b Kahi liseanc Kwx osavkamc rpet ta ktrnvakwi.
     /p káč·i ləs·iáne, kó·x ɔ·s·áhkame é·p·i·t tá=á· kte·nha·k·ó·wi.
     /t But if you (sg.) do, your father who is in heaven will not reward you.
     /k otherwise ye have no reward of your Father which is in heaven.

Text, Transcription, and Translation

Mt 6.2 /b Kata krkw nuxpufwfranc, kahi vetami pwtatufvun pwtathekun,

[⟨Kata⟩ for ⟨Kavta⟩]

/p káhta- kéku -naxpankunké·ane, káči hítami po·t·a·t·ánkhan po·t·a·č·í·k·an,
/t When you (sg.) want to give a present to someone, don't first blow a trumpet,
/k Therefore when thou doest thine alms, do not sound a trumpet before thee,

/b rvlinumivtet krvakevokrthek, cntu mycvuluf; ok lawotrnyc
/p ehəli·namíhti·t kehahki·hɔke·č·i·k énta-ma·éhəlank ɔ́·k la·wo·t·é·naye,
/t as the hypocrites (*lit.*, deceivers) do in the synagogue and in the middle of town,
/k as the hypocrites do in the synagogues and in the streets,

/b wunhi a wrmi awrni xifwrlumwkvwetet.
/p wə́nči-=á· wé·mi awé·ni -xinkwe·ləmukhwíti·t.
/t so that everyone would think a lot of them.
/k that they may have glory of men.

/b Kehe ktclwvwmw; wtrnvrnrw.
/p khičí·i ktəllúhəmɔ: wte·nhe·né·ɔ.
/t Truly I say to you (pl.): their account is even.
/k Verily I say unto you, They have their reward.

Mt 6.3 /b Jwk nuxpufwnseanc, kahi lrlintufvun ktunorvaun lri kumununheun rlrk,
/p šúkw naxpankunsiáne, káči le·ləntánkhan ktənne·há·ɔn lé·i kəmənančí·ɔn é·le·k,
/t But when you (sg.) give presents, don't let your right hand do what your left hand does,
/k But when thou doest alms, let not thy left hand know what thy right hand doeth:

Mt 6.4 /b wunhih nuxpufwnseanc mutu wavko;
/p wə́nči-=č naxpankunsiáne máta -wwáhkɔ.
/t so that when you give presents it is not known.
/k That thine alms may be in secret:

/b nuh Kwx, mutu nrvqwset, ktrnvakwn cntu nrvkwtuk.
/p ná=č kó·x, máta ne·ykwə́s·i·t, kte·nhá·k·o·n énta-ne·ykɔ́t·ək.
/t Then your father, who is unseen, will reward you where it is seen.
/k and thy Father which seeth in secret himself shall reward thee openly.

Mt 6.5 /b Patamanc, kahi lisevun krvakevokrt rlset [⟨-anc⟩ for /-á·ane/; or pa·tamáne]
/p pa·tamá·ane, káči ləs·í·han kehahki·hɔke·t é·lsi·t.
/t When you (sg.) pray, don't do what the hypocrite does.
/k And when thou prayest, thou shalt not be as the hypocrites are:

129

/b rli nrk wivifi patamaok, cntu mycvuluf, ok lawtrnyc
/p é·li né·k wihínki-pa·tamá·ɔk énta-ma·éhəlank ɔ́·k la·wo·t·é·naye,
/t For they always like to pray in the synagogue and in the middle of town,
/k for they love to pray standing in the synagogues and in the corners of the streets,

/b wunhi rli nrvqevtet wrmi awrni.
/p wə́nči é·li-ne·ykwíhti·t wé·mi awé·ni.
/t because of how everyone sees them.
/k that they may be seen of men.

/b Kehe ktclwvwmw rnvrok.
/p khičí·i ktəllúhəmɔ, e·nhé·ɔk.
/t Truly I say to you (pl.), their account is even.
/k Verily I say unto you, They have their reward.

Mt 6.6 /b Jwk ke patamanc, eku amc cntu tavhrk,
/p šúkw kí· pa·tamá·ane, íka á·me énta-tahčé·k.
/t But when *you* (sg.) pray, go into a narrow place.
/k But thou, when thou prayest, enter into thy closet,

/b kpavumanc, nuh kpatamaon Kwx mutu awrn nrot,
/p kpahəmáne, ná=č kpa·tamáɔ·n kó·x, máta awé·n né·ɔ·t.
/t When you shut the door, then you shall pray to your father, who no one sees.
/k and when thou hast shut thy door, pray to thy Father which is in secret;

/b nrkumuh ktrnvakwn wunhih nrvqwseun.
/p né·k·əma=č kte·nhá·k·o·n, wə́nči-=č -ne·ykwə́s·ian.
/t *He* will reward you, so that you shall be seen.
/k and thy Father which seeth in secret shall reward thee openly.

Mt 6.7 /b Patamanc, kahi nwhqc xrlaptwnrvun mulaji nrlwawset rlset,
/p "pa·tamá·ane, káči nó·čkwe xe·la·pto·né·han málahši ne·lo·wá·wsi·t é·lsi·t.
/t "When you (sg.) pray, don't pointlessly speak with many words, as the pagan does.
/k But when ye pray, use not vain repetitions, as the heathen do:

/b rli letrvat mpuntakch wunhi xrltwnvrt,
/p é·li-li·t·é·ha·t, 'mpəntá·k·e=č,' wə́nči-xe·ltó·nhe·t.   [*lit.*, 'I will be heard.']
/t Because they think they will be heard is why they speak a lot.
/k for they think that they shall be heard for their much speaking.

Mt 6.8 /b kahi nuni lisevrq rlsevtet;
/p káči nə́ni ləs·í·he·kw e·lsíhti·t,
/t Don't do what they do,   [you (pl.)]
/k Be not ye therefore like unto them:

	/b	rli Kwxwu wataq krkw krtatmun nrlumu nrtoxtaoot.
	/p	é·li- kó·x·əwa -wwá·ta·kw kéku ke·t·á·t·aman né·ləma ne·t·o·xtaó·ɔt.
	/t	for your (pl.) father knows what you (sg.) desire before you ask him for it.
	/k	for your Father knoweth what things ye have need of, before ye ask him.

Mt 6.9 /b Nulh bni rlenako ktcli pataman.
        /p nál=č yó·ni e·li·ná·k·ɔ ktə́li-pá·tama·n:
        /t This is the way you (sg.) must pray: [*lit.*, 'this is how it must be that you pray']
        /k After this manner therefore pray ye:

        /b Wrtwxumulrf rpeun osavkamc. Xifoxkunemvkotkch ktclwenswakun.
            [⟨xk⟩ for /hk/; ⟨wens⟩ for ⟨wcns⟩]
        /p "we·t·o·x·əmə́lenk, é·p·ian ɔ·s·áhkame, xinkɔhkəni·mkɔ́tkeč ktələwensəwá·k·an.
        /t "You who are our father, who are in heaven, may your name be praised.
        /kl Our Father which art in heaven, Hallowed be thy name.

Mt 6.10 /b Prrekch ksakemaokun.   [⟨ksakemao|kun⟩]
        /p pe·e·í·k·eč ksa·k·i·ma·ó·k·an.
        /t May your kingdom come.
        /kl Thy kingdom come.

        /b Ktetrvrokun lrkch xqetvakameqc, rlkeqi lrk tali osavkamc.
        /p kti·t·e·he·ó·k·an lé·k·eč xkwi·thakamí·k·we, e·lkí·kwi-lé·k táli ɔ·s·áhkame.
        /t May your will be done on earth, to the same degree that it is done in heaven.
        /kl Thy will be done in earth, as it is in heaven.

Mt 6.11 /b Melenrn bqc kejqek tcpi metherf:
        /p mi·lí·ne·n yúkwe kí·škwi·k tépi mí·č·ienk.
        /t Give us today enough for us to eat.
        /kl Give us this day our daily bread.

Mt 6.12 /b ok pavketrlintamaenrn nhanawswakuninu, rlkqi nelwnu pavketatamarf nrk hihanelaiqifek,
        /p ɔ́·k pahki·t·e·ləntamaí·ne·n nčana·wsəwa·k·anə́na,
            e·lkí·kwi- ni·ló·na -pahki·t·a·t·amáenk né·k čəčani·laehkwénki·k,
        /t And forgive our misdeeds for us, as *we* forgive those that mistreat *us*.
        /kl And forgive us our debts, as we forgive our debtors.
        /cp And forgive us our trespasses, as we forgive them that trespass against us.

Mt 6.13 /b ok kahi paevif avqrhetwakunif, jwk pale linenrn wunhi mrtvikif.
        /p ɔ́·k káči pa·í·henk ahkwe·č·ihtəwá·k·anink, šúkw palí·i ləní·ne·n wə́nči me·thíkink.
        /t And may we not come into temptation; but remove us from evil.
        /kl And lead us not into temptation, but deliver us from evil:

	/b	Rli ke nuni sakemaokun ok ktclswakun, ok taloeliswakun rvalumakumek.
		[⟨ok ta-⟩ for ⟨ok kta-⟩; ⟨rvalumaku-‖mek⟩]
	/p	é·li kí· nə́ni sa·k·i·ma·ɔ́·k·an, ɔ́·k ktəlsəwá·k·an, ɔ́·k ktaləwí·i-ləs·əwá·k·an, ehaləmá·kami·k.
	/t	For *yours* is the kingdom, and your power and your superiority, forever.
	/kl	For thine is the kingdom, and the power, and the glory, for ever.
(p. 45)	/b	Nanc lrkch.
	/p	ná=nə lé·k·eč.
	/t	May it be that way.
	/kl	Amen.
Mt 6.14	/b	Puketatumaotc, awrn honawswakun,
	/p	pahki·t·a·t·amaɔ́t·e awé·n čona·wsəwá·k·an,
	/t	If you (sg.) forgive someone's misdeeds for them,
	/k	For if ye forgive men their trespasses,
	/b	Kwx osavkamc, nu ok nc tclsen kpuketatumakwnh khanawswakun.
	/p	kó·x ɔ·s·áhkame ná ɔ́·k nə́ tə́lsi·n; kpak·i·t·a·t·amá·k·o·n=č kčana·wsəwá·k·an.
	/t	your father in heaven then also does that; he will forgive your misdeeds for you.
	/k	your heavenly Father will also forgive you:
Mt 6.15	/b	Jwk ke mutu paketatumaootc awrn honawswakun,
	/p	šúkw kí· máta pahki·t·a·t·amaɔ·ɔ́t·e awé·n čona·wsəwá·k·an,
	/t	But if *you* (sg.) do not forgive someone's misdeed for them,
	/k	But if ye forgive not men their trespasses,
	/b	taa ok nu Kwx osavkamc kpuketatamakwun khanawswakun.
	/p	tá=á· ɔ́·k ná kó·x ɔ·s·áhkame kpak·i·t·a·t·ama·k·ó·wən kčana·wsəwá·k·an.
	/t	your father in heaven will also not forgive you for your misdeed.
	/k	neither will your Father forgive your trespasses.
Mt 6.16	/b	Ave wli mutu kutu metseonc, kahi lisevun krvakevokrt rlset,
	/p	"áhi-wə́li máta káhta-mi·tsí·ɔne, káči ləs·í·han kehahki·hɔ́ke·t é·lsi·t.
	/t	"When you (sg.) fast, don't do what the hypocrite does.
	/k	Moreover when ye fast, be not, as the hypocrites, of a sad countenance:
	/b	rli vufq rlavkevtet, wunhi xrli awrn letrvat kehe ta wli muta kavta metsei.
	/p	é·li-=hánkw -e·lahkíhti·t, wənči- xé·li awé·n -li·t·é·ha·t, 'khiči·i=tá wə́li máta káhta-mi·tsí·i.'
	/t	For they paint their faces, so that many people think, 'He truly is fasting.'
	/k	for they disfigure their faces, that they may appear unto men to fast.
	/b	Kehe ktclwvwmw, rnvrok.
	/p	khiči·i ktəllúhəmɔ, e·nhé·ɔk.

/t   Truly I say to you (pl.): their account is even.
/k   Verily I say unto you, They have their reward.

Mt 6.17 /b   Jwk ke ave wli mutu kavtu metseonc, wletwmc kel okh kijextwn kijkifq,
/p   šúkw kí· áhi-wəli máta káhta-mi·tsí·ɔne, wəli·tó·me kí·l, ó·k=č kkəš·í·xto·n kə́škinkw,
/t   But *you* (sg.), when you fast, fix your hair (*lit.*, your head), and you must wash your face,
/k   But thou, when thou fastest, anoint thine head, and wash thy face;

Mt 6.18 /b   wunhih muta awrn letrvawun ncrt ktclsen, jwk Kwx mutu nenrvqwset,
/p   wwə́nči-=č máta awé·n -li·t·e·há·wən, nə́=ét ktə́lsi·n, šúkw kó·x máta ni·ne·ykwə́s·i·t.
/t   so that no one will think that you must be doing that, except your father who is never seen.
/k   That thou appear not unto men to fast, but unto thy Father which is in secret:

/b   nrkumah ktrnvakwn cntuh nrvqwseun.
/p   né·k·əma=č kte·nhá·k·o·n énta=č -ne·ykwə́s·ian.
/t   *He* will reward you where you will be seen.
/k   and thy Father, which seeth in secret, shall reward thee openly.

Mt 6.19 /b   Kahi myrnumwvrq lathrswakun xqetvakameqc,
/p   "káči ma·e·nəmó·he·kw lač·e·s·əwá·k·an xkwi·thakamí·k·we,
/t   "Do not gather possessions on earth,   [you (pl.)]
/k   Lay not up for yourselves treasures upon earth,

/b   cntu a moxrsuk pekjimevtet, ok a cntu muxalituk,   [⟨muxal-⟩ for ⟨muxkal-⟩]
/p   énta-=á· mo·x·wé·s·ak -pi·kšəmíhti·t, ó·k=á· énta-maxkalə́t·ək,   [⟨ox⟩ for /o·x·w/]
/t   where insects would cut them up and they would rust,
/k   where moth and rust doth corrupt,

/b   cntu a kevkumwtkrthek tufjrnumevtet kumwtkctet.   [⟨kevk-⟩ for ⟨kcvk-⟩]
/p   énta-=á· kehkəmo·tké·č·i·k -tunkše·nəmíhti·t, -kəmo·tkéhti·t.
/t   and where thieves would open and steal them.
/k   and where thieves break through and steal:

Mt 6.20 /b   Jwk marnumwq lathrswakun li osavkamc,
/p   šúkw ma·é·nəmo·kw lač·e·s·əwá·k·an lí ɔ·s·áhkame,
/t   But gather possessions in heaven,
/k   But lay up for yourselves treasures in heaven,

/b   cntu a mutu mwxrsuk paletwvtet, jitu muxalituk,   [⟨muxal-⟩ for ⟨muxkal-⟩]
/p   énta-=á· máta mo·x·wé·s·ak -pali·túhti·t, ší=tá -maxkalə́t·ək,
/t   where insects would not destroy them, or they would not rust,
/k   where neither moth nor rust doth corrupt,

	/b	ok a cntu mutu krvkumwtkchek tufjrnumitet, kumwtkcvtet;
	/p	ɔ́·k=á· énta- máta kehkəmo·tké·č·i·k -tunkše·nəmíhti·t, -kəmo·tkéhti·t.
	/t	and where thieves would not open and steal them.
	/k	and where thieves do not break through nor steal:

Mt 6.21 /b rli ktclathrswakun rtrk, nuh ok nc ktri topen.   [⟨ktri⟩ for ⟨ktr⟩]
         /p é·li ktəlač·e·s·əwá·k·an é·te·k, ná=č ɔ́·k nə́ kté· tɔ́p·i·n.
         /t For where your possessions are, that will be where your heart also is.
         /k For where your treasure is, there will your heart be also.

Mt 6.22 /b Oxrr voky wunhi wujkifq,
         /p ɔ·x·é·e· hɔ́k·ay wə́nči wə́škinkw;
         /t The body is lit by the eye.
         /k The light of the body is the eye:

         /b nunc jwk lisetc kijkifq msithrih oxrr kvaky.
         /p ná=nə šúkw lǝs·í·t·e kə́škinkw, məsəč·é·i=č ɔ·x·é·e· khák·ay.
         /t If that's all your eye does, your whole body will be *lit*.
         /k if therefore thine eye be single [RSV: sound], thy whole body shall be full of light.

Mt 6.23 /b Jwk mahi lisetc kijkifq, misthrih kvaky peskrr.   [⟨misthri⟩ for ⟨msithri⟩]
         /p šúkw máhči-lǝs·í·t·e kə́škinkw, məsəč·é·i=č khák·ay pi·ské·e·.
         /t But if your eye is evil, your whole body will be a dark place.
         /k But if thine eye be evil, thy whole body shall be full of darkness.

         /b Nanc jekunh koxrrkum, mrhi peskrr, ave xifwi peskuntqrr!
         /p ná=nə ší·kanč kɔ·x·e·é·k·əm: mé·či pi·ské·e·; áhi·xínkwi-pi·skəntkwé·e·.
         /t That's all for your light: it is now dark; it is an extremely dark place inside.
         /k If therefore the light that is in thee be darkness, how great is that darkness!

Mt 6.24 /b Ta awrn koski mekumosuntamaoeu neju nevlalkwkc,   [⟨-kc⟩ for /-k·i/]
         /p "tá=á· awé·n kɔ́ski-mi·kəmɔ·s·əntamaɔ·í·ɔ ní·š·a nehəla·lkúk·i.
         /t "No one can work for two masters.
         /k No man can serve two masters:

         /b rli mawselw jifalatc, ok maoselw avolatc,
         /p é·li ma·wsí·lu šinka·lá·t·e, ɔ́·k ma·wsí·lu ahɔ·lá·t·e,   [confused; see next line]
         /t For if he hates one, and if he loves the other,
         /k for either he will hate the one, and love the other;

         /b jita mawselw wlsitaol, ok takoki mavtrlumatc.
         /p ší=tá ma·wsí·lu o·lsət·aɔ́·ɔl, ɔ́·k takɔ́·ki mahte·ləmá·t·e.   [confused]
         /t or he listens to one, and if he scorns the other.
         /k for else he will hold to the one, and despise the other.

	/b	Ta koski mekintamaoeu Krtanitwelethi, nuxpi avoprokun.
	/p	tá=á· kóski-mi·kəntamaɔ·í·ɔ ke·tanət·o·wi·li·č·i náxpi ahɔ·p·e·ó·k·an.
	/t	He would not be able to work for God having (*lit.*, with) wealth.
	/k	Ye cannot serve God and mammon.

Mt 6.25 /b Nanc wunhi lilrq: Kahi kumr punyrlintufvrq wcntawserq,
/p ná=nə wə́nči-lə́le·kw: káči nkəmé·i pəna·eləntánkhe·kw wenta·wsíe·kw,
/t That's why I say to you (pl.): Do not always think about what you live from,
/k Therefore I say unto you, Take no thought for your life,

/b krkw a ta metherq, ‖ ok a mrnrrq, ok a qeaqi kvakif rtaon.
/p kéku=á·=tá mí·č·ie·kw, ó·k=á· me·né·e·kw, ó·k=á· kwiá·kwi khák·enk é·taɔn.
/t what you would eat or drink, nor yet what you would put on your body.
/k what ye shall eat, or what ye shall drink; nor yet for your body, what ye shall put on.

(p. 46) /b Mutu vuh lrlrxrokun aloe lri, methwakun rlrk,
/p máta=háč lehəle·x·e·ó·k·an aləwí·i-lé·i mi·č·əwá·k·an é·le·k,
/t Is not life more than food,
/k Is not the life more than meat,

/b ok wavtwvrpi aloe lri rvaqif rlrk?
/p ó·k wahtuhé·p·i aləwí·i-lé·i éhahkwink é·le·k?
/t and the body more than clothing?
/k and the body than raiment?

Mt 6.26 /b Punw hwlinsuk prmapanek; Mutu vakevreuk, takw wewlataeuk,
/p pənó· čo·lə́nsak pe·má·p·ani·k; máta haki·he·í·ɔk, takó· wi·wəla·ta·í·ɔk.
/t Look at the birds of the air; they do not plant and never put up food,
/k Behold the fowls of the air: for they sow not, neither do they reap, nor gather into barns;

/b jwk vufq Kwxwu osavkamc texamao.   [⟨tex-⟩ for ⟨tox-⟩]
/p šúkw=hánkw kó·x·əwa o·s·áhkame tɔx·amá·ɔ.
/t But your father in heaven feeds them.
/k yet your heavenly Father feedeth them.

/b Mutu vuh kelwu kumifasri lisevwmw nrk rlsevtet?
/p máta=háč ki·ló·wa kəminkahsé·i-ləs·i·húmɔ né·k e·lsíhti·t?
/t Are *you* not better than they are?
/k Are ye not much better than they?

Mt 6.27 /b Awrn vuh kelwu koski unhi sakevao vokyu koti srksetuf, letrvatc?
/p awé·n=háč ki·ló·wa kóski-ánči-shaki·há·ɔ hókaya kwə́t·i se·ksí·t·ank, li·t·e·há·t·e?
/t Who of you can lengthen his body by one foot if he wants to?
/k Which of you by taking thought can add one cubit unto his stature?

Mt 6.28 /b ok krkw wunhi natrlintamrq rqerq?
         /p ɔ·k kéku wə́nči-na·te·ləntame·kw é·k·wie·kw?
         /t And why do you take thought for your clothing?
         /k And why take ye thought for raiment?

         /b Punamwq otyrsul lckveqi wlekun.—
         /p pənámo·kw ɔ·taé·s·al ləkhíkwi-wəlí·k·ən.   (Cf. Lk 12.27.)
         /t Look at how beautifully flowers grow.
         /k Consider the lilies of the field, how they grow;

         /b Takw mekumoseeuk; ok takw pemunatreuk.
         /p takó· mi·kəmɔ·s·i·í·ɔk, ɔ́·k takó· pi·məna·te·í·ɔk.
         /t They do not work, and they do not make thread.
         /k they toil not, neither do they spin:

Mt 6.29 /b Ktclwvwmw; Salumunu, nale wtaloeliswakun. mutu telukveqi owluvkonkwunrp rlkeqi bl wlatyrek.
         /p ktəllúhəmɔ, †sa·lamána nahəlí·i wtaləwí·i-ləs·əwá·k·an máta tilləkhíkwi-owəlahkɔnk·ó·wəne·p e·lkí·kwi- yó·l -wəla·taé·i·k.
         /t I tell you, even Solomon was never clothed by his "glory" (lit., power) as beautifully as their blossoms are.
         /k And yet I say unto you, That even Solomon in all his glory was not arrayed like one of these.

Mt 6.30 /b Kejrlumwrt avkonifc b vake wunhi skeko, bqc kejqek wlekifc, alupu lwsasekc;
         /p ki·š·e·ləmúwe·t ahkɔnínke yú hák·i wə́nči skí·kɔ, yúkwe kí·škwi·k wəli·k·ínki, aláp·a lo·s·a·s·í·k·i,   [⟨-fc⟩ for /-nki/; ⟨-kc⟩ for /-k·i/]
         /t If God clothes this earth with grass, which today grows nicely and tomorrow is burned up,
         /k Wherefore, if God so clothe the grass of the field, which to day is, and to morrow is cast into the oven,

         /b mutu ksi kelwu aloe ktlevkwewu?
         /p máta=ksí ki·ló·wa aləwí·i ktəlihko·wíwwa?
         /t ought he not then to treat you better?
         /k shall he not much more clothe you,

         /b O tatxuntw kwlsitamwrokunwu.
         /p ó·, ta·txə́ntu ko·lsət·amwe·ɔ·k·anúwa.
         /t Oh, you have not much faith.
         /k O ye of little faith?

Mt 6.31 /b Nc wunhi kahi kumr punyrlintwfvun krkw metheun, ok mrnrun,
                                         [⟨-wfvun⟩ for ⟨-ufvun⟩]
         /p nə wə́nči káči nkəmé·i pəna·eləntánkhan kéku mí·č·ian ɔ́·k me·né·an,

Text, Transcription, and Translation

/t Therefore do not always think about what you eat or drink,
/k Therefore take no thought, saying, What shall we eat? or, What shall we drink?

/b jitu krkw rqeun.
/p ší=tá kéku é·k·wian.
/t or what you wear.
/k or, Wherewithal shall we be clothed?

Mt 6.32 /b Wrmi bl nrlwawsethek, jwk notwnaminru.
/p wé·mi yó·l ne·lo·wa·wsí·č·i·k šúkw nɔt·o·namené·ɔ.
/t All these things only the heathen seek.
/k (For after all these things do the Gentiles seek:)

/b Osavkumc nu Kwx watwn cntxi katatumun nrl krkw.
/p ɔ·s·áhkame ná kó·x o·wá·to·n éntxi-kahtá·t·aman né·l kéku.
/t In heaven your father knows how much you desire of those things.
/k for your heavenly Father knoweth that ye have need of all these things.

Mt 6.33 /b Vetami ntwnamwq Kejrlumwrt wsakemaokun, ok wjaxakawswakun,
/p hítami ntó·namo·kw ki·š·e·ləmúwe·t wsa·k·i·ma·ɔ́·k·an ɔ́·k wšaxahka·wsəwá·k·an.
/t First seek God's kingdom and his righteousness.
/k But seek ye first the kingdom of God, and his righteousness;

/b ktapih bl wrmi melqwsenrw.
/p ktá·pi·=č yó·l wé·mi -mi·lkwəs·i·né·ɔ.
/t You (pl.) will be given all these things in the bargain.
/k and all these things shall be added unto you.

Mt 6.34 /b Ncni wunhi kahi punyrlintufvun, wunhi alupu,
/p nəni wə́nči káči pəna·eləntánkhan wə́nči aláp·a,
/t Therefore do not think about tomorrow,
/k Take therefore no thought for the morrow:

/b rli alupu tcpi punyrlintamun lupi nc kejqek.   [⟨tcpi⟩ for /wtépi-/]
/p é·li aláp·a wtépi-pəna·eləntamən lápi nə́ kí·škwi·k.
/t for tomorrow thinks enough about the next day.
/k for the morrow shall take thought for the things of itself.

/b Kwti kejqek trpevulr sukwrlintamun.
/p kwə́t·i kí·škwi·k te·p·íhəle· sak·we·ləntaman.
/t One day is enough for you to be troubled about.
/k Sufficient unto the day is the evil thereof.

Mt 7.1	/b	Kahi avkunemerkuh, tclih mutu krpi avkrkvokrwun; [⟨krpi⟩ for ⟨krpc⟩ 11x]
	/p	"káči ahkəni·mié·k·ač, ktə́li-=č máta ké·pe -ahke·kho·k·é·wən. [⟨t-⟩ for /kt-/]
	/t	"Do not pronounce judgment on them, so that you, too, will not be judged.
	/k	Judge not, that ye be not judged.

Lk 6.37	/b	mutu awrn avkrkvootc, ta awrn avkunemkwun.
	/p	máta awé·n ahke·khɔ·ót·e, tá=á· awé·n ahkəní·mko·wan.
	/t	If you do not judge anyone, there will be no one that pronounces judgment on you.
	/k	Judge not, and ye shall not be judged: condemn not, and ye shall not be condemned:

	/b	Paketatumaotc, krpch kpuketatumakc.
	/p	pahki·t·a·t·amaót·e, ké·pe=č kpak·i·t·a·tamák·e.
	/t	If you forgive them, you, too, will be forgiven.
	/k	forgive, and ye shall be forgiven:

Mt 7.2	/b	Nul nc ktatekun rrkreun nunulh nc qwtatekrn; [⟨reu⟩ for /é·a/]
	/p	nál nə́ kwta·tí·k·an e·e·ké·an, nánal=č nə́ kkwət·a·tí·k·e·n.
	/t	The same measure that you use will be what you measure with.
	/k	... with what measure ye mete, it shall be measured to you again.

Lk 6.38	/b	melatc, krpch kumelkwn,
	/p	mi·lát·e, ké·pe=č kəmí·lko·n.
	/t	If you give to him, he will give it to you, too.
	/k	Give, and it shall be given unto you;

	/b	wli qtatakreunc kuskekvatasekc, ok qwthwkounivifc, palejevulrh;
		[⟨qtatakr-⟩ for ⟨qtatekr-⟩ (cf. Mt 7.2); ⟨reu⟩ for /é·a/; ⟨-koun-⟩ for ⟨-kon-⟩]
	/p	wə́li-kwta·ti·k·é·ane, †kaski·khata·s·í·k·e ɔ́·k kwčuk·ɔnihínke, palí·i šíhəle·=č.
	/t	If you measure well, if it is tamped down(?) and shaken, it will overflow.
	/k	good measure, pressed down, and shaken together, and running over,

	/b	nunih ktcli melkrn.
	/p	nə́ni=č ktə́li-mí·lke·n."
	/t	That is how it will be given to you."
	/k	shall men give into your bosom.

Lk 6.39	/b	Tclau rnuntvakrokun. Kuski vuh ‖ a krkrpifot savkaqwnr krkrpifolethi?
	/p	təlá·ɔ e·nənthake·ɔ́·k·an: káski·=háč =á· ke·k·e·p·ínkɔ·t -sahká·kwəne· ke·k·e·p·inkɔ·lí·č·i?
	/t	He told them a parable: Can a blind person lead a blind person?
	/k	And he spake a parable unto them, Can the blind lead the blind?

(p. 47)	/b	mutu vuh a rlee eku levelreuk cntu keskalavku?
	/p	máta=háč=á· ellí·i íka lihəle·í·ɔk énta-ki·ská·lahka?

| | /t | Wouldn't both of them fall into a ditch? |
| | /k | shall they not both fall into the ditch? |

Lk 6.40 /b Rkrkemqwset takw tolwelisewunu rkrkemathel,
/p e·k·e·ki·mkwə́s·i·t takó· tɔləwí·i-ləs·í·wəna e·k·e·ki·má·č·i·l.
/t The disciple (one taught) is not greater than his teacher (*lit.*, the one he teaches!).
/k The disciple is not above his master:

/b jwk wrmi cntxi myailiset, tupisqih tclsen rvakrkifrt.
/p šúkw wé·mi éntxi-mayá·i-lə́s·i·t, tpə́skwi=č tə́lsi·n ehahke·kínke·t.
/t But everyone who is the way he should be will be just like a teacher.
/k but every one that is perfect shall be as his master.

Lk 6.41 /b Koh wunhi punamun cntu suprtek kematis wijkifq,
/p kóč wə́nči-pənáman énta-sap·é·t·i·k kí·mahtəs wə́škinkw,
/t How come you look at the little spot your brother's eye has,
/k And why beholdest thou the mote that is in thy brother's eye,

/b jwk mutu ktamuntumwun taxun nuni eku rtrk kijkifwf.
/p šúkw máta ktamantamó·wən tá·x·an nə́ni íka é·te·k kəškínkunk?
/t but you do not feel the piece of wood that is in your eye?
/k but perceivest not the beam that is in thine own eye?

Lk 6.42 /b Jita, ta vuh a kwnhi kuski lan kematis,
/p ší=tá, tá=háč=á· kúnči-káski-lá·n kí·mahtəs,
/t Or, how could you say to your brother,
/k Either how canst thou say to thy brother,

/b lavupu futunimun pulalekaxqtit kijkifwf
/p 'lahápa nkət·ənə́mən pəlali·k·á·xkwtət kəškínkunk,'
/t 'Let me pull out the little splinter in your eye,'
/k Brother, let me pull out the mote that is in thine eye,

/b xifwi taxun eku vatrkc kijkifwf?
/p xínkwi-tá·x·an íka hat·é·k·e kəškínkunk?
/t when there is a large piece of wood in your eye?
/k when thou thyself beholdest not the beam that is in thine own eye?

/b Rvakevokrt, vetami palelini xifwi taxun kijkifwf,
/p ehahki·hɔ́ke·t, hítami palí·i lə́ni xínkwi-tá·x·an kəškínkunk.
/t You hypocrite, first remove the large piece of wood in your eye.
/k Thou hypocrite, cast out first the beam out of thine own eye,

/b   nuh kuski wli nrmun tufiti krkw ekali kematis wijkifwf.
/p   ná=č kkáski-wə́li-né·mən tankíti kéku íkali kí·mahtəs wəškínkunk.
/t   Then you will be able to see well the little bit of a thing in your brother's eye.
/k   and then shalt thou see clearly to pull out the mote that is in thy brother's eye.

Mt 7.6   /b   Kahi eku lanivmawerkuh mykunruk krkw wli pelvik,
/p   "káči íka lanihəmawié·k·ač mwe·k·ané·ɔk kéku wə́li-pí·lhik,
/t   "Do not throw something really holy to the dogs,
/k   Give not that which is holy unto the dogs,

/b   ok krkw mrxifootek kahi kwjkwjuk cku lanivmawerkuh,
/p   ɔ́·k kéku me·x·inkɔ́·ɔhti·k, káči kwəškwə́š·ak íka lanihəmawié·k·ač,
/t   and something of great value, do not throw to the hogs,
/k   neither cast ye your pearls before swine,
/n   (The chiasmus in the translation is not in the original.)

/b   rli a tamsc vupvekamevtet wunhi wsetwaif,
/p   é·li-=á· tá·mse -haphikamíhti·t wə́nči wsi·t·əwá·ink,
/t   for they might trample on it with their feet,
/k   lest they trample them under their feet,

/b   nu a ok eku tcli qwlwpenru kmy twxkumwkwn.
/p   ná=á· ɔ́·k íka tə́li-kwələp·i·né·ɔ, kəmái-to·xkamúk·o·n.
/t   and then they would turn on you and tear you apart.   ['on you': *lit.*, 'there']
/k   and turn again and rend you.

Mt 7.7   /b   Wenwranch, nuh kumelkrn.
/p   wi·nəwé·ane=č, ná=č kəmí·lke·n.
/t   If you ask, it will be given to you.
/k   Ask, and it shall be given you;

/b   Ntwnu, kumuxkamunh.
/p   ntó·na; kəmáxkamən=č.
/t   Seek it; you shall find it.
/k   seek, and ye shall find;

/b   Pwpwvetrva, ktufjrnumakrnh;
/p   pəp·uhhitéha; ktunkše·nəmá·k·e·n=č.
/t   Knock on the door; it shall be opened for you.
/k   knock, and it shall be opened unto you:

Mt 7.8   /b   rli wrmi cntxi wenwrt, mijinif,
/p   é·li- wé·mi éntxi-wí·nəwe·t -məšə́nink,
/t   For everyone that asks receives it,
/k   For every one that asketh receiveth;

/b ok awrn ntonufc, muxkamunh;
/p ɔ́·k awé·n nto·nánke, móxkamən=č,
/t and if someone seeks it, he will find it,
/k and he that seeketh findeth;

/b ok awrn pwpwvetcvufc twfjrnumaonh.
/p ɔ́·k awé·n pəp·uhhitehánke, tunkše·nəmáɔ·n=č.
/t and if someone knocks on the door, it shall be opened for them.
/k and to him that knocketh it shall be opened.

Mt 7.9
/b Awrn vuh a kelwu wenwumkwkc wnehanu avpon, mwelao asin?
/p awé·n=háč=á· ki·ló·wa wi·nəwamkúk·e wəni·č·á·na ahpɔ́·n, mwi·lá·ɔ ahsə́n?
/t Who of you, if his child asks him for bread, would give them a stone?
/k Or what man is there of you, whom if his son ask bread, will he give him a stone?

Mt 7.10
/b jitu ntwxtaqkc namrsu mwelao vuh a xkwku.
/p ší=tá nto·xtá·kwke namé·s·a, mwi·lá·ɔ=háč=á· xkó·k·a?
/t Or, if they ask him for a fish, would give them a snake?
/k Or if he ask a fish, will he give him a serpent?

Mt 7.11
/b Kumuthilisi, jwk kuski ktumakrlumu kunehan wenowumkonc,
/p kəmáči-lə́s·i, šúkw kkáski-ktəma·k·é·ləma kəní·č·a·n wi·nəwamkɔ́ne.
/t You are evil, but you are able to take pity on your child when they ask you.
/k If ye then, being evil, know how to give good gifts unto your children,

/b mutu vuh a Kwx osavkamc qwtumakrlumaeu, wenwumkwkc,   [⟨-kc⟩ for /-k·i/]
/p máta=háč=á· kó·x o·s·áhkame kwət·əma·k·e·ləma·í·ɔ wi·nəwamkúk·i,
/t Would your father in heaven not take pity on those that ask him
/k how much more shall your Father which is in heaven

/b ok mwelaeu krkw wrlvik?
/p ɔ́·k mwi·la·í·ɔ kéku wé·lhik?
/t and not give them good things?
/k give good things to them that ask him?

Mt 7.12
/b nani wunhi, nuh nc wrmi krkw ktclevan awrnek, krkw rletrvaun qwlu ntclevkrn.
/p nə́ni wə́nči ná=č nə wé·mi kéku ktəlí·ha·n awé·ni·k, kéku e·li·t·e·há·an, 'kwə́la ntəlíhke·n',
/t Therefore that is everything you must do to people, the things you want to be done to you,   [*lit.*, 'things of which you think, "I wish it was done to me."']
/k Therefore all things whatsoever ye would that men should do to you, do ye even so to them:

	/b	Rli nuni lexifup lomwc nwhi, ok nrnekanewrwsetpanifu toptwnakunwu.
	/p	é·li- nə́ni -li·x·ínkəp ló·məwe núči, ɔ́·k nehəni·k·a·ní·i-we·wsi·tpanínka tɔ·pto·na·k·anúwa.
	/t	for that has been the rule since long ago, and the law of the prophets.
	/k	for this is the law and the prophets.

Mt 7.13 /b Nrli al tufrtek skontif.
/p "né·li á·l tanké·t·i·k skɔ́ntenk,
/t "Go in the small door,
/k Enter ye in at the strait gate:

/b Rli xifwrk skonty, ok xifwi talalavku nc wunhi eku pchi ufulwakunif, ‖
/p é·li-xínkwe·k skɔ́ntay ɔ́·k -xínkwi-talá·lahka, nə́ wə́nči íka péči ankələwá·k·anink
/t for the doorway is large and there is a big hole by which to go to death.
/k for wide is the gate, and broad is the way, that leadeth to destruction,

(p. 48) /b ok xrli nc wuntaqi rathek.
/p ɔ́·k xé·li nə́ wə́ntahkwi e·á·č·i·k.
/t and many are the ones that go that way.
/k and many there be which go in thereat:

Mt 7.14 /b Skonty somi tufrtw ok nc tumakun tufvakrxuntw rlvakrxif pumawswakunif
/p skɔ́ntay sɔ́·mi-tanké·t·u, ɔ́·k nə́ təmá·k·an tankhake·x·ə́ntu e·lhaké·x·ink pəma·wsəwá·k·anink;
/t The doorway is very small, and the road is small that leads to life;
/k Because strait is the gate, and narrow is the way, which leadeth unto life,

/b ncni wunhi tatxiti mrxkufek.
/p nə́ni wə́nči ta·txíti me·xkánki·k.
/t that is why there are not many that find it.
/k and few there be that find it.

Mt 7.15 /b Nuxalwmc mrmrmunsethek, atcli a toxkwn mrkesavqethek, [⟨atcli⟩ for ⟨ktcli⟩]
/p naxa·ló·me me·me·mantsí·č·i·k, ktə́li-=á· -tɔ́xko·n mekisahkwí·č·i·k,
/t Watch out for soothsayers to be coming to you in sheep clothes,
/k Beware of false prophets, which come to you in sheep's clothing,

/b jwk lamwfwc kehe tumr tclsen.
/p šúkw la·múnkwe khičí·i tə́me tə́lsi·n.
/t but inside to be really a wolf.
/k but inwardly they are ravening wolves.

Mt 7.16 /b Kwavaokh wunhi tclswakunwu.
/p ko·wa·há·ɔk=č wə́nči təlsəwa·k·anúwa.
/t You will know them by their actions.
/k Ye shall know them by their fruits.

/b Kuski vuh a wesavkem kejekun kawunjakwf tali,
/p káski-=háč=á· wísahki·m -ki·š·í·k·ən ka·wənšá·kunk táli,
/t Could grapes grow on a thorn bush,
/k Do men gather grapes of thorns,

/b ok vuh a kuski krkw jwkulepwko wunheyw kavwruf.
/p ó·k=háč=á· káski- kéku šo·k·əli·pó·k·ɔ -wənčí·ayu kahəwé·yunk.
/t or could something sweet come from "itch weed"?
/k or figs of thistles?

Mt 7.17
/b Aphi nc lrw,
/p á·pči nə̂ lé·w:
/t That is always so: [apparently misunderstood]
/k Even so

/b jeki vetkwf wifuf wunheyw,
/p ší·ki-hítkunk wínkank wənčí·ayu,
/t from a good tree comes good-tasting fruit,
/k every good tree bringeth forth good fruit;

/b ok maheqi vetkwf mahepwko wunheyw,
/p ó·k mahčí·kwi-hítkunk mahči·pó·k·ɔ wənčí·ayu.
/t and from a bad tree comes bad-tasting fruit.
/k but a corrupt tree bringeth forth evil fruit.

Mt 7.18
/b jeki vetkwf, ta kuski mavhepwko wunheyee,
/p ší·ki-hítkunk tá=á· káski- mahči·pó·k·ɔ -wənči·aí·i,
/t From a good tree bad-tasting fruit cannot come,
/k A good tree cannot bring forth evil fruit,

/b ok mavheqi vetkwf ta kuski wifuf wunheyee,
/p ó·k mahčí·kwi-hítkunk tá=á· káski- wínkank -wənči·aí·i.
/t and from a bad tree good-tasting fruit cannot come.
/k neither can a corrupt tree bring forth good fruit.

Mt 7.19
/b wrmi vetkwk cntxi mutu wifuf wcnheyeq keskvoh tuntrufh laneven.
                                              [⟨wcnh-⟩ for /wənč-/]
/p wé·mi hítko·k éntxi- máta wínkank -wənčí·ai·kw, kí·skhɔ·=č, tənté·yunk=č laníhi·n.
/t All trees that good-tasting fruit does not come from will be cut down and will be thrown into the fire.   [lit., 'as many as what is good-tasting does not come from']
/k Every tree that bringeth not forth good fruit is hewn down, and cast into the fire.

Mt 7.20
/b Kwatwnruh wunhi nc wunhekif.
/p ko·wa·to·né·ɔ=č wənči nə̂ wənčí·k·ink.
/t You shall know it by what grows from it.
/k Wherefore by their fruits ye shall know them.

Lk 6.45	/b	Wrliliset awrn, wtrvif kumr wrlvik wunheyw;
	/p	wé·li-ləs·i·t awé·n wté·hink nkəmé·i wé·lhik wənčí·ayu,
	/t	From a good person's heart always comes good,
	/k	A good man out of the good treasure of his heart bringeth forth that which is good;
	/b	ok mrhiliset awrn, wtrvif kumr mrtvik wunheyw.
	/p	ó·k méči-ləs·i·t awé·n wté·hink nkəmé·i mé·thik wənčí·ayu,
	/t	and from a bad person's heart always comes evil,
	/k	and an evil man out of the evil treasure of his heart bringeth forth that which is evil:
	/b	Rli rlavpelet wtrva, wtwnif kumr wunhevlr.
	/p	é·li e·lahpí·li·t wté·ha wtó·nink nkəmé·i wənčíhəle·.
	/t	for the way his heart is always comes out of his mouth.
	/k	for of the abundance of the heart his mouth speaketh.
Lk 6.46	/b	Krkw vuh wcnhi lwrun, Nrvlaliun, Nrvlaliun nu wrnu mutu ktclsewun rlwru.
	/p	kéku=háč wénči-luwé·an, 'nehəlá·lian, nehəlá·lian,' ná wé·na máta ktəlsí·wən e·ləwé·a.
	/t	Why do you say, 'My Lord, my Lord,' and then still you don't do what I say?
	/k	And why call ye me, Lord, Lord, and do not the things which I say?
Mt 7.21	/b	Takw ta wrmi awrn tumekrwun osavkamce sakemaokun rlet Nrvlaliun, Nrvlaliun, [⟨t-⟩ for /wt-/]
	/p	takó·=tá wé·mi awé·n wtəmi·k·é·wən ɔ·s·ahkame·í·i-sa·k·i·ma·ó·k·an é·li·t, 'nehəlá·lian, nehəlá·lian,'
	/t	Everyone who says to me, 'My Lord, my Lord,' does not enter the kingdom of heaven,
	/k	Not every one that saith unto me, Lord, Lord, shall enter into the kingdom of heaven;
	/b	jwk bk rlsethek Nwx osavkamce rletrvat.
	/p	šúkw yó·k e·lsí·č·i·k nó·x ɔ·s·ahkame·í·i e·li·t·é·ha·t.
	/t	but only those that do what my father in heaven wants done.
	/k	but he that doeth the will of my Father which is in heaven.
Mt 7.22	/b	Xrlwkh rlethek nuni kejqek. Nrvlaliun, Nrvlaliun,
	/p	xé·lo·k=č e·lí·č·i·k nə́ni kí·škwi·k, 'nehəlá·lian, nehəlá·lian,
	/t	There will be many who say to me that day, 'My Lord, my Lord,
	/k	Many will say to me in that day, Lord, Lord,
	/b	mutu vuh mpumtwnvatamwnrnap ktclswakun,
	/p	máta=háč mpəmto·nha·t·amo·wəné·na·p ktəlsəwá·k·an?
	/t	haven't we preached about your power?
	/k	have we not prophesied in thy name?

/b mutu vuh ok pale ntclskaoewnapanek mavtuntwuk wunhi ktclswakun,
/p máta=háč ɔ́·k palí·i ntəlskaɔ·i·wəná·p·ani·k mahtant·ó·wak wə́nči ktəlsəwá·k·an?
/t Haven't we also driven away devils by your power?
/k and in thy name have cast out devils?

/b mutu vuh ok nc ktclswakun nwnhi xrlrnaovki li kunjyvosewunrnap?
/p máta=háč ɔ́·k nə́ ktəlsəwá·k·an núnči- xe·lennáɔhki -kanšaehɔ·s·i·wəné·na·p?'
/t Haven't we performed many kinds of miracles by your power?'
/k and in thy name done many wonderful works?

Mt 7.23
/b Nuh ntclan.Takw vuji kwavlwvwmw paleaq b wunhi amutalokaserq.
/p ná=č ntə́la·n, 'takó· háši ko·wahəlúhəmɔ; palí·i á·kw yú wə́nči, amat·alo·ká·s·ie·kw.
/t Then I will say to them, 'I never knew you; go away from here, you who do bad deeds.
/k And then will I profess unto them, I never knew you: depart from me, ye that work iniquity.

Mt 7.24
/b Bqc puna awrn puntufc b ntaptonakun,
/p "yúkwe pənáh, awé·n pəntánke yú nta·pto·ná·k·an,
/t "Now, if someone heeds my words,
/l Therefore, whosoever cometh to me, and heareth these sayings of mine, and doeth them,
/k Therefore whosoever heareth these sayings of mine, and doeth them,

Lk 6.47
/b ktalwvwmwlin rlenakset.   [⟨ktalw-|vwm̥wlin⟩; ⟨m⟩ broken]
/p ktaluhəmó·lən e·li·ná·kwsi·t
/t I'll show you what he is like:
/l I will shew you to what he is like.
/k I will shew you to whom he is like:

Lk 6.47, Mt 7.24
/b Mulaji lrpot lino kavtu wekvr, mwnvamun arsin rtrkh weket.   [⟨arsin⟩ for ⟨avsin⟩]
/p málahši lép·ɔ·t lə́nu káhta-wí·khe·, mmo·nhámən ahsə́n é·te·k=č wí·k·i·t.
/t As if a wise man wants to build a house, and he digs down to rock where his house is to be.
/l He is like unto a wise man, which built an house, and digged deep, and laid the foundation on a rock:

Mt 7.25, Lk 6.48.
/b Kejekvutc ‖
/p ki·š·i·khá·t·e,
/t After he finished building his house,
/l [no text]

(p. 49)
    /b nu krjelufc, xaqexun
    /p ná, ke·š·i·lánke, xa·kwí·x·ən
    /t then, when it rained heavily, there was a flood,
    /l and when the rain descended, and the flood arose,

    /b ok kjwpcvulc ave wekwam rtrk
    /p ó·k kšəp·éhəle· áhi wí·k·əwam é·te·k,
    /t and the water flowed very fast where the house was,
    /l the stream beat vehemently upon that house,

    /b ok ave kjuxun,
    /p ó·k áhi-kšáx·ən,
    /t and the wind blew very hard,
    /l and the winds blew, and beat upon that house,

Lk 6.48
    /b jwk mutu kuski qhwqevulri, rli avsinif xqihi vatrk.
    /p šúkw máta káski-kwčuk·wihəlé·i, é·li- ahsə́nink xkwíči -hát·e·k.
    /t but it could not be shaken, because it was set on top of a rock.
    /k and could not shake it: for it was founded upon a rock.

Mt 7.26
    /b Jwk awrn puntufc b ntaptwnakun, mutu nc lisetc,
    /p "šúkw awé·n pəntánke yú nta·pto·ná·k·an, máta nə́ ləs·í·t·e,
    /t "But if someone hears these words of mine and does not act accordingly,
    /kl And every one that heareth these sayings of mine, and doeth them not,
    /k But he that heareth, and doeth not,   (Lk 6.49)

    /b mulajih krphat linw; wekvatup cntu lrkwek.
    /p málahši=č ké·pča·t lə́nu wi·khá·t·əp énta-le·k·ó·wi·k.
    /t it will be like a foolish man who built his house in a sandy place.
    /k shall be likened unto a foolish man, which built his house upon the sand,
    /l (L. adds "without a foundation" from Lk 6.49.)

Mt 7.27, Lk 6.49.
    /b Nu krjelufc, prtaqexnwp, ok kjaxunwp,
    /p ná ke·š·i·lánke pe·t·a·kwí·x·əno·p, ó·k kšáx·əno·p,
    /t Then, when it rained heavily, a flood came, and there was wind,
    /l And the rain descended, and the floods came, and the winds blew,

    /b ok kjwpcvulrp nc wekwam rtrk,
    /p ó·k kšəp·éhəle·p nə́ wí·k·əwam é·te·k;
    /t and the water flowed fast where the house was.
    /l and the stream did beat vehemently upon that house,

	/b	nu jac lwkevulrp, ave pale lrw.
	/p	ná šá·e lo·k·íhəle·p, áhi-palí·i lé·w."
	/t	Then it immediately broke apart and was utterly destroyed."
	/l	and immediately it fell, and great was the fall of it.

Mt 7.28	/b	Nhesus mrhi kejaptwnrtc wrmi bl aptwnakunu,
	/p	nčí·sas mé·či ki·š·a·pto·né·t·e wé·mi yó·l a·pto·ná·k·ana,
	/t	After Jesus had finished all these talks,
	/k	And it came to pass, when Jesus had ended these sayings,

	/b	ave kanjrlintamwpanek wrmi cntxetpanek wunhi rlavkrkifrtup,
	/p	áhi-kanše·ləntamó·p·ani·k wé·mi entxi·tpáni·k wənči e·lahke·kinké·t·əp,
	/t	all those who had been present were greatly astonished by what he had taught,
	/k	the people were astonished at his doctrine:

Mt 7.29	/b	rli pumitwnvalatup ok rli mulaji nevlatamat, rli mutu liset rvlrkvekrthek rlsevtet.
	/p	é·li-pəmət·o·nha·lá·t·əp ó·k é·li- málahši -nihəlá·t·ama·t, é·li- máta -ləs·i·t ehəle·khi·k·é·č·i·k e·lsíhti·t.
	/t	as he had preached to them as if also having authority, not doing as the scribes do.
	/k	For he taught them as one having authority, and not as the scribes.

Chapter 27 (p. 49). [L. section 26.] (Matthew 8.1-4, Mark 1.45 [beginning], Luke 5.15 [end], 16)

Mt 8.1	/b	Mrhi punusetc eku wunhi ovhwf, xrli awrn wtrkaopani.
	/p	mé·či pənas·í·t·e íka wənči ɔhčúnk, xé·li awé·n o·t·e·kaɔ́·p·ani.
	/t	After he came down from the mountain, many people followed him.
	/kl	When he was come down from the mountain, great multitudes followed him.

Mt 8.2	/b	Puna, linw wtxapani neskufulukup, nrotc Nhesusu,
	/p	pənáh, lənu o·txá·p·ani ni·skankəlɔ́k·əp, ne·ɔ́·t·e nči·sás·a,
	/t	And here a man with the nasty disease came to Jesus, when he saw him,
	/k	And, behold, there came a leper

	/b	wnejetqetaopani rlifwcxenulet, ok wenwumapani,
	/p	wəni·š·i·tkwi·taɔ́·p·ani e·linkwe·x·í·nəli·t, ɔ́·k wwi·nəwamá·p·ani,
	/t	and he knelt before him and begged him,
	/k	and worshipped him,

	/b	lwrp Nrvlaliun, wifi a liseunc, kuski a pelevi.
	/p	lúwe·p, "nehəlá·lian, wínki-=á· -ləs·iáne, kkáski-=á· -pi·lí·hi."
	/t	saying, "My Lord, if you're willing to, you could make me clean."
	/k	saying, Lord, if thou wilt, thou canst make me clean.

Mt 8.3 /b Nu Nhesus eku tclenxkrn, lwrp nunc ntclsen ktclih pelsen,
/p ná nčí·sas íka təlí·nxke·n, lúwe·p, "ná=nə ntə́lsi·n, ktə́li-=č -pí·lsi·n."
/t Then Jesus stretched out his hand to him and said, "That's what I do for you to be clean."
/k And Jesus put forth his hand, and touched him, saying, I will; be thou clean.

/b nunc jwk tclwrn nu jai qekrn nu wneskufulwakun.
/p ná=nə šúkw tə́ləwe·n, ná šá·e kwí·k·e·n nə́ wəni·skankələwá·k·an.
/t No sooner had he said that than he was cured of his nasty disease.
[*lit.*, 'That's what he only said, and then immediately he was cured ...']
/k And immediately his leprosy was cleansed.

Mt 8.4 /b Nhesus tclao, alumskal jwk kahi lerkuh awrn.
/p nčí·sas təlá·ɔ, "alə́mska·l, šúkw káči lié·k·ač awé·n.
/t Jesus said to him, "Go, but don't tell anyone.
/k And Jesus saith unto him, See thou tell no man; but go thy way,

/b My punwntul kvaky wcvevwfrt,
/p mái-pənúntəl khák·ay wehi·húnke·t,
/t Go and show yourself to a priest,
/k shew thyself to the priest,

/b ok wevwfr, rlextakup Mwjiju, wunhi wrmi awrn avrlintuf.
/p ó·k wi·húnke, e·li·xtá·k·əp mo·šə́š·a, wə́nči- wé·mi awé·n -ahe·lə́ntank.
/t and make sacrifice, as Moses established, so that everyone honors it.
/k and offer the gift that Moses commanded, for a testimony unto them.

Mk 1.45 /b Jwk rlumskatc, nu tolumi lathemwen wrmi nc tali.
/p šúkw e·ləmská·t·e, ná tóləmi-la·č·í·mwi·n wé·mi nə́ táli.
/t But when he left he then began to tell what had happened to him all over.
/k But he went out, and began to publish it much, and to blaze abroad the matter,

/b Nanc wunhi Nhesus, mutu koski heh eku awun wtrnif wrotasekc,
/p ná=nə wə́nči nčí·sas máta kóski- čí·č íka -á·wən o·té·nink, we·ɔ·ta·sí·k·e,
/t For that reason Jesus was no longer able to go into the town after it was known,
/k insomuch that Jesus could no more openly enter into the city, ...

Lk 5.15 /b rli xrli pavtet krtu puntaothek, ok krtu kekrvunhek, wrmi polswakunwu;
/p é·li- xé·li -páhti·t ké·t·a-pəntaɔ́·č·i·k, ó·k ké·t·a-ki·k·e·hə́nči·k wé·mi pɔ·lsəwa·k·anúwa.
/t as many came who wanted to hear him and who wanted to be cured of all their diseases.
/k ... and great multitudes came together to hear, and to be healed by him of their infirmities.

Lk 5.16 /b jwk trkunu rp, ok patamap. ‖
         /p šúkw té·kəna é·p, ɔ́·k pá·tama·p.
         /t But he went into the wilderness and prayed.
         /k And he withdrew himself into the wilderness, and prayed.

Chapter 28 (p. 50). [L. section 27.] (Luke 7.1[end]-10, Matthew 8.7, 11-13)

Lk 7.1   /b Lupi Nhesus rp Kpunium,   [⟨Kpunium⟩ for ⟨Kupunium⟩]
(p. 50)   /p lápi nčí·sas é·p †kapəniam.
          /t Jesus again went to Capernaum.
          /l [*Thereupon*] Jesus entered into Capernaum.

Lk 7.2   /b nc tali Krkyimvrt tolwkakunu rvolathi ave palselw,
          /p nə́ táli-ke·kayəmhe·t tɔlo·ká·k·ana ehɔ·lá·č·i áhi-pa·lsí·lu,
          /t The servant of a ruler there, whom he loved, was very sick;
          /k And a certain centurion's servant, who was dear unto him, was sick,

          /b kavti uful.
          /p káhti-ánkəl.
          /t he was almost dead.
          /k and ready to die.

Lk 7.3   /b Nani Krkyimvrt puntufc tcli Nhesus pan
          /p náni ke·kayəmhe·t pəntánke táli- nčí·sas -pá·n,
          /t When that ruler heard that Jesus had come,
          /k And when he heard of Jesus,

          /b eku lalwkalrp Nhwe Krkyimvrlethi Nhesusif,
          /p íka lalo·ká·le·p nčo·wí·i-ke·kayəmhe·lí·č·i nči·sás·ink,
          /t he sent some Jewish leaders to Jesus,
          /k he sent unto him the elders of the Jews,

          /b wcnhemao, li a my kekrvalen tolwkakunu.
          /p wwenči·má·ɔ, lí-=á· -mái-ki·k·e·há·li·n tɔlo·ká·k·ana.
          /t and called on him to come, so that his servant would be cured.
          /k beseeching him that he would come and heal his servant.

Lk 7.4   /b Eku pravtetc, tove lawao, kwcnhemwq xifwrlumwkset.
          /p íka pe·ahtí·t·e, tɔ́hi-lawwá·ɔ, "kəwenčí·mukw xinkwe·ləmúkwsi·t,
          /t When they got there, they implored him, "Someone is calling for you to come who is highly regarded,
          /k And when they came to Jesus, they besought him instantly, saying, That he was worthy for whom he should do this:

Blanchard's Harmony of the Gospels

Lk 7.5   /b   Rli ktavolkwnu rlvakreufq, kmanetakwnu patamwrekaon.
            /p   é·li ktahɔ·lkó·na e·lhaké·iankw; kəmanni·ta·k·ó·na pa·tamwe·i·k·á·ɔn."
            /t   for he loves us, of our tribe; he built us a house of worship.
            /k   For he loveth our nation, and he hath built us a synagogue.

Mt 8.7   /b   Nhesus lwrp ekuh ntav numy kekrvan,
            /p   nčí·sas lúwe·p, "íka=č ntá, nəmái-ki·k·é·ha·n."
            /t   Jesus said, "I will go there to cure him."
            /k   And Jesus saith unto him, I will come and heal him.

Lk 7.6   /b   nu tolomi wehrvkwnrop.
            /p   ná tólemi-wi·č·e·yko·né·ɔ·p.
            /t   Then he started off with them.
            /k   Then Jesus went with them.

            /b   Mrhi mutu ovlumupetc nc wunhi weket,
            /p   mé·či máta ɔhələmap·í·t·e nə́ wə́nči wí·k·i·t,
            /t   And when he was already not far from his house,
            /k   And when he was now not far from the house,

            /b   nu krkyimvrt eku tulalwkalanrp wetesu, tcli lan,
            /p   ná ke·kayə́mhe·t íka təlalo·ka·lá·ne·p wi·t·í·s·a, tə́li-lá·n,
            /t   the ruler sent his friend to tell him,
            /k   the centurion sent friends to him, saying unto him,

            /b   Nrvlaliun, kahi mekwmoswkrvan kvaky,
            /p   "nehəlá·lian, káči mi·kəmɔ·s·o·ké·han khák·ay,
            /t   "My Lord, don't trouble yourself,
            /k   Lord, trouble not thyself:

            /b   rli mutu tcpi liseo ktcli a kuski tumekrn;
            /p   é·li- máta -tépi-ləs·í·ɔ, ktə́li-=á· -káski-təmí·k·e·n.
            /t   as I am not worthy enough for you to come in.
            /k   for I am not worthy that thou shouldest enter under my roof:

Lk 7.7   /b   ok mutu ntetrvai ntcpi lisen ktcli a toxulun, jwk lwrl,
            /p   ɔ́·k máta nti·t·e·há·i, ntépi-ləs·i·n ktə́li-=á· -tɔ́x·ələn, šúkw lúwe·l,
            /t   And I don't think I'm worthy to come to you, but only say so,
            /k   Wherefore neither thought I myself worthy to come unto thee: but say in a word,

            /b   nuh qekrn ntalwkakun.
            /p   ná=č kwí·k·e·n ntalo·ká·k·an.
            /t   and then my servant will be cured.
            /k   and my servant shall be healed.

Lk 7.8 /b Lenwavkuset nrpc nvaky, Sohuluk frnavkeva.
/p linnuwahkǝs·i·t né·pe nhák·ay; sɔ́·čǝlak nke·nahkí·ha.
/t I, too, am one of authority; I have soldiers under me.
/k For I also am a man set under authority, having under me soldiers,

/b Kwti lukc eku aul, eku rw, ok lukc kwti wuntuxal, wuntaxrw, [⟨aul⟩ for ⟨al⟩]
/p kwǝt·i lák·e, 'íka á·l,' íka é·w; ɔ́·k lák·e kwǝt·i, 'wǝntax á·l,' wǝntax é·w.
/t If I say to one, 'Go there,' he goes there; and if I say to another, 'Come here,' he comes here.
/k and I say unto one, Go, and he goeth; and to another, Come, and he cometh;

/b ok ntalwkakun lukc blisel nani tclsen. [⟨bli-|sel⟩ for ⟨b lisel⟩]
/p ɔ́·k ntalo·ká·k·an lák·e, 'yú lǝs·i·l,' náni tǝlsi·n."
/t And if I say to my servant, 'Do this,' that's what he does.
/k and to my servant, Do this, and he doeth it.

Lk 7.9 /b Mrhi Nhesus bni puntufc wlrlumrlintumwp,
/p mé·či nčí·sas yó·ni pǝntánke, wǝle·lǝme·lǝ́ntamo·p.
/t After Jesus heard this, he was astonished.
/k When Jesus heard these things, he marvelled at him,

/b eku li qulwpep, tclaol wrmi naolwkki, kehe ktclwvwmw,
/p íkali kwǝlǝp·i·p, tǝlá·ɔl wé·mi na·ɔlúkwki, "khičí·i ktǝllúhǝmɔ,
/t He turned to all those following him and said to them, "Truly I say to you,
/k and turned him about, and said unto the people that followed him, I say unto you,

/b takw vuji numuxkumwi lukveqi xifwi nvakatamwrokun tali Islilif.
/p takó· háši nǝmaxkamó·wi lǝkhíkwi-xínkwi-nhaka·t·amwe·ɔ́·k·an táli †isǝlǝ́link.
/t never have I found such a great faith in Israel.
/k I have not found so great faith, no, not in Israel.

Mt 8.11 /b Ok ktclwvwmw, xrlih prok wcnhi khifwcvulak, ok rvliwsekak wunhi,
/p ɔ́·k ktǝllúhǝmɔ, xé·li=č pé·ɔk wénči-kčinkwéhǝla·k ɔ́·k éhǝli-wsí·ka·k wǝ́nči,
/t And I say to you: Many shall come from the east and from the west,
/k And I say unto you, That many shall come from the east and west,

/b wetvwqrpemawaoh Rpulivamu. Ok Ysuku, ok Nhrkwpu eku osavkmc sakemaokunif.
/p wwi·thukwe·p·i·mawwá·ɔ=č †e·pǝliháma, ɔ́·k †aisáka, ɔ́·k †nče·kǝ́pa íka ɔ·s·áhkame sa·k·i·ma·ɔ́·k·anink.
/t and they shall sit with Abraham, and Isaac, and Jacob in the kingdom of heaven.
/k and shall sit down with Abraham, and Isaac, and Jacob, in the kingdom of heaven.

Mt 8.12   /b   Jwk bk sakemaomeminsuk kohwmifh lanevenuk cntu ave peskrk,
           /p   šúkw yó·k sa·k·i·ma·ɔmi·mə́nsak kɔ́čəmink=č lanihí·nak énta-áhi-pí·ske·k,
           /t   But the king's children will be thrown outside into utter darkness,
           /k   But the children of the kingdom shall be cast out into outer darkness:

           /b   cntuh amuxavolamwivtet, ok kukamwkuntamivtet wepetwao.
           /p   énta-=č -amax·ahɔla·mwíhti·t, ɔ́·k -kək·amo·kantamíhti·t wi·p·i·t·əwá·ɔ."
           /t   where they will scream loudly and 'gnash' their teeth."
           /k   there shall be weeping and gnashing of teeth.

[added]   /b   Prp ok nu krkyimvrt Nhesusif.
           /p   pé·p ɔ́·k ná ke·kayə́mhe·t nči·sás·ink.
           /t   The ruler also came to Jesus.
           /l   And the centurion came to Jesus,

Mt 8.13   /b   Nhesus tclaol mahel,
           /p   nčí·sas təlá·ɔl, "má·č·i·l.
           /t   Jesus said to him, "Go home.
           /l   and Jesus said unto him, Go thy way,
           /k   And Jesus said unto the centurion, Go thy way;

           /b   lrkch rletrvaan qwlu b lrk, rli nvakalian.
           /p   lé·k·eč e·li·t·e·há·an, 'kwə́la yú lé·k,' é·li-nhaká·lian."
           /t   And what you wished to happen, let it happen, what you relied on me to do.
           /kl and as thou hast believed, so be it done unto thee.

           /b   Nu jai tolwkakanu wexkaohi qekrlen.
           /p   ná šá·e tɔlo·ká·k·ana wi·xkaɔ́či kwi·k·é·li·n.
           /t   And then right away his servant was suddenly cured.
           /k   And his servant was healed in the selfsame hour.

Lk 7.10   /b   Avpahevtetc alwkakunuk wnroapani   [⟨Avp-⟩ for ⟨Ap-⟩]
           /p   a·p·a·č·ihtí·t·e alo·ká·k·anak, wəne·ɔ́·p·ani;
           /t   When the servants returned home, they saw him.
           /k   And they that were sent, returning to the house, found

           /b   alwkakun palsetup mrhi wlumalsw. ‖
           /p   alo·ká·k·an pa·lsí·t·əp mé·či wəlamálsu.
           /t   the servant that had been sick was now well.
           /k   the servant whole that had been sick.

Chapter 29 (p. 51). [L. section 28.] (Mark 1.21-28; cf. Luke 4.31, 33; Matthew 7.28-29 [cf. p. 49])

Mk 1.21   /b   Eku rpetc Kupuniumif,

(p. 51) /p íka e·p·í·t·e †kapəniámink,
/t When he was in Capernaum,
/k And they went into Capernaum;

/b alaxemwe kejqekc rp cntu mycvuluf moi akrkemapani, [⟨ak-⟩ for ⟨avk-⟩]
/p ala·x·i·məwí·i-ki·škwí·k·e, é·p énta-ma·éhəlank, mɔ́i-ahke·ki·má·p·ani.
/t on the day of rest, he went to the synagogue to teach them.
/k and straightway on the sabbath day he entered into the synagogue, and taught.

Mk 1.22 /b kanjrlintamwpanek wunhi avkrkifrokun;
/p kanše·ləntamó·p·ani·k wənči ahke·kinke·ɔ́·k·an,
/t They were astonished by the teaching,
/k And they were astonished at his doctrine: (Cf. Mt 7.28-29.)

/b rli rlavkrkifrt mulaji xifwiliset, mutu nc liset, rlsitet rvlrkvekrsuk.
/p é·li e·lahke·kínke·t málahši xínkwi-lə́s·i·t, máta nə́ -lə́s·i·t e·lsíhti·t ehəle·khi·k·é·s·ak.
/t as the way he taught was like one with authority, and he did not do what the scribes did.
/k for he taught them as one that had authority, and not as the scribes.

Mk 1.23 /b Eku avpwp linw cntu mycvuluf neski manitwet, amuxavolamwp
/p íka ahpó·p lə́nu énta-ma·éhəlank ní·ski-manət·ó·wi·t, amax·ahɔlá·mo·p,
/t In the synagogue there was a man who had an unclean spirit, and he screamed
/k And there was in their synagogue a man with an unclean spirit; and he cried out,

Mk 1.24 /b rlwrtc, Konulenyenrn,
/p e·ləwé·t·e, "kɔ́na li·naí·ne·n.
/t when he said, "Let us alone.
/k Saying, Let us alone;

/b krkw vuh ktcli elwvunu, ke Nasulutet Nhesus? [⟨ktcli el-⟩ for ⟨ktclivl-⟩]
/p kéku=háč ktəlihəlúhəna, kí· †nasəlát·i·t nčí·sas?
/t What did we do to you, you Jesus the Nazarene?
/k what have we to do with thee, thou Jesus of Nazareth?

/b Kwnhi vuh pan kwmyi palevenu?
/p kúnči-=háč -pá·n, kəmái-pali·híhəna?
/t Did you come to destroy us?
/k art thou come to destroy us?

/b Kwavlwvnu awrniun, ke Krtanitwet Pwelsetamu.
/p ko·wahəlúhəna awé·nian, kí· ke·tanət·ó·wi·t pwi·lsí·t·əma."
/t We know who you are, you holy one of God."
/k I know thee who thou art, the Holy One of God.

Mk 1.25 /b Jwk Nhesus qetulao, tclao, Hetqwsel, vokif wunhi khel.
/p šúkw nčí·sas kkwi·tǝlá·ɔ, tǝlá·ɔ, "či·tkwǝ́s·i·l, hɔ́k·enk wǝ́nči-kčí·l."
/t But Jesus admonished him, saying to him, "Be quiet, and come out of his body."
/k And Jesus rebuked him, saying, Hold thy peace, and come out of him.

Mk 1.26 /b Mrhi neskanitwet twxkanatc, ok amaxavolamw nu eku wunhi khen.
/p mé·či ni·skanǝt·ó·wi·t to·xkǝná·t·e, ɔ́·k amax·ahɔlá·mu; ná íka wwǝ́nči-kči·n.
/t After the unclean spirit had torn him, he also screamed; and then he came out of him.
/k And when the unclean spirit had torn him, and cried with a loud voice, he came out of him.

Mk 1.27 /b Nunc rlsetc, nu wrmi kanjrlintamwpanek, ntwtwmaotwpanek,
/p nǝ́ni e·lsí·t·e, ná wé·mi kanše·lǝntamóp·ani·k, nto·t·ǝma·ɔhtóp·ani·k,
/t When he did that, everyone was amazed and asked each other,
/k And they were all amazed, insomuch that they questioned among themselves, saying,

/b Krkw vuh ct lrw? Krkw ta bv wuskif avkrkintwakun.
/p "kéku=háč=ét lé·w? kéku=tá yúh wǝ́skink ahke·kǝntǝwá·k·an?
/t "What happened, I wonder? And what is this new teaching?
/k What thing is this? what new doctrine is this?

/b Rli ave nevlahi qetulaol neski manitwul,
/p é·li áhi-nihǝláči kkwi·tǝlá·ɔl ní·ski-manǝt·ó·wal,
/t For, completely on his own he admonished the unclean spirit (or spirits),
/k for with authority commandeth he even the unclean spirits,

/b nu jai qwlsitakwn.
/p ná šá·e kwǝlsǝt·á·k·o·n.
/t and it (or they) then immediately obeyed him.
/k and they do obey him.

Mk 1.28 /b Wrmi b rlrk jai puntakotwp avpami Faluleuf.
/p wé·mi yú é·le·k šá·e pǝntákɔhto·p ahpá·mi †nka·lalí·yunk.
/t All of this that happened was immediately heard about all around Galilee.
/k And immediately his fame spread abroad throughout all the region round about Galilee.

Chapter 30 (pp. 51-52). [L. section 29.] (Mark 1.29-34; Luke 4.41; Matthew 8.16 [part]-17)

Mk 1.29 /b Mrhi rlumskavtetc wunhi cntu mycvuluf
/p mé·či e·lǝmskahtí·t·e wǝ́nči énta-ma·éhǝlank,
/t After they left the synagogue,
/k And forthwith, when they were come out of the synagogue,

/b eku rpanek Symun weket ok Antulws, Nhim ok Nhan wehroapani.
/p íka é·p·ani·k †sáiman wí·k·i·t, ɔ́·k †ántəlo·s; nčím ɔ́·k nčá·n wwi·č·e·ɔ́·p·ani.
/t they went to Simon's house, and Andrew's; Jim and John went with them.
/k they entered into the house of Simon and Andrew, with James and John.

Mk 1.30
/b Symun wehrohi kovrsu jcfexenwp rli palset ave kjulrxen,
/p †sáiman wi·č·e·ɔ́·č·i kɔhé·s·a šenki·x·í·no·p, é·li-pá·lsi·t; áhi-kšəléx·i·n.
/t Simon's wife's mother was lying down, as she was sick; she had a high fever.
/k But Simon's wife's mother lay sick of a fever,

/b nu jai tclanro,
/p ná šá·e təla·né·ɔ.
/t Then right away they told him.
/k and anon they tell him of her.

Mk 1.31
/b nu eku tonan wnuxkelet tomwekunao,
/p ná íka tónna·n wənaxkí·li·t, tɔ·mwi·kəná·ɔ.
/t Then he took her hand, and he raised her up.
/k And he came and took her by the hand, and lifted her up;

/b nu jai wnukavtumun polswakun,
/p ná šá·e wənəkahtə́mən pɔ·lsəwá·k·an;
/t Then she immediately left behind her disease;
/k and immediately the fever left her,

/b amwetc mwekintamaopani.
/p a·mwí·t·e, mwi·kəntamaɔ́·p·ani.
/t and when she got up, she did things for them.
/k and she ministered unto them.

Mk 1.32
/b Wrlakorkc mrhi wsekakc,
/p we·la·k·əwé·k·e, mé·či wsi·ká·k·e,
/t That evening after sunset,
/k And at even, when the sun did set,

/b nu prjwanrop wrmi cntxrnaoki lufulukek, ok nrk mavtuntwethek,
/p ná pe·š·əwa·né·ɔ·p wé·mi entxennáɔhki-lankələ́k·i·k, ɔ́·k né·k mahtant·o·wí·č·i·k.
/t then people with all sorts of diseases were brought, and those possessed by devils.
/k they brought unto him all that were diseased, and them that were possessed with devils.

Mk 1.33
/b ok wrmi wrtwtrnyethek myrvlrpanek eku skontrf.
/p ɔ́·k wé·mi we·t·o·t·e·naí·č·i·k ma·ehəlé·p·ani·k íka skɔ́ntenk.
/t And all the townspeople gathered at the door.
/k And all the city was gathered together at the door.

Mk 1.34 /b Qekrvapani xrli palselethi, ok qutskaopani xrli mavtuntwul.
 /p kwi·k·e·há·p·ani xé·li pa·lsi·lí·č·i, ɔ́·k kwətskaɔ́·p·ani xé·li mahtant·ó·wal.
 /t He cured many that were sick and drove out many devils.
 /k And he healed many that were sick of divers diseases, and cast out many devils; ...
 /l [L. text of this section differs.]

Lk 4.41 /b Mawsw mavtuntw tclao, Ke Klyst Krtanitwet qesul.
 /p má·wsu mahtánt·u təlá·ɔ, "kí· kəláist, ke·tanət·ó·wi·t kkwí·s·al."
 /t One devil said to him, "You are Christ, the son of God."
 /k And devils also came out of many, crying out, and saying, Thou art Christ the Son of God.

 /b Jwk qetulapani tcli a ‖ krkw lwrlen, rli watwlet tcli Klysten.
 /p šúkw kkwi·təlá·p·ani tɔ́li-=á· kéku -luwé·li·n, é·li-wwa·tó·li·t təli-kəláisti·n.
 /t But he forbade him (or them) to say anything, since he (or they) knew that he was Christ.
 /k And he rebuking them suffered them not to speak: for they knew that he was Christ.

Mt 8.16 /b Qekrvapani wrmi palselethi;
(p. 52) /p kwi·k·e·há·p·ani wé·mi pa·lsi·lí·č·i.
 /t He cured all that were sick.
 /k ... he ... healed all that were sick:

Mt 8.17 /b wunhi pavkunhi lrk rlwrtup nrnekanewrwsetpanu Esrusu.
 /p wónči-pahkánči-lé·k e·ləwé·t·əp nehəni·k·a·ní·i-we·wsi·tpána †i·se·yós·a:
 /t so that it would happen exactly as the prophet Esaias said:
 /k That it might be fulfilled which was spoken by Esaias the prophet, saying,

 /b Wrtunimun kjawswakuninu, ok kpalswakuninu.
 /p wwe·t·ənómən kšawsəwa·k·anóna ɔ́·k kpa·lsəwa·k·anóna.
 /t He took our infirmities and our illnesses.
 /k Himself took our infirmities, and bare our sicknesses.

Chapter 31 (pp. 52-53). [L. section 30.] (Mark 1.35-39 [beginning], 4.36, 37, 38[parts], 39; Matthew 8.18-22, 25-26; Luke 8.22 [end], 25 [end])

Mk 1.35 /b Nrlumu prtapunwep amwetc, eku rp cntu xwva patamat.
 /p né·ləma pe·t·a·p·anó·wi·p a·mwí·t·e, íka é·p énta- xó·ha -pá·tama·t.
 /t Dawn had not yet come when he got up and went to where he prayed alone.
 /k And in the morning, rising up a great while before day, he went out, and departed into a solitary place, and there prayed.

Mk 1.36 /b Symun, ok wehrotpanek wnaolawao.
 /p †sáiman ɔ́·k wi·č·e·ɔ·tpáni·k wəna·ɔlawwá·ɔ.

| | /t | Simon and ones that were with him followed after him. |
| | /k | And Simon and they that were with him followed after him. |

Mk 1.37 /b Mrxkaovtetc, tclawao, Wrmi awrn kprvwq.
/p me·xka‿htí·t·e, təlawwá·ɔ, "wé·mi awé·n kpé·hukw."
/t When they found him, they said to him, "Everyone is waiting for you."
/k And when they had found him, they said unto him, All men seek for thee.

Mk 1.38 /b Jwk tclao, Eku atumwq pchi mukunexif wtrny
/p šúkw təlá·ɔ, "íka á·t·amo·kw péči-məkəní·x·ink o·t·é·nay,
/t But he said to them, "Let's all go to the next town,
/k And he said unto them, Let us go into the next towns,

/b ntclih ok nc tali pumitwnvrn; rli nani wunhi pan;   [⟨wunhi⟩ for ⟨nwnhi⟩]
/p ntəli-=č ɔ́·k nə́ táli -pəmət·ó·nhe·n, é·li nə́ni núnči-pá·n.
/t so that I may preach there also, as that is why I came.
/k that I may preach there also: for therefore came I forth.

Mk 1.39 /b pumitwnvrp cntu mycvuluf wrmi avpami Faluleuf.
/p pəmət·ó·nhe·p énta-ma·éhəlank wé·mi ahpá·mi †nka·lalí·yunk.
/t He preached in the synagogues all over Galilee.
/k And he preached in their synagogues throughout all Galilee, ...

Mt 8.18 /b Nhesus nrotc tcli xrli awrni toxkwn,
/p nčí·sas ne·ɔ́·t·e təli- xé·li awé·ni -tɔ́xko·n,
/t When Jesus saw many people coming to him,
/k Now when Jesus saw great multitudes about him,

/b tclao kamif atumwq munwprkwf.
/p təlá·ɔ, "ká·mink á·t·amo·kw mənəp·é·k·unk."
/t he said to them, "Let's all go to the other side of the sea."
/k he gave commandment to depart unto the other side.

Mt 8.19 /b Wtxwkw kwti rvrlrkvekrlethi tclkw rvavkrkifrs, kwethrwul tutu raun.
/p o·txúk·u kwə́t·i ehəle·khi·k·e·lí·č·i, təlku, "ehahke·kínke·s, kəwi·č·é·wəl tətá e·á·an."
/t A certain scribe came to him and said to him, "Teacher, I'll go with you wherever you go."
/k And a certain scribe came, and said unto him, Master, I will follow thee whithersoever thou goest.

Mt 8.20 /b Nhesus tclao, Oqsuk wolavkwuk, ok hwlinsuk wojexywuk
/p nčí·sas təlá·ɔ, "ɔ́·kwsak wɔ·lahkúwak, ɔ́·k čo·lə́nsak wɔši·x·ayúwak,
/t Jesus said to him, "Foxes have holes, and birds have nests,
/k And Jesus saith unto him, The foxes have holes, and the birds of the air have nests;

/b jwk linw Wrqesif, takw vatri tutu a rtaq wel.
/p šúkw lə́nu we·k·wí·s·ink takó· hat·é·i tə́ta=á· é·ta·kw wí·l."
/t but the man who is the Son does not have any place where he could lay his head."
/k but the Son of man hath not where to lay his head.

Mt 8.21
/b Takoki rkrkemathi tclkw,
/p takó·ki e·k·e·ki·má·č·i tə́lku,
/t Another of his disciples said to him,
/k And another of his disciples said unto him,

/b Rkrkifrs luvupu ne vetami ntalumskan nmyi pvokvakcvon nwx.
/p "e·k·e·kínke·s, lahápa ní· hítami ntaləmska·n, nəmái-phɔkhakého·n nó·x.
/t "Teacher, let me first go and bury my father."
/k Lord, suffer me first to go and bury my father.

Mt 8.22
/b Jwk Nhesus tclao, Wehrel; lrlum rvafulukek, pokvakcvonro rfulilethi.
/p šúkw nčí·sas təlá·ɔ, "wi·č·é·i·l; lé·ləm ehankələk·i·k ppɔ·khakehɔ·né·ɔ enkələlí·č·i."
/t But Jesus said to him, "Come with me; let those that have died bury the dead."
/k But Jesus said unto him, Follow me; and let the dead bury their dead.

Mk 4.36
/b Nunu wnukalan wrmi rpelethi, mwxolif li pwswpanek,
/p nána wənək·ala·n wé·mi e·p·i·lí·č·i, mux·ó·link lí-po·s·ó·p·ani·k.
/t Then he left all those that were there, and they got aboard a boat.
/kl And when they had sent away the multitude, they took him even as he was in the ship.

/b ok takokek tufamwxoltitif avpwpanek wehroapani;
/p ɔ́·k takó·ki·k tankamux·o·ltə́t·ink ahpó·p·ani·k, wwi·č·e·ɔwwá·p·ani.
/t And others were in small boats accompanying him.
/kl And there were also with him other little ships.

Lk 8.22
/b nu tolumelavtanrop.
/p ná tɔləmilahta·né·ɔ·p.
/t And then they started out in the boat.
/kl ... And they launched forth.

Mk 4.37
/b Jwk alumi ave kjaxunwp munwprkwf
/p šúkw áləmi-áhi-kšáx·əno·p mənəp·é·k·unk,
/t But a strong wind began to blow on the sea,
/kl And there arose a great storm of wind, and a great tempest in the sea,

Mk 4.37, Mt 8.24, Lk 8.23
/b alwe mumjalwvlrp tkwv nc mwxwlif.
/p aləwí·i †məmšalúhəle·p tkú nə́ mux·ó·link.

/t and increasingly the crests of the waves were breaking into the boat.
/l insomuch that the ship was covered with the waves, and the waves beat into the ship, so that it was now full, and they were in jeopardy.

Mk 4.38 /b Nhesus wtifaltri tali kaep.
/p nčí·sas wtenka·lté·e táli-kaí·p.
/t Jesus was asleep in the stern of the boat.
/kl And he was in the hinder part of the ship, asleep on a pillow;

Mt 8.25 /b Rkrkemathel moi twkunwkw, tclaol
/p e·k·e·ki·má·č·i·l mói-to·kənúk·u, təlá·ɔl,
/t His disciples went and woke him up, and (one) said to him,
/kl And his disciples came to him, and awoke him, saying,

/b Rvakrkifrs, Wetyvrmenrn.
/p "ehahk·e·kínke·s, wi·t·a·he·mí·ne·n.
/t "Teacher, help us.
/kl (2) Lord, save us: or we perish.   [numbers = sequence in L.]

Mk 4.38 /b mutuh vuh krkw lri ufulcfc.
/p máta=č=háč kéku lé·i ankəlénke."
/t Will it be of no consequence if we (exc.) die?"   [*lit.*, 'Will nothing happen?']
/kl (1) Master, carest thou not that we perish?

Mt 8.26 /b Tclao, Ktufiti nvakrwsevmw, krkw wunhi wejaserq?
/p təlá·ɔ, "ktankíti-nhake·wsíhəmɔ; kéku wə́nči-wi·š·á·s·ie·kw?"
/t He said to them, "You have little faith; why are you afraid?"
/kl And he saith unto them, Why are ye fearful, O ye of little faith? ...

Mk 4.39, Mt 8.26, Lk 8.24
/b Amwetc, qetulituminrp krjxif ok cntu tkwek, ‖ lwr Kulumuvpeq,
/p a·mwí·t·e, kkwi·tələt·əmə́ne·p ké·šxink ó·k énta-tkó·wi·k, lúwe·, "kəlámahpi·kw."
/t After getting up, he admonished the wind and the waves, saying, "Be still."
/l Then he arose, and rebuked the winds, and the raging of the water, and said unto the sea, Peace, be still.

Mk 4.39 /b nu jai alu kjaxunwp, ok munwprq klumivulrp.
(p. 53) /p ná šá·e ála-kšáx·əno·p, ó·k mənə́p·e·kw kəlamíhəle·p.
/t Then immediately the wind ceased, and the sea became calm.
/kl And the wind ceased, and there was a great calm.

Mk 4.41, Lk 8.25
/b Wrmi nc rpetpanek wejaswpanek, ok kanjrlintumwpanek lwrpanek,
/p wé·mi nə́ e·p·i·tpáni·k wi·š·a·s·ó·p·ani·k ó·k kanše·ləntamó·p·ani·k, luwé·p·ani·k,
/t Everyone who was there was frightened and astonished, and they said,
/l But the men feared exceedingly, and marvelled. and said one to another,

Mk 4.41 /b Awrn ct tu wu linw?
/p "awé·n=ét=tá wá lə́nu?
/t "Who can this man be?
/kl What manner of man is this!

Lk 8.25, Mk 4.41
/b Rli aptwnatuf krjxif, ok munwprq ok jai wlsitakwn.
/p é·li-a·pto·ná·t·ank ké·šxink ɔ́·k mənə́p·e·kw, ɔ́·k šá·e o·lsət·á·k·o·n.
/t For he speaks to the wind and the sea, and they immediately obey him.
/l for he commandeth even the winds and water, even the wind and the sea obey him?

Chapter 32 (pp. 53-54). [L. section 31.] (Matthew 8.28-29, 33; Luke 8.27 [part], 34 [part], 35, 37; Mark 5.3 [end]-13, 16-20; cf. Matthew 8.31, Mark 5.15)

Mk 5.1, Mt 8.28
/b Mrhi xkovkavtetc munwprq, nokeskawao neju linwu
/p mé·či xkɔhkahtí·t·e mənə́p·e·kw, nɔk·i·skaɔwwá·ɔ ní·š·a lə́nəwa
/t After they had crossed the sea, they met two men,
/l And they came over unto the other side of the sea,... And .. there met him two

Mt 8.28 /b rpetaqkek mavtuntwu,
/p e·p·i·tá·kwki·k mahtant·ó·wa.
/t who had devils in them.
/kl possessed with devils,

/b mavhekameqekri pipumenwpanek.
/p mahči·k·ami·k·wi·ké·i pihpəminnó·p·ani·k.
/t They always stayed among the graves.
/kl coming out of thc tombs,

/b Ave manwfswpanek, wunhi mutu kekski awrn eku pumuskat.
/p áhi-manunksúwak, wə́nči- máta -ki·kski- awé·n íka -pəmə́ska·t.
/t They were very fierce, which is why no one was ever able to go there.
/kl exceeding fierce, so that no man might pass by that way.

Lk 8.27 /b Mawsw lomwc wnwhi nc lisen.
/p má·wsu lɔ́·məwe wənúči- nə́ -lə́s·i·n.
/t One had been that way a long time.
/l *One of them* had devils long time, ...

Mk 5.3 /b Takw awrn qekski kaxpelaeo taoni swswkulasu.
/p takó· awé·n kwí·kski-kaxpi·la·í·ɔ, tá·ɔni so·so·k·ahəlá·s·a.
/t No one was ever able to tie him up, even with chains.
/kl And no man could bind him, no, not with chains:

Mk 5.4 /b Tevtumeki kaxpeswp sukasinu vwekatif ok swswkavlasu,
        /p tihtəmí·ki kaxpí·s·o·p səkahsə́na hwiká·t·ink, ɔ́·k so·so·k·ahəlá·s·a,
        /t He had often been bound with irons on his legs, and chains,
        /kl Because that he had been often bound with fetters and chains,

        /b jwk vufq pwpxkunapani swswkalasu
        /p šúkw=hánkw pupxkəná·p·ani so·so·k·ahəlá·s·a,
        /t but he would break apart the chains
        /kl and the chains had been plucked asunder by him,

        /b ok sukasinu vwekatif myai vufq pwpxkunimun.
        /p ɔ́·k səkahsə́na hwiká·t·ink mayá·i=hánkw pupxkənə́mən.
        /t and the irons on his legs he would simply break.
        /kl and the fetters broken in pieces:

        /b Takw awrn koski tkawswkrwunu.
        /p takó· awé·n kɔ́ski-tkawso·ké·wəna.
        /t No one was able to make him be gentle.
        /kl neither could any man tame him.   [B. skips some of L.]

Mk 5.5 /b Fumri vufq qwnitpwq ok qwnikejwq ovhwf avpwp,
        /p nkəmé·i=hánkw kwə́ni-tpó·kw ɔ́·k kwə́ni-kí·š·ukw ɔhčúnk ahpó·p,
        /t He was always in the hills, night and day,
        /kl And always, night and day, he was in the mountains,   [Mk "And", L. "but"]

        /b ok mahekameqekri, amuxavolamw, ok qekeskjao vokyu.
        /p ɔ́·k mahči·k·ami·k·wi·ké·i amax·ahɔlá·mu, ɔ́·k kwi·ki·skšá·ɔ hɔ́kaya.
        /t and he screamed among the graves and cut himself up,
        /kl and in the tombs, crying, and cutting himself with stones.

Mk 5.6 /b Nrotc Nhesusu ovlumi li
        /p ne·ɔ́·t·e nči·sás·a ɔ́həlomi lí,
        /t When he saw Jesus at a distance,
        /k But when he saw Jesus afar off,   [he: L. "they"]

        /b eku jevelr; eku tclaneven voky;
        /p íka šíhəle·, íka təlaníhi·n hɔ́k·ay.
        /t he ran to him and threw himself down to him.
        /k he ran and worshipped him,   [he: L. "they"]

Mk 5.7 /b amufexswp rlwrtc,
        /p amankí·xso·p, e·ləwé·t·e,
        /t In a loud voice he said,   [*lit.*, 'He talked loud when he said, ..']
        /k And cried with a loud voice, and said,

	/b	Krkw vuh ktclevul ke Nhesus Xifwrlumwkset Krtanitwet Qesu?
	/p	"kéku=háč ktəlí·həl, kí· nčí·sas, xinkwe·ləmúkwsi·t ke·tanət·ó·wi·t kkwí·s·a?
	/t	"What did I do to you, you Jesus, son of the highly honored God?
	/k	What have I to do with thee, Jesus, thou Son of the most high God? ... [L. "we"]

Mt 8.29
/b Kwnhi vuh pan kmy amuxavelyvi nrlumu tpisqevulak.
/p kúnči-=háč -pá·n, kəmái-amax·ahi·laéhi né·ləma tpəskwíhəla·k?
/t Do you come in order to torment me before it is time?
/kl art thou come hither to torment us before the time?

Mk 5.7
/b Qetclil nuxpi Krtanitwet ktcli a mutu amuxavelyvewun.
/p kkwí·tələl, náxpi ke·tanət·ó·wi·t, ktəli-=á· máta -amax·ahi·laehí·wən."
/t I admonish you, by God, that you not "torment" me."
/kl ... I adjure thee by God, that thou torment me not.

Mk 5.8
/b Rli mrhi keji lat, Kthel nc wunhi neski manitw.
/p é·li- mé·či -kíši-lá·t, "kčí·l nə wənči, ní·ski-manət·u."
/t For he had said to him, "Come out of there, unclean spirit."
/k For he said unto him, Come out of the man, thou unclean spirit.

Mk 5.9
/b Nhesus tclao, Krkw vuh ktclwcnsi?
/p nčí·sas təlá·ɔ, "kéku=háč ktələwénsi?"
/t Jesus said to him, "What is your name?"
/k And he asked him, What is thy name?

/b Lwr Ntclwcnsi palrnaxtxun tclintxapki, rli xrlrf.
/p lúwe·, "ntələwénsi 'palé·naxk-txə́n télən-txá·pxki', é·li-xé·lenk."
/t He said, "My name is Five-Thousand', for there are many of us."
/k And he answered, saying, My name is Legion: for we are many.

Mk 5.10
/b Nu mavtuntwuk tove wenwumanro
/p ná mahtant·ó·wak tóhi-wi·nəwama·né·ɔ,
/t Then the devils pleaded with him
/k And he besought him much

/b tcli a mutu paleliskakwunro nc wunhi vakif.
/p təli-=á· máta palí·i -ləska·k·o·wəné·ɔ nə wənči hák·ink.
/t that he would not drive them away from that country.
/k that he would not send them away out of the country.

Mk 5.11
/b Avpwpanek xrli kwjkwjuk kexki xifwi ovhwf nrteasethek.
/p ahpó·p·ani·k xé·li kwəškwə́š·ak, kí·xki xínkwi-ɔhčúnk ne·t·ia·s·í·č·i·k.
/t And there were many hogs that were feeding near the mountain.
/k Now there was there nigh unto the mountains a great herd of swine feeding.

Mk 5.12	/b	Nu wrmi mavtuntwuk tclanro, Konulenaenrn ‖ ekuntanrn kwjkwjekri
	/p	ná wé·mi mahtant·ó·wak təla·né·ɔ, "kɔ́na li·naí·ne·n, íka ntá·ne·n kwəškwəš·i·ké·i,
	/t	And then all the devils said to him, "Release us to go among the hogs,
	/k	And all the devils besought him, saying, Send us into the swine,

(p. 54)	/b	ntclih ekali punhenrn.
	/p	ntə́li-=č íkali -pənčí·ne·n."
	/t	in order for us to enter into them."
	/k	that we may enter into them.

Mk 5.13	/b	Nu jai konutclenaon eku tonro.
	/p	ná šá·e kɔ́na təli·naɔ·n, íka tɔ·né·ɔ.
	/t	Then right away he released them to go there.
	/kl	And forthwith Jesus gave them leave. (L. adds "and said unto them, Go.")

	/b	Nu mavtuntwuk qhenro wunhi linwf,
	/p	ná mahtant·ó·wak kwəč·i·né·ɔ wə́nči lə́nunk.
	/t	Then the devils went out of the man.
	/kl	And the unclean spirits went out,

	/b	eku jevulanro k kwjkwjekri ok ekali punhevulrok. [⟨jevulanro k⟩! for ⟨jevulrok⟩]
	/p	íka šihəlé·ɔk kwəškwəš·i·ké·i, ɔ́·k íkali pənčihəlé·ɔk.
	/t	They rushed to the hogs and entered into them.
	/kl	and entered into the swine:

Mt 8.32	/b	Nu wexkaohi kwjkwjuk tolumi qevlinro
	/p	ná wi·xkaɔ́či kwəškwə́š·ak †tɔ́ləmi-kwihələné·ɔ, [see: kwihəl-(?)]
	/t	Then immediately the hogs began to [jump up(?)],
	/kl	And, behold, the whole herd of swine

	/b	ave kjevulrok ekali cntu keskaufrk
	/p	áhi-kšihəlé·ɔk íkali énta-ki·ska·ɔ́nke·k,
	/t	and they ran rapidly over a cliff,
	/kl	ran violently down a steep place into the sea,

Mk 5.13	/b	munwprkwf cntu aptwpctet.
	/p	mənəp·é·k·unk énta-a·ptəp·éhti·t.
	/t	where they drowned in the sea.
	/k	and were choked in the sea. [KJV "choked" also in Lk 8.33]
	/kl	and perished in the waters. (Mt 8.32)

Mk 5.13	/b	Avpami ct nejcn tclin txapxkswuk.
	/p	ahpá·mi=ét ní·š·ən télən txa·pxksúwak. [*lit.*, 'two times ten hundred']
	/t	There were maybe about two thousand of them.
	/kl	... (they were about two thousand;) ...

Lk 8.34, Mt 8.33.
- /b Krnavkevathek kwjkwju wtrnif lijemwuk nrmvetetc rlrk,
- /p ke·nahki·há·č·i·k kwəškwə́š·a o·t·é·nink ləš·í·məwak, ne·mhití·t·e é·le·k,
- /t Those who looked after the hogs fled to the town, when they saw what happened,
- /l And when they that fed the swine saw what was done, they fled, and went their ways into the city,

- /b ok tclathemwenrop wrmi avpami wtrnif,
- /p ó·k təla·č·i·mwi·né·ɔ·p wé·mi ahpá·mi o·t·é·nink,
- /t and they told all about it around the town,
- /l and told every thing in the city and in the country.

- /b ok tclathemwenrop rlevunt nu linw rpetaqkwp mavtuntwu.
- /p ó·k təla·č·i·mwi·né·ɔ·p e·lí·hənt ná lə́nu e·p·i·tá·kwkəp mahtant·ó·wa.
- /t and they told what had been done to the man the devils had been in,
- /l and what was befallen to the possessed of the devils.

Mt 8.34, Lk 8.35
- /b Wrmi rpethek wtrnif prpanek moi punamunro rlrk,
- /p wé·mi e·p·í·č·i·k o·t·é·nink pé·p·ani·k, mɔ́i-pənaməné·ɔ é·le·k.
- /t All those who were in the town came to see what happened.
- /l And behold the whole city came out .. to see what it was that was done.
- /k Then they went out to see what was done;

Lk 8.35
- /b ok Nhesusif rpanek, tuntu nronro linwu
- /p ó·k nči·sás·ink é·p·ani·k, tə́nta-ne·ɔ·né·ɔ lə́nəwa
- /t And they came to Jesus and saw there the man
- /l And they came to Jesus, and found the man,

- /b wcnhi kthetetup mavtuntwuk.
- /p wénči-kčihtí·t·əp mahtant·ó·wak.
- /t the devils had gone out of.
- /kl out of whom the devils were departed,

Mk 5.15
- /b Mrhi eku pravtetc Nhesusif, wnrowao
- /p mé·či íka pe·ahtí·t·e nči·sás·ink, wəne·ɔwwá·ɔ
- /t After they had come to Jesus, they saw
- /k And they come to Jesus, and see him
- /l and saw him

- /b rpetaqkwp mavtuntwu, lrmuvtupet,
- /p e·p·i·tá·kwkəp mahtant·ó·wa, le·mahtáp·i·t.
- /t the one the devils had been in, who was sitting there.
- /l that had the legion, sitting at the feet of Jesus, clothed, and in his right mind:

Text, Transcription, and Translation

Mk 5.15, Lk 8.35
- /b ave wejaswuk.
- /p áhi-wi·š·á·s·əwak.
- /t They were very afraid.
- /kl and they were afraid.

Mk 5.16
- /b Nrkek eku rpetpanek tohemwlxawao wrmi rlrk
- /p né·ki·k íka e·p·i·tpáni·k tɔ·č·i·mo·lxawwá·ɔ wé·mi é·le·k.
- /t Those that had been there recounted to others everything that happened,
- /k And they that saw it told them how it befell
- /l And they that saw it told them by what means he that was possessed of the devils was healed, and also concerning the swine. (Includes Lk 8.36.)

- /b rli linw avpetaqkwp mavtuntwu, ok wunhi kwjkwjuk.
- /p é·li- lə́nu -ahpi·tá·kwkəp mahtant·ó·wa, ɔ́·k wə́nči kwəškwə́š·ak.
- /t how the man had devils in him, and also about the hogs.
- /k to him that was possessed with the devil, and also concerning the swine.

Lk 8.37
- /b Nu wrmi nrk Fatulensuk tove lawaol, pale al b wunhi.
- /p ná wé·mi né·k †nka·talí·ns·ak tóhi-lawwá·ɔl, "palí·i á·l yú wə́nči."
- /t Then all those Gadarenes implored him to go away from there.
- /kl Then the whole multitude of the country of the Gadarenes round about besought him to depart from them; (Omits some of L.)

Mk 5.18
- /b Mrhi Nhesus lupi ekali pwsetc mwxwlif,
- /p mé·či nčí·sas lápi íkali po·s·í·t·e mux·ó·link,
- /t After Jesus had again gotten into the boat,
- /kl And when he was come into the ship,

- /b nani linw mavtuntwu rpetaqkwp tove kavta wehroo.
- /p náni lə́nu mahtant·ó·wa e·p·i·tá·kwkəp tóhi-káhta-wi·č·e·ó·ɔ.
- /t that man that the devils had been in pleaded to go along with him.
  [*lit.*, 'very much wanted to go along with him']
- /k he that had been possessed with the devil prayed him that he might be with him.
- /l the man out of whom the devils were departed besought him that he might be with him.

Mk 5.19
- /b Alwt Nhesus mutu tclrlumaeo, tclao Mahel li ketesekri,
- /p aló·t nčí·sas máta tələ·ləma·í·ɔ, təlá·ɔ, "má·č·i·l lí ki·t·i·s·i·ké·i.
- /t Jesus, however, would not let him, saying to him, "Go home to your friends.
- /k Howbeit Jesus suffered him not, but saith unto him, Go home to thy friends,
- /l (L. adds to this from Luke.)

/b   lul nrk rlkeqi Nrvlalkon xifwi levkon nckc krtumakrlumwkonc.
/p   ləl né·k e·lkí·kwi- nehəlá·lkɔn -líhkən néke ke·t·əma·k·e·ləmúk·ɔne.
/t   Tell them what a great thing your Lord did for you the time he took pity on you."
/k   and tell them how great things the Lord hath done for thee, and hath had compassion on thee.   [L. replaces "the Lord" with "God".]

Mk 5.20   /b   Nu tolumskan, tolumi lwrn tali Tclin-wtrnif
/p   ná tɔləmska·n, tɔ́ləmi-lúwe·n táli télən-o·t·é·nink
/t   Then he departed and in Ten-City began telling
/k   And he departed, and began to publish in Decapolis
/l   (L. adds to this.)

/b   rlkeqi Nhesus xifwi levat,
/p   e·lkí·kwi- nčí·sas -xínkwi-lí·ha·t.
/t   what a great thing Jesus had done for him.
/k   how great things Jesus had done for him:

/b   wrmi kanjrlintamwk.
/p   wé·mi kanše·ləntamo·k.
/t   And all were astonished.
/kl   and all men did marvel.

Chapter 33 (pp. 54-55). [L. section 32.] (Mark 5.21; Luke 8.40; Mark 2.1-2, 4 [part]-5, 8 [part], 9-12; Luke 5.17-19, 20, 22 [part], 25-26; Matthew 9.2)

Mk 5.21   /b   Mrhi lupi qrxkavkatc,
/p   mé·či lápi kwe·xkahká·t·e,
/t   After he crossed over again,
/k   And when Jesus was passed over again by ship unto the other side, ...

Lk 8.40   /b   wifi nrowapani rli pwrvawapani.
/p   wwínki-ne·ɔwwá·p·ani, é·li pwe·hawwá·p·ani.
/t   they were glad to see him, as they waited for him.
/k   ... the people gladly received him: for they were all waiting for him.

Mk 2.1   /b   Eku rp lupi Kupunium.
/p   íka é·p lápi †kapə́niam.
/t   He went again to Capernaum.
/k   And again he entered into Capernaum,...;

/b   Puntametetc tcli wekwamif avpen,
/p   pəntamihtí·t·e tə́li- wi·k·əwáhəmink -ahpí·n,
/t   When they heard that he was in the house,
/k   and it was noised that he was in the house.

Mk 2.2 /b xrli awrn mycvulrp,
/p xé·li awé·n ma·éhəle·p.
/t many people gathered.
/k And straightway many were gathered together,

/b jwk ‖ ok xrli awrn mutu kuski tumekri,
/p šúkw ó·k xé·li awé·n máta káski-təmi·k·é·i;
/t But also many were not able to come in;
/k insomuch that there was no room to receive them,

(p. 55) /b takw nuxpunc kuski kexki skuntr preok,
/p takó· náxpəne káski- kí·xki skónte -pe·í·ɔk.
/t they were not even able to come near the door.
/k no, not so much as about the door:

/b nu pumtwnvalan.
/p ná pwəmto·nhá·la·n.
/t And then he preached to them.
/k and he preached the word unto them.

Lk 5.17 /b Nrli pumitwnvrtup eku avpwpanek Paluseuk, ok lrpothek,
/p né·li-pəmət·o·nhé·t·əp, íka ahpó·p·ani·k †pa·ləsi·í·ɔk ó·k le·p·ó·č·i·k,
/t While he preached, there were sitting there Pharisees and wise men,
/k ... as he was teaching, ... there were Pharisees and doctors of the law sitting by,

/b wunhi wrmi wtrnif Faluleuf, ok Nhwteuf, ok Nhelwsulum wunheyethek.
/p wənči wé·mi o·t·é·nink †nka·lalí·yunk, ó·k nčo·tí·yunk, ó·k †nči·ló·sələm wənči·aí·č·i·k.
/t from all the towns in Galilee and Judaea, and ones from Jerusalem.
/k which were come out of every town of Galilee, and Judaea, and Jerusalem:

/b Nrvlalkofq tolweliswakun vokif vatrlwp,
/p nehəlá·lkɔnkw tɔləwí·i-ləs·əwá·k·an hók·enk hat·é·lo·p,
/t And the power of our Lord was present in him,
/k and the power of the Lord was present

/b wunhi xrli kekrvat palselethi.
/p wənči- xé·li -ki·k·é·ha·t pa·lsi·lí·č·i.
/t by which he cured many who were sick.
/k to heal them.

Lk 5.18, Mt 9.2, Mk 2.3
/b Nu punu, nrwu linwuk pwrjwanro palselethi
/p ná pənáh, né·wa lónəwak pwe·š·əwa·né·ɔ pa·lsi·lí·č·i,
/t Then here there came four men bringing a sick person,
/l And behold, men came unto him, bringing a man sick of the palsy,

	/b	trxunekunif tuntu kulinawao.
	/p	te·x·əní·k·anink tə́nta-kələnawwá·ɔ.
	/t	carrying him on a litter.
	/l	lying on a bed, which was borne of four.

Lk 5.18
- /b Kwhi eku lwxolawao Nhesusif li wekwavmif.
- /p kkwə́či- íka -lo·x·ɔlawwá·ɔ nči·sás·ink lí wi·k·əwáhəmink.
- /t They tried to bring him to Jesus in the house.
- /k and they sought means to bring him in, and to lay him before him.

Mk 2.4, Lk 5.19
- /b Mrhi alyi eku lwxolavtetc nu xqetakc tonro
- /p mé·či á·lai- íka -lo·x·ɔlahtí·t·e, ná xkwi·t·á·k·e tɔ·né·ɔ.
- /t After they had been unable to bring him to him, they then went onto the roof,
- /l And when they could not come nigh unto him .., nor find by what way they might bring him in .., they went upon the housetop,

Mk 2.4
- /b twfjrnumunro cntu avkonrkvasek
- /p wtunkše·nəməné·ɔ énta-ahkɔne·khá·s·i·k.
- /t and they opened a hole in the roof covering.
- /k they uncovered the roof where he was: (See next (Lk 5.19): "tiling.")

Lk 5.19
- /b nu eku tcli pununanro vapi nc trxunekun lrlyi rlifwrxif Nhesus.
- /p ná íka tə́li-pənəna·né·ɔ hápi nə́ te·x·əní·k·an le·lá·i e·linkwé·x·ink nčí·sas.
- /t Then they let him down, with the litter, in the middle of it before Jesus.
- /k and let him down through the tiling with his couch into the midst before Jesus.

Lk 5.20
- /b Nhesus nrfc rlkeqi nvakalunt tclao,
- /p nčí·sas nénke e·lkí·kwi-nhaká·lənt, təlá·ɔ,
- /t When Jesus saw how much trust was placed in him, he said to him,
- /k And when he saw their faith, he said unto him,   [L. expands "him".]

- /b Linw mrhi kumutawswakun kpuketatumakrn,
- /p "lə́nu, mé·či kəmat·a·wsəwá·k·an kpak·i·t·a·t·amá·k·e·n.
- /t "Man, your sins have now been forgiven for you.
- /k Man, thy sins are forgiven thee. [L. omits "Man" and puts this line after the next.]

Mt 9.2
- /b fwes nvakrlintu.
- /p nkwí·s, nhake·e·lə́nta."
- /t Son, be hopeful."
- /k Son, be of good cheer; ...

Lk 5.21
- /b Rvlrkvekrthek ok Paluseuk nu tolumi punyrlintumunro. Letrvrok,
- /p ehəle·khi·k·é·č·i·k ɔ́k †pa·ləsi·í·ɔk, ná tɔ́ləmi-pəna·eləntaməné·ɔ, li·t·e·hé·ɔk,

	/t	The scribes and the Pharisees then began to reflect, thinking,
	/k	And the scribes and the Pharisees began to reason, saying,
Mk 2.6	/k	But there were certain of the scribes sitting there, and reasoning in their hearts,

	/b	Awrn vuh ct wu linw aptwnrtaq Krtanitwet toptwnakun?
	/p	"awé·n=háč=ét wá lə́nu a·pto·né·ta·kw ke·tanət·ó·wi·t tɔ·pto·ná·k·an?
	/t	"Who could this man be who speaks the word of God?
	/kl	Who is this which speaketh blasphemies?
Mk 2.7	/k	Why doth this man thus speak blasphemies?

	/b	Awrn vuh a kuski puketatumasw mutawswakun, Krtanitwet jwk xwva.
	/p	awé·n=háč=á· káski-pahki·t·a·t·amá·s·u mahta·wsəwá·k·an, ke·tanət·ó·wi·t šúkw xó·ha?
	/t	Who would be able to forgive sin except God alone?"
	/kl	Who can forgive sins, but God alone?

Mk 2.8, Lk 5.22

	/b	Jai Nhesus watwnrp rletrvalet, tclao; Krkw vuh wunhi nc letrvarq?
	/p	šá·e nčí·sas o·wa·tó·ne·p e·li·t·e·há·li·t, təlá·ɔ, "kéku=háč wə̂nči- nə́ -li·t·e·há·e·kw?
	/t	Jesus immediately knew what they were thinking, and he said to them. "Why do you think that?"
	/l	And immediately, [when] Jesus [perceived in his spirit, that they so reasoned within themselves], knowing their thoughts; [he, answering,] said unto them, Why reason ye these things! [Wherefore think ye evil in your hearts?]
Mk 2.8	/k	And immediately when Jesus perceived in his spirit that they so reasoned within themselves, he said unto them, Why reason ye these things in your hearts?
Lk 5.22	/k	But when Jesus perceived their thoughts, he answering said unto them, What reason ye in your hearts?

Mk 2.9	/b	Ta vuh nc alwei apwat lintc palset, Kumutawswakun kpuketatumakrn,
	/p	tá=háč nə́ aləwí·i á·p·əwat, lə́nte pá·lsi·t, 'kəmat·a·wsəwá·k·an kpak·i·t·a·t·amá·k·e·n,'
	/t	Which is easier, if a sick person is told, 'Your sins are forgiven,'
	/k	Whether is it easier to say to the sick of the palsy, Thy sins be forgiven thee;

	/b	jitu lintc, Amwel, wrtuni rnunsiun pumuskal?
	/p	ší=tá lə́nte, 'á·mwi·l, wé·t·əni e·nánsian, pəmə́ska·l'?
	/t	or if they are told, 'Get up, pick up your bed, and walk'?
	/k	or to say, Arise, and take up thy bed, and walk?

Mk 2.10	/b	Jwk kwnhih watwnro
	/p	šúkw kúnči-=č -wwa·to·né·ɔ,
	/t	But you (pl.) will hereby know
	/k	But that ye may know

/b linw wrqesif tcpi liset poketatamasen mutawswakun b tali xqetvakameqc,
/p lə́nu we·k·wí·s·ink tépi-lə́s·i·t pɔk·i·t·a·t·amá·s·i·n mahta·wsəwá·k·an yú táli xkwi·thakamí·k·we," —
/t that the man who is the Son is one capable of forgiving sin here on earth," —
/k that the Son of man hath power on earth to forgive sins,

/b (tclao palselethi linwu,)
/p təlá·ɔ pa·lsi·lí·č·i lə́nəwa,
/t and speaking to the sick man,
/k (he saith to the sick of the palsy,)

Mk 2.11 /b Amwel wrtuni ktupeny, mathel.
/p "á·mwi·l, wé·t·əni ktap·í·nay, má·č·i·l."
/t "Get up, pick up your bed, and go home."
/k I say unto thee, Arise, and take up thy bed, and go thy way into thine house.

Mk 2.12, Lk 5.25
/b Nu jai tomwen wrtunimun topeny rnunset,
/p ná šá·e tó·mwi·n, wwe·t·ənəmən tɔp·í·nay, e·nánsi·t.
/t Then he immediately got up and picked up his bed, where he lay.
/l And immediately he rose up before them, and took up his bed,

Lk 5.25 /k ... and took up that whereon he lay,

Lk 5.25 /b nu mohen, qrnamao Krtunitwelethi.
/p ná mó·č·i·n, kwe·na·má·ɔ ke·tanət·o·wi·lí·č·i.
/t Then he went home, thanking God.
/k ... and departed to his own house, glorifying God.
/l (L. has additions.)

Lk 5.26 /b Nu wrmi kanjrlintamwpanek, ok qrnamawapani Krtanitwelethi, ok wejaswuk;
/p ná wé·mi kanše·ləntamóp·ani·k, ɔ́·k kwe·na·mawwá·p·ani ke·tanət·o·wi·lí·č·i, ɔ́·k wi·š·á·s·əwak;
/t Then everyone was astonished, and gave thanks to God, and were afraid;
/k And they were all amazed, and they glorified God, and were filled with fear,

/b lwrpanek Kanjilenamwvnu bqc kejqek. ‖
/p luwé·p·ani·k, "kkánši-li·namúhəna yúkwe kí·škwi·k."
/t they said, "Today we have seen something wonderful."
/k saying, We have seen strange things to day.

Chapter 34 (pp. 56-57). [L. section 33.] (Luke 5.27-30, 33-37, 39; Matthew 9.9, 12-17; Mark 2.14-16, 19-22)

Mt 9.9   /b Nc wunhi alumskatc
(p. 56)   /p nə́ wə́nči-aləmská·t·e,

/t When he went away from there,
/l And as he passed forth from thence,

Mt 9.9, Lk 5.27
/b Nhesus nrr linwu lwcnsw Matws
/p nčí·sas né·e· lə́nəwa, luwénsu '†má·to·s'
/t Jesus saw a man named Matthew
/l he saw a publican, named Matthew

Mk 2.14
/b ok Lepy Alpius qesu wlumutupenrp cntu evrnvwnt moni.
/p ɔ́·k '†lí·pay,' †a·lpías kkwí·s·a, wələmahtap·í·ne·p énta-ihé·nhunt mɔ́ni.
/t or Levi, the son of Alphaeus, sitting where he was paid money.
/l *or* Levi *the son* of Alphaeus, sitting at the receipt of custom,

Lk 5.27
/b Tclao, Wtrkyel.
/p təlá·ɔ, "wté·kai·l."
/t He said to him, "Follow me."
/kl and he said unto him, Follow me.

Lk 5.28
/b Nu posqen, wrmi krkw wnukavtimun; nu tolumi naolan.
/p ná pɔ́skwi·n, wé·mi kéku wənəkahtə́mən; ná tɔ́ləmi-ná·ɔla·n.
/t And he then got to his feet, leaving everything behind, and followed him away.
/kl And he left all, rose up, and followed him.

Lk 5.29
/b Ok Lepy monetwn li xifi metsavten tali weket;
/p ɔ́·k †lí·pay mɔnní·to·n lí-xínkwi-mi·tsáhti·n táli wí·k·i·t.
/t And Levi gave a great feast in his house.   [*lit.*, 'made there be great eating']
/kl And Levi made him a great feast in his own house: ...

/b xrlwpanek mrmyrnifek moni, ok peli awrnek wehi metswpanek,
/p xe·ló·p·ani·k mehəma·e·nínki·k mɔ́ni, ɔ́·k pí·li awé·ni·k wíči-mi·tsó·p·ani·k.
/t There were many tax-collectors, and other people ate along with them,
/k and there was a great company of publicans and of others that sat down with them.
/kl ... publicans and sinners came and sat down ... (Mt 9.10)

Mk 2.15
/b ok Nhesus ok rkrkemathi rli xrlwk wrtrkaotpanek.
/p ɔ́·k nčí·sas ɔ́·k e·k·e·ki·má·č·i, é·li xé·lo·k we·t·e·kaɔ·tpáni·k.
/t and Jesus and his disciples, for there were many that followed him.
/k ... together with Jesus and his disciples: for there were many, and they followed him.
/l also with him and his disciples: for there were many, and they followed him.

Mk 2.16 /b Nrovtetc rvlrkvekrthek ok Paluseuk
         /p ne·ɔhtí·t·e ehəle·khi·k·é·č·i·k ɔ́·k †pa·ləsi·í·ɔk,
         /t When the scribes and Pharisees saw
         /k And when the scribes and Pharisees saw him   [L. has "But" from Lk 5.30]

         /b tcli Nhesus ok rkrkemathe wepwmanro mrtawselethi, ok mrvmynumulethi moni,
         /p táli- nčí·sas ɔ́·k e·k·e·ki·má·č·i -wi·po·ma·né·ɔ me·t·a·wsi·lí·č·i ɔ́·k
             mehəma·e·nəməlí·č·i móni,
         /t Jesus and his disciples eating with sinners and tax-collectors,
         /kl eat with publicans and sinners,

Lk 5.30 /b kwvkalwmawao, tclawao   [⟨kwvk-⟩ for ⟨kwk-⟩]
         /p kwək·a·lo·mawwá·ɔ, təlawwá·ɔ,
         /t they berated them, saying to them,
         /l they murmured against his disciples, saying,

         /b koh vuh wepwmrq mrtawsethek, ok mrvmynifek moni.
         /p "kóč=háč wi·pó·me·kw me·t·a·wsí·č·i·k ɔ́·k mehəma·e·nínki·k móni?"
         /t "Why do you eat with sinners and tax-collectors?"
         /k Why do ye eat and drink with publicans and sinners?   (L. adds from Mk 2.16.)

Mt 9.12 /b Nhesus puntufc tclapani,
         /p nčí·sas pəntánke, təlá·p·ani,
         /t When Jesus heard it, he said to them,
         /k But when Jesus heard that, he said unto them,   (L. adds "answering.")

         /b Awrn wlamalsetc, takw kavtalri ntaktulu; palsethek jwk.
         /p "awé·n wəlamalsí·t·e, takó· kahta·lé·i nta·ktəla; pa·lsí·č·i·k šúkw.
         /t "When someone is well, they have no need of a doctor; only the sick (do).
         /kl They that be whole need not a physician, but they that are sick.

Mt 9.13 /b Alwei nwifatum ktumakrlintwakun, nwntyi wevwfrokun;
         /p aləwí·i nəwinká·t·am ktəma·k·e·lәntəwá·k·an, nuntá·i wi·hunke·ɔ́·k·an,
         /t I like mercy (received) more, sacrifice (performed) less.
         /kl (2) I will have mercy, and not sacrifice: [numbers = sequence in L.]

         /b my nunwstamwq myai rlwif.
         /p mái-nəno·stámo·kw mayá·i é·ləwenk.
         /t Go and understand what is truly said.
         /kl (1) But go ye and learn what that meaneth, ...

         /b Takw nwnhi pawun ntcli a ntwman jaxakawsethek,
         /p takó· núnči-pá·wən ntəli-=á· -ntó·ma·n šaxahka·wsí·č·i·k,
         /t I did not come to summon the righteous,
         /kl for I am not come to call the righteous,

	/b	jwk mrtawsethek wunhih qulwpevtet.
	/p	šúkw me·t·a·wsí·č·i·k, wə́nči-=č -kwələp·íhti·t."
	/t	but sinners, for them to repent."
	/kl	but sinners to repentance.

Mt 9.14
- /b   Nhan rkrkemathi eku prok, tclawao,
- /p   nčá·n e·k·e·ki·má·č·i íka pé·ɔk, təlawwá·ɔ,
- /t   John's disciples came there and said to them,
- /k   Then came to him the disciples of John, saying,   (L. adds words.)

- /b   Krkw wunhi nelwnu, ok Paluseuk tevtumeki wli mutu kuvtu metserf,
- /p   "kéku wə́nči- ni·ló·na ɔ́·k †pa·ləsi·i·ɔk tihtəmí·ki -wə́li- máta -káhta-mi·tsíenk,
- /t   "Why do we and the Pharisees often fast,
- /k   Why do we and the Pharisees fast oft,   [L. changes and adds words.]

- /b   na wrnu kelwu mutu,
- /p   ná wé·na ki·ló·wa máta,
- /t   while you (pl.) do not,
- /kl   but thy disciples fast not?

Lk 5.33
- /b   jwk, kmemetsivumw ok kmemuncvmw?
- /p   šúkw kəmihəmi·tsíhəmɔ ɔ́·k kəmihəmənéhəmɔ?"
- /t   but you eat and drink?"
- /k   ... but thine eat and drink?   [L. omits "thine"]

Mk 2.19
- /b   Nhesus tclaol,
- /p   nčí·sas təlá·ɔl,
- /t   Jesus said to them,
- /kl   And Jesus said unto them, ...

- /b   Kuski vuh a awrn wenhemuntc wunhi cntu metsavtif mutu metsee,
- /p   "káski-=háč=á· awé·n, wenči·mɔ́nte wə́nči énta-mi·tsáhtink, máta -mi·tsí·i,
- /t   "Would someone, when they are invited to a feast, be able not to eat,
- /k   Can the children of the bridechamber fast,   [L. combines Lk 5.34 and Mt 9.15]

Mt 9.15
- /b   nrli avpet wcnhifrt?
- /p   né·li-ahpí·t wenčínke·t?
- /t   while the host is there?
- /kl   as long as the bridegroom is with them?

Mk 2.20
- /b   Jwkh kejqek prrekc mutu awrn kavtu wcnhematc bl;
- /p   šúkw=č kí·škwi·k pe·e·í·k·e, máta awé·n káhta-wenči·má·t·e yó·l,
- /t   But when the day comes when no one will want to invite them,
- /kl   But the days will come, when the bridegroom shall be taken away from them, ...

                                                          (Also Mt 9.15, Lk 5.35.)

| | /b | nuh mutu kotu metsewunro.
| | /p | ná=č máta kót·a-mi·tsi·wəné·ɔ.
| | /t | then they will not want to eat.
| | /kl | and then shall they fast in those days.

Lk 5.36 /b Rnwnvakrokun tclapani,
/p e·nunthake·ó·k·an təlá·p·ani,
/t He told them a parable,
/kl And he spake also a parable unto them; (Cf. Mt 9.16.)

Mk 2.21 /b Takw awrn xoakvwqeonif, tufiti wwskaqeon pxufwekri,
/p "takó· awé·n xuwa·khuk·wí·ɔnink tankíti wəskahkwí·ɔn pxankhwi·k·é·i.
/t "No one puts a patch of a little bit of new cloth on an old coat.
/kl No man seweth a piece of new cloth on an old garment; ... (Cf. Mt 9.16. Lk 5.36.)

/b nuni a lisetc, toxkevulru li okai, alwe a lukvekolavkevlr
/p nə́ni=á· ləs·í·t·e, to·xkihəlé·ɔ lí ɔ·ká·i, aləwí·i=á· ləkhikɔ·lahkíhəle·,
/t If he does that, they would tear around the edge, and the hole become bigger,
/kl else the new piece that filled it up taketh away from the old, and the rent is made worse.

Lk 5.36 /b rli pufriti wwskavqeon ta wlexunwi.
/p é·li panke·íti wəskahkwí·ɔn tá=á· wəli·x·ənó·wi.
/t for the little piece of new cloth would not be right.
/kl and the piece that was taken out of the new agreeth not with the old.

Lk 5.37 /b Ok ta wwskif wyn xwi pwtalasif, vatwun
/p ɔ́·k tá=á· wə́skink wáin xúwi-po·t·a·lá·s·ink hat·ó·wən.
/t And new wine would not be put in an old skin bag.
/k And no man putteth new wine into old bottles; ... (Cf. Mt 9.17, Mk 2.22.)

/b ok a nc awrn lisetc, ‖ nc a wyn twxkvekaoo pwtalasu, ok a swkavlr,
/p ɔ́·k=á· nə́ awé·n ləs·í·t·e, nə́=á· wáin to·xkhikaɔ́·ɔ po·t·a·lá·s·a, ɔ́·k=á· so·k·áhəle·.
/t And if anyone did that, the wine would tear the skin bag and spill,
/k else the new wine will burst the bottles, and be spilled,

(p. 57) /b ok a palelisw nu pwtalas.
/p ɔ́·k=á· palí·i ləs·u ná po·t·á·la·s.
/t and the skin bag would be destroyed.
/k and the bottles shall perish.

Lk 5.38 /b Jwk a wwskif wyn wwski pwtalasif vatwfc, nu rle a wlilreo.   [⟨lreo⟩ for /lé·ɔ/]
/p šúkw=á· wə́skink wáin wə́ski-po·t·a·lá·s·ink hat·únke, ná ellí·i=á· wə́li-lé·ɔ.
/t But if new wine is put in a new skin bag, then both would be in good shape.
/k But new wine must be put into new bottles; and both are preserved.

Lk 5.39 /b Ok awrn xwrk wyn munrte, ta jai wifi munri wwskif;
/p ɔ́·k awé·n xúwe·k wáin məné·t·e, tá=á· šá·e winki-məné·i wə́skink.
/t And if someone drinks old wine, he will not immediately like to drink the new.
/k No man also having drunk old wine straightway desireth new:

/b ok xan a lwr xowrk alwe w*lit.*
/p ɔ́·k=xán=á· lúwe·, 'xúwe·k aləwí·i wələ́t.'"
/t But rather he would say, 'The old is better.'"
/k for he saith, The old is better.

Chapter 35 (pp. 57-58). [L. section 34.] (Matthew 9.18-19, 22-23 [part]; Mark. 5.22-23, 25-31, 33, 35-43; Luke 8.41-43, 46-47)

Mt 9.18 /b Nrli nc lwrtup Nhesus,
/p né·li- nə́ -luwé·t·əp nčí·sas,
/t While Jesus was saying that,
/kl While he spake these things unto them,

Mk 5.22 /b mwxkevlrp linw lwcnsw Hrlus, nekanexif cntu mycvuluf.
/p mo·xkíhəle·p lə́nu, luwénsu †čé·ləs, ni·k·a·ní·x·ink énta-ma·éhəlank,
/t there emerged (from the crowd) a man named Jairus, a leader in the synagogue,
/k behold, there cometh one of the rulers of the synagogue, Jairus by name;

/b Vakif tclaneven voky
/p hákink təlaníhi·n hɔ́k·ay.
/t and he threw himself down.
/k and ... he fell at his feet,
/l [and when he saw him,] he fell down at Jesus' feet, ...

Mk 5.23 /b moxifokuemao lwr, Mrhi kavti uful ntanis;   [⟨-kuem-⟩ for ⟨-kunem-⟩]
/p mɔx·inkɔhkəni·má·ɔ, lúwe·, "mé·či káhti-ánkəl ntá·nəs.
/t He praised him and said, "My daughter is now almost dead.
/k And besought him greatly, saying, My little daughter lieth at the point of death:
 (Cf. Mt 9.18 "worshipped him"; L. passage has both verbs in a longer, repetitive text.)

Mt 9.18 /b jwk wuntu xal my kekrvaw.
/p šúkw wə́ntax á·l, mái-ki·k·é·haw."
/t But come and cure her."
/k ... but come and lay thy hand upon her, and she shall live.   (Cf. Mk 5.23 [longer].)

Lk 8.42 /b Nu tcli mawselen avpami ct tclin ok neju kavtinumw.
/p nə́ tə́li-ma·wsí·li·n; ahpá·mi=ét télən ɔ́·k ní·š·a kahtənámu.
/t She was the only one he had; she must have been about twelve years old.
/kl For he had one only daughter, about twelve years of age, ...

Mt 9.19 /b Nhesus paswqe tolumi wehroo ok rkrkemathi,
/p nčí·sas pahsúk·wi·, tɔ́ləmi-wi·č·e·ɔ́·ɔ, ɔ́·k e·k·e·ki·má·či.
/t Jesus got up and followed after him, and (so did) his disciples.
/kl And Jesus arose, and followed him, and so did his disciples.

Lk 8.42 /b jwk nrlwxwrt tohekawao.
/p šúkw ne·ló·x·we·t, tɔčikaɔwwá·ɔ.
/t But as he went, they crowded up to him.
/k But as he went the people thronged him. (L. adds words.)

Lk 8.43 /b Avpwp nc tali xqr tclin ok neju txi kavtin nwhi mvwqenrp.
/p ahpó·p nɔ́ táli xkwé·; télən ɔ́·k ní·š·a txí-kahtən núči-mhukwí·ne·p.
/t There was a woman there, and she had had the bloody flux for twelve years.
/k And a woman having an issue of blood twelve years, ... (Cf. Mk 5.25.)

Mk 5.26 /b Wrmi krkw cntxi wlataq noxpi nvakrwsen;
/p wé·mi kéku éntxi-wəlá·ta·kw nɔ́xpi-nhaké·wsi·n.
/t She sought help using (*lit.*, 'with') everything she had.
/k ... and had spent all that she had,
/k which had spent all her living upon physicians, ... (Lk 8.43; cf. L.)

Lk 8.43 /b takw kuski wlevai
/p takó· káski-wəli·há·i.
/t She could not be made well,
/kl ... neither could be healed of any,
/k ... and was nothing bettered, ... (Mk 5.26)

Mk 5.26 /b jwk fumri alwe lamalsw.
/p šúkw nkəmé·i aləwí·i-lamálsu.
/t but she was always worse.
/kl ... but rather grew worse,

Mk 5.27 /b Mrhi punufc krkw wunhi Nhesus, [⟨punufc⟩ for ⟨puntufc⟩]
/p mé·či pəntánke kéku wə́nči nčí·sas,
/t When she heard something about Jesus,
/kl When she had heard of Jesus,

/b nu eku ton larnac vwpxonelet wunhi eku pr, [⟨px⟩ for ⟨pxk⟩]
/p ná íka tó·n †la·é·nae hupxkɔní·li·t wə́nči, íka pé·,
/t she went in the middle of the crowd behind him and came to him,
/k came in the press behind, .. (L. adds from Lk 8.44.)

Mk 5.28 /b rli lwrt, eli a kuski jwk eku alinamanc rqet nwlamalsih.
/p é·li-lúwe·t, "illi=á· káski- šúkw íka -alənəmá·ne é·k·wi·t, no·lamálsi=č."
/t as she said, "Even if I could just touch his clothes, I will be well."
/k For she said, If I may touch but his clothes, I shall be whole.

Mk 5.29 /b Mrhi nanc rlsetc, wlamalswp ok tove wlamuntumun msihri voky.
/p mé·či ná=nə e·lsí·t·e, wəlamálso·p, ɔ́·k tɔ́hi-wəlamántamən məsəč·é·i hɔ́k·ay.
/t After she did that, she was well, and she felt very good all over her body.
/kl And straightway the fountain of her blood was dried up; and she felt in her body that she was healed of that plague.

Mk 5.30 /b Nhesus jai nevelahi watwn li kekrvwrokun vokif wunhivulr,
/p nčí·sas šá·e nihəláči o·wá·to·n lí- ki·k·ehəwe·ɔ́·k·an hɔ́k·enk -wənčíhəle·,
/t Jesus spontaneously knew right away that curing power had gone out of his body,
/kl And Jesus, immediately knowing in himself that virtue had gone out of him,

/b eku lwqr lwri awrn tcli eku alinamun rqeu?
/p íka lɔ́·kwe·, lúwe·, "awé·n tɔ́li- íka -alɔ́nəmən é·k·wia?"
/t He looked there and said, "Who was it that touched my clothes?"
/kl turned him about in the press, and said, Who touched my clothes?

Mk 5.31 /b Rkrkemathi tclkw, Kunrmun vun xavrlin ktuhekakc
/p e·k·e·ki·má·č·i tɔ́lku, "kəné·mən=xán xahé·lən, ktačiká·k·e,
/t His disciples said to him, "Although you see the crowd pressing around you,
/k And his disciples said unto him, Thou seest the multitude thronging thee,
(L. adds words.)

/b nu wrnu knatwxton awrn ta rli kekunwkon.
/p ná wé·na kənat·ó·xto·n, awé·n=tá é·li-ki·kənúk·ɔn."
/t you still ask who was it that touched you."
/kl and sayest thou, Who touched me?

Lk 8.46 /b Nhesus lwr, Kehe ta awrn fkekunwq
/p nčí·sas lúwe·, "khičí·i=tá awé·n nkí·kənukw,
/t Jesus said, "Truly someone touched me,
/kl And Jesus said, Somebody hath touched me:

/b rli ntamutamun li kekrvwrokun nvakif wcnhivulr.   [⟨ntamut-⟩ for ⟨ntamunt-⟩]
/p é·li ntamántamən lí- ki·k·ehəwe·ɔ́·k·an nhák·enk -wənčíhəle·.
/t for I felt curing power go out of my body.
/kl for I perceive that virtue is gone out of me.

Lk 8.47 /b Nu xqr nrfc tcli mutu kuski kuntvatwun, eku rp nufevlrp,
/p ná xkwé· nénke tɔ́li- máta -káski-kanthatɔ́·wən, íka é·p, nankíhəle·p.
/t That woman, when she saw she could not hide it, went to him, trembling.
/k And when the woman saw that she was not hid, she came trembling, ...

Mk 5.33 /b wli watwn rlevkwkup
/p ó·li-wwá·to·n e·lihkúk·əp.
/t She well knew what he had done to her.
/kl [fearing and trembling,] knowing what was done in her, ...

Lk 8.47 /b wnejetqetaopani, ok kjexathemwp wrmi awrn rlifwrxif
/p wəni·š·i·tkwi·taɔ́·p·ani, ɔ́·k kši·x·a·č·í·mo·p wé·mi awé·n e·linkwé·x·ink
/t She knelt down before him and made clear, before everyone, (L. adds.)
/k ... and falling down before him, she declared unto him before all the people

/b wunhi patup, ok rlkeqi jai kekrt. ‖
/p wə́nči-pá·t·əp, ɔ́·k e·lkí·kwi- šá·e -kí·k·e·t.
/t why she had come, and how immediately she was cured.
/kl for what cause she had touched him and how she was healed immediately.

Mt 9.22 /b Nu Nhesus tclan, Nvakrrlintu ntanis rli nvakatamwrokun kekrvkon.
(p. 58) /p ná nčí·sas tɔ́lan, "nhake·e·lə́nta, ntá·nəs, é·li- nhaka·t·amwe·ɔ́·k·an -ki·k·éhkɔn."
/t Then Jesus said to her, "Be hopeful, my daughter, for faith has cured you."
/k and .. he said, Daughter, be of good comfort; thy faith hath made thee whole. ...
/l (L. adds before and after.)

Mk 5.35 /b Nrli krkw lwrtup
/p né·li- kéku -luwé·t·əp,
/t While he was speaking,
/kl While he yet spake,

/b mwxkevlrpanek linwuk wunhi, xifwrlumwkset weket.
/p mo·xkihəlé·p·ani·k lə́nəwak wə́nči xinkwe·ləmúkwsi·t wí·k·i·t.
/t there appeared men from the house of the highly regarded man.
/kl there came from the ruler of the synagogue's house certain

/b Tclawapani, Ktanes mrhi uful, koh vuh a ekalisi nvakalat Rkrkemvkon?
/p təlawwá·p·ani, "ktá·nəs mé·či ánkəl; kɔ́č=háč=á· ikalísi nhaká·lat e·k·e·kí·mkɔn?
/t They said to him, "Your daughter has died; why would you need help from your teacher anymore?"
/k which said, Thy daughter is dead: why troublest thou the Master any further?
/k saying to him, Thy daughter is dead; ... (Lk 8.49)

Mk 5.36 /b Nhesus mrhi puntufc nc aptwnakun nc rlaptwncf,
/p nčí·sas mé·či pəntánke nɔ́ a·pto·ná·k·an nɔ́ e·la·ptó·nenk,
/t As soon as Jesus heard the words that were spoken,
/k As soon as Jesus heard the word that was spoken,

/b tclao nrl xifwrlumwkselethi, kahi wejasevan, jwk nvakali.
/p təlá·ɔ né·l xinkwe·ləmukwsi·lí·č·i, "káči wi·š·a·s·í·han; šúkw nhaká·li."
/t he said to the highly regarded man, "Don't be afraid; just believe in (rely on) me."
/k he saith unto the ruler of the synagogue, Be not afraid, only believe. (L. adds.)

Mk 5.37 /b Takw tclrlumaeo awrni wehrvkwn, jwk Petul ok Nhim ok Nhan wemavtu Nhim.
/p takó· təle·ləma·í·ɔ awé·ni wwi·č·é·yko·n, šúkw †pí·təl ɔ́·k nčím, ɔ́·k nčá·n, wí·mahta nčím.

| | /t | He allowed no one to go with him except Peter and Jim, and John, Jim's brother. |
| | /k | And he suffered no man to follow him, save Peter, and James, and John the brother of James. (L. has "to go in" and adds words.) |

Mt 9.23 /b Eku pravtetc weket nu mrxifwrlumwkset, nrotc rpeqrlethi
/p íka pe·ahtí·t·e wí·k·i·t ná me·x·iŋkwe·ləmúkwsi·t, ne·ɔ́·t·e e·p·i·k·we·lí·č·i
/t When they came to the house of the highly regarded man and saw the musicians,
/k And when Jesus came into the ruler's house, and saw the minstrels ... (L. adds.)

Mk 5.38 /b ave lupukwk ok salamwuk;
/p áhi-ləpák·o·k ɔ́·k salá·məwak.
/t they wept loudly and cried out.
/k ... and them that wept and wailed greatly.

Mk 5.39 /b mrhi trmekrtc, tclaol nrl,
/p mé·či te·mi·k·é·t·e, təlá·ɔl né·l,
/t After he had come in, he said to them,
/k And when he was come in, he saith unto them,

/b Krkw wunhi nc liserq, ok lupukrq, bvleq,
/p "kéku wə́nči- nɔ́ -lɔ́s·ie·kw, ɔ́·k -ləpák·e·kw?—yúh lí·kw.
/t "Why are you doing that, and weeping?—Tell me this.
/k Why make ye this ado, and weep? (L. adds.)

/b wu xqrhih mutu ufulwi, jwk kawe.
/p wá xkwé·čəč máta ankəlɔ́·wi, šúkw kawí·.
/t This girl is not dead, but only sleeping."
/k the damsel is not dead, but sleepeth.

Mk 5.40 /b Nu wrvrmwalanro rli mavtrlumavtet.
/p ná wwehe·məwa·la·né·ɔ, é·li-mahte·ləmáhti·t.
/t Then they laughed at him, as they had contempt for him.
/kl And they laughed him to scorn.

/b Mrhi wrmi kohumif rlskaotc;
/p mé·či wé·mi kɔ́čəmink e·lskaɔ́·t·e,
/t After he had shown them all out,
/kl But when he had put them all out,

/b wehrou wxo ok nrl kovrsu nu xqrhih, ok nrl wehrvkwki
/p wwi·č·e·ɔ́·ɔ ɔ́·x·ɔ ɔ́·k né·l kɔhé·s·a ná xkwé·čəč, ɔ́·k né·l wi·č·e·ykúk·i,
/t he took the girl's father and mother with him, and those that came with him,
/kl he taketh the father and the mother of the damsel, and them that were with him,

/b eku li tumekrok xqrhih jcfexif,
/p íkali təmi·k·é·ɔk xkwé·čəč šenkí·x·ink.
/t and they went in to where the girl lay.
/kl and entereth in where the damsel was lying.

Mk 5.41
/b nu eku tonan wnaxkelet xqrhihu, tclao, Amwel ktclil.
/p ná íka tónna·n wənaxkí·li·t xkwe·čə́č·a, təlá·ɔ, "á·mwi·l, ktə́ləl."
/t Then he took the girl by her hand and said to her, "Get up, I tell you."
/kl And he took the damsel by the hand, and said unto her, Talitha cumi; which is, being interpreted, Damsel, I say unto thee, arise.

Mk 5.42
/b Nu jai nu xqrhih tomwen ok pumiskr, rli tclin ok neju kavtinamwp,
/p ná šá·e ná xkwé·čəč tó·mwi·n, ɔ́·k pəmə́ske·, é·li télən ɔ́·k ní·š·a kahtənámo·p
/t Then the girl immediately got up and walked, as she was twelve years old.
/k And straightway the damsel arose, and walked; for she was of the age of twelve years.   (L. adds.)

/b ave vwsku kanjrlintamwk;
/p áhi-hwə́ska kanše·lə́ntamo·k.
/t They were extremely astonished.
/k And they were astonished with a great astonishment.   (L. adds "her parents".)

Mk 5.43
/b tclao melw krkw mehet, ok kahi awrn watulavrq.
/p təlá·ɔ, "mí·lo· kéku mí·č·i·t, ɔ́·k káči awé·n wwa·təlá·he·kw."
/t He said to them, "Give her something to eat, and don't let anyone know."
/k And he charged them straitly that no man should know it; and commanded that something should be given her to eat.   (L. rearranges.)

Mt 9.26
/b Jwk wrmi li puntakot rlamrk nu vake.
/p šúkw wé·mi lí-pəntá·k·ɔt e·lá·me·k nə́ hák·i.
/t But news of it went the whole length of the land.
/k And the fame hereof went abroad into all that land.

Chapter 36 (pp. 58-59). [L. section 35.] (Matthew 9.27-34)

Mt 9.27
/b Mrhi rlumskatc nc wunhi, neju linwuk krkrpifothek wnaolawao,
/p mé·či e·ləmská·t·e nə́ wə́nči, ní·š·a lə́nəwak ke·k·e·p·inkɔ́·č·i·k wəna·ɔlawwá·ɔ.
/t After he had departed from there, two men who were blind followed him.
/k And when Jesus departed thence, two blind men followed him,   (L. "went from".)

/b popaketaowao, tclawao, O Ntrpit Qesu ktumakrlumenrn.
/p pɔ·pa·k·i·taɔwwá·ɔ, təlawwá·ɔ, "ó·, †nté·pit kkwí·s·a, ktəma·k·e·ləmí·ne·n."
/t They cried out to him, saying, "O son of David, have mercy on us."
/kl crying, and saying, Thou Son of David, have mercy on us.

Mt 9.28	/b	Wekwamif pratc krkrpifothek wtxawao,
	/p	wi·k·əwáhəmink pe·á·t·e, ke·k·e·p·inkɔ́·č·i·k o·txawwá·ɔ.
	/t	When he arrived in the house, the blind men came to him.
	/k	And when he was come into the house, the blind men came to him:

/b nu Nhesus tclan kwlamvetamunro vuh ntcli kuski ni lisen?
/p ná nčí·sas tɔ́la·n, "ko·la·mhitamɔné·ɔ=háč ntɔ́li-káski- ní -lɔ́s·i·n?"
/t Then Jesus said to them, "Do you believe that I can do that?"
/k and Jesus saith unto them, Believe ye that I am able to do this?

/b Tclawao, Kovan Nrvlaliun.
/p təlawwá·ɔ, "kɔhán, nehəlá·lian.
/t They said to him, "Yes, my Lord."
/k They said unto him, Yea, Lord.

Mt 9.29 /b Nu qekinimaon wijkifqelet, tclao Krkw nrkatumrq na nuni lrkch.
/p ná kwi·kənəmáɔ·n wəškinkwí·li·t, təlá·ɔ, "kéku ne·ká·t·ame·kw, ná=nɔ́ni lé·k·eč."
/t Then he touched their eyes and said, "What you have faith in, let it be like that."
/k Then touched he their eyes, saying, According to your faith be it unto you.

Mt 9.30 /b Nu wijkifwao twfjrlrlw.
/p ná wəškinkəwá·ɔ tunkšehəlé·lu.
/t Then their eyes opened.
/k And their eyes were opened;

/b Nhesus qehe lao kahi awrn watwveh.   [⟨wa-‖twveh⟩]
/p nčí·sas kwi·čí·i-lá·ɔ, "káči awé·n wwa·tó·hi·č."
/t Jesus strongly admonished them, "Don't let anyone know about it."
/k and Jesus straitly charged them, saying, See that no man know it.

Mt 9.31 /b Jwk kenh rlumskavtetc wrmi awrni tohemwlxawapani wrmi nu tali.
(p. 59) /p šúkw kɔ́nč e·ləmskahtí·t·e, wé·mi awé·n tɔ·č·i·mo·lxawwá·p·ani wé·mi nɔ́ táli.
/t But as soon as they departed, they told everyone all over.
/k But they, when they were departed, spread abroad his fame in all that country.

Mt 9.32 /b Mrhi nc wunhi khetetc,
/p mé·či nɔ́ wɔ́nči-kčihtí·t·e,
/t After they had gone out of there,
/k As they went out,

/b puna pwrjwawaol mutu kekski krkw lwrlet lunwu;
/p pənáh, pwe·š·əwawwá·ɔl máta kí·kski- kéku -luwé·li·t lɔ́nəwa,
/t why, here they brought a man who was never able to say anything,
/k behold, they brought to him a dumb man

182 Blanchard's Harmony of the Gospels

  /b rpetakwk mavtuntwu.
  /p e·p·i·tá·k·uk mahtant·ó·wa.
  /t who had a devil in him.
  /k possessed with a devil.

Mt 9.33 /b Mrhi paleliskamwntc mavtuntwu nu kcnh koski krkw lwrn.
  /p mé·či palí·i ləskamúnte mahtant·ó·wa, ná kə́nč kóski- kéku -lúwe·n.
  /t As soon as the devil had been driven away from him, he was able to speak.
  /k And when the devil was cast out, the dumb spake:

  /b Wrmi eku rpethek kanjrlintamwk;
  /p wé·mi íka e·p·í·č·i·k kanše·lə́ntamo·k,
  /t Everyone who was there was astonished,
  /k and the multitudes marvelled,

  /b lwrpanek, Takw vuji lrep Islilif tali.
  /p luwé·p·ani·k, "takó· háši lé·i·p †isələ́link táli."
  /t and they said, "It never happened before in Israel."
  /k saying, It was never so seen in Israel.

Mt 9.34 /b Jwk Paluseuk lwrpanek
  /p šúkw †pa·ləsi·í·ɔk luwé·p·ani·k,
  /t But the Pharisees said,
  /k But the Pharisees said,

  /b qwtskao mavtuntwul wunhi xifwi mavtuntw.
  /p "kwətskaɔ́·ɔ mahtant·ó·wal wə́nči xínkwi-mahtánt·u."
  /t "He drives out devils by means of the great devil."
  /k He casteth out devils through the prince of the devils.

Chapter 37 (pp. 59-62). [L. section 36.] (Matthew 9.35-38, 10.1-42, 11.1; Luke 8.1-3; cf. Mark 9.41)

Mt 9.35 /b Nu Nhesus wrmi btu tonrp rlwtrnyek avkrkifrp cntu mycvluf
  /p ná nčí·sas wé·mi=yú=tá tó·ne·p e·lo·t·é·nai·k, ahke·kínke·p énta-ma·éhəlank.
  /t Then Jesus went to all the towns, and he taught in the synagogues.
  /k And Jesus went about all the cities and villages, teaching in their synagogues,

  /b pumtwnvatumirp wrlvik aptwnakun rlwe lrk, [⟨umirp⟩ for ⟨uminrp⟩]
  /p pwəmto·nha·t·amə́ne·p wé·lhik a·pto·ná·k·an e·ləwí·i-lé·k.
  /t He preached the gospel (*lit.*, good word) of the better life (*lit.*, what is greater).
  /k and preaching the gospel of the kingdom,

  /b ok qekrvapani wrmi palselethi wrmi krkw rlufulilethi,
  /p ɔ́·k kwi·k·e·há·p·ani wé·mi pa·lsi·lí·č·i, wé·mi kéku e·lankələlí·č·i.

Text, Transcription, and Translation

/t   And he healed all the sick, who suffered from every disease.
/k   and healing every sickness and every disease among the people.

Lk 8.1
/b   nrk tclin ok neju wethrotpanek,
/p   né·k télən ɔ́·k ní·š·a wi·č·e·ɔ·tpáni·k,
/t   The twelve were the ones who went with him,
/k   ... and the twelve were with him,

Lk 8.2
/b   ok alintc xqrok kekrvunhek wrvokyetpanek mavtuntwakun.
/p   ɔ́·k a·lə́nte xkwé·ɔk ki·k·e·hə́nči·k, we·hɔk·ai·tpáni·k mahtant·uwwá·k·an.
/t   and also some women who were cured, who had been possessed by evil power.
/k   And certain women, which had been healed of evil spirits and infirmities,

/b   Mawsw lwcnsw Mrli lwivulap Maktulen; vokif wunhi khelwu nejaj mavtuntwul,
/p   má·wsu luwénsu mé·li, luwíhəla·p †má·ktali·n, hɔ́k·enk wə́nči-kčí·ləwa ní·š·a·š mahtant·ó·wal,
/t   One was named Mary, called Magdalene; seven devils came out of her.
/k   Mary called Magdalene, out of whom went seven devils,

Lk 8.3
/b   ok Nhwanu Kwsi wekemathel Vclut krnavketaqki, ok Swsanu ok xrli peli awrnek
/p   ɔ́·k †nčo·wá·na, †kó·si wi·k·i·má·č·i·l, hélat ke·nahki·tá·kwki, ɔ́·k †so·sána, ɔ́·k xé·li pí·li awé·ni·k.
/t   and Joanna, the wife of Chuza, who took care of things for Herod, and Susanna, and many other people.
/k   And Joanna the wife of Chuza Herod's steward, and Susanna, and many others,

/b   topalawapani li lathrswakunif.
/p   tɔp·a·lawwá·p·ani lí lač·e·s·əwá·k·anink.
/t   They took care of him in goods.
/k   which ministered unto him of their substance.
                          [RSV: "who provided for them out of their means"]

Mt 9.36
/b   Jwk nrotc macvlalethi qwtumakrlumao rli jawusetet,
/p   šúkw ne·ɔ́·t·e ma·ehəla·lí·č·i, kwət·əma·k·e·ləmá·ɔ, é·li-šawəs·íhti·t.
/t   But when he saw the ones gathered together, he pitied them, as they were infirm,
/k   But when he saw the multitudes, he was moved with compassion on them, because they fainted,   [RSV: "because they were harassed and helpless"]

/b   rli avsrlavtet mulaji mrkesuk mutu awrn krnavkevavtc.   [⟨-vavtc⟩ for ⟨-vatc⟩]
/p   é·li-ahsehəláhti·t málahši mekí·s·ak máta awé·n ke·nahki·há·t·e.
/t   and as they scattered the way sheep do when no one is taking care of them.
/k   and were scattered abroad, as sheep having no shepherd.

Mt 9.37	/b	Tclao rkrkemathi, Xifwi cntu a mwnjsqif jwk tatxetwuk mekumosethek;
	/p	təláꞏɔ eꞏkꞏeꞏkiꞏmáꞏčꞏi, "xínkwi énta-=áꞏ -múnšskwenk, šúkw taꞏtxíꞏtꞏəwak miꞏkəmɔꞏsꞏíꞏčꞏiꞏk.
	/t	He said to his disciples, "Great would be the harvest, but few are the workers.
	/k	Then saith he unto his disciples, The harvest truly is plenteous, but the labourers are few;

Mt 9.38	/b	wenowumw nrvlatuf mwnjskosek tcli a qeaqi alwkalan mekumoselethi.
	/p	wiꞏnəwámoꞏ nehəláꞏtꞏank munšskhɔ́ꞏsꞏiꞏk, təĺi-=áꞏ kwiáꞏkwi -aloꞏkáꞏlaꞏn miꞏkəmɔꞏsꞏiꞏlíꞏčꞏi.
	/t	Ask the one in charge of the harvest to hire still more workers.
	/k	Pray ye therefore the Lord of the harvest, that he will send forth labourers into his harvest.

Mt 10.1	/b	Nrtwmatc nrl tclin ok neju rkrkemathi,
	/p	neꞏtꞏoꞏmáꞏtꞏe néꞏl télən ɔ́ꞏk níꞏšꞏa eꞏkꞏeꞏkiꞏmáꞏčꞏi,
	/t	After he called those twelve disciples of his to come,
	/k	And when he had called unto him his twelve disciples,

	/b	mwelao alweliswakun wunhi kuski ktiskumevtet mavtuntwakun,
	/p	mwiꞏláꞏɔ aləwíꞏiꞏləsꞏəwáꞏkꞏan wənči-káski-ktəskamíhtiꞏt mahtantꞏuwwáꞏkꞏan,
	/t	he gave them the power by which they could drive out evil spirits
	/k	he gave them power against unclean spirits, to cast them out,

	/b	ok kekrvatet palselethi ok wrmi tclenrokunelet.
	/p	ɔ́ꞏk -kiꞏkꞏeꞏháhtiꞏt paꞏlsiꞏlíꞏčꞏi, ɔ́ꞏk wéꞏmi təliꞏneꞏɔꞏkꞏaníꞏliꞏt.
	/t	and cure the sick and all their diseases.
	/k	and to heal all manner of sickness and all manner of disease.

Mt 10.2	/b	Nrk atux neju rlwkalinhek; vetami Symun Petul ok wemavtu Antulwsu,
	/p	néꞏk átax níꞏšꞏa eꞏloꞏkaꞏlənčiꞏk: hítami †sáiman-píꞏtəl ɔ́ꞏk wíꞏmahta, †antəlóꞏsꞏa;
	/t	Those twelve apostles were: first Simon Peter and his brother Andrew,
	/k	Now the names of the twelve apostles are these; The first, Simon, who is called Peter, and Andrew his brother;

	/b	Nhim ‖ Scpute qesul ok Nhanu wemavtu,
	/p	nčím, †sépati kkwíꞏsꞏal, ɔ́ꞏk nčáꞏna, wíꞏmahta;
	/t	Jim, Zebedee's son, and his brother John;
	/k	James the son of Zebedee, and John his brother;

Mt 10.3	/b	Pilups, ok Mpatalumw, Tamas ok Matws, nu mcmarnif moni, ok Nhim Alpius quesu, ok Lipius Nhwtus, [⟨qu-⟩ for ⟨q-⟩]
(p. 60)	/p	†pílaps ɔ́ꞏk †mpaꞏtáꞏlamu; †támas ɔ́ꞏk †máꞏtoꞏs, ná mehəmaꞏéꞏnink móni; ɔ́ꞏk nčím, †aꞏlpias kkwíꞏsꞏa, ɔ́ꞏk †ləpías-nčóꞏtas;

	/t	Philip and Bartholemew; Thomas and Matthew, the tax collector; and Jim, the son of Alphaeus, and Lebbaeus Judas;
	/k	Philip, and Bartholomew; Thomas, and Matthew the publican; James the son of Alphaeus, and Lebbaeus, whose surname was Thaddaeus;
Mt 10.4	/b	ok Symun Krnunif wunheywp, ok Nhwtus Iskaliut krthevlalat.
	/p	ɔ́·k †sáiman †ké·nanink wənčí·ayo·p; ɔ́·k †nčó·tas †iská·liat, ke·č·íhəlala·t.
	/t	and Simon from Canaa; and Judas Iscariot, who exposed him.
	/k	Simon the Canaanite, and Judas Iscariot, who also betrayed him.
Mt 10.5	/b	Nrk atux neju Nhesus tolwkalapani
	/p	né·k átax ní·š·a, nčí·sas tɔlo·ka·lá·p·ani,
	/t	Those twelve Jesus sent as messengers,
	/k	These twelve Jesus sent forth, and commanded them,
	/b	tclao Kahi eku avrq awrnvakreki; [⟨-eki⟩ for ⟨-ekri⟩]
	/p	təlá·ɔ, "káči íka á·he·kw awe·nhake·i·ké·i;
	/t	saying to them, "Do not go among foreigners.
	/k	saying, Go not into the way of the Gentiles,
	/b	ok kahi eku avrq Sumrlieuk wtwtrnywaif
	/p	ɔ́·k káči íka á·he·kw †same·lií·ɔk wto·t·e·nayəwá·ink.
	/t	And do not go to the towns of the Samaritans.
	/k	and into any city of the Samaritans enter ye not:
Mt 10.6	/b	jwk toxw mrkesuk trofulukek Isliluk.
	/p	šúkw tɔ́x·o· mekí·s·ak te·ɔnkələ́k·i·k, †isəlɔ́lak.
	/t	But (only?) go to the lost sheep, the Israelites.
	/k	But go rather to the lost sheep of the house of Israel.
Mt 10.7	/b	Nrlwxrrq, pumitwnvrq; lwrq osavkomre sakemaokun prxwthevulr. [⟨ko⟩ for ⟨ka⟩]
	/p	ne·lo·x·wé·e·kw, pəmət·ó·nhe·kw, lúwe·kw, "ɔ·s·ahkame·í·i·sa·k·i·ma·ɔ́·k·an pe·x·o·č·íhəle·."
	/t	As you go, preach, saying, "The kingdom of heaven is becoming near."
	/k	And as ye go, preach, saying, The kingdom of heaven is at hand.
Mt 10.8	/b	Kekrvw palsethek, pelevw neskufulukek, amwekunw rfulukek, ktiskw mavtuntwuk;
	/p	ki·k·é·ho· pa·lsí·č·i·k, pi·lí·ho· ni·skankələ́k·i·k, a·mwí·kəno· enkələ́ki·k, ktə́sko· mahtant·ó·wak.
	/t	Heal the sick, cleanse those with the nasty disease, raise up the dead, drive out devils.
	/k	Heal the sick, cleanse the lepers, raise the dead, cast out devils:

/b knwhi melinro ok nwhi mrkwq.
/p kənó·čkwe-milləné·ɔ, ɔ́·k nó·čkwe-mé·k·o·kw.
/t I gave it to you freely, and you, give it freely.
/k freely ye have received, freely give.

Mt 10.9
/b Kahi kulinifvrq fwl, jita moni, jita muxkasin kpuntasunakunwaif
/p káči kələnínkhe·kw nkó·l, ší=tá móni, ší=tá máxkahsən kpəntahsəna·k·anəwá·ink,
/t Don't carry gold, or silver, or copper in your bags (*lit.*, tobacco pouches),
/k Provide neither gold, nor silver, nor brass in your purses,

Mt 10.10
/b jita nwtrs, jita neju jakvoqeonu jitu hepavko jita alavwn;
/p ší=tá nó·t·e·s, ší=tá ní·š·a ša·khuk·wí·ɔna, ší=tá čípahkɔ, ší=tá alá·ho·n;
/t or a knapsack, or two coats, or shoes, or a cane;
/k Nor scrip for your journey, neither two coats, neither shoes, nor yet staves:

/b rli mcmekumoset aeavi nemat methwakun.
/p é·li- mehəmi·kəmɔ́·s·i·t -a·yáhi·ní·ma·t mi·č·əwá·k·an.
/t as a worker already has food with him.
/k for the workman is worthy of his meat.

Mt 10.11
/b Eku parqc xifwi wtrnif jitu line wtrnif, ntoxumwmoc wrliliset linw;
/p íka pa·é·k·we xínkwi-o·t·é·nink ší=tá ləní·i-o·t·é·nink, nto·x·əmo·mɔ́·e wé·li-lɔ́s·i·t lɔ́nu;
/t When you come to a large town or an ordinary town, ask for a good man.
/k And into whatsoever city or town ye shall enter, enquire who in it is worthy;

/b nuh nc ksaki avpenro lupi kavtu alumskarqc.
/p ná=č nɔ́ ksá·ki-ahpi·né·ɔ lápi káhta-aləmska·é·k·we.
/t That is where you must stay until you intend to leave again.
/k and there abide till ye go thence.

Mt 10.12
/b Tumekrqc wekwamif ofonsemoc.   [⟨r⟩ for ⟨rr⟩]
/p təmi·k·e·é·k·we wi·k·əwáhəmink, ɔnkunsi·mɔ́·e.
/t When you enter a house, give greetings.
/k And when ye come into an house, salute it.

Mt 10.13
/b Eku avpetetc wrlilisethek nuni lrkch kwlufwnswakunwu.
/p íka ahpihtí·t·e wé·li-ləs·í·č·i·k, nɔ́ni lé·k·eč ko·lankunsəwa·k·anúwa.
/t If good people are there, let your friendship be like that.
/k And if the house be worthy, let your peace come upon it: ...

Mt 10.14
/b Awrn jifi wlulqrqc, jitu jifi klistufc ktaptwnakunwu,
/p awé·n šínki-wəlalkwé·k·we, ší=tá šínki-kələstánke kta·pto·na·k·anúwa,
/t If someone is unwilling to put you up (*lit.*, keep you), or is unwilling to listen to your words,
/k And whosoever shall not receive you, nor hear your words,

Text, Transcription, and Translation

/b alumskarqc nc wunhi weket, jitu wtrnif, paetrxtwmoc pwfq ksetwaif.
/p aləmska·é·k·we nə́ wənči wí·k·i·t, ší=tá o·t·é·nink, pai·te·xto·mɔ́·e púnkw ksi·t·əwá·ink.
/t when you leave that house of his, or town, knock off the dust on your feet.
/k when ye depart out of that house or city, shake off the dust of your feet.

Mt 10.15
/b Kehe ktclwvwmw, Satumeuk, ok Fomaloeuk
/p khičí·i ktəllúhəmɔ, †sa·tamí·ɔk ɔ́·k †nkɔma·lɔí·ɔk,
/t Truly I say to you, the people of Sodom and of Gomorrha,　　　[numbers =
/kl (1)Verily I say unto you, (3) the land of Sodom and Gomorrha,　sequence in L.]

/b rlkeqi avkrkvutwe kejqek　　　　　　　　　　　　　[⟨-kvut-⟩ for ⟨-kvwt-⟩]
/p e·lkí·kwi-ahke·kho·t·əwí·i-kí·škwi·k,
/t at the time of the Day of Judgment,
/k (4) in the day of judgment,

/b mifasrh lenamwk rlkeqih bk lenamevtet.
/p mínkahse=č lí·namo·k e·lkí·kwi-=č yó·k -li·namíhti·t.
/t will have it better than those people will.
/k (2) it shall be more tolerable for (5) than for that city.

Mt 10.16
/b Puna ktalwkalwvmw, mulaji mrkesuk cntu tumrekrk;
/p "pənáh, ktalo·kallúhəmɔ málahši mekí·s·ak énta-təme·í·ke·k.
/t "Here, I send you forth like sheep among wolves.
/k Behold, I send you forth as sheep in the midst of wolves:

/b nuni wunhi lipoq mulaji xkwk rlkeqi lipot,
/p nə́ni wənči ləpɔ́·kw málahši xkó·k e·lkí·kwi-ləpɔ́·t,
/t Therefore, be as wise as a snake is,
/k be ye therefore wise as serpents,

/b ok wliliseq mulaji mrmrtvakrmw rlset,
/p ɔ́·k wə́li-lə́s·i·kw málahši me·me·thaké·mu é·lsi·t.
/t and be as well-behaved as a dove.
/k and harmless as doves.

Mt 10.17
/b nuxalwmc nrk linwuk, rli a tamsi ekulwxolwkon cntu athemwlsif,
/p naxa·ló·me né·k lə́nəwak, é·li-=á· tá·mse íka -lo·x·ɔlúk·ɔn énta-a·č·i·mó·lsink,
/t Watch out for those men (you sg.), for they would perhaps take you to the councils,
/k But beware of men: for they will deliver you up to the councils,

/b ok a ktcli sisukavtrvwkwn cntu mycvuluf,
/p ɔ́·k=á· ktə́li-səsəkahtehó·k·o·n énta-ma·éhəlank.
/t and then they would whip you (sg.) in the synagogues.
/k and they will scourge you in their synagogues;

Mt 10.18	/b	ktalumwxolukch li krkyimvrtif ok sakemawf wunhi ne	[⟨sake-‖mawf⟩]
(p. 61)	/p	ktaləmo·x·ɔlək·e=č lí ke·kayəmhé·t·ink ɔ́·k sa·k·i·má·unk wə́nči ní·,	
	/t	You (sg.) shall be brought to governors and kings because of me,	
	/k	And ye shall be brought before governors and kings for my sake,	

/b ktclih punwntulanro, ok nrk nrlwawsethek.
/p ktə́li-=č -pənuntəla·né·ɔ, ɔ́·k né·k ne·lo·wa·wsí·č·i·k.
/t for you (pl.) to testify about it to them, and to the heathen.
/k for a testimony against them and the Gentiles.

[RSV: "to bear testimony before them"]

Mt 10.19 /b Alumwxolukrrqc kahi punyrlintufvrq krkwh ta rlwrrq eku parqc,
/p aləmo·x·ɔlək·e·é·k·we, káči pəna·eləntánkhe·kw, kéku=č=tá e·ləwé·e·kw íka pa·é·k·we.
/t When you are brought, don't think about what you will say when you get there.
/k But when they deliver you up, take no thought how or what ye shall speak:

/b rli nuh kumelkrnro krkwh rlwrrq,
/p é·li ná=č kəmi·lke·né·ɔ kéku=č e·ləwé·e·kw,
/t For what you will say will be given to you then,
/k for it shall be given you in that same hour what ye shall speak.

Mt 10.20 /b rli muta nevlahi krkw lwrrq, jwk montwakun Kwxwu aptwnrtarq.
/p é·li- máta=á· nihəláči kéku -luwé·e·kw, šúkw mɔnt·uwwá·k·an kó·x·əwa a·pto·né·tae·kw.
/t as you would not speak yourselves, but what you speak is the spiritual power of your father.
/k For it is not ye that speak, but the Spirit of your Father which speaketh in you.

Mt 10.21 /b Kwti wemavtu eku tclwxolauh cntuh nvelalif,
/p kwə́t·i wí·mahta íka təlo·x·ɔlú·ɔ-č ə́nta-nhilá·link,
/t One brother will bring the other to where he will be slain, [lit., 'one .. his brother']
/k And the brother shall deliver up the brother to death,

/b ok wrtwxif wnehanu nuni tclevan;
/p ɔ́·k we·t·ó·x·ink wəni·č·á·na nə́ni təlí·ha·n;
/t and that's what the father will do to his child;
/k and the father the child:

/b ok meminsuk paswqeokh ekali qekybbmwaif
/p ɔ́·k mi·mə́nsak pahsuk·wí·ɔk=č íkali kwi·kayo·yəməwá·ink
/t and children will stand up against their parents;
/k and the children shall rise up against their parents,

/b motavkunemawaoh rli kavtwnalwkvetet.
/p mɔtahkəni·mawwá·ɔ=č, é·li-kahto·nalukhwíti·t.

| | /t | they will denounce them, because they (obv., i.e. the parents) seek to slay them. |
| | /k | and cause them to be put to death. |

Mt 10.22 /b Wrmih awrn kjifalkwu wunhi ne ntclswakun.
/p wé·mi=č awé·n kšinka·lkúwa wə́nči ní· ntəlsəwá·k·an.
/t Everyone will hate you because of *my* doing.
/k And ye shall be hated of all men for my name's sake:

/b Jwk awrn wlilisetc heme, eku pchi ufulukc, khwvalah.
/p šúkw awé·n wəli-ləs·í·t·e či·mí·i, íka péči ankələk·e, kčo·há·la·=č.
/t But if anyone is well behaved forever, until the time they die, they shall be saved.
/k but he that endureth to the end shall be saved.

Mt 10.23 /b Tamsc bni wtrnif tali kavtwnalukrrqc, pale lijemwemoc,
/p tá·mse yó·ni o·t·é·nink táli-kahto·nalək·e·é·k·we, palí·i ləš·i·mwi·mó·e.
/t If perhaps your lives are theatened in this town, flee to another (*lit.*, away).
/k But when they persecute you in this city, flee ye into another:

/b rli kehe ktclwvwmw,
/p é·li, khičí·i ktəllúhəmɔ,
/t For, truly I say to you,
/k for verily I say unto you,

/b Nrlumuh wrmi arq Islilukk wtwtrnywaif nuh Wrqesif pon.
/p né·ləma-=č wé·mi -á·e·kw †isəlɔ́lak wto·t·e·nayəwá·ink, ná=č we·k·wí·s·ink pó·n.
/t before you go to all the towns of the Israelites, the Son shall come.
/k Ye shall not have gone over the cities of Israel, till the Son of man be come.

Mt 10.24 /b Rkrkemqwset takw tolwe lisewunu rvakrkifrsu,
/p e·k·e·ki·mkwə́s·i·t takó· tɔləwí·i-ləs·í·wəna ehahke·kinké·s·a, [-ləs·í·wən below]
/t The student is not more than the teacher,
/k The disciple is not above his master,

/b ok alwkakun takw tolwe lisewun nrvlalkwkel.
/p ɔ́·k alo·ká·k·an takó· tɔləwí·i-ləs·í·wən nehəla·lkúk·i·l. [-ləs·í·wəna above]
/t and the servant is not more than his lord.
/k nor the servant above his lord.

Mt 10.25 /b Tcpi rkrkemqwset lisen rkrkemkwki rlselet, [⟨tcpi⟩ for /wtépi-/]
/p wtépi- e·k·e·ki·mkwə́s·i·t -ləs·i·n e·k·e·ki·mkúk·i e·lsí·li·t,
/t It is enough for the student to be as his teacher is,
/k It is enough for the disciple that he be as his master,

	/b	ok tcpi alwkakun lisen nrvlalkwki rlselet.	[⟨tcpi⟩ for /wtépi-/]
	/p	ɔ́·k wtépi- alo·ká·k·an -ləs·i·n nehəla·lkúk·i e·lsí·li·t.	
	/t	and it is enough for the servant to be as his master is.	
	/k	and the servant as his lord.	

	/b	Lwevlavtetc wrekethek mavtuntwe sakema,	
	/p	luwihəlahtí·t·e we·i·k·í·č·i·k 'mahtant·o·wí·i-sa·k·í·ma',	[obscurely recast]
	/t	If the house-owners name him 'Chief of the Devils,'	
	/k	If they have called the master of the house Beelzebub,	

	/b	mutu vuh ok nc tclwevulawunro wrekelethi.
	/p	máta=háč ɔ́·k nɔ́ tələwihəla·wəné·ɔ we·i·k·i·lí·č·i?
	/t	do they not also name the house-owners that?
	/k	how much more shall they call them of his household?

Mt 10.26	/b	Kahi qxwerkrq,
	/p	"káči kxwié·k·e·kw.
	/t	"Do not fear them.
	/k	Fear them not therefore:

	/b	rli wrmi krkw mrtavkovmevtet, wlih nrvkot,
	/p	é·li wé·mi kéku metahkɔhəmíhti·t wə́li-=č -né·ykɔt,
	/t	For, everything they cover over shall be properly seen,
	/k	for there is nothing covered, that shall not be revealed;

	/b	ok wrmi krkw kuntvatwvtet wlih wavkot.
	/p	ɔ́·k wé·mi kéku kanthatúhti·t wə́li-=č -wwáhkɔt.
	/t	and everything they hide shall be properly known.
	/k	and hid, that shall not be known.

Mt 10.27	/b	Krkw kemc rlrq kclwuh wrmi awrn ktclanro,
	/p	kéku ki·mí·i élle·kw, ki·ló·wa=č wé·mi awé·n ktəla·né·ɔ.
	/t	What I tell you in secret, *you* must tell everyone.
	/k	What I tell you in darkness, that speak ye in light:

	/b	krkw kvetaokwaif puntamrq pumitwnvatumwq tali xqetakc.
	/p	kéku khitaɔk·əwá·ink pɔ́ntame·kw, pəmət·o·nhá·t·amo·kw táli xkwi·t·á·k·e.
	/t	What you hear in your ears, preach on the rooftop.
	/k	and what ye hear in the ear, that preach ye upon the housetops.

Mt 10.28	/b	Kahi qvetaealerkrq ninvelwrthek, jwk hehufo ta koski nvelaewao;
	/p	káči khwitaya·lié·k·e·kw nenhiləwé·č·i·k, šúkw či·čánkɔ tá=á· kɔ́ski-nhila·iwwá·ɔ.
	/t	Do not be afraid of those who are murderers, but they cannot kill the soul.
	/k	And fear not them which kill the body, but are not able to kill the soul:

/b jwk alwe qvetaealw nrkuma wnevlan rlee hehufo ok watovrpi tali mavtuntwf.
/p šúkw aləwí·i-khwitayá·lo· né·k·əma wəníhla·n ellí·i či·čánkɔ ɔ́·k wahtuhé·p·i táli mahtánt·unk.
/t But fear more that *he* destroy (*lit.*, kill) both soul and body in Hell.
/k but rather fear him which is able to destroy both soul and body in hell.

Mt 10.29 /b Mutu vuh neju hwlintituk koti sens laoteeok?   [⟨sens⟩ for ⟨scns⟩]
/p máta=háč ní·š·a čo·ləntət·ak kwət·i séns la·ɔhti·í·ɔk?
/t Aren't two little birds priced at one cent?
/k Are not two sparrows sold for a farthing?

/b Ok koti nrk ta punevulri li vakif mutu Kwxwa letrvatc.
/p ɔ́·k kwət·i né·k tá=á· pənihəlé·i lí hák·ink, máta kó·x·əwa li·t·e·há·t·e.
/t And one of those will not fall to the ground if your father does not wish it so.
/k and one of them shall not fall on the ground without your Father.

Mt 10.30 /b Jwk wrmi kmexlwau kelwawf wrmi avkintasw.   [⟨xl⟩ for ⟨lx⟩; ⟨-sw⟩: read ⟨-swu⟩]
/p šúkw wé·mi kəmi·lxəwá·ɔ ki·ləwá·unk wé·mi ahkəntá·s·u.   [-s·u: read -s·əwa]
/t But all your hairs on your heads are all counted,
/k But the very hairs of your head are all numbered.

Mt 10.31 /b Nuni wunhi kahi wejasevrq, rli alwe ktclaotevmw xrli ‖ hwlintituk.
/p nəni wənči, káči wi·š·a·s·í·he·kw, é·li aləwí·i ktəla·ɔhtíhəmɔ xé·li čo·ləntət·ak.
/t So, do not be afraid, as you are worth more than many little birds.
/k Fear ye not therefore, ye are of more value than many sparrows.

Mt 10.32 /b Awrn mutu paswrqc nvaky, nrpc ta npaswrwun tali Nwxif Osavkamc.
    [⟨np-⟩ for ⟨mp-⟩]
(p. 62) /p awé·n máta pahsəwé·k·we nhák·ay, né·pe tá=á· mpas·əwé·wən táli nó·x·ink ɔ·s·áhkame.
/t If anyone does not deny me, I also will not deny him before my father in heaven.
/k Whosoever therefore shall confess me before men, him will I confess also before my Father which is in heaven.

Mt 10.33 /b Jwk awrn paswrte nvaky bni cntu lawset, nrpch npuswrn voky Nwxif tali osavkamc.
/p šúkw awé·n pahsəwé·t·e nhák·ay yó·ni entalá·wsi·t, né·pe=č mpás·əwen hók·ay nó·x·ink táli ɔ·s·áhkame.   [⟨np-⟩ for ⟨mp-⟩]
/t But if anyone denies me here on earth, I will also deny him before my father in heaven.
/k But whosoever shall deny me before men, him will I also deny before my Father which is in heaven.

Mt 10.34 /b Kahi letrvavrq lufwntwakun ct mprtw b cntu lawsif, [⟨luf-⟩ for ⟨wluf-⟩]
/p "káči li·t·e·há·he·kw, wəlankuntəwá·k·an=ét mpé·t·u yú entalá·wsink.
/t "Don't assume that I must be bringing peace here on earth.
/k Think not that I am come to send peace on earth:

/b takw nwnhi pawn wlufwntwakun numy lenamwi, jwk tufamekun.
/p takó· núnči-pá·wən, wəlankuntəwá·k·an nəmái-li·namó·wi, šúkw tankamí·k·an.
/t I did not come because of it, not to experience peace but a sword.
/k I came not to send peace, but a sword.

Mt 10.35 /b Nwnhi pan tclih jifalan linw wxo,
/p núnči-pá·n, təli-=č -šinká·la·n lənu ó·x·ɔ,
/t I have come so that a man will hate his father,
/k For I am come to set a man at variance against his father,

/b ok wunhih xqr jifalan kovrsu, ok wunhi xqr jifalan vwswqesu.
/p ó·k wwə́nči-=č xkwé· -šinká·la·n kɔhé·s·a, ó·k wwə́nči- xkwé· -šinká·la·n wsuk·wí·s·a.
/t and so a woman will hate her mother, and a woman will hate her mother-in-law.
/k and the daughter against her mother, and the daughter in law against her mother in law.

Mt 10.36 /b Awrn jifalkon nevlahi weket wnheyw.
/p "awé·n šinká·lkɔn nihəláči wí·k·i·t wənčí·ayu. [wí·k·i·t s.b. wí·k·ian]
/t "The person who hates you comes from his own house. ['his' should 'your']
/k And a man's foes shall be they of his own household.

Mt 10.37 /b Awrn wxo jitu kovrsu alwe avolatc rlkqi ne avolet takw ne nakalkwi;
[⟨rlkqi⟩ for ⟨rlkeqi⟩]
/p awé·n ó·x·ɔ šī=tá kɔhé·s·a aləwí·i ahɔ·lá·t·e e·lkí·kwi- ní· -ahó·li·t, takó· ní· nna·ka·lkó·wi.
/t If someone loves his father or mother more than *me*, he does not trust in *me*.
/k He that loveth father or mother more than me is not worthy of me:

/b ok awrn qesu jitu tonu alwe avolatc rlkeqi ne avolet, takw ne nakalkwi,
/p ó·k awé·n kkwí·s·a šī=tá tó·na aləwí·i ahɔ·lá·t·e e·lkí·kwi- ní· -ahó·li·t, takó· ní· nna·ka·lkó·wi.
/t And if someone loves his son or daughter more than *me*, he does not trust in *me*.
/k and he that loveth son or daughter more than me is not worthy of me.

Mt 10.38 /b awrn mutu alwvekufc luxyevtwakun, ok naolekxaletc,
/p awé·n máta aluhikánke †laxaihtəwá·k·an, ó·k †na·ɔli·kxa·lí·t·e,
/t If someone does not overcome hindrances and follow after me,
/k And he that taketh not his cross, and followeth after me,

	/b	takw ne nakalkwi.
	/p	takó· ní· nna·ka·lkó·wi.
	/t	he does not trust in *me*.
	/k	is not worthy of me.

Mt 10.39 /b Awrn ntwnufc bni lrlrxrokun tofvetwnh wlrlrxrokun.
/p awé·n nto·nánke yó·ni lehəle·x·e·ɔ́·k·an, tɔnkhíto·n=č wəlehəle·x·e·ɔ́·k·an.
/t If someone seeks this life, he shall lose his life.
/k He that findeth his life shall lose it:

/b Jwk awrn ufvetaqc bni lrlrxrokun ne wunhi, moxkamunh.
/p šúkw awé·n ankhitá·k·we yó·ni lehəle·x·e·ɔ́·k·an ní· wə́nči, mɔ́xkamən=č,
/t But if someone loses this life for my sake, he shall find it.
/k and he that loseth his life for my sake shall find it.

Mt 10.40 /b Awrn wifalkon, ok nrpi nwifalwq;
/p awé·n winká·lkɔn ɔ́·k né·pe nəwinká·lukw.
/t Anyone who is welcoming to you is also welcoming to me.
/k He that receiveth you receiveth me,

/b ok awrn wifaletc ok wifalao prtalwkalelethi;
/p ɔ́·k awé·n winka·lí·t·e, ɔ́·k wwinka·lá·ɔ pe·t·alo·ka·li·lí·č·i.
/t And if anyone is welcoming to me, they are also welcoming to him who sent me.
/k and he that receiveth me receiveth him that sent me.

Mt 10.41 /b ok awrn wifalaoh nrnekanewrwselethi rli nrnekanewrwselet,
/p ɔ́·k awé·n wwinka·lá·ɔ=č nehəni·k·a·ní·i-we·wsi·lí·č·i
é·li-nehəni·k·a·ní·i-we·wsí·li·t,
/t Also, someone will welcome a prophet as a prophet,
/k He that receiveth a prophet in the name of a prophet

/b mwjinumunh nrkumu nrnekanewrwset wtrnvaotwakun,
/p mwəš·ənə́mən=č né·k·əma nehəni·k·a·ní·i-wé·wsi·t wte·nha·ohtəwá·k·an.
/t and he will himself receive a prophet's reward
/k shall receive a prophet's reward;

/b ok awrn wifalaoh jaxakawselethi rli jaxakawselet,
/p ɔ́·k awé·n wwinka·lá·ɔ=č šaxahka·wsi·lí·č·i é·li-šaxahka·wsí·li·t,
/t And someone will welcome a righteous one as a righteous one,
/k and he that receiveth a righteous man in the name of a righteous man

/b mwjinumunh jaxakawset wtrnvaotwakun;
/p mwəš·ənə́mən=č šaxahká·wsi·t wte·nha·ohtəwá·k·an.
/t and they will receive a righteous person's reward.
/k shall receive a righteous man's reward.

Mt 10.42	/b	ok awrn mrnvwkon mawsw tufrlinserq, jwk mpi rli rkrkemut	[2s, 2p, 2s]
	/p	ɔ·k awé·n me·nhó·k·ɔn má·wsu tanke·lə́nsie·kw šúkw mpí é·li e·k·e·kí·mat	
	/t	And someone who gives one of you humble ones only water as one you teach,	
	/k	And whosoever shall give to drink unto one of these little ones a cup of cold water only in the name of a disciple,	

	/b	kehe ktclwvwmw ta tofvetwun trnvaotwakun.	
	/p	khičí·i ktəllúhəmɔ, tá=á· tɔnkhitó·wən wte·nha·ɔhtəwá·k·an."	[⟨t-⟩ for /wt-/]
	/t	I tell you truly, he will not lose his reward."	
	/k	verily I say unto you, he shall in no wise lose his reward.	

Mt 11.1	/b	Nhesus keji latc nrl tclin ok neju rkrkemathi wrmi bl aptwnakunul,
	/p	nčí·sas kíši-lá·t·e né·l télən ɔ́·k ní·š·a e·k·e·ki·má·č·i wé·mi yó·l a·pto·ná·k·anal,
	/t	After Jesus had finished telling his twelve disciples all these sayings,
	/k	And it came to pass, when Jesus had made an end of commanding his twelve disciples,

	/b	alumskrp nc wunhi, akrkifrp ok pumitwnvrp wrmi tali cntxif wtrnyu.
	/p	aləmske·p nə́ wə́nči; ahke·kínke·p ɔ́·k pəmət·ó·nhe·p wé·mi táli éntxink o·t·é·naya.
	/t	he departed from there; he taught and preached in all the towns there were.
	/k	he departed thence to teach and to preach in their cities.

Chapter 38 (pp. 62-63). [L. section 37.] (Luke 7.11-18)

Lk 7.11	/b	Rlavparkc eku rp wtrnif lwcntaswp Nrun,
	/p	e·lahpa·é·k·e, íka é·p o·t·é·nink luwentá·s·o·p †né·yən,
	/t	The next day, he went to a town called Nain,
	/k	And it came to pass the day after, that he went into a city called Nain;

	/b	ok ‖ xrli rkrkemathi wethrvkw, ok xrli navkoi awrnek.
	/p	ɔ́·k xé·li e·k·e·ki·má·č·i wwi·č·é·yku, ɔ́·k xé·li nahkɔ́·i awé·ni·k.
	/t	and many of his disciples went with him, and many ordinary people.
	/k	and many of his disciples went with him, and much people.

Lk 7.12	/b	Kexki pravtetc nc skontramrnxkif,
(p. 63)	/p	kí·xki pe·ahtí·t·e nə́ skɔnte·amé·nxkink,
	/t	When they got near the gate in the wall,
	/k	Now when he came nigh to the gate of the city,

	/b	punu, linwuk pwchi ktwxolawao rfululethi,
	/p	pənáh, lə́nəwak pwéči-kto·x·ɔlawwá·ɔ enkələlí·č·i,
	/t	why here, men were bringing a dead body out.
	/k	behold, there was a dead man carried out,

/b na tcli kwtwnjrlenrp kovrsu ok kotvww.   [⟨na⟩ for ⟨nu⟩ /nə́/ (see lí (1))]
/p nə́ tə́li-kwət·unše·lí·ne·p kɔhé·s·a, ɔ́·k kɔ·thó·u.
/t He had been his mother's only child, and she was a widow.
/k the only son of his mother, and she was a widow:

/b Xrli wrtwtrnyethek wethroao.
/p xé·li we·t·o·t·e·naí·č·i·k wwi·č·e·ɔwwá·ɔ.
/t Many townspeople were with her.
/k and much people of the city was with her.

Lk 7.13 /b Nrotc Nhesus qwtumakrlumao; tclao kahi lupukvun.
/p ne·ɔ́·t·e nčí·sas, kwət·əma·k·e·ləmá·ɔ, təlá·ɔ, "káči ləpákhan."
/t When Jesus saw her, he took pity on her, saying, "Do not weep."
/k And when the Lord saw her, he had compassion on her, and said unto her, Weep not.

Lk 7.14 /b Nu eku tclenxkrn trxunekunif,
/p ná íka təlí·nxke·n te·x·əní·k·anink,
/t Then he reached out his hand to the litter,
/k And he came and touched the bier:

/b nrk krnathek navkevlrok.
/p ne·k kenná·č·i·k nahkihəlé·ɔk.
/t and the ones carrying him stopped.
/k and they that bare him stood still.

/b Lwrp, Skenw ktclul amwel.
/p lúwe·p, "skínnu, ktə́ləl, á·mwi·l."
/t He said, "Young man, I tell you, get up."
/k And he said, Young man, I say unto thee, Arise.

Lk 7.15 /b Nunu rfulukup tomwen, nu ok tolumi krkw lwrn.
/p ná ná enkəlák·əp tɔ́·mwi·n; ná ɔ́·k tɔ́ləmi- kéku -lúwe·n.
/t Then the one who had been dead got up; and then he also began to speak.
/k And he that was dead sat up, and began to speak.

/b Nu mwelan wrnehanelethi.
/p ná mwí·la·n we·ni·č·a·ni·lí·č·i.
/t And then he turned him over to his mother.
/k And he delivered him to his mother.

Lk 7.16 /b Wejaswakun toxkwk wrmi rpethek,
/p wi·š·a·s·əwá·k·an tɔ́xko·k wé·mi e·p·í·č·i·k.
/t Fear came over everyone there.
/k And there came a fear on all:

/b ok moxifovkunemawao Krtanitwelethi; lwrpanek,
/p ɔ́·k mɔx·inkɔhkəni·mawwá·ɔ ke·tanət·o·wi·lí·č·i, luwé·p·ani·k,
/t And they praised God and said,
/k and they glorified God, saying,

/b Mrhi xifwi nrnekanewrwset avpw, ok Krtanitwet pwnyrlumapani wtunaprbmu.
/p "mé·či xínkwi-nehəni·k·a·ní·i-wé·wsi·t ahpú, ɔ́·k ke·tanət·ó·wi·t pwənae·ləmá·p·ani wtənna·p·é·yəma."
/t "A great prophet is now here, and God has thought about his people."
/k That a great prophet is risen up among us; and, That God hath visited his people.

Lk 7.17
/b Bni konjyvoswakun jai puntavkotwp wrmi li Nhwteuf
/p yó·ni kɔnšaehɔ·s·əwá·k·an šá·e pəntákɔhto·p wé·mi lí †nčo·tí·yunk,
/t This miracle of his was immediately heard about all over Judaea,
/k And this rumour of him went forth throughout all Judaea,

/b ok wrmi okai rlekvatif;
/p ɔ́·k wé·mi ɔ·ká·i e·li·khátink.
/t and in all the surrounding settlements.
/k and throughout all the region round about.

Lk 7.18
/b ok Nhan rkrkemathi wrmi tclahemwlxwkwnrp.
/p ɔ́·k nčá·n e·k·e·ki·má·č·i wé·mi təla·č·i·mo·lxuk·ó·ne·p.
/t And John's diciples told him about all of that.
/k And the disciples of John shewed him of all these things.

Chapter 39 (pp. 63-66). [L. section 38.] (Luke 7.19-35; Matthew 11.11-15, 20-30)

Lk 7.19
/b Nu Nhan wcnhemapani neju rkrkemathi, eku tulalwkalapani Nhesusif
/p ná nčá·n wwenči·má·p·ani ní·š·a c·k·c·ki·má·č·i, íka təlalo·ka·lá·p·ani nči·sás·ink,
/t Then John called two of his disciples to him and sent them to Jesus,
/k And John calling unto him two of his disciples sent them to Jesus,

/b tcli my lanro; Ke vuh prvqwseun, ji vuh peli awrn prvqwset?
/p táli-mái-la·né·ɔ, "kí=háč pehkwəs·ian, ší=háč pí·li awé·n pehkwəs·i·t?"
/t to go and ask him, "Are *you* the one expected to come, or is someone else the one expected?"
/k saying, Art thou he that should come? or look we for another?

Lk 7.20
/b Eku pravtetc Nhesusif tclawao,
/p íka pe·ahtí·t·e nči·sás·ink, təlawwá·ɔ,
/t When they came to Jesus, they said to him,
/k When the men were come unto him, they said,

/b Nhan hchopunwrt ntcli prtalwkalkwnrn ktcli my ntwxtwlinrn,
/p "nčá·n čečhɔ·pwənúwe·t ntə́li-pe·t·alo·ka·lkó·ne·n, ktə́li-mái-nto·xtó·lǝne·n,
/t "It's John the Baptist who sends us to ask you,
/k John Baptist hath sent us unto thee, saying,

/b Ke vuh prvqwseun, ji vuh peli awrn tcli prvqwsen?
/p kí·=háč pehkwə́s·i·an, ší=háč pí·li awé·n tə́li-pehkwə́s·i·n?"
/t Are *you* the one expected to come, or is it someone else that is the one expected?"
/k Art thou he that should come? or look we for another?

Lk 7.21
/b Nc tupisqi qekrvapani xrli rlufululethi, ok palselethi
/p nə́ tpə́skwi kwi·k·e·há·p·ani xé·li e·lankəláli·č·i, ɔ́·k pa·lsi·lí·č·i,
/t At the same time he cured ones with many afflictions, and the sick,
/k And in that same hour he cured many of their infirmities and plagues,

/b ok neski manetwlehi,   [⟨manetwlehi⟩ for ⟨manitwelehi⟩]
/p ɔ́·k ní·ski-manət·o·wi·lí·č·i,
/t and ones with unclean spirits;
/k and of evil spirits;

/b ok xrli krkrpifolethi mwelapani wunhi kuski wlapuntumalet.
/p ɔ́·k xé·li ke·k·e·p·inkɔ·lí·č·i mwi·lá·p·ani wə́nči-káski-wəla·p·antamá·li·t.
/t and he gave many blind people the ability to see properly.
/k and unto many that were blind he gave sight.

Lk 7.22
/b Nu Nhesus noxkwmao, Tclao my lw Nhan krkw rlenamrq, ok puntamrq
/p ná nčí·sas nɔxko·má·ɔ, təlá·ɔ, "mái-ló· nčá·n kéku e·lí·name·kw, ɔ́·k pə́ntame·kw,
/t Then Jesus answered them, saying, "Go tell John what you have seen and heard,
/k Then Jesus answering said unto them, Go your way, and tell John what things ye have seen and heard;

/b tcli krkrpifothek nrmanro ok kwkwlwqevlathek tcli wli pumuskanro, ok neskufulukek tcli pelsenro ok krkrpxathek tcli puntamunro, ok rfulukek tcli amwenro ok krtumaksethek li wrlvik pumitwnvatumaonro;   [⟨kr-‖tumaksethek⟩]
/p tə́li- ke·k·e·p·inkɔ́·č·i·k -ne·ma·né·ɔ,
    ɔ́·k kuk·wəluk·wihəlá·č·i·k tə́li-wə́li-pəməska·né·ɔ,
    ɔ́·k ni·skankəlák·i·k tə́li-pi·lsi·né·ɔ,
    ɔ́·k ke·k·e·pxá·č·i·k tə́li-pəntamǝné·ɔ,
    ɔ́·k enkəlák·i·k tə́li-a·mwi·né·ɔ,
    ɔ́·k ke·t·əma·ksí·č·i·k lí- wé·lhik -pəmət·o·nha·t·amaɔ·né·ɔ.
/t that the blind see, and the lame walk, and those with the nasty disease are cleansed, and the deaf hear, and the dead rise, and to the poor is preached the good (word).
/k how that the blind see, the lame walk, the lepers are cleansed, the deaf hear, the dead are raised, to the poor the gospel is preached.

Lk 7.23 /b wrlapcnset awrn, takw nvakif wunhi muvtrlintumwi.
(p. 64) /p we·la·p·énsi·t awé·n, takó· nhák·enk wə́nči-mahte·ləntamó·wi."
/t A blessed person is not offended because of me."
/k And blessed is he, whosoever shall not be offended in me.

Lk 7.24 /b Mrhi rlumskavtetc Nhan rvalwkalathi,
/p mé·či e·ləmskahtí·t·e nča·n ehalo·ka·lá·č·i,
/t After the messengers John sent had left,
/k And when the messengers of John were departed,

/b nu tolumi krkw lan eku rpelethi, wunhi Nhan;
/p ná tóləmi- kéku -lá·n íka e·p·i·lí·č·i wə́nči nča·n.
/t he then began to speak to the people there about John.
/k he began to speak unto the people concerning John,

/b Krkw vuh kumy nrmvwmw trkunu li?
/p "kéku=háč kəmái-ne·mhúmɔ té·kəna lí?
/t "What did you go to the wilderness to see?
/k What went ye out into the wilderness for to see?

/b Wekunusq vuh wunhi rli quthwqevlak cntu kjaxif?   [⟨quth-⟩ for /kwč-/]
/p wí·kənaskw=háč wə́nči é·li-kwčuk·wíhəla·k énta-kšáx·ink?
/t Was it because of a reed as it shook in the wind?
/k A reed shaken with the wind?

Lk 7.25 /b Krkw vuh mri punamrq?
/p kéku=háč mé·i-pənáme·kw?
/t What did you (pl.) go to see?
/k But what went ye out for to see?

/b Kutu vuh nro linw wrwulavqet?
/p kkát·a-=háč -né·ɔ lə́nu we·wə́lahkwi·t?
/t Did you (sg.) want to see a man wearing fine clothes?
/k A man clothed in soft raiment?

/b Punw nrk, sakemawf wekwavmif rpethek.
/p pənó· né·k sa·k·i·má·unk wi·k·əwáhəmink e·p·í·č·i·k.
/t Look at those who are at the king's, in the house.
/k Behold, they which are gorgeously apparelled, and live delicately, are in kings courts.

Lk 7.26 /b Jwk krkw vuh mri punamrq? Nrnekanewrwset vuh?
/p šúkw kéku=háč mé·i-pənáme·kw? nehəni·k·a·ní·i-wé·wsi·t=háč?
/t But what did you go to see? Was it a prophet?
/k But what went ye out for to see? A prophet?

	/b	Pejik kta ne. Kehe ktclwvmw, Alwe liset nrnekanewrwset rlset,	[⟨A⟩ for ⟨R⟩]
	/p	píši=k ktá, ní· khičí·i ktəllúhəmɔ, e·ləwí·i-lə́s·i·t nehəni·k·a·ní·i-wé·wsi·t é·lsi·t.	
	/t	Yes, indeed, in fact (*I* tell you truly) one greater than a prophet is.	
	/k	Yea, I say unto you, and much more than a prophet.	

Lk 7.27
  /b Rli nunul ta wuni wunhi lrkvaswp,
  /p é·li nánal=tá wáni: wə́nči-le·khá·s·o·p,
  /t For this is who he is: it was written of him,
  /k This is he, of whom it is written,

  /b Punw, Awrn ntalwkalu knekanetamwkwn
  /p 'pənó·, awé·n ntalo·ká·la, kəni·k·a·ni·tamúk·o·n;
  /t 'Behold, I send a messenger to go ahead of you;
  /k Behold, I send my messenger before thy face,

  /b rlifwrxenun moi wletwn tumakun raunh.
  /p e·linkwe·x·í·nan mói-wəlí·to·n təmá·k·an e·á·an-č.'
  /t he goes before you to make a road for you to go on.
  /k which shall prepare thy way before thee.

Lk 7.28
  /b Rli kehe ktclwvmw;
  /p é·li khičí·i ktəllúhəmɔ,
  /t For truly I say to you,
  /k For I say unto you,   (Mt 11.11: Verily I say unto you,)

  /b wrmi cntxi xqrwf wunhi kejeket nrnekanewrwset
  /p wé·mi éntxi- xkwé·yunk -wə́nči-ki·š·í·k·i·t nehəni·k·a·ní·i-wé·wsi·t,
  /t of all the prophets who have been born of women,
  /k Among those that are born of women

	/b	takw talwe lisewunu Nhan Hchopunwrt.	[⟨tal-⟩ for ⟨tol-⟩]
	/p	takó· tɔləwí·i-ləs·í·wəna nčá·n čečhɔ·pwənúwe·t.	
	/t	none has been greater than John the Baptist.	
	/k	there is not a greater prophet than John the Baptist:	

  /b Jwk Kejrlumwrt sokemaokunif tali nwntyi rlset alwee lisw nrku rlkeqi liset.
  /p šúkw ki·š·e·ləmúwe·t sɔ·k·i·ma·ó·k·anink táli nuntá·i é·lsi·t aləwí·i-lə́s·u né·k·a e·lkí·kwi-lə́s·i·t.
  /t But he that is least in the kingdom of God (the creator) is greater than he is.
  /k but he that is least in the kingdom of God is greater than he.

Mt 11.12
	/b	Ncki pratc Nhan hchopunwrt bqi pchi	[⟨Ncki⟩ for /néke/; ⟨bqi⟩ for /yúkwe/]
	/p	néke pe·á·t·e nčá·n čečhɔ·pwənúwe·t yúkwe péči	
	/t	From the time when John the Baptist came until now	
	/k	And from the days of John the Baptist until now	

/b tahekasw osavkamce sakemaokun,
/p tahči·ká·s·u ɔ·s·ahkame·í·i-sa·k·i·ma·ó·k·an,
/t the kingdom of heaven has been oppressed,
/k the kingdom of heaven suffereth violence,

/b ok bk wejuksethe amunhe tumekrok. [⟨-sethe⟩ for ⟨-sethek⟩]
/p ó·k yó·k wi·šəksí·č·i·k amənčí·i təmi·k·é·ɔk.
/t and these violent ones have forced their way in.
/k and the violent take it by force.

Mt 11.13
/b Wrmi nrnekanewrwsepanifu toptwnakunwu, ok bl
    xwi aptwnakunu xifwrlintaswpani eku pchi Nhan rpetc.   [⟨-sepan-⟩ for ⟨-setpan-⟩]
/p wé·mi nehəni·k·a·ní·i-we·wsi·tpanínka tɔ·pto·na·k·anúwa, ó·k yó·l
    xúwi-a·pto·ná·k·ana xinkwe·lənta·s·ó·p·ani íka péči nčá·n e·p·í·t·e.
/t The words of all the ancient prophets and the laws (*lit.*, old sayings) were greatly
    esteemed until the time of John.
/k For all the prophets and the law prophesied until John.

Mt 11.14
/b Wlistamrqc, nul ta wuni Elyus prvuntup.
/p wələstamé·k·we, nál=tá wáni †i·láyas pe·hə́ntəp.
/t If you believe them, this is Elias, who was expected to come.
/k And if ye will receive it, this is Elias, which was for to come.

Mt 11.15
/b Awrn wrvetaoket krski krkw puntuf, puntufch.
/p awé·n we·hitaɔ́k·i·t, ké·ski- kéku -pə́ntank, pəntánkeč."
/t Anyone who has ears and can hear things, let him hear it."
/k He that hath ears to hear, let him hear.

Lk 7.29
/b Wrmi cntxi puntufek, ok moni mcmyrnifek wlamvetawao
/p wé·mi éntxi-pəntánki·k ó·k móni mehəma·e·nínki·k o·la·mhitaɔwwá·ɔ
/t All those that heard, and the tax-collectors, believed
/k And all the people that heard him, and the publicans, justified   [i.e., 'credited'?]

/b Kejrlwmwrlethi, hvopunatup Nhan hvopunwntwakunif.
                                                    [⟨hvopunwnt-⟩ for ⟨vwhovopwnunt-⟩]
/p ki·š·e·ləməwe·lí·č·i čhɔ·pwəná·t·əp nčá·n wčɔhɔ·pwənəntəwá·k·anink.
/t God was who had baptized them in John's baptism.
/k God, being baptized with the baptism of John.

Lk 7.30
/b Jwk, Paluseuk, ok lrpothek motrlintaminro Kejrlumwrt rlextaq li vokywauf,
/p šúkw †pa·ləsi·í·ɔk ó·k le·p·ó·č·i·k mɔt·e·ləntaməné·ɔ ki·š·e·ləmúwe·t e·lí·xta·kw lí
    hɔk·ayəwá·unk,
/t But the Pharisees and wise men scorned what God had set for them,
/k But the Pharisees and lawyers rejected the counsel of God against themselves,
                [RSV "rejected the purpose of God for themselves"]

    /b rli mutu hvopunukrun wunhi nrkumu.
/p é·li- máta -čhɔ·pwənək·é·an wə́nči né·k·əma.   [/-ək·e·an/ or neg. /-ək·e·ɔn/]
/t as you (sg.) were not baptized by him.   [an apparent misunderstanding]
/k being not baptized of him.

Lk 7.31 /b Nrvlalwrt lwrp, Ta vuh if la rlenaqset b rlvakret?
/p nehəlá·ləwe·t lúwe·p, "tá=háč=ínk=láh e·li·ná·kwsi·t yú e·lhaké·i·t?
/t The Lord said, "What could I say this tribe is like?
/kl And the Lord said, Whereunto then shall I liken the men of this generation? and to what are they like?

Lk 7.32 /b Mulaji memisuk lrmuvtupethek cntu mumvalumwntif, rltevtet.   [⟨is⟩ for ⟨ins⟩]
/p málahši mi·mə́nsak le·mahtap·í·č·i·k énta-memhalamúntink e·ltíhti·t.
/t It is like what children who sit in the market say to each other.
/k They are like unto children sitting in the marketplace, and calling one to another,

/b Tclao ktupekwlvwmunu jwk mutu kintkavwmw,   [⟨ktupekwlvwmu-‖nu⟩]
/p təlá·ɔ, 'ktap·i·k·o·lhúmana, šúkw máta kkəntka·húmɔ,
/t One says to the other, 'We played music for you, but you did not dance,
/k and saying, We have piped unto you, and ye have not danced;

(p. 65) /b ok kjerlumulvwmunu jwk kaksenvakrvwmw.
/p ɔ́·k kši·e·ləməlhúmana, šúkw kka·ksi·nhakéhəmɔ.'
/t and we grieved for you but you were indifferent.'
/k we have mourned to you, and ye have not wept.
    [RSV "we wailed, and you did not weep"]

Lk 7.33 /b Nhan takw navkoi krkw wifi methee ok memunri;
/p nčá·n takó· nahkɔ́·i kéku wínki-mi·č·í·i ɔ́·k mi·məné·i.
/t John did not like to eat ordinary things and never drank.
/k For John the Baptist came neither eating bread nor drinking wine;

/b Lwrok mavtuntw ta wuni.
/p luwé·ɔk, 'mahtánt·u=tá wáni.'
/t They said, 'He is a devil.'
/k and ye say, He hath a devil.

Lk 7.34 /b Wrqesif linw memetsw, ok mevmunri.
/p we·k·wí·s·ink lə́nu mihəmí·tsu ɔ́·k míhəməne·.
/t The man who is the Son eats and drinks.
/k The Son of man is come eating and drinking;

/b Lwrok, Punw mrxulrteat, ok wyn mcvmunrt,
/p luwé·ɔk, 'pənó· me·x·alé·t·ia·t ɔ́·k wáin méhəməne·t.
/t They say, 'Look at the glutton and wine-drinker.
/k and ye say, Behold a gluttonous man, and a winebibber,

	/b	moni mrvmyrnumulehi ok mrhiliselethi wetesu.
	/p	móni mehəma·e·nəməlí·č·i ɔ́·k méči-ləs·i·lí·č·i wi·t·í·s·a.
	/t	Tax-collectors and sinners are his friends.'
	/k	a friend of publicans and sinners!

Lk 7.35 /b Jwk cntxi lipothik wlenumunro lipwrokun.
/p šúkw éntxi-ləpɔ́·č·i·k o·li·naməné·ɔ ləpwe·ɔ́·k·an."
/t But all who are wise admire wisdom."
/k But wisdom is justified of all her children.

Mt 11.20 /b Nu tolumi kjaptwnalan wrtwtrnyelet
/p ná tɔ́ləmi-kša·pto·ná·la·n we·t·o·t·e·naí·li·t
/t Then he began to scold the people of the towns
/k Then began he to upbraid the cities

/b cntu alwe kanjyvosetup
/p énta-aləwí·i-kanšaehɔ·s·í·t·əp,
/t where he had done most of his miracles,
/k wherein most of his mighty works were done,

/b rli mutu qwlwpevtet.
/p é·li- máta -kwələp·íhti·t.
/t because they did not repent.
/k because they repented not:

Mt 11.21 /b Avoth ke Kolrsun! Avoth ke Pctsriti!
/p "áhɔt=č kí·, †kɔlé·sən! áhɔt=č kí·, †petsé·iti!
/t "It will be hard for you, Chorazin! It will be hard for you, Bethsaida!
/k Woe unto thee, Chorazin! woe unto thee, Bethsaida!

/b Rli Tyulif, ok Sytunif rpcthck lenamevtetpani konjyvoswakun, rlkeqi krpwu lenumrq [⟨-ni⟩ for /-ne/]
/p é·li †táyalink ɔ́·k †sáitanink e·p·í·č·i·k li·namihti·tpáne kanšaehɔ·s·əwá·k·an e·lkí·kwi- ké·pəwa -lí·name·kw,
/t For if the citizens of Tyre and Sidon had seen miracles as great as you have seen,
/k for if the mighty works, which were done in you, had been done in Tyre and Sidon,

/b lelomwc a qlpwpenrop. [⟨qlpwp-⟩ for ⟨qwlp-⟩]
/p li·lɔ́·məwe=á· kkwəlpi·né·ɔ·p. (Cf. Lk 10.13.)
/t it would have been long ago that they repented.
/k they would have repented long ago in sackcloth and ashes.

Mt 11.22 /b Jwk ktclwvwmw mifasrih lro rlkeqi avkrkvwtwe kejqek Tyul ok Sytun kelwuh rlenamrq,
/p šúkw ktəllúhəmɔ, minkahsé·i=č lé·w e·lkí·kwi-ahke·kho·t·əwí·i-kí·škwi·k táyal ɔ́·k †sáitan, ki·ló·wa=č e·lí·name·kw.
/t But I tell you, at the time of the Day of Judgment it will be better for Tyre and Sidon than what you will experience.
/k But I say unto you, It shall be more tolerable for Tyre and Sidon at the day of judgment, than for you.

Mt 11.23 /b ok ke Kupuniun, qen kpmitwnvalkrn, [⟨kpmit⟩ for ⟨kpimt⟩]
/p ɔ́·k kí·, †kapə́niam, kwí·n kpəmto·nhá·lke·n,
/t And you, Capernaum, long have you been preached to,
/k And thou, Capernaum, which art exalted unto heaven,

/b Jwkh kehe vakifh ktclanrvmalkc;
/p šúkw=č khičí·i, hákink=č ktəlanehəmá·lke,
/t but truly you shall be thrown down,
/k shalt be brought down to hell:

/b rli konjyvoswakun lenumunup Satumif rlrkup, qeaqi vatr pchi bqi kejqek.
/p é·li- kanšaehɔ·s·əwá·k·an -li·namánəp †sá·tamink e·lé·k·əp, kwiá·kwi hát·e· péči yúkwe kí·škwi·k.
/t for you have seen the miracles that happened in Sodom; it still exists until today. [a misunderstanding]
/k for if the mighty works, which have been done in thee, had been done in Sodom, it would have remained until this day.

Mt 11.24 /b Jwk ktclwvwmw, mifasrih lro rlkeqi avkrkvwtwe kejqek keh rlenamun.
/p šúkw ktəllúhəmɔ, minkahsé·i=č lé·w e·lkí·kwi-ahke·kho·t·əwí·i-kí·škwi·k, kí·=č e·lí·naman."
/t But I tell you, it will be better at the time of the Day of Judgment than what *you* will experience."
/k But I say unto you, That it shall be more tolerable for the land of Sodom in the day of judgment, than for thee.

Mt 11.25 /b Nu ma Nhesus tclwrn, O wuniji Nwxa, nevlatumun osavkamc, ok prmakamekrk
/p ná=máh nčí·sas tə́ləwe·n, "ó·, wanə́š·i, núxa·, nihəlá·t·aman ɔ·s·áhkame ɔ́·k pe·mhakamí·k·e·k,
/t Then Jesus said, "Oh, thank you, Father, lord of heaven and earth,
/k At that time Jesus answered and said, I thank thee, O Father, Lord of heaven and earth,

/b ktcli kuntvatwn b krkw wunhi lrpothek, ok lipwrlinsethek, [⟨rl⟩ for ⟨rrl⟩]
/p ktə́li-kantháto·n yú kéku wə́nči le·p·ɔ́·č·i·k ɔ́·k ləpwe·e·lənsí·č·i·k,
/t for hiding these things from the wise and those that think they are wise,
/k because thou hast hid these things from the wise and prudent,

/b ok ktcli watulan ktcli tomeminsumen.
/p ɔ·k ktə́li-wwá·tələn ktə́li-tɔmi·mə́nsəmi·n.
/t and for letting them know that they are your children.   [a misunderstanding]
/k and hast revealed them unto babes.

Mt 11.26 /b Nani lro Nwxa, rli nani ke ketrva.   [⟨ketrva⟩ for ⟨ktetrva⟩ (or ⟨ktetrvan⟩?)]
/p ná=ní lé·w, núxa·, é·li ná=ní kí· kti·t·é·ha.
/t That is so, Father, as that is what *you* wish.
/k Even so, Father: for so it seemed good in thy sight.

Mt 11.27 /b Wrmi krkw nevlatumun wunhi Nwxif;
/p wé·mi kéku nnihəlá·t·amən wə́nči nó·x·ink.
/t I am lord over everything because of my father.
/k All things are delivered unto me of my Father:

/b ok mutu awrn wavaeu Wrqesifc nu jwk Wrtwxumut,   [⟨-c⟩ for /-i/; ⟨-ut⟩ for ⟨-unt⟩]
/p ɔ·k máta awé·n o·wa·ha·í·ɔ we·k·wi·s·ínki, ná šúkw we·t·ó·x·əmənt,
/t And no one knows the Son except the Father,
/k and no man knoweth the Son, but the Father;

/b ok mutu awrn wavaeu Wrtwxifi nu jwk Wrqesif,
/p ɔ·k máta awé·n o·wa·ha·í·ɔ we·t·o·x·ínki, ná šúkw we·k·wí·s·ink,
/t and no one knows the Father except the Son,
/k neither knoweth any man the Father, save the Son,

/b ok Wrqesif letrvatc awrnih watulan.
/p ɔ·k we·k·wí·s·ink li·t·e·há·t·e, awé·ni=č o·wá·tələn.
/t and if the Son wants to, he will make it known to people.
/k and he to whomsoever the Son will reveal him.

Mt 11.28 /b Toxeq wrmi mekumoserq ok qrskoserq,
/p "tóx·i·kw wé·mi mi·kəmɔ́·s·ie·kw ɔ·k kwe·skwə́s·ie·kw;
/t "Come to me, all you who work and are heavy;   [a misunderstanding]
/k Come unto me, all ye that labour and are heavy laden,

/b neh ktalaxemwvalwvwmw.
/p ní·=č ktala·x·i·mo·hallúhəmɔ.
/t *I* will give you rest.
/k and I will give you rest.

Mt 11.29 /b Kavptekrnro a favptekun, ok knetatwnroh wunhi ne,
/p kkaxpti·k·e·né·ɔ=á· nkaxptí·k·an, ɔ·k kəni·ta·t·o·né·ɔ=č wə́nči ní·.
/t You should tie on my "yoke," and you shall learn from me.
/k Take my yoke upon you, and learn of me;

/b rli ntukawuse, ok ‖ ntufrlinsi,
/p é·li ntək·awə́s·i ɔ́·k ntanke·lə́nsi.
/t For I am gentle and meek.
/k for I am meek and lowly in heart:

(p. 66)
/b nuh kumuxkumun wunhih khehufum alaxemwet.
/p ná=č kəmáxkamən wə́nči-=č kči·čánkəm -ala·xí·mwi·t.
/t Then you shall find the means for your soul to have rest.
/k and ye shall find rest unto your souls.

Mt 11.30
/b Rli favptekun apwat, ok nweajwn lufun. [⟨ea⟩ for /í·ɔh/]
/p é·li nkaxptí·k·an á·p·əwat, ɔ́·k nəwí·ɔhšo·n lánkan.
/t For my "yoke" is easy, and my pack (bundle) is light.
/k For my yoke is easy, and my burden is light.

Chapter 40 (pp. 66-67). [L. section 39.] (Luke 7.36-50)

Lk 7.36
/b Mawsw Palisee kutatumun wepwmkwn,
/p má·wsu †pa·ləsí·i kɔt·á·t·amən wwi·pó·mko·n.
/t A certain Pharisee wanted to have him eat with him.
/k And one of the Pharisees desired him that he would eat with him.

/b ekali tumekrp Palisee weket, mjakr tcli a metsen.
/p íkali təmí·k·e·p †pa·ləsí·i wí·k·i·t, məšá·ke· tə́li-=á· -mí·tsi·n.
/t And he entered the Pharisee's house and sat down to eat.
/k And he went into the Pharisee's house, and sat down to meat.

Lk 7.37
/b Puna avpwp xqr mrhiliset nu tali wtrnif;
/p pənáh, ahpó·p xkwé· méči-lə́s·i·t nə́ táli o·t·é·nink.
/t Now, there was a woman who was a sinner in that town.
/k And, behold, a woman in the city, which was a sinner,

/b wrotaqc tcli Nhesus metsen Palisee weket tali,
/p we·ɔ·tá·k·we tə́li- nčí·sas -mí·tsi·n †pa·ləsí·i wí·k·i·t táli,
/t When she knew that Jesus was eating in the Pharisee's house,
/k when she knew that Jesus sat at meat in the Pharisee's house,

/b eku prtw opasine sekaxqtit hwvotrk mpeswn;
/p íka pé·t·o· ɔpahsəní·i-si·k·á·xkwtət čuhóte·k mpí·s·o·n,
/t she brought there a white-stone box full of medicine
/k brought an alabaster box of ointment,

Lk 7.38 /b kexki wsetif tcli nepyen ok lupuq,
/p kí·xki wsí·t·ink tə́li-ní·p·ai·n, ɔ́·k ləpákw,
/t and she went and stood near his feet and wept,
/k And stood at his feet behind him weeping,

/p ɔ́·k tɔ́ləmi-kši·xtáɔ·n wsí·t·a wə́nči wsəp·ínkɔ, ɔ́·k wči·skhamáɔ·n, mwí·laxk tɔé·ke·n.
/b ok tolumi kjextaon wsetu wunhi wswpifo ok wtheskvamaon mwelaxk torkrn.
/t and then she began to wash his feet with her tears and wiped them using her hair.
/k and began to wash his feet with tears, and did wipe them with the hairs of her head,

/b ok mwstwnamao wsetif, nu ok eku tcli jwvwmaon mpeswn.
/p ɔ́·k mmo·sto·na·má·ɔ wsí·t·ink, ná ɔ́·k íka tə́li-šuhəmáɔ·n mpí·s·o·n.
/t And she kissed him on the feet, and then she also smeared them with the medicine.
/k and kissed his feet, and anointed them with the ointment.

Lk 7.39 /b Nani Palisee wcnhematup nrlenufc letrvrw,
/p náni †pa·ləsí·i wenči·má·t·əp ne·li·nánke, li·t·é·he·w,
/t As that Pharisee who had invited him watched, he thought,
/k Now when the Pharisee which had bidden him saw it, he spake within himself, saying,

/b nrnekane a wrwsetc watwna nu xqr rlset; rli muvtawset.
/p "nehəni·k·a·ní·i=á· -we·wsí·t·e, o·wá·to·n=á· ná xkwé· é·lsi·t, é·li-mahtá·wsi·t."
/t "If he is a prophet, he would know what kind of a woman she is, as she is a sinner."
/k This man, if he were a prophet, would have known who and what manner of woman this is that toucheth him: for she is a sinner.

Lk 7.40 /b Nu Nhesus tclan, Symun, kutu krkw lil.
/p ná nčí·sas tə́la·n, "†sáiman, kkát·a- kéku -lə́l."
/t Then Jesus said to him, "Simon, I want to tell you something."
/k And Jesus answering said unto him, Simon, I have somewhat to say unto thee.

/b Nu tclkwn Rvakrkifrs nani lisel.
/p ná tə́lko·n, "ehahke·kínke·s, ná=ní lə́s·i·l."
/t And then he said to him, "Teacher, tell me that."
/k And he saith, Master, say on.

Lk 7.41 /b Avpwp linw, nejelw rlrkvamuothi, ⟨muo⟩ for ⟨mao⟩]
/p "ahpó·p lə́nu, ni·š·í·lu e·le·khamáɔ·č·i.
/t "There was a man who had two debtors.
/k There was a certain creditor which had two debtors:

Text, Transcription, and Translation

/b maoselw tulrkvamaopani palrnax txapuxki rlaotek. Kahi mawselw palrnax
txenxkc; [⟨-x⟩ for /-xk/ 2x; ⟨puxk⟩ for /pxk/]
/p ma·wsí·lu təle·khamaɔ́·p·ani palé·naxk txá·pxki e·lá·ɔhti·k, káč·i ma·wsí·lu palé·naxk txí·nxke.
/t One owed him the value of five hundred, and the other fifty.
/k the one owed five hundred pence, and the other fifty.

Lk 7.42
/b mrhi qelu rnvrtc, nu noxpufwmkwn rlee.
/p mé·či kwí·la-e·nhé·t·e, ná nɔxpankó·mko·n, ellí·i.
/t After each was unable to pay, he made a gift of it to him, both of them.
/k And when they had nothing to pay, he frankly forgave them both.

/b Bqc ta lel, ta vuh nrl alwe tovolao?
/p yúkwe=tá lí·l, tá=háč né·l aləwí·i tɔhɔ·lá·ɔ?"
/t Now tell me, which one does he love more?" [misunderstood]
/k Tell me therefore, which of them will love him most?

Lk 7.43
/b Symun tclao, Wretet ct nunul li nrl rlwe txi nuxpufwmkwki. [⟨nunul li⟩ for nanáli]
/p †sáiman təlá·ɔ, "we·í·t·ət=ét nanáli né·l e·ləwí·i-txí-naxpanko·mkúk·i."
/t Simon said, "I suppose it was the one that gave him the most." [misunderstood]
/k Simon answered and said, I suppose that he, to whom he forgave most.

/b Tclao kwlamwc nani lro.
/p təlá·ɔ, "ko·lá·məwe; ná=ní lé·w."
/t He said to him, "You are right; that is true."
/k And he said unto him, Thou hast rightly judged.

Lk 7.44
/b Nu eku tcli qwlwpen nc xqruf, tclao Symunu, Kunrw vuh wu xqr?
/p ná íka təli-kwələp·i·n nə́(?) xkwé·yunk, təlá·ɔ †sáimana, "kəné·ɔ=háč wá xkwé·?
/t Then he turned to the woman, and he said to Simon, "Do you see this woman?
/k And he turned to the woman, and said unto Simon, Seest thou this woman?

/b Ntumekrn wekiun, takw kumele mpi wunhi a kjextao nsetul;
/p ntəmí·k·e·n wí·k·ian; takó· kəmi·lí·i mpí wə́nči·=á· -kši·xtáɔ nsí·t·al.
/t I came into your house, and you did not give me water for me to wash my feet.
/k I entered into thine house, thou gavest me no water for my feet:

/b jwk nrku qwjextwnu nsetu wunhi wswpifo, ok wtheskvamunu wunhi mwelaxk.
/p šúkw né·k·a kwəš·i·xtó·na nsí·t·a wə́nči wsəp·ínkɔ, ɔ́·k wči·skhámana wə́nči mwí·laxk.
/t But *she* washed my feet with her tears, and wiped them with her hair.
/k but she hath washed my feet with tears, and wiped them with the hairs of her head.

207

Lk 7.45 /b Takw kmwstwname,
         /p takó· kəmo·sto·na·mí·i.
         /t You did not kiss me.
         /k Thou gavest me no kiss:

         /b jwk wuni xqr srkc pchi tumekru mutu ntalu mwnstwnamkwi nsetif.
                                                              [⟨mwns-⟩ for /mo·s-/]
         /p šúkw wáni xkwé·, sé·ki-péči-təmi·k·é·a, máta ntála-mo·sto·na·mkó·wi nsí·t·ink.
         /t But this woman, from the time I came in, has not stopped kissing me on the feet.
         /k but this woman since the time I came in hath not ceased to kiss my feet.

Lk 7.46 /b Takw kjumvwqrnee nuxpuni prmi,
         /p takó· kšamhukwe·ní·i náxpəne pəmí,
         /t You did not anoint my head even with oil,
         /k My head with oil thou didst not anoint:

         /b jwk wuni jumunimunu nsetu wunhi ‖ mpeswn.
         /p šúkw wáni šomənəména nsí·t·a wə́nči mpí·s·o·n.
         /t but she anointed my feet with medicine.
         /k but this woman hath anointed my feet with ointment.

Lk 7.47 /b Nuni wunhi ktclul,
(p. 67) /p nə́ni wə́nči ktə́ləl,
         /t Therefore I say to you,
         /k Wherefore I say unto thee,

         /b Motaoswakun, alwt xrlit, mrhi mpuketatamaon rli ave avolet,
         /p mɔt·a·wsəwá·k·an, aló·t xé·lət, mé·či mpak·i·t·a·t·amáɔ·n, é·li-áhi-ahɔ́·li·t.
         /t her sins, though many, I have forgiven her for, as she loves me greatly.
         /k Her sins, which are many, are forgiven; for she loved much:

         /b jwk awrn mavtiti mpuketamaon, nul nu mavtiti avolet.   [⟨-puket-⟩ for ⟨-puketat-⟩]
         /p šúkw awé·n mahtíti mpak·i·t·a·t·amáɔ·n, nál ná mahtíti ahɔ́·li·t."
         /t But let me forgive little to someone, and he is one who loves me little."
         /k but to whom little is forgiven, the same loveth little.

Lk 7.48 /b Nu tclan nrl xqru, Kmutawswakun kpuketatumakrn.
         /p ná tə́la·n né·l xkwé·ɔ, "kəmat·a·wsəwá·k·an kpak·i·t·a·t·amá·k·e·n."
         /t Then he said to that woman, "Your sins are forgiven."
         /k And he said unto her, Thy sins are forgiven.

Lk 7.49 /b Nu wepwmathi tolumi lwrnro, Awrn vuh wu prketatumaset mutaoswakun?
         /p ná wi·po·má·č·i tóləmi-luwe·né·ɔ, "awé·n=háč wá pe·k·i·t·a·t·amá·s·i·t mahta·wsəwá·k·an?"

	/t	Then those he ate with began to say, "Who is this one who forgives sins?"
	/k	And they that sat at meat with him began to say within themselves, Who is this that forgiveth sins also?

Lk 7.50 /b Jwk tclao xqru, Knakatamwrakun kuthwvalkwn,   [⟨-rakun⟩ for ⟨-rokun⟩]
/p šúkw təláːɔ xkwéːɔ, "kənaˑkaˑtˑamweˑíˑkˑan kkəčˑoˑháˑlkoˑn.
/t But he said to the woman, "Your faith has saved you.
/k And he said to the woman, Thy faith hath saved thee;

/b alumskal, wlufwntwakun ktupetaq.
/p aləmskaˑl; wəlankuntəwáˑkˑan ktapˑíˑtaˑkw."
/t Depart; peace is with you."
/k go in peace.

Chapter 41 (pp. 67-68). [L. section 40.] (Luke 6.1, 5; Matthew 12.2-6, 8; Mark 2.27-28.)

Lk 6.1 /b Mrhi nejun alaxemwre kejqekc mukune alaxemwre kejqekc,
(p. 67) /p méˑči níˑšˑən alaˑxˑiˑməweˑíˑiˑkiˑškwíˑkˑe, məkəníˑi-alaˑxˑiˑməweˑíˑiˑkiˑškwíˑkˑe,
/t After two days of rest, on the last day of rest,
/k And it came to pass on the second sabbath after the first,

/b ekali hwpwep vwet-vakevakunif,
/p íkali čə́pˑwiˑp hwiˑthakiˑháˑkˑanink.
/t he passed through the wheat fields.
/k that he went through the corn fields;   [RSV: "grainfields"]

/b rkrkemathi tolomi pupxkanimunro nc vwet,
/p eˑkˑeˑkiˑmáˑčˑi tóləmi-pəpxkənəménéˑɔ nə́ hwíˑt.
/t And his disciples began plucking the wheat.
/k and his disciples plucked the ears of corn,

/b srki pokvamanro wnaxkwaif nu methenro.   [⟨me-⟩ for /mwiˑ-/]
/p séˑkiˑ-[...], ppɔˑkhamaˑnéˑɔ wənaxkəwáˑink, ná mwiˑčˑiˑnéˑɔ.   [word missing]
/t And as [they did?], they broke it up in their hands and ate it.
/k and did eat, rubbing them in their hands.

Mt 12.2 /b Alintc Paliseuk nc rlenamevtetc tclawo,
/p aˑlə́nte †paˑləsiˑíˑɔk nə́ eˑliˑnamihtíˑtˑe, təlawwáˑɔ,
/t When some of the Pharisees saw it, they said to him,
/k But when the Pharisees saw it, they said unto him,

/b Punaw rkrkemuthek, takw wlexunwi rlsevtet alavlmwre kejkw.   [⟨vlm⟩ for ⟨xem⟩]
/p "pənáw eˑkˑeˑkiˑmáˑčˑiˑk; takóˑ wəliˑxˑənóˑwi eˑlsíhtiˑt; alaˑxˑiˑməweˑíˑiˑkíˑšku."
/t "Look at your disciples; what they are doing is not lawful; it is a day of rest."
/k Behold, thy disciples do that which is not lawful to do upon the sabbath day.

Mt 12.3 /b Jwk tclao, mutu vuh vuji ktukintumwnro
         /p šúkw təláˑɔ, "máta=háč háši ktakˑəntamoˑwənéˑɔ
         /t But he said to them, "Have you never read about
         /k But he said unto them, Have ye not read

         /b Ntrpitu rlsetup krtopwetc ok nukavkc wehrotpanek?
         /p †nteˑpítˑa eˑlsítˑəp keˑtˑoˑpˑwíˑtˑe, ɔ́ˑk nəkáhke wiˑčˑeˑɔˑtpániˑk?
         /t what David did when he was hungry, he and those who were with him?
         /k what David did, when he was an hungred, and they that were with him;

Mt 12.4 /b rli patamwrekaonif rpanek ok mevthenrap nu pelvik avpon,
                                                                          [⟨mevth-⟩ for /mwiˑč-/]
         /p éˑli paˑtamweˑiˑkˑáˑɔnink éˑpˑaniˑk, ɔ́ˑk mwiˑčˑiˑnéˑɔˑp nə́ píˑlhik ahpɔ́ˑn.
         /t For they went to the temple and ate the holy bread.
         /k How he entered into the house of God, and did eat the shewbread,

         /b takw wlexunw navkoi awrn mwethen wrvevwfrthek xwva.   [⟨-w⟩ for /-óˑu/]
         /p takóˑ wəliˑxˑənóˑu nahkɔ́ˑi awéˑn mwíˑčˑiˑn, wehiˑhunkéˑčˑiˑk xóˑha.
         /t It was not lawful for just anyone to eat it, only the priests.
         /k which was not lawful for him to eat, neither for them which were with him, but
             only for the priests?

Mt 12.5 /b Ok vuh mutu vuji ktukintamonro xwi aptwnakunif
         /p ɔ́ˑk=háč máta háši ktakˑəntamoˑwənéˑɔ xúwi-aˑptoˑnáˑkˑanink
         /t Or have you never read in the law (lit., in the old word(s))
         /k Or have ye not read in the law,

         /b krkw rvrlisetetup wrvevwfrthek alaxemwre kejqekc, patamwrekaonif,
         /p kéku ehələsˑihtíˑtˑəp wehiˑhunkéˑčˑiˑk alaˑxˑiˑməweˑíˑi-kiˑškwíˑkˑe
             paˑtamweˑiˑkˑáˑɔnink;
         /t about the things done by the priests on the day of rest, in the tenple;
         /k how that on the sabbath days the priests in the temple profane the sabbath,

         /b ok takw krkw eli haneliseepanek.
         /p ɔ́ˑk takóˑ kéku ílli čáni-ləsˑiˑíˑpˑaniˑk.
         /t and they did not even do anything wrong.
         /k and are blameless?

Mt 12.6 /b Ktclwvwmw, avpw awrn bni tali alwe rlkeluk patamwrekaon rlkeqif.
         /p ktəllúhəmɔ, ahpú awéˑn yóˑni táli aləwíˑi eˑlkíˑlək paˑtamweˑiˑkˑáˑɔn eˑlkíˑkwink.
         /t I tell you, there is someone in this place greater than the temple.
         /k But I say unto you, That in this place is one greater than the temple.

Mt 12.7 /b Jwk watarqi krkw ta rlwrf,   [⟨-qi⟩ for /-kˑwe/]
         /p šúkw wwaˑtaéˑkˑwe kéku=tá éˑləwenk,

/t But if you knew what it means to say, [*lit.*, 'what one says']
/k But if ye had known what this meaneth,

/b Nwlenamun qwtumakrlintwakun, jwk wevwfrokun mutu;
/p 'no·lí·namən kwət·əma·k·e·ləntəwá·k·an, šúkw wi·hunke·ɔ́·k·an máta,'
/t 'I admire his mercy, but not sacrifice,'
/k I will have mercy, and not sacrifice,

/b ta khanemaeok bk javakawsehek.
/p tá=á· kčani·ma·í·ɔk yó·k šaxahka·wsí·č·i·k."
/t you would not criticize these righteous ones."
/k ye would not have condemned the guiltless.

Mk 2.27 /b Tclao alaxemwre kejqek manetaswp wunhi wrmi awrn,
/p təlá·ɔ, "ala·x·i·məwe·í·i-kí·škwi·k manni·tá·s·o·p wə́nči wé·mi awé·n,
/t He said to them, "The day of rest was made for everyone,
/k And he said unto them, The sabbath was made for man,

/b ok wrmi awrn mutu nc wunhi manevawun alaxemre kejqek. [⟨manev-‖awun⟩]
/p ɔ́·k wé·mi awé·n máta nə́ wə́nči-manni·há·wən ala·x·i·məwe·í·i-kí·škwi·k.
/t and everyone was not made for the day of rest.
/k and not man for the sabbath:

Mt 12.8 /b Linw Wrqesif Nevlatuf alaxemwre kejqek.
(p. 68) /p lə́nu we·k·wí·s·ink nihəlá·t·ank ala·x·i·məwe·í·i-kí·škwi·k."
/t The man who is the Son is the Lord of the day of rest.
/k For the Son of man is Lord even of the sabbath day.

Chapter 42 (pp. 68-69). [L. section 41.] (Matthew 12.9, 11-12, 15-21; Luke 6.6 [part]-11; Mark 3.6)

Mt 12.9 /b Nu wunhi alumskatc eku rp cvcntu myrvuluf.
/p nə́ wə́nči-aləmská·t·e, íka é·p ehə́nta-ma·éhəlank.
/t When he departed from there, he went to a synagogue.
/k And when he was departed thence, he went into their synagogue:

Lk 6.6 /b Ok avkrkifrp.
/p ɔ́·k ahke·kínke·p.
/t And he taught.
/k ... and taught:

/b Avpwp linw wtunrvaon swnswktr.
/p ahpó·p lə́nu, wtənne·há·ɔn sunsó·kte·.
/t And there was a man, (and) his right hand was "withered."
/k ... and there was a man whose right hand was withered.

Lk 6.7
/b Nu rlrkvekrthek, ok Paliseuk qrnavkevanro,
/p ná ehəle·khi·k·é·č·i·k ó·k †pa·ləsi·í·ɔk kwe·nahki·ha·né·ɔ,
/t Then the scribes and Pharisees watched him,
/k And the scribes and Pharisees watched him,

/b kavunch qekrva alaxemwre kejqek;　　　　　　　[⟨-va⟩ /-há·a/ for usual ⟨-vao⟩ /-há·ɔ/]
/p ká·xəne=č kwi·k·e·há·a ala·x·i·məwe·í·i-kí·škwi·k.
/t to see whether he would heal him on a day of rest.
/k whether he would heal on the sabbath day;

/b rli kutu muxkamunro krkw a rli hanemavtet.　　　　　　　[⟨kutu⟩ for /kót·a/]
/p é·li kót·a-maxkamənéɔ kéku=á· é·li-čani·máhti·t.
/t For they wanted to find some way they could accuse him.
/k that they might find an accusation against him.

Lk 6.8
/b Jwk wavapani rletrvalet,
/p šúkw o·wa·há·p·ani e·li·t·e·há·li·t.
/t But he knew what they were thinking.
/k But he knew their thoughts,

/b ok tclaw nrl linwu swnswktrlek wnaxk
/p ó·k təlá·ɔ né·l lənəwa sunso·kté·li·k wənáxk,
/t And he said to the man whose hand was withered,
/k and said to the man which had the withered hand,

/b paswkwel, eku lrlyi my nepyel.
/p "pahsúk·wi·l, íka le·lá·i mái-ní·p·ai·l."
/t "Get up, and go stand in the middle."
/k Rise up, and stand forth in the midst.

/b Nu posqenrp my eku nepwp.
/p ná pɔskwí·ne·p, mái- íka -ní·p·o·p.
/t Then he got up and went and stood there.
/k And he arose and stood forth.

Lk 6.9
/b Nhesus tclaol nrl, kwtrnaoki krkw knatoxtwlvwmw.
/p nčí·sas təlá·ɔl né·l, "kwət·ennáɔhki kéku kənat·o·xto·lhúmɔ.
/t Jesus said to them, "I ask you one thing.
/k Then said Jesus unto them, I will ask you one thing;

/b Wlexun vuh alaxemwre kejqekc awrn wlevan, jita mahevan?
/p wəlí·x·ən=háč ala·x·i·məwe·í·i-kí·škwi·k awé·n wəlí·ha·n, ší=tá mahčí·ha·n?
/t Is it lawful on a day of rest for someone to be treated well, or to be treated ill?
/k Is it lawful on the sabbath days to do good, or to do evil?

/b Lrlrxrmvalan jitu palevan?
/p lehəle·x·e·mhá·la·n, ší=tá palí·ha·n?
/t To have their life saved, or to be destroyed?
/k to save life, or to destroy it?

Mt 12.11 /b Awrn vuh a kelwu
/p awé·n=háč=á· ki·ló·wa,
/t Who of you,
/k ... What man shall there be among you,

/b mrkesu tolumwnsu kwti eku levelaletc cntu keskalavku alaxemwre kejqekc
/p mekí·s·a tɔləmúnsa kwə́t·i íka lihəla·lí·t·e énta-ki·ská·lahka ala·x·i·məwe·í·i-ki·škwí·k·e,
/t if one of his sheep fell into a pit on a day of rest,
/k that shall have one sheep, and if it fall into a pit on the sabbath day,

/b mutu vuh a jai qutinaeu?
/p máta=háč=á· šá·e kwət·əna·í·ɔ?
/t would not immediately take it out?
/k will he not lay hold on it, and lift it out?

Mt 12.12 /b Ta vuh alwe lisw linw, ok mrkes?
/p tá=háč aləwí·i-lə́s·u lə́nu ɔ́·k méki·s?
/t How much better is a man than a sheep?
/k How much then is a man better than a sheep?

/b Nc wunhi puna wlexun awrn wlevan alaxemwre kejqek.
/p nə́ wə́nči pənáh, wəlí·x·ən awé·n wəlí·ha·n ala·x·i·məwe·í·i-kí·škwi·k.
/t Therefore consider, it is lawful for someone to be well treated on a day of rest.
/k Wherefore it is lawful to do well on the sabbath days.

Lk 6.10 /b Mrhi wrmi b tu rlvwqrtc nu tclan nu linw jepenxkc;
/p mé·či wé·mi yú tá e·lhukwé·t·e, ná tə́la·n ná lə́nu, "ši·p·í·nxke."   [prox. for obv.]
/t After he had looked all around, then he said / that man, "Hold out your hand."
/k And looking round about upon them all, he said unto the man, Stretch forth thy hand.

/b nu nuni tclsen; ok wnaxk msithr, lupi mulaji takok.
/p ná nə́ni tə́lsi·n, ɔ́·k wənáxk məsəč·é·e, lápi málahši táko·k.
/t Then that's what he did; and his hand was whole, again like the other one.
/k And he did so: and his hand was restored whole as the other.

Lk 6.11 /b Paliseeuk ave manwfswuk
/p †pa·ləsi·í·ɔk áhi-manunksúwak.
/t The Pharisees were very angry.
/k And they were filled with madness; ...

Mt 12.14 /b nu tolumi kthenro
/p ná tóləmi-kči·né·ɔ,
/t Then they went out,
/k Then the Pharisees went out,

/b my wehi ahemwlswuk Vclutif wunheyethek rli a nvelavtet.
/p mái-wíči-a·č·i·mo·lsúwak †hélatink wənči·aí·č·i·k, é·li-=á· -nhiláhti·t.
/t and people from Herod went to hold a council with them, about how they could kill him.
/k and held a council against him, how they might destroy him.

Mt 12.15 /b Nhesus wrotaqc pale ton nu wunhi
/p nči·sas we·ɔ·tá·k·we, palí·i tó·n nɔ́ wə́nči.
/t When Jesus knew it, he went away from there.
/k But when Jesus knew it, he withdrew himself from thence:

/b xavrlwk naolathek, ok wrmi qekrvapani.
/p xahé·lo·k na·ɔlá·č·i·k; ɔ́·k wé·mi kwi·k·e·háp·ani.
/t There were many who followed him; and he healed them all.
/k and great multitudes followed him, and he healed them all;

Mt 12.16 /b Jwk qetulapani wunhi mutu khevlalwkwk.
/p šúkw kkwi·təlá·p·ani wə́nči- máta -kčihəlalúk·o·kw,
/t But he admonished them so that they would not expose him,
/k And charged them that they should not make him known:

Mt 12.17 /b Wunhi pavkunhi lrk nrnekanewrwsetpanu Esrusu rlwrtc;   [missing ⟨rlwrtup⟩]
/p wə́nči-pahkánči-lé·k nehəni·k·a·ní·i-we·wsi·tpána †i·se·yə́s·a [e·ləwé·t·əp] e·ləwé·t·e,
/t so that it was fulfilled [what] the prophet Esaias [said] when he said,
/k That it might be fulfilled which was spoken by Esaias the prophet, saying,

Mt 12.18 /b Punw ntalokakun, pepenaok, rvoluk, vokif wunhi wlrlintum whehufum.
                                                          [⟨wh-⟩ for ⟨nh-⟩]
/p "pənó· ntalo·ká·k·an, pi·p·í·naɔk, ehɔ́·lak; hɔ́k·enk wə́nči-wəle·lə́ntam nči·čánkəm.
/t "Behold my servant, whom I chose and whom I love; my soul rejoices because of him.
/k Behold my servant, whom I have chosen; my beloved, in whom my soul is well pleased:

/b Vokifh ntatwn numuntwakun, ok wlamwreokunh pwnwntulan rkvokrelethi.
/p hɔ́k·enk=č ntá·to·n nəmant·uwwá·k·an, ɔ́·k wəla·məwe·ɔ́·k·an=č pwənúntəla·n e·khɔke·i·lí·č·i.
/t I shall put my spiritual power in him, and he shall show truth to the nations.
/k I will put my spirit upon him, and he shall shew judgment to the Gentiles.

Mt 12.19 /b Ta pumenrvekri okh ta kanjalamwei
/p tá=á· pəmi·nehi·k·é·i, ɔ́·k=č tá=á· kanšala·mwí·i,
/t He will not quarrel, and he will not shout,
/k He shall not strive, nor cry;   [RSV "wrangle or cry aloud"]

/b ok ta vuji awrn ‖ tumakunif tuntu puntamwun rlwrtaset.   [⟨-taset⟩ for ⟨-taqset⟩]
/p ɔ́·k tá=á· háši awé·n təmá·k·anink tɔ́nta-pəntamó·wən e·ləwe·tá·kwsi·t.
/t and no one would ever hear his voice in the streets.
/k neither shall any man hear his voice in the streets.

Mt 12.20 /b Wekonusq jopunimun mutuh kutu pwqelavtwnro. [⟨jo-⟩ for /šɔɔ-/; ⟨ku-⟩ for /kɔ́-/]
(p. 69) /p wí·kənaskw[=č] šɔɔp·ənɔ́mən, máta=č kɔ́t·a-po·kwilahto·wəné·ɔ.
/t He [will] bend the reed; they will not try to snap it in two.
/k A bruised reed shall he not break,

/b Takw kovtu weqri qrjatrek osulrnekun   [⟨kovtu⟩ for /káhta/]
/p takó· káhta-wi·kwé·i kwe·šaté·i̯·k ɔ·s·əle·ní·k·an.
/t The smoking wick is not going to end.
/k and smoking flax shall he not quench,

/b eku pchi kcnjhinao wlamwrokun patavwrokunif,
/p íka péči-kənččəná·ɔ wəla·məwe·ɔ́·k·an pa·tahəwe·ɔ́·k·anink.
/t Truth is sent to victory.
/k till he send forth judgment unto victory.

Mt 12.21 /b okh rkvokrethek nokatamunro wtclswukun.
/p ɔ́·k=č e·khɔke·í·č·i·k nɔ·ka·t·aməné·ɔ wtəlsəwá·k·an."
/t And the nations shall rely on his power."
/k And in his name shall the Gentiles trust.

Chapter 43 (pp. 69-72). [L. section 42.] (Mark 3.20-21, 23-26; Matthew 12.22-24, 26 [part], 27, 29-50; Luke 11.20-21, 23, 27-28)

Mk 3.20 /b Lupi mrxrlkek eku pruk   [B. omits a sentence (the end of Mk 3.19).]
/p lápi me·x·é·lki·k íka pé·ɔk,
/t Again the multitudes came there,
/k And the multitude cometh together again,

/b ok tuhvekaoau wunhi a mutu nuxpunc kushi metsevtet.   [⟨kushi⟩ for ⟨kuski⟩]
/p ɔ́·k tɔčhikaɔwwá·ɔ, wə́nči-=á· máta náxpəne -káski-mi·tsíhti·t.
/t and they crowded up against them, so that they could not even eat.
/k so that they could not so much as eat bread.

Mk 3.21 /b Mrhi puntamevtetc rlafomathek wrmi nc rlrk, eku ruk naolawau, [⟨ao⟩ for /ɔ·ɔ/]
         /p mé·či pəntamihtí·t·e e·lanko·má·č·i·k wé·mi nə́ é·le·k, íka é·ɔk, nɔ·ɔlawwá·ɔ.
         /t After his neighbors and relatives heard all that happened, they went there and followed him.
         /k And when his friends heard of it, they went out to lay hold on him:

         /b rli letrvrok, kpithruful ct. [⟨ru⟩ for /e·ɔ́/]
         /p é·li li·t·e·hé·ɔk, "kpəč·e·ɔ́nkəl=ét."
         /t For they thought, "He must be out of his mind."
         /k for they said, He is beside himself.

Mt 12.22 /b Nu prtaon kwti rpetakwk mavtuntwu,
         /p ná pé·t·aɔ·n kwə́t·i e·p·i·tá·k·uk mahtant·ó·wa;
         /t Then there was brought to him one who had a devil in him;
         /k Then was brought unto him one possessed with a devil,

         /b avkrpifwr, ok mutu kekski krkw lwri.
         /p ahke·p·ínkwe· ɔ́·k máta kí·kski- kéku -luwé·i.
         /t he was blind and was never able to say anything.
         /k blind, and dumb:

         /b Qekrvao cntu avkrpifolet, ok cntu mutu kekski krkw lwrlet,
         /p kwi·k·e·há·ɔ énta-ahke·p·inkɔ́·li·t, ɔ́·k énta- máta -kí·kski- kéku -luwé·li·t,
         /t He healed him in his blindness and in his total muteness.
                     [lit., 'where he was blind and where he was never able to speak']
         /k and he healed him, insomuch that the blind and dumb

         /b wunhi nrmat, ok wunhi kuski krkw lwrt.
         /p wə́nči-né·ma·t, ɔ́·k wə́nči-káski- kéku -lúwe·t.
         /t so that he saw, and so that he was able to speak.
         /k both spake and saw.

Mt 12.23 /b Kanjrlintamwp wrmi awrn.
         /p kanše·lə́ntamo·p wé·mi awé·n.
         /t Everyone was amazed.
         /k And all the people were amazed,

         /b Lwrpanek, mutu vuh wu Ntrpit Qesu.
         /p luwé·p·ani·k, "máta=háč wá †nté·pit kkwí·s·a?"
         /t They said, "Isn't he the son of David?"
         /k and said, Is not this the son of David?

Mt 12.24 /b Jwk Paliseeuk mrhi putamevtetc, lwrpanek,
         /p šúkw †pa·ləsi·í·ɔk mé·či pəntamihtí·t·e, luwé·p·ani·k,
         /t But after the Pharisees heard about it, they said,
         /k But when the Pharisees heard it, they said,

/b Sakemae mavtuntwu jwk wunhi kuski ktiskaon mavtuntwu.
/p "saˑkˑiˑmaˑíˑi-mahtantˑóˑwa šúkw wwə́nči-káski-ktə́skaɔˑn mahtantˑóˑwa."
/t "The king of devils is the only reason he is able to cast out devils."
/k This fellow doth not cast out devils, but by Beelzebub the prince of the devils.

Mt 12.25 /b Nhesus wrotaqc rletrvatet   [⟨-vatet⟩ for ⟨-valet⟩]
/p nčíˑsas weˑɔˑtáˑkˑwe eˑliˑtˑeˑháˑliˑt,
/t When Jesus knew what they were thinking,
/k And Jesus knew their thoughts, ...

Mk 3.23 /b wenhemapani, mormopani, rncntvokrokun tclapani, lwro,
         [⟨wenh-⟩ for ⟨wcnh-⟩; ⟨mormo-⟩ for /mɔˑeˑmáˑ-/; ⟨-tvo-⟩ for /-tha-/; ⟨-ro⟩ for /-eˑw/]
/p wwenčiˑmáˑpˑani, mɔˑeˑmáˑpˑani, eˑnənthakeˑóˑkˑan təláˑpˑani, lúweˑw,
/t he called for them to come and gather together, and he told them a parable, saying,
/k And he called them unto him, and said unto them in parables,

/b Ta vuh wunhi kuski ktiskaon mavtuntw mavtuntwu.
/p táˑháč wwə́nči-káski-ktə́skaɔˑn mahtántˑu mahtantˑóˑwa.
/t "How does a devil cast out devils?
/k How can Satan cast out Satan?

Mk 3.24 /b Sakemaokun cntxi nevlahi mavtakrbek, takw kuski hetani lri.
/p saˑkˑiˑmaˑóˑkˑan éntxi- nihəláči -mahtaˑkeˑyóˑwiˑk, takóˑ káski-číˑtˑani-léˑi.
/t Any kingdom that fights by itself (on its own) cannot stand firm.
                                                                [a misunderstanding]
/k And if a kingdom be divided against itself, that kingdom cannot stand.

Mk 3.25 /b Ok a wekwam nevlahi muvtavkrbekc, ta kuski hetani lri.
/p óˑk=áˑ wíˑkˑəwam nihəláči mahtaˑkeˑyoˑwíˑkˑe, tá=áˑ káski-číˑtˑani-léˑi.
/t And if a house fights by itself, it would not be able to stand firm.   [as in 3.24]
/k And if a house be divided against itself, that house cannot stand.

Mk 3.26 /b Mavtuntw a mutakalatc vokyu ta kuski hetani lisee,
/p mahtántˑu=áˑ mahtaˑkaˑláˑtˑe hókaya, tá=áˑ káski-číˑtˑani-ləsˑíˑi.
/t If the devil fought against himself, he would not be able to stand strong.
/k And if Satan rise up against himself, [and be divided,] he cannot stand, [but hath an end.]

Mt 12.26 /b ta vuh a hetanisetwn sakemaokun.   [⟨sak-⟩ for /sɔˑkˑ-/]
/p tá=háč=áˑ [wə́nči-]čiˑtˑanəsˑíˑtoˑn sɔˑkˑiˑmaˑóˑkˑan?   [word missing]
/t How would his kingdom be made strong?
/k ... how shall then his kingdom stand?

Mt 12.27 /b Ne a ktiskaokc mavtuntwuk wunhi nu sakema mavtuntw,
/p ní·=á· ktəskaɔ́k·e mahtant·ó·wak wə́nči ná sa·k·í·ma mahtánt·u,
/t If I cast out devils by the king devil,
/k And if I by Beelzebub cast out devils,

/b awrni vuh ct wunhi kuski ktiskaoau mavtuntwu nrk knehanwaok?
/p awé·ni=háč=ét wwə́nči-káski-ktəskaɔwwá·ɔ mahtant·ó·wa né·k kəni·č·a·nəwá·ɔk?
/t by whom do you imagine your children are able to cast out devils?
/k by whom do your children cast them out?

/b Nani wunhi nrkumao kekejavkunemavumw.
/p nə́ni wə́nči / ne·k·əmá·ɔ / kkihkišahkəni·máhəmɔ(?)   [intended form uncertain]
/t Therefore / *they* / you are the judges of [indef. object missing].   [garbled]
/k therefore they shall be your judges.   (also Lk 11.19)

Lk 11.20 /b Jwk ne ktiskaok mavtuntwuk wunhi Krtanitwet muntwakun   [⟨-aok⟩ for ⟨-aokc⟩]
/p šúkw ní· ktəskaɔ́k·e mahtant·ó·wak wə́nči ke·tanət·ó·wi·t mɔnt·uwwá·k·an,
/t But if *I* cast out devils by the spiritual power of God,
/k But if I with the finger of God cast out devils,

/b javakia Krtanitwet sokemaokun prxosekakwnro.   [⟨prxoseka-‖kwnro⟩ for ⟨kp-⟩]
/p šáxahki=á· ke·tanət·ó·wi·t sɔ·k·i·ma·ɔ́·k·an kpe·x·o·shika·k·o·né·ɔ.
/t it would certainly be true that the kingdom of God has come near you.
/k no doubt the kingdom of God is come upon you.

Mt 12.29 /b Jita ta vuh a wunhi kuski awrn tumekrn hetaniset linw weket
/p ší=tá, tá=háč=á· wwə́nči-káski- awé·n -təmí·k·e·n či·t·anə́s·i·t lə́nu wí·k·i·t
(p. 70) /t Or, how would anyone be able to enter the house of a strong man
/k Or else how can one enter into a strong man's house,

/b ok paletaon tclathrswakun?
/p ɔ́·k -palí·taɔ·n təlač·e·s·əwá·k·an?
/t and destroy his possessions?
/k and spoil his goods,

/b Kcnh a vetami kavpelintc nu hetaniset linw, nu kcnh kuski paletaon.
/p kə́nč=á· hítami kaxpi·lə́nte ná či·t·anə́s·i·t lə́nu, ná kə́nč káski-palí·taɔ·n.
/t Only if the strong man was first tied up, then they could be destroyed.
/k except he first bind the strong man? and then he will spoil his house.

Lk 11.21 /b Hetaniset linw krkw kulinifc wunhi kuski wli krnavketaq weket,
/p či·t·anə́s·i·t lə́nu kéku kələnínke wə́nči-káski-wə́li-ke·nahkí·ta·kw wí·k·i·t,
/t If the strong man carries something with which he can keep his house secure,
/k When a strong man armed keepeth his palace,

/b wli a lrlw tclathrswukun.
/p wə́li-=á· -lé·lu təlač·e·s·əwá·k·an.
/t his possessions would be safe.
/k his goods are in peace:

Lk 11.22
/b Jwk a alwe hetaniselethi qelwtaqkc,
/p šúkw=á· aləwí·i či·t·anəs·i·lí·č·i kwi·lo·t·á·kwke,
/t But if he is attacked by someone stronger,
/k But when a stronger than he shall come upon him, and overcome him,

/b nuh wthekwnwkwn nrkatufwp okh tukrkvamun lathrswakun. [⟨kwnw⟩ for /k·ənú/]
/p ná=č wči·k·ənúk·o·n ne·ka·t·ánkəp, ó·k=č tək·e·khámən lač·e·s·əwá·k·an.
/t then he will take away from him what he relied on and select some of the possesions.
/k he taketh from him all his armour wherein he trusted, and divideth his spoils.

Mt 12.30
/b Awrn mutu wifrlumet, nunul ta jifalet.
/p awé·n máta winké·ləmi·t, nánal=tá šinká·li·t.
/t Anyone who does not like me is one who hates me.
/k He that is not with me is against me;   (also Lk 11.23)

/b Ok awrn mutu wehi marnifc myrnasekc, nul ta jwk tusrlavtwn.   [⟨-kc⟩ for /-k·i/]
/p ó·k awé·n máta wíči-ma·e·nínke, ma·e·na·s·í·k·i, nál=tá šúkw tɔs·élahto·n.
/t And if anyone does not join in the harvest of what is harvested, he just scatters it.
/k and he that gathereth not with me scattereth abroad.   (Lk 11.23 without "abroad")

Mt 12.31
/b Nani wunhi ktclwvwmw,
/p nə́ni wə́nči ktəllúhəmɔ,
/t Therefore I say to you,
/k Wherefore I say unto you,

/b wrmi cntxrnaoki mutawswukun kuskih pavketrlintaw, ok mavtaptwnrokunu.
                                                              [⟨-taw⟩ for ⟨-tasw⟩]
/p wé·mi entxennáɔhki mahta·wsəwá·k·an káski-=č -pahki·t·e·ləntá·s·u, ó·k mahta·pto·ne·ó·k·ana.
/t All kinds of sins will possibly be forgiven, and also evil utterances.
/k All manner of sin and blasphemy shall be forgiven unto men:

/b Jwk awrn mavtaptwnrtc wunhi Pelset Manitw, ta pavketatamaoi.
/p šúkw awé·n mahta·pto·né·t·e wə́nči pí·lsi·t manə́t·u, tá=á· pahki·t·a·t·amaɔ́·i.
/t But if someone speaks evilly regarding the Holy Spirit, he would not be forgiven.
/k but the blasphemy against the Holy Ghost shall not be forgiven unto men.

Mt 12.32 /b Awrn hanaptwnalatc Wrqesifc linwu,
/p awé·n čana·pto·na·lá·t·e we·k·wi·s·ínki lə́nəwa,
/t If anyone speaks ill of the Son who is a man,
/k And whosoever speaketh a word against the Son of man,

/b kuskih puvketatumaon.
/p káski-=č -pahki·t·a·t·amáɔ·n.
/t it will be possible for him to be forgiven for it.
/k it shall be forgiven him:

/b Jwk awrn hanaptwnalatc Pelselethi Manitwu,
/p šúkw awé·n čana·pto·na·lá·t·e pi·lsi·lí·č·i manət·ó·wa.
/t But if anyone speaks ill of the Holy Spirit,
/k but whosoever speaketh against the Holy Ghost,

/b ta puvketatamaon b tali cntu lawsif jitu takok cntu lawsif,   [⟨-on⟩ for /-ɔ́·wən/]
/p tá=á· pahki·t·a·t·amaɔ́·wən yú táli entalá·wsink, ší=tá tákɔ·k entalá·wsink.
/t he will not be forgiven for it, in this world or in the next (*lit.*, other) world.
/k it shall not be forgiven him, neither in this world, neither in the world to come.

Mk 3.29 /b avih lenum rlumwqwnuku:
/p áhi-=č -lí·nam e·ləmo·k·wənák·a."
/t Bad things will happen to him for eternity."
/l but he is in danger of eternal damnation:

Mk 3.30 /b nuni tclan, rli lwrpanek Ktopetakw mavtuntwu.   [⟨Kt-⟩ for ⟨T-⟩]
/p nə́ni tə́la·n, é·li luwé·p·ani·k, "tɔp·i·tá·k·u mahtant·ó·wa."
/t He said that to them because they said, "He has a devil in him."
/kl Because they said, He hath an unclean spirit.

Mt 12.33 /b Wlisetc vetwq wlit eku wcnhckif.
/p "wələs·í·t·e hít·ukw, wələ́t íka wenčí·k·ink.
/t "If a tree is good, what grows from it is good.
/k Either make the tree good, and his fruit good;

/b Jitu mavheqi vetwq maheqi eku wcnhekif
/p ší=tá mahčí·kwi hít·ukw, mahčí·kwi íka wenčí·k·ink.
/t Or (if) a tree is bad, what grows from it is bad.
/k or else make the tree corrupt, and his fruit corrupt:

/b rli vetwq wavqwsw wunhi ni wunhekif.
/p é·li hít·ukw wwahkwə́s·u wə́nči ní wənčí·k·ink.
/t For a tree is known by what grows from it.
/k for the tree is known by his fruit.

Mt 12.34 /b Kelwu qejkomwruk tclvakrevmw;
/p ki·ló·wa kwi·škamǝwé·ɔk ktǝlhake·íhǝmɔ.
/t You are of the tribe of copperheads.
/k O generation of vipers,

/b Ta vuh a kwnhi kuski wrlvik krkw lwrn nrli mavhi liseun?
/p tá=háč=á· kúnči-káski- wé·lhik kéku -lúwe·n, né·li-máhči-lǝs·ian?
/t How would you (sg.) be able to say something good, when you are evil?
/k how can ye, being evil, speak good things?

/b Rli tuktu krkw awrn hwvatrlek wtrvif na nuni tclaptwnrn.   [⟨va⟩ for /hɔ/]
/p é·li tákta kéku awé·n čuhɔté·li·k wté·hink, ná=nǝni tǝla·ptó·ne·n.
/t For whatever fills someone's heart, that is how he speaks.
/k for out of the abundance of the heart the mouth speaketh.

Mt 12.35 /b Wrli liset linw wtrvif wrlvik rtrk wrlvik vufq wunheyw,
/p wé·li-lǝs·i·t lǝnu wté·hink wé·lhik é·te·k, wé·lhik=hánkw wǝnčí·ayu,
/t From the good that is in a good man's heart comes good,
/k A good man out of the good treasure of the heart bringeth forth good things:

/b ok mrhi liset linw wtrvif mrtvik rtrk, mrtvik vufq wunheyw;
/p ɔ·k méči-lǝs·i·t lǝnu wté·hink mé·thik é·te·k, mé·thik=hánkw wǝnčí·ayu.
/t and from the evil that is in a bad person's heart comes evil.
/k and an evil man out of the evil treasure bringeth forth evil things.

Mt 12.36 /b jwk ok ktclwvwmw,
/p šúkw ɔ́·k ktǝllúhǝmɔ,
/t But I also say to you,
/k But I say unto you,

/b wrmih cntxi awrn nwhqc aptwnalet ntwtamaonh rlkeqi mrkuni-kejqek.
     [⟨am⟩ for /ǝm/; ⟨mrk⟩ for /mǝk/]
|| /p wé·mi=č éntxi- awé·n nó·čkwe -a·pto·ná·li·t, ntɔ·t·ǝmáɔ·n=č
e·lkí·kwi-mǝkǝni-kí·škwi·k.
/t Every frivolous thing anyone says about me they will be asked about at the time of the last day.
/k That every idle word that men shall speak, they shall give account thereof in the day of judgment.

Mt 12.37 /b Rli ktaptwnakunu kwunhi wli lenumun,   [⟨kwunhi⟩ for ⟨kwnhi⟩ (below)]
/p é·li kta·pto·ná·k·ana kúnči-wǝli-lí·namǝn.
/t For because of your words good things happen to you,
/k For by thy words thou shalt be justified,

/b ok ktaptwnakunu a kwnhi avi lenamun. ‖
/p ó·k kta·pto·ná·k·ana=á· kúnči-áhi-lí·namən."
/t and because of your words bad things would happen to you."
/k and by thy words thou shalt be condemned.

Mt 12.38 /b Nu alintc rlrkvekrthek ok Paliseeuk tclawao.
(p. 71) /p ná a·lə́nte ehəle·khi·k·é·č·i·k ó·k †pa·ləsi·í·ok təlawwá·ɔ.
/t Then some of the scribes and Pharisees said to him,
/k Then certain of the scribes and of the Pharisees answered, saying,

/b Futu nrmvwmnu krkw nata wunheyek wunhih myairlintamrf.
/p "nkát·a-ne·mhúmǝna kéku ná·ta wǝnčí·ai·k, wə́nči-=č -maya·e·lə́ntamenk."
/t "We'd like to see something from you by which we will be certain."
/k Master, we would see a sign from thee.

Mt 12.39 /b Jwk Nhesus tclao
/p šúkw nčí·sas təlá·ɔ,
/t But Jesus said to them,
/k But he answered and said unto them,

/b Kelwu mrtaprethek rlvakrerq, nrtwnamrq myairlintamwakun;
/p "ki·ló·wa me·ta·p·e·í·č·i·k e·lhaké·ie·kw, ne·t·ó·name·kw maya·e·ləntaməwá·k·an.
/t "You of the tribe of evil people are ones who seek a confirmation (or assurance).
/k An evil and adulterous generation seeketh after a sign;

/b jwk takw peli myairlintamwakun mwelaeu;
/p šúkw takó· pí·li maya·e·ləntaməwá·k·an mwi·la·í·ɔ,
/t But he gave no other confirmation (or assurance) to them,
/k and there shall no sign be given to it,

/b nrnekanewrwsetpanu Nhonusu rlsetup xwva.
/p nehəni·k·a·ní·i-we·wsi·tpána †nčɔ·nás·a e·lsí·t·əp xó·ha.
/t except only what the prophet Jonas did.
/k but the sign of the prophet Jonas:

Mt 12.40 /b Nhonusu nuxi kejqc, ok nuxi tpwkwc xifwi namrsif lamavtc avpwp,
/p †nčɔ·nás·a náxi-kí·škwe ó·k náxi-tpó·kəwe xínkwi-namé·s·ink lá·mahte ahpó·p.
/t Jonas was in the belly of a whale (lit., large fish) for three days and three nights.
/k For as Jonas was three days and three nights in the whale's belly;

/b nuh ok nc tcli linw wrqesif nuxi kejqc, ok nuxi tpwkwc lamvakec avpen.
/p ná=č ó·k nə́
      təli- lənu we·k·wí·s·ink náxi-kí·škwe ó·k náxi-tpó·kəwe la·mhákie -ahpí·n.
/t In that same way also shall the man who is the Son be inside the earth for three days and three nights.
/k so shall the Son of man be three days and three nights in the heart of the earth.

Mt 12.41 /b Mckuni-kejqekc Niniprewfu kotinh ktalumi amwenru
/p məkə́ni-ki·škwí·k·e †ninipe·i·yúnka kwə́t·ən=č ktáləmi-a·mwi·né·ɔ.
/t On the last day the ancient Ninevites and you shall rise up all at the same time.
/k The men of Nineveh shall rise in judgment with this generation,

/b kmexunemkwaukh,
/p kəmi·x·ani·mkəwá·ɔk=č,
/t They shall shame you by what they say,
/k and shall condemn it:

/b rli wlistaotetup Nhonusu,
/p é·li-wələstaɔhtí·t·əp †nčɔ·nás·a,
/t as they believed Jonas,
/k because they repented at the preaching of Jonas;

/b jwk nu b topen rlweliset Nhonusu.
/p šúkw ná=yú tɔ́p·i·n e·ləwí·i-lə́s·i·t †nčɔ·nás·a.
/t but here there is one who is greater than Jonas.
/k and, behold, a greater than Jonas is here.

Mt 12.42 /b Sakemaxqru jaonruf kwehih amwemkwu mckunr-kejqekc   [⟨-nr⟩ for ⟨-ni⟩]
/p "sa·k·i·ma·xkwé·ɔ ša·ɔné·yunk kəwíči-=č -a·mwi·mkúwa məkə́ni-ki·škwí·k·e,
/t "The queen in the south will rise up along with you on the last day
/k The queen of the south shall rise up in the judgment with this generation,

/b kmexunemkwuh,
/p kəmi·x·ani·mkúwa=č,
/t and will shame you,
/k and shall condemn it:

/b rli wekvokamekrk wifup moi puntufup Salomunu wlipwrokun,
/p é·li- wi·khɔkamí·k·e·k -wínkəp, mɔ́i-pəntánkəp †sa·lamána wələp·we·ɔ́·k·an.
/t for she came from the ends of the earth to hear the wisdom of Solomon,
/k for she came from the uttermost parts of the earth to hear the wisdom of Solomon;

/b jwk nu b topen rlweliset Solamunu.
/p šúkw ná=yú tɔ́p·i·n e·ləwí·i-lə́s·i·t †sa·lamána.
/t but here is one who is greater than Solomon.
/k and, behold, a greater than Solomon is here.

Mt 12.43 /b Neski manitw krthetc wunhi awrnif
/p "ní·ski-manə́t·u ke·č·í·t·e wə́nči awé·nink,
/t "When an unclean spirit goes out of someone,
/k When the unclean spirit is gone out of a man,

	/b	nu lovwmun cntu pifvokrk tcli a alaxemwen, jwk qelalisw;	[⟨l-⟩ for /wəl-/]
	/p	ná wəlo·hómən énta-penkhóke·k, tə́li-=á· -ala·x·í·mwi·n, šúkw kwí·la-lə́s·u.	
	/t	he (the spirit) passes by dry land, in order to rest, but is unsuccessful.	
	/k	he walketh through dry places, seeking rest, and findeth none.	

Mt 12.44 /b nu tclwrn eku ntcli ktuke wrmu,
/p ná tə́ləwe·n, 'íka ntə́li-ktə́k·i wé·ma.'
/t Then he says, 'I'm going back where I came from.'
/k Then he saith, I will return into my house from whence I came out;

/b eku pratc wnrmun li alaxut, hekvasw, ok wletasw.
/p íka pe·á·t·e, wəné·mən lí-aláx·at, -či·khá·s·u, ó·k -wəli·tá·s·u.
/t When he gets there, he sees it that it is empty, swept out, and fixed up.
/k and when he is come, he findeth it empty, swept, and garnished.

Mt 12.45 /b Nu pwrjwaun nejaj rlweliselethi manitwuk,   [⟨-aun⟩ for /-a·n/]
/p ná pwé·š·əwa·n ní·š·a·š e·ləwí·i-ləs·i·lí·č·i manət·ó·wak.
/t Then he brings seven greater devils.
/k Then goeth he, and taketh with himself seven other spirits more wicked than himself,

/b tavqe ekali punheuk, nunu wekenru;
/p tahkwí·i íkali pənčí·ɔk, ná=nə wwi·k·i·né·ɔ.
/t They go in together, and there they live.
/k and they enter in and dwell there:

/b nu kcnh nu linw alwe muvhi lro vokif rlrkup vetami.
/p ná kə́nč ná lə́nu aləwí·i máhči-lé·w hók·enk e·lé·k·əp hítami.
/t Then it is worse in that man's body than it had been at first.
/k and the last state of that man is worse than the first.

/b Nuh ok nc lrih bni mutapret rlvakret.   [⟨lri⟩ for /lé·=/; ⟨mut-⟩ for ⟨mrt-⟩]
/p ná=č ó·k ná lé·=č yó·ni me·t·a·p·é·i·t e·lhaké·i·t."
/t That is also how it shall be for this wicked tribe."
/k Even so shall it be also unto this wicked generation.

Lk 11.27 /b Nrli krkw lwrtup, mawsw xqr amufexswp tclaol,
/p né·li- kéku -luwé·t·əp, má·wsu xkwé· amankí·xso·p, təlá·ɔl,
/t As he was speaking, a certain woman raised her voice and said to him,
/k ... as he spake these things, a certain woman of the company lifted up her voice, and said unto him,

/b Wlapcnsw lamavtc ke rpeanup, ok nwnakunu ke nwnatamunrp.   [⟨-nrp⟩ for ⟨-nup⟩]
/p "wəla·p·ensó·u lá·mahte kí· e·p·iánəp, ó·k no·ná·k·ana kí· no·na·t·amánəp."
/t "Blessed is the womb *you* were in, and the breasts *you* nursed from."
/k Blessed is the womb that bare thee, and the paps which thou hast sucked.

Lk 11.28	/b	Jwk lwr, alwt alwe bk puntufek Krtanitwet toptonakun, ok wrlvataqek.
	/p	šúkw lúwe·, "aló·t aləwí·i yó·k pəntánki·k ke·tanət·ó·wi·t tɔ·pto·ná·k·an, ɔ́·k we·lhatá·k·wi·k."
	/t	But he said, "Actually, moreso these who hear the word of God and keep it."
	/k	But he said, Yea rather, blessed are they that hear the word of God, and keep it.

Mt 12.46	/b	Nrli qeaqi krkw lat rpelethi,
	/p	né·li- kwiá·kwi kéku -lá·t e·p·i·lí·č·i,
	/t	While he was still talking to those who were there,
	/k	While he yet talked to the people,

	/b	puna kovrsu, ok wemavteny weqrlif nepwuk kotu nrvkw.
	/p	pənáh, kɔhé·s·a, ɔ́·k wi·mahtí·nay †wi·kwé·link ni·p·ó·wak, kót·a-né·yku.
	/t	well, here his mother and also his brothers were standing outside and wanted to see him.
	/k	behold, his mother and his brethren stood without, desiring to speak with him.

Mt 12.47	/b	Nu awrn tclan,
	/p	ná awé·n təla·n,
	/t	Then someone said to him,
	/k	Then one said unto him,

	/b	Kavrs ta ekali ok kxesmusuk weqrlif kutu nrvkwk.	[⟨we-‖qrlif⟩]
	/p	kkáhe·s=tá íkali ɔ́·k kxi·s·əməs·ak †wi·kwe·link kkát·a-né·yko·k.	
	/t	"Your mother and your younger brothers outside want to see you.	
	/k	Behold, thy mother and thy brethren stand without, desiring to speak with thee.	

Mt 12.48	/b	Jwk navkwmao tclao,
(p. 72)	/p	šúkw nɔxko·má·ɔ, təlá·ɔ,
	/t	But he answered him and said to him,
	/k	But he answered and said unto him that told him,

	/b	Awrn vuh nu favrs? Ok awrnek vuh nuxesmusuk?
	/p	"awé·n=háč ná nkáhe·s? ɔ́·k awé·ni·k=háč naxi·s·əməs·ak?"
	/t	"Who is my mother? And who are my younger brothers?"
	/k	Who is my mother? and who are my brethren?

Mt 12.49	/b	Nu tcli tpavon rkrkemathi, lwri	[⟨lwri⟩ for /lúwe·/]
	/p	ná təli-tpáhɔ·n e·k·e·ki·má·č·i, lúwe·,	
	/t	And with that he pointed to his disciples, and he said,	
	/k	And he stretched forth his hand toward his disciples, and said,	

	/b	Jr nu favrs ok nuxesmusuk!
	/p	"šé· ná nkáhe·s ɔ́·k naxi·s·əməs·ak.
	/t	"There is my mother and my brothers.
	/k	Behold my mother and my brethren!

Mt 12.50 /b Rli cntxi nc lisethek rletrvat Nwx rpet osavkamc,
/p é·li éntxi- nə́ -ləs·í·č·i·k e·li·t·é·ha·t nó·x é·p·i·t ɔ·s·áhkame,
/t For, as many as do what my father who is inheaven wants done,
/k For whosoever shall do the will of my Father which is in heaven,

/b nunulek nrk nemavtisuk ok ntoxqrbmuk, ok favrs.
/p nanáli·k né·k ni·mahtəs·ak, ɔ́·k ntuxkwé·yəmak, ɔ́·k nkáhe·s."
/t they are my brothers, and my sisters, and my mother."
/k the same is my brother, and sister, and mother.

Chapter 44 (pp. 72-77). [L. section 43.] (Matthew 13.1-58; Luke 8.11 [part]; Mark 4.26-58, 6.5 [part]-6; cf. Mark 4.14ff, Luke 8.11ff.)

Mt 13.1 /b Na ncki kejqek Nhesus krthetc wunhi wekwavmif,
/p ná-néke kí·škwi·k nčí·sas ke·č·í·t·e wə́nči wi·k·əwáhəmink,
/t That same day, after Jesus went out of the house,
/k The same day went Jesus out of the house,

/b eku lumutupwp eapri munwprkwf.
/p íka ləmátahpo·p ya·p·é·i mənəp·é·k·unk.
/t he sat on the shore of the sea.
/k and sat by the sea side.

Mt 13.2 /b Xrli awrn eku macvlrp, wunhi mwxolif li pwsen nanc wlumuvtupen;
/p xé·li awé·n íka ma·éhəle·p, wwə́nči- mux·ó·link -pó·s·i·n, ná=nə wələmahtáp·i·n.
/t Many people gathered there, so he got into a boat and sat there.
/k And great multitudes were gathered together unto him, so that he went into a ship, and sat;

/b ok nrk mrxrlkek eapri ncpwpanck.
/p ɔ́·k né·k me·x·é·lki·k ya·p·é·i ni·p·ó·p·ani·k
/t And the crowd stood on the shore.
/k and the whole multitude stood on the shore.

Mt 13.3 /b Nu xrlrnovk krkw tclapani nrl rnwntvakrokun; [⟨xrlrnovk⟩ for ⟨xrlrnaovki⟩]
/p ná xe·lennáɔhki kéku təlá·p·ani né·l e·nunthake·ó·k·an,
/t Then he told those people many things as parables,
/k And he spake many things unto them in parables,

/b lwrp punu srnevet my srnevep;
/p lúwe·p, "pənáh, se·níhi·t mái-se·níhi·p.
/t saying, "Now, a sower went to sow.
/k saying, Behold, a sower went forth to sow;

Mt 13.4	/b	nrli srnevet alintc xkunem muvtrxun joexkunai;
	/p	né·li-se·níhi·t, a·lə́nte xkáni·m mahté·x·ən šɔi·xkanáe.
	/t	As he sowed, some seeds fell at the side of the road.
	/k	And when he sowed, some seeds fell by the way side,
	/b	nu hwlinsuk ponro mwkinvomunro.
	/p	ná čo·lə́nsak pɔ·né·ɔ, mwək·ənhaməné·ɔ.
	/t	Birds then came and picked them all up.
	/k	and the fowls came and devoured them up:
Mt 13.5	/b	Alintc muvtrxun cntu asinekri cntu mutu kvwpavkexif vaki,
	/p	a·lə́nte mahté·x·ən énta ahsəni·ké·i, énta- máta -khupahkí·x·ink hák·i,
	/t	Some landed where it was stony, where the earth was not deep (*lit.*, thick),
	/k	Some fell upon stony places, where they had not much earth:
	/b	ok apwe sakun, rli mutu kvwpukexif vake.
	/p	ɔ́·k á·p·əwi-sá·k·ən, é·li- máta -khupahkí·x·ink hák·i.
	/t	and they easily sprouted, as the earth was not deep.
	/k	and forthwith they sprung up, because they had no deepness of earth:
Mt 13.6	/b	Jwk mrhi alumi vwqruf tuntakc nu jaosktr,
	/p	šúkw mé·či é·ləmi- hukwé·yunk -təntá·k·e, ná šaɔ́skte·, [⟨alumi⟩ for ⟨rlumi⟩]
	/t	But after the sun began to get high in the sky, they wilted.
	/k	And when the sun was up, they were scorched;
	/b	ok xun takw hwpvikwe nani wunhi jaosktr.
	/p	ɔ́·k=xán takó· čəphiko·wí·i, ná=ní wə́nči-šaɔ́skte·.
	/t	They had no roots, see, and that is why they wilted.
	/k	and because they had no root, they withered away.
Mt 13.7	/b	Ok alintc muvtrxun cntu kawnjekrk;
	/p	ɔ́·k a·lə́nte mahté·x·ən énta-ka·wənší·ke·k.
	/t	And some landed among brambles.
	/k	And some fell among thorns;
	/b	nu nrk kawunjuk rlumevkevtetc, tolsqrkamunro. [⟨-mevkevt-⟩ for ⟨-mekevt-⟩]
	/p	ná né·k ka·wə́nšak e·ləmi·k·ihtí·t·e, tɔlskwe·kaməné·ɔ.
	/t	And then when those brambles grew, they smothered(?) them.
	/k	and the thorns sprung up, and choked them:
Mt 13.8	/b	Jwk alintc muvtrxun cntu wlituk vaki, ok alumekun xuntki kejekun,
	/p	šúkw a·lə́nte mahté·x·ən énta-wəlɔ́t·ək hák·i, ɔ́·k aləmí·k·ən, xántki ki·š·í·k·ən.
	/t	But some landed where the ground was good and, growing up, eventually ripened.
	/k	But other fell into good ground, and brought forth fruit,

/b alintc kotxapxki txunw, ok alintc kotaj txentkc txunw, ok alintc xenxkc txunw.
             [⟨kotxapxki⟩ for ⟨kotapxki⟩; ⟨txentkc⟩: for ⟨txenxkc⟩]
/p a·lə́nte kwət·á·pxki txə́nu, ɔ́·k a·lə́nte kwə́t·a·š txí·nxke txə́nu, a·lə́nte xí·nxke txə́nu.
/t Of some there was a hundred (times?), and of some sixty, and of some thirty.
/k some an hundredfold, some sixtyfold, some thirtyfold.

Mt 13.9 /b Cntxi awrn vwetaoket puntufch.
/p éntxi- awé·n -hwitaɔ́k·i·t pəntánkeč."
/t Let everyone who has ears hear it."
/k Who hath ears to hear, let him hear.

Mt 13.10 /b Rkrkemathi wtxwkw, tclkw krkw vuh wunhi lat rnenvakrokun? [⟨en⟩ for /ənt/]
/p e·k·e·ki·má·č·i o·txúk·u, tə́lku, "kéku=háč wə́nči-lát e·nənthake·ɔ́·k·an?"
/t His disciples came to him, saying to him, "Why do you tell them a parable?"
/k And the disciples came, and said unto him, Why speakest thou unto them in parables?

Mt 13.11 /b Noxkwmao tclao, ok xun kwatulukrnro avkrkuntwakun osavkamri sakemaokanif;
/p nɔxko·má·ɔ, təlá·ɔ, "ɔ́·k=xán ko·wa·tələk·e·né·ɔ ahke·kəntəwá·k·an ɔ·s·ahkaméi-sa·k·i·ma·ɔ́·k·anink,
/t He answered them, saying to them, "See, you have also been allowed to know teachings about the kingdom of heaven,
/k He answered and said unto them, Because it is given unto you to know the mysteries of the kingdom of heaven,

/b Jwk bk mutu watwnro.   [⟨wn⟩ for /-o·wən-/]
/p šúkw yó·k máta o·wa·to·wəné·ɔ.
/t but these people do not know them.
/k but to them it is not given.

Mt 13.12 /b Rli cntxi awrn wlataoq, qeaqch xrli mela   [⟨taoq⟩ for /-ta·kw/]
/p é·li éntxi- awé·n -wəlá·ta·kw, kwiá·kwi=č xé·li mí·la·.
/t For, anyone who has (something) shall be given still much more.
/k For whosoever hath, to him shall be given, and he shall have more abundance:

/b ok cntxi awrn mutu wlataoq hekunanh cntxi wlataq.   [⟨taoq⟩ for /-ta·kw/]
/p ɔ́·k éntxi- awé·n máta -wəlá·ta·kw, čí·k·əna·n=č éntxi-wəlá·ta·kw.
/t And anyone who does not have (something) shall be deprived of all that he has.
/k but whosoever hath not, from him shall be taken away even that he hath.

Mt 13.13 /b Nanc ‖ uwnhi lan rnwntvakrokun,   [⟨ṳwnhi⟩ for ⟨nwnhi⟩]
/p ná=nə núnči-lá·n e·nunthake·ɔ́·k·an.
/t That is why I speak parables to them.
/k Therefore speak I to them in parables:

(p. 73) /b rli nrmvetet takw wnrmwnro, [⟨mwn⟩ for /moˑwən/]
 /p éˑliˑneˑmhítiˑt, takóˑ wəneˑmoˑwənéˑɔ,
 /t In seeing it they do not see it,
 /k because they seeing see not;

 /b ok puntametet takw pwntamwnro, [⟨-metet⟩ for ⟨-mevtet⟩]
 /p óˑk -pəntamíhtiˑt, takóˑ pwəntamoˑwənéˑɔ.
 /t and in hearing it, do not hear it.
 /k and hearing they hear not,

 /b ok takw wncnwstamwnro.
 /p óˑk takóˑ wənənoˑstamoˑwənéˑɔ.
 /t And they do not understand it.
 /k neither do they understand.

Mt 13.14 /b Vokywaif pokunhextwn ncnekanaptwnrtup Esrusu, cntu lwrtup;
 /p hɔkˑayəwáˑink pɔkˑančíˑxtoˑn nehəniˑkˑaˑnaˑptoˑnéˑtˑəp †iˑseˑyə́sˑa, éntaˑluwéˑtˑəp,
 /t In them Esaias fulfills his prophecy, where he said,
 /k And in them is fulfilled the prophecy of Esaias, which saith,

 /b Nrxpi puntamrq, kpuntamunrok jwk taa knunwstamunro,
    [⟨-nrok⟩ for ⟨-nroh⟩; ⟨-amunro⟩ probably for ⟨-amwnro⟩]
 /p néˑxpi-pəntameˑkw, kpəntamənéˑɔ=č, šúkw táˑáˑ kənənoˑstamoˑwənéˑɔ.
 /t With what you hear it with you shall hear it, but you will not understand it.
 /k By hearing ye shall hear, and shall not understand;

 /b ok nrxpi nrmrq knrmunroh, jwk ta kwli nrmwnro.
 /p óˑk néˑxpiˑnéˑmeˑkw, kəneˑmənéˑɔ=č, šúkw tá=áˑ kóˑliˑneˑmoˑwənéˑɔ.
 /t And with what you see it with you shall see it, but you will not see it clearly.
 /k and seeing ye shall see, and shall not perceive:

Mt 13.15 /b Rli bk wtrvwao alumi wthahselw, [⟨th⟩ for /č/; ⟨hs⟩ for /ts/ (or possibly /čs/)]
 /p éˑli yóˑk wtehəwáˑɔ álǝmi-wčaˑtsíˑlu,
 /t For the hearts of these people become hard,
 /k For this people's heart is waxed gross,

 /b ok vwetaoqaif jvot krkw pwntamunro, ok svopifwrxenwk [⟨q⟩ for /kˑəw/]
 /p óˑk hwitaɔkˑəwáˑink šhɔ́t kéku pwəntamənéˑɔ, óˑk shɔpinkweˑxˑíˑnoˑk,
 /t and there is a weakness in their ears for them to hear things, and they have their eyes closed,
 /k and their ears are dull of hearing, and their eyes they have closed;

 /b tclih mutu nrmaonro, ok tclih mutu puntamaonro,
 /p tə́li-=č máta -neˑmaˑwənéˑɔ, óˑk tə́li-=č máta -pəntamaˑwənéˑɔ,
 /t such that they will not see, and such that they will not hear,
 /k lest at any time they should see with their eyes, and hear with their ears,

	/b	ok tclih mutu nunwstamwnro,
	/p	ɔ·k tɔ́li-=č máta -nəno·stamo·wəné·ɔ,
	/t	and such that they will not understand,
	/k	and should understand with their heart,

	/b	ok tclih mutu wlamvetamwnro, ok ntclih mutu kekrvawun.
	/p	ɔ́·k tɔ́li-=č máta -wəla·mhitamo·wəné·ɔ, ɔ́·k ntɔ́li-=č máta -ki·k·e·há·wən.
	/t	and such that they will not believe, and such that I will not heal them.
	/k	and should be converted, and I should heal them.

Mt 13.16	/b	Jwk wlapcnswbu kijkifwao, rli wlapuntamarq,
	/p	"šúkw wəla·p·ensó·yəwa kəškinkəwá·ɔ, é·li-wəla·p·antamá·e·kw,
	/t	"But blessed are your eyes, for you can see well,
	/k	But blessed are your eyes, for they see:

	/b	ok kvetaoqao, rli wli puntamarq.	[⟨-q-⟩ for /k·əw/]
	/p	ɔ́·k khitaɔk·əwá·ɔ, é·li-wɔ́li-pəntamá·e·kw.	
	/t	and your ears, for you can hear well.	
	/k	and your ears, for they hear.	

Mt 13.17	/b	Rli kehe ktclwvwmw,
	/p	é·li khičɨ́·i ktəllúhəmɔ,
	/t	For, I tell you truly,
	/k	For verily I say unto you,

	/b	rli nrnekane wrwsetpanifu, ok jaxakawsetpanifu kotu nrmunro, krkw kelwu rlenamrq,	[⟨rli⟩ for ⟨xrli⟩ (KJV "many")]
	/p	xé·li nehəni·k·a·nɨ́·i-we·wsi·tpanínka ɔ́·k šaxahka·wsi·tpanínka kɔ́t·a-ne·mənéɔ kéku ki·ló·wa ehəlí·name·kw,	
	/t	Many ancient prophets and righteous ones desired to see the things that *you* see,	
	/k	That many prophets and righteous men have desired to see those things which ye see,	

	/b	jwk takw koski lenamwnro
	/p	šúkw takó· kɔ́ski-li·namo·wəné·ɔ,
	/t	but they were unable to see them,
	/k	and have not seen them;

	/b	ok kotu puntamunro krkw kelwu puntamrq;
	/p	ɔ́·k kɔ́t·a-pəntamənéɔ kéku ki·ló·wa pə́ntame·kw,
	/t	and they desired to hear the things *you* hear,
	/k	and to hear those things which ye hear,

	/b	jwk takw koski puntamwnro.
	/p	šúkw takó· kɔ́ski-pəntamo·wəné·ɔ.

| | /t | but were unable to hear them. |
| | /k | and have not heard them. |

Mt 13.18 /b Puntyeq bqc rncntvakrokun wunhi srneve.
/p "pə́ntai·kw yúkwe e·nənthake·ɔ́·k·an wə́nči se·níhi.
/t "Hear from me now the parable about the sower.
/k Hear ye therefore the parable of the sower.

Lk 8.11 /b Nuni xkunem toptwnakun Krtanitwet.
/p nə́ni xkáni·m tɔ·pto·ná·k·an ke·tanət·ó·wi·t.
/t That seed is the word of God.
/k ... The seed is the word of God.

Mt 13.19 /b Tamsi awrn puntufc nc aptwnakun, mutu nunwstamwqc;
/p tá·mse awé·n pəntánke nə́ a·pto·ná·k·an, máta nəno·stamó·k·we,
/t If someone sometime hears the word and does not understand it,
/k When any one heareth the word of the kingdom, and understandeth it not,

/b nu mavtuntw pon wrtunimun krkw mrtrxif.
/p ná mahtánt·u pɔ́·n, wwe·t·ənə́mən kéku me·t·é·x·ink.
/t then the devil comes and takes what falls to the ground.
/k then cometh the wicked one, and catcheth away that which was sown in his heart.

/b Nul nuni xkunem mrtrxif joexkunac.
/p nál nə́ni xkáni·m me·t·é·x·ink šɔi·xkanáe.
/t That is the seed that lands on the side of the road.
/k This is he which received seed by the way side.

Mt 13.20 /b Jwk nuni xkunem mrtrxif cntu asinekrk
/p šúkw nə́ni xkáni·m me·t·é·x·ink énta-ahsəní·ke·k,
/t But that seed that lands where it was stony,
/k But he that received the seed into stony places,

/b nul ok nuni, awrn puntufc nc aptwnakun nani avkrxkumi wrtunumun,
/p nál ɔ́·k nə́ni, awé·n pəntánke nə́ a·pto·ná·k·an, náni ahké·xkami wwe·t·ənə́mən.
/t that is the word that, when someone hears it, they immediately accept it,
/k the same is he that heareth the word, and anon with joy receiveth it;

[KJV "anon": RSV "immediately"]

Mt 13.21 /b nrlumu mulaji nevlahi hwpvikwei tali wtrvif.
/p né·ləma málahši nihəláči čəphiko·wí·i táli wté·hink,
/t It has not yet, as it were, taken root in his own heart,
/k Yet hath he not root in himself,

/b   Takiti jwk kulrlintuf.
/p   thakíti šúkw kəle·ləntank.
/t   what he holds to for only a little while.
/k   but dureth for a while:

/b   Jwk rlumi avatrkc sukwelyvtwakun wunhi nc aptwnakwn,
/p   šúkw é·ləmi-ahhaté·k·e sak·wi·laehtəwá·k·an wə́nči nə́ a·pto·ná·k·an,
/t   But when there begin to be persecutions because of the word,
/k   for when tribulation or persecution ariseth because of the word,

/b   nu jai motrlintumun.
/p   ná šá·e mɔt·e·ləntamən.
/t   then he suddenly has a negative opinion of it.
/k   by and by he is offended.

Mt 13.22 /b   Ok nc mrtrxif cntu kawunjekrk mulaji awrn puntufc nc aptwnakun
/p   "ɔ́·k nə́ me·t·é·x·ink énta-ka·wənší·ke·k málahši awé·n pəntánke nə́ a·pto·ná·k·an,
/t   "And that which lands among the brambles is as if someone hears the word,
/k   He also that received seed among the thorns is he that heareth the word;

/b   jwk somi wrmi krkw b ‖ tali xqetakameqc ok avoprokun tavi punyrlintamun
/p   šúkw sɔ́·mi wé·mi kéku yú táli xkwi·thakamí·k·we ɔ́·k ahɔ·p·e·ɔ́·k·an tɔ́hi-pəna·eləntamən,
/t   but he thinks much too much about everything here on earth and about wealth,
/k   and the care of this world, and the deceitfulness of riches, choke the word,

(p. 74) /b   wunhi mutu kuski wlekunwi nc aptwnakun.
/p   wə́nči máta káski-wəli·k·ənó·wi nə́ a·pto·ná·k·an.
/t   so that the word cannot grow well.
/k   and he becometh unfruitful.

Mt 13.23 /b   Jwk nc xkunem mrtrxif cntu wlituk vaki,
/p   šúkw nə́ xkáni·m me·t·é·x·ink énta-wəlát·ək hák·i,
/t   But the seed that lands where the ground is good,
/k   (1) But he that received seed into the good ground   [numbers = sequence in L.]

/b   ok kejekifc alintc kotapxki txunw, ok alintc kwtaj txenkc txunw, ok alintc xenxkc txunw,   [⟨txenkc⟩: for ⟨txenxkc⟩]
/p   ɔ́·k ki·š·i·k·ínke, a·lə́nte kwət·á·pxki txə́nu, ɔ́·k a·lə́nte kwə́t·a·š txí·nxke txə́nu, ɔ́·k a·lə́nte xí·nxke txə́nu,
/t   and when it is ripe, of some there is a hundred, and of some sixty, and of some thirty,
/k   (3) which also beareth fruit, and bringeth forth, some an hundredfold, some sixty, some thirty.

/b nul nuni awrn puntufc nc aptwakun, ok nunwstufc ok nanc rlsetc.
/p nál nə́ni awé·n pəntánke nə́ a·pto·ná·k·an, ɔ́·k nəno·stánke, ɔ́·k ná=nə e·lsí·t·e."
/t that is when someone hears the word, and understands it, and does that."
/k (2) is he that heareth the word, and understandeth it;

Mt 13.24 /b Lupi rnwntrakrokun tclao, lwri   [⟨tra⟩ for ⟨tva⟩; ⟨lwri⟩ for /lúwe·/]
/p lápi e·nunthake·ɔ́·k·an təlá·ɔ, lúwe·,
/t He told them another parable, saying,
/k Another parable put he forth unto them, saying,

/b osavkamri sakemaokun mulaji linw srnevet tokevakunif wrltuk xkunem,
/p "ɔ·s·ahkamé·i-sa·k·i·ma·ɔ́·k·an málahši lə́nu se·níhi·t tɔ·ki·há·k·anink wé·ltək xkáni·m.
/t "The kingdom of heaven is like a man who sowed good seed in his field.
/k The kingdom of heaven is likened unto a man which sowed good seed in his field:

Mt 13.25 /b jwk nrli kaet
/p šúkw né·li-kaí·t,
/t But while he slept,
/k But while men slept,

/b jifalkwki prlw ekali srnevelw maheqi xkunem, nu tcli pale an.
/p šinka·lkúk·i pé·lu, íkali se·nihí·lu mahčí·kwi-xkáni·m, ná təli- palí·i -á·n.
/t his enemy came and sowed bad seed there, and then he went away.
/k his enemy came and sowed tares among the wheat, and went his way.

Mt 13.26 /b Jwk mrhi sakifc nu vwet ok rlumi kejekefc,
/p šúkw mé·či sa·k·ínke nə́ hwí·t, ɔ́·k é·ləmi-ki·š·i·k·ínke,
/t But after the wheat had come up, and when it began to get ripe,
/k But when the blade was sprung up, and brought forth fruit,

/b nu ok alumi nrvkot nc maheqi xkunem.
/p ná ɔ́·k áləmi-né·ykɔt nə́ mahčí·kwi-xkáni·m.
/t then the bad seed also began to be visible.
/k then appeared the tares also.

Mt 13.27 /b Tamsi nu wrtvakevakunet wtxwkwn tolwkakunu, tclkw,
/p tá·mse ná we·thaki·há·k·ani·t o·txúk·o·n tɔlo·ká·k·ana, tə́lku,
/t At some point then the servants of the field owner came to him and said to him,
/k So the servants of the householder came and said unto him,

/b mutu vuh ksrnevei wrltuk xkunem ktakevakunif?
/p "máta=háč kse·nihí·i wé·ltək xkáni·m kta·ki·há·k·anink?
/t "Didn't you sow good seed in your field?
/k Sir, didst not thou sow good seed in thy field?

/b   Ta vuh nc wunheyw nrl maheqi skeko?
/p   tá=háč nə́ wənčí·ayu né·l mahčí·kwi-skí·kɔ?"
/t   Where did those weeds (*lit.*, bad grass) come from?"
/k   from whence then hath it tares?

Mt 13.28 /b   Tclao jifalet tcletwn.
/p   təlá·ɔ, "šinká·li·t təlí·to·n."
/t   He said to them, "My enemy (*lit.*, one who hates me) did it."
/k   He said unto them, An enemy hath done this.

/b   Tolwkakunu tclkw, Konu vuh a nmy pwpvwnimunrn.
/p   tɔlo·ká·k·ana, tə́lku, "kóna=háč=á· nəmái-pəphwə́nəmə́ne·n?"
/t   His servants said to him, "Would it be alright if we went and pulled them up?"
/k   The servants said unto him, Wilt thou then that we go and gather them up?

Mt 13.29 /b   Tclao ta,
/p   təlá·ɔ, "tá=á·,
/t   He said to them, "No,
/k   But he said, Nay;

/b   rli a tamsi pvwnumrqc nrl maheqi skeko vapi pvwnumrq nc vwet.
/p   é·li-=á· tá·mse, phwənəmé·k·we né·l mahčí·kwi-skí·kɔ, -hápi-phwə́nəme·kw nə́ hwí·t.
/t   for when you pull up the weeds, you could sometimes pull up the wheat with them.
/k   lest while ye gather up the tares, ye root up also the wheat with them.

Mt 13.30 /b   Konulenamwq, rle alumekunw eku pchi rlkeqi tomsjasek;   [⟨tomsj-⟩ for /təmš-/]
/p   kóna lí·namo·kw ellí·i aləmí·k·ənu íka péči e·lkí·kwi-təmšá·s·i·k.
/t   Let them both continue growing until the time when they are reaped.
/k   Let both grow together until the harvest:

/b   nunih lukveqi rlkeqi tomsjasek, ntclaokh tctomujifek,
                                     [⟨tomsj-⟩ for /təmš-/; ⟨-tomuj-⟩ for /-təməš-/]
/p   nə́ni=č ləkhíkwi e·lkí·kwi-təmšá·s·i·k, ntəlá·ɔk=č tehtəməš·ínki·k,
/t   At that time when they are reaped, I will say to the reapers,
/k   and in the time of harvest I will say to the reapers,

/b   Macvmwq vetami nrl maheqi skeko
/p   "ma·éhəmo·kw hítami né·l mahčí·kwi-skí·kɔ.
/t   "First gather the weeds.
/k   Gather ye together first the tares,

/b   kukxptwnroh ktclih lwsamunro;   [⟨sam⟩ for /s·əm/]
/p   kkəkxpto·né·ɔ=č, ktə́li-=č -lo·s·əməné·ɔ.

	/t	You must tie them in bundles in order to burn them.
	/k	and bind them in bundles to burn them:

	/b	jwk macvnumwq nc vwet li vwetekaonif. [for ⟨marnumwq⟩ (see *Glossary*)]
	/p	šúkw ma·é·nəmo·kw nə́ hwí·t lí hwi·ti·k·á·ɔnink."
	/t	But gather the wheat into the granary."
	/k	but gather the wheat into my barn.

Mk 4.26
- /b Lupi rnwnvakrokun tclao, lwri,
- /p lápi e·nunthake·ó·k·an təlá·ɔ, lúwe·,
- /t He told them another parable, saying,
- /k And he said,

- /b bqc bni rlenako osavkamri sakemaokun,
- /p "yúkwe yó·ni e·li·ná·k·ɔ ɔ·s·ahkamé·i·sa·k·i·ma·ó·k·an:
- /t "This is what the kingdom of heaven is like:
- /k So is the kingdom of God,

- /b mulaji linw vakevrtc xkunem tali vakif.
- /p málahši lə́nu haki·hé·t·e xkáni·m táli hák·ink,
- /t like a man when he plants seed in the earth,
- /k as if a man should cast seed into the ground;

Mk 4.27
- /b Nu peskrwune kawe ok kejqwne twke,
- /p ná pi·ske·wəní·i kawí·, ó·k ki·škwəní·i tó·ki·.
- /t Then by night he sleeps, and by day he is awake.
- /k And should sleep, and rise night and day,

- /b nu xkunem alumi sakun ok wlekun,
- /p ná xkáni·m áləmi-sá·k·ən, ó·k wəlí·k·ən.
- /t And then the seed sprouts up and grows well,
- /k and the seed should spring and grow up,

- /b jwk mutu myai watwn rlexif wunhi sakif;
- /p šúkw máta mayá·i o·wá·to·n e·lí·x·ink wə́nči-sá·k·ink.
- /t but he does not rightly know what was the reason why it sprouted.
- /k he knoweth not how.

Mk 4.28
- /b rli vaki vokif wunhi krkw kejekif;
- /p é·li- hák·i hɔ́k·enk wə́nči kéku -ki·š·í·k·ink,
- /t For things grow from the body of the earth,
- /k For the earth bringeth forth fruit of herself;

	/b	vetami puna kumpavko, nu kenh ketakw, nu kcnh otarw, nu ‖ kcnh kejekun vwet.
	/p	hítami pənáh kə́mpahkɔ, ná kə́nč khitá·kɔ, ná kə́nč ɔ·taé·yu, ná kə́nč ki·š·í·k·ən hwí·t.
	/t	first here are the leaves, then ears(?), then it blooms, then the wheat ripens.
	/k	first the blade, then the ear, after that the full corn in the ear.

Mk 4.29 /b Mrhi kejekifc nu jai tumjasw rli mrhi tpisqevlak. [⟨tum-|jasw⟩]
(p. 75) /p mé·či ki·š·i·k·ínke, ná šá·e təmšá·s·u, é·li- mé·či -tpəskwíhəla·k."
/t After it is ripe, then right away it is reaped, for the time has come."
/k But when the fruit is brought forth, immediately he putteth in the sickle, because the harvest is come.

Mt 13.31 /b Lupi peli rnwntvakrokun tclao lwr,
/p lápi pí·li-e·nunthake·ɔ́·k·an təlá·ɔ, lúwe·,
/t He told them yet another parable, saying,
/k Another parable put he forth unto them, saying,

/b osavkumri sakemakun, mulaji mostute mifqtit
/p "ɔ·s·ahkamé·i-sa·k·i·ma·ɔ́·k·an málahši †mɔstatí·i-mínkwtət
/t "The kingdom of heaven is like a little mustard seed,
/k The kingdom of heaven is like to a grain of mustard seed,

/b linw vakevrtc tali tokevakunif.
/p lə́nu haki·hé·t·e táli tɔ·ki·há·k·anink.
/t if a man plants it in his field.
/k which a man took, and sowed in his field:

Mt 13.32 /b Nul nuni mrkuni tufrtek xkunem wrmi cntxif xkunem,
/p nál nə́ni mé·k·əni-tanké·t·i·k xkáni·m wé·mi éntxink xkáni·m.
/t That is the smallest seed of all seeds.
/k Which indeed is the least of all seeds:

/b jwk kejekifc nul nuni alwe xifwi wrmi cntxif skeko,
/p šúkw ki·š·i·k·ínke, nál nə́ni aləwí·i xínkwi wé·mi éntxink skí·kɔ,
/t But when it is grown, that is the largest of all grasses,
/k but when it is grown, it is the greatest among herbs,

/b mulaji vetkwtit wunhi kuski hwlinsuk naovlavtet twvuntitif. [⟨vunt⟩ for ⟨vnut⟩]
/p málahši hitkwə́t·ət, wə́nči-káski- čo·lə́nsak -naɔhəláhti·t tuhənət·ə́t·ink."
/t like a small tree, so that birds can alight on the little branches."
/k and becometh a tree, so that the birds of the air come and lodge in the branches thereof.

Mt 13.33 /b Lupi peli rnwnvakrokun tclao lwri
/p lápi pí·li-e·nunthake·ɔ́·k·an təlá·ɔ, lúwe·,

/t He told them another parable, saying,
/k Another parable spake he unto them;

/b osavkamri sakemaokun mulaji pcpastrk
/p "ɔ·s·ahkamé·i-sa·k·i·ma·ɔ́·k·an málahši pehpá·ste·k,
/t "The kingdom of heaven is like yeast,
/k The kingdom of heaven is like unto leaven,

/b xqr wrtunifc eku vataqc cntu nuxrnaoki vatrk lwkut,
/p xkwé· we·t·ənínke, íka hatá·k·we énta- naxennáɔhki -hát·e·k ló·kat,
/t when a woman takes it and puts it in three batches of flour,
/k which a woman took, and hid in three measures of meal,

/b na wrmi pastro.
/p ná wé·mi pa·sté·ɔ."
/t and then they all rise."
/k till the whole was leavened.

Mt 13.34 /b Wrmi bl lwrokunu rncntvakrokun Nhesus tclanrp
/p wé·mi yó·l luwe·ɔ́·k·ana e·nənthake·ɔ́·k·an nčí·sas təlá·ne·p;
/t All these sayings Jesus told them as parables;
/k All these things spake Jesus unto the multitude in parables;

/b tcxi jwk rncntvakrokun tclapanek.   [⟨tclapanek⟩ for ⟨tclapanel⟩]
/p téxi šúkw e·nənthake·ɔ́·k·an təlá·p·ani·l,
/t he only ever told them parables,
/k and without a parable spake he not unto them:

[The corner is torn off pages 75-76 (affecting Mt 13.35-42, 47-54); the text was taken from this and the 1906 reprint, later checked against the KHS copy.]

Mt 13.35 /b Wunhi pavkunhi lrk nrnekanewrwsetpani toptwnaknu rlwrtc;
                                    [⟨-pani⟩ for ⟨-panu⟩; ⟨-knu⟩ for ⟨-kunu⟩]
/p wənči-pahkánči-lé·k nehəni·k·a·ní·i-we·wsi·tpána tɔ·pto·ná·k·ana, e·ləwé·t·e,
/t so that the words of the prophet were fulfilled, when he said,
/k That it might be fulfilled which was spoken by the prophet, saying,

/b Ntaptwnc rnwntvakrokunu;
/p "nta·ptó·ne e·nunthake·ɔ́·k·ana;
/t "I speak parables;
/k I will open my mouth in parables;

/b ok ntukunwtumunh, mutu vuji awrn wrotaq wewuntvakameq.
/p ɔ́·k ntak·ənó·t·əmən=č, máta háši awé·n we·ɔ́·ta·kw wi·wənthákami·kw."
/t and I shall tell what no one has ever known since the beginning of the world."
/k I will utter things which have been kept secret from the foundation of the world.

Mt 13.36 /b　Mrhi Nhesus marvlalethi rlatc luxwrxwrq, nu wekwavmif ton.
　　　　/p　mé·či nčí·sas ma·ehəla·lí·č·i e·lá·t·e, "laxwé·x·we·kw," ná wi·k·əwáhəmink tó·n.
　　　　/t　After Jesus told those gathered to disperse, he went to the house.
　　　　/k　Then Jesus sent the multitude away, and went into the house:

　　　　/b　Rkrkemathi wtxwkw tclawao,
　　　　/p　e·k·e·ki·má·č·i o·txúk·u, təlawwá·ɔ,
　　　　/t　His disciples went to him, and they said to him,
　　　　/k　and his disciples came unto him, saying,

　　　　/b　Wrehextwl nc rnwnvakrokun, maheqi skeq hakevakunif.
　　　　/p　we·i·č·í·xto·l nɔ́ e·nunthake·ɔ́·k·an mahčí·kwi·skí·kw haki·há·k·anink."
　　　　/t　"Explain the parable of the weeds in the field."
　　　　/k　Declare unto us the parable of the tares of the field.　　　　[RSV "Explain to us"]

Mt 13.37 /b　Nhesus noxkwmao, tclao.
　　　　/p　nčí·sas nɔxko·má·ɔ, təlá·ɔ,
　　　　/t　Jesus answered them, saying to them,
　　　　/k　He answered and said unto them,

　　　　/b　Nani srnevet wrltuk xkunem nul nuni linw wrqesif,
　　　　/p　"náni se·níhi·t wé·ltək xkáni·m, nál náni lɔ́nu we·k·wí·s·ink.
　　　　/t　"The one who sowed the good seed, that is the man who is the Son.
　　　　/k　He that soweth the good seed is the Son of man;

Mt 13.38 /b　nuni vakevakun nul nuni prmvakamekrk
　　　　/p　nə́ni haki·há·k·an, nál nə́ni pe·mhakamí·k·e·k;
　　　　/t　the field, that is the world;
　　　　/k　The field is the world;

　　　　/b　nuni wrltuk xkunem nunulck nrk wrlilisthek,　　　　[⟨-listh-⟩ for ⟨-liseth-⟩]
　　　　/p　nə́ni wé·ltək xkáni·m, nanáli·k né·k wé·li·ləs·í·č·i·k;
　　　　/t　the good seed, that is the righteous;　　　　　　　　　[lit., 'those are']
　　　　/k　the good seed are the children of the kingdom;

　　　　/b　ok nc maheqi xkunem, nunulek nrk mrtawsethek.
　　　　/p　ɔ́·k nɔ́ mahčí·kwi-xkáni·m, nanáli·k né·k me·t·a·wsí·č·i·k.
　　　　/t　and the bad seed, that is the sinners.　　　　　　　　　[lit., 'those are']
　　　　/k　but the tares are the children of the wicked one;

Mt 13.39 /b　Nrli jifalkwki srnivet nu nul nu mavtuntw,　　　　[⟨nu nul⟩ for ⟨nunul⟩]
　　　　/p　né·li šinka·lkúk·i se·níhi·t, nánal ná mahtánt·u;
　　　　/t　The enemy of the sower, that is the devil;
　　　　/k　The enemy that sowed them is the devil;

/b rlkeqi tumjasek nul nuni rlkeqih alu vatrk vaki,
/p e·lkí·kwi-təmšá·s·i·k, nál nəni e·lkí·kwi-=č -ála-hát·e·k hák·i;
/t the time when it is reaped, that is the time when the world shall cease to exist;
/k the harvest is the end of the world;

/b nrk tctomujifek, nu nulek nrk osavkamri rvalokalinhek.
/p né·k tehtəməš·ínki·k, nanáli·k né·k ɔ·s·ahkamé·i ehalo·ka·lə́nči·k.
/t the ones that reap it, those are the heavenly messengers (angels).
/k and the reapers are the angels.

Mt 13.40 /b Rlkeqi myrvasek nrl maheqi skeko ok lwsasek
/p e·lkí·kwi-ma·ehá·s·i·k né·l mahčí·kwi-skí·kɔ ɔ́·k -lo·s·á·s·i·k,
/t In the same way that the weeds are gathered and burned,
/k As therefore the tares are gathered and burned in the fire;

/b nunih lro rlkeqi alu vatrk b prmvakamekrk.
/p nəni=č lé·w e·lkí·kwi-ála-hát·e·k yú pe·mhakamí·k·e·k.
/t that is what shall happen at the time this world ceases to exist.
/k so shall it be in the end of this world.

Mt 13.41 /b Linw Wrqesif pwrtalwkalaoh rvalwkalathi
/p lə́nu we·k·wí·s·ink pwe·t·alo·ka·lá·ɔ=č ehalo·ka·lá·č·i;
/t The man who is the Son shall send down his angels;
/k The Son of man shall send forth his angels,

/b mocvowaoh wunhi wsakemaokunif
/p mɔ·ehɔwwá·ɔ=č wə́nči wsa·k·i·ma·ɔ́·k·anink
/t they shall gather from his kingdom
/k and they shall gather out of his kingdom

/b wrmi cntxi pepalalwkaselethi ok mrtawselethi.
/p wé·mi éntxi-pihpalalo·ka·s·i·li·č·i ɔ́·k me·t·a·wsi·lí·č·i,
/t all the criminals and sinners,
/k all things that offend, and them which do iniquity;

Mt 13.42 /b Tclih eku lanevenro tuntre-kaonif,   [⟨lane-‖venro⟩]
/p tə́li-=č íka -lanihi·né·ɔ tənte·i·k·á·ɔnink,
/t in order to cast them into a "furnace,"
/k And shall cast them into a furnace of fire:

(p. 76) /b cntuh muxavolamwitet, ok cntuh kukamwkuntamivtet wepetwao.
/p énta-=č -maxahɔla·mwíhti·t, ɔ́·k énta-=č -kək·amo·kantamíhti·t wi·p·i·t·əwá·ɔ.
/t where they will scream loudly, and where they will "gnash" their teeth.
/k there shall be wailing and gnashing of teeth.

Mt 13.43 /b Nuh nrk javakaosethek wosulrxenunro,
/p ná=č né·k šaxahka·wsí·č·i·k wɔ·s·əle·x·i·nəné·ɔ,
/t Then the righteous shall shine,
/k Then shall the righteous shine forth,

/b mulajih kejwx eku wsavkamaokun Wxwao.   [⟨-savkam-⟩ for ⟨-sakem-⟩]
/p málahši=č kí·š·o·x íka wsa·k·i·ma·ɔ́·k·an o·x·əwá·ɔ.
/t like the sun on their father's kingdom.
/k as the sun in the kingdom of their Father.

/b Awrn wrvetaoket puntufch.
/p awé·n we·hitaɔ́k·i·t pəntánkeč.
/t Let anyone who has ears hear it.
/k Who hath ears to hear, let him hear.

Mt 13.44 /b Lupi, Osavkamri sakemaokun, mulaji kuntvatwfc lahrswakun vakevakunif;
/p "lápi, ɔ·s·ahkamé·i-sa·k·i·ma·ɔ́·k·an málahši kanthatúnke lač·e·s·əwá·k·an haki·há·k·anink.
/t "Again, the kingdom of heaven is like when possessions are hidden in a field.
/k Again, the kingdom of heaven is like unto treasure hid in a field;

/b tamsi vufq linw mrxkufc hetkwsw vufq
/p tá·mse=hánkw lə́nu me·xkánke, či·tkwə́s·u=hánkw.
/t When at some point a man has found it, he keeps silent.
/k the which when a man hath found, he hideth,

/b ta tclwrwun, rli ave wlenuf
/p tá=á· tələwé·wən é·li-áhi-wəlí·nank.
/t He won't talk about how he admires it a lot.
/k and for joy thereof

/b my mvalumaon wrmi krkw nrvlatuf, nu namovlemun nc vakevakun.   [⟨na-|mo⟩]
/p mái-mhalamáɔ·n wé·mi kéku nehəlá·t·ank; nána mɔ́həlamən nə́ haki·há·k·an.
          [⟨nu na-|⟩: nána (1) 'then']
/t He goes and sells everything he owns; and then he buys that field.
/k goeth and selleth all that he hath, and buyeth that field.

Mt 13.45 /b Lupi, Osavkamri sakemaokun mulaji mcmvalamwut   [⟨-mwut⟩ for ⟨-mwnt⟩]
/p "lápi, ɔ·s·ahkamé·i-sa·k·i·ma·ɔ́·k·an málahši memhálamunt
/t "Again, the kingdom of heaven is like a merchant
/k Again, the kingdom of heaven is like unto a merchant man,

/b nrtwnufc krkw rvooteki;
/p ne·t·o·nánke kéku ehɔ·ɔhtí·k·i.
/t when he looked for things of great value.
/k seeking goodly pearls:

Text, Transcription, and Translation

Mt 13.46 /b   mrhi mrxkufc koti, nu my mvalumaon wrmi krkw nrvlatuf
         /p   mé·či me·xkánke kwɔ́t·i, ná mái-mhalamɔ́·n wé·mi kéku nehəlá·t·ank;
         /t   After he found one, then he went and sold everything he owned;
         /k   Who, when he had found one pearl of great price, went and sold all that he had,

         /b   nu movlumun.
         /p   ná mɔ́hǝlamǝn.
         /t   and then he bought it.
         /k   and bought it.

Mt 13.47 /b   Lupi, Osavkamri sakemaokun mulaji, avkonekun rlanivif munwprkwf
         /p   "lápi, ɔ·s·ahkamé·i-sa·k·i·ma·ɔ́·k·an málahši ahkɔ·ní·k·an e·laníhink mǝnǝp·é·k·unk.
         /t   "Again, the kingdom of heaven is like a net that is thrown into the sea.
         /k   Again, the kingdom of heaven is like unto a net, that was cast into the sea,

         /b   wrmi cntxrnaokisethek namrsuk tovwnwkwnro,
         /p   wé·mi entxennaɔhkǝs·í·č·i·k namé·s·ak tɔhwǝnuk·o·né·ɔ.
         /t   It caught fish of every kind.
         /k   and gathered of every kind:

Mt 13.48 /b   mrhi hovatrkc nu eapri lwxotwn,
         /p   mé·či čuhɔté·k·e, ná ya·p·é·i lúxɔhto·n.
         /t   After it was full, then it was pulled to the shore.
         /k   Which, when it was full, they drew to shore,

         /b   nu mrjvakrvtetc pwepenanro, namrsu   [namrsu (KHS); reprint ⟨na nrsu⟩]
         /p   ná me·šhakehtí·t·e pwi·p·i·na·né·ɔ namé·s·a.
         /t   Then, after they sat down, they looked over the fish to select them.
         /k   and sat down,

         /b   wrlselethi tovulanro rvalavtet, ok mutu wrlselethi pokelawao.
                                                 [mutu | wrlselethi (KHS); reprint ⟨mutu wrise⟩]
         /p   we·lsi·lí·č·i tɔhǝla·né·ɔ ehhaláhti·t, ɔ́·k máta we·lsi·lí·č·i pɔk·i·lawwá·ɔ.
         /t   The good ones they put in what they always put them in, and the bad ones they discarded.
         /k   and gathered the good into vessels, but cast the bad away.

Mt 13.49 /b   Nuni lenakot weqrkc vaki,
         /p   "nɔ́ni li·ná·k·ɔt wi·kwé·k·e hák·i.
         /t   "That is what it is like when the world ends.
         /k   So shall it be at the end of the world:

/b   prokh rvalwkalinhek wunhi osavkumc,
/p   pé·ɔk=č ehalo·ka·lə́nči·k wə́nči ɔ·s·áhkame;
/t   Angels shall come from heaven;
/k   the angels shall come forth,

/b   wthipunawaoh mrtaoselethi wunhi cntu javakakawsif,
/p   wčəp·ənawwá·ɔ=č me·t·a·wsi·lí·č·i wə́nči énta-šaxahká·wsink.
/t   they shall separate the sinners from where the righteous are.
/k   and sever the wicked from among the just,

Mt 13.50 /b   ekuh lanevenuk nrk tuntre-kaonif,
/p   íka=č lanihí·nak né·k tənte·i·k·á·ɔnink,
/t   Those shall be cast into the "furnace,"
/k   And shall cast them into the furnace of fire:

/b   cntuh muxavolamwevtet, okh cntu kukamwkuntamevtet wepetwao.
/p   énta-=č -maxahɔla·mwíhti·t, ɔ́·k=č énta-kək·amo·kantamíhti·t wi·p·i·t·əwá·ɔ."
/t   where they will scream loudly, and where they will 'gnash' their teeth."
/k   there shall be wailing and gnashing of teeth.

Mt 13.51 /b   Nhesus tclapani kninwstamunro vuh wrmi bl rnwntvokrokunu?
/p   nčí·sas təlá·p·ani, "kənəno·staməné·ɔ=háč wé·mi yó·l e·nunthake·ɔ́·k·ana?"
/t   Jesus said to them, "Did you understand all these parables?"
/k   Jesus saith unto them, Have ye understood all these things?

/b   Tclawao, Kovun Nrvlaleif.
/p   təlawwá·ɔ, "kɔhán, nehəlá·lienk."
/t   They said to him, "Yes, Master."
/k   They say unto him, Yea, Lord.

Mt 13.52 /b   Nu tclan. Nu wunhi   [Nu wunhi (KHS)]
/p   ná tə́la·n, "nə́ wə́nči
/t   Then he said to them, "Therefore,
/k   Then said he unto them, Therefore

/b   cntxi rvakifrs rkrkemuntup li osavkamce sakemaokunif,
/p   éntxi ehahke·kínke·s e·k·e·ki·mə́ntəp lí ɔ·s·ahkame·í·i-sa·k·i·ma·ɔ́·k·anink,
/t   every teacher that has been trained for the kingdom of heaven,   [lit., 'taught']
/k   every scribe which is instructed unto the kingdom of heaven   [RSV "trained for"]

/b   nrku mulaji wrlekrt linw prnwntvekrt tclathrswakunu wwskifc, ok xwrkc.
                              [⟨-fc⟩ for /-nki/; ⟨-kc⟩ for /-k·i/]
/p   né·k·a málahši we·lí·k·e·t lə́nu pe·nunthíke·t təlač·e·s·əwá·k·ana, wəskínki ɔ́·k xuwé·k·i."

| | /t | he is like a man with a nice house who shows his possessions, new and old." |
| | /k | is like unto a man that is an householder, which bringeth forth out of his treasure things new and old. |

Mt 13.53 /b Mrhi lwi lrkc, Nhesus kejetaqc bl rnwmtvakrokunu, nu pale ton.
/p mé·či ló·wi-lé·k·e, nčí·sas ki·š·i·tá·k·we yó·l e·nunthake·ɔ́·k·ana, ná palí·i tɔ́·n.
/t After it was over and Jesus had finished these parables, then he went away.
/k And it came to pass, that when Jesus had finished these parables, he departed thence.

Mt 13.54 /b Eku pravtc cntu lufwntuf, pumtwnvalapani tali cntu mycvluf,   [⟨-avtc⟩ for ⟨-atc⟩]
/p íka pe·á·t·e énta-lankúntank, pwəmto·nha·lá·p·ani táli énta-ma·éhəlank.
/t When he came to his home country, he preached to them in the synagogue.
/k And when he was come into his own country, he taught them in their synagogue,

/b nu wunhi ‖ kanjrlintamunro; lwrpanek,
/p nə́ wwə́nči-kanše·ləntaməné·ɔ, luwé·p·ani·k,
/t They were astonished by it, and they said,
/k insomuch that they were astonished, and said,

(p. 77) /b Ta vuh ct wunheyw wu linw wlipwrokun, ok b konjyvoswakun?
/p "tá=háč=ét wənčí·ayu wá lə́nu wələp·we·ɔ́·k·an, ɔ́·k yú kɔnšaehɔ·s·əwá·k·an?
/t "Where can this man's wisdom come from, and these miraculous deeds of his?
/k Whence hath this man this wisdom, and these mighty works?

Mt 13.55 /b Mutu vuh wu wevekvrs qesu?   [⟨weve-⟩ for ⟨wcve-⟩]
/p máta=háč wá wehí·khe·s kkwí·s·a?
/t Isn't this the carpenter's son?
/k Is not this the carpenter's son?

/b Mutu vuh kovrsu lwcnselei Mrli?
/p máta=háč kɔhé·s·a luwensi·lí·i 'mé·li'?
/t Isn't his mother's name Mary?
/k is not his mother called Mary?

/b Ok xwesmusu, Nhim, ok Nhosis, ok Symun, ok Nhwtus?
/p ɔ́·k xwi·s·əmə́s·a nčím, ɔ́·k †nčó·səs, ɔ́·k †sáiman, ɔ́·k †nčó·tas?
/t And his younger brothers Jim, and Joses, and Simon, and Judas.
/k and his brethren, James, and Joses, and Simon, and Judas?

Mt 13.56 /b Ok wtoxqrbmenu, mutu vuh qetavpemkwewunanuk?
/p ɔ́·k wtuxkwe·yəmí·na, máta=háč kəwitahpi·mko·wi·wəná·nak?
/t And his sisters, are they not sitting with us?
/k And his sisters, are they not all with us?

/b Ta vuh wuntcn b lipwrakun ok konjyvoswakun?
/p tá=háč wwə́ntən yú ləpwe·ɔ́·k·an, ɔ́·k kɔnšaehɔ·s·əwá·k·an?"
/t Where does he get this wisdom from, and his miracles?"
/k Whence then hath this man all these things?

Mt 13.57
/b Nu puna mutrlumawaul.
/p ná pənáh mɔt·e·ləmawwá·ɔl.
/t Well, then they felt contempt for him.
/k And they were offended in him.   [RSV "they took offense at him"]

/b Jwk Nhesus tclao, Nrnekanewrwset takw mutu xifwrlumuksei,
/p šúkw nčí·sas təlá·ɔ, "nehəni·k·a·ní·i-wé·wsi·t takó· máta xinkwe·ləmukwsí·i
/t But Jesus said to them, "A prophet does not fail to be thought highly of,
/k But Jesus said unto them, A prophet is not without honour,

/b cntu lafwntuf jwk tali mutu ok weket.
/p énta-lankúntank šúkw táli máta, ɔ́·k wí·k·i·t."
/t except not in his home country and in his house."
/k save in his own country, and in his own house.

Mt 13.58
/b Nu tali takw xrli li kanjyvosei, rli mutu wlamvetaowunt.
/p nə́ táli takó· xé·li lí-kanšaehɔ·s·í·i, é·li- máta -wəla·mhitaó·wənt,
/t He did not do many miracles there, because he was not believed,
/k And he did not many mighty works there because of their unbelief.

Mk 6.5
/b Alwt krxu palselethi eka lenxkr nu qekrvan.
/p alót ké·x·a pa·lsi·lí·č·i, íka lí·nxke·, ná kwi·k·é·ha·n.
/t although for a few sick people, he reached out his hand to them and healed them.
/k ... save that he laid his hands upon a few sick folk, and healed them.

Mk 6.6
/b Kanjrlintam rli mutu klistakwk,
/p kanše·lɔ́ntam, é·li- máta -kələstá·k·uk.
/t He was astonished that they did not believe him.
/k And he marvelled because of their unbelief.

/b nu okai rli wvwtrnyekrthek tcli pumitwnvrn.
/p ná ɔ·ká·i ϯé·li-uho·t·e·nai·k·é·č·i·k, tə́li-pəmət·ó·nhe·n.
/t And then he preached, going to those who lived in the villages around there.
/k And he went round about the villages, teaching.

Chapter 45 (pp. 77-79). [L. section 44.] (Matthew 14.1-2, 5 [part], 12 [part], 14 [part]; Mark 6.15-34; John 6.5-14.) (L.: Matt. 14.1-21; Mark 6.14-44; Luke 11.7-17; John 6.1-14. But L. differs considerably from the text B. translates.)

Text, Transcription, and Translation

Mt 14.1   /b   Ncki lukveqi sakema Vclut. Nclutu qesu, puntufc   [⟨-t. Nclutu⟩ for ⟨-t, Vclutu⟩]
             /p   néke ləkhíkwi sa·k·í·ma †hélat, †helát·a kkwí·s·a, pəntánke
             /t   At that time, when king Herod, the son of the late Herod, heard of
             /k   At that time Herod the tetrarch heard of

             /b   rlrlumwkset Nhesus,
             /p   e·le·ləmúkwsi·t nčí·sas,
             /t   how Jesus was regarded,
             /k   the fame of Jesus,

Mt 14.2   /b   tclao rvalwkalathi Nul ta wu Nhan Hihopunwrt   [⟨Hih-⟩ for ⟨Hch-⟩]
             /p   təlá·ɔ ehalo·ka·lá·č·i, "nál=tá wá nčá·n čečhɔ·pwənúwe·t,
             /t   he said to his servants, "This is John the Baptist,
             /k   And said unto his servants, This is John the Baptist;   (Cf. Mark 6.14.)

             /b   amwet ta wunhi ufulwakunif,
             /p   á·mwi·t=tá wənči ankələwá·k·anink.
             /t   who has risen up from death.
             /k   he is risen from the dead;

             /b   nani kta wunhi kanjyvoswakun punwntvekrn vokif wunhi;
             /p   nəni=ktá wənči- kanšaehɔ·s·əwá·k·an -pənunthíke·n hɔ́k·enk wənči."
             /t   That, rather, is why miracles are manifested from him."
             /k   and therefore mighty works do shew forth themselves in him.

Mk 6.15   /b   jwk alintc lwrok Elyusu ta,
             /p   šúkw a·lə́nte luwé·ɔk, "†i·layás·a=tá."
             /t   But some said, "He is Elias."
             /k   Others said, That it is Elias.

             /b   ok alintc lwrok, nekane ta wrwset,
             /p   ɔ́·k a·lə́nte luwé·ɔk, "ni·k·a·ní·i-=tá -wé·wsi·t,
             /t   And some said, "He's a prophet,
             /k   And others said, That it is a prophet,

             /b   jita maosw nrnekanewrwsetpanu.
             /p   ší=tá má·wsu nehəni·k·a·ní·i-we·wsi·tpána."
             /t   or one of the ancient prophets."
             /k   or as one of the prophets.

Mk 6.16   /b   Jwk Vclut puntufc lwrp nul ta wu Nhan keskekojakwp,
             /p   šúkw †hélat pəntánke, lúwe·p, "nál=tá wá nčá·n, ki·skikɔhšák·əp.
             /t   But when Herod heard about it, he said, "This is John, who I beheaded.
             /k   But when Herod heard thereof, he said, It is John, whom I beheaded:

	/b	amwe ta wunhi ufulwakun.
	/p	á·mwi·=tá wə́nči ankələwá·k·an."
	/t	He has risen up from death."
	/k	he is risen from the dead.

Mk 6.17 /b Nul nu Vclut rlwkrmwetwp li Nhan tvwnan, li kaxpelan, ok li kpavon,
/p nál ná †hélat e·lo·ke·mwí·t·əp lí- nčá·n -thwə́na·n, lí-kaxpí·la·n, ɔ́·k lí-kpáhɔ·n,
/t It was Herod who had ordered that John be arrested, bound, and imprisoned,
/k For Herod himself had sent forth and laid hold upon John, and bound him in prison

/b wunhi Vclotiusu Wematu Pilupsu wethrotup
/p wə́nči †helɔ·tiás·a, wí·mahta †pilápsa wi·č·e·ɔ́·t·əp,
/t because of Herodias, who had been the wife of his brother Philip,
/k for Herodias' sake, his brother Philip's wife:

/b rli Vclut manoxqrrtup Vclotiusu.
/p é·li- †hélat -manuxkwe·é·t·əp †helɔ·tiás·a.
/t as Herod had taken Herodias as his wife.
/k for he had married her.

Mk 6.18 /b Rli Nhan latup takw wlexwnw ktcli a wehron kemavtis wehrohi.   [⟨-w⟩ for /-ó·u/]
/p é·li- nčá·n -lá·t·əp, "takó· wəli·x·ənó·u ktə́li-=á· -wi·č·é·ɔ·n kí·mahtəs wi·č·e·ɔ́·č·i."
/t For John had said to him, "It is not lawful for you to marry your brother's wife."
/k For John had said unto Herod, It is not lawful for thee to have thy brother's wife.

Mk 6.19 /b Nuni wunhi Vclotius mahi punyrluman tcli a nvelan,
/p nə́ni wwə́nči- †helɔ́·tias -máhči-pənaé·ləma·n, tə́li-=á· -nhíla·n,
/t For that reason, Herodias had evil thoughts about him, that she would kill him,
/k Therefore Herodias had a quarrel against him, and would have killed him;

/b jwk mutu kuski,
/p šúkw máta káski,
/t but she could not,
/k but she could not:

Mk 6.20 /b rli Vclut kxotup Nhanu,
/p é·li- †hélat -kxɔ́·t·əp nčá·na.
/t as Herod had feared John.
/k For Herod feared John, ...

Mt 14.5 /b ok koxapani wrmi awrn rli letrvatet nrnekane ct wrwset.
                              [⟨awrn⟩ for /awé·ni/; ⟨letrvatet⟩ for /-li·t·e·há·li·t/]
/p ɔ́·k kɔx·á·p·ani wé·mi awé·ni, é·li-li·t·e·há·li·t, nehəni·k·a·ní·i-=ét -wé·wsi·t.
/t And he feared everyone, as they thought he must be a prophet.
/k And ... he feared the multitude, because they counted him as a prophet.

Mk 6.20 /b Wavao tcli javakawselen ok pelawselen, ok wlrlumapani,   [⟨pelaw-‖selen⟩]
/p o·wa·há·ɔ tɔ́li-šaxahka·ws·í·li·n ɔ́·k -pi·la·wsí·li·n, ɔ́·k o·le·ləmá·p·ani.
/t He knew that he was righteous and holy, and he thought well of him.
/k ... knowing that he was a just man and an holy, and observed him;
    [RSV "and kept him safe." (Cf. the next line.)]

(p. 78) /b pcntaotc xrlraovki nani tclsen, ok krnavkevao.   [⟨-lra-⟩ for ⟨-lrna-⟩; ⟨kr-⟩ for ⟨qr-⟩]
/p pentaɔ́·t·e xe·lennáɔhki, ná=ní tɔ́lsi·n, ɔ́·k kwe·nahki·há·ɔ.
/t When he heard various things about him, that's what he did, and he watched out for him.
/k and when he heard him, he did many things, and heard him gladly.

Mk 6.21 /b Lupi tpisqevlakc Vclut rlkeqi kejeketup,
/p lápi tpəskwihəlá·k·e †hélat e·lkí·kwi-ki·š·i·k·í·t·əp,
/t When Herod's birthday (*lit.*, the time when he had been born) came again,
/k And when a convenient day was come, that Herod on his birthday

/b nu muxifwi wepwmvkwn wrmi wtelybmenu, ok wrmi Falule elaok.
/p ná mɔx·ínkwi-wi·pó·mko·n wé·mi wti·la·yəmí·na, ɔ́·k wé·mi †nka·lalí·i-i·lá·ɔk.
/t then all his officers and all the officers of Galilee attended a great feast with him.
/k made a supper to his lords, high captains, and chief estates of Galilee;

Mk 6.22 /b Vclotius tonu pchi tumekrletc, nu tcli kintkan.
/p †helɔ́·tias tɔ́·na péči-təmi·k·e·lí·t·e, ná tɔ́li-kɔ́ntka·n.
/t When Herodias's daughter came in, she danced.
/k And when the daughter of the said Herodias came in, and danced,

/b Vclut wlenaopani ok wrmi wepwmathek.
/p †hélat o·li·naɔ́·p·ani, ɔ́·k wé·mi wi·po·má·č·i·k.
/t Herod admired her, as did all who ate with him.
/k and pleased Herod and them that sat with him,

/b Nu sakema tclao nrl skexqro,
/p ná sa·k·í·ma təlá·ɔ né·l ski·xkwé·ɔ,
/t Then the king said to the girl,
/k the king said unto the damsel,

/b Wenwumel tuktu krkw rletrvaun, nuh kmelin.
/p "wi·nəwámi·l tákta kéku e·li·t·e·há·an, ná=č kəmíllən."
/t "Ask me for whatever you want, and I will give it to you."
/k Ask of me whatsoever thou wilt, and I will give it thee.

Mk 6.23 /b Qetaptwnalan, tuktu krkw wenwumeunh, kmelinh,
/p kwi·ta·pto·ná·la·n, "tákta kéku wi·nəwamían=č, kəmíllən=č,
/t And he swore to her, "Whatever you shall ask me for, I will give to you,
/k And he sware unto her, Whatsoever thou shalt ask of me, I will give it thee,

248 Blanchard's Harmony of the Gospels

/b taoni a pase nsakemaokun.
/p tá·ɔni=á· pahsí·i nsa·k·i·ma·ɔ́·k·an."
/t though it would be half my kingdom."
/k unto the half of my kingdom.

Mk 6.24 /b Nu eku tcli kthen kovrsif, tclao kovrsu, Krkwh vuh nwenwc?
/p ná íka tə́li-kčí·n kɔhé·s·ink, təlá·ɔ kɔhé·s·a, "kéku=č=háč nəwí·nəwe?"
/t Then she went out to her mother and said to her mother, "What shall I ask for?"
/k And she went forth, and said unto her mother, What shall I ask?

/b Tclao Wel Nhan Hchopunwrt.
/p təlá·ɔ, "wí·l nča·n čečhɔ·pwənúwe·t."
/t She said to her, "The head of John the Baptist."
/k And she said, The head of John the Baptist.

Mk 6.25 /b Nu jai tumekaman sakemao, nu notoxtwn, tclao, [⟨tum-⟩ for /wtəm-/]
/p ná šá·e wtəmí·k·ama·n sa·k·i·má·ɔ, ná nɔt·ó·xto·n, təlá·ɔ,
/t Then she immediately came in to the king, and then she asked for it, saying to him,
/k And she came in straightway with haste unto the king, and asked, saying,

/b Nanc ntclse [⟨ntclse⟩ for ⟨ntclsen⟩]
/p "ná=nə ntə́lsi·n,
/t "What I want (*lit.*, do) [idiom?]
/k I will

/b ktclih melen nakyrkc Nhan Hchopunwrt wel lokcnsif.
/p ktə́li-=č -mí·li·n na·k·a·é·k·e nčá·n čečhɔ·pwənúwe·t wí·l lɔ·k·énsink.
/t is for you to give me, after a while, the head of John the Baptist on a plate.
/k that thou give me by and by in a charger the head of John the Baptist.

Mk 6.26 /b Nu kehe ave jrlintum sakema; [⟨jrl-⟩ for ⟨jerl-⟩]
/p ná khičí·i áhi-ši·e·lə́ntam sa·k·í·ma.
/t Then the king was truly very upset.
/k And the king was exceeding sorry;

/b jwk rli Ketaptwnalat, ok wunhi bk wepwmathek takw jwelaovtet.
/p šúkw é·li-khita·pto·ná·la·t, ɔ́·k wə́nči- yó·k wi·po·má·č·i·k takó· -šhwi·laɔ́hti·t.
/t But as he had promised her, and for those who ate with him not to lose heart,
/k yet for his oath's sake, and for their sakes which sat with him, he would not reject her.

Mk 6.27 /b Nu sakema tolwkalan ncnvelwrlethi, tclao. Kprtwnh wel,
/p ná sa·k·í·ma tɔlo·ká·la·n nenhiləwe·lí·č·i, təlá·ɔ, "kpé·t·o·n=č wí·l."

	/t	then the king sent an executioner, telling him, "You must bring his head."
	/k	And immediately the king sent an executioner, and commanded his head to be brought:

	/b	nu eku ton cntu kpavwtif, nu tcli keskeqcvon,
	/p	ná íka tó·n énta-kpahó·t·ink, ná tə́li-ki·ski·k·wéhɔ·n,
	/t	Then he went to the prison and proceeded to chop his head off.
	/k	and he went and beheaded him in the prison,

Mk 6.28	/b	ok pwrtwn ne wel lokensif, mwelan nrl skexqro, [⟨kens⟩ for ⟨kcns⟩]
	/p	ó·k pwé·t·o·n nə́ wí·l lɔ·k·énsink, mwí·la·n né·l ski·xkwé·ɔ.
	/t	And he brought the head on a plate and gave it to the girl.
	/k	And brought his head in a charger, and gave it to the damsel:

	/b	nanu mwelan kovrsu.
	/p	ná=nə mwí·la·n kɔhé·s·a.
	/t	And she gave that to her mother.
	/k	and the damsel gave it to her mother.

Mk 6.29	/b	Rkrkemahi pantamevtetc, prok wrtunimanro voky
		[⟨pant-⟩ for ⟨punt-⟩; ⟨-man-⟩ for ⟨-mun-⟩]
	/p	e·k·e·ki·má·č·i pəntamihtí·t·e, pé·ɔk, wwe·t·ənəməné·ɔ hɔ́k·ay,
	/t	When his disciples heard about it, they came and took his body
	/k	And when his disciples heard of it, they came and took up his corpse, ...

Mt 14.12	/b	pokvakrvmunro nu tolumskanro moi lanro Nhesusu.
	/p	ppɔ·khakehəməné·ɔ; ná tɔləmska·né·ɔ, mɔ́i-la·né·ɔ nči·sás·a.
	/t	and buried it; then they departed, going to tell Jesus.
	/k	... and buried it, and went and told Jesus.

Mk 6.30	/b	Rvalokalinhek tavqe wtxawao Nhesusu,
	/p	ehalo·ka·lə́nči·k tahkwí·i o·txawwá·ɔ nči·sás·a,
	/t	The apostles went to Jesus together
	/k	And the apostles gathered themselves together unto Jesus,

	/b	tclanro wrmi krkw rlsevtet, ok rli avkrkifcvtet.
	/p	təla·né·ɔ wé·mi kéku e·lsíhti·t ó·k é·li-ahke·kinkéhti·t.
	/t	and told him everything they did and how they taught.
	/k	and told him all things, both what they had done, and what they had taught.

Mk 6.31	/b	Tclao, Eku aaq entuh xwva, alaxemwerq; [⟨aaq⟩ for /á·kw/]
	/p	təlá·ɔ, "íka á·kw énta-=č xó·ha -ala·x·í·mwie·kw."
	/t	He said to them, "Go to where you will be alone and rest."
	/k	And he said unto them, Come ye yourselves apart into a desert place, and rest a while:

/b rli xrli prathek, ok xrli rlumskathek,
/p é·li xé·li pe·á·č·i·k, ó·k xé·li e·ləmská·č·i·k,
/t For, there were many that came, and many that went,
/k for there were many coming and going,

/b wunhi mutu kuski nuxpuni metsewunro.
/p wwə́nči- máta -káski- náxpəne -mi·tsi·wəné·ɔ.
/t so that they were not even able to eat.
/k and they had no leisure so much as to eat.

Mk 6.32 /b Nu eku tcli pwsenro moxwlif keme.
/p ná íka tə́li-po·s·i·né·ɔ mux·ó·link ki·mí·i.
/t Then they secretly got on board a boat.
/k And they departed into a desert place by ship privately.

Mk 6.33 /b Nrli rlumelavtetc,   [⟨lavt⟩ for ⟨lavtavt⟩]
/p né·li e·ləmilahtahtí·t·e,
/t When they departed yonder in the boat,
/k And the people saw them departing,

/b alintc wnroa, ok alintc wnunaoau.   [⟨-a⟩ and ⟨-au⟩ for /-á·a/ (for /-á·ɔ/)]
/p a·lə́nte wəne·ɔwwá·a, ó·k a·lə́nte wənənaɔwwá·a.
/t some people saw them (or him), and some recognized them (or him).
/k and many knew him,

/b Nu tolumi mvetamerlanro wunhi wrmi wtrnyekri,   [⟨-merl-⟩ for ⟨-mcvl-⟩]
/p ná tɔ́ləmi-mhita·mehəla·né·ɔ wə́nči wé·mi o·t·e·nai·ké·i,
/t Then they began to run along on land out of all the towns,
/k and ran afoot thither out of all cities,

/b naomawao, cku marvlrok.   [⟨naom-⟩ for ⟨noom-⟩]
/p †nɔɔmawwá·ɔ, íka ma·ehəlé·ɔk.
/t and they outran them and gathered together over there.
/k and outwent them, and came together unto him.

Mk 6.34 /b Nhesus mrhi krpatc xrli awrni nrr,
/p nčí·sas mé·či ke·p·á·t·e, xé·li awé·ni né·e·.
/t After Jesus came ashore, he saw many people.
/k And Jesus, when he came out, saw much people,

/b tove ktumakrlumao, rli mulaji mrkesuk, mutu awrn knavkevat.
                                                [⟨mrke-∥suk⟩; ⟨kn-⟩ for ⟨krn-⟩]
/p tóhi-ktəma·k·e·ləmá·ɔ, é·li málahši mekí·s·ak, máta awé·n ke·nahkí·ha·t.
/t He pitied them greatly, as being like sheep with no one looking after them.
/k and was moved with compassion toward them, because they were as sheep not having a shepherd:

(p. 79)   /b Xrli krkw tclakemapane,   [⟨tclakem⟩ for ⟨tclavkrkem⟩]
          /p xé·li kéku təlahke·ki·má·p·ani,
          /t He taught them about many things,
          /k and he began to teach them many things.

Mt 14.14 /b ok qekrvao palselethi.
          /p ɔ́·k kwi·k·e·há·ɔ pa·lsi·lí·č·i.
          /t and he healed the sick.
          /k ... and he healed their sick.

Mt 14.15 /b Mrhi loqekc rkrkremathi moi lwkw,
          /p mé·či lɔ·k·wí·k·e, e·k·e·ki·má·č·i mɔ́i-lúk·u,
          /t After it had become evening, his disciples came and said to him,
          /k And when it was evening, his disciples came to him, saying,

          /b Laxwrvoctetch marvlathek wunhih kuski vulumevtet krkw mehevtet,
                              [⟨-rvoc-⟩ for /-e·x·we-/; ⟨vul-⟩ for ⟨mvul-⟩]
          /p "laxwe·x·wehtí·t·eč ma·ehəlá·č·i·k, wə́nči-=č -káski-mhalamíhti·t kéku mi·č·íhti·t,
          /t "Let the crowd disperse, so that they will be able to buy something to eat,
          /k ... send the multitude away, that they may ... buy themselves victuals.

Mk 6.36   /b rli mutu wlavtwvlet krkw mehevtet.   [⟨wlavtwvlet⟩ for ⟨wlatwvtet⟩]
          /p é·li- máta -wəla túhti·t kéku mi·č·íhti·t."
          /t for they do not have anything to eat."
          /k for they have nothing to eat.

Mt 14.16 /b Jwk Nhesus tclao, Nwhqi a palerok, xamw.
          /p šúkw nčí·sas təlá·ɔ, "nó·čkwe=á· palí·i é·ɔk; xámo·."
          /t But Jesus said to them, "There would be no point in them going away; feed them."
          /k But Jesus said unto them, They need not depart; give ye them to eat.

Jn 6.5   /b Nu Nhesus notwxtaon Pilupsu, tclao,
          /p ná nčí·sas nɔt·o·xtáɔ·n †pilápsa, təlá·ɔ,
          /t Then Jesus asked Philip, saying,
          /k ... Jesus then ... saith unto Philip,

          /b Tuh vuh ktcntu mvalaminrn avpon bk a methevtet?
          /p "tá=č=háč ktə́nta-mhalamə́ne·n ahpó·n, yó·k=á· mi·č·íhti·t?"
          /t "Where shall we buy bread which these people could eat?"
          /k Whence shall we buy bread, that these may eat?

Jn 6.6   /b Jwk wunhi nc lan kotu watwn, krkwj ta rlwrtet,
          /p šúkw wwə́nči- nə́ -lá·n, kɔ́t·a-wwá·to·n, kéku=š=tá e·ləwéhti·t,
          /t But the reason he said that to him was, he wanted to know what they would say,
          /k And this he said to prove him:

	/b	rli wataoq nevlahi rnumevteth.	[⟨wataoq⟩ for /wwá·ta·kw/]
	/p	é·li-wwá·ta·kw nihəláči ennəmíhti·t=č.	
	/t	as he himself knew what they would do.	
	/k	for he himself knew what he would do.	

Jn 6.7   /b   Pilups tclao, Nejenxkc ok nejaj rlaovtek,
         /p   †pílaps təlá·ɔ, "ni·š·í·nxke ɔ́·k ní·š·a·š e·lá·ɔhti·k
         /t   Philip said to him, "Twenty-seven dollars' worth
         /k   Philip answered him, Two hundred pennyworth of bread   (i.e., 200 silver denarii)

	/b	takw tepi wunhi nuxpunc pupvakreti xamaonro.	[⟨tepi⟩ for ⟨tcpi⟩]
	/p	takó· tépi wənči- náxpəne pəphake·íti -xama·wəné·ɔ."	
	/t	is not enough for them to be given even little pieces to eat."	
	/k	is not sufficient for them, that every one of them may take a little.	

Mk 6.38 /b   Nu tclao, Ta vuh txi avponu vatr?
         /p   ná təlá·ɔ, "tá=háč txí ahpɔ́·na hát·e·?"
         /t   Then he said to them, "How many loaves of bread are there?"
         /k   He saith unto them, How many loaves have ye? ...

Jn 6.8   /b   Kwti rkrkemathi lwcnsw Antlws, Symun Petul wemavtul tclao,
         /p   kwə́t·i e·k·e·ki·má·č·i, luwénsu †ántəlo·s, †sáiman-pí·təl wí·mahtal, təlá·ɔ,
         /t   One of his disciples, named Andrew, Simon Peter's brother, said to him,
         /k   One of his disciples, Andrew, Simon Peter's brother, saith unto him,

Jn 6.9   /b   Skenwtit eku avpw palrnax avpona wlatw ok neju namrtitu,
         /p   "skinnó·t·ət íka ahpú, palé·naxk ahpɔ́·na wəlá·to·, ɔ́·k ní·š·a name·t·ə́t·a,
         /t   "There is a young fellow here who has five loaves of bread and two small fish,
         /k   There is a lad here, which hath five barley loaves, and two small fishes:

         /b   alwt krkw vuh a laprmkotw cntu xrlif.
         /p   aló·t, kéku=háč=á· la·p·e·mkɔ́t·u énta-xé·link?"
         /t   What use would they be, though, in a large crowd?"
         /k   but what are they among so many?

Jn 6.10 /b   Nhesus tclao, Lw lumutavpeq.
         /p   nčí·sas təlá·ɔ, "ló·, 'ləmátahpi·kw.'"
         /t   Jesus said to them, "Tell them to sit down."
         /k   And Jesus said, Make the men sit down.

         /b   Ave wluskavtwp nu tali.
         /p   áhi-wəláskahto·p nə́ táli.
         /t   There was a lot of nice grass there.
         /k   Now there was much grass in the place.

/b Nu wrmi linwuk wlumavtupenro
/p ná wé·mi lə́nəwak wələmahtap·i·né·ɔ.
/t Then all the men sat down.
/k So the men sat down, ...

Mk 6.40 /b jijaxakufwrpwuk
/p šəšaxahkankwé·p·əwak.
/t They sat in rows.
/k And they sat down in ranks, ...

Jn 6.10 /b avpami ct palrnax txapxkswuk. [⟨txapxk-⟩: for ⟨txun tclin txapxk-⟩ 'thousand' 4x]
/p ahpá·mi=ét palé·naxk [txə́n télən] txa·pxksúwak.
/t There were maybe about five thousand of them.   [B. has 'five hundred']
/k ... in number about five thousand.

Jn 6.11 /b Nu Nhesus wrtanimun nrl avponu,
/p ná nčí·sas wwe·t·ənə́mən né·l ahpɔ́·na.
/t Then Jesus picked up the loaves.
/k And Jesus took the loaves;

/b mrhi krnamwetc, nu popvakrnumun, nu qwlintulan rkrkremathi,
/p mé·či ke·na·mwí·t·e, ná puphaké·nəmən, ná kwəlɔ́ntəla·n e·k·e·ki·má·č·i,
/t After giving thanks, he tore pieces off them and handed them out to his disciples,
/k and when he had given thanks, he distributed to the disciples,

/b tclih kulintulanro wrmi lrmuvtupelethi,
/p tɔ́li-=č -kələntəla·né·ɔ wé·mi le·mahtap·i·lí·č·i.
/t for them to hand out to everyone who was sitting,
/k and the disciples to them that were set down;

/b nu ok namrsu.
/p ná ɔ́·k namé·s·a.
/t and then also the fish.
/k and likewise of the fishes as much as they would.

Mk 6.42 /b Nu methenro, wrmi kespwuk.   [⟨me-⟩ for ⟨mwe-⟩]
/p ná mwi·č·i·né·ɔ, wé·mi ki·spúwak.
/t Then they ate them, and all were filled.
/k And they did all eat, and were filled.

Jn 6.12 /b Mrhi wrmi kespwetetc, tclao rkrkemathi.
/p mé·či wé·mi ki·spwihtí·t·e, təlá·ɔ e·k·e·ki·má·č·i,
/t After all were filled, he said to his disciples,
/k When they were filled, he said unto his disciples,

	/b	Mukinvamwq wrmi pupvakreti peontasek, wnhih mutu krkw taofunwq.
	/p	"məkənhámo·kw wé·mi pəphake·íti pi·ontá·s·i·k, wə́nči-=č máta kéku -taónkəno·kw.
	/t	"Gather up all the little pieces left uneaten, so that nothing will be lost."
	/k	Gather up the fragments that remain, that nothing be lost.
Jn 6.13	/b	Nu morvmunro tali kotrnaovki,
	/p	ná mɔ·ehəməné·ɔ táli kwət·ennáɔhki.
	/t	Then they gathered them in a single place.
	/k	Therefore they gathered them together,
	/b	owvhwvotwnro tclin ok neju tufvakunu nrl rlwevlaki nrl avponu
	/p	ɔwčuhɔto·né·ɔ télən ó·k ní·š·a tankhá·k·ana né·l e·ləwihəlá·k·i né·l ahpó·na.
	/t	They filled twelve baskets with what was left over of the loaves.
	/k	and filled twelve baskets with the fragments of the five barley loaves, which remained over and above unto them that had eaten.
Mt 14.21	/b	vapi nrk palrnax txun tclin txapxki linwuk
	/p	hápi né·k palé·naxk txə́n télən txá·pxki lə́nəwak,
	/t	Along with the five thousand men,
	/k	And they that had eaten were about five thousand men,
	/b	ok xqruk ok meminsuk tavqe nc methenro.
	/p	ó·k xkwé·ɔk ó·k mi·mə́nsak tahkwí·i nə́ mwi·č·i·né·ɔ.
	/t	women and children also ate that food with them.
	/k	beside women and children.
Jn 6.14	/b	Nrk linwuk nrmvetetc nu konjyvoswakun, rlsetup Nhesus, lwrpanek,
	/p	né·k lə́nəwak ne·mhití·t·e nə́ kanšaehɔ·s·əwá·k·an e·lsí·t·əp nčí·sas, luwé·p·ani·k,
	/t	When those men saw the miracle that Jesus had done, they said,
	/k	Then those men, when they had seen the miracle that Jesus did, said,
	/b	Nunul ta wuni nrnekanowrwset, prath b xqetvakameqc. ‖ [⟨-now-⟩ for ⟨-new-⟩]
	/p	"nánal=tá wáni nehəni·k·a·ní·i-wé·wsi·t pé·a·t=č yú xkwi·thakamí·k·we.
	/t	"This is the prophet who is to come to this world."
	/k	This is of a truth that prophet that should come into the world.

Chapter 46 (p. 80). [L. section 45.] (Mark 6.45, 47-48, 50-52, 54-55; John 6.15, 19; Matthew 14.28-29, 33-36; cf. Matthew 14.22-27)

Mk 6.45	/b	Nu jai tclalwkalan rkrkemathi
(p. 80)	/p	ná šá·e təlalo·ká·la·n e·k·e·ki·má·č·i
	/t	Then he immediately ordered his disciples
	/k	And straightway he constrained his disciples

	/b	moxwlif tcli a nekanelen li kamif Mpctsrytc
	/p	mux·ó·link tə́li-=á· -ni·k·a·ní·li·n lí ká·mink †mpetsáite
	/t	to go ahead in a boat to the other side to Bethsaida
	/k	to get into the ship, and to go to the other side before unto Bethsaida,

	/b	nrli lat wtcnaprmul luxwvwrq.	[⟨-xwvw-⟩ for ⟨-xwrxw-⟩]
	/p	né·li-lá·t wtənna·p·é·yəmal, "laxwé·x·we·kw."	
	/t	while he told his people to disperse.	
	/k	while he sent away the people.	

Jn 6.15 /b Jwk mrhi Nhesus nrfc li kavta sakemaovrn
/p šúkw mé·či nčí·sas nénke lí-káhta-sa·k·i·má·whe·n,
/t But after Jesus saw that there was a desire to make him king,
/k When Jesus therefore perceived that they would [come and take him by force, to] make him a king,

	/b	alumskrp, ovhwf rp xwva, moi patamap.	[⟨moi⟩ for /mái/]
	/p	alə́mske·p, ɔhčúnk é·p xó·ha, mái-pá·tama·p.	
	/t	he departed, and went alone to a mountain, going to pray.	
	/k	he departed again into a mountain himself alone.	

Mk 6.47 /b Mrhi peskrkc, moxwl wlc laetunc mwnwprkwf,
/p mé·či pi·ské·k·e, múx·o·l wəlé la·í·tane mənəp·é·k·unk,
/t After night had fallen, the boat was out in the middle of the sea,
/k And when even was come, the ship was in the midst of the sea,

	/b	kahi nrkuma xwva ovhwf avpwp.
	/p	káč·i né·k·əma xó·ha ɔhčúnk ahpó·p.
	/t	but *he* was alone on the mountain.
	/k	and he alone on the land.

Mk 6.48 /b Ok wnro, ave mekumoswok ave hemrok, rli avpetxunclavtet. [⟨avp-⟩ for ⟨apv-⟩]
/p ó·k wəne·ó·ɔ; áhi-mi·kəmó·s·əwak, áhi-či·mé·ɔk, é·li-a·phitxənehəláhti·t.
/t And he saw them; they were laboring hard, rowing hard, as they were rowing into the wind.
/k And he saw them toiling in rowing; for the wind was contrary unto them: ...

Jn 6.19 /b Avpami ct nrwa mylif lckvekqi avpwuk.
/p ahpá·mi=ét né·wa máilink ləkhíkwi ahpúwak.
/t They were at a distance of maybe about four miles.
/k (2) when they had rowed about five and twenty or thirty furlongs, ...

Mk 6.48 /b Mrhi kexki opun nu wtxan xqespc prmwskr, [⟨prm-⟩ for ⟨pum-⟩]
/p mé·či kí·xki ɔ́·p·an, ná ɔ́·txa·n, xkwí·spe pəmə́ske·.
/t It was already nearly dawn, and then he came to them, walking on the water.
/k (1) And about the fourth watch of the night he cometh unto them, (3) walking upon the sea,

/b koti lwenu.
/p kɔ́ti-lo·wí·na.
/t He almost went past them,
/k and would have passed by them.

Mt 14.26 /b Jwk nrovtetc xqespc prmisr, [⟨prmisr⟩ for ⟨pumiskr⟩]
/p šúkw ne·ɔhtí·t·e, xkwí·spe pəmə́ske·,
/t but when they saw him walking on the water,
/k And when the disciples saw him walking on the sea, ...

Mk 6.49 /b letrvrok hepy ct, nu momxavolamwenro,
/p li·t·e·hé·ɔk, "čí·p·ay=ét"; ná mumxahɔla·mwi·né·ɔ,
/t they thought it must be a ghost; and then they cried out loudly,
/k ... they supposed it had been a spirit, and cried out:

Mk 6.50 /b rli wrmi nrovtet, ave sukwrlintamwk.
/p é·li- wé·mi -ne·ɔ́hti·t, áhi-sak·we·lə́ntamo·k.
/t as they all saw him, and they were very distressed.
/k For they all saw him, and were troubled.

/b Nu jai krkw tclan, lwr Ne ta kah kwxevrq. [⟨kah⟩ for ⟨kahi⟩]
/p ná šá·e kéku tə́la·n, lúwe·, "ní·=tá; káči kxwí·he·kw.
/t Then immediately he spoke to them, saying, "It's me; don't be afraid of me."
/k And immediately he talked with them, and saith unto them, ... it is I; be not afraid.

Mt 14.28 /b Petul tclao kehe ke Nevlatet, lel, wuntux al li xqespc. [⟨-atet⟩ for ⟨-alet⟩]
/p †pí·təl təlá·ɔ, "khiči·i kí·, nehəlá·li·t, lí·l, 'wə́ntax á·l lí xkwí·spe.'"
/t Peter said to him, "If it is truly you, my Lord, tell me to come on the water."
/k And Peter answered him and said, Lord, if it be thou, bid me come unto thee on the water.

Mt 14.29 /b Nu Nhesus tclan, Wuntax al.
/p ná nčí·sas tə́la·n, "wə́ntax á·l."
/t Then Jesus said to him, "Come here."
/k And he said, Come.

/b Petul mrhi krthetc wunhi moxwlif xqespc pumiskr.
/p †pí·təl, mé·či ke·č·í·t·e wə́nči mux·ɔ́·link, xkwí·spe pəmə́ske·.
/t Peter, after getting out of the boat, walked on the water.
/k And when Peter was come down out of the ship, he walked on the water, ...

Mt 14.30 /b Jwk nrfc li avi kjavun qetaminrp,
/p šúkw nénke lí-áhi-kšáx·ən, kkwi·taməne·p.
/t But when he saw that the wind was blowing strongly, he was fearful of it.
/k But when he saw the wind boisterous, he was afraid;

/b nu tolumi qtaevlan amaxavulamo, lwr Nrvlaliun tumakrlumi. [⟨tum-⟩ for /ktəm-/]
/p ná tóləmi-kwtaíhəla·n, amax·ahɔlá·mu, lúwe·, "nehəlá·lian, ktəma·k·é·ləmi."
/t Then he began to sink, and he shouted, saying, "My Lord, take pity on me."
/k and beginning to sink, he cried, saying, Lord, save me.

Mt 14.31 /b Nu jai Nhesus eku tclenxkun eku tunao tclao, [⟨-xkun⟩ for ⟨-xkrn⟩]
/p ná šá·e nčí·sas íka təlí·nxke·n, íka tɔnná·ɔ, təlá·ɔ,
/t Then Jesus immediately reached out his hand and caught him, saying to him,
/k And immediately Jesus stretched forth his hand, and caught him, and said unto him,

/b O tfrtw knakatamwrokun krkw wunhi jwrlumweun. [⟨tfrtw⟩ for ⟨tufrtw⟩]
/p "ó·, tanké·t·u kəna·ka·t·amwe·ɔ́·k·an! kéku wɔ́nči-šhwe·ləmwían?"
/t "Oh, slight is your faith! Why do you doubt?"
/k O thou of little faith, wherefore didst thou doubt?

Mk 6.51 /b Nu eku ton moxwlif, ok alu kjwxun. [⟨kjwxun⟩ for ⟨kjuxun⟩ (or ⟨kjaxun⟩)]
/p ná íka tó·n mux·ó·link, ɔ́·k ála-kšáx·ən.
/t Then he went up into the boat, and the wind stopped blowing.
/k And he went up unto them into the ship; and the wind ceased:

/b Ave wejaswuk ok kanjrlintamok.
/p áhi-wi·š·á·s·əwak ɔ́·k kanše·lə́ntamo·k.
/t They were very frightened and amazed.
/k and they were sore amazed in themselves beyond measure, and wondered.

Mk 6.52 /b Rli mutu punyrlintumevtet rlrkup avponu; rli ovtami punyrlintamevtet.
/p é·li- máta -pəna·eləntamíhti·t e·lé·k·əp ahpó·na, é·li-ɔ·wtámi-pəna·eləntamíhti·t.
/t For they did not think of what had happened with the loaves, as they were slow in thought.
/k For they considered not the miracle of the loaves: for their heart was hardened.
[*hardened*: i.e., 'obtuse'; Greek idiom also in Mk 8.17]

Mt 14.33 /b Nu wrmi moxwlif rpethek moxifokunemanro lwrpanek,
/p ná wé·mi mux·ó·link e·p·í·č·i·k mɔx·inkɔhkəni·ma·né·ɔ, luwé·p·ani·k,
/t Then everyone who was in the boat praised him and said,
/k Then they that were in the ship came and worshipped him, saying,

	/b	Kehe ta ke Krtaniwet Qesu.	[⟨-niwet⟩ for ⟨-nitwet⟩]
	/p	"khičí·i=tá kí· ke·tanət·ó·wi·t kkwí·s·a."	
	/t	"Truly you are the son of God."	
	/k	Of a truth thou art the Son of God.	

Mt 14.34 /b Mrhi qrxkakatetc nu eku ponrop Huncsulite vakif.
          /p mé·či kwe·xkahkahtí·t·e, ná íka pɔ·né·ɔ·p †čanesalití·i-hák·ink.
          /t After they crosed over, they then came to the land of Gennesaret.
          /k And when they were gone over, they came into the land of Gennesaret.

Mk 6.54   /b Nu tcli kupanro wunhi moxwlif;
          /p ná təli-kahpa·né·ɔ wənči mux·ó·link.
          /t And they proceeded to disembark from the boat.
          /k And when they were come out of the ship,

          /b nu jai wavanro kexki prmekrthe   [⟨prmekrthe⟩ for ⟨prmekrthek⟩]
          /p ná šá·e o·wa·ha·né·ɔ kí·xki pe·mi·k·é·č·i·k,
          /t Then right away those dwelling nearby knew who he was,
          /k straightway they knew him,

Mk 6.55   /b ok wrmi tujevlanro,
          /p ó·k wé·mi təš·ihəla·né·ɔ.
          /t and they ran everywhere.
          /k And ran through that whole region round about,

          /b wrmi palselethi eku tclwxalawao tutu rli puntamevtet rpet Nhesus.
          /p wé·mi pa·lsi·lí·č·i íka təlo·x·ɔlawwá·ɔ tətá é·li-pəntamíhti·t é·p·i·t nčí·sas.
          /t They took all the sick people to wherever they heard Jesus was.
          /k and began to carry about in beds those that were sick, where they heard he was,

Mt 14.36 /b Wenwumanro tcli a cka alinamanro rqlet.   [⟨rqlet⟩ for ⟨rqelet⟩]
          /p wwi·nəwama·né·ɔ, təli-=á· íka -alənəmaɔ·né·ɔ e·k·wí·li·t.
          /t And they asked him if they could touch his garment.
          /k And besought him that they might only touch the hem of his garment:

          /b Ok wrmi cntxi eka alinifek myai msithri wlumalswuk. ‖
          /p ó·k wé·mi éntxi- íka -alənínki·k mayá·i məsəč·é·i wəlamalsúwak.
          /t And all those that touched it were perfectly whole and well.
          /k and as many as touched were made perfectly whole.

Chapter 47 (pp. 81-84). [L. section 46.] (John 6.22-71)

Jn 6.22   /b Lupi opufc nrk mrxrlkek kamif rpethek nrmvetetc
(p. 81)   /p lápi ɔ·p·ánke, né·k me·x·é·lki·k ká·mink e·p·í·č·i·k ne·mhití·t·e,

/t   The next day, when the crowd on the other side saw
/k   The day following, when the people which stood on the other side of the sea saw

/b   li mutu peli mwxwl vatri,
/p   lí máta pí·li múx·o·l hat·é·i,
/t   that there was no other boat,
/k   that there was none other boat there,

/b   nu jwq kwti rkrkemathi pwswpanek,
/p   nɔ́ šúkw kwət·i, e·k·e·ki·má·č·i po·s·ó·p·ani·k,
/t   except that one, and his disciples were getting on board,
/k   save that one whereinto his disciples were entered,

/b   ok Nhesus mutu wethrvkwepani rkrkematpani,
/p   ó·k nčí·sas máta wwi·č·e·yko·wí·p·ani e·k·e·ki·ma·tpáni,
/t   and Jesus's disciples were not with him,
/k   and that Jesus went not with his disciples into the boat,

/b   jwq rkrkematpani xwvu kamif lelavtapanek.
/p   šúkw e·k·e·ki·ma·tpáni xó·ha ká·mink lilahtá·p·ani·k
/t   but his disciples were crossing in the boat alone
/k   but that his disciples were gone away alone;

Jn 6.23 /b   Alwt peli mwxwlu wunhevlrpani Typeliusif
/p   (aló·t pí·li mux·ó·la wənčihəlé·p·ani †taipi·liás·ink
/t   (although other boats came from Tiberias
/k   (Howbeit there came other boats from Tiberias

/b   kexki cntu avpon methevtetup, mrhi krnamatc Nrvlalkofwi.
/p   kí·xki énta- ahpó·n -mi·č·ihtí·t·əp, mé·či ke·na·má·t·e nehəla·lkónkwi.)
/t   to a place near where they had eaten bread after he had given thanks to our Lord)
/k   nigh unto the place where they did eat bread, after that the Lord had given thanks:)

Jn 6.24 /b   Mrhi mrxrlkek nrmvetetc tcli mutu avpewun,
/p   mé·či me·x·é·lki·k ne·mhití·t·e tɔ́li- máta -ahpí·wən,
/t   After the crowd saw that he was not there,
/k   When the people therefore saw that Jesus was not there,

/b   ok rkrkematpani navle mutu avpeepanek
/p   ó·k e·k·e·ki·ma·tpáni nahəlí·i máta ahpi·í·p·ani·k,
/t   and his disciples were not there either,
/k   neither his disciples,

/b nu nrk mrxrlkek pwsepanek eku prpanek Kupuniumif,
/p ná né·k me·x·é·lki·k po·s·í·p·ani·k, íka pé·p·ani·k †kapəniámink,
/t that crowd of people got into boats and came to Capernaum,
/k they also took shipping, and came to Capernaum,

/b notwnaowapani Nhesusu.
/p nɔt·o·naɔwwá·p·ani nči·sás·a,
/t looking for Jesus.
/k seeking for Jesus.

Jn 6.25
/b Mrhi mrxkaotetc, munwprkwf tali kamif, tclawapani,
/p mé·či me·xkaɔhtí·t·e mənəp·é·k·unk táli ká·mink, təlawwá·p·ani,
/t After they had found him on the other side of the sea, they said to him,
/k And when they had found him on the other side of the sea, they said unto him,

/b Rvakrkifrs hifc ct ta kpepavump?
/p "ehahke·kínke·s, čínke=ét=tá kpi·p·á·həmp?"
/t "Teacher, when did you come here?"
/k Rabbi, when camest thou hither?

Jn 6.26
/b Nhesus tclapani, kehe ktclwvmw,
/p nčí·sas təlá·p·ani, "khičí·i ktəllúhəmɔ,
/t Jesus said to them, "I tell you truly,
/k Jesus answered them and said, Verily, verily, I say unto you,

/b mutu kwnhi ntwnaewunro rli nrmrkup funjyrvoswakunu,
/p máta kúnči-nto·nai·wəné·ɔ é·li-ne·mé·k·əp nkanšaehɔ·s·əwá·k·ana,
/t you do not seek me because you saw my miracles,
/k Ye seek me, not because ye saw the miracles,

/b jwq rli metherkup nrl avponu, ok kespwenropani.
/p šúkw é·li-mi·č·ié·k·əp né·l ahpɔ́·na, ɔ́·k kki·spwi·ne·ɔ́·p·ani.
/t but because you ate the loaves of bread and were filled by them.
/k but because ye did eat of the loaves, and were filled.

Jn 6.27
/b Kahi kavtatufvun alituk a methwakun.
/p káči kahta·t·ánkhan alət·ək=á· mi·č·əwá·k·an,
/t Do not desire the food that would rot,
/k Labour not for the meat which perisheth,

/b jwq a nc methwakun wlitukh rvalamakamek pumawswakun.
/p šúkw=á· nə́ mi·č·əwá·k·an wələt·ək=č, ehaləmá·kami·k pəma·wsəwá·k·an.
/t but rather the food that will be good, eternal life.
/k but for that meat which endureth unto everlasting life,

Text, Transcription, and Translation

/b Nul nuni linw Wrqesif kmelkwnroh;
/p nál nə́ni lə́nu we·k·wí·s·ink kəmi·lko·né·ɔ=č,
/t That is what the man who is the Son will give you,
/k which the Son of man shall give unto you:

/b rli nuni kejemat Krtanitwet Wrtwxumunt.
/p é·li- nə́ni -ki·š·í·ma·t ke·tanət·ó·wi·t we·t·ó·x·əmənt."
/t for that is what God the Father assigned to him."
/k for him hath God the Father sealed.   [RSV "on him .. set his seal"]

Jn 6.28
/b Nu tclawapani; Tuh vuh ntclsenrn
/p ná təlawwá·p·ani, "tá=č=háč ntəlsí·ne·n,
/t Then they said to him, "What shall we do,
/k Then said they unto him, What shall we do,

/b wcnhih mekintumrf Krtanitwet mwekwmoswakun?
/p wénči-=č -mi·kə́ntamenk ke·tanət·ó·wi·t mwi·kəmɔ·s·əwá·k·an?"
/t that we may do the work of God?"
/k that we might work the works of God?

Jn 6.29
/b Nhesus tclapani; jr nuni Krtanitwet mwekwmoswakun,
/p nčí·sas təlá·p·ani, "šé· nə́ni ke·tanət·ó·wi·t mwi·kəmɔ·s·əwá·k·an,
/t Jesus said to him, "This is the work of God,
/k Jesus answered and said unto them, This is the work of God,

/b ktclih wlistaonro Krtanitwet prtalwkalatpani.
/p ktə́li-=č -wələstaɔ·né·ɔ ke·tanət·ó·wi·t pe·t·alo·ka·la·tpáni."
/t for you to listen to the one that God has sent."
/k that ye believe on him whom he hath sent.

Jn 6.30
/b Tclawapani; Ta vuh lenakot kekenwlwakun bqc prnwntvekrun,
/p təlawwá·p·ani, "tá=háč li·ná·k·ɔt khiki·no·ləwá·k·an yúkwe pe·nunthiké·an,
/t They said to him, "What kind of a sign are you now revealing,
/k They said therefore unto him, What sign shewest thou then,

/b wunhih nrmrf, ok wunhih wlamvetumrf;
/p wə́nči-=č -né·menk, ɔ́·k wə́nči-=č -wəla·mhítamenk?
/t so that we will see it and believe it?
/k that we may see, and believe thee?

/b krkw vuh ktclsi?
/p kéku=háč ktə́lsi?
/t What are you doing?
/k what dost thou work?

Jn 6.31
/b Nwxunanifu krkw methwpanek jwkulepwko trkunu tali,
/p no·x·əna·nínka kéku mi·č·ó·p·ani·k šo·k·əli·pó·k·ɔ té·kəna táli,
/t Our forefathers ate something sweet in the wilderness,
/k Our fathers did eat manna in the desert;

/b rli nuni lrkvasekup,
/p é·li- nə́ni -le·kha·s·í·k·əp:
/t as that is what was written:
/k as it is written,

/b Melapanek osavkamc wunhi avpon wcnhi metsevtetup. ‖
/p mi·lá·p·ani·k ɔ·s·áhkame wə́nči ahpɔ́·n wénči-mi·tsihtí·t·əp."
/t from heaven they were given bread for them to eat."
/k He gave them bread from heaven to eat.

Jn 6.32
(p. 82)
/b Nu Nhesus tclanrp; Kehe kehe ktclinro;
/p ná nčí·sas təlá·ne·p, "khičí·i, khičí·i, ktəlləné·ɔ,
/t Then Jesus said to them, "Truly, truly, I say to you,
/k Then Jesus said unto them, Verily, verily, I say unto you,

/b Mwjiju mutu melqrkup nc avpon osavkamc wunhi,
/p mo·šə́š·a máta mi·lkwé·k·əp nə́ ahpɔ́·n ɔ·s·áhkame wə́nči,
/t Moses is not the one who gave you that bread from heaven,
/k Moses gave you not that bread from heaven;

/b jwq nuni Nwx kumelkwnro myai osavkamre avpon.
/p šúkw náni nó·x kəmi·lko·né·ɔ mayá·i-ɔ·s·ahkame·í·i-ahpɔ́·n.
/t but it is my father that gives you the true bread of heaven.
/k but my Father giveth you the true bread from heaven.

Jn 6.33
/b Rli Krtanitwet toponum, nul wuni osavkamc wunheyet,
/p é·li ke·tanət·ó·wi·t tɔp·ɔ́·nəm, nál wáni ɔ·s·áhkame wənčí·ai·t.
/t For the bread of God is this one who came from heaven.
/k For the bread of God is he which cometh down from heaven,

/b ok melanroh pumawswakun b cntu lawsethek.
/p ɔ́·k mi·la·né·ɔ=č pəma·wsəwá·k·an yú entala·wsí·č·i·k."
/t And life shall be given to the people of this world (*lit.* 'the ones living here')."
/k and giveth life unto the world.

Jn 6.34
/b Nu tclanrop; Nrvlalerf aphih ktaxamenrn b avpon.
/p ná təla·né·ɔ·p, "nehəlá·lienk, á·pči=č ktax·amí·ne·n yú ahpɔ́·n."
/t Then they said to him, "Master, you must feed us this bread forever."
/k Then said they unto him, Lord, evermore give us this bread.

Jn 6.35 /b Nu Nhesus tclanrp; Ne ta nuni pumawswek avpon:
         /p ná nčí·sas təlá·ne·p, "ní·=tá nəni pəma·wsó·wi·k ahpɔ́·n.
         /t Then Jesus said to them, "I am the living bread.
         /k And Jesus said unto them, I am the bread of life:

         /b awrn toxetc, mutuh vaji kavtwpwei,
         /p awé·n tɔx·í·t·e, máta=č háši kahto·p·wí·i.
         /t If anyone comes to me, they will never be hungry.
         /k he that cometh to me shall never hunger;

         /b wlistyetc mutuh vuji kutwsumwei.
         /p wələstaí·t·e, máta=č háši kahto·s·əmwí·i.
         /t If they believe in me, they will never be thirsty.
         /k and he that believeth on me shall never thirst.

Jn 6.36 /b Jwq mrhi ktclinrop, ktcli nrenro, qeaqi nrsko kulsityevwmw.
         /p šúkw mé·či ktəlləné·ɔ·p ktə́li-ne·i·né·ɔ, kwiá·kwi né·skɔ kkəlsət·ai·húmɔ.
         /t But I have told you that you see me, and still you do not yet believe me.
         /k But I said unto you, That ye also have seen me, and believe not.

Jn 6.37 /b Wrmi cntxi Nwx melethi nwtxwkwk
         /p wé·mi éntxi- nó·x -mi·lí·č·i no·txúk·o·k,
         /t All those that my father gave me come to me,
         /k All that the Father giveth me shall come to me;

         /b ok awrn toxetc taa tu ekali ntclskaoi.
         /p ɔ́·k awé·n tɔx·í·t·e, tá=á·=tá íkali ntəlskaɔ́·i.
         /t and if anyone comes to me I will not drive him away.
         /k and him that cometh to me I will in no wise cast out.

Jn 6.38 /b Rli osavkamc nwmvwmp,
         /p é·li ɔ·s·áhkame nó·mhəmp.
         /t For, I came from heaven.
         /k For I came down from heaven,

         /b takw nevlahi rletrvau ntclsewun, jwq nrkuma prtalwkaletup wtetrvrokun.
         /p takó· nihəláči e·li·t·e·há·a ntəlsí·wən, šúkw né·k·əma pe·t·alo·ka·lí·t·əp wti·t·e·he·ɔ́·k·an.
         /t I do not do what I want to do, but the will of the one who has sent me here.
         /k not to do mine own will, but the will of him that sent me.

Jn 6.39 /b Jr ncni prtalwkaletup Wrtxwxumunt wtetrvokun,
                     [⟨-txwx-⟩ for ⟨-twx-⟩; ⟨-trvo-⟩ for ⟨-trvro-⟩]
         /p šé· nə́ni pe·t·alo·ka·lí·t·əp we·t·ó·x·əmənt wti·t·e·he·ɔ́·k·an,
         /t That is what the Father that has sent me wants,
         /k And this is the Father's will which hath sent me,

/b   wnhih mutu krkw afvetwu cntxi meletup
/p   wə́nči-=č máta kéku -ankhitó·wa éntxi-mi·lí·t·əp.
/t   so that I do not lose anything of all that he gave me.
/k   that of all which he hath given me I should lose nothing,

/b   jwqh ntamwekunaok mckuni-kejqekc.
/p   šúkw=č nta·mwi·kəná·ɔk məkə́ni-ki·škwí·k·e.
/t   But I shall raise them up on the last day.
/k   but should raise it up again at the last day.

Jn 6.40   /b   Ok jr ncni prtalwkaletup wtetrvrokun;
              /p   ɔ́·k šé· nə́ni pe·t·alo·ka·lí·t·əp wti·t·e·he·ɔ́·k·an,
              /t   And that is what the one that has sent me wants,
              /k   And this is the will of him that sent me,

/b   Tclih wrmi cntxi nrothek Wrqesifi ok wlamvetaovtetc
/p   tə́li-=č wé·mi éntxi-ne·ɔ́·č·i·k we·k·wi·s·ínki, ɔ́·k wəla·mhitaɔhtí·t·e,
/t   that everyone who sees the Son, if they also believe him,
/k   that every one which seeth the Son, and believeth on him,

/b   koskiih wlatwnro rvalumakumek pumawswakun: [⟨koski-|ih⟩: better /-káski-=č/:
/p   -káski-=č -wəla·to·né·ɔ ehaləmá·kami·k pəma·wsəwá·k·an, [*i.e.*, tə́li-=č .. -káski-=č]
/t   will be able to have eternal life,
/k   may have everlasting life:

/b   ok ntamwekunaokh mckuni-kejqekc.
/p   ɔ́·k nta·mwi·kəná·ɔk=č məkə́ni-ki·škwí·k·e."
/t   and I shall raise them up on the last day."
/k   and I will raise him up at the last day.

Jn 6.41   /b   Nhwuk honsitaowao, rli lwrtup,
              /p   nčó·wak čɔns·ət·aɔwwá·ɔ, é·li-luwé·t·əp,
              /t   The Jews took what he said amiss when he said,
              /k   The Jews then murmured at him, because he said,

/b   ne ta nc avpon osavkumc wcnheyek.
/p   "ní·=tá nə́ ahpɔ́·n ɔ·s·áhkame wenčí·ai·k."
/t   "I am the bread that came from heaven."
/k   I am the bread which came down from heaven.

Jn 6.42   /b   Lwrpanek, mutu vuh nul wuni Nhesus Nhosipu wrqesumwkwk,
              /p   luwé·p·ani·k, "máta=háč nál wáni nčí·sas, †nčo·sə́p·a we·k·wi·s·əmúk·wək?
              /t   They said, "Isn't this Jesus, who is the son of Joseph?
              /k   And they said, Is not this Jesus, the son of Joseph,

Text, Transcription, and Translation

/b wxol, ok kovrsul kavni nevnrownu.
/p óxˑɔl ɔ́ˑk kɔhéˑsˑal, káˑxəne nnihəneˑɔ́ˑwəna."
/t Haven't we long known his father and his mother?"
/k whose father and mother we know? ...

Jn 6.43
/b Nc wunhi Nhesus lanrp; Kahi tu hanistaevrq.
/p nə́ wwə́nči- nčíˑsas -láˑneˑp, "káči=tá čanəstaíˑheˑkw.
/t Because of that, Jesus said to them, "Do not take what I say amiss.
/k Jesus therefore answered and said unto them, Murmur not among yourselves.

Jn 6.44
/b Takw a awrn fuski toxkwi, kcnh a Wrtwxumunt prtalwkaletup natcnatc;
/p takóˑ=áˑ awéˑn nkáski-tɔxkóˑwi, kə́nč=áˑ weˑtóˑxˑəmənt peˑtaloˑkaˑlíˑtˑəp naˑtˑənáˑtˑe,
/t No one would be able to come to me, unless the Father who sent me takes him,
/k No man can come to me, except the Father which hath sent me draw him:

/b nulh nuni ntamwekunu mukuni-kejqekc.
/p nál=č náni ntaˑmwíˑkəna məkə́ni-kiˑškwíˑkˑe.
/t *Him* I shall raise up in the last day.
/k and I will raise him up at the last day.

Jn 6.45
/b Nrnekanewrwsetpanifu jr b tclrkvekasenrop;
/p nehəniˑkˑaˑníˑi-weˑwsiˑtpanínka, šéˑ yú təleˑkhiˑkˑaˑsˑiˑnéˑɔˑp:
/t This is what the prophets of old have written:
/k It is written in the prophets,

/b Wrmih Krtanitwet ktalrpomkwu.
/p wéˑmi=č keˑtanətˑóˑwiˑt ktaleˑpˑɔˑmkúwa.
/t 'God will give all of you advice.'
/k And they shall be all taught of God.

/b Wrmi cntxi puntaothek krtanitwelethi, ok watulwqvetet Wrtwxumunhi, [⟨watu-‖lwqvetet⟩]
/p wéˑmi éntxi-pəntaɔ́ˑčˑiˑk keˑtanətˑoˑwiˑlíˑčˑi ɔ́ˑk -wwaˑtəlukhwítiˑt weˑtˑoˑxˑəmə́nči,
/t Everyone who hears God and is taught by the Father,
/k Every man therefore that hath heard, and hath learned of the Father,

(p. 83)
/b nul ekh nrk ntcli toxkwnro. [⟨nul ekh⟩ for ⟨nulekh⟩]
/p náliˑk=č néˑk ntə́li-tɔxkoˑnéˑɔ.
/t those are the ones who shall come to me.
/k cometh unto me.

Jn 6.46
/b Jwq takw vuji awrn, wnroepani Wrtwxuminthi,
/p šúkw takóˑ háši awéˑn wəneˑɔˑíˑpˑani weˑtˑoˑxˑəmə́nči.
/t But no one has ever seen the Father.
/k Not that any man hath seen the Father,

/b   nul wuni xwva Krtanitwetif wunheyet wnropani Wrtwxumunthi.
/p   nál wáni xó·ha ke·tanət·o·wí·t·ink wənčí·ai·t wəne·ó·p·ani we·t·o·x·əmə́nči.
/t   It is only he who comes from God who has seen the Father.
/k   save he which is of God, he hath seen the Father.

Jn 6.47
/b   Kehe kehe ktclwvwmw awrn nvakaletc, rvalumakamekh pumawswakun topetakwn.
/p   khičí·i, khičí·i, ktəllúhəmɔ, awé·n nhaka·lí·t·e, ehaləmá·kami·k=č pəma·wsəwá·k·an tɔp·i·tá·k·o·n.
/t   Truly, truly, I tell you, if anyone relies on me, eternal life will be in him.
/k   Verily, verily, I say unto you, He that believeth on me hath everlasting life.

Jn 6.48
/b   Ne tu kehe prmawswek avpon.
/p   ní·=tá khičí·i pe·ma·wsó·wi·k ahpɔ́·n.
/t   I am truly the living bread.
/k   I am that bread of life.

Jn 6.49
/b   Kwxwawfu methwpanek krkw jwkul e pwko trkunu tali,
                               [⟨jwkul e|pwko⟩ for ⟨jwkulepwko⟩]
/p   ko·x·əwa·únka mi·č·ó·p·ani·k kéku šo·k·əli·pó·k·ɔ té·kəna táli,
/t   Your forefathers ate something sweet in the wilderness,
/k   Your fathers did eat manna in the wilderness,

/b   ok mrhi wekowswfu.
/p   ó·k mé·či wi·kɔ·wsúnka.
/t   and now their lives have ended.
/k   and are dead.

Jn 6.50
/b   Bni avpon osavkamc wcnheyek
/p   yó·ni ahpɔ́·n ɔ·s·áhkame wenčí·ai·k,
/t   This bread that comes from heaven,
/k   This is the bread which cometh down from heaven,

/b   ncni awrn methetc, ta tu wekowsei.
/p   nə́ni awé·n mi·č·í·t·e, tá=á·=tá wi·kɔ·wsí·i.
/t   if anyone eats that, their life will not end.
/k   that a man may eat thereof, and not die.

Jn 6.51
/b   Ne ta ncni avpon osavkamc wcnheyek;
/p   ní·=tá nə́ni ahpɔ́·n ɔ·s·áhkame wenčí·ai·k.
/t   *I* am the bread that came from heaven.
/k   I am the living bread which came down from heaven:

/b   tamsc awrn bni avpon methetc, rvalumakumekh pumawsw;
/p   tá·mse awé·n yó·ni ahpɔ́·n mi·č·í·t·e, ehaləmá·kami·k=č pəmá·wsu.

/t If anyone should eat this bread, he will live forever.
/k if any man eat of this bread, he shall live for ever:

/b ncni avpon melukh, nul nuni nwwsum
/p nə́ni ahpɔ́·n mí·lak=č, nál nə́ni no·ó·s·əm.
/t That bread that I shall give you, that is my flesh.
/k and the bread that I will give is my flesh,

/b nmrkunh wcnhih pumawswvalqevtet b cntu lawsethek.
/p nəmé·k·ən=č, wénči-=č -pəma·wso·ha·lkwíhti·t yú entala·wsí·č·i·k."
/t I shall give it, so that it shall save the lives of the people of this world."
/k which I will give for the life of the world.

Jn 6.52 /b Nuni wunhi Nhwuk nevlahi litenrop, lwrpanek,
/p nə́ni wwə́nči- nčó·wak nihəláči -lət·i·né·ɔ·p, luwé·p·ani·k,
/t Because of that the Jews spoke among themselves, saying,
/k The Jews therefore strove among themselves, saying,

/b Ta vuh a mct ktcli melkwnrn wwsum wunhi a methiufq;
/p "tá=háč=á·m=ét ktə́li-mi·lkó·ne·n o·ó·s·əm, wə́nči-=á· -mí·č·iankw?"
/t "How would he possibly give us his flesh, so that we would eat it?"
/k How can this man give us his flesh to eat?

Jn 6.53 /b Nu Nhesus tclanrp; Kehe kehe ktclwvumw,
/p ná nčí·sas təlá·ne·p, "khičí·i, khičí·i, ktəllúhəmɔ,
/t Then Jesus said to them, "Truly, truly, I say to you,
/k Then Jesus said unto them, Verily, verily, I say unto you,

/b mutuh metherqc Wrqesumunt linw wwsum, ok munrrqc mwkum,
/p máta=č mi·č·ié·k·we we·k·wí·s·əmənt lə́nu o·ó·s·əm, ɔ́·k məne·é·k·we mmó·kəm,
/t if you do not eat the flesh of the man who is the Son, and drink his blood,
/k Except ye eat the flesh of the Son of man, and drink his blood,

/b ta tcxi pumawsswakun ktupetakwnro.   [⟨pumaws-|swakun⟩ for ⟨pumawswakun⟩]
/p tá=á· téxi pəma·wsəwá·k·an ktap·i·ta·k·o·wəné·ɔ.
/t you would have no life at all in you.
/k ye have no life in you.

Jn 6.54 /b Awrn nwwsum methetc, ok nmwkum munrtc,
/p awé·n no·ó·s·əm mi·č·í·t·e ɔ́·k nəmó·kəm məné·t·e,
/t If anyone eats my flesh and drinks my blood,
/k Whoso eateth my flesh, and drinketh my blood,

	/b	nulh nuni rvalumakumek pumawswakun topetakwn,
	/p	nál=č náni ehaləmá·kami·k pəma·wsəwá·k·an tɔp·i·tá·k·o·n,
	/t	*he* shall have eternal life in him,
	/k	hath eternal life;

	/b	okh ntamwekunu mukuni-kejqekc.
	/p	ɔ́·k=č nta·mwí·kəna məkə́ni-ki·škwí·k·e.
	/t	and I shall raise him up on the last day.
	/k	and I will raise him up at the last day.

Jn 6.55
	/b	Rli nwwsum kehe methwakun, ok nmwkum kehe munrokun.
	/p	é·li no·ó·s·əm khičí·i mi·č·əwá·k·an, ɔ́·k nəmó·kəm khičí·i məne·ó·k·an.
	/t	For my flesh is truly food, and my blood is truly drink.
	/k	For my flesh is meat indeed, and my blood is drink indeed.

Jn 6.56
	/b	Awrn nwwsum methetc, ok nmwkum munrtc,
	/p	awé·n no·ó·s·əm mi·čí·t·e ɔ́·k nəmó·kəm məné·t·e,
	/t	If anyone eats my flesh and drinks my blood,
	/k	He that eateth my flesh, and drinketh my blood,

	/b	nul nuni ntupetaq ok ntupetao.
	/p	nál náni ntap·í·ta·kw, ɔ́·k ntap·í·taɔ.
	/t	*he* is in *me*, and I am in him.
	/k	dwelleth in me, and I in him.

Jn 6.57
	/b	Rlkeqi prtalwkaletup prmawswet Wrtwxumunt,
	/p	e·lkí·kwi-pe·t·alo·ka·lí·t·əp pe·má·wsi·t we·t·ó·x·əmənt,
	/t	The time when the living Father sent me here,
	/k	As the living Father hath sent me,

	/b	ok wrtwxumunt, ntcli pumawswvalkwn
	/p	ɔ́·k we·t·ó·x·əmənt ntə́li-pəma·wso·há·lko·n.
	/t	the Father was also the one who gave me life.
	/k	and I live by the Father:

	/b	na ok nc nrpc ntclkeqih pumawswvalan awrn methetc nwwsum.
	/p	ná ɔ́·k nə́ né·pe ntəlkí·kwi-=č -pəma·wso·há·la·n awé·n mi·čí·t·e no·ó·s·əm.
	/t	That is also the time when I, too, shall give life to anyone if he eats my flesh.
	/k	so he that eateth me, even he shall live by me.

Jn 6.58
	/b	Jr ncni avpon osavkamc wunheyek,
	/p	šé· nə́ni ahpó·n ɔ·s·áhkame wənčí·ai·k,
	/t	That is the bread that comes from heaven,
	/k	This is that bread which came down from heaven:

/b mutu ncni rlenako krkw methevtetup kwxwawfu, ok wekoswpanifu;
/p máta nə́ni e·li·ná·k·ɔ kéku mi·č·ihtí·t·əp ko·x·əwa·únka, ɔ́·k wi·kɔ·wso·p·anínka;
/t not the kind that your forefathers ate, and their lives ended.
/k not as your fathers did eat manna, and are dead:

/b bni avpon methevtc awrn, rvalumakumekh pumawsw.   [⟨pumaw-‖sw⟩]
/p yó·ni ahpɔ́·n mi·č·í·t·e awé·n, ehaləmá·kami·k=č pəmá·wsu."
/t If anyone eats *this* bread he shall live forever."
/k he that eateth of this bread shall live for ever.

Jn 6.59 /b Bni tclaptwnrnrp cntu mycluf cntu avkrkifrtc Kupuniumif tali.
(p. 84) /p yó·ni təla·pto·né·ne·p énta-ma·éhəlank énta-ahke·kinké·t·e †kapəniámink táli.
/t This is what he said when he taught in the synagogue in Capernaum.
/k These things said he in the synagogue, as he taught in Capernaum.

Jn 6.60 /b Nc wunhi xrli rkrkematpani puntametetc, lwrpanek
/p nə́ wənči, xé·li e·k·e·ki·ma·tpáni pəntamihtí·t·e, luwé·p·ani·k,
/t Because of that, when many of his disciples heard it, they said,
/k Many therefore of his disciples, when they had heard this, said,

/b avot ta bni aptwnakun;
/p "áhɔt=tá yó·ni a·pto·ná·k·an.
/t "These words are difficult.
/k This is an hard saying;

/b awrn nc va mct koski puntamun?
/p awé·n=néh=á·m=ét kɔ́ski-pə́ntamən?"
/t Who would possibly be able to understand them?"
/k who can hear it?

Jn 6.61 /b Nhesus mrhi nevlahi wrovatc rkrkematpani tcli litenro, nu tclanrp,
/p nčí·sas mé·či nihəláči we·ɔ·há·t·e e·k·e·ki·ma·tpáni tɔ́li-lət·i·né·ɔ, ná təlá·ne·p,
/t After Jesus himself realized his disciples were talking together, he said to them,
/k When Jesus knew in himself that his disciples murmured at it, he said unto them,

/b Ncni vuh kwnhi hanistamunro?
/p "nə́ni=háč kúnči-čanəstaməné·ɔ?
/t "Is that the reason you take it amiss?
/k Doth this offend you?

Jn 6.62	/b	Tuh vuh lrw nrrqc linw Wrqesumunt tcli uspen li vwqrwf wunheyet?
	/p	tá=č=háč lé·w ne·é·k·we lónu we·k·wí·s·əmənt tóli-áspi·n lí hukwé·yunk, wənčí·ai·t?
	/t	What will happen if you see the man who is the Son ascend to heaven, where he came from?
	/k	What and if ye shall see the Son of man ascend up where he was before?

Jn 6.63	/b	Montwakun a pumawswvalwrbw, wwsum muta krkw laprmkotwi;
	/p	mɔnt·uwwá·k·an=á· pəma·wso·ha·ləwe·yó·u; o·ó·s·əm máta=á· kéku la·p·e·mkɔt·ó·wi.
	/t	His spiritual power would give life; his flesh would not be good for anything.
	/k	It is the spirit that quickeneth; the flesh profiteth nothing: ...

Jn 6.64	/b	jwq alintc kelwu mutu kulsitamwnro.
	/p	šúkw a·lónte ki·ló·wa máta kkəlsət·amo·wəné·ɔ."
	/t	But some of you do not believe it."
	/k	But there are some of you that believe not.

	/b	Rli nevnwhi wavat awrni mutu wrlsitumileqc, [⟨-qc⟩ for /-k·wi/]
	/p	é·li- nihənúči -wwá·ha·t awé·ni máta we·lsət·aməlí·k·wi,
	/t	For he knew from the beginning who did not believe,
	/k	For Jesus knew from the beginning who they were that believed not,

	/b	okh awrn mrvlamwnt.
	/p	ó·k=č awé·n méhəlamunt.
	/t	and who would sell him out.
	/k	and who should betray him.

Jn 6.65	/b	Lwrp Nhesus, nanc kwnhi lilinrop,
	/p	lúwe·p nčí·sas, "ná=nə kúnči-lələné·ɔ·p,
	/t	Jesus said, "That is why I said to you,
	/k	And he said, Therefore said I unto you,

	/b	ntcli a muta awrn kuski toxkwun
	/p	ntóli-=á· máta awé·n -káski-tɔxkó·wən.
	/t	that no one would be able to come to me.
	/k	that no man can come unto me,

	/b	kcnh a Nwx melatc kenh fuski toxwq. [⟨kenh⟩ for ⟨kcnh⟩]
	/p	kə́nč=á· nó·x mi·lá·t·e, kə́nč nkáski-tóx·ukw."
	/t	Only if my father grants it to them, then he would be able to come to me."
	/k	except it were given unto him of my Father.

| Jn 6.66 | /b | Nanc wunhi xrli rkrkematpani qtukelen, |
| | /p | ná=nə wwə́nči- xé·li e·k·e·ki·ma·tpáni -kwtək·í·li·n, |

/t Because of that many of his disciples turned back,
/k From that time many of his disciples went back,

/b ok mutu heh wethrvkwepani.
/p ɔ́·k máta čí·č wwi·č·e·yko·wí·p·ani.
/t and they no longer went with him.
/k and walked no more with him.

Jn 6.67
/b Na Nhesus tclanrp nrl tclin ok neju;
/p ná nčí·sas təlá·ne·p né·l télən ɔ́·k ní·š·a,
/t Then Jesus said to the twelve,
/k Then said Jesus unto the twelve,

/b ok vuh krpwu kutu pale avmw?
/p "ɔ́·k=háč ké·pəwa kkát·a- palí·i -áhəmɔ?"
/t "Do you also want to go away?"
/k Will ye also go away?

Jn 6.68
/b Symun Petul tclapani; Nrvlaleun awrnif vuh a ntavnu?
/p †sáiman-pí·təl təlá·p·ani, "nehəlá·lian, awé·nink=háč=á· ntáhəna?
/t Simon Peter said to him, "My Lord, who would we go to?
/k Then Simon Peter answered him, Lord, to whom shall we go?

/b Ke xwva kwlvatwn rvalumakumek pumawswek aptwnakun;
/p kí· xó·ha ko·lháto·n ehaləmá·kami·k pəma·wsó·wi·k a·pto·ná·k·an.
/t You alone have the eternal, living words.
/k thou hast the words of eternal life.

Jn 6.69
/b ok nwatwnrn ktcli ke kehe Klysten
/p ɔ́·k no·wa·tó·ne·n, ktə́li- kí· khičí·i -kəláisti·n,
/t And we know that *you* are truly Christ,
/k And we believe and are sure that thou art that Christ,

/b ktcli qesumwkwn prmawswet Krtanitwet.
/p ktə́li-kkwi·s·əmúk·o·n pe·ma·wsó·wi·t ke·tanət·ó·wi·t."
/t that you are the son of the living God."
/k the Son of the living God.

Jn 6.70
/b Nhesus tclapani, mutu vuh kelwu kpepenwlwvwmwp,
/p nčí·sas təlá·p·ani, "máta=háč ki·ló·wa kpi·p·i·no·lo·húmɔ·p,
/t Jesus said to them, "Have I not chosen *you*,
/k Jesus answered them, Have not I chosen you twelve,

	/b	jwq mawsw njifalwq?
	/p	šúkw má·wsu nšinká·lukw?"
	/t	though one is my enemy?" [*lit.*, 'hates me']
	/k	and one of you is a devil?

Jn 6.71 /b Nhwtus Iskaliut Symun qesul wunhi nuni lwrn,
/p †nčó·tas †iská·liat, †sáiman kkwí·s·al, wwə́nči- nə́ni -lúwe·n,
/t Judas Iscariot, the son of Simon, was the reason he said that,
/k He spake of Judas Iscariot the son of Simon:

/b rli nunulh mclamwnt, nrk mawsw tclcn ok neju cntxethek.
/p é·li nánal=č méhəlamunt, né·k má·wsu télən ɔ́·k ní·š·a entxí·č·i·k.
/t for he was to be the one who sold him out, he being one of those twelve.
/k for he it was that should betray him, being one of the twelve.

Chapter 48 (pp. 84-86). [L. section 47.] (Mark 7.1-5, 13, 16-20; Matthew 15.3-11, 15-20, 12-14.)

Mk 7.1 /b Nu wtxanrop Paluseok, ok alintc rvlrkvekrthek
/p ná o·txa·né·ɔ·p †pa·ləsi·í·ɔk ɔ́·k a·lə́nte ehəle·khi·k·é·č·i·k
/t Then there came to him Pharisees and some scribes
/k Then came together unto him the Pharisees, and certain of the scribes,

/b Nhelwsulum wcnheyethek.
/p †nči·ló·sələm wenči·aí·č·i·k.
/t from Jerusalem.
/k which came from Jerusalem.

Mk 7.2 /b Nu wnronro rkrkemkwselethi,
/p ná wəne·ɔ·né·ɔ e·k·e·ki·mkwəs·i·lí·č·i
/t And then they saw the disciples
/k And when they saw some of his disciples

/b tcli avpon methelen nrsko krjelinhrlet mothwtumaonro. [⟨krje-‖linhrlet⟩]
/p tə́li- ahpɔ́·n -mi·č·í·li·n né·sko ke·š·i·lənčé·li·t, mɔč·o·t·əmaɔ·né·ɔ.
/t eating bread before washing their hands, and they criticized them for it.
/k eat bread with defiled, that is to say, with unwashen, hands, they found fault.

Mk 7.3 /b Rli Paluseok, ok wrmi Nhwuk, mutu tumeki hvopulinhrqc
(p. 85) /p é·li †pa·ləsi·í·ɔk ɔ́·k wé·mi nčó·wak, máta təmí·ki čhɔ·pwələnčé·k·we, [3s for 3p]
/t For the Pharisees and all Jews, if they do not dip their fingers in water often,
/k For the Pharisees, and all the Jews, except they wash their hands oft,

/b ta wifi metseeok,
/p tá=á· wínki-mi·tsi·í·ɔk.

| | /t | would be unwilling to eat. |
| | /k | eat not, |

	/b	krkyimvrte aptwnakun qwnimanro.
	/p	ke·kayəmhe·t·í·i-a·pto·ná·k·an kwənnəməné·ɔ.
	/t	They hold fast to the laws of the rulers.
	/k	holding the tradition of the elders.

Mk 7.4
	/b	Ok cntu mvalamaotif mwk ta hvopwenxkrtetc, ta metseeok,
	/p	ɔ́·k énta-mhalamá·ɔhtink mmó·k, tá=á· čhɔ·pwi·nxkehtí·t·e, tá=á· mi·tsi·í·ɔk.
	/t	And they come from the market and will not eat if they do not rinse their hands.
	/k	And when they come from the market, except they wash, they eat not.

	/b	ok xrlrnaoki peli krkw wrtunimunro tclih nanc lisenro,
	/p	ɔ́·k xe·lennáɔhki pí·li kéku wwe·t·ənəməné·ɔ, táli-=č ná=nə -ləs·i·né·ɔ,
	/t	And they adopt many different kinds of things, for them to do that way,
	/k	And many other things there be, which they have received to hold,
		[RSV "and there are many other traditions which they observe"]

	/b	cntu hvopunasek pyntul, ok seskwu vwsuk, ok wesaosin vwsuk, ok cntulepwifi.
	/p	énta-čhɔ·pwəná·s·i·k paíntal, ɔ́·k si·skəwahó·s·ak, ɔ́·k wi·s·a·ɔhsənhó·s·ak, ɔ́·k entali·p·wínki.
	/t	when cups are washed, and earthen pots, and brass kettles, and tables.
	/k	as the washing of cups, and pots, brasen vessels, and of tables.

Mk 7.5
	/b	Nu Paluseok ok rlrkvekrthek notwtumaonrop
	/p	ná †pa·ləsi·í·ɔk ɔ́·k ehəle·khi·k·é·č·i·k nɔt·o·t·əmaɔ·né·ɔ·p,
	/t	Then the Pharisees and scribes asked him
	/k	Then the Pharisees and scribes asked him,

	/b	wunhi mutu rkrkemathi nanc liselet krkyimvrthek toptwnakunwaif,
	/p	wə́nči- máta e·k·e·ki·má·č·i ná=nə -ləs·í·li·t ke·kayəmhé·č·i·k tɔ·pto·na·k·anəwá·ink,
	/t	why that was not what his disciples did within the laws of the rulers,
	/k	Why walk not thy disciples according to the tradition of the elders,

	/b	jwq avpon methwuk nrsko hvopwenxkctet?
	/p	šúkw ahpó·n mí·č·əwak né·skɔ čhɔ·pwi·nxkéhti·t.
	/t	but they ate bread before dipping their hands in water.
	/k	but eat bread with unwashen hands?

Mt 15.3
	/b	Nu tclanro, Krkw vuh wunhi krpwu haniliserq
	/p	ná təla·né·ɔ, "kéku=háč wə́nči- ké·pəwa -čáni-lə́s·ie·kw
	/t	Then he said to them, "Why do you also do wrong
	/k	But he answered and said unto them, Why do ye also transgress

	/b	Krtanitwet toptwnakun kelwu ktaptwnakunwaif wunhi?
	/p	ke·tanət·ó·wi·t tɔ·pto·ná·k·an ki·ló·wa kta·pto·na·k·anəwá·ink wə́nči?
	/t	regarding the laws of God by *your* traditions?
	/k	the commandment of God by your tradition?

Mt 15.4 /b Rli Krtunitwet lwrtup, Xifwrlumw kwxwu, ok kavrswu,
/p é·li- ke·tanət·ó·wi·t -luwé·t·əp, 'xinkwé·ləmo· kó·x·əwa ɔ́·k kkahé·s·əwa.
/t For God said, 'Respect your (pl.) father and your mother.
/k For God commanded, saying, Honour thy father and mother:

/b awrn mavtaptwnalatc wxo jitu kovrsu
/p awé·n mahta·pto·na·lá·t·e ó·x·ɔ ší=tá kɔhé·s·a,
/t If anyone speaks evilly about their father or their mother,
/k and, He that curseth father or mother,   [RSV "who speaks evil of"]

/b ktclrlifrnh tofulin tali cvcntu nveltif.
/p ktəle·línke·n=č tɔ́nkələn táli ehə́nta-nhíltink.'
/t you shall let him die in the place of execution.'
/k let him die the death.

Mt 15.5 /b Jwk kelwu ktclwcvmw Awrnh latc wxo jitu kovrsu
/p šúkw ki·ló·wa ktələwéhəmɔ, 'awé·n=č lá·t·e ó·x·ɔ ší=tá kɔhé·s·a,
/t But you say, 'If anyone says to their father or mother,
/k But ye say, Whosoever shall say to his father or his mother,

/b nuxpufwman ta Krtanitwet cntxi krkw katatumun;
/p "nnaxpankó·ma·n=tá ke·tanət·ó·wi·t éntxi- kéku -kahtá·t·aman,"
/t "I make a gift to God of as much as you want,"
/k It is a gift, by whatsoever thou mightest be profited by me;

Mt 15.6 /b nuh mutu krkw lri mutu wlistaokqc wxo jitu kovrsu.   [⟨kq⟩ for /k·w/]
/p ná=č máta kéku lé·i, máta wəlɔstaɔ́·k·we ó·x·ɔ ší=tá kɔhé·s·a.
/t then there will be no problem if he does not listen to his father or mother.'
/k And honour not his father or his mother, he shall be free.

/b Jr pnna kpaletwnro Krtanitwet toptwnakun, ktaptwnawaif wunhi;
                              [⟨pnna⟩ for ⟨puna⟩; ⟨nawa⟩ for ⟨nakunwa⟩]
/p šé· pənáh kpali·to·né·ɔ ke·tanət·ó·wi·t tɔ·pto·ná·k·an, kta·pto·na·k·anəwá·ink wə́nči.
/t See here how you destroy the law of God by your tradition.
/k Thus have ye made the commandment of God of none effect by your tradition.

Mk 7.13 /b Ok xrlrnaoki rlenako krkw ktclsevmw.
/p ɔ́·k xe·lennáɔhki e·li·ná·k·ɔ kéku ktəlsíhəmɔ.
/t And you do many kinds of similar things.
/k ... and many such like things do ye.

Mt 15.7 /b Rvakekvorthek kelwu.
/p ehahki·hɔké·č·i·k ki·ló·wa,
/t You hypocrites,
/k Ye hypocrites,

/b Tcpi tu Esrusu nekanaptwnatufpanu, lwrp
/p tépi-=tá ɫi·se·yə́s·a, ni·k·a·na·pto·na·t·ankpána, -lúwe·p,
/t Esaias, who prophesied about it, could rightly say,
/k well did Esaias prophesy of you, saying,

Mt 15.8 /b bk awrnek pcxwsekaethek wtwnwaif wunhi,
/p 'yó·k awé·ni·k pe·x·o·shikaí·č·i·k wto·nəwá·ink wə́nči,
/t 'These people who come near me with their mouths,
/k This people draweth nigh unto me with their mouth,

/b ok xifwrlumevtetc wjrtwnwaif wunhi, jwk ovolumupeletc wtrvuwao.
/p ɔ́·k xinkwe·ləmihtí·t·e wše·t·o·nəwá·ink wə́nči, šúkw ɔhələmap·i·lí·t·e wtehəwá·ɔ,
/t if they also praise me with their lips but their hearts are far away,
/k and honoureth me with their lips; but their heart is far from me.

Mt 15.9 /b Nwhqc a mpatamakwk rli linwu toptwnakunlet alrpomqevtet. [⟨-nlet⟩ for ⟨-nelet⟩]
/p nó·čkwe=á· mpa·tamá·k·o·k, é·li- lə́nəwa tɔ·pto·na·k·aní·li·t -ale·p·ɔ·mkwíhti·t.'"
/t they would pray to me in vain, as they are taught by men the laws of men.'"
/k But in vain they do worship me, teaching for doctrines the commandments of men.

Mt 15.10 /b Mrhi nrtwmatc nrl mrxrlilehi, tclapani, Klistaeq, ok nunwstumwq.
/p mé·či ne·t·o·má·t·e né·l me·x·e·ləlí·č·i, təlá·p·ani, "kələstái·kw, ɔ́·k nəno·stámo·kw.
/t After he had summoned the crowd, he said to them, "Hear me and understand.
/k And he called the multitude, and said unto them, Hear, and understand:

Mt 15.11 /b Takw krkw vatri ktwnwaif a neskvalqrq,
/p takó· kéku hat·é·i kto·nəwá·ink=á· ni·skhá·lkwe·kw,
/t There is nothing that would defile you in your mouths,
/k Not that which goeth into the mouth defileth a man;

/b jwq ncni krkw eku wcnhevlak ktwnwaif ncni wlava kneskvalkwnro.
/p šúkw nə́ni kéku íka wenčíhəla·k kto·nəwá·ink, nə́ni wəláha kəni·skha·lko·né·ɔ.
/t but those things that come out of your mouths, that is rather what defiles you.
/k but that which cometh out of the mouth, this defileth a man.

Mk 7.16 /b Cntxi vwetaokerq puntamwq.
/p éntxi-hwitaɔ́k·ie·kw, pə́ntamo·kw."
/t All of you who have ears, hear!"
/k If any man have ears to hear, let him hear.

Mk 7.17 /b Mrhi trmekrtc li ‖ wekwavmif eku wcfc cntu xrlif;
/p mé·či te·mi·k·é·t·e lí wi·k·əwáhəmink, íka wénke énta-xé·link,
/t After he had entered the house, when he came from the crowd,
/k And when he was entered into the house from the people,

(p. 86) /b nu notwtumakwn rkrkemathi nc rnwntvakrokun.
/p ná nɔt·o·t·əmá·k·o·n e·k·e·ki·má·č·i nə́ e·nunthake·ɔ́·k·an.
/t his disciples asked him about the parable.
/k his disciples asked him concerning the parable.

Mk 7.18 /b Nu tclan; Krpwu vuh mutu knunwstamwnro?
/p ná tə́la·n, "ké·pəwa=háč máta kənəno·stamo·wəné·ɔ?
/t Then he said to them, "Do you also not understand?
/k And he saith unto them, Are ye so without understanding also?

/b Mutu vuh kwatwnro tcli wtwnwaif tuktu krkw punhevlak, ta wneskvalkwunro,
/p máta=háč ko·wa·to·wəné·ɔ, tə́lí wto·nəwá·ink tákta kéku pənčíhəla·k, tá=á·wəni·skha·lko·wəné·ɔ?
/t Do you not know that whatever enters their mouths will not defile them?
/k Do ye not perceive, that whatsoever thing from without entereth into the man, it cannot defile him;

Mk 7.19 /b rli mutu wtrvwaif mutrxif, jwq mwtywaif mutrxun,
/p é·li- máta wtehəwá·ink -mahté·x·ink, šúkw mmo·t·ayəwá·ink mahté·x·ən,
/t For it does not end up (*lit.*, land) in their hearts, but it ends up in their stomachs,
/k Because it entereth not into his heart, but into the belly,

/b nu ok nc wunhi eka li levlr.
/p ná ɔ́·k nə́ wə́nči íkali líhəle·."
/t and from there it goes away."
/k and goeth out into the draught, purging all meats?

Mk 7.20 /b Lwr,
/p lúwe·,
/t He said,
/k And he said, ...

Mt 15.18 /b Jwq krkw wtwnif wcnhevlak wtrvif wunheyb,
/p "šúkw kéku wtó·nink wenčíhəla·k wté·hink wənčí·ayu;
/t "But what issues from his mouth comes from his heart;
/k But those things which proceed out of the mouth come forth from the heart;

/b nul ncni wneskvalkwn;
/p nál nə́ni wəni·skhá·lko·n.
/t that is what defiles him.
/k and they defile the man.

Mt 15.19 /b rli wtrvif wunheyek maheqi punarlintumwakun, nveltwakun, wepcfrokun kumwtkrokun, kulwnrokun ok amutaptwnrokun.
/p é·li- wté·hink -wənčí·ai·k mahčí·kwi-pəna·eləntaməwá·k·an, nhiltəwá·k·an, wi·penke·ó·k·an, kəmo·tke·ó·k·an, kəlo·ne·ó·k·an, ó·k amat·a·pto·ne·ó·k·an.
/t For from the heart come evil thinking, murder, adultery, theft, lying, and blasphemy (*lit.*, saying evil things).
/k For out of the heart proceed evil thoughts, murders, adulteries, fornications, thefts, false witness, blasphemies:

Mt 15.20 /b Nunul li nrl wneskvalkwnu awrn.
/p nanáli né·l wəni·skha·lkó·na awé·n."
/t Those are the things that defile a person."
/k These are the things which defile a man: ...

Mt 15.12 /b Rkrkemunhek tclawao,
/p e·k·e·ki·mə́nči·k təlawwá·ɔ,
/t The disciples said to him,
/k ... his disciples ... said unto him,

/b Kwatwn vuh tcli Palseuk mutu wlrlintumwnro puntamevtetc bl aptwnakunu?
/p "ko·wá·to·n=háč tə́li- †pa·ləsi·í·ɔk máta -wəle·ləntamo·wəné·ɔ pəntamihtí·t·e yó·l a·pto·ná·k·ana?"
/t "Do you know that the Pharisees were not pleased when they heard these words?"
/k Knowest thou that the Pharisees were offended, after they heard this saying?

Mt 15.13 /b Jwq tclao, Wrmi cntxrnaoki Nwx osavkumc rpet mutu vakevrt wrmih pvwnasw.
/p šúkw təlá·ɔ, "wé·mi entxennáɔhki- nó·x ɔ·s·áhkame é·p·i·t máta -hakí·he·t, wé·mi=č phwəná·s·u.
/t But he said to them, "Every kind of thing that my father who is in heaven did not plant shall all be pulled up.
/k But he answered and said, Every plant, which my heavenly Father hath not planted, shall be rooted up.

Mt 15.14 /b Konulenw,
/p kɔ́na lí·no·.
/t Leave them alone.
/k Let them alone:

/b krkrpifohek tolwmoxolanro krkrpifolethi.
/p ke·k·e·p·inkɔ́·č·i·k tɔləmo·x·ɔla·né·ɔ ke·k·e·p·inkɔ·lí·č·i.
/t Let the blind lead the blind.
/k they be blind leaders of the blind.

/b   Krkrpifot alumwxalatc krkrpifolethi
/p   ke·k·e·p·ínkɔ·t alǝmo·x·ɔlá·t·e ke·k·e·p·inkɔ·lí·č·i,
/t   If a blind person leads a blind person,
/k   And if the blind lead the blind,

/b   rle a eku levlrok cntu kesalavku.   [⟨kes-⟩ for ⟨kesk-⟩]
/p   ellí·i=á· íka lihǝlé·ɔk énta-ki·ská·lahka."
/t   both will fall into a ditch."
/k   both shall fall into the ditch.

Chapter 49 (pp. 86-87). [L. section 48.] (Mark 7.24, 30; Matthew 15.21-28)

Mt 15.21   /b   Nu Nhesus tolumskan
              /p   ná nčí·sas tɔlǝmska·n,
              /t   Then Jesus departed
              /k   Then Jesus went thence, ...

Mk 7.24   /b   tonrp Tyulif ok Sytunif, eku li tumekrp wekwavmif,
             /p   tɔ́·ne·p †táyalink ɔ́·k †sáitanink, íkali tǝmí·k·e·p wi·k·ǝwáhǝmink.
             /t   and went to Tyre and Sidon, and he entered into a house.
             /k   ... and went into the borders of Tyre and Sidon, and entered into an house,

/b   takw kotatumwnrp awrni wavkwn, jwq takw kuski kuntavpeep;
/p   takó· kɔt·a·t·amó·wǝne·p awé·ni o·wáhko·n, šúkw takó· káski-kantahpí·i·p;
/t   He did not want anyone to know about him, but he was not able to stay hidden,
/k   and would have no man know it: but he could not be hid.

Mt 15.22   /b   rli Krnexqr nunc wunheyet mai lupuketaotup, tclapani
              /p   é·li- †ke·ní·xkwe nǝ́ni wǝnčí·ai·t -mái-lǝpak·i·taɔ́·t·ǝp, tǝlá·p·ani,
              /t   as a Canaanite woman from there came and wept before him, and she said to him,
              /k   And, behold, a woman of Canaan came out of the same coasts, and cried unto him, saying,

/b   Ktumakrlumel O Nrvlaliun qesu Ntatpiu;   [⟨Ntatpiu⟩ for ⟨Ntrpitu⟩]
/p   "ktǝma·k·é·lǝmi·l, ó· nehǝlá·lian, kkwí·s·a †nte·pít·a.
/t   "Have mercy on me, my Lord, son of David.
/k   Have mercy on me, O Lord, thou Son of David;

/b   ntanis ave kwphrwnwkw mavtuntwu.
/p   ntá·nǝs áhi kupče·wǝnúk·u mahtant·ó·wa."
/t   My daughter is very much driven mad by the devil."
/k   my daughter is grievously vexed with a devil.

Mt 15.23   /b   Jwq takw krkw tclaeo.
              /p   šúkw takó· kéku tǝla·í·ɔ.

	/t	But he said nothing to her.
	/k	But he answered her not a word.

/b Rkrkemathi tclkw, Ekali liskaw,
/p eˑkˑeˑkiˑmáˑčˑi tə́lku, "íkali lə́skaw,"
/t His disciples said to him, "Send her away,"
/k And his disciples came and besought him, saying, Send her away;

/b rli lupuketakwk.
/p éˑli-ləpakˑiˑtáˑkˑuk.
/t as she was weeping before him.
/k for she crieth after us.

Mt 15.24
/b Jwq tclao, Takw peli ntclalwkalkri
/p šúkw təláˑɔ, "takóˑ píˑli ntəlaloˑkaˑlkéˑi,
/t But he said to her, "I was not sent to anywhere else,
/k But he answered and said, I am not sent

/b xwva jwq mrkesuk trofulukek w̨unhi Isliul weket.
/p xóˑha šúkw mekíˑsˑak teˑɔnkələ́kˑiˑk wə́nči †isəlíal wíˑkˑiˑt."
/t but only the lost sheep from the house of Israel."
/k but unto the lost sheep of the house of Israel.

Mt 15.25
/b Nu tonhi wenwrn, lwr, Nrvlaliun wethumel.
/p ná tə́nči-wíˑnəweˑn, lúweˑ, "nehəláˑlian, wíˑčˑəmiˑl.
/t Then she renewed her plea, saying, "Lord, help me."
/k Then came she and worshipped him, saying, Lord, help me.

Mt 15.26
/b Jwq tclao takw wlexunwi wrtunnumaon meminsuk toponwu,
/p šúkw təláˑɔ, "takóˑ wəliˑxˑənóˑwi weˑtˑənəmáɔˑn miˑmə́nsak tɔpˑɔ́ˑnəwa,
/t But he said to her, "It is not right to take the children's bread from them
/k But he answered and said, It is not meet to take the children's bread,

/b xaman morkunrok.
/p xámaˑn mweˑkˑanéˑɔk."
/t and feed it to dogs."
/k and to cast it to dogs.

Mt 15.27
/b Tclao, ‖ Kwlamwc Nrvlaliun,
/p təláˑɔ, "koˑláˑməwe, nehəláˑlian.
/t She said to him, "You are right, my Lord.
/k And she said, Truth, Lord:

(p. 87)	/b	Jwqh morkunreuk mwimethenro punevlak nrvlalqevtethi tcvcntulepwifumif.
	/p	šúkw=č mwe·k·ané·ɔk mwihəmi·č·i·né·ɔ pəníhəla·k nehəla·lkwihtí·č·i tehəntali·p·wínkəmink."
	/t	But the dogs will eat what falls at their master's table."
	/k	yet the dogs eat of the crumbs which fall from their masters' table.
Mt 15.28	/b	Nu Nhesus noxkwman tclao,
	/p	ná nčí·sas nɔxkó·ma·n, təlá·ɔ,
	/t	Then Jesus answered her, saying to her,
	/k	Then Jesus answered and said unto her,
	/b	O xqr xifwi knakatamwrokun!
	/p	"ó· xkwé·, xínkwi kəna·ka·t·amwe·ó·k·an.
	/t	"O woman, your faith is great.
	/k	O woman, great is thy faith:
	/b	Lrwh rletrvaun.
	/p	lé·w=č e·li·t·e·há·an.
	/t	It shall be as you wish.
	/k	be it unto thee even as thou wilt.
	/b	Nu ncni lukveqi jai wlamalselen tonu.
	/p	ná nə́ni ləkhíkwi šá·e o·lamalsí·li·n tó·na.
	/t	Then at that moment her daughter was immediately well.
	/k	And her daughter was made whole from that very hour.
Mk 7.30	/b	Eku pratc weket moxkao tcli mavtuntw pale an;
	/p	íka pe·á·t·e wí·k·i·t, mɔxkaó·ɔ tə́li- mahtánt·u palí·i -á·n.
	/t	When she got to her house, she found that the devil had gone away.
	/k	And when she was come to her house, she found the devil gone out,
	/b	wnro tonu jcfexif avpencf.
	/p	wəne·ó·ɔ tó·na šenkí·x·ink ahpí·nenk.
	/t	She saw her daughter lying on a bed.
	/k	and her daughter laid upon the bed.

Chapter 50 (p. 87). [L. section 49.] (Mark 7.31-36; Matthew 15.30-31)

Mk 7.31	/b	Lupi rlumskatc wunhi Tyul ok Sytun lwetc Tclin wtrnif,
	/p	lápi e·ləmská·t·e wə́nči †táyal ó·k †sáitan, lo·wí·t·e télən-o·t·é·nink,
	/t	After he again departed from Tyre and Sidon and passed through Ten-City,
	/k	(1) And again, departing from the coasts of Tyre and Sidon, (3) through the midst of the coasts of Decapolis, [numbers = sequence in L.]

/b nu eku ponrp Falule munwprkwf.
/p ná íka pó·ne·p †nka·lalí·i-mənəp·é·k·unk.
/t he came to the sea of Galilee.
/k (2) he came unto the sea of Galilee,

Mk 7.32
/b Nu eku prtaon krkrpxalethi ok mutu keski krkw lwrlethi. [⟨keski⟩ for ⟨kekski⟩]
/p ná íka pé·t·aɔ·n ke·k·e·pxa·lí·č·i, ɔ́·k máta kí·kski- kéku -luwe·lí·č·i.
/t Then there was brought to him someone that was deaf and never said anything.
/k And they bring unto him one that was deaf, and had an impediment in his speech;

/b Nu wenwumanro tcli a eku lenxkrn.
/p ná wwi·nəwama·né·ɔ, tə́li-=á· íka -lí·nxke·n.
/t Then they asked him to reach out his hand to him.
/k and they beseech him to put his hand upon him.

Mk 7.33
/b Nu pale tclwxolan wunhi cntu xrlif,
/p ná palí·i təló·x·ɔla·n wə́nči énta-xé·link,
/t Then he took him away from where the crowd was,
/k And he took him aside from the multitude,

/b ok eku li punhenxkr vwetaokelet, ok wswkvolao welanwelet.
/p ɔ́·k íkali pənčí·nxke· hwitaɔk·í·li·t, ɔ́·k wsukhɔ·lá·ɔ wi·lanəwí·li·t.
/t and he put his fingers into his ears, and he spat on his tongue.
/k and put his fingers into his ears, and he spit, and touched his tongue;

Mk 7.34
/b Eku rli uspwqrtc osavkamc, muntum, lwr Twfjrvlakch.
/p íka é·li-asphukwé·t·e ɔ·s·áhkame, mə́ntam, lúwe·, "tunkšehəlá·k·eč."
/t Looking up to heaven, he sighed and said, "Let them open."
/k And looking up to heaven, he sighed, and saith unto him, Ephphatha, that is, Be opened.

Mk 7.35
/b Nu jai twfjrvlro wvetaoku, ok welanw khaxkevlr ok wlexsw.
/p ná šá·e tunkšehəlé·ɔ hwitaɔ́k·a, ɔ́·k wí·lanu kčaxkíhəle·, ɔ́·k wəlí·xsu.
/t The immediately his ears opened, and his tongue came loose, and he spoke plainly.
/k And straightway his ears were opened, and the string of his tongue was loosed, and he spake plain.

Mk 7.36
/b Qetulaol tcli a awrni lanro;
/p kkwi·təlá·ɔl, tə́li-=á· awé·ni -la·né·ɔ.
/t And he forbade them to tell anyone.
/k And he charged them that they should tell no man:

/b   taoni qetulao, jwq amunhe watvekrnro.
/p   tá·ɔni kkwi·təlá·ɔ, šúkw amənčí·i o·wa·thike·né·ɔ.
/t   But even though he forbade them, they made it known regardless.
/k   but the more he charged them, so much the more a great deal they published it;

Mt 15.30 /b   Ok mrxrlulethi wtxwkw, pwrjwawao
/p   ɔ́·k me·x·e·ləlí·č·i o·txúk·u; pwe·š·əwawwá·ɔ
/t   And a great crowd came to him; they brought
/k   And great multitudes came unto him, having with them

/b   mutu keksk pumiskalethi, krkrpifolethi, ok mutu kekski krkw lwrlethi, ok jaofulilethi,   [⟨keksk⟩ for ⟨kekski⟩]
/p   máta kí·kski-pəməska·lí·č·i, ke·k·e·p·inkɔ·lí·č·i, ɔ́·k máta kí·kski- kéku -luwe·lí·č·i, ɔ́·k šaɔnkələlí·č·i.
/t   people who could never walk, who were blind, and who could never speak, and who were infirm.
/k   those that were lame, blind, dumb, maimed, and many others,

/b   eku lanevenuk Nhesus wsetif;
/p   íka lanihí·nak nčí·sas wsí·t·ink.
/t   They were deposited at Jesus's feet.
/k   and cast them down at Jesus' feet;

/b   qekrvao wrmi,
/p   kwi·k·e·há·ɔ wé·mi,
/t   And he healed them all,
/k   and he healed them:

Mt 15.31 /b   wunhi mrxlkek kanjrlintumunro,   [⟨mrxlkek⟩ for ⟨mrxrlkek⟩]
/p   wwə́nči- me·x·é·lki·k -kanše·ləntaməné·ɔ,
/t   because of which the crowd was amazed,
/k   Insomuch that the multitude wondered,

/b   nrovtetc mutu keksk krkw lwrt tcli kuski krkw lwrn,   [⟨keksk⟩ for ⟨kekski⟩]
/p   ne·ɔhtí·t·e máta kí·kski- kéku -lúwe·t tə́li-káski- kéku -lúwe·n,
/t   when they saw the one never able to say anything be able to speak,
/k   when they saw the dumb to speak,

/b   ok jaofulukek tcli hetanisenro, ok mutu keksi pumiskat tcli pumiskan,
                                                                      [⟨keksi⟩ for ⟨kekski⟩]
/p   ɔ́·k šaɔnkəlák·i·k tə́li-či·t·anəs·i·né·ɔ, ɔ́·k máta kí·kski-pəmə́ska·t tə́li-pəmə́ska·n,
/t   and the infirm to be strong, and the one never able to walk, walk,
/k   the maimed to be whole, the lame to walk,

/b   ok krkrpifot tcli nrman,
/p   ɔ́·k ke·k·e·p·ínkɔ·t tə́li-né·ma·n.

/t   and the one who was blind, see.
/k   and the blind to see:

/b   nu moxifovkunemanro Krtanitwelethi Islilu.
/p   ná mɔx·inkɔhkəni·ma·né·ɔ ke·tanət·o·wi·lí·č·i †isəlɔ́la.
/t   Then they praised the God Israel.
/k   and they glorified the God of Israel.

Chapter 51 (pp. 87-88). [L. section 50.] (Mark 8.1-7; Matthew 15.37-39.)

Mk 8.1   /b   Nu nckc kejqek mrxrlkek ave xrlwpanek ok ‖ qelu krkw methwpanek,
         /p   ná-néke kí·škwi·k me·x·é·lki·k áhi xe·ló·p·ani·k ɔ́·k kwí·la- kéku -mi·č·ó·p·ani·k.
         /t   That same day the crowd was very large, and they had nothing to eat.
         /k   In those days the multitude being very great, and having nothing to eat,

         /b   Nhesus wcnhemapani rkrkemathi, tclao
(p. 88) /p   nčí·sas wwenči·má·p·ani e·k·e·ki·má·č·i, təlá·ɔ,
         /t   Jesus called his disciples to him and said to them,
         /k   Jesus called his disciples unto him, and saith unto them,

Mk 8.2   /b   futumakrlumaok bk mrxrlkek,
         /p   "nkət·əma·k·e·ləmá·ɔk yó·k me·x·é·lki·k,
         /t   "I pity the people in this crowd,
         /k   I have compassion on the multitude,

         /b   rli mrhi bqi nuxi kejqc wetuvpemevtet, ok mutu krkw methevtet,
         /p   é·li- mé·či yúkwe náxi-kí·škwe -witahpi·míhti·t, ɔ́·k máta kéku -mi·č·íhti·t.
         /t   for they have now been with me for three days without eating anything.
         /k   because they have now been with me three days, and have nothing to eat:

Mk 8.3   /b   bqc a alumskaokc li nevlahi wekevtet jawuswuk a nrli pumiskavtet,
         /p   yúkwe=á· aləmskaɔ́k·e lí nihəláči wi·k·íhti·t, šawɔ́s·əwak=á· né·li-pəməskáhti·t,
         /t   If I send them away now to their own houses, they would become weak as they walk,
         /k   And if I send them away fasting to their own houses, they will faint by the way:

         /b   rli alintc ovolumi wunheyevtet.
         /p   é·li- a·lɔ́nte ɔ́hələmi -wənči·aíhti·t.
         /t   as some of them come from far away.
         /k   for divers of them came from far.

Mk 8.4   /b   Rkrkemathi tclkw,
         /p   e·k·e·ki·má·č·i tɔ́lku,
         /t   His disciples said to him,
         /k   And his disciples answered him,

/b Ta vuh a wunhi awrn kuski xaman bl trkunu tali nuxpunc avpon.
/p "tá=háč=á· wwə́nči- awé·n -káski-xáma·n yó·l té·kəna táli náxpəne ahpɔ́·n."
/t "How would anyone be able to feed these people in the wilderness even bread?"
/k From whence can a man satisfy these men with bread here in the wilderness?

Mk 8.5
/b Nu notwxtaon krxa vuh avponu kwlvatwmw?
/p ná nɔt·o·xtáɔ·n, "ké·x·a=háč ahpɔ́·na ko·lhatúhəmɔ?"
/t Then he asked them, "How many loaves of bread do you have?"
/k And he asked them, How many loaves have ye?

/b Tclawao, Nejaj.
/p təlawwá·ɔ, "ní·š·a·š."
/t They told him, "Seven."
/k And they said, Seven.

Mk 8.6
/b Nu tclan mrxrlulethi, Vakif li mijakrq.
/p ná tə́la·n me·x·e·ləlí·č·i, "hák·ink lí-məšá·ke·kw."
/t The he said to the crowd, "Sit down on the ground."
/k And he commanded the people to sit down on the ground:

/b Nu wrtunimun nrl avponul, nu tcli krnamwen
/p ná wwe·t·ənə́mən né·l ahpɔ́·nal, ná tə́li-ke·ná·mwi·n.
/t Then he took the loaves and proceeded to give thanks.
/k and he took the seven loaves, and gave thanks,

/b ok pwekunimunu, ok mwelan rkrkemathi
/p ɔ́·k pwi·k·ənəmə́na, ɔ́·k mwí·la·n e·k·e·ki·má·č·i,
/t And he tore them into small pieces and gave them to his disciples,
/k and brake, and gave to his disciples

/b tcli a eku vataonro rlifwrxenulet mrxrlulethi;
/p tə́li-=á· íka -hataɔ·né·ɔ e·linkwe·x·í·nəli·t me·x·e·ləlí·č·i.
/t for them to put before the people in the crowd.
/k to set before them; and they did set them before the people.

Mk 8.7
/b ok krxa wlavlrpanek namrtitul.
/p ɔ́·k ké·x·a wəlahəlé·p·ani·k name·t·ə́t·al.
/t And they had a few small fish.
/k And they had a few small fishes:

/b Krnamwetc, nu tclan eku ok bk valw.
/p ke·na·mwí·t·e, ná tə́la·n, "íka ɔ́·k yó·k hálo·."
/t After giving thanks, he told them, "Put these before them (*lit.*, there) also."
/k and he blessed, and commanded to set them also before them.

Mt 15.37 /b Wrmi metswuk, ok wrmi kespwuk:
/p wé·mi mi·tsúwak, ɔ́·k wé·mi ki·spúwak.
/t All ate, and all were filled.
/k And they did all eat, and were filled:

/b nu peontasek wrtunimunro nejaj tufvakunif hwi.
/p ná pi·ɔntá·s·i·k wwe·t·ənəməné·ɔ, ní·š·a·š tankhá·k·anink čúwi.
/t Then they picked up what was left over, filling seven baskets.
/k and they took up of the broken meat that was left seven baskets full.

Mt 15.38 /b Nrkek metsethek avpami ct nrwun tclintxapki,   [⟨tclintxapki⟩ for ⟨tclin txapxki⟩]
/p né·ki·k mi·tsí·č·i·k ahpá·mi=ét né·wən télən txá·pxki.
/t Those that ate were maybe about four thousand.
/k And they that did eat were four thousand men,

/b takw avkemqwseeok xqrok ok meminsuk.
/p (takó· ahki·mkwəs·i·í·ɔk xkwé·ɔk ɔ́·k mi·mə́nsak.)
/t (Women and children were not counted.)
/k beside women and children.

Mt 15.39 /b Mrhi lrxwrxrutetc, nrk mrxrlkek,   [⟨-xrut-⟩ for ⟨-xrvt-⟩ (for /-x·weht-/)]
/p mé·či le·x·we·x·wehtí·t·e né·k me·x·é·lki·k,
/t After the crowd had dispersed,
/k And he sent away the multitude,

/b nu mwxwlif tcli pwsenrp, eku lelavtap kexki Maktrlu.
/p ná mux·ó·link təli-po·s·í·ne·p, íka lílahta·p kí·xki †ma·kté·la.
/t then he got into a boat and went to near Magdala.
/k and took ship, and came into the coasts of Magdala,

Chapter 52 (pp. 88-90). [L. section 51.] (Matthew 16.1-4, 11-12; Mark 8.13 [end]-20, 22-26)

Mt 16.1 /b Paluseok ok Satuseok wtxawapani Nhesusul, koqrhevawapani;
/p †pa·ləsi·í·ɔk ɔ́·k †sa·tasí·ɔk o·txawwá·p·ani nči·sás·al, kɔk·we·č·i·hawwá·p·ani,
/t Pharisees and Sadducees came to Jesus and tested him,
/k The Pharisees also with the Sadducees came, and tempting

/b tclawapani, punwntulenrn kekenwlwakun wunhi osavkamc.
/p təlawwá·p·ani, "pənuntəlí·ne·n khiki·no·ləwá·k·an wə́nči ɔ·s·áhkame."
/t saying to him, "Show us a sign from heaven."
/k desired him that he would shew them a sign from heaven.

Mt 16.2 /b Jwq tclao, ktclwcvumw, Tokunrh ta, rli mwjvaq muxkrk loqwne;
/p šúkw təláˑɔ, "ktələwéhəmɔ, 'tókˑaneˑ=č=tá, éˑli- móˑšhakw -máxkeˑk lɔˑkˑwəníˑi.'
/t But he said to them, "You say, 'It will be mild weather, for the sky is red in the evening.'
/k He answered and said unto them, When it is evening, ye say, It will be fair weather: for the sky is red.

Mt 16.3 /b ok alupae vufq ktclwcmw mavhih rli mwjvaq muxkrk ok aof.
/p ɔ́ˑk alapˑaˑíˑi=hánkw ktələwéhəmɔ, 'máhči=č, éˑli- móˑšhakw -máxkeˑk ɔ́ˑk -aɔ́nk.'
/t and in the morning you say, 'It will be bad, as the sky is red and it's foggy.'
/k And in the morning, It will be foul weather to day: for the sky is red and lowring.

/b Kelwu rvakevokrthek; kuski a watwnro rlenako mwjvaq,
/p kiˑlóˑwa ehahkiˑhɔkéˑčˑiˑk, kkáskiˑ=áˑ -wwaˑtoˑwənéˑɔ eˑliˑnáˑkˑɔ móˑšhakw,
/t You hypocrites, you would be able to recognize what kind of sky it is,
/k O ye hypocrites, ye can discern the face of the sky;

/b jwq mutu kwatwnro rlenako bqc b rlrk, krkw vuh wunhi?
/p šúkw máta koˑwaˑtoˑwənéˑɔ eˑliˑnáˑkˑɔ yúkwe yú éˑleˑk. kéku=háč wə́nči?
/t but you do not recognize what kinds of things are happening now. How come?
/k but can ye not discern the signs of the times?

Mt 16.4 /b Mrtawsethek, wrvepifrthek, rlvakrerq kutatumunro kvekenwlwakun. [⟨kuta-‖tum⟩]
/p meˑtˑaˑwsíˑčˑiˑk, wehiˑpenkéˑčˑiˑk, eˑlhakéˑieˑkw kkatˑaˑtˑamənéˑɔ khikiˑnoˑləwáˑkˑan.
/t Sinners and fornicators, you of your tribe want the sign.
/k A wicked and adulterous generation seeketh after a sign;

(p. 89) /b Jwq ta kvekenwlwakun melaeok, jwq nu kvekenwlwakun Nhonusu nrnekanewrwsetpanu.
/p šúkw táˑ=áˑ khikiˑnoˑləwáˑkˑan miˑlaˑíˑɔk, šúkw nə́ khikiˑnoˑləwáˑkˑan †nčɔˑnásˑa nehəniˑkˑaˑníˑi-weˑwsiˑtpána."
/t But they will not be given a sign, except the sign of Jonas, the prophet."
/k and there shall no sign be given unto it, but the sign of the prophet Jonas.

/b Nu wnukalan, palerp;
/p ná wənə́kˑalaˑn, palíˑi éˑp.
/t Then he left them and went away.
/k And he left them, and departed.

Mk 8.13 /b lupi mwxolif li pwswp kamif rp.
/p lápi muxˑóˑlink líˑpóˑsˑoˑp, káˑmink éˑp.
/t He again went aboard a boat and went across to the other side.
/k [And he left them, and] entering into the ship again departed to the other side.

Mk 8.14 /b Rkrkemathi wunenro tcli a klinumunro avpon
/p e·k·e·ki·má·č·i wwani·né·ɔ, tóli-=á· -kələnəməné·ɔ ahpó·n,
/t His disciples forgot that they should take bread with them,
/k Now the disciples had forgotten to take bread,

/b ok takw nuxpunc alwe koti avpon vatri.
/p ó·k takó· náxpəne aləwí·i kwə́t·i ahpó·n hat·é·i.
/t and there was no more than just a single loaf. [*lit.*, 'not even more than one']
/k neither had they in the ship with them more than one loaf.

Mk 8.15 /b Nu Nhesus tclan, Trku tu nuxatumwmoc Palusei pastrk, ok Vclute pastrk.
/p ná nčí·sas tóla·n, "té·ka=tá, naxa·t·amo·mó·e †pa·ləsi·í·i-pá·ste·k,
ó·k †helat·í·i-pá·ste·k.
/t Then Jesus said to them, "Watch out! Beware of Pharisee yeast and Herod yeast."
/k And he charged them, saying, Take heed, beware of the leaven of the Pharisees, and of the leaven of Herod.

Mk 8.16 /b Nu nevlahi pwnarlintumunro lwrok
/p ná nihəláči pwəna·eləntaməné·ɔ, luwé·ɔk,
/t Then they thought to themselves and said,
/k And they reasoned among themselves, saying,

/b wunhi ct rli mutu wlatwfq avpon. [⟨-twfq⟩ for ⟨-twufq⟩]
/p "wə́nči=ét é·li- máta -wəla·tó·wankw ahpó·n."
/t "I guess it's because we have no bread."
/k It is because we have no bread.

Mk 8.17 /b Nhesus wrotaqc tclapani
/p nčí·sas we·ɔ·tá·k·we, təlá·p·ani,
/t When Jesus knew it, he said to them,
/k And when Jesus knew it, he saith unto them,

/b Krkw vuh wunhi punarlintamrq rli mutu toponumerq?
/p "kéku=háč wə́nči-pəna·eləntame·kw, é·li- máta -tɔp·ɔ·nəmíe·kw?
/t "Why do you think about having no bread?
/k Why reason ye, because ye have no bread?

/b Takw vuh knrmwnro, ok knunwstamwnro?
/p takó·=háč kəne·mo·wəné·ɔ, ó·k kənəno·stamo·wəné·ɔ?
/t Do you not see and understand it?
/k perceive ye not yet, neither understand?

/b Qeaqi vuh ktrwu hetanisw?
/p kwiá·kwi=háč ktéhəwa či·t·anə́s·u?
/t Are your hearts still obtuse? [See note to Mk 6.52.]
/k have ye your heart yet hardened?

Mk 8.18 /b Wrjkifwet mutu vuh nrmai?
/p we·škínkwi·t, máta=háč ne·má·i?
/t The one with eyes, does he not see?
/k Having eyes, see ye not?

/b Wrvetaoket mutu vuh puntamai?
/p we·hitaɔk·i·t, máta=háč pəntamá·i?
/t The one with ears, does he not hear?
/k and having ears, hear ye not?

/b Ok takw vuh kumijatumwnro?
/p ɔ́·k takɔ́·=háč kəməš·a·t·amo·wəné·ɔ?
/t And do you not remember it?
/k and do ye not remember?

Mk 8.19 /b Nckc palrnaxk avponu pupvakrnumanc
/p néke palé·naxk ahpɔ́·na pəphake·nəmá·ne
/t The time I broke five loaves in pieces
/k When I brake the five loaves

/b cntu palrnaxk txun tclin txapxki txitetc,
/p énta- palé·naxk txɔ́n télən txá·pxki -txihtí·t·e,
/t when there were five thousand,
/k among five thousand,

/b krxa vuh tufvakunif peontaswp?
/p ké·x·a=háč tankhá·k·anink pi·ɔntá·s·o·p?"
/t in how many baskets were there uneaten leftovers?"
/k how many baskets full of fragments took ye up?

/b Tclawao tclin ok neju.
/p təlawwá·ɔ, "télən ɔ́·k ní·š·a."
/t They said to him, "Twelve."
/k They say unto him, Twelve.

Mk 8.20 /b Ok Nckc nejaj cntu nrwun tclin txapxki txitetc,
/p "ɔ́·k néke ní·š·a·š énta- né·wən télən txá·pxki -txihtí·t·e,
/t "And the time with seven when there were four thousand,
/k And when the seven among four thousand,

/b krxa vuh tufvakunif peontaswp?
/p ké·x·a=háč tankhá·k·anink pi·ɔntá·s·o·p?"
/t in how many baskets were there uneaten leftovers?"
/k how many baskets full of fragments took ye up?

/b Tclawao, nejaj.
/p təlawwá·ɔ, "ní·š·a·š."
/t They said to him, "Seven."
/k And they said, Seven.

Mt 16.11
/b Tclao Krkw vuh wunhi mutu kuski nunwstumwrq
/p təlá·ɔ, "kéku=háč wə́nči- máta -káski-nəno·stamó·we·kw,
/t He said to them, "Why are you not able to understand
/k How is it that ye do not understand

/b ktcli mutu akunwtumwlwnro avpon pastrk nckc rlrqc, [⟨avpon⟩ for ⟨avpone⟩;
/p ktə́li- máta -ahkəno·t·əmo·lo·wəné·ɔ ahpɔ·ní·i-pá·ste·k néke ellé·k·we, [see 16.12]
/t that I was not speaking to you about the yeast of bread when I said to you,
/k that I spake it not to you concerning bread,

/b Trku tu nuxatumwmoc Palusei pastrk, ok Vclute pastrk?
/p 'té·ka=tá, naxa·t·amo·mɔ́·e †pa·ləsi·í·i-pá·ste·k, ɔ́·k †helat·í·i-pá·ste·k'?"
/t 'Watch out! Beware of Pharisee yeast and Herod yeast.'?"
/k that ye should beware of the leaven of the Pharisees and of the Sadducees?

Mt 16.12
/b Nu wnunwstaonro,
/p ná wənəno·staɔ·né·ɔ,
/t Then they understood
/k Then understood they

/b tcli mutu avpone pastrk wunhi lwkwnrop, trkuta nuxatumwmac,
[⟨-mac⟩ for ⟨-moc⟩]
/p tə́li- máta ahpɔ·ní·i-pá·ste·k -wə́nči-luk·o·wəné·ɔ·p, "té·ka=tá, naxa·t·amo·mɔ́·e,"
/t that it was not about the yeast for bread that he had told them, 'Watch out! Beware of it!',
/k how that he bade them not beware of the leaven of bread,

/b jwq Paluse, ok Vclute avkrkifrokunu.
/p šúkw †pa·ləsi·í·i- ɔ́·k †helat·í·i-ahke·kinke·ɔ́·k·ana.
/t but about the teachings of the Pharisees and Herod.
/k but of the doctrine of the Pharisees and of the Sadducees.

Mk 8.22
/b Eku prp Mpetsritr.
/p íka pé·p †mpi·tsé·ite·.
/t He came to Bethsaida.
/k And he cometh to Bethsaida;

/b Prtao krkrpifolethi linwu kavtatamaon tcli a eku a linan. [⟨a linan⟩ for ⟨alinan⟩]
/p pé·t·aɔ· ke·k·e·p·inkɔ·lí·č·i lə́nəwa, kahta·t·amáɔ·n tə́li-=á· íka -alə́na·n.
/t And there was brought to him a blind man, and it was desired that he touch him.
/k and they bring a blind man unto him, and besought him to touch him.

Mk 8.23 /b Nhesus eku tonao wnaxkelet sokaqwnao eku wunhi wtrnif.
/p nčí·sas íka tɔnná·ɔ wənaxkí·li·t, sɔk·a·kwəná·ɔ íka wə́nči o·t·é·nink.
/t Jesus put his hand on his hand and led him away from the town.
/k And he took the blind man by the hand, and led him out of the town;

/b Mrhi keji swkvolatc wujkifwelet ok eku tonao,
/p mé·či kíši-sukhɔ·lá·t·e wəškinkwí·li·t, ɔ́·k íka tɔnná·ɔ.
/t After he had spit on his eyes, he also put his hands on him.
/k and when he had spit on his eyes, and put his hands upon him,

/b nu notwtwmaon tcli a krkw nrmulen?
/p ná nɔt·o·t·əmáɔ·n, tə́li-=á· kéku -né·məli·n.
/t Then he asked him if he could see anything.
/k he asked him if he saw ought.

Mk 8.24 /b Apvwqrtc, lwr linwuk nro mulaji vetkwk avpamskrok.
/p a·phukwé·t·e, lúwe·, "lə́nəwak nné·ɔ, málahši hítko·k ahpa·mské·ɔk."
/t When he looked up, he said, "I see men as if trees are walking about."
/k And he looked up, and said, I see men as trees, walking.

Mk 8.25 /b Lupi eku tonao wijkifwelet
/p lápi íka tɔnná·ɔ wəškinkwí·li·t,
/t He again put his hands on his eyes,
/k After that he put his hands again upon his eyes,

/b ok lupi apvwqrtc wli ‖ krkw kuski nrm.
/p ɔ́·k lápi a·phukwé·t·e, wə́li- kéku -káski-né·m.
/t and when he looked up again, he could see things well.
/k and made him look up: and he was restored, and saw every man clearly.

Mk 8.26 /b Nu tolumskaon li wekelet,
(p. 90) /p ná tɔləmskáɔ·n lí wi·k·í·li·t.
/t Then he sent him away to his house.
/k And he sent him away to his house,

/b tclao kahi avan wtrnif ok kahi awrn lerkuh.
/p təlá·ɔ, "káči á·han o·t·é·nink, ɔ́·k káči awé·n lié·k·ač."
/t He said to him, "Don't go to the town, and don't tell anyone."
/k saying, Neither go into the town, nor tell it to any in the town.

Chapter 53 (pp. 90-93). [L. section 52.] (John 7.1-53.)

Jn 7.1 /b Na nuni Nhesus pupamskanrp avpani Fclule
⟨pup-⟩ for /pup·-/; ⟨avpani⟩ for ⟨avpami⟩]
/p ná nə́ni nčí·sas pup·a·mská·ne·p, ahpá·mi †nkélali·.

/t   And then that is where Jesus went walking, around Galilee.
/k   After these things Jesus walked in Galilee:

/b   rli mutu wifi avpamskrep Nhwtewf rli Nhwuk kavtwnalavtetup.
/p   é·li máta wínki-ahpa·mské·i·p †nčo·tí·yunk, é·li- nčó·wak -kahto·nalahtí·t·əp.
/t   For, he did not want to go walking in Judaea, since the Jews wanted to kill him.
/k   for he would not walk in Jewry, because the Jews sought to kill him.

Jn 7.2   /b   Mrhi prxothevlakc Nhwuk tcli kawunjrekaonif tali tavqepwenro.
/p   mé·či pe·x·o·č·ihəlá·k·e nčó·wak təli- ka·wənše·i·k·á·ɔnink -táli-tahkwi·p·wi·né·ɔ.
/t   The time was now near for the Jews to feast in booths of brush.   [*lit.*, brambles]
/k   Now the Jews' feast of tabernacles was at hand.

Jn 7.3   /b   Xwesmusu tclkw, Alumskal b wunhi eku al Nhwtebf
/p   xwi·s·əməs·a tálku, "aləmska·l yú wənči; íka á·l †nčo·tí·yunk,
/t   His younger brothers said to him, "Go away from here; go to Judaea,
/k   His brethren therefore said unto him, Depart hence, and go into Judaea,

/b   rli nrk rkrkemuthek tcli nrmunro ktclyvoswakun rlseun.
/p   é·li né·k e·k·e·ki·máč·i·k, táli-ne·məné·ɔ ktəlaehɔ·s·əwá·k·an e·lsían.
/t   for those are your disciples, for them to see your deeds, that you do.
/k   that thy disciples also may see the works that thou doest.

Jn 7.4   /b   Rli mutu awrn keme krkw larvoset, krtu wavkwsetc.
/p   é·li- máta awé·n ki·mí·i kéku -laehɔ́·s·i·t, ké·t·a-wwahkwəs·í·t·e.
/t   For no one does anything secretly when they want to be known.
/k   For there is no man that doeth any thing in secret, and he himself seeketh to be known openly.

/b   Mrhi a bni liseunc, wavkwsel b cntu lawsif.
/p   mé·či=á· yó·ni ləs·iáne, wwahkwəs·i·l yú entalá·wsink."
/t   If you would now do this, make yourself known in the world."
/k   If thou do these things, shew thyself to the world.

Jn 7.5   /b   Rli mutu nuxpunc xwesmusu wlamvetakweo.
/p   é·li máta náxpəne xwi·s·əməs·a o·la·mhita·k·o·wí·ɔ.
/t   For, not even his brothers believed him.
/k   For neither did his brethren believe in him.

Jn 7.6   /b   Nhesus tclao nrsko ntupsqelavtai, jwq kelwu kumri ktupsqelavtavmw.
/p   nčí·sas təlá·ɔ, "né·skɔ ntəpskwilahtá·i, šúkw ki·ló·wa nkəmé·i ktəpskwilahtáhəmɔ.
/t   Jesus said to them, "My time has not yet come, but it is always *your* time.
/k   Then Jesus said unto them, My time is not yet come: but your time is alway ready.

Jn 7.7 /b B cntu lawsethek takw kuski jifalkweok;
       /p yú entala·wsí·č·i·k takó· kkáski-šinka·lko·wí·ɔk.
       /t People cannot hate you (sg.).
       /k The world cannot hate you;

       /b jwq ne njifalkwk rli luk rlsevtet, rli mavhi lisevtet.
       /p šúkw ní· nšinká·lko·k, é·li-lák e·lsíhti·t, é·li-máhči-ləs·íhti·t.
       /t But they hate *me,* because I say what they do, as they do evil.
       /k but me it hateth, because I testify of it, that the works thereof are evil.

Jn 7.8 /b Eku aq bqc b cntu metsavtif,
       /p íka á·kw yúkwe yú énta-mi·tsáhtink.
       /t Go now to this feast.
       /k Go ye up unto this feast:

       /b nrsko ne futu eku ai, rli nrsko mpukunhi tpisqelavtai.
       /p né·skɔ ní· nkát·a- íka -á·i, é·li né·skɔ mpak·ánči-tpəskwilahtá·i.
       /t *I* do not want to go yet, as my time has not yet fully come.
       /k I go not up yet unto this feast; for my time is not yet full come.

Jn 7.9 /b Mrhi nc rlatc qeaqi Falulebf avpwp.
       /p mé·či nə́ e·lá·t·e, kwiá·kwi †nka·lalí·yunk ahpó·p.
       /t After he told them that, he still stayed in Galilee.
       /k When he had said these words unto them, he abode still in Galilee.

Jn 7.10 /b Jwq mrhi xwesmusu eku raletc,
       /p šúkw mé·či xwi·s·əmə́s·a íka e·a·lí·t·e,
       /t But after his brothers had gone there,
       /k But when his brethren were gone up,

       /b nu ok nrkumu eku tonrp cntu metsavtif,
       /p ná ɔ́·k nc̓·k·əma íka tɔ́·nc·p énta-mi·tsáhtink.
       /t then *he* also went to the feast.
       /k then went he also up unto the feast,

       /b jwq mutu wavkweo, malaji kemei.
       /p šúkw máta o·wahko·wí·ɔ, málahši ki·mí·i.
       /t But they did not know about him, as if it was secret.
       /k not openly, but as it were in secret.

Jn 7.11 /b Nu Nhwuk notwnoanro tali cntu metsatif, lwrok Ta vuh nu? [⟨-noa-⟩ for ⟨-nao-⟩]
       /p ná nčó·wak nɔt·o·naɔ·né·ɔ táli énta-mi·tsáhtink, luwé·ɔk, "tá=háč ná?"
       /t Then the Jews looked for him at the feast, asking, "Where is he?"
       /k Then the Jews sought him at the feast, and said, Where is he?

Jn 7.12
/b Ave pumenrvwtwuk cntu xrlif;
/p áhi-pəmi·nehó·t·əwak énta-xé·link.
/t The people in the crowd argued greatly.
/k And there was much murmuring among the people concerning him:

/b alintc lwrok, Wli tu lisw nu linw,
/p a·lə́nte luwé·ɔk, "wə́li-=tá -lə́s·u ná lə́nu."
/t Some said, "He is a good man."
/k for some said, He is a good man:

/b ok alintc lwrok Takw tu rli keolat linapro.
/p ɔ́·k a·lə́nte luwé·ɔk, "takó·=tá, é·li-kí·ɔla·t ləna·p·é·ɔ."
/t And some said, "No, for he deceives the people."
/k others said, Nay; but he deceiveth the people.

Jn 7.13
/b Alwt mutu awrn tokunemaeo cntu a wavko, rli qetumunrop Nhwuk.
/p aló·t máta awé·n tɔk·əni·ma·í·ɔ énta-=á· -wwáhkɔ, é·li kkwi·taməné·ɔ·p nčó·wak.
/t Yet no one spoke of him where it would be known, as the Jews were afraid of it.
/k Howbeit no man spake openly of him for fear of the Jews. [misunderstood]

Jn 7.14
/b Rlumi lrlaevlakc cntu metsavtif,
/p é·ləmi-le·la·ihəlá·k·e énta-mi·tsáhtink,
/t When the feast was midway through,
/k Now about the midst of the feast

/b nu wexkaohi Nhesus eku tonrp patamwrekaonif tuntu avkrkifrn.
/p ná wi·xkaóči nčí·sas íka tó·ne·p pa·tamwe·i·k·á·ɔnink, tə́nta-ahke·kínke·n.
/t Jesus abruptly went to the temple and taught there.
/k Jesus went up into the temple, and taught.

Jn 7.15
/b Nhwuk kanjrlintamwk lwrok,
/p nčó·wak kanše·lə́ntamo·k, luwé·ɔk,
/t The Jews were astonished, saying,
/k And the Jews marvelled, saying,

/b Ta vuh wunhi wu linw wavan lrkvekunu,
/p "tá=háč wwə́nči- wá lə́nu -wwá·ha·n le·khí·k·ana?
/t "How does this man know the writings (law, doctrines)?
/k How knoweth this man letters,

/b rli takw wuntamaoi?
/p é·li takó· wəntamaɔ́·i."
/t For he was not taught."
/k having never learned?

Jn 7.16 /b Nhesus noxkwmao, tclao
/p nčí·sas nɔxko·má·ɔ, təlá·ɔ,
/t Jesus answered, saying to them,
/k Jesus answered them, and said,

/b Ntukrkifrokun, takw ne nevlahi, jwq nu prtalwkalet   [⟨Ntukrk-‖ifrokun⟩]
/p "ntak·e·kinke·ɔ́·k·an, takó· ní· nihəláči, šúkw ná pe·t·alo·ká·li·t.
/t "My doctrine is not my own, but of the one that sent me.
/k My doctrine is not mine, but his that sent me.

Jn 7.17 /b Liserqc awrn, nrkumu rletrvat,
(p. 91) /p ləs·ié·k·we awé·n né·k·əma e·li·t·é·ha·t,
/t If any of you does what *he* wishes done,
/k If any man will do his will,

/b watwnh li Krtanitwete, jitu li ne nevlahi.
/p o·wá·to·n=č lí ke·tanət·o·wi·t·í·i, ší=tá lí ní· nihəláči.
/t he will know that it is God's, or that it is my own.
/k he shall know of the doctrine, whether it be of God, or whether I speak of myself.

[Page 91 was creased when printed and later flattened; a diagonal white space distorts some letters in Jn 7.18 through Jn .7.25. These were checked against the KHS copy.]

Jn 7.18 /b Awrn nevlahi krkw rlwrt, notwnamun nevlahi xifwrlinswakun;
/p awé·n nihəláči kéku é·ləwe·t nɔt·ó·namən nihəláči xinkwe·lənsəwá·k·an,
/t Anyone who speaks of things that pertain to himself seeks glory for himself,
/k He that speaketh of himself seeketh his own glory:

/b jwq a awrn xifwrlumatc petalwkalkwki,
/p šúkw=á· awé·n xinkwe·ləmá·te pe·t·alo·ka·lkúk·i,
/t but if anyone praises (glorifies) the one who sent him,
/k but he that seeketh his glory that sent him,

/b nul nu wlamwr, ok takw hanawswakun vokcf vatri
/p nál ná wəlá·məwe·, ɔ́·k takó· čana·wsəwá·k·an hók·enk hat·é·i.
/t he is the one who tells the truth, and there is no sin in him.
/k the same is true, and no unrighteousness is in him.

Jn 7.19 /b Mutu vuh Mwjiju kumelkwewap qetulitwakun?   [⟨qet-⟩ for /khwit-/]
/p máta=háč mo·šə́š·a kəmi·lko·wíwwa·p khwitələt·əwá·k·an?
/t Didn't Moses give you a law?
/k Did not Moses give you the law,

/b Ok takw kelwu awrn wlamvetamwun.
/p ɔ́·k takó· ki·ló·wa awé·n o·la·mhitamó·wən.

/t And none of you heed it?
/k and yet none of you keepeth the law?

/b Koh vuh avpamskarq, li kavtwnalerq?
/p kóč=háč ahpa·mská·e·kw, lí-kahto·nalíe·kw?"
/t Why do you go about wanting to kill me?"
/k Why go ye about to kill me?

Jn 7.20 /b Rpethek noxkwmawao, tclawao,
/p e·p·í·č·i·k nɔxko·mawwá·ɔ, təlawwá·ɔ,
/t The people there answered him, saying,
/k The people answered and said,

/b Jcv mavtunw ct ktupetaq,
/p šéh, mahtánt·u=ét ktap·í·ta·kw.
/t "Look, there must be a devil in you.
/k Thou hast a devil:

/b awrn vuh tcli avpamskan ktcli a nvlkwn? [⟨nvl-⟩ for ⟨nvel-⟩]
/p awé·n=háč təli-ahpá·mska·n, ktəli-=á· -nhílko·n?"
/t Who is it that's going about to kill you?"
/k who goeth about to kill thee?

Jn 7.21 /b Nhesus tclaol Kotrnaoki feji lisi, ok kanjrlintamwvmw.
/p nčí·sas təlá·ɔl, "kwət·ennáɔhki nkíši-lə́s·i, ɔ́·k kkanše·ləntamúhəmɔ.
/t Jesus said to them, "I have done one thing, and you are astonished.
/k Jesus answered and said unto them, I have done one work, and ye all marvel.

Jn 7.22 /b Mwjiju kmelkwap ncni okajaokun,
/p mo·šə́š·a kəmi·lkúwa·p nə́ni ɔ·ka·š·a·ɔ́·k·an.
/t Moses gave you what is circumcision.
/k (1) Moses therefore gave unto you circumcision; [numbers = sequence in L.]

/b kelwu vufq kokrjawu pelaihih taoni alaxemwe kejkw
/p ki·ló·wa=hánkw kɔ·ka·š·áwwa pi·laéčəč, tá·ɔni ala·x·i·məwí·i-kí·šku.
/t *You* circumcise the boy even though it is the day of rest,
/k (3) ye on the sabbath day circumcise a man.

/b rli mutu wunhi Mwjijn wunheyeq, jwq kwxwawfu. [⟨Mwjijn⟩ for ⟨Mwjiju⟩]
/p é·li- máta wə́nči mo·šə́š·a -wənčí·ai·kw, šúkw ko·x·əwa·únka.
/t because it did not come from Moses, but from your forefathers. [misunderstood]
/k (2) (not because it is of Moses, but of the fathers;) and ...

Jn 7.23   /b   Pelaihih a okrjwntc taoni a alaxemwe kejkw
          /p   pi·laéčəč=á· ɔ·ka·š·únte, tá·ɔni=á· ala·x·i·məwí·i-kí·šku,
          /t   If a boy would be circumcised, even though it would be the day of rest,
          /k   If a man on the sabbath day receive circumcision,

          /b   wunhi a mutu hanexif Mwjiju qetalitwakun;
          /p   wə́nči-=á· máta -čaní·x·ink mo·šə́š·a kkwi·tələt·əwá·k·an,
          /t   so that the law of Moses would not be broken,
          /k   that the law of Moses should not be broken;

          /b   ktavelwvmw vun rli kekrvuk linw nrli alaxemwe kejqek?   [⟨vun⟩ for ⟨vuh⟩]
          /p   ktahihəlúhəmɔ=háč é·li-ki·k·é·hak lə́nu né·li-ala·x·i·məwí·i-kí·škwi·k?
          /t   do I make you angry by curing a man during the day of rest?
          /k   are ye angry at me, because I have made a man every whit whole on the sabbath
               day?

Jn 7.24   /b   Kahi orlintamwvrq rli nrmrq, jwq orlintamwq jaxakrk orlintamwakun.
          /p   káči †ɔ·e·ləntamó·he·kw é·li-né·me·kw, šúkw †ɔ·e·ləntamo·kw šáxahke·k
               †ɔ·e·ləntaməwá·k·an."
          /t   Do not be convinced because you see it, but be convinced of an honest
               conviction."
          /k   Judge not according to the appearance, but judge righteous judgment.

Jn 7.25   /b   Nu alintc Nhelwsulumeok tclwrnro; Mutu vuh nul wu krtwnalint?
          /p   ná a·lə́nte †nči·lo·sələmí·ɔk tələwe·né·ɔ, "máta=háč nál wá ke·t·ó·nalənt?
          /t   Then some of those from Jerusalem said, "Isn't this the one they wanted to kill?
          /k   Then said some of them of Jerusalem, Is not this he, whom they seek to kill?

Jn 7.26   /b   Punu, kseni hetani krkw lwr,
          /p   pənáh, ksí·ni čí·t·ani-kéku lúwe·.
          /t   Look how he speaks powerful things unconcernedly.
          /k   But, lo, he speaketh boldly, and they say nothing unto him.

          /b   wavawao vuh krkyimvrthek tcli nul wu kehe Klyst?
          /p   o·wa·hawwá·ɔ=háč ke·kayəmhé·č·i·k, tə́li=á· nál wá khičí·i kəláist?
          /t   Do the authorities know that this is truly Christ?
          /k   Do the rulers know indeed that this is the very Christ?

Jn 7.27   /b   jwmwh nwavawunu wa linw wcnheyet,
          /p   šəmúč no·wa·há·wəna wá lə́nu wenčí·ai·t,
          /t   What's more, we know where this man comes from.
          /k   Howbeit we know this man whence he is:

          /b   Klyst patc mutuh awrn wavaeo wcnheyelet.
          /p   kəláist pá·t·e, máta=č awé·n o·wa·ha·í·ɔ wenči·aí·li·t."

Text, Transcription, and Translation

/t   When Christ comes, no one will know where he comes from."
/k   but when Christ cometh, no man knoweth whence he is.

Jn 7.28
/b   Nu Nhesus patamwrekaonif tali amafexsw rlwrtc,
/p   ná nčí·sas pa·tamwe·i·k·á·ɔnink táli-amankí·xsu e·ləwé·t·e,
/t   Then Jesus spoke with a loud voice in the temple when he said,
/k   Then cried Jesus in the temple as he taught, saying,

/b   Knunaevmw, ok kwatwnro wenheyeu;   [⟨wenh-⟩ for ⟨wcnh-⟩]
/p   "kənənaíhəmɔ, ɔ́·k ko·wa·to·né·ɔ wenči·aía.
/t   "You know who I am, and you know where I come from.
/k   Ye both know me, and ye know whence I am:

/b   takw nevlahi mpai, jwq nrku nu prtalwkalet wlamwr;
/p   takó· nihəláči mpá·i, šúkw né·k·a, ná pe·t·alo·ká·li·t, wəlá·məwe·;
/t   I did not come on my own; but *he*, the one who sent me, speaks the truth.
/k   and I am not come of myself, but he that sent me is true,

/b   nul nu mutu wrovarq.
/p   nál ná máta we·ɔ·há·e·kw.
/t   He is the one you do not know.
/k   whom ye know not.

Jn 7.29
/b   Nwava rli nrku nu vokif wnhekeu, ok nrku nu mprtalwkalwq.
/p   no·wá·ha, é·li- né·k·a ná hók·enk -wənčí·k·ia, ɔ́·k né·k·a ná mpe·t·alo·ká·lukw.
/t   I know him, because *his* body is what I am from, and *he* is who sent me.
/k   But I know him: for I am from him, and he hath sent me.

Jn 7.30
/b   Nu kotu twnaro   [⟨twnaro⟩ for ⟨twnanro⟩]
/p   ná kɔ́t·a-thwəna·né·ɔ,
/t   Then they wanted to arrest him,
/k   Then they sought to take him:

/b   jwq takw awrn eku tonaeo, rli nrsko tpisqelakwp.
/p   šúkw takó· awé·n íka tɔnna·í·ɔ, é·li- né·skɔ -tpəskwihəlá·k·əp.
/t   but no one laid a hand on him, as his time was not yet come.
/k   but no man laid hands on him, because his hour was not yet come.

Jn 7.31
/b   Jwq rpethek xrli wlamvetaoao, lwrok;   [⟨wlamveta-‖oao⟩]
/p   šúkw e·p·í·č·i·k xé·li o·la·mhitaɔwwá·ɔ, luwé·ɔk,
/t   But many of the people there believed him, and they said,
/k   And many of the people believed on him, and said,

(p. 92) /b Patch Klyst alweh vuh lukveqi kanjyvosw wu rlyvoset?
/p "pá·t·e=č kəláist, aləwí·i=č ləkhíkwi-kanšaehó·s·u, wá e·laehó·s·i·t?
/t "When Christ comes, will he do greater miracles than this man does?
/k When Christ cometh, will he do more miracles than these which this man hath done?

Jn 7.32 /b Mrhi Paluseok puntamevtetc rlwcvtet wunhi Nhesus,
/p mé·či †pa·ləsi·í·ɔk pəntamihtí·t·e e·ləwéhti·t wə́nči nčí·sas,
/t After the Pharisees heard what they said about Jesus,
/k The Pharisees heard that the people murmured such things concerning him;

/b nu myai wcvevufrthek ok Paluseok tolwkalanro elao
/p ná mayá·i-wehi·hunké·č·i·k ó·k †pa·ləsi·í·ɔk tɔlo·ka·la·né·ɔ i·lá·ɔ,
/t then the chief priests and the Pharisees sent officers
/k and the Pharisees and the chief priests sent officers

/b tcli a mai twnanro.
/p tə́li-=á· -mái-thwəna·né·ɔ.
/t to go and arrest him.
/k to take him.

Jn 7.33 /b Nu Nhesus tclan,
/p ná nčí·sas tə́la·n,
/t Then Jesus said to them,
/k Then said Jesus unto them,

/b Heh takiti qetavpemlwvmw, ekuh nta wcntalwkalif.   [⟨qe-⟩ for /kəwi-/]
/p "čí·č thakíti kəwitahpi·məlúhəmɔ, íka=č ntá wentalo·ká·link.
/t "I am with you a little while longer, and I shall go to where I was sent from.
/k Yet a little while am I with you, and then I go unto him that sent me.

Jn 7.34 /b Knutwnaevmwh jwq ta kmuxkyevwmw.
/p kənat·o·naíhəmɔ=č, šúkw tá=á· kəmaxkai·húmɔ.
/t You will seek me, but you shall not find me.
/k Ye shall seek me, and shall not find me:

/b Rpeu ta kuski pawnro.
/p é·p·ia, tá=á· kkáski-pa·wəné·ɔ."
/t Where I am, you will not be able to come."
/k and where I am, thither ye cannot come.

Jn 7.35 /b Nu Nhwuk tclwrnro, Tuh vuh ct ton wunhih mutu kuski muxkaoufq?
/p ná nčó·wak tələwe·né·ɔ, "tá=č=háč=ét tɔ́·n, wə́nči-=č máta -káski-maxkaó·ankw?
/t Then the Jews said, "Where could he go so that we won't be able to find him?
/k Then said the Jews among themselves, Whither will he go, that we shall not find him?

/b Ekuh vuh ct rw vusrxwrthek rpevtet
    [⟨vus-⟩ 2x for ⟨uvs-⟩ 1x (Blanchard [and Journeycake] 1842: ⟨avs-⟩ 1x)]
/p íka=č=háč=ét é·w ahse·x·wé·č·i·k e·p·íhti·t,
/t Will he maybe go to where the people who scattered are,
/k will he go unto the dispersed among the Gentiles,

/b cntu weumxkapevtet peli rlvakrelethi,
/p énta-wiamxkahpíhti·t pí·li e·lhake·i·lí·č·i,
/t where they and other tribes live mixed together,
/k —

/b ok tokrkemao rlvakrelethi.
/p ó·k tɔk·e·ki·má·ɔ e·lhake·i·lí·č·i?
/t and teach (those other) tribes?
/k and teach the Gentiles?

Jn 7.36
/b Ta vuh ct lenakot b lwrokun cntu lwkofq.
/p tá=háč=ét li·ná·k·ɔt yú luwe·ó·k·an énta-lúk·ɔnkw,
/t What kind of a saying could it have been it when he told us,
/k What manner of saying is this that he said,

/b Knatwnaevmwh, jwq ta kmuxkaevwmw, rpeu ta kuski pawnro?
/p 'kənat·o·naíhəmɔ=č, šúkw tá=á· kəmaxkai·húmɔ; é·p·ia, tá=á· kkáski-pa·wəné·ɔ.'"
/t You will seek me, but you shall not find me; where I am, you will not be able to come."
/k Ye shall seek me, and shall not find me: and where I am, thither ye cannot come?

Jn 7.37
/b Mrhi nc mckuni kejqek kavti lwelrkc cntu metsavtif,
/p mé·či nə məkə́ni-kí·škwi·k, káhti-ló·wihəlé·k·e énta-mi·tsáhtink,
/t On the last day, when the feast was almost over,
/k In the last day, that great day of the feast,

/b Nhesus nepwp amufexswp rlwrtc,
/p nčí·sas ní·p·o·p, amankí·xso·p e·ləwé·t·e,
/t Jesus stood and spoke in a loud voice when he said,
/k Jesus stood and cried, saying,

/b Awrn Krtwsumwet toxetch munrw.
/p "awé·n ke·t·ó·s·əmwi·t, tɔx·í·t·e=č məné·w.
/t "Someone who is thirsty, if he comes to me, he will drink."
/k If any man thirst, let him come unto me, and drink.

Jn 7.38
/b Awrn nrkalet nanc lrkvekun tclwrn,
/p awé·n ne·ká·li·t, le·khí·k·an tə́ləwe·n,
/t Anyone who relies on me, the scripture says,
/k He that believeth on me, as the scripture hath said,

	/b	Vokifh wunhi ktuprvlro sepw prmawswek mpi. [⟨sepw⟩ 'river' for pl. ⟨sepwu⟩]
	/p	'hók·enk=č wə́nči-ktəp·ehəlé·ɔ sí·p·əwa pe·ma·wsó·wi·k mpí.'"
	/t	'Rivers of living water shall flow out of him.'"
	/k	out of his belly shall flow rivers of living water.
Jn 7.39	/b	Jwq nc tokunwtuminrp nanitwakun
	/p	šúkw nə́ tɔk·əno·t·amə́ne·p manət·uwwá·k·an—
	/t	But he was speaking about that spiritual power—
	/k	(But this spake he of the Spirit,
	/b	cntxih awrn nvakalet mwjinuminh,
	/p	éntxi-=č awé·n -nhaká·li·t mwəš·ənə́mən=č— ['me' for 'him']
	/t	everyone that relies on me will get it—
	/k	which they that believe on him should receive:
	/b	rli Pelselet Hehufo nrsko melawunt,
	/p	é·li- pi·lsí·li·t či·čánkɔ né·skɔ -mi·lá·wənt,
	/t	as he had not yet been given the Holy Spirit,
	/k	for the Holy Ghost was not yet given;
	/b	rli Nhesus nrsko xifovkunemkwswvalaep.
	/p	é·li nčí·sas né·skɔ xinkɔhkəni·mkwəs·o·ha·lá·i·p.
	/t	for Jesus had not yet been glorified.
	/k	because that Jesus was not yet glorified.)
Jn 7.40	/b	Rpethek puntamevtetc b aptwnakun lwrok
	/p	e·p·í·č·i·k pəntamihtí·t·e yú a·pto·ná·k·an, luwé·ɔk,
	/t	When people there heard these words, they said,
	/k	Many of the people therefore, when they heard this saying, said,
	/b	nul tu wu nrnekanewrwset,
	/p	"nál=tá wá nehəni·k·a·ní·i-wé·wsi·t."
	/t	"He is a prophet."
	/k	Of a truth this is the Prophet.
Jn 7.41	/b	kahi alintc lwrok nul tu wu Klyst.
	/p	káč·i a·lə́nte luwé·ɔk, "nál=tá wá kəláist."
	/t	But some said, "He is Christ."
	/k	Others said, This is the Christ.
	/b	Jwq alintc lwrok, Faluleufh vuh wunheyw Klyst?
	/p	šúkw a·lə́nte luwé·ɔk, "†nka·lalí·yunk=č=háč wənčí·ayu kəláist?
	/t	But some said, "Is Christ going to come out of Galilee?
	/k	But some said, Shall Christ come out of Galilee?

Jn 7.42	/b	Mutu vuh lrkvekun lwrep, Ntrpitifh wunheyw Klyst,
	/p	máta=háč le·khí·k·an luwé·i·p, †nte·pít·ink=č wənčí·ayu kəláist,
	/t	Hasn't the scripture said, Christ shall come from David,
	/k	Hath not the scripture said, That Christ cometh of the seed of David,

	/b	ok wtrnif Avpone wtrnif rpetup Nirpitu? [⟨Nirpitu⟩ for ⟨Ntrpitu⟩]
	/p	ó·k o·t·é·nink ahpo·ní·i-o·t·é·nink, e·p·í·t·əp †nte·pít·a?"
	/t	and from the town of Bread Town, where David had been?"
	/k	and out of the town of Bethlehem, where David was? [lit., house of bread]

Jn 7.43	/b	hihprlintwpanek wunhi nrkuma [⟨hihprlintwpanek⟩ for ⟨hihprlintamwpanek⟩]
	/p	čəčpe·ləntamó·p·ani·k wə́nči né·k·əma.
	/t	There was a difference of opinion among them because of him.
	/k	So there was a division among the people because of him.

Jn 7.44	/b	Alintc kotu tvwnawao, jwq takw awrn tovwnaeo.
	/p	a·lə́nte kót·a-thwənawwá·ɔ, šúkw takó· awé·n tɔhwəna·í·ɔ.
	/t	Some wanted to arrest him, but no one arrested him.
	/k	And some of them would have taken him; but no man laid hands on him.

Jn 7.45	/b	Nu eku pravtetc wrvevwfrtif elaok; tclawao
	/p	ná íka pe·ahtí·t·e wehi·hunké·t·ink i·lá·ɔk, təlawwá·ɔ,
	/t	Then when officers came to the priests, they (the priests) said to them,
	/k	Then came the officers to the chief priests and Pharisees; and they said unto them,

	/b	krkw vuh wunhi mutu prjwarq.
	/p	"kéku=háč wə́nči- máta -pe·š·əwá·e·kw?"
	/t	"Why haven't you brought him?"
	/k	Why have ye not brought him?

Jn 7.46	/b	Elaok, lwrok, tukw vuji awrn tealaptwnrwn wuni linw rlset! ‖ [⟨teal-⟩ for /till-/]
	/p	i·lá·ɔk luwé·ɔk, "takó· háši awé·n tilla·pto·né·wən wáni lə́nu é·lsi·t."
	/t	The officers said, "No one has ever spoken as this man does."
	/k	The officers answered, Never man spake like this man.

Jn 7.47 (p. 93)	/b	Paluseok tclawao krpwu vuh ok kukeolwkwu?
	/p	†pa·ləsi·í·ɔk təlawwá·ɔ, "ké·pəwa=háč ó·k kkak·i·ɔlúk·əwa?
	/t	The Pharisees said to them, "Has he deceived you also?
	/k	Then answered them the Pharisees, Are ye also deceived?

Jn 7.48	/b	Avpw vuh krkyimvrt jitu Paluse wrlamvetaot?
	/p	ahpú=háč ke·kayə́mhe·t ší=tá †pá·lasi we·la·mhítaɔ·t?
	/t	Is there a ruler or a Pharisee who believes him?
	/k	Have any of the rulers or of the Pharisees believed on him?

Jn 7.49 /b jwq bk mutu wrotaqek aptwnakun ktumakswuk.
         /p šúkw yó·k máta we·ɔ·tá·k·wi·k a·pto·ná·k·an ktəma·ksúwak."
         /t But these people who do not know the scripture are pitiful."
         /k But this people who knoweth not the law are cursed.

Jn 7.50 /b Nikutemus wrtxatup Nhesusu peskrwune
         /p †nikɔtí·mas, we·txá·t·əp nči·sás·a pi·ske·wəní·i,
         /t Nicodemus, who had come to Jesus at night,
         /k Nicodemus ..., (he that came to Jesus by night, ...)

         /b nul nu wehi eku avpwp, tclaol,
         /p nál ná wíči- íka -ahpó·p, təlá·ɔl,
         /t he was one among those present, and he said to them,
         /k ... saith unto them, (... being one of them,)

Jn 7.51 /b Fwetulitwakuninu vuh lexun
         /p "nkwi·tələt·əwa·k·anəna=háč lí·x·ən,   [our (exc.)!]
         /t "Does our law provide that   [*lit.*, is set, laid down]
         /k Doth our law judge

         /b li a palevan awrn nrsko puntaownt ok wraovawunt krkw tu rlset?   [⟨rao⟩ for ⟨ro⟩]
         /p lí-=á· -palí·ha·n awé·n né·skɔ pəntaɔ́·wənt, ɔ́·k -we·ɔ·há·wənt kéku=tá é·lsi·t?"
         /t someone be destroyed before he is heard or before it is known what he has done?"
         /k any man, before it hear him, and know what he doeth?

Jn 7.52 /b Noxkwmawao, tclawao Faluleet vuh ok krpc?
         /p nɔxko·mawwá·ɔ, təlawwá·ɔ, "†nka·lalí·i·t=háč ɔ́·k ké·pe?
         /t They answered him by saying to him, "Are you also a Galilean?
         /k They answered and said unto him, Art thou also of Galilee?

         /b Wli ntwnu kwlih punamun,
         /p wə́li-ntó·na. kó·li-=č -pənámən.
         /t Search diligently for it. You must examine it well.
         /k Search, and look:

         /b rli Falulebf ta wunheyeq nrnekanewrwset.
         /p é·li †nka·lalí·yunk, tá=á· wənčí·ai·kw nehəni·k·a·ní·i-wé·wsi·t."
         /t For from Galilee there will not come a prophet."
         /k for out of Galilee ariseth no prophet.

Jn 7.53 /b Nu wrmi mahepanek li nevlahi wekevtet.
         /p ná wé·mi ma·č·í·p·ani·k lí nihəláči wi·k·íhti·t.
         /t Then everyone went home to their own houses.
         /k And every man went unto his own house.

Chapter 54 (pp. 93-97). [L. section 53.] (John 8.1-46, 47 [part], 48-59)

Jn 8.1
/b   Nhesus rp Olipe ovhwf;
/p   nčí·sas é·p †ɔlipí·i-ɔhčúnk.
/t   Jesus went to Olive Mountain.
/k   Jesus went unto the mount of Olives.

Jn 8.2
/b   ave alupae eku prp patamwrekaonif, ok wrmi awrnek wtxawapani,
/p   áhi-alap·a·í·i íka pé·p pa·tamwe·i·k·á·ɔnink, ɔ́·k wé·mi awé·ni·k o·txawwá·p·ani.
/t   Very early in the morning he came to the temple, and the people all came to him.
/k   And early in the morning he came again into the temple, and all the people came unto him;

/b   mrhi lrmutavpetc avkrkifrp.
/p   mé·či le·matahpí·t·e, ahke·kínke·p.
/t   After he sat down, he taught.
/k   and he sat down, and taught them.

Jn 8.3
/b   Nu rvrlrvekrthek ok Paluseok eku pwrjwanro xqro   [⟨rvrlrvek-⟩ for ⟨rvlrkvek-⟩]
/p   ná ehəle·khi·k·é·č·i·k ɔ́·k †pa·ləsi·í·ok íka pwe·š·əwa·né·ɔ xkwé·ɔ.
/t   Then the scribes and the Pharisees brought a woman there.
/k   And the scribes and Pharisees brought unto him a woman

/b   tovwnawao nrli keme wepcfrlet,
/p   tɔhwənawwá·ɔ né·li- ki·mí·i -wi·penké·li·t.
/t   They arested her while she was committing adultery.
/k   taken in adultery;

/b   nu lawuntc tovlanro;
/p   ná la·wə́nte tɔhəla·né·ɔ.
/t   Then they set her in the middle of the floor.
/k   and when they had set her in the midst,

Jn 8.4
/b   tclawao, Rkrkifrs, wu xqr twna cntu keme wepcfrt
/p   təlawwá·ɔ, "e·k·e·kínke·s, wá xkwé· thwə́na· énta- ki·mí·i -wi·pénke·t,
/t   And they said to him, "Teacher, this woman was arrested committing adultery,
/k   They say unto him, Master, this woman was taken in adultery,

/b   nrli nc liset.
/p   né·li- nə́ -ləs·i·t.
/t   while in the act of doing it.
/k   in the very act.

Jn 8.5 /b Mwjiju qetulitwakun ntclkwnrn
/p mo·šə́š·a kkwi·tələt·əwá·k·an ntəlkó·ne·n,
/t The law of Moses tells us,
/k Now Moses in the law commanded us,

/b b rlset avsinh pavkuma kxunkih nvela;
/p yú é·lsi·t ahsə́n=č pahkáma·, kxántki=č nhíla·.
/t one who does this is to have stones (*lit.*, a stone) thrown at them, until they are killed.
/k that such should be stoned:

/b krkw vuh ke ktclwe?
/p kéku=háč kí· ktə́ləwe?"
/t What do *you* say?"
/k but what sayest thou?

Jn 8.6 /b Wunhi lanro rli avqrhevavtet wunhih hanemavtet.
/p wwə́nči-la·né·ɔ, é·li-ahkwe·č·i·háhti·t, wə́nči-=č -čani·máhti·t.
/t They said that to him because they were testing him, in order to accuse him.
/k This they said, tempting him, that they might have to accuse him.

/b Jwq Nhesus vatrvlrp vakif tali kseni lrkvekrp tilwvekun torkrn.
/p šúkw nčí·sas hatéhəle·p, hák·ink táli ksí·ni le·khí·k·e·p, təlo·hí·k·an tɔé·ke·n.
/t But Jesus stooped down and unconcernedly wrote on the ground, using his forefinger.
/k But Jesus stooped down, and with his finger wrote on the ground, as though he heard them not.

Jn 8.7 /b Jwq amunhei notwtumawao,
/p šúkw amənčí·i nɔt·o·t·əmaɔwwá·ɔ.
/t But they asked him insistently.
/k So when they continued asking him,

/b Nhesus apaqep, ok tclao;
/p nčí·sas †a·p·á·kwi·p, ɔ́·k təlá·ɔ,
/t Jesus raised up and said to them,
/k he lifted up himself, and said unto them,

/b Kelwu awrn mutu mrvtawset vetamih asin pukuma.   [⟨pu|-kuma⟩ for /kpák·ama/]
/p "ki·ló·wa awé·n máta me·t·á·wsi·t, hítami=č ahsə́n kpák·ama.
/t "Anyone of you who has not sinned should be the first to throw a stone at her."
/k He that is without sin among you, let him first cast a stone at her.

Jn 8.8 /b Nu lupi vatrep li vakif lrkvekrp.
/p ná lápi haté·i·p lí hák·ink, le·khí·k·e·p.

| | /t | Then he stooped down again to the ground and wrote. |
| | /k | And again he stooped down, and wrote on the ground. |

Jn 8.9 /b Nrk puntaothek alumi mexaniswuk wunhi nevlahi pwnarlintumwukunwu,
/p né·k pəntaɔ́·č·i·k áləmi-mi·x·anə́s·əwak wə́nči nihəláči pwəna·eləntaməwa·k·anúwa.
/t Those who heard him became ashamed because of their own thoughts.
/k And they which heard it, being convicted by their own conscience,

/b nun kwti ktheok. krkyethek vetami kxunki pavkunhi.
/p †nənk·wə́ti kčí·ɔk, ke·kaí·č·i·k hítami, kxántki pahkánči.
/t One by one they went out, the oldest first and eventually completely.
/k went out one by one, beginning at the eldest, even unto the last:

/b Nhesus falap xwva,
/p nčí·sas nkála·p xó·ha,
/t Jesus was left by himself,
/k and Jesus was left alone,

/b ok nu xqr nepwp lawuntc.
/p ɔ́·k ná xkwé· ní·p·o·p la·wə́nte.
/t and the woman was standing in the middle of the floor.
/k and the woman standing in the midst.

Jn 8.10 /b Nhesus apaqetc takw awrni nrri jwq nrl xqro, tclao;
/p nčí·sas †a·p·a·kwí·t·e, takó· awé·ni ne·é·i šúkw né·l xkwé·ɔ, təlá·ɔ,
/t When Jesus raised himself up, he saw no one but the woman, and he said to her.
/k When Jesus had lifted up himself, and saw none but the woman, he said unto her,

/b Xqr ‖ taneka kc vuh bkavkc mrtavkunemkonek?
/p "xkwé·, ta·nikáhke=háč yukáhke metahkəni·mkóni·k?
/t "Woman, where are those accusers of yours that were here?
/k Woman, where are those thine accusers?

(p. 94) /b takw vuh awrn kuntrlumwkwi?
/p takó·=háč awé·n kkənte·ləmuk·ó·wi?"
/t Did no one condemn you?"
/k hath no man condemned thee?

Jn 8.11 /b tclkw, Takw awrn Nrvlalian.
/p tə́lku, "takó· awé·n, nehəlá·lian."
/t She said to him, "No one, my Lord."
/k She said, No man, Lord.

/b   Nhesus tclao. Ok nrpc mutu kuntrlumulwi,
/p   nčí·sas tǝlá·ɔ, "ɔ́·k né·pe máta kkǝnte·lǝmǝló·wi.
/t   Jesus said to her, "And I, also, do not condemn you.
/k   And Jesus said unto her, Neither do I condemn thee:

/b   alumska kahi heh mavhi lisevun.
/p   alǝ́mska; káči čí·č máhči-lǝs·í·han."
/t   Go, and don't be bad anymore."
/k   go, and sin no more.

Jn 8.12 /b   Nu lupi krkw tclan Nhesus, tclaol;
/p   ná lápi kéku tǝla·n nčí·sas, tǝlá·ɔl,
/t   Then Jesus spoke again and said to them.
/k   Then spake Jesus again unto them, saying,

/b   Ne tu bv noxrkamun cntu lawsif,
/p   "ní·=tá yúh nɔ·x·é·kamǝn entalá·wsink.
/t   "It is *I* who light this world.
/k   I am the light of the world:

/b   awrnh naolet, ta pumiskri peskrkif.
/p   awé·n=č ná·ɔli·t, tá=á· pǝmǝské·i pi·ské·k·ink,
/t   Whoever follows me will not walk in darkness,
/k   he that followeth me shall not walk in darkness,

/b   jwqh noxpawsen prmawswek oxrrk.
/p   šúkw=č nɔxpá·wsi·n pe·ma·wsó·wi·k ɔ·x·é·e·k."
/t   but he shall have (*lit.*, live with) the living light."
/k   but shall have the light of life.

Jn 8.13 /b   Nc wunhi Paluseok lanro,
/p   nǝ́ wwǝ́nči- †pa·lǝsi·í·ɔk -la·né·ɔ,
/t   Because of that the Pharisees said to him,
/k   The Pharisees therefore said unto him,

/b   Ktukunwtumun nevlahi kvuky, takw kwlamwri.
/p   "ktak·ǝnó·t·ǝmǝn nihǝláči khák·ay; takó· ko·la·mǝwé·i."
/t   "You tell of yourself, and you do not tell the truth."
/k   Thou bearest record of thyself; thy record is not true.

Jn 8.14 /b   Nhesus tclan,
/p   nčí·sas tǝ́la·n,
/t   And Jesus said to them,
/k   Jesus answered and said unto them,

/b avkunwtumanc a nevlahi nvaky, jwq a eaphi nwlamwc,
/p "ahkəno·t·əmá·ne·á· nihəláči nhák·ay, šúkw·á· i·á·pči no·lá·məwe,
/t "If I do tell of my own self, still I would only tell the truth,
/k Though I bear record of myself, yet my record is true:

/b rli nevlahi watao wrmu, ok tutuh rau;
/p é·li- nihəláči -wwá·taɔ wé·ma, ɔ́·k tətá=č e·á·a.
/t for I, myself, know where I came from and where I shall go.
/k for I know whence I came, and whither I go;

/b jwq kelwu mutu kwavevwmw wrmu, ok tutu ta rau.
/p šúkw ki·ló·wa máta ko·wa·hi·húmɔ wé·ma, ɔ́·k təta=tá e·á·a.
/t But *you* do not know where I came from and where I go.
/k but ye cannot tell whence I come, and whither I go.

Jn 8.15 /b Kelwu, kejavkunemrq linei, ne mutu awrn fejavkunemai;
/p ki·ló·wa kišahkəní·me·kw ləní·i; ní· máta awé·n nkišahkəni·má·i.
/t *You* judge (i.e., pronounce sentence on) them in the ordinary way; *I* judge no one.
/k Ye judge after the flesh; I judge no man.

Jn 8.16 /b ok a kejavkunemakc fejavkunemwakun wlamwrw,   [⟨-rw⟩ for /-e·yó·u/; cf. 8.17]
/p ɔ́·k=á· kišahkəni·mák·e, nkišahkəni·məwá·k·an wəla·məwe·yó·u,
/t And if I did judge them, my judgment would be true,
/k And yet if I judge, my judgment is true:

/b rli mutu mawseo, rli ne ok Nwx Prtalwkalet.
/p é·li- máta -ma·wsí·ɔ, é·li ní· ɔ́·k nó·x pe·t·alo·ká·li·t.
/t for I am not one, as it is I and my father who sent me.
/k for I am not alone, but I and the Father that sent me.

Jn 8.17 /b Ok nanc lrkvasw qetuletwakunwu,
/p ɔ́·k ná=nə le·khá·s·u kkwi·tələt·əwa·k·anúwa:
/t And that is how your law is written:
/k It is also written in your law,

/b nejevtetch linwuk toptwnakunwu wlamwrbwh.
/p ni·š·ihtí·t·e=č lə́nəwak, tɔ·pto·na·k·anúwa wəla·məwe·yó·u=č.
/t if there are two men, their word shall be true.
/k that the testimony of two men is true.

Jn 8.18 /b Ne numawsi, nevlahi ntukunwtumun nvaky,
/p ní· nəmá·wsi; nihəláči ntak·ənó·t·əmən nhák·ay.
/t I am one; I tell of my own self.
/k I am one that bear witness of myself,

          /b   ok Nwx prtalwkalet ntukunemwq.
          /p   ó·k nó·x pe·t·alo·ká·li·t ntak·əní·mukw."
          /t   And my father who sent me tells of me."
          /k   and the Father that sent me beareth witness of me.

Jn 8.19   /b   Tclawao, Tani vuh nu Kwx?
          /p   təlawwá·ɔ, "tá·ni=háč ná kó·x?"
          /t   They said to him, "Where is your father?"
          /k   Then said they unto him, Where is thy Father?

          /b   Nhesus tclao, Takw kwavevwmw, ok kwavaewu Nwx,
          /p   nčí·sas təlá·ɔ, "takó· ko·wa·hi·húmɔ, ó·k ko·wa·ha·íwwa nó·x.
          /t   Jesus said to them, "You do not know me, and you do not know my father.
          /k   Jesus answered, Ye neither know me, nor my Father:

          /b   Waverqc a, kwavawu a Nwx.
          /p   wwa·hié·k·we=á·, ko·wa·háwwa=á· nó·x."
          /t   If you knew me, you would know my father."
          /k   if ye had known me, ye should have known my Father also.

Jn 8.20   /b   Nuni tuntxi Nhesus akunwtuminrp
          /p   ná=ní tə́ntxi- nčí·sas -ahkəno·t·əmə́ne·p
          /t   Those were all the things Jesus talked about
          /k   These words spake Jesus

          /b   patamwrekaonif nc rvatwf mwni, cntu avkrkifrtc,
          /p   pa·tamwe·i·k·á·ɔnink, nə́ ehhátunk mɔ́ni, énta-ahke·kinké·t·e.
          /t   when he taught in the temple at the place where money is put.
          /k   in the treasury, as he taught in the temple:

          /b   ok takw awrn tovwnaepani rli nrlumu tpisqevlalkup.   [⟨-lalkup⟩ for ⟨-lakup⟩]
          /p   ó·k takó· awé·n tɔhwəna·í·p·ani, é·li- né·ləma -tpəskwihəlá·k·əp.
          /t   And no one arrested him, as his time had not yet come.
          /k   and no man laid hands on him; for his hour was not yet come.

Jn 8.21   /b   Nu lupi Nhesus tclanrp,
          /p   ná lápi nčí·sas təlá·ne·p,
          /t   Then again Jesus said to them,
          /k   Then said Jesus again unto them,

          /b   Paleh natav,   [⟨natav⟩ for ⟨ntav⟩: /ntá(h)/]
          /p   "palí·i=č ntá.
          /t   "I shall go away.
          /k   I go my way,

	/b	knatwnaevmwh nuxpufulrqch kmutawswakunwu,
	/p	kənat·o·naíhəmɔ=č, naxpankəlé·k·we=č kəmat·a·wsəwa·k·anúwa.
	/t	You will look for me when you die with your sins.
	/k	and ye shall seek me, and shall die in your sins:

	/b	tutu rau ta kuski pawunro.
	/p	tətá e·á·a, tá=á· kkáski-pa·wəné·ɔ."
	/t	Where I may go you will not be able to come."
	/k	whither I go, ye cannot come.

Jn 8.22	/b	Nu Nhwuk tclwrnro, Wnevlaoh vuh ct vokyu?
	/p	ná nčó·wak tələwe·né·ɔ, "wənihəlá·ɔ=č=háč=ét hókaya?
	/t	Then the Jews said, "Is he maybe going to kill himself?
	/k	Then said the Jews, Will he kill himself?

	/b	rli lwrt rauh ta kuski paonro.
	/p	é·li-lúwe·t, 'e·á·a=č tá=á· kkáski-pa·wəné·ɔ.
	/t	For he said, 'Where I am going you will not be able to come.'"
	/k	because he saith, Whither I go, ye cannot come.

Jn 8.23	/b	Tclao, Kelwu vakif kwnheyevmw, ne vwqrwf nwnheyi;
	/p	təlá·ɔ, "ki·ló·wa hákink kunči·aíhəmɔ; ní· hukwé·yunk nunčí·ai.
	/t	He said to them, "*You* are from below; *I* am from above.
	/k	And he said unto them, Ye are from beneath; I am from above:

	/b	kelwu b cntu, lawsif kwnheyevmw, ne mutu b cntu lawsif nwnheyei. ‖
	/p	ki·ló·wa yú entalá·wsink kunči·aíhəmɔ; ní· máta yú entalá·wsink nunči·aí·i.
	/t	*You* are from this world; *I* am not from this world.
	/k	ye are of this world; I am not of this world.

Jn 8.24	/b	Nc wunhi lilrq, nuxpufulrqch kmutawswakunwu.
(p. 95)	/p	nə́ wənči-ləĺe·kw, 'naxpankəlé·k·we=č kəmat·a·wsəwa·k·anúwa.'
	/t	That's why I say to you, 'When you die with your sins.'
	/k	I said therefore unto you, that ye shall die in your sins:

	/b	rli mutu wlamvetamwrq ntcli ne lisen,
	/p	é·li- máta -wəla·mhitamó·we·kw ntə́li- ní· -lə́s·i·n,
	/t	For if you do not believe that I am me,
	/k	for if ye believe not that I am he,

	/b	knuxpufululinro kmutawswakunwu.	[⟨-ufululin-⟩ for ⟨-ufulin-⟩]
	/p	kənaxpankələné·ɔ kəmat·a·wsəwa·k·anúwa."	
	/t	you die with your sins."	
	/k	ye shall die in your sins.	

Jn 8.25	/b	Nu tclanro, Awan vuh ke?	[⟨Awan⟩ for ⟨Awrn⟩]
	/p	ná təla·né·ɔ, "awé·n=háč kí·?"	
	/t	Then they said to him, "Who are you?"	
	/k	Then said they unto him, Who art thou?	

/b Nhesus tclao, Nunul tu nuni nrtami lilrkup bqc qeaqi ntclwrn.
/p nčí·sas təlá·ɔ, "nánal=tá nə́ni né·tami-lǝlé·k·əp, yúkwe kwiá·kwi ntə́ləwe·n.
/t Jesus said to them, "It's the same thing I first said to you, and I still say it now.
/k And Jesus saith unto them, Even the same that I said unto you from the beginning.

Jn 8.26 /b Xrlrnaovki krkw kutu li avkunemulwvmw, cntu mutu wlelarverq;
/p xe·lennáɔhki kéku kkát·a-ahkəni·məlúhəmɔ, énta- máta -wəli·lae·hí(·)e·kw.
/t There are many things I want to say about you in which you do not please me.
/k I have many things to say and to judge of you:

/b jwq nu prtalwkalet wlamwr;
/p šúkw ná pe·t·alo·ká·li·t wəlá·məwe·.
/t But he that sent me speaks the truth.
/k but he that sent me is true;

/b cntxi puntaokwp anvwqi ntclanro b cntu lawsethek.
/p éntxi-pəntaɔ́k·əp, a·nhúkwi ntəla·né·ɔ yú entala·wsí·č·i·k."
/t Everything I heard from him I tell in turn to the people of this world."
/k and I speak to the world those things which I have heard of him.

Jn 8.27 /b Takw wninwstamwnro li avkuneman Wrtwxumunt.
/p takó· wənəno·stamo·wəné·ɔ lí-ahkəní·ma·n we·t·ó·x·əmənt.
/t They did not understand that the Father was being talked about.
/k They understood not that he spake to them of the Father.

Jn 8.28 /b Nu Nhesus tclan, Mrhih linw Wrqesif uspunrqc,
/p ná nčí·sas tə́la·n, "mé·či=č lə́nu we·k·wí·s·ink aspəné·k·we,
/t Then Jesus said to them, "After you have lifted up the man who is the Son,
/k Then said Jesus unto them, When ye have lifted up the Son of man,

/b nuh kwavenro ntcli ne lisen, ok ntcli mutu krkw nevlahi lisewun,
/p ná=č ko·wa·hi·né·ɔ, ntə́li- ní· -lə·s·i·n, ɔ́·k ntə́li- máta kéku nihəláči -lə·s·í·wən.
/t then you will know that I am me, and that I do nothing on my own.
/k then shall ye know that I am he, and that I do nothing of myself;

/b jwq Nwx rvlukrkemet nanc krkw rlwranup.
/p šúkw nó·x ehəlak·e·kí·mi·t, ná=nə kéku e·ləwe·á·nəp.
/t But as my father taught me, those are the things I have said.
/k but as my Father hath taught me, I speak these things.

Jn 8.29
/b Nrku prtalwkalet nwetavpemwq,
/p né·k·a pe·t·alo·ká·li·t nəwitahpí·mukw.
/t The one that sent me is himself with me.
/k And he that sent me is with me:

/b mutu Wrtwxumunt nuxwvrxkalkwi;
/p máta we·t·ó·x·əmənt nnax·o·he·xka·lkó·wi,
/t The Father has not left me all alone,
/k the Father hath not left me alone;

/b rli aphi liseu rli wlrlintamaet.
/p é·li- á·pči -lás·ia é·li-wəle·ləntamái·t."
/t for I always act in such a way that he is pleased with me."
/k for I do always those things that please him.

Jn 8.30
/b Nc rlwrtc xrli wlamvetaowao.
/p nə́ e·ləwé·t·e, xé·li o·la·mhitaɔwwá·ɔ.
/t When he said that, many believed him.
/k As he spake these words, many believed on him.

Jn 8.31
/b Nhesus tclao bl Nhwu
/p nčí·sas təlá·ɔ yó·l nčó·wa,
/t Jesus said to these Jews,
/k Then said Jesus to those Jews

/b wrlamvetaerq, heme avperqe ntaptwnakunif,
/p "we·la·mhitaíe·kw, či·mí·i ahpié·k·we nta·pto·ná·k·anink,
/t "You that believe me, if you abide in my word permanently,
/k which believed on him, If ye continue in my word,

/b nuh rkrkemukek kehe;
/p ná=č e·k·e·ki·mák·i·k khičí·i.
/t then it's truly as my disciples.
/k then are ye my disciples indeed;

Jn 8.32
/b okh kwatwnro wlamwrokun,
/p ɔ́·k=č ko·wa·to·né·ɔ wəla·məwe·ɔ́·k·an,
/t And you shall know the truth,
/k And ye shall know the truth,

/b nc wlamwrokun knevlatamwrvalkwnroh.
/p nə́ wəla·məwe·ɔ́·k·an kənihəla·t·amwe·ha·lko·né·ɔ=č."
/t and the truth shall make you free."
/k and the truth shall make you free.

Jn 8.33
/b Tclawao. Nelwnu tu Rplivamif nwnhekevnu,
/p təlawwá·ɔ, "ni·ló·na=tá †e·pəlihámink nunči·k·íhəna.
/t They said to him, "*We* are born from Abraham.
/k They answered him, We be Abraham's seed,

/b takw vuji awrn nwtulwkakunumkwewunu,
/p takó· háši awé·n no·t·alo·ka·k·anəmko·wí·wəna.
/t We have never been the servants of anyone.
/k and were never in bondage to any man:

/b ta vuh kwnhi lwrn, Knevlatumwrvalkwnroh?
/p tá=háč kúnči-lúwe·n, 'kənihəla·t·amwe·ha·lko·né·ɔ=č.'"
/t Why do you say that it shall make us free?"
/k how sayest thou, Ye shall be made free?

Jn 8.34
/b Nhesus tclao, Kehe kehe ktclwvmw,
/p nčí·sas təlá·ɔ, "khičí·i, khičí·i, ktəllúhəmɔ,
/t Jesus said to them, "Truly, truly, I say to you,
/k Jesus answered them, Verily, verily, I say unto you,

/b awrnh mavtawsetc, nul nc wtalwkakunumkwn motawswakun.
/p awé·n=č mahta·wsí·t·e, nál nə́ o·t·alo·ka·k·anəmko·n mot·a·wsəwá·k·an.
/t if anyone sins, that sin of his is what he is the servant of.
/k Whosoever committeth sin is the servant of sin.

Jn 8.35
/b Alwkakun takw heme kwtrnaoki eavpei
/p alo·ká·k·an takó· či·mí·i kwət·ennáɔhki i·ahpí·i,
/t A servant never stays in one place forever,
/k And the servant abideth not in the house for ever:

/b jwq wrqesif aphih nc topen.
/p šúkw we·k·wí·s·ink á·pči=č nə́ tɔ́p·i·n.
/t but the Son will stay there always.
/k but the Son abideth ever.

Jn 8.36
/b Wrqesif a nevlatamwrvolkonc, knevlatamu a kehe.
/p we·k·wí·s·ink=á· nihəla·t·amwe·hɔ·lkóne, kənihəlá·t·ama=á· khičí·i.
/t If the Son makes you free, you would be truly free.
/k If the Son therefore shall make you free, ye shall be free indeed.

Jn 8.37
/b Nwatwn tu ktcli Rplivamif wcnheyenro
/p no·wá·to·n=tá ktə́li- †e·pəlihámink -wənči·ai·né·ɔ,
/t I know that you were born from Abraham,
/k I know that ye are Abraham's seed;

/b　jwq kutwnalevmw rli ntaptwnakun mutu kuski avpetakwrq.
/p　šúkw kkat·o·nalíhəmɔ é·li- nta·pto·ná·k·an máta -káski-ahpi·ta·k·ó·we·kw.
/t　but you want to kill me because you are unable to have my word in you.
/k　but ye seek to kill me, because my word hath no place in you.

Jn 8.38
/b　Ntclaptwnrn krkw rlenumakup Nwxif;
/p　ntəla·ptó·ne·n kéku e·li·namá·k·əp nó·x·ink.
/t　I speak of things I have seen at my father's.
/k　I speak that which I have seen with my Father:
　　　　　　　[RSV "of what I have seen with my Father."]

/b　ktclsenro rlenamrq kwxwawf.
/p　ktəlsi·né·ɔ e·lí·name·kw ko·x·əwá·unk."
/t　You do what you have seen at your father's.
/k　and ye do that which ye have seen with your father.
　　　　　　　[RSV "you do what you have heard from your father."]

Jn 8.39
/b　Tclawao, Rplivamu tu nwxunanu.
/p　təlawwá·ɔ, "†e·pəliháma=tá no·x·əná·na."
/t　They said to him, "Abraham is our father."
/k　They answered and said unto him, Abraham is our father.

/b　Nhesus tclao, Wnehanumwqrqpanc a Rplivamu ‖
/p　nčí·sas təlá·ɔ, "wəni·č·a·nəmuk·we·kwpáne=á· †e·pəliháma,
/t　Jesus said to them, "If you had been children of Abraham,
/k　Jesus saith unto them, If ye were Abraham's children,

(p. 96)
/b　na nc ktclsenro rlsetup.
/p　ná=nə ktəlsi·né·ɔ e·lsí·t·əp.
/t　you would do the same thing he did.
/k　ye would do the works of Abraham.

Jn 8.40
/b　Jwq bqc, kutwnalevmw,
/p　šúkw yúkwe kkat·o·nalíhəmɔ,
/t　But now you want to kill me,
/k　But now ye seek to kill me,

/b　mrhi rlrqc wlamwrokun nu mpuntaonrp Krtanitwet;
/p　mé·či ellé·k·we wəla·məwe·ó·k·an, nə́ mpəntaó·ne·p ke·tanət·ó·wi·t
/t　after I have told you the truth, and I have heard that from God.
/k　a man that hath told you the truth, which I have heard of God:

/b　mutu tu nc tclsewunrp Rplivamu.
/p　máta=tá nə́ təlsí·wəne·p †e·pəliháma.
/t　Abraham did not do that.
/k　this did not Abraham.

Jn 8.41 /b Ktclsenro rlset kwxwu.
         /p ktəlsi·né·ɔ é·lsi·t kó·x·əwa.
         /t You do what your father did.
         /k Ye do the deeds of your father.

         /b Tclawao; Takw ta keme wepifrokunif nwnhi kejekevwmnu,
         /p təlawwá·ɔ, "takó·=tá ki·mí·i·wi·penke·ɔ́·k·anink núnči-ki·š·i·k·i·húməna.
         /t They said to him, "We were not born from adultery.
         /k Then said they to him, We be not born of fornication;

         /b koti nwtwxivunu nul nu Krtanitwet.
         /p kwət·i no·t·o·x·íhəna; nál ná ke·tanət·ó·wi·t.
         /t We have one father; it is God.
         /k we have one Father, even God.

Jn 8.42 /b Nhesus tclao, Krtanitwet a vwtwxerqc, ktavolevmw a,
         /p nčí·sas təlá·ɔ, "ke·tanət·ó·wi·t=á· wto·x·ié·k·we, ktahɔ·líhəmɔ=á·.
         /t Jesus said to them, "If God were your father, you would love me.
         /k Jesus said unto them, If God were your Father, ye would love me:

         /b rli Krtanitwetif wenhekeu, ok eku mu,
         /p é·li- ke·tanət·o·wí·t·ink -wənčí·k·ia, ɔ́·k íka -mmá.
         /t For I was born from God and came from him.
         /k for I proceeded forth and came from God;

         /b ok mutu nevlahi, mpai, jwq mprtalwkalwq.
         /p ɔ́·k máta nihəláči mpá·i, šúkw mpe·t·alo·ká·lukw.
         /t And I did not come on my own, but he sent me.
         /k neither came I of myself, but he sent me.

Jn 8.43 /b Koh vuh mutu nunwstamwrq ntaptwnakun?
         /p kɔ́č=háč máta nəno·stamó·we·kw nta·pto·ná·k·an?
         /t Why do you not understand my words?
         /k Why do ye not understand my speech?

         /b wunhi rli mutu a kuski puntamwrq ntaptwnakun.
         /p wənči é·li- máta=á· -káski-pəntamó·we·kw nta·pto·ná·k·an.
         /t It's because you cannot understand my words.
         /k even because ye cannot hear my word.

Jn 8.44 /b Kelwu ktclsenro rlset kwxwu mavtuntw,
         /p ki·ló·wa ktəlsi·né·ɔ é·lsi·t kó·x·əwa, mahtánt·u.
         /t *You* are the way your father is, the devil.
         /k Ye are of your father the devil,

/b nu kwxwu mavheqi pwnarlintumwakun krpwu nc kutu lisenro:
/p ná kó·x·əwa mahčí·kwi pwəna·eləntaməwá·k·an, ké·pəwa nə́ kkát·a-ləs·i·né·ɔ.
/t The thoughts of that father of yours are evil, and you also desire to be that way.
/k and the lusts of your father ye will do.

/b nrtami nvlwrtup ok bqc nc tclsen, [⟨nvl-⟩ for ⟨nvel-⟩]
/p né·tami-nhiləwé·t·əp, ɔ́·k yúkwe nə́ tə́lsi·n.
/t He was the first to commit murder, and he also does that now.
/k He was a murderer from the beginning,

/b mutu vuji wlamwrokunif pumenei
/p máta háši wəla·məwe·ɔ́·k·anink pəminní·i,
/t He never dwells in the truth,
/k and abode not in the truth,

/b rli mutu nuxpunc vuji wlamwrokun vokif vatrk,
/p é·li máta náxpəne háši wəla·məwe·ɔ́·k·an hɔ́k·enk hát·e·k.
/t as there is never even any truth in him.
/k because there is no truth in him.

/b krkulwnrtc, nevlahi toptwnakun tokunwtumun,
/p ke·k·əlo·né·t·e, nihəláči tɔ·pto·ná·k·an tɔk·ənó·t·əmən,
/t When he lies, he speaks his own words,
/k When he speaketh a lie, he speaketh of his own:

/b rli krkulwnrt: ok kulwnrokunuk wxwao.
/p é·li ke·k·əlo·́ne·t, ɔ́·k kəlo·ne·ɔ́·k·anak o·x·əwá·ɔ.
/t as he is a liar and the father of lies.
/k for he is a liar, and the father of it.

Jn 8.45 /b Rli lilrq wlamwrokun mutu kwlamevtaevwmw. [⟨mevt⟩ for ⟨mvet⟩]
/p é·li-lɔ́le·kw wəla·məwe·ɔ́·k·an, máta ko·la·mhitai·húmɔ.
/t Because I tell you the truth, you do not believe me.
/k And because I tell you the truth, ye believe me not.

Jn 8.46 /b Cntxi avperq, awrn vuh a kuski myaohemw ntcli muvtawsen?
/p éntxi-ahpíe·kw, awé·n=háč=á· káski-maya·ɔ·č·í·mu ntɔ́li-mahtá·wsi·n?
/t Of all of you here, who would be able to testify that I sin.
/k Which of you convinceth me of sin? [RSV "convicts me"]

/b lilrqc a wlamwrokun. koh vuh a mutu wlamvetaerq?
/p lɔlé·k·we=á· wəla·məwe·ɔ́·k·an, kɔ́č=háč=á· máta wəla·mhitaíe·kw?
/t If I tell you the truth, why would you not believe me?
/k And if I say the truth, why do ye not believe me?

Jn 8.47 /b Krtanetwete awrn qulsitamun vufq Katanitwet toptwnakun.
             [⟨Krtanet-⟩ for ⟨Krtanit-⟩; ⟨Kat-⟩ for ⟨Krt-⟩]
/p ke·tanət·o·wi·t·í·i-awé·n kwəlsə́t·amən=hánkw ke·tanət·ó·w·i·t tɔ·pto·ná·k·an."
/t A person of God hears God's words."
/k He that is of God heareth God's words: [ye therefore hear them not, because ye are not of God.]

Jn 8.48 /b Nhwuk tclawao, mutu vuh ktcpi lilwvumnu
/p nčó·wak təlawwá·ɔ, "máta=háč ktépi-lǝlo·húmǝna,
/t The Jews said to him, "Can we not rightly say of you,
/k Then answered the Jews, and said unto him, Say we not well

/b Sumclei kvaky, ktupetaq mavtuntw?
/p †samelí·i khák·ay, ktap·í·ta·kw mahtánt·u?"
/t that you are a Samaritan and have a devil in you?"
/k that thou art a Samaritan, and hast a devil?

Jn 8.49 /b Nhesus tclao, Takw ta ne nmavtuntwei: nmuxifwrlumu Nwx.
/p nčí·sas təlá·ɔ, "takó·=tá ní· nəmahtant·o·wí·i; nəmax·inkwé·ləma nó·x.
/t Jesus said to them, "I am not a devil; I honor my father.
/k Jesus answered, I have not a devil; but I honour my Father,

/b kahi kelwu kmutrlumevmw.
/p káč·i ki·ló·wa kəmat·e·ləmíhəmɔ.
/t But *you* think little of me.
/k and ye do dishonour me.

Jn 8.50 /b Takw natwnamwun nevlahi xifwrlinswakun;
/p takó· nnat·o·namó·wən nihəláči xinkwe·lənsəwá·k·an.
/t I do not seek glory for myself.
/k And I seek not mine own glory:

/b jwq avpw nrtwnamwnt, ok kejavkunemunt.
/p šúkw ahpú ne·t·ó·namunt ó·k kišahkəní·mənt.
/t But there is one that it is sought for and judged.   [misunderstood]
/k there is one that seeketh and judgeth.

Jn 8.51 /b Kehe kehe ktclwvmw
/p khičí·i, khičí·i, ktəllúhəmɔ,
/t Truly, truly, I tell you,
/k Verily, verily, I say unto you,

/b awrnh krnavketaqc rlwru ta vuji wnrmwun wfulwakun.   [⟨wf-⟩ for ⟨uf-⟩]
/p awé·n=č ke·nahki·tá·k·we e·ləwé·a, tá·á· háši wəne·mó·wən ankələwá·k·an."
/t if anyone shall keep what I say, he would never see death."
/k If a man keep my saying, he shall never see death.

Text, Transcription, and Translation 317

Jn 8.52 /b Nu tclanro Nhwuk; Mrhi bqc nwatwnrn ktcli ke mavtuntwen.
         /p ná təla·né·ɔ nčó·wak, "mé·či yúkwe no·wa·tó·ne·n ktə́li- kí· -mahtant·ó·wi·n.
         /t Then the Jews said to him, "Now we know that *you* are a devil.
         /k Then said the Jews unto him, Now we know that thou hast a devil.

         /b Rplivamu ufulu, ok ncnekanewrwsetpanifu ufulwfu;   [⟨ncnekan-‖e⟩]
         /p †e·pəliháma ánkəla, ɔ́·k nehəni·k·a·ní·i-we·wsi·tpanínka ankəlúnka.
         /t Abraham is dead, and the ancient prophets are dead.
         /k Abraham is dead, and the prophets;

(p. 97) /b ke ktclwc awrnh krnavketaq rlwru ta vuji ufulwi.
         /p kí· ktə́ləwe, 'awé·n=č ke·nahkí·ta·kw e·ləwé·a tá·á· háši ankəló·wi.
         /t And *you* say, 'Someone who keeps what I say would never die.'
         /k and thou sayest, If a man keep my saying, he shall never taste of death.

Jn 8.53 /b Ktalwe vuh lisen nmwxwmsunanu Rplivamu?
         /p ktaləwí·i-=háč -lə́s·i·n nəmux·o·msəná·na †e·pəliháma
         /t Are you greater than our grandfather of old, Abraham,
         /k Art thou greater than our father Abraham, which is dead?

         /b ok nrnekanewrwsetpanifu?
         /p ɔ́·k nehəni·k·a·ní·i-we·wsi·tpanínka?
         /t and the prophets of old?
         /k and the prophets are dead:

         /b awrnif vuh ktclrlumu kvaky?
         /p awé·nink=háč ktəlé·ləma khák·ay?"
         /t Who do you consider yourself to be like?"
         /k whom makest thou thyself?

Jn 8.54 /b Nhesus tclao, Ne a nevlahi xifwrlinseanc, taa nmuxifwi lisei.
         /p nčí·sas təlá·ɔ, "ní·=á· nihəláči xinkwe·lənsiá·ne, tá=á· nəmax·ínkwi-ləs·í·i.
         /t Jesus said to them, "If I think *myself* great, I would not be great.
         /k Jesus answered, If I honour myself, my honour is nothing:

         /b Nwx kta nmuxifwrlumwq,
         /p nó·x=ktá nəmax·inkwé·ləmukw.
         /t It is rather my father that thinks highly of me.
         /k it is my Father that honoureth me;

         /b nu nul nu krpwu rlwrrq Kejrlumwqrf,
         /p nánal ná ké·pəwa e·ləwé·e·kw, 'ki·š·e·ləmúk·wenk.'
         /t He is the one of whom you also say, 'Our God'.
         /k of whom ye say, that he is your God:

Jn 8.55 /b jwq mutu kwavaewu, ne nwava;
/p šúkw máta ko·wa·ha·íwwa; ní· no·wá·ha.
/t But you don't know him; *I* know him.
/k Yet ye have not known him; but I know him:

/b lwranc a, takw nwavai fukulwnc a mulaji a kelwu rlserq;
/p luwe·á·ne=á·, 'takó· no·wa·há·i,' nkak·əló·ne=á·, málahši=á· ki·ló·wa e·lsíe·kw.
/t If I said, 'I don't know him,' I would be a liar, like the way *you* are.
/k and if I should say, I know him not, I shall be a liar like unto you:

/b jwq nwava ok fulsitao krkw rlet.
/p šúkw no·wá·ha, ó·k nkəlsət·ao é·li·t.
/t But I know him, and I obey what he tells me.
/k but I know him, and keep his saying.

Jn 8.56 /b Kwxwao Rplivamu wlrlintamwp nrfc fejkweum,   [⟨eu⟩ for /yə/; elsewhere ⟨b⟩]
/p ko·x·əwá·ɔ †e·pəliháma wəle·ləntamo·p nénke nki·škó·yəm.
/t Your father of old Abraham was glad when he saw my day.
/k Your father Abraham rejoiced to see my day:

/b wnrmunrp ok wlrlintumwp.
/p wəné·məne·p ó·k wəle·ləntamo·p."
/t He saw it and was glad."
/k and he saw it, and was glad.

Jn 8.57 /b Nhwuk tclawao, Nrsko ct palrnuxk txenxkc kutinamei,
/p nčó·wak təlawwá·ɔ, "né·skɔ=ét palé·naxk txí·nxke kkat·ənamí·i,
/t The Jews said to him, "You can't yet be fifty years old,
/k Then said the Jews unto him, Thou art not yet fifty years old,

/b ok vuh knevnro Rplivamu?
/p ó·k=háč kənihəné·ɔ †e·paliháma?"
/t and have you seen Abraham?"
/k and hast thou seen Abraham?

Jn 8.58 /b Nhesus tclao, Kvehe kvehe ktclwvmw nrsko rpeqc Rplivamu, ne nenwhi.
/p nčí·sas təlá·ɔ, "khičí·i, khičí·i ktəllúhəmɔ, né·skɔ e·pí·k·we †e·pəliháma, ní· ni·núči."
/t Jesus said to them, "Truly, truly, I tell you, before Abraham was, *I* did from the beginning."
/k Jesus said unto them, Verily, verily, I say unto you, Before Abraham was, I am.

Jn 8.59 /b Nu wrtunimunro avsinul tcli a puvkamanro,
/p ná wwe·t·ənəməné·ɔ ahsənal, tóli-=á· -pahkama·né·ɔ.
/t Then they picked up stones to throw them at him.
/k Then took they up stones to cast at him:

/b jwq Nhesus nevlahi kuntavpw,
/p šúkw nčí·sas nihəláči kántahpu,
/t But Jesus hid by himself.
/k but Jesus hid himself,

/b patamwrekaonif wcnhi kthetc, hwpwep li cntu xrlif rjei li lwep.
/p pa·tamwe·i·k·á·ɔnink wə́nči kčí·t·e, čə́p·wi·p lí énta-xé·link, e·š·í·i lí-ló·wi·p.
/t When he went out of the temple, he slipped into the crowd, passing through.
/k and went out of the temple, going through the midst of them, and so passed by.

Chapter 55 (pp. 97-101). [L. section 54.] (John 9.1-41; John 10.1-21.)

Jn 9.1
/b Rjetc wnro linwu,
/p e·š·í·t·e, wəne·ɔ́·ɔ lə́nəwa.
/t When he went through, he saw a man.
/k And as Jesus passed by, he saw a man

/b kejeketc nenwhi avkrpifwrp.
/p ki·š·i·k·í·t·e ni·núči ahke·p·ínkwe·p.
/t He had been blind from the time he was born.
/k which was blind from his birth.

Jn 9.2
/b Rkrkemathi notwtumakw tclkw,
/p e·k·e·ki·má·č·i nɔt·ó·t·əma·kw, tə́lku,
/t His disciples asked him, saying to him,
/k And his disciples asked him, saying,

/b Awrn vuh tcli muvtawsen wunhi wu linw avkrpifot?
/p "awé·n=háč tə́li-mahtá·wsi·n, wə́nči- wá lə́nu -ahke·p·ínkɔ·t?
/t "Who was the sinner, because of which this man is blind?
/k Master, who did sin, [this man, or his parents,] that he was born blind?

/b nrku vuh ji nc qekybbmu?
/p né·k·a=háč, ší=néh kwi·kayó·yəma?"
/t Was it him, or was it his parents?"
/k this man, or his parents ...?

Jn 9.3
/b Nhesus tclao, Takw tu rli muvtawsen wunhi ok mutu qekybbmu;
/p nčí·sas təlá·ɔ, "takó·=tá é·li-mahtá·wsi·n wə́nči, ɔ́·k máta kwi·kayó·yəma,
/t Jesus said to them, "It was not because he sinned, and not his parents,
/k Jesus answered, Neither hath this man sinned, nor his parents:

	/b	jwq wunhih tclswakun Krtanitwet vokif wunhi nrvkot.
	/p	šúkw wə́nči-=č təlsəwá·k·an ke·tanət·ó·wi·t hók·enk wə́nči -né·ykɔt.
	/t	but so that the deed (or power) of God would be seen coming from him.
	/k	but that the works of God should be made manifest in him.

Jn 9.4   /b   Neh tu ntclsen rletrvat prtalwkalet nrli kejqek,
              /p   ní·=č=tá ntə́lsi·n e·li·t·é·ha·t pe·t·alo·ká·li·t né·li-kí·škwi·k.
              /t   *I* must do what the one who sent me wants done while it is daytime.
              /k   I must work the works of him that sent me, while it is day:

              /b   rli nakyrkih nc peskrk, cntu mutu awrn kuski mekumoset.   [⟨-kih⟩ for /-keč/]
              /p   é·li- na·k·a·é·k·e=č nə́ -pí·ske·k, énta- máta awé·n -káski-mi·kəmó·s·i·t.   [nə́ (?)]
              /t   For, after a while, it will be dark, when no one is able to work.
              /k   the night cometh, when no man can work.

Jn 9.5   /b   Srki avpeu b entu lawsif, b entu lawslf noxrkamun.   [⟨-slf⟩ for ⟨-sif⟩]
              /p   sé·ki-ahpía yú entalá·wsink, yú entalá·wsink nɔ·x·é·kamən."
              /t   As long as I am in this world, I light this world."
              /k   As long as I am in the world, I am the light of the world.

Jn 9.6   /b   Mrhi nc rlwrtc, vakif li swkwp vwswqenakun wunhi seskwvrn,
              /p   mé·či nə́ e·ləwé·t·e, hák·ink lí-súk·o·p, wsuk·wi·ná·k·an wwə́nči-si·skó·he·n,
              /t   After saying that, he spat on the ground and made clay from his spit,
              /k   When he had thus spoken, he spat on the ground, and made clay of the spittle,

              /b   wujkifwf tcli jwvmaon seskw nrl krkrpifolethi,
              /p   wəškínkunk tə́li-šuhəmáɔ·n sí·sku né·l ke·k·e·p·inkɔ·lí·č·i.
              /t   and he rubbed the clay on the eyes of that blind man.
              /k   and he anointed the eyes of the blind man with the clay,

Jn 9.7   /b   tclao, ‖ Mai ksifwrl Rvalwkalinte munwprqtitif.
              /p   təlá·ɔ, "mái-ksínkwe·l ehalo·ka·ləntí·i-mənəp·e·kwtə́t·ink."
              /t   He said to him, "Go wash your face in the pool of the messenger (*lit.*, one sent)."
              /k   And said unto him, Go, wash in the pool of Siloam, (which is by interpretation, Sent.)

(p. 98)   /b   Nu eku ton ok ksifwr prhi nrman.   [⟨prhi⟩ for /pwéči-/]
              /p   ná íka tɔ́·n, ɔ́·k ksínkwe·, pwéči-né·ma·n.
              /t   Then he went there and washed his face, and then he came back seeing.
              /k   He went his way therefore, and washed, and came seeing.

Jn 9.8   /b   Nrvnrothek bl krkrpifolethi lwrok,
              /p   nehəne·ɔ́·č·i·k yó·l ke·k·e·p·inkɔ·lí·č·i luwé·ɔk,
              /t   The ones that used to see this blind man said,
              /k   The neighbours therefore, and they which before had seen him that he was blind, said,

/b Mutu vuh nul wu lrvlumutupet cventu wenwrufq? [⟨cve-⟩ for ⟨cvc-⟩]
/p "máta=háč nál wá lehələmátahpi·t ehə́nta-wi·nəwé·ankw?"
/t "Isn't this the one that used to sit where we always beg?"
/k Is not this he that sat and begged?

Jn 9.9
/b Alintc lwrok; Nul tu wu,
/p a·lə́nte luwé·ɔk, "nál=tá wá."
/t Some said, "This is him."
/k Some said, This is he:

/b alintc lwrok eku lenaqsw.
/p a·lə́nte luwé·ɔk, "íka li·ná·kwsu."
/t Some said, "He is like him."
/k others said, He is like him:

/b Jwq lwr, Ne tu.
/p šúkw lúwe·, "ní·=tá."
/t But he said, "It's me."
/k but he said, I am he.

Jn 9.10
/b Tclawao, Ta vuh lrw wunhi nrmaun.
/p təlawwá·ɔ, "tá=háč lé·w wə́nči-ne·má·an?"
/t They said to him, "What happened so that you can see?"
/k Therefore said they unto him, How were thine eyes opened?

Jn 9.11
/b Noxkwmao tclao, Linw tu lwcnsw Nhesus,
/p nɔxko·má·ɔ, təlá·ɔ, "lə́nu=tá luwénsu nčí·sas.
/t He answered them, saying to them, "It was a man named Jesus.
/k He answered and said, A man that is called Jesus

/b seskwvrp eku ntcli jwvmakwn nijkifwf,
/p si·skó·he·p, íka ntə́li-šuhəmá·k·o·n nəškínkunk.
/t He made clay and rubbed it on my eyes.
/k made clay, and anointed mine eyes,

/b ntclwq. Eku tu al Rvulwkalinte munwprqtitif my ksifwc:
/p ntə́lukw, 'íka=tá á·l ehalo·ka·lə̆ntí·i-mənəp·e·kwtə́t·ink, mái-ksínkwe.
/t He said to me, "Go to the pool of the messenger and wash your face.
/k and said unto me, Go to the pool of Siloam, and wash:

/b eku ntu ok fusifwc,
/p íka ntá, ɔ́·k nkəs·ínkwe.
/t I went there and washed my face.
/k   and I went and washed,

	/b	nu eku wrmanc naohe ntalumi nrman.
	/p	ná íka we·má·ne, naɔč·í·i ntáləmi-né·ma·n.
	/t	Then when I came from there, on the way I began to see."
	/k	and I received sight.

Jn 9.12
	/b	Nu tclanro, Tan eku vuh?
	/p	ná təla·né·ɔ, "ta·níka=háč."
	/t	Then they said to him, "Where is he?"
	/k	Then said they unto him, "Where is he?"

	/b	Tclao, tuk tani.
	/p	təlá·ɔ, "taktá·ni."
	/t	He said to them, "I don't know."
	/k	He said, I know not.

Jn 9.13
	/b	Nu eku tclwxolanro nrl krkrpifoletup Paluseekri.
	/p	ná íka təlo·x·ɔla·né·ɔ né·l ke·k·e·p·inkɔ·lí·t·əp †pa·ləsi·i·ké·i.
	/t	Then they took the man who had been blind to the Pharisees.
	/k	They brought to the Pharisees him that aforetime was blind.

Jn 9.14
	/b	Na nckc Nhesus seskwvrp ok qekrvapani wijkifwf,
	/p	ná-néke nčí·sas si·skó·he·p ɔ́·k kwi·k·e·há·p·ani wəškínkunk.
	/t	At that time Jesus had made clay and healed him in his eyes.
	/k	[And it was the sabbath day] when Jesus made the clay, and opened his eyes.

	/b	na nckc alaxemwe kejkwp.
	/p	ná-néke ala·x·i·məwí·i-kí·ško·p.
	/t	And at that time it had been the day of rest.
	/k	And it was the sabbath day ...

Jn 9.15
	/b	Nu lupi Paluseok notwtomanro nrl wuski nrmalethi,
	/p	ná lápi †pa·ləsi·í·ɔk nɔt·o·t·əma·né·ɔ né·l wəski-ne·ma·lí·č·i,
	/t	Then the Pharisees asked the newly seeing one again,
	/k	Then again the Pharisees also asked him

	/b	tu vuh lr wunhi kuski nrmaun?
	/p	"tá=háč lé·, wənči-káski-ne·má·an?"
	/t	"What happened so that you are able to see?"
	/k	how he had received his sight.

	/b	Tclao, Seskw eku ntcnumakwp nijkifwf, nu fusifwrn nu nrman.
	/p	təlá·ɔ, "sí·sku íka ntənnəmá·k·əp nəškínkunk, ná nkəs·ínkwe·n, ná nné·ma·n."
	/t	He said to them, "He put clay on my eyes; then I washed my face; then I saw."
	/k	He said unto them, He put clay upon mine eyes, and I washed, and do see.

Jn 9.16
/b Nu alintc Paluseok lwrok, Nu linw takw Krtanitwete,
/p ná a·lə́nte †pa·ləsi·í·ɔk luwé·ɔk, "ná lə́nu takó· ke·tanət·o·wi·t·í·i,
/t Then some Pharisees said, "That man is not of God,
/k Therefore said some of the Pharisees, This man is not of God,

/b rli mutu krnavketaq alaxemwe kejqek;
/p é·li- máta -ke·nahkí·ta·kw ala·x·i·məwí·i-kí·škwi·k."
/t as he does not keep the day of rest."
/k because he keepeth not the sabbath day.

/b ok alintc lwrok,
/p ɔ́·k a·lə́nte luwé·ɔk,
/t And some said,
/k Others said,

/b Ta vuh a wunhi kuski mrtawset linw bni li kunjyvosen?
/p "tá=háč=á· wwə́nči-káski- me·t·á·wsi·t lə́nu yó·ni -lí-kanšaehɔ́·s·i·n?"
/t "How would a sinful man be able to do a miracle like this?"
/k How can a man that is a sinner do such miracles?

/b Hihpetrvrok.
/p čəčpi·t·e·hé·ɔk.
/t They had a difference of opinion.
/k And there was a division among them.

Jn 9.17
/b Lupi tclawao krkrpifoletup,
/p lápi təlawwá·ɔ ke·k·e·p·inkɔ·lí·t·əp,
/t Again they said to the one who had been blind,
/k They say unto the blind man again,

/b Krkw vuh ke ktclavkunemu rli nrmwrvalkon?
/p "kéku=háč kí· ktəlahkəní·ma é·li-ne·mwe·há·lkɔn?"
/t "What do *you* say about how he made you see?"
/k What sayest thou of him, that he hath opened thine eyes?

/b Lwr Nrnekanewrwset tu.
/p lúwe·, "nehəni·k·a·ní·i-wé·wsi·t=tá,"
/t He said, "He is a prophet."
/k He said, He is a prophet.

Jn 9.18
/b Nhwuk takw wlamvetamwunro tcli, kvehe avkrpifonrp,
/p nčó·wak takó· o·la·mhitamo·wəné·ɔ tə́li- khičí·i -ahke·p·inkó·ne·p,
/t The Jews did not believe that he had truly been blind
/k But the Jews did not believe concerning him, that he had been blind,

```
           /b   ok li nrmwrvalan
           /p   ɔ·k lí-ne·mwe·há·la·n,
           /t   and had been made to see,
           /k   and received his sight,

           /b   kxuntki wcnhemaok qekybbmu.
           /p   kxántki wenči·má·ɔk kwi·kayó·yəma.
           /t   until his parents were summoned.
           /k   until they called the parents of him that had received his sight.

Jn 9.19    /b   Notwtumaowao, tclawao,
           /p   nɔt·o·t·əmaɔwwá·ɔ, təlawwá·ɔ,
           /t   They asked them, saying to them,
           /k   And they asked them, saying,

           /b   Nul vuh wu qeswu, rlwrrq noxpeken kokrpifon?
           /p   "nál=háč wá kkwí·s·əwa, e·ləwé·e·kw, 'nɔxpí·k·i·n kɔk·e·p·ínkɔ·n'?
           /t   "Is this your son, who you say was born being blind?
           /k   Is this your son, who ye say was born blind?

           /b   Ta vuh lrw wunhi bqc kuski nrmat?
           /p   tá=háč lé·w wə́nči- yúkwe -káski-né·ma·t?"
           /t   What happened so that he is now able to see?"
           /k   how then doth he now see?

Jn 9.20    /b   Qekybbmu lwrok,
           /p   kwi·kayó·yəma luwé·ɔk,
           /t   His parents said,
           /k   His parents answered them and said,

           /b   Nwatwnrn nul tu wu fwesunu, ok noxpeken kokrpifon;
           /p   "no·wa·tó·ne·n, nál=tá wá nkwí·s·əna, ɔ·k nɔxpí·k·i·n kɔk·e·p·ínkɔ·n.
           /t   "We know that this is our son, and he was born being blind.
           /k   We know that this is our son, and that he was born blind:

Jn 9.21    /b   jwq mutu nwatwnrn wcnhi bqc nrmat,
           /p   šúkw máta no·wa·tó·wəne·n wénči- yúkwe -né·ma·t,
           /t   But we do not know the reason why he now can see,
           /k   But by what means he now seeth, we know not;

           /b   jitu awrn kekrvat mutu nwavaewunu,
           /p   ší=tá awé·n ki·k·é·ha·t, máta no·wa·ha·í·wəna.
           /t   nor do we know who healed him.
           /k   or who hath opened his eyes, we know not:
```

/b mrhi ‖ nevlatama
/p mé·či nihəlá·t·ama·.
/t He is now his own man.
/k he is of age;

(p. 99)
/b knatwtumaou a, nevlahih krkw lwr.
/p kənat·o·t·əmaɔ́wwa=á·; nihəláči=č kéku lúwe·."
/t You should ask him; he will speak for himself."
/k ask him: he shall speak for himself.

Jn 9.22
/b Qekybbmu wcnhi nc lwrlen rli kxotet Nhwu;   [⟨wcnhi⟩ for /wwə́nči/]
/p kwi·kayó·yəma wwə́nči- nə́ -luwé·li·n, é·li-kxɔ́hti·t nčó·wa,
/t His parents said that because they feared the Jews,
/k These words spake his parents, because they feared the Jews:

/b rli mrhi Nhwuk tavqe lwcvtet,
/p é·li- mé·či nčó·wak tahkwí·i -luwéhti·t,
/t as the Jews had already agreed among themselves,
/k for the Jews had agreed already,

/b Awrnh lwrtc nul tu nu Kylist ktiskaoh wunhi cventu mycvluf.   [⟨cve-⟩ for ⟨cvc-⟩]
/p "awé·n=č luwé·t·e, nál=tá ná kəláist, ktə́skaɔ·=č wə́nči ehə́nta-ma·éhəlank."
/t "If anyone says he is Christ, he shall be driven out of the synagogue."
/k that if any man did confess that he was Christ, he should be put out of the synagogue.

Jn 9.23
/b Nunc wunhi lwrlen qekybbmu, nevlatama ta ntwtumw.
/p ná=nə wwə́nči-luwé·li·n kwi·kayó·yəma, "nihəlá·t·ama·=tá; ntó·t·əmo·.
/t That is why his parents said, "He is his own man; ask him."
/k Therefore said his parents, He is of age; ask him.

Jn 9.24
/b Nu lupi notwmanro nrl linwu krkrpifoletup, tclawao,
/p ná lápi nɔt·o·ma·né·ɔ né·l lə́nəwa ke·k·e·p·inkɔ·lí·t·əp, təlawwá·ɔ,
/t Then again they summoned the man who had been blind and said to him,
/k Then again called they the man that was blind, and said unto him,

/b Krnam Krtanitwet;
/p "ké·na·m ke·tanət·ó·wi·t;
/t "Give thanks to God;
/k Give God the praise:

/b nwavawunu nu tcli muvtawsen.
/p no·wa·há·wəna ná tə́li-mahtá·wsi·n."
/t we know that that one is a sinner."
/k we know that this man is a sinner.

Jn 9.25 /b Tclao Takw, nwavai tcli ct tu muvtawsen;
         /p təlá·ɔ, "takó· no·wa·há·i, tə́li-=ét=tá -mahtá·wsi·n.
         /t He said to them, "I don't know whether he is a sinner.
         /k He answered and said, Whether he be a sinner or no, I know not:

         /b kotrnaovki nwatwn fukrpifovwmp, bqc nrmu.
         /p kwət·ennáɔhki no·wá·to·n: nkak·e·p·inkɔ́·həmp, yúkwe nné·ma."
         /t I know one thing: I was blind and now I see."
         /k one thing I know, that, whereas I was blind, now I see.

Jn 9.26 /b Lupi tclawao, Krkw vuh ktclevwq?
         /p lápi təlawwá·ɔ, "kéku=háč ktəlí·hukw?
         /t Again they said to him, "What did he do to you?
         /k Then said they to him again, What did he to thee?

         /b Ta vuh tunimun cntu wletakon kijkifo?
         /p tá=háč tənnə́mən énta-wəli·tá·k·ɔn kəškínkɔ?"
         /t What did he do when he fixed your eyes for you?"
         /k how opened he thine eyes?

Jn 9.27 /b Tclao Mrhi keji lilunro, ok mutu kpuntyivwmw;
         /p təlá·ɔ, "mé·či kkíši-lələné·ɔ, ɔ́·k máta kpəntai·húmɔ.
         /t He said to them, "I have already told you, and you didn't hear me.
         /k He answered them, I have told you already, and ye did not hear:

         /b lupi vuh katu puntamunro?
         /p lápi=háč kkát·a-pəntaməné·ɔ?
         /t Do you want to hear it again?
         /k wherefore would ye hear it again?

         /b Krpwu vuh ok kutu wlistaou.
         /p ké·pəwa=háč ɔ́·k kkát·a-wələstaɔ́wwa?"
         /t Do you also want to become his adherents?"
         /k will ye also be his disciples?

Jn 9.28 /b Nu wrvrmwalanro tclawao Ke kta kwlisitao,   [⟨kwlisit-⟩ for ⟨kwlsit-⟩]
         /p ná wwehe·məwa·la·né·ɔ, təlawwá·ɔ, "kí·=ktá ko·lsət·aɔ,
         /t Then they made fun of him, saying to him, "*You* are his adherent,
         /k Then they reviled him, and said, Thou art his disciple;

         /b jwq nelwnu Mwjiju nwlsitaownu.
         /p šúkw ni·ló·na †mo·šə́š·a no·lsət·aɔ́·wəna.
         /t but *we* are adherents of Moses.
         /k but we are Moses' disciples.

Jn 9.29
/b Nwatwn tcli Krtanitwet krkw lanrp Mwjijifu,
/p no·wá·to·n tə́li- ke·tanət·ó·wi·t kéku -lá·ne·p †mo·šəš·ínka.
/t I know that God spoke to Moses.
/k We know that God spake unto Moses:

/b jwq wuni awrn tuk ct tu tcxi wunheyet.
/p šúkw wáni awé·n, ták=ét=tá téxi wənčí·ai·t."
/t But as for this person, I have no idea at all where he comes from."
/k as for this fellow, we know not from whence he is.

Jn 9.30
/b Nu linw lwr Krvalu tu wlrlumi lri
/p ná lə́nu lúwe·, "kéhəla=tá wəlé·ləmi-lé·,
/t The man said, "It's really odd,
/k The man answered and said unto them, Why herein is a marvellous thing,

/b rli mutu wavarq wcf, jwq eaphi fekrvwq nijkifwf.
/p é·li- máta -wwa·há·e·kw wénk, šúkw i·á·pči nki·k·é·hukw nəškínkunk.
/t as you don't know where he came from, but still he healed me in my eyes.
/k that ye know not from whence he is, and yet he hath opened mine eyes.

Jn 9.31
/b Bqc punu, kwatwnrn tcli Krtanitwet mutu klistaoun mrtawselethi.
/p yúkwe pənáh, ko·wa·tó·ne·n tə́li- ke·tanət·ó·wi·t máta -kələstaɔ́·wən me·t·a·wsi·lí·č·i.
/t Now consider, we all know that God does not listen to sinners.
/k Now we know that God heareth not sinners:

/b Jwq awrn prvpatamaot Krtanitwelethi ok liset rletrvat
/p šúkw awé·n pehpa·tamáɔ·t ke·tanət·o·wi·lí·č·i ɔ́·k lə́s·i·t e·li·t·é·ha·t,
/t But someone who prays to God and does what he wants done,
/k but if any man be a worshipper of God, and doeth his will,

/b nuli nrl qwlsitao.
/p náli né·l kwəlsə́t·aɔ.
/t he is one he listens to.
/k him he heareth.

Jn 9.32
/b Wewuntvakamek takw vuji awrn pwuntamwun li lwrn
/p wi·wənthákami·kw takó· háši awé·n pwəntamó·wən lí-lúwe·n,
/t Since the world began no one ever heard it said
/k Since the world began was it not heard

/b linw qekrvao nrxpekelet kokrpifon.
/p lə́nu kwi·k·e·há·ɔ ne·xpi·k·í·li·t kək·e·p·ínkɔ·n.
/t that a man healed one who was born blind.
/k that any man opened the eyes of one that was born blind.

Jn 9.33	/b	Nu linw mutu Krtanitweteqc ta kuski krkw lisei.
	/p	ná lə́nu máta ke·tanət·o·wi·t·í·k·we, tá=á· káski- kéku -lǝs·í·i."
	/t	If that man is not of God, he would not be able to do anything."
	/k	If this man were not of God, he could do nothing.

Jn 9.34	/b	Tclawao Mutawswakunif tcxi jwq kwnheki,
	/p	tǝlawwá·ɔ, "mahta·wsǝwá·k·anink téxi šúkw kunčí·k·i;
	/t	They said to him, "You were utterly born in sin;
	/k	They answered and said unto him, Thou wast altogether born in sins,

	/b	kutu vuh avkrkemevnu?
	/p	kkát·a-=háč -ahke·ki·míhǝna?"
	/t	do you wish to teach us?"
	/k	and dost thou teach us?

	/b	Nu sakvcskaon.
	/p	ná †sa·khə́skaɔ·n.
	/t	Then he was expelled.
	/k	And they cast him out.

Jn 9.35	/b	Nhesus puntufc li sakvcskaon, mrhi mrxkaotc, tclao,
	/p	nčí·sas pǝntánke lí-†sa·khə́skaɔ·n, mé·či me·xkaɔ́·t·e, tǝlá·ɔ,
	/t	When Jesus heard that he was expelled, after he had found him, he said to him,
	/k	Jesus heard that they had cast him out; and when he had found him, he said unto him,

	/b	Knakalu vuh Krtanitwet Qesu?
	/p	"kǝna·ká·la=háč ke·tanǝt·ó·wi·t kkwí·s·a?"
	/t	"Do you believe in the son of God?"
	/k	Dost thou believe on the Son of God?

Jn 9.36	/b	tclkw, Awrn vuh nu, Nrvlaliun ntcli a kuski nvakalan?
	/p	tǝ́lku, "awé·n=háč ná, nehǝlá·lian, ntə́li-=á· -káski-nhaká·la·n?" ‖
	/t	He said to him in reply, "Who is he, my Lord, so that I could believe in him?"
	/k	He answered and said, Who is he, Lord, that I might believe on him?

Jn 9.37	/b	Nhesus tclao, Knrop ok nul nu bqc krkw alwkon.
(p. 100)	/p	nčí·sas tǝlá·ɔ, "kǝné·ɔ·p, ɔ́·k nál ná yúkwe kéku allúk·ɔn."
	/t	Jesus said to him, "You have seen him, and he is the one speaking to you now."
	/k	And Jesus said unto him, Thou hast both seen him, and it is he that talketh with thee.

Jn 9.38	/b	Tclkw Nrvlaliun, knakalil, ok krnamul.
	/p	tə́lku. "nehǝlá·lian, kǝna·ká·lǝl ɔ́·k kke·ná·mǝl."
	/t	He said to him in reply, "My Lord, I believe in you, and I give thanks to you."
	/k	And he said, Lord, I believe. And he worshipped him.

Jn 9.39	/b	Nhesus lwr, Avkrkvwtwakun nwnhi pan bqc b cntu lawsif;
	/p	nčí·sas lúwe·, "ahke·kho·t·əwá·k·an núnči-pá·n yúkwe yú entalá·wsink,
	/t	Jesus said, "I come into this world for judgment,
	/k	And Jesus said, For judgment I am come into this world,
	/b	tclih nrk mutu nrmathek nrmanro,
	/p	tə́li-=č né·k máta ne·má·č·i·k -ne·ma·né·ɔ,
	/t	so that those who do not see shall see,
	/k	that they which see not might see;
	/b	ok tclih nrk nrmathek mutu nrmawnro.
	/p	ɔ́·k tə́li-=č né·k ne·má·č·i·k máta -ne·ma·wəné·ɔ."
	/t	and so that those that see shall not see."
	/k	and that they which see might be made blind.
Jn 9.40	/b	Alintc Paluseok eku rpethek puntastehek tclawao, [⟨-astehek⟩ for ⟨-asethek⟩]
	/p	a·lə́nte †pa·ləsi·í·ɔk íka e·p·í·č·i·k pənta·s·í·č·i·k təlawwá·ɔ,
	/t	Some of the Pharisees who were there listening said to him,
	/k	And some of the Pharisees which were with him heard these words, and said unto him,
	/b	Nrpunu vuh ok fukrpifovnu?
	/p	"né·pəna=háč ɔ́·k nkak·e·p·inkɔ́həna?"
	/t	"Are we blind, too?"
	/k	Are we blind also?
Jn 9.41	/b	Nhesus tclao, Avkrpiforqc a, tau kumutawsevwmw,
	/p	nčí·sas təlá·ɔ, "ahke·p·inkɔ·é·k·we=á·, tá=á· kəmat·a·wsi·húmɔ.
	/t	Jesus said to them, "If you were blind, you would not be sinners.
	/k	Jesus said unto them, If ye were blind, ye should have no sin:
	/b	jwq bqc ktclwcvmw, Nrmavnu,
	/p	šúkw yúkwe ktələwéhəmɔ, "nne·máhəna."
	/t	But now you say, "We see."
	/k	but now ye say, We see;
	/b	nc wunhi kumutawswakunwu wetavpemqrq.
	/p	nɔ́ wə́nči- kəmat·a·wsəwa·k·anúwa -witahpí·mkwe·kw.
	/t	Because of that your sins remain with you.
	/k	therefore your sin remaineth.
Jn 10.1	/b	Kvehe kvehe ktclwvmw;
	/p	khičí·i, khičí·i, ktəllúhəmɔ:
	/t	Truly, truly I tell you,
	/k	Verily, verily, I say unto you,

	/b	Awrn a mutu tumekrtc wunhi skontr mrkesuk rvpevtet, [⟨rvpevt-⟩ for ⟨rpevt-⟩]
	/p	awé·n=á· máta təmi·k·é·t·e wə́nči skónte mekí·s·ak e·p·íhti·t,
	/t	if someone does not enter the place where the sheep are by the door
	/k	He that entereth not by the door into the sheepfold,

	/b	pale lukwsetc,
	/p	palí·i lak·o·s·í·t·e,
	/t	and climbs up another way,
	/k	but climbeth up some other way,

	/b	nul tu nu, krvkumwtkrt ok ncnvelwrt.
	/p	nál=tá ná kehkəmó·tke·t ó·k nenhíləwe·t.
	/t	he is a thief and a murderer.
	/k	the same is a thief and a robber.

Jn 10.2 /b Jwq trmekrt skontr wunhi, nul tu nu krnavkevat mrkesu.
/p šúkw te·mí·k·e·t skónte wə́nči, nál=tá ná ke·nahkí·ha·t mekí·s·a.
/t But the one who enters by the door, he is the one who takes care of the sheep.
/k But he that entereth in by the door is the shepherd of the sheep.

Jn 10.3 /b Nwheskontyrt vwtwfjrnumaon, mwrkesumu pwuntawao rlwrtaqselet
/p no·č·i·skóntae·t wtunkše·nəmáɔ·n, mwekí·s·əma pwəntaɔwwá·ɔ e·ləwe·ta·kwsí·li·t.
/t The door-keeper opens the door to him, and his sheep hear his voice.
/k To him the porter openeth; and the sheep hear his voice:

/b ok notwmao mwrkesumu rlwcnselet ok qutwxolao.
/p ó·k nɔt·o·má·ɔ mwekí·s·əma e·ləwensí·li·t, ó·k kwət·o·x·ɔlá·ɔ.
/t And he calls his sheep by their names and leads them out.
/k and he calleth his own sheep by name, and leadeth them out.

Jn 10.4 /b Mrhi krtwxolatc mwrkesumu alumi nekane, ok mrkesuk nolawao,
/p mé·či ke·t·o·x·ɔlá·t·e mwekí·s·əma, áləmi-ni·k·á·ni·, ó·k mekí·s·ak nɔ·ɔlawwá·ɔ,
/t After he has led his sheep out, he goes on ahead and the sheep follow him,
/k And when he putteth forth his own sheep, he goeth before them, and the sheep follow him:

/b rli wavtwvtet rlwrtaqset.
/p é·li-wwa·túhti·t e·ləwe·tá·kwsi·t.
/t as they know his voice.
/k for they know his voice.

Jn 10.5 /b Jwq ta wnaolaewao pale wcnheyelethi;
/p šúkw tá=á· wəna·ɔla·iwwá·ɔ palí·i wenči·ai·lí·č·i.
/t But they will not follow someone from another place.
/k And a stranger will they not follow,

/b wjemawao a rli mutu wavtwvtet rlwrtaqselet pale wcnheyelethi. [⟨avt⟩ for ⟨at⟩]
/p o·š·i·mawwá·ɔ=á·, é·li- máta -wwa·túhti·t e·ləwe·ta·kwsí·li·t palí·i wenči·ai·lí·č·i."
/t They would run away from him, as they do not know the voice of one from another place."
/k but will flee from him: for they know not the voice of strangers.

Jn 10.6 /b Bni rnwntvakrokun tclanrp Nhesus;
/p yó·ni e·nunthake·ó·k·an təlá·ne·p nčí·sas,
/t Jesus told them this parable,
/k This parable spake Jesus unto them:

/b jwq takw wnunwstakweo, krkw rlat.
/p šúkw takó· wənəno·sta·k·o·wí·ɔ kéku é·la·t.
/t but they did not understand what he was saying to them.
/k but they understood not what things they were which he spake unto them.

Jn 10.7 /b Nu lupi Nhesus tclan, Kvehe kvehe ktclwvmw,
/p ná lápi nčí·sas tɔ́la·n, "khičí·i, khičí·i ktəllúhəmɔ,
/t Then again Jesus said to them, "Truly, truly I say to you,
/k Then said Jesus unto them again, Verily, verily, I say unto you,

/b ne tu skonty mrkese.
/p ní·=tá skɔ́ntay meki·s·í·i.
/t I am the door of the sheep.
/k I am the door of the sheep.

Jn 10.8 /b Wrmi cntxi nekanetumethek, krvkumwtkrthek ok mcvmavhevwrthek;
/p wé·mi éntxi-ni·k·a·ni·tamí·č·i·k, kehkəmo·tké·č·i·k ɔ́·k mehəmahčihəwé·č·i·k.
/t All those that came before me were thieves and doers of violence.
/k All that ever came before me are thieves and robbers:

/b jwq mrkesuk takw qwlsitaoewapani.
/p šúkw mekí·s·ak takó· kwəlsət·aɔ·iwwá·p·ani.
/t But the sheep did not listen to them.
/k but the sheep did not hear them.

Jn 10.9 /b Ne tu skonty;
/p ní·=tá skɔ́ntay
/t I am a door.
/k I am the door:

/b awrn tumekrtc, lclrxrmvalah;
/p awé·n təmi·k·é·t·e, lehəle·x·e·mhá·la·=č.
/t If anyone enters, he shall be restored to life.
/k by me if any man enter in, he shall be saved,

/b   tumekrtch, ok khetc aphih muxkum krkw methet.
/p   təmi·k·é·t·e=č ɔ́·k kčí·t·e, á·pči=č máxkam kéku mí·č·i·t.
/t   When he goes in and goes out, he will always find something to eat.
/k   and shall go in and out, and find pasture.

Jn 10.10   /b   Krkumwtkrt tcxi jwq wunhi pan tcli a kumwtkrn, ok tcli a nvelwrn, ok tcli a palevwrn.
/p   kehkəmó·tke·t téxi šúkw wwə́nči-pá·n tə́li-=á· -kəmó·tke·n, ɔ́·k tə́li-=á· -nhíləwe·n, ɔ́·k tə́li-=á· -palíhəwe·n.
/t   A thief comes to do nothing but to steal, and to kill, and to destroy.
/k   The thief cometh not, but for to steal, and to kill, and to destroy:

/b   Ne, mpu wunhih lclrxrtet alwei.
/p   ní· mpá wə́nči-=č -lehəle·x·éhti·t aləwí·i.
/t   *I* came so that they might have more life.
/k   I am come that they might have life, and that they might have it more abundantly.

Jn 10.11   /b   Ne tu wrli liset ncnwtumat mrkesu.   [⟨ncnw-‖tumat⟩]
/p   ní·=tá wé·li-lə́s·i·t nehənó·t·əma·t mekí·s·a.
/t   I am the good shepherd (*lit.*, watcher of sheep).
/k   I am the good shepherd:

(p. 101)   /b   Wrli liset ncnwtumat mwrkun wlclrxrokun wunhi mrkesuk.
/p   wé·li-lə́s·i·t nehənó·t·əma·t mwé·k·ən wəlehəle·x·e·ɔ́·k·an wə́nči mekí·s·ak.
/t   A good shepherd gives his life for the sheep.
/k   the good shepherd giveth his life for the sheep.

Jn 10.12   /b   Jwq nu rlwkalint takw myai mrkesu nwtwmat, mutu wrtalumwnset mrkesu,
/p   šúkw ná e·lo·ká·lənt, takó· mayá·i mekí·s·a nó·t·əma·t, máta we·t·aləmúnsi·t mekí·s·a,
/t   But the hired hand, who is not the real shepherd, not the owner of the sheep,
/k   But he that is an hireling, and not the shepherd, whose own the sheep are not,

/b   tamsc a nrotc tumc prat,
/p   tá·mse=á· ne·ɔ́·t·e, təme pé·a·t
/t   if sometime he sees there is a wolf coming,
/k   seeth the wolf coming,

/b   na awnukalan mrkesu, nu a tcli wjemwen,   [⟨na awnuk-⟩ for ⟨na a wnuk-⟩]
/p   ná=á· wənə́k·ala·n mekí·s·a, ná=á· tə́li-wší·mwi·n.
/t   he would then abandon the sheep; he would then run away.
/k   and leaveth the sheep, and fleeth:

/b   nu a nc tali tvwnan ok luxwrskaon.
/p   ná=á· nə́ táli-thwə́na·n ɔ́·k -laxwé·skaɔ·n.

| | /t | Then they would be caught there and scattered. |
| | /k | and the wolf catcheth them, and scattereth the sheep. |

Jn 10.13 /b Rlwkalint wjemw rli alwkalint,
/p eˑloˑkáˑlənt wšíˑmu éˑli-aloˑkáˑlənt,
/t "The hired hand runs away because he is a hired hand,
/k The hireling fleeth, because he is an hireling,

/b rli mutu krkw tclrlumaeo mrkesu.
/p éˑli máta kéku tələ-ləmaˑíˑɔ mekíˑsˑa.
/t as he has no thought for the sheep.
/k and careth not for the sheep.

Jn 10.14 /b Ne tu wrli liset ncnwtumat, ok nunaok numrkesumuk, ok nunakwk.
/p níˑ=tá wéˑli-ləsˑiˑt nehənóˑtˑəmaˑt, ɔ́ˑk nnənaɔ́ˑɔk nəmekíˑsˑəmak ɔ́ˑk nnənáˑkˑoˑk.
/t I am the good shepherd, and I know my sheep and they know me.
/k I am the good shepherd, and know my sheep, and am known of mine.

Jn 10.15 /b Rlkeqi Wrtwxwmunt wavet, nrpc ntclkeqi wavan Wrtwxwmunt.
/p eˑlkíˑkwi- weˑtˑóˑxˑəmənt -wwáˑhiˑt, néˑpe ntəlkíˑkwi-wwáˑhaˑn weˑtˑóˑxˑəmənt.
/t To the same extent that the father knows me, I also know the father.
/k As the Father knoweth me, even so know I the Father:

/b Ok nevlahih ntuful wunhi mrkesuk.
/p ɔ́ˑk nihəláči=č ntánkəl wənči mekíˑsˑak.
/t Also, I shall die myself for the sheep.
/k and I lay down my life for the sheep.

Jn 10.16 /b Ok peli numrkesumuk, mutu b wcnheyehek.
/p ɔ́ˑk píˑli nəmekíˑsˑəmak máta yú wenčiˑaíˑčˑiˑk.
/t And other sheep of mine are not ones from here.
/k And other sheep I have, which are not of this fold:

/b Okh nrk mprjwaok, okh pwntamunro rlwrtaqseu,
/p ɔ́ˑk=č néˑk mpeˑšˑəwáˑɔk, ɔ́ˑk=č pwəntamənéˑɔ eˑləweˑtaˑkwsía.
/t I shall bring them also, and they shall hear my voice.
/k them also I must bring, and they shall hear my voice;

/b nuh kwtrnaovki topenro, okh kwti nwtumat.
/p náˑ=č kwətˑennáɔhki təpˑiˑnéˑɔ, ɔ́ˑk=č kwə́tˑi nóˑtˑəmaˑt,
/t Then they shall stay in one place, and one (shepherd) shall watch over them.
/k and there shall be one fold, and one shepherd.

Jn 10.17	/b	Nani nwnhi Nwx avolkwn rli nwifi uful
	/p	ná=ní núnči- nóˑx -ahóˑlkoˑn, éˑli nəwínki-ánkəl,
	/t	That's the reason why my father loves me, as I am willing to die,
	/k	Therefore doth my Father love me, because I lay down my life,
	/b	ok ntclih lupi lclrxrn.
	/p	óˑk ntə́li-=č lápi -lehəléˑxˑeˑn.
	/t	and in order for me to live again.
	/k	that I might take it again.
Jn 10.18	/b	Ta awrn koski wrtunimwun lclrxrokun.
	/p	tá=áˑ awéˑn kóski-weˑtˑənəmóˑwən llehəleˑxˑeˑóˑkˑan.
	/t	No one would be able to take my life.
	/k	No man taketh it from me, ['my life': Jn 10.17]
	/b	Neh nevlahi vakif ntatwn
	/p	níˑ=č nihəláči hákink ntáˑtoˑn.
	/t	I shall lay it down myself.
	/k	but I lay it down of myself.
	/b	Nevlatumun ntclih vakif vatwn,
	/p	nnihəláˑtˑamən ntə́li-=č hákink -hátˑoˑn,
	/t	I have the power to lay it down,
	/k	I have power to lay it down,
	/b	ok ne nevlatumun ntclih lupi wrtunimun.
	/p	óˑk nnihəláˑtˑamən ntə́li-=č lápi -weˑtˑənə́mən.
	/t	and I have the power to take it up again,
	/k	and I have power to take it again.
	/b	Rli nunc letup Nwx.
	/p	éˑli- ná=nə -líˑtˑəp nóˑx."
	/t	for that is what my father told me to do."
	/k	This commandment have I received of my Father.
Jn 10.19	/b	Nu lupi hanencvwtwuk Nhwuk wunhi nrl aptwnakunul.
	/p	ná lápi čaniˑnehóˑtˑəwak nčóˑwak wə́nči néˑl aˑptoˑnáˑkˑanal.
	/t	Then the Jews again disputed among themselves regarding those statements.
	/k	There was a division therefore again among the Jews for these sayings.
Jn 10.20	/b	Xrli lwrok, mavtuntwe krphrofuluk;
	/p	xéˑli luwéˑɔk, "mahtantˑoˑwíˑi-kepčeˑónkələk.
	/t	Many said, "He's someone with devil madness.
	/k	And many of them said, He hath a devil, and is mad;

/b krkw wcnhi klistarq?
/p kéku wénči-kələstáe·kw?"
/t Why do you listen to him?"
/k why hear ye him?

Jn 10.21
/b Aluntc lwrok, nrl aptwnakunu takw mavtuntwet toptwnakun.
/p a·lə́nte luwé·ɔk, "né·l a·pto·ná·k·ana takó· mahtant·ó·wi·t tɔ·pto·ná·k·an.
/t Some said, "Those words are not the saying of one who is a devil.
/k Others said, These are not the words of him that hath a devil.

/b Kuski vuh a mavtuntw taxkifwrnr krkrpifolethi.
/p káski-=háč=á· mahtánt·u -ta·xkinkwé·ne· ke·k·e·p·inkɔ·lí·č·i?"
/t Would a devil be able to open the eyes of a blind person?"
/k Can a devil open the eyes of the blind?

Chapter 56 (pp. 101-103). [L. section 55.] (John 10.22-42.)

Jn 10.22
/b Nu nckc lwunwp Nhelwsulumif cntu tpisqevlakc li metsavten;
/p ná-néke ló·wano·p, †nči·lo·sələ́mink énta-tpəskwihəlá·k·e lí-mi·tsáhti·n.
/t At that time it had been winter, when it was the time for a feast in Jerusalem.
/k And it was at Jerusalem the feast of the dedication, and it was winter.

Jn 10.23
/b Nhesus avpamskrp patamwrekaonif cntu alwekvaonik Salumunu tolwekvaonif.
/p nčí·sas ahpá·mske·p pa·tamwe·i·k·á·ɔnink énta-aləwi·khá·ɔni·k, †sa·lamána tɔləwi·khá·ɔnink.
/t And Jesus had walked around the porch of the temple, on Solomon's porch.
/k And Jesus walked in the temple in Solomon's porch.

Jn 10.24
/b Nhwuk wokrkaowao, tclawao,
/p nčó·wak wɔ·ke·kaɔwwá·ɔ, təlawwá·ɔ,
/t Jews came around him and said to him,
/k Then came the Jews round about him, and said unto him,

/b Tah vuh ksaki hihanelarmenrn?
/p "tá=č=háč ksá·ki·čəčani·lae·mí·ne·n?
/t "How long will you keep us in doubt?
/k How long dost thou make us to doubt? [RSV "keep us in suspense"]

/b Ke Klysteunc, myai lenrn.
/p kí· kəlaistiáne, mayá·i lí·ne·n." ‖
/t If you are Christ, tell us straight out."
/k If thou be the Christ, tell us plainly.

Jn 10.25 /b Nhesus tclao, Ktclinrop jwq mutu kwlamvetyevwmw.
(p. 102) /p nčí·sas təlá·ɔ, "ktəlləné·ɔ·p, šúkw máta ko·la·mhitai·húmɔ.
         /t Jesus said to them, "I told you, but you don't believe me.
         /k Jesus answered them, I told you, and ye believed not:

         /b Nrl ntclyvoswakunu rlyvoseu, wunhi Nwx tclswakun,
         /p né·l ntəlaehɔ·s·əwá·k·ana e·laehó·s·ia wə́nči nó·x təlsəwá·k·an,
         /t The deeds I have done by my father's power,
         /k the works that I do in my Father's name,

         /b nunul le a nrl nwnhi wavkrn.   [⟨nunul le⟩ for /nanáli/]
         /p nanáli=á· né·l núnči-wwáhke·n.
         /t those are what I would be known by.
         /k they bear witness of me.

Jn 10.26 /b Jwq kwnhi mutu wlamvetamwnro
         /p šúkw kúnči- máta -wəla·mhitamo·wəné·ɔ
         /t But the reason you do not believe it
         /k But ye believe not,

         /b rli mutu ne mwrkesumeo kvakybu,
         /p é·li- máta ní· -mweki·s·əmí·ɔ khak·ayúwa.
         /t is because you are not my sheep.
         /k because ye are not of my sheep,

         /b na nuni ktclinrop.
         /p ná=nəni ktəlləné·ɔ·p.
         /t That is what I told you.
         /k as I said unto you.

Jn 10.27 /b Numrkesumuk vufq pwuntamunro rlwrtaqseu, ok naolwkwk;
         /p nəmekí·s·əmak=hánkw pwəntaməné·ɔ e·ləwe·ta·kwsía, ɔ́·k nna·ɔlúk·o·k.
         /t My sheep hear my voice and follow me.
         /k My sheep hear my voice, and I know them, and they follow me:

Jn 10.28 /b ok numelaok nrk rvalumakumek pumawswakun.
         /p ɔ́·k nəmi·lá·ɔk né·k ehaləmá·kami·k pəma·wsəwá·k·an.
         /t And I give them eternal life.
         /k And I give unto them eternal life;

         /b Ta vuji ufulweok, ok muta a vuji awrn ntamunhevkwunu.
         /p tá=á· háši ankəlo·wí·ɔk, ɔ́·k máta=á· háši awé·n ntamənčihkó·wəna.
         /t They would never die, and no one would ever force them away from me.
         /k and they shall never perish, neither shall any man pluck them out of my hand.

Jn 10.29 /b Nwx rli melet, xifwi lisw,
          /p nó·x, é·li-mí·li·t, xínkwi-lə́s·u,
          /t My father, the one who gave them to me, is great,
          /k My Father, which gave them me, is greater than all;

          /b ok ta awrn koski amunhevaeo.
          /p ó·k tá=á· awé·n kóski-amənči·ha·í·ɔ.
          /t and no one would be able to force him to do anything.
          /k and no man is able to pluck them out of my Father's hand.

Jn 10.30 /b Ne ok Nwx nmawswevnu.
          /p ní· ó·k nó·x nəma·wso·wíhəna."
          /t I and my father are one."
          /k I and my Father are one.

Jn 10.31 /b Nu Nhwuk lupi wrtunimunro asinu tcli a pavkumanro.
          /p ná nčó·wak lápi wwe·t·ənəməné·ɔ ahsə́na, tɔ́li-=á· -pahkama·né·ɔ.
          /t Then the Jews again picked up stones to throw at him.
          /k Then the Jews took up stones again to stone him.

Jn 10.32 /b Nhesus tclao, Xrli wlyvoswakun kpunwntulilvwmw Nwxif wunhi;
          /p nčí·sas təlá·ɔ, "xé·li wəlaehɔ·s·əwá·k·an kpənuntələlhúmɔ nó·x·ink wə́nči.
          /t Jesus said to them, "I have shown you many good deeds from my father.
          /k Jesus answered them, Many good works have I shewed you from my Father;

          /b ta vuh nrl rlenako lyvoswakunu wunhi kavtu puvkumerq?
          /p tá=háč né·l e·li·ná·k·ɔ laehɔ·s·əwá·k·ana wə́nči-káhta-pahkámie·kw?"
          /t For which of those deeds do you intend to stone me?"
          /k for which of those works do ye stone me?

Jn 10.33 /b Nhwuk tclawao,
          /p nčó·wak təlawwá·ɔ,
          /t The Jews said to him,
          /k The Jews answered him, saying,

          /b Takw tu wlyvoswakun kwnhi kavtu puvkumwlwvwmunu;
          /p "takó·=tá wəlaehɔ·s·əwá·k·an kúnči-káhta-pahkaməlo·húməna,
          /t "It's not for a good deed that we intend to stone you,
          /k For a good work we stone thee not;

          /b jwq rli muvtuvkunemut Krtanitwet,   [⟨muvtuvk-⟩ for ⟨muvtuk-⟩]
          /p šúkw=tá é·li-mahtak·əní·mat ke·tanət·ó·wi·t,
          /t but it's because you say bad things about God,
          /k but for blasphemy;

	/b	ok rli ke, line linw tpisqrlinseun Krtanitwetif.
	/p	ɔ·k é·li- kí·, lǝní·i-lǝ́nu, -tpǝskwe·lǝ́nsian ke·tanǝt·o·wí·t·ink."
	/t	and because you, an ordinary man, consider *yourself* equal to God."
	/k	and because that thou, being a man, makest thyself God.

Jn 10.34 /b Tclao, Mutu vuh ktclrkvekunwaif tu lrkvasei cntu lwrf,
/p tǝlá·ɔ, "máta=háč ktǝle·khi·k·anǝwá·ink tale·kha·s·í·i énta-lúwenk,
/t He said to them, "Isn't it written in your law where it is said,
/k Jesus answered them, Is it not written in your law,

/b Ntclwrvump kmantwevmw?
/p 'ntǝlǝwé·hǝmp, "kǝmant·o·wíhǝmɔ."'?
/t 'I said, "You are gods."'?
/k I said, Ye are gods?

Jn 10.35 /b Lwevlatetpanc a manitwuk nukavke wrtxwqvetetup Krtanitwet toptwnakun,
/p luwihǝlahti·tpáne=á· 'manǝt·ó·wak' nǝkáhke we·txukhwití·t·ǝp ke·tanǝt·ó·wi·t tɔ·pto·ná·k·an—
/t If they called those ancients to whom the word of God came 'gods'—
/k If he called them gods, unto whom the word of God came,

/b ok a mutu kuski puvkelaewu nu xwi lrkvekun;
/p ɔ·k=á· máta kkáski-pahki·la·íwwa ná xúwi-le·khí·k·an—
/t and you would not be able to discard the ancient scripture—
/k and the scripture cannot be broken;

Jn 10.36 /b ta vuh kwnhi lenro kmutaptwnalu Krtanitwet
/p tá=háč kúnči-li·né·ɔ, 'kǝmat·a·pto·ná·la ke·tanǝt·ó·wi·t,'
/t why do you say to me, 'You speak evilly about God,'
/k Say ye of him, [whom the Father hath sanctified, and sent into the world,] Thou blasphemest;

/b lwranc, ne qesu Krtanitwet,
/p luwe·á·ne, 'ní· kkwí·s·a ke·tanǝt·ó·wi·t.'
/t when I say, 'I am the son of God.'
/k because I said, I am the Son of God?

/b ne Wrtwxumunt ntcli kejexumwkwn,
/p ní· we·t·ó·x·ǝmǝnt ntǝ́li-ki·š·i·x·ǝmúk·o·n,
/t *I* am the one the father made ready (for his purpose)
/k ... whom the Father hath sanctified,   [RSV: "consecrated"]

/b ok ntcli prtalwkalkwn b cntu lawsif.
/p ɔ·k ntǝ́li-pe·t·alo·ká·lko·n yú entalá·wsink.
/t and sent here into the world.
/k and sent into the world, ...

Jn 10.37 /b Mutuh liseonc Nwx tclyvoswakun, kahi wlamvetyevrq.
/p máta=č ləs·i·ɔ́·ne nóˑx təlaehɔ·s·əwá·k·an, káči wəla·mhitaí·he·kw.
/t If I don't do my father's deeds, don't believe me.
/k If I do not the works of my Father, believe me not.

Jn 10.38 /b Jwq liseanc, muta wlamvetyerqc, jwq wlamvetamwq nc lyvoswakun;
/p šúkw ləs·iá·ne, máta=áˑ wəla·mhitaié·k·we, šúkw wəla·mhítamo·kw nə́ laehɔ·s·əwá·k·an,   [-ié·k·we: or -i·é·k·we (if this was distinct)]
/t But if I do them, and if you don't believe me, just believe the deeds,
/k But if I do, though ye believe not me, believe the works:

/b wunhih kuski watyerq ok wlamvetyerq
/p wə́nči-=č -káski-wwa·taíe·kw, ɔ́·k -wəla·mhitaíe·kw
/t so that you will be able to know and believe
/k that ye may know, and believe,

/b ntcli Wrtwxumunt avpetakwn ok ntcli nrpc avpetaon.
/p ntə́li- we·t·ɔ́·x·əmənt -ahpi·tá·k·o·n, ɔ́·k ntə́li- né·pe -ahpí·taɔ·n."
/t that the father is in me, and that I, too, am in him."
/k that the Father is in me, and I in him.

Jn 10.39 /b Nc wunhi kavta tvwnanro, jwq tolyi   [⟨tvwnan-‖ro⟩]
/p nə́ wwə́nči-káhta-thwəna·né·ɔ, šúkw tɔ́·lai.
/t Because of that they desired to arrest him, but they failed.
/k Therefore they sought again to take him: but he escaped out of their hand,

Jn 10.40 /b palerp lupi Nhutunif kamif; cntu Nhanu hihvopwnwrtup vetamc, [⟨-mc⟩ for /-mi/]
(p. 103) /p palí·i é·p lápi †nčátanink ká·mink, énta- nčá·na -čičhɔ·pwənəwé·t·əp hítami.
/t He went away again to the other side of the Jordan, where John had baptized people first.
/k And went away again beyond Jordan into the place where John at first baptized;

/b nanc pumenenru.   [⟨pum-⟩ for /pwəm-/]
/p ná=nə pwəminni·né·ɔ,
/t And they stayed there.
/k and there he abode.

Jn 10.41 /b Xrli awrni eku wtxwkw
/p xé·li awé·ni íka o·txúk·u.
/t Many people came to him there.
/k And many resorted unto him,

/b lwrok takw kanjyvosepanu Nhanu   [⟨-sepanu⟩ for ⟨-setpanu⟩]
/p luwé·ɔk, "takó· kanšaehɔ·s·i·tpána nčá·na,
/t They said, "John was not one who did miracles,
/k and said, John did no miracle:

/b jwq wrmi cntxi lathemwetup wunhi wu linw wlamwrp.
/p šúkw wé·mi éntxi-la·č·i·mwí·t·əp, wá lə́nu wəlá·məwe·p."
/t but in everything he told about, this man told the truth." [misunderstood]
/k but all things that John spake of this man were true.

Jn 10.42
/b Xrli nani tuntu wlamvetakwn.
/p xé·li ná=ní tə́nta-wəla·mhitá·k·o·n.
/t And many believed him there.
/k And many believed on him there.

Chapter 57 (pp. 103-104). [L. section 56.] (Matthew 16.13-28; Mark 8.38 [part]. L. also includes much from Luke 9.18-27, but Blanchard follows Matthew.)

Mt 16.13
/b Nhesus mrhi patc avpami Sisuleuf Pilupae,
/p nčí·sas mé·či pá·t·e ahpá·mi †sisəlí·yunk †pilápai,
/t After Jesus arrived around Caesarea Philippi,
/k When Jesus came into the coasts of Caesarea Philippi,

/b notwxtao rkrkematpani, tclao
/p nɔt·o·xtaɔ́·ɔ e·k·e·ki·ma·tpáni, təlá·ɔ,
/t he asked his disciples (*lit.*, the ones he had taught), saying to them,
/k he asked his disciples, saying,

/b krkw vuh b cntu lawsethek lwrok
/p "kéku=háč yú entala·wsí·č·i·k luwé·ɔk,
/t "What do people say
/k Whom do men say

/b cntu lwcvtet awmia ne, Wrqlsif linw?   [⟨awmia⟩ for ⟨awrnia⟩]
/p énta-luwéhti·t awé·nia ní·, we·k·wí·s·ink lə́nu?"
/t when they say who I am, the man who is the Son?"
/k that I the Son of man am?

Mt 16.14
/b Tclawao, alintc lwrok Nhanu hihvopwnwrtup, ok alintc lwrok Esrusu,
/p təlawwá·ɔ, "a·lə́nte luwé·ɔk 'nčá·na čičhɔ·pwənəwé·t·əp,' ɔ́·k a·lə́nte luwé·ɔk '†i·se·yə́s·a,'
/t They said to him, "Some say 'John the Baptist,' some say 'Esaias,'
/k And they said, Some say that thou art John the Baptist: some, Elias;

/b ok alintc lwrok Hclemyusu jitu mawsw nrnekanewrwsetpanifu.   [⟨wrw|set⟩]
/p a·lə́nte luwé·ɔk '†čeli·mayás·a,' ší=tá má·wsu nehəni·k·a·ní·i-we·wsi·tpanínka."
/t and some say Jeremiah or one of the ancient prophets."
/k and others, Jeremias, or one of the prophets.

Mt 16.15 /b Nhesus tclao, kahi kelwu, krkw vuh ktclwilevmw?
/p nčí·sas təlá·ɔ, "káč·i ki·ló·wa, kéku=háč ktələwihəlíhəmɔ?"
/t Jesus said to them, "But what name do *you* give me?"
/k He saith unto them, But whom say ye that I am?

Mt 16.16 /b Symun Petul tclao, ke tu Klyst, prmawswet Krtaniswet Qesu.   [⟨-nis-⟩ for ⟨-nit-⟩]
/p †sáiman-pí·təl təlá·ɔ, "kí·=tá kəláist, pe·ma·wsó·wi·t ke·tanət·ó·wi·t kkwí·s·a.
/t Simon Peter said to him, "You are Christ, the son of the living god."
/k And Simon Peter answered and said, Thou art the Christ, the Son of the living God.

Mt 16.17 /b Nhesus tclao, Kwlapcnsi Symun Nhonu qesu,
/p nčí·sas təlá·ɔ, "ko·la·p·énsi, †sáiman, nčó·na kkwí·s·a,
/t Jesus said to him, "You are blessed, Simon, son of Jonah,
/k And Jesus answered and said unto him, Blessed art thou, Simon Barjona:

/b rli wews ok mvwq mutu vuji lwkwun, jwq Nwx osavkamc rpet.
/p é·li- wió·s ɔ́·k mhúkw máta háši -luk·ó·wan, šúkw nó·x ɔ·s·áhkame é·p·i·t.
/t for flesh and blood never told you, but my father who is in heaven.
/k for flesh and blood hath not revealed it unto thee, but my Father which is in heaven.

Mt 16.18 /b Ktclil ke tu avsin, okh bni asinif ntuvulan nmcmarvlasumuk
/p ktə́ləl, kí·=tá ahsə́n, ɔ́·k=č yó·ni ahsə́nink ntáhəla·n nəmehəma·ehəlá·s·əmak,
/t I say to you, You are a rock, and on this rock I shall place my congregation,
/k And I say also unto thee, That thou art Peter, and upon this rock I will build my church;

/b okh mutu vuji mavtuntwe punyrlintumwakun potavkwnro.
/p ɔ́·k=č máta háši mahtant·o·wí·i-pəna·eləntaməwá·k·an pɔ·tahko·wəné·ɔ.
/t and the devil's schemes shall never conquer them.
/k and the gates of hell shall not prevail against it.

Mt 16.19 /b Osavkamri savkamaokune twfjrkokun kumelilh,   [⟨savkam-⟩ for ⟨sakem-⟩]
/p ɔ·s·ahkamé·i-sa·k·i·ma·ɔ·k·aní·i-tunkše·kó·k·an kəmí·ləl=č.
/t The heavenly-kingdom key I shall give you.
/k And I will give unto thee the keys of the kingdom of heaven:

/b okh tuktu krkw rli qetvekrun bni tali cntu lawsif okh li wlrlintasw tali osavkamc.
/p ɔ́·k=č tákta kéku é·li-khwithiké·an yó·ni táli entalá·wsink, ɔ́·k=č lí-wəle·ləntá·s·u táli ɔ·s·áhkame.
/t And whatever you forbid here on earth, shall also be acceptable to do in heaven.
     [The second verb should be negative.]
/k and whatsoever thou shalt bind on earth shall be bound in heaven:

	/b	Okh tuktu krkw konu rlenasean, okh li wlrlintasw osavkamc tali.
	/p	ɔ·k=č tákta kéku kɔ́na e·li·ná·s·ian, ɔ́·k=č lí-wəle·ləntá·s·u ɔ·s·áhkame táli."
	/t	And whatever you shall allow, shall also be acceptable to do in heaven."
	/k	and whatsoever thou shalt loose on earth shall be loosed in heaven.

Mt 16.20
- /b Nu rkrkemathi tclan
- /p ná e·k·e·ki·má·č·i təla·n
- /t Then he told his disciples
- /k Then charged he his disciples

- /b tcli a mutu awrni lawunro tcli nrkumu Nhesus Pepenwnt.
- /p tə́li-=á· máta awé·ni -la·wəné·ɔ, tə́li nék·əma nčí·sas pi·p·í·nunt.
- /t that they should not tell anyone that he was Jesus the chosen one.
- /k that they should tell no man that he was Jesus the Christ.

Mt 16.21
- /b Na nckc wnwhi lanrp Nhesus rkrkematpani,
- /p ná-néke wənúči-lá·ne·p nčí·sas e·k·e·ki·ma·tpáni,
- /t From that time on Jesus began to tell his disciples,
- /k From that time forth began Jesus to shew unto his disciples,

- /b yaskamih eku nta Nhelwsalumif
- /p "ayá·skami=č íka ntá †nči·lo·sələmink.
- /t "I must go to Jerusalem.
- /k how that he must go unto Jerusalem,

- /b xavrlrnaokih krkw nwnhi amuxavrlintum wunhi krkyimvrthek, ok wcvevwfrthek, ok rvrlrkvekrthek,   [⟨amuxavrlintum⟩: has ⟨ì⟩]
- /p xahe·lennáɔhki=č kéku núnči-amax·ahe·ləntam wə́nči ke·kayəmhé·č·i·k, ɔ́·k wehi·hunké·č·i·k, ɔ́·k ehəle·khi·k·é·č·i·k,
- /t I shall suffer greatly from many things at the hands of the rulers and priests and scribes,
- /k and suffer many things of the elders and chief priests and scribes,

- /b ok ntclih nvelkwn ok ntclih nuxwqunakvakc lupi amwen.
- /p ɔ́·k ntə́li-=č -nhílko·n, ɔ́·k ntə́li-=č naxo·k·wənakháke lápi -á·mwi·n."
- /t for them also to kill me, and for me to rise up again after three days."
- /k and be killed, and be raised again the third day.

Mt 16.22
- /b Nu Petul ‖ pale tclwxolan, nu tolumi qvetulan tclao,
- /p ná †pí·təl palí·i təlɔ́·x·ɔla·n, ná tɔ́ləmi-khwítəla·n, təlá·ɔ,
- /t Then Peter took him aside, and then he began to admonish him, saying to him,
- /k Then Peter took him, and began to rebuke him, saying,

(p. 104)
- /b Nrvlaliun; Krtanitwet nathevkonch, wcnhih mutu nuni lrk.
- /p "nehəlá·lian, ke·tanət·ó·wi·t na·čihkɔ́neč, wénči-=č máta nɔ́ni -lé·k."

	/t	"My lord, may God concern himself with you, so that that will not happen."
	/k	Be it far from thee, Lord: this shall not be unto thee.

Mt 16.23 /b Jwq pale wuntaqi li qulwpe tclao, Petulu.
/p šúkw palí·i wə́ntahkwi lí-kwələp·i·, təlá·ɔ †pí·təla,
/t But he turned away and said to Peter,
/k But he turned, and said unto Peter,

/b Nwtcf al qcqvetvekrun rli eku kupekapai rau,   [⟨Nwtcf⟩ for ⟨Vwtcf⟩]
/p "wténk á·l, kwekhwithiké·an, é·li íka kkəp·i·k·á·p·ai e·á·a.
/t "Get behind me, you admonisher, as you stand blocking the way I am going.
/k Get thee behind me, Satan: thou art an offence unto me:

/b ok mutu kpunyrlintamwun Krtanitwetif wunheyek,
/p ɔ́·k máta kpəna·eləntamó·wən ke·tanət·o·wí·t·ink wənčí·ai·k,
/t And you are not thinking about what comes from God,
/k for thou savourest not the things that be of God,

/b jwq bni cntu lawsif.
/p šúkw yó·ni entalá·wsink."
/t but about this world."
/k but those that be of men.

Mt 16.24 /b Nu Nhesus tclan rkremathi,
/p ná nčí·sas tə́la·n e·k·e·ki·má·č·i,
/t Then Jesus said to his disciples,
/k Then said Jesus unto his disciples,

/b Awrnh kavtu naoletc tofrlintumunh voky,
/p "awé·n=č káhta-na·ɔlí·t·e, tɔnke·ləntamən=č hɔ́k·ay.
/t "If anyone wants to follow me, he must think little of himself,
/k If any man will come after me, let him deny himself,

/b ok taoni a xrli suqrlintamwakun noxpwxwrnh,
/p ɔ́·k tá·ɔni=á· xé·li sak·we·ləntaməwá·k·an, nɔxpó·x·we·n=č,
/t and although there is much suffering, he must take it with him
/k and take up his cross,

/b amunheh naolwq.
/p amənčí·i=č nná·ɔlukw.
/t and must follow me despite that.
/k and follow me.

Mt 16.25 /b Awrn rvotuf wlclrxrokun, tofvetwnh;
/p awé·n ehɔ́·t·ank wəlehəle·x·e·ɔ́·k·an tɔnkhíto·n=č.
/t Anyone who loves his life shall lose it.
/k For whosoever will save his life shall lose it:

/b ok awrn wlclrxrokun afvetaqc ne wunhi, lupih moxkamun.
/p ɔ́·k awé·n wəlehəle·x·e·ɔ́·k·an ankhitá·k·we ní· wə́nči, lápi=č mɔ́xkamən.
/t And if anyone loses his life for my sake, he shall find it again.
/k and whosoever will lose his life for my sake shall find it.

Mt 16.26 /b Krkw ksi a awrn tclapcntamun,
/p kéku=ksí=á· awé·n təla·p·éntamən?
/t What benefit would it then be to someone?
/k For what is a man profited,

/b taoni a msithri wnelatumun bni cntu lawsif; taofulilwu a vwhehufumu?
/p tá·ɔni=á· məsəč·é·i wənihəlá·t·amən yó·ni entalá·wsink, taɔnkəlɔ́ləwa=á· wči·čánkəma?
/t Even though they (indef.) would own the whole world, their soul would be lost.
/k if he shall gain the whole world, and lose his own soul?

/b ji vuh krkw vatri wunhi a ajwntrnat vwhe hufumu.
                                [⟨vatri⟩ for /hát·e·/; ⟨vwhe hufumu⟩ for ⟨vwhehufumu⟩]
/p ší=háč kéku hát·e· wə́nči-=á· -a·š·unté·na·t wči·čánkəma?
/t Or what is there that they (indef.) would trade their soul for?
/k or what shall a man give in exchange for his soul?

Mk 8.38 /b Awrnh mexanaletc ji tu ntaptwnakun cntu wcvepcfrekri mrtawsetekri tali
                                                        [⟨rek⟩ for ⟨rtek⟩]
/p awé·n=č mi·x·ana·lí·t·e, ší=tá nta·pto·ná·k·an, énta wehi·penke·t·i·ké·i, me·t·a·wsi·t·i·ké·i táli,
/t If anyone is ashamed of me or my words, while among the fornicators and sinners,
/k Whosoever therefore shall be ashamed of me and of my words in this adulterous and sinful generation;

/b nul nuni linw Wrqesif lupi patc mwexanalaoh.
/p nál náni, lənu we·k·wí·s·ink lápi pá·t·e, mwi·x·ana·lá·ɔ=č.
/t they are one that, when the man who is the Son returns, he will be ashamed of.
/k of him also shall the Son of man be ashamed, when he cometh ...

Mt 16.27 /b Rli kveheh prw linw Wrqesif, ok wehih rvalwkalinhek, Wxo tclswakuneleth
/p é·li khiči·i=č pé·w lənu we·k·wí·s·ink, ɔ́·k wíči=č ehalo·ka·lənči·k, ɔ́·x·ɔ təlsəwa·k·aní·li·t=č.
/t For truly the man who is the Son shall come, and with him angels, and his father's power.
/k For the Son of man shall come in the glory of his Father with his angels;

	/b	nuh wrmi awrn rnvaon tuktu krkw mekintufup.
	/p	ná=č wé·mi awé·n e·nháɔ·n tákta kéku mi·kəntánkəp.
	/t	Then everyone shall be paid for whatever they had done.
	/k	and then he shall reward every man according to his works.

Mt 16.28 /b Kvehe ktlwvmw alintc bk nepyethek   [⟨kt-|lwvmw⟩ for ⟨ktclwvmw⟩]
         /p khičí·i ktəllúhəmɔ, a·lənte yó·k ni·p·aí·č·i·k
         /t Truly, I say to you, some standing here
         /k Verily I say unto you, There be some standing here,

         /b ta ufulweok nrlumu nrmvetet linw Wrqesif sokemaokun.
         /p tá=á· ankəlo·wí·ɔk né·ləma-ne·mhíti·t lə́nu we·k·wí·s·ink sɔ·k·i·ma·ɔ́·k·an."
         /t will not die before seeing the kingdom of the man who is the Son."
         /k which shall not taste of death, till they see the Son of man coming in his kingdom.
                                        (Cf. Mk 9:1: ... the kingdom of God ...)

Chapter 58 (pp. 104-105). [L. section 57.] (Matthew 17.1-3, 13; Luke 9.31 [end]-36 [beginning]; Mark 9.9-13; cf. Mark 9.2ff., Luke 9.27ff.)

Mt 17.1 /b Nu wunhi kwtaj cntxwqunakvakc,
        /p nə́ wə́nči kwə́t·a·š entxo·k·wənakháke,
        /t Six days after that,
        /k And after six days

        /b Nhesus tclwxolan xwvu Petulu, ok Nhim, ok wemavtu Nhanu cntu muxutif.
        /p nčí·sas təló·x·ɔla·n xó·ha †pí·təla, ɔ́·k nčím, ɔ́·k wí·mahta nčá·na énta-maxát·ink.
        /t Jesus took Peter, Jim, and his brother John to a high mountain by themselves.
        /k Jesus taketh Peter, James, and John his brother, and bringeth them up into an high mountain apart,

Lk 9.29 /b Nanc tuntu pataman
        /p ná=nə tə́nta-pá·tama·n.
        /t There he prayed.
        /k ... and went up into a mountain to pray.

Mt 17.2 /b nu wexkaohi peli tclenaqsen rlifwrxenvetet.
        /p ná wi·xkaóči pí·li təli·ná·kwsi·n e·linkwe·x·i·nhíti·t.
        /t Then suddenly his appearance became different before their eyes.
        /k And was transfigured before them:

        /b Wwjkifq lukveqi sapulrr kejwxif, ok rqethi kvehe ave opulrxunw.
        /p wə́škinkw ləkhíkwi-sa·p·əlé·e· ki·š·ó·x·ink, ɔ́·k e·k·wí·č·i khičí·i áhi·ɔ·p·əlé·x·ənu.
        /t His face was as bright as the sun, and his clothes truly shone intensely white.
        /k and his face did shine as the sun, and his raiment was white as the light.

Mt 17.3	/b	Nu ok wexkaohi neju linwfu wihi eku avpenro Mwjiju ok Elyusu.
	/p	ná ɔ́·k wi·xkaɔ́či ní·š·a lənúnka wwíči- íka -ahpi·né·ɔ, †mo·šə́š·a ɔ́·k †i·layə́s·a.
	/t	Then suddenly two departed men were also sitting there with him, Moses and Elias.
Mt 17.3	/k	And, behold, there appeared unto them [Moses and Elias talking with him.]
Lk 9.30	/k	[And, behold, there talked] with him two men, which were Moses and Elias:

Lk 9.31	/b	Tokunwtumunro ‖ nveltwakun rlrkh Nhelwsalumif tali.
	/p	tɔk·əno·t·əməné·ɔ nhiltəwá·k·an, é·le·k=č †nči·lo·səlɔ́mink táli.
	/t	They talked about the killing, which would occur in Jerusalem.
	/k	[Who appeared in glory,] and spake of his decease which he should accomplish at Jerusalem.

Lk 9.32	/b	Jwq Petul, ok wethrvkwki ave kavtwfomwk,
(p. 105)	/p	šúkw †pí·təl ɔ́·k wi·č·e·ykúk·i áhi-kahtunkɔ́·mo·k.
	/t	But Peter and his companions were very sleepy.
	/k	But Peter and they that were with him were heavy with sleep:

	/b	mrhi twkevlatetc wnrawao rlenaqselet [⟨ra⟩ for invariant /e·ɔ/]
	/p	mé·či to·kihəlahtí·t·e, wəne·ɔwwá·ɔ e·li·na·kwsí·li·t,
	/t	After they woke up, they saw how he looked,
	/k	and when they were awake, they saw his glory,

	/b	ok neju linwfu wehi eku avpwuk.
	/p	ɔ́·k ní·š·a lənúnka wíči- íka -ahpúwak.
	/t	and the two departed men were sitting with him there.
	/k	and the two men that stood with him.

Lk 9.33	/b	Mrhi rlumi alumskavtetc nukavkc linwfu,
	/p	mé·či é·ləmi-aləmskahtí·t·e nəkáhke lənúnka,
	/t	When those men began to leave,
	/k	And it came to pass, as they departed from him,

	/b	Petul tclao Nhesusu Wlexun a na b avpeufwc,
	/p	†pí·təl təlá·ɔ nči·sás·a, "wəlí·x·ən=á· ná=yú ahpiánkwe.
	/t	Peter said to Jesus, "It would be good for us all to be here. ['us all' = 'us (inc.)']
	/k	Peter said unto Jesus, Master, it is good for us to be here:

	/b	manetwtamwq nuxu wekwamtitu,
	/p	manni·tó·t·amo·kw naxá wi·k·əwamtə́t·a:
	/t	Let's all make three little houses:
	/k	and let us make three tabernacles;

	/b	ke a kwti, ok a mwfif kwti, ok a Elyus kwti;
	/p	kí·=á· kwə́t·i, ɔ́·k=á· mó·šəš kwə́t·i, ɔ́·k=á· †i·láyas kwə́t·i."

Text, Transcription, and Translation 347

/t one would be for you, one would be for Moses, and one would be for Elias."
/k one for thee, and one for Moses, and one for Elias:

/b takw wutamwi wcnhi nc lwrt.
/p takó· wwa·t·amó·wi, wénči- nə́ -lúwe·t.
/t He was unaware of himself, which is why he said that.
/k not knowing what he said.

Lk 9.34
/b Nrli nc lwrtup, kwmvwq wokrkakwnro,
/p né·li- nə́ -luwé·t·əp, kəmhɔkw wɔ·ke·ka·k·o·né·ɔ.
/t As he said that, a cloud surrounded them.
/k While he thus spake, there came a cloud, and overshadowed them:

/b wejaswuk rli lamwfwc avpevtet.
/p wi·š·á·s·əwak, é·li- la·múnkwe -ahpíhti·t.
/t They were afraid, being inside.
/k and they feared as they entered into the cloud.

Lk 9.35
/b Eku wunhevlr aptwnakun nc kumvokwf, lwrtakot
/p íka wənčíhəle· a·pto·ná·k·an nə́ kəmhɔ́kunk, luwe·tá·k·ɔt,
/t A voice came out of the cloud, being heard to say,
/k And there came a voice out of the cloud, saying,

/b nunul wu rvoluk Fwes; klistw.
/p "nánal wá ehɔ́·lak nkwí·s; kələ́sṭo·."
/t "This is my son, who I love; listen to him."
/k This is my beloved Son: hear him.

Lk 9.36
/b Mrhi nc lwrokun lwxwrekc, nu Nhesus jwq xwvu topen.   [⟨lw-⟩ for /lo·o·-/]
/p mé·či nə́ luwe·ɔ́·k·an lo·o·x·we·í·k·e, ná nčí·sas šúkw xó·ha tɔ́p·i·n.
/t After the voice had gone past, then just Jesus was there alone.
/k And when the voice was past, Jesus was found alone. ...

Mk 9.9
/b Mrhi punusevtetc eku wunhi ovhwf, Nhesus qetulao, tclao,
/p mé·či pənas·ihtí·t·e íka wə́nči ɔhčúnk, nčí·sas kkwi·təlá·ɔ, təlá·ɔ,
/t After they had come down from the mountain, Jesus admonished them, saying to them,
/k And as they came down from the mountain, he charged them

/b Kahi vuji awrn lerkrq
/p "káči háši awé·n lié·k·e·kw,
/t "Never tell anyone,
/k that they should tell no man what things they had seen,

	/b	kcnh amwetc linw Wrqesif wunhi ufulwakunif,
	/p	kə́nč a·mwí·t·e lə́nu we·k·wí·s·ink wə́nči ankələwá·k·anink."
	/t	until the man who is the Son rises from death."
	/k	till the Son of man were risen from the dead.

Mk 9.10 /b wlvatwnro nuni lwrokun,
/p o·lhato·né·ɔ nə́ni luwe·ɔ́·k·an.
/t They kept that statement to themselves.
/k And they kept that saying with themselves,

/b ntwtumaovtwpanek litwpanek
/p nto·t·əma·ɔhtó·p·ani·k, lət·ó·p·ani·k,
/t They asked each other, saying to each other,
/k questioning one with another

/b krkw nc vct b rlwcf, amwetch wunhi ufulwakunif.
/p "kéku=néh=ét yú é·ləwenk, 'a·mwí·t·e=č wə́nči ankələwá·k·anink.'?"
/t "What could this possibly mean, 'When he rises from death.'?"
/k what the rising from the dead should mean.

Lk 9.36 /b Nunu nckc takw vuji awrni tclawunro krkw rlenamevtetup.
/p ná ná-néke takó· háši awé·ni təla·wəné·ɔ kéku e·li·namihtí·t·əp.
/t At that time then they never told anyone the things they had witnessed.
/k ... And they kept it close, and told no man in those days any of those things which they had seen.

Mk 9.11 /b Nu notwxtaonro tclawao,
/p ná nɔt·o·xtaɔ·né·ɔ, təlawwá·ɔ,
/t Then they asked him, saying to him,
/k And they asked him, saying,

/b Krkw vuh wcnhi rlvrkvekrthek evlwcvtet, vetamih Elyus pr?   [⟨rlv-⟩ for ⟨rvl-⟩]
/p "kéku=háč wénči- ehɔle·khi·k·é·č·i·k -ihɔləwéhti·t, 'hítami=č ʈi·láyas pć·.'?
/t "Why do the scribes always say, 'Elias shall come first.'?"
/k Why say the scribes that Elias must first come?

Mk 9.12 /b Tclao, Kvehe tu vetamih Elyus pr okh wrmi krkw tonhetwn,
/p təlá·ɔ, "khičí·i=tá hítami=č ʈi·láyas pé·, ɔ́·k=č wé·mi kéku tɔnčí·to·n.
/t He said to them, "Truly Elias shall come first, and he shall restore everything.
/k And he answered and told them, Elias verily cometh first, and restoreth all things;

/b nuh kcnh linw Wrqesif, rli na nuni lrkvasek,
/p ná=č kə́nč lə́nu we·k·wí·s·ink, é·li- ná=nə́ni -le·khá·s·i·k,
/t Only then shall the man who is the Son, because that is what is written,
/k and how it is written of the Son of man,

	/b	okh tcli xrlrnaovki krkw wunhi amuxavrlintumun
	/p	ɔ·k=č tə́li- xe·lennáɔhki kéku -wə́nči-amax·ahe·ləntamən,
	/t	and also so that he shall suffer greatly from many things,
	/k	that he must suffer many things,

	/b	okh li mavtrluman.
	/p	ɔ́·k=č lí-mahté·lǝma·n.
	/t	and so that he shall be despised.
	/k	and be set at nought.

Mk 9.13 /b Jwq kctlwvmw Elyus mrhi peprp   [⟨kctlwvmw⟩ for ⟨ktclwvmw⟩]
        /p šúkw ktǝllúhǝmɔ, †i·láyas mé·či pí·p·e·p,
        /t But I say to you, Elias has already come some time ago,
        /k But I say unto you, That Elias is indeed come,

        /b ok mrhi qeji levanro krkw krta levavtet,
        /p ɔ́·k mé·či kwíši-li·ha·né·ɔ kéku ké·t·a-li·háhti·t,
        /t and they have already done to him what they wanted to do to him,
        /k and they have done unto him whatsoever they listed,

        /b ok na nuni lrkvuswp.
        /p ɔ́·k ná=nǝni le·khá·s·o·p."
        /t and that is what is written."
        /k as it is written of him.

Mt 17.13 /b Nu rkrkemathi wnunwstakwn tcli avkuneman Nhanu hchvopunwrletup.
         /p ná e·k·e·ki·má·č·i wǝnǝno·stá·k·o·n, tə́li-ahkǝní·ma·n nčá·na čečhɔ·pwǝnǝwe·lí·t·ǝp.
         /t Then his disciples understood him to be talking about John the Baptist.
         /k Then the disciples understood that he spake unto them of John the Baptist.

Chapter 59 (pp. 105-107). [L. section 58.] (Luke 9.37 [part], 38 [part], 42 [part]-45; Mark 9.14 [part]-25, 28; Matthew 17.20-21)

Lk 9.37 /b Nu nckc pchi punusevtetc, nu rlavparkc
        /p ná·néke péči-pǝnas·ihtí·t·e, ná e·lahpa·é·k·e,
        /t At the time they came down from the height, on that next morning,
        /k And it came to pass, that on the next day, when they were come down from the hill, ...

Mk 9.14 /b eku ‖ pratc rpelet rkrkemathi, wnro xrli awrni eku okai.
        /p íka pe·á·t·e e·p·í·li·t e·k·e·ki·má·č·i, wǝne·ɔ́·ɔ xé·li awé·ni íka ɔ·ká·i.
        /t when he came to where his disciples were, he saw many people around them.
        /k And when he came to his disciples, he saw a great multitude about them, ...

Mk 9.15	/b	Mrhi mrxrlkek nrovtetc kanjrlintamwpanek
(p. 106)	/p	mé·či me·x·é·lki·k ne·ɔhtí·t·e, kanše·ləntamó·p·ani·k.
	/t	After the crowd saw him, they were amazed.
	/k	And straightway all the people, when they beheld him, were greatly amazed,

	/b	nu eku tujevlanro moi ofwmawao.
	/p	ná íka təš·ihəla·né·ɔ, mɔ́i-ɔnko·mawwá·ɔ.
	/t	Then they ran to him, going to greet him.
	/k	and running to him saluted him.

Mk 9.16	/b	Tclao rvlrkvekrthek, Krkw vuh nrtwtamarq?
	/p	təlá·ɔ, ehəle·khi·k·é·č·i·k, "kéku=háč ne·t·o·t·əmáe·kw?"
	/t	He said to them, regarding the scribes, "What are you asking them about?"
	/k	And he asked the scribes, What question ye with them?

Mk 9.17	/b	Nu mawsw nrk mrxrlkek noxkwman lwr
	/p	ná má·wsu né·k me·x·é·lki·k nɔxkó·ma·n, lúwe·,
	/t	Then one from the crowd answered him, saying,
	/k	And one of the multitude answered and said,

	/b	rvavkrkifrs kprtwlin fwes
	/p	"ehahke·kínke·s, kpe·t·ó·lən nkwí·s;
	/t	"Teacher, I brought my son to you.
	/k	Master, I have brought unto thee my son,

	/b	mutu kekski krkw lwri manutwakun avpetaq.
	/p	máta kí·kski- kéku -luwé·i; manət·uwwá·k·an ahpí·ta·kw.
	/t	He is never able to say anything; he has a power in him.
	/k	Master, I have brought unto thee my son, which hath a dumb spirit;

Lk 9.38	/b	Ave qwlu kpunaonro, rli nuli mawset nehan. [⟨nuli⟩ for /nə́ -lí-/]
	/p	áhi-kwə́la kpənaɔ·né·ɔ, é·li- nə́ -lí-má·wsi·t nní·č·a·n.
	/t	I greatly wish for you to look at him, for he is my only child. ['you (pl.)']
	/k	... I beseech thee, look upon my son: for he is mine only child.

Mk 9.18	/b	Tutu rlwxolatc, vwtoxkunao, [⟨toxk-⟩ for ⟨twxk-⟩ 6x]
	/p	tətá e·lo·x·ɔlá·t·e, wto·xkəná·ɔ,
	/t	Wherever it takes him, it tears him,
	/k	And wheresoever he taketh him, he teareth him:

	/b	amuxavolamw petrwv vwtwnr kwkumwkuntaminu,
		[⟨petrwv vwtwnr⟩ for ⟨petrwvtwnr⟩ (Mk 9.20)]
	/p	amax·ahɔlá·mu, pi·te·wtó·ne·, kwək·amo·kantamə́na ⟨wi·pí·ta⟩. [word missing]
	/t	he screams loudly, foams at the mouth, and 'gnashes' [his teeth].
	/k	and he foameth, and gnasheth with his teeth,

/b avealwkw.
/p áhi-a·ló·ku."
/t he's doing very poorly."
/k and pineth away:

/b Notwxtaonrp rkrkemkwselehi tcli a kekrvanro jwq toly.
/p nɔt·o·xtaɔ́·ne·p e·k·e·ki·mkwəs·i·lí·č·i, tə́li-=á· -ki·k·e·ha·né·ɔ, šúkw tɔ́·lai.
/t He had asked the disciples to heal him, but they failed.
/k and I spake to thy disciples that they should cast him out; and they could not.

Mk 9.19
/b Nhesus noxkwmao lwr, O mutu wrlamvetufek rlvakrerq,
/p nčí·sas nɔxko·má·ɔ, lúwe·, "ó·, máta we·la·mhitánki·k e·lhaké·ie·kw,
/t Jesus answered them, saying, "Oh, you tribe of unbelievers!
/k He answereth him, and saith, O faithless generation,

/b ta vuh ksaki wetavpemulinro?
/p tá=háč ksá·ki-witahpi·mələné·ɔ?
/t How long will I be with you?
/k how long shall I be with you?

/b ta vuh ksaki luxyevlinro?
/p tá=háč ksá·ki-laxaihələné·ɔ?
/t How long will I annoy you?
/k how long shall I suffer you?

/b Wuntavlwxotyel qes.
/p wə́ntax luxɔhtái·l kkwí·s."
/t Bring your son to me."
/k bring him unto me.

Mk 9.20
/b Nu eku tulwxotaon,
/p ná íka təluxɔhtáɔ·n;
/t Then he brought him there to him.
/k And they brought him unto him:

/b mrhi nrotc, nu jac manutw vwtwxkunan vakif tcli kaevlan,
/p mé·či ne·ɔ́·t·e, ná šá·e manə́t·u wtó·xkəna·n, hák·ink tə́li-kaíhəla·n.
/t When he had seen him, then immediately the spirit tore him, and he fell to the ground.
/k and when he saw him, straightway the spirit tare him; and he fell on the ground,

/b nanc pwpamxqsen, ok petrwvtwnr.
/p ná=nə pup·á·mxkwsi·n, ɔ́·k pi·te·wtó·ne·.
/t And there he crawled around, foaming at the mouth.
/k and wallowed foaming.

Mk 9.21
/b Nu Nhesus notwxtaon wrqeselehe, tutu rlkeqi nwhe nc liselet?
/p ná nčí·sas nɔt·o·xtáɔ·n we·k·wi·s·i·lí·č·i, tətá e·lkí·kwi-núči- nə́ -ləs·í·li·t.
/t Then Jesus asked the one whose son he was, since when he had been like that.
/k And he asked his father, How long is it ago since this came unto him?

/b Tclkw rmeminsetc.
/p tə́lku, "e·mi·mənsí·t·e."
/t He said to him, "Since he was a child."
/k And he said, Of a child.

Mk 9.22
/b Tumeki vufq tuntrewf tclanevenu, ok mpif, tcli a nvelan,
/p təmí·ki=hánkw tənté·yunk təlanihí·na, ɔ́·k mpínk, tə́li-=á· -nhíla·n.
/t It often throws him into the fire, and into the water, in order to kill him.
/k And ofttimes it hath cast him into the fire, and into the waters, to destroy him:

/b bqc kuski liseunc, ktumakrlumenrn wetavrmenrn.
/p yúkwe káski-lǝs·iáne, ktəma·k·e·ləmí·ne·n, wi·t·a·he·mí·ne·n."
/t If you are able to now, take pity on us and help us."
/k but if thou canst do any thing, have compassion on us, and help us.

Mk 9.23
/b Nhesus tclao, Nvakaleane a,
/p nčí·sas təlá·ɔ, "nhaka·liáne=á·,
/t Jesus said to him, "If you believe in me,
/k Jesus said unto him, If thou canst believe,

/b rli awrn nrkaletc, wrmi krkw apwe lenuf,   [⟨nrkaletc⟩: em. to ⟨nvakaletc⟩]
/p é·li-, awé·n nhaka·lí·t·e, wé·mi kéku -á·p·əwi-lí·nank."
/t for, if someone believes in me, he easily does everything."
/k all things are possible to him that believeth.

Mk 9.24
/b Nu jac wrqeselet wlwpuvketakwn tclkw
/p ná šá·e we·k·wi·s·í·li·t wələpahki·tá·k·o·n, tə́lku,
/t Then immediately the one whose son he was wept before him, saying to him,
/k And straightway the father of the child cried out, and said with tears,

/b Nrvlaleun knakalil, wetyvrmel knakalin.
/p "nehəlá·lian, kəna·ká·ləl, wi·t·a·hé·mi·l kəna·kállən."
/t "My lord, I believe in you; help me to believe in you."
/k Lord, I believe; help thou mine unbelief.

Mk 9.25
/b Mrhi Nhesus nrotc mrxrlulehi tcli ekali marvlalen,
/p mé·či nčí·sas ne·ɔ́·t·e me·x·e·ləlí·č·i tə́li- íkali -ma·ehəlá·li·n,
/t After Jesus saw the crowd running together there,
/k When Jesus saw that the people came running together,

/b nu qetulan neski manutwu, tclao,
/p ná kwítəla·n ní·ski-manət·ó·wa, təlá·ɔ,
/t then he admonished the unclean spirit, saying to it,
/k he rebuked the foul spirit, saying unto him,

/b Mutu keksi krkw lwrt ok krkrpxat   [⟨keksi⟩ for ⟨kekski⟩]
/p "máta kí·kski- kéku -lúwe·t ɔ́·k ke·k·é·pxa·t,
/t "You who never say anything and are deaf,
/k Thou dumb and deaf spirit,

/b eku wunhi khel, ok kahi heh ekali punhevan.
/p íka wə́nči-kčí·l, ɔ́·k káči čí·č íkali pənčí·han."
/t come out of him, and don't ever go in him again."
/k I charge thee, come out of him, and enter no more into him.

Mk 9.26 /b Nu mwmxavolamwen ok tovi twxkunao ok eku wunhi khe;
/p ná mumxahɔlá·mwi·n ɔ́·k tɔ́hi-to·xkəná·ɔ, ɔ́·k íka wə́nči-kčí·.
/t Then it cried out loudly and tore him greatly, and it came out of him.
/k And the spirit cried, and rent him sore, and came out of him:

/b nu mulaji tofulin, wunhi xrli awrn lwrn, Mrhi ta ufulu.
/p ná málahši tónkələn, wwə́nči- xé·li awé·n -lúwe·n, "mé·či=tá ánkəla."
/t Then he was as if dead, causing many people to say, "He has died."
/k and he was as one dead; insomuch that many said, He is dead.

Mk 9.27 /b Jwq Nhesus eku tonao wnaxkelet tospunao, nu tomwen,
/p šúkw nčí·sas íka tɔnná·ɔ wənaxkí·li·t, tɔspəná·ɔ, ná tó·mwi·n.
/t But Jesus took him by the hand and lifted him, and then he got up.
/k But Jesus took him by the hand, and lifted him up; and he arose.

Lk 9.42 /b nu mwelan wrnehanelethi.
/p ná mwí·la·n we·ni·č·a·ni·lí·č·i.
/t Then he turned him over to the one whose child he was.
/k ... and delivered him again to his father.

Lk 9.43 /b Ave kanjrlintamwk wcnhi nc Krtanitwet tolweliswakun. ‖   [⟨lin⟩: ⟨i⟩ lacks dot]
/p áhi-kanše·ləntamo·k wə́nči ná ke·tanət·ó·wi·t tɔləwí·i-ləs·əwá·k·an.
/t They were greatly amazed by the power of God.
/k And they were all amazed at the mighty power of God.

(p. 107) /b Jwq nrli kanjrlintamevtet wunhi rlyvosetup Nhesus, tclao rkrkemathi
/p šúkw né·li-kanše·ləntamíhti·t wə́nči e·laehɔ·s·í·t·əp nčí·sas, təlá·ɔ e·k·e·ki·má·č·i,
/t But while they wondered because of what Jesus had done, he said to his disciples,
/k But while they wondered every one at all things which Jesus did, he said unto his disciples,

Lk 9.44
/b bqc bni lwrokun hetani kulrlintamwq,
/p "yúkwe yó·ni luwe·ó·k·an čí·t·ani-kəle·lə́ntamo·kw:
/t "Hold this statement firmly in your minds:
/k Let these sayings sink down into your ears:

/b Linw Wrqesifi uskih melanro cntu lawsehek.
/p lə́nu we·k·wi·s·ínki áski=č mi·la·né·ɔ [yú] éntala·wsí·č·i·k."   [word missing]
/t The man who is the Son must be turned over to the people of [this] world."
/k for the Son of man shall be delivered into the hands of men.

Lk 9.45
/b Jwq mutu wnunwstamwnro wcnhi nc lwrt,
/p šúkw máta wənəno·stamo·wəné·ɔ wénči- nə́ -lúwe·t.
/t But they did not understand why he said that,
/k But they understood not this saying,

/b rli kuntvataonro wunhih mutu nrmvetet.
/p é·li kanthataɔ·né·ɔ, wə́nči-=č máta -ne·mhíti·t.
/t as it was hidden from them, so that they would not see it.
/k and it was hid from them, that they perceived it not:

/b Qetaealanro notwxtaonro.
/p kkwi·taya·la·né·ɔ nɔt·o·xtaɔ·né·ɔ.
/t And they were afraid to ask him about it.
/k and they feared to ask him of that saying.

Mk 9.28
/b Nhesus mrhi wekwavmif pratc, nu rkrkemathi notwxtakwn kemei,
/p nčí·sas mé·či wi·k·əwáhəmink pe·á·t·e, ná e·k·e·ki·má·č·i nɔt·o·xtá·k·o·n ki·mí·i,
/t After Jesus had come to the house, his disciples asked him confidentially,
/k And when he was come into the house, his disciples asked him privately,

/b tclkw, Krkw vuh wcnhi mutu kuski ktiskaorf nu manutw?
/p tə́lku, "kéku=háč wénči- máta -káski-ktəskaɔ·enk ná manə́t·u?"
/t saying to him, "Why were we unable to drive out that spirit?"
/k saying to him, Why could not we cast him out?

Mt 17.20
/b Nhesus tclao, Rlik mutu nvakrwserq
/p nčí·sas təlá·ɔ, "é·li=k máta -nhake·wsí(·)e·kw.
/t Jesus said to them, "Well, because you have no faith.
/k And Jesus said unto them, Because of your unbelief:

/b lenakvokc a knakatamwrokunwu mustute mifwf,
/p li·na·khɔ́ke=á· kəna·ka·t·amwe·ɔ·k·anúwa †mɔstatí·i-mínkunk,
/t If your faith is like a mustard seed,
/k ... If ye have faith as a grain of mustard seed,

/b lrqc a bni ovhwv,
/p lé·k·we=á· yó·ni ɔhčú,
/t and if you say to this mountain,
/k ye shall say unto this mountain,

/b Qsel b wunhi ekali li, nu a jac eku vatr,
/p 'kwsí·l yú wə́nči íkali lí,' ná=á· šá·e íka hát·e·.
/t 'Move from here over to there,' then immediately it would be there.
/k Remove hence to yonder place; and it shall remove;

/b ta krkw kpoi lisevwmw.
/p tá=á· kéku kpɔ́·i-ləs·i·húmɔ.
/t Nothing would be impossible for you to do.
/k and nothing shall be impossible unto you.

Mt 17.21 /b Alwt nuni rlenaqset ta pale ktclskaoewu
/p aló·t nə́ni e·li·ná·kwsi·t, tá=á· palí·i ktəlskaɔ·íwwa,
/t Although one of that kind, you will not drive away
/k Howbeit this kind goeth not out

/b kcnh ave patamarqc ok mutu metserqc.
/p kə́nč áhi-pa·tama·é·k·we, ɔ́·k máta mi·tsié·k·we."
/t unless you pray hard, or if you don't eat."
/k but by prayer and fasting.

Chapter 60 (pp. 107-111). [L. sections 59-60.] (Mark 9.30-32, 48-50; Matthew 17.24-27, 18.1-5, 7-34; Mark 9.33 [part]-35, 39, 41-42, 44/46; Luke 9.49-50)

Mk 9.30 /b Nc wcnhi alumskatc Falulewf wlwen,
/p nə́ wénči-aləmská·t·e, †nka·lalí·yunk wəló·wi·n.
/t When he departed from there, he went through Galilee.
/k And they departed thence, and passed through Galilee;

/b takw kotatamwun awrn watwn.
/p takó· kɔt·a·t·amó·wən, awé·n o·wá·to·n.
/t He did not want anyone to know it.
/k and he would not that any man should know it.

Mk 9.31 /b Rli rkrkemathi lat, tclao
/p é·li- e·k·e·ki·má·č·i -lá·t, təlá·ɔ,
/t For he spoke to his disciples, saying to them,
/k For he taught his disciples, and said unto them,

/b Linwu Wrqesifi mrhi melanro b cntu lawsethek
/p "lə́nəwa we·k·wi·s·ínki mé·či mi·la·né·ɔ yú entala·wsí·č·i·k,
/t "The man who is the Son has already been turned over to the people of this world
/k The Son of man is delivered into the hands of men,

/b tclih nvelanro,
/p tə́li-=č -nhila·né·ɔ,
/t for them to kill him.
/k and they shall kill him;

/b mrhih nvelintc, nuxwqunakvakch amwe.
/p mé·či=č nhilə́nte, naxo·k·wənakháke=č á·mwi·."
/t After he is killed, in three days he shall rise up."
/k and after that he is killed, he shall rise the third day.

Mk 9.32 /b Jwq mutu wnunwstumwnro nc lwrokun, jwq qetu ntwxtaonro.
/p šúkw máta wnəno·stamo·wəné·ɔ nə́ luwe·ɔ́·k·an, šúkw kkwí·ta-nto·xtaɔ·né·ɔ.
/t But they did not understand that statement, only they feared to ask him about it.
/k But they understood not that saying, and were afraid to ask him.

Mt 17.24 /b Mrhi eku pravtetc Kpunium moni mcvmarnifek otxawao Petulu,
/p mé·či íka pe·ahtí·t·e †kapə́niam, mə́ni mehəma·e·nínki·k o·txawwá·ɔ †pí·təla,
/t After they had come to Capernaum, some tax-collectors came to Peter
/k And when they were come to Capernaum, they that received tribute money came to Peter,

/b tclawao, Rkrkemkon vuh ok evrnvr,
/p təlawwá·ɔ, "e·k·e·kí·mkɔn=háč ɔ́·k ihé·nhe·?"
/t and said to him, "Does your teacher also pay (tribute)?"
/k and said, Doth not your master pay tribute?

Mt 17.25 /b lwr Kovan.
/p lúwe·, "kɔhán."
/t He said, "Yes."
/k He saith, Yes.

/b Mrhi Petul trmekrtc, Nhesus nomao tclao,
/p mé·či †pí·təl te·mi·k·é·t·e, nčí·sas †nɔɔmá·ɔ, təlá·ɔ,
/t After Peter came in, Jesus anticipated him and said to him,
/k And when he was come into the house, Jesus prevented him, saying,

/b Krkw vuh ktetrva Symun?
/p kéku=háč kti·t·é·ha, †sáiman?
/t "What do you think, Simon?"
/k What thinkest thou, Simon?

/b Bk sakemaok b cntu lawsif, ta vuh wunhi mijinumunro rnvaotwakun,
/p yó·k sa·k·i·má·ɔk yú entalá·wsink, tá=háč wwə́nči-məšənəməné·ɔ
e·nha·ɔhtəwá·k·an?
/t These kings of the world, where do they get payment (of tribute) from?
/k of whom do the kings of the earth take custom or tribute?

/b nevlahi vuh wnehanwao ji vuh peli awrni?
/p nihəláči=háč wəni·č·a·nəwá·ɔ, ší=háč pí·li awé·ni?"
/t Is it their own children, or is it someone else?"
/k of their own children, or of strangers?

Mt 17.26 /b Petul tclao, Peli awrni.
/p †pí·təl təlá·ɔ, "pí·li awé·ni."
/t Peter said to him, "Someone else."
/k Peter saith unto him, Of strangers.

/b Nhesus tclao, jr punu wnehanwao mutu.
/p nčí·sas təlá·ɔ, "šé· pənáh, wəni·č·a·nəwá·ɔ máta.
/t Jesus said to him, "See, not their children.
/k Jesus saith unto him, Then are the children free.

Mt 17.27 /b Jwq eaphi wcnhih mutu hamemevtet,   [⟨hamem-⟩ for ⟨hanem-⟩]
/p šúkw i·á·pči, wénči-=č máta -čani·míhti·t,
/t But still, so that they do not accuse me,
/k Notwithstanding, lest we should offend them,

/b eku al munwprkwf, amunh khovoponeven,   [⟨munw-‖prkwf⟩]
/p íka á·l mənəp·é·k·unk, á·man=č kčɔhɔ·pɔníhi·n.
/t go to the sea, and you must cast a fishhook into the water.
/k go thou to the sea, and cast an hook,

(p. 108) /b kavpalwmc nrtami tvontuf ktwftwnrnuh,
/p kahpaló·me né·tami-thɔ́ntank, ktunktɔ·né·na=č.
/t Haul out the first one that bites it, and you must open its mouth.
/k and take up the fish that first cometh up; and when thou hast opened his mouth,

/b nuh nc ktuntu muxkamun monetit,
/p ná=č nə́ ktə́nta-máxkamən mɔní·t·ət.
/t There you will find a coin.
/k thou shalt find a piece of money:

/b kwrtunimunh nuh nc kmelan wunhi ne ok krpc.
/p kəwe·t·ənə́mən=č, ná=č nə́ kəmí·la·n wə́nči ní· ɔ́·k ké·pe."
/t You must take it, and that's what you must give to them from me and you, also."
/k that take, and give unto them for me and thee.

[L. section 60.]

Mk 9.33 /b Nrli wekwamif avpetup rkrkemathi notwxtao tclao,
/p né·li- wi·k·əwáhəmink -ahpí·t·əp, e·k·e·ki·má·č·i nɔt·o·xtaɔ́·ɔ, təlá·ɔ,
/t While he was in the house, he asked his disciples a question, saying to them,
/k ... and being in the house he asked them,
/l At the same time, being in the house, he asked them,

/b Krkw vuh wcnhi hihanencvwterq naohei b wrmufqc?
/p "kéku=háč wénči-čəčani·nehó·t·ie·kw naɔč·í·i yú we·mánkwe?"
/t "What did you argue with each other about on our way here?"
/k What was it that ye disputed among yourselves by the way?

Mk 9.34 /b Jwq hetquswuk,
/p šúkw či·tkwə́s·əwak,
/t But they kept silent,
/k But they held their peace:

/b rli wunhi hanencvwtenro naohi rli a awrn xifwrlumwqset.
/p é·li wwə́nči-čani·neho·t·i·né·ɔ naɔ́č·i, é·li-=á· awé·n -xinkwe·ləmúkwsi·t.
/t as they had argued on the way about who would be thought great.
/k for by the way they had disputed among themselves, who should be the greatest.

Mk 9.35 /b Nu mwjvakrn, nu tuli ntwman nrl tclin ok neju; tclao,
/p ná mwəšháke·n, ná tə́li-ntó·ma·n né·l télən ɔ́·k ní·š·a, təlá·ɔ,
/t Then he sat down and called the twelve to come, saying to them,
/k And he sat down, and called the twelve, and saith unto them,

/b Awrn kavtu nekanexifc, nrkumuh vwtif avpwv okh tolwkakunen.
/p "awé·n káhta-ni·k·a·ni·x·ínke, né·k·əma=č wténk ahpú, ɔ́·k=č tɔlo·ká·k·ani·n."
/t "If anyone desires to be first, he shall be behind and shall be a servant."
/k If any man desire to be first, the same shall be last of all, and servant of all.

Mt 18.1 /b Nu tclanro,
/p ná təla·né·ɔ,
/t Then they said to him,
/k At the same time came the disciples unto Jesus, saying,

/b Awrnh ksela, rli xifwrlumwqset b osavkamre sakemaokunif tali.
/p "awé·n=č=ksí=láh é·li-xinkwe·ləmúkwsi·t yú ɔ·s·ahkame·í·i-sa·k·i·ma·ɔ́·k·anink táli.
/t "So then, who will be the one (most) honored in this kingdom of heaven?
/k Who is the greatest in the kingdom of heaven?

Mt 18.2 /b Nu Nhesus wcnheman menintitu, nanc lrlai tovlan.   [⟨menintitu⟩ for ⟨memintitu⟩]
/p ná nčí·sas wwenčí·ma·n mi·məntə́t·a, ná=nə le·lá·i tóhəla·n.

/t Then Jesus called over a little child and set him in the middle there.
/k And Jesus called a little child unto him, and set him in the midst of them,

Mt 18.3 /b Tclao, Kvehe ktclwvmw, mutuh liserqc wu memintit rlset,
/p təláːɔ, "khičíˑi ktəllúhəmɔ, máta=č ləsˑiéˑkˑwe wá miˑmə́ntət éˑlsiˑt,
/t He said to them, "Truly I say to you, if you do not become as this child is,
/k And said, Verily I say unto you, Except ye be converted, and become as little children,

/b ta kuski avpewunro nc osavkumre sakemaokunif.
/p táːáˑ kkáskiˑahpiˑwəné ɔ nɔ́ ɔˑsˑahkameˑíˑiˑsaˑkˑiˑmaˑɔ́ˑkˑanink.
/t you will not be able to be in the kingdom of heaven.
/k ye shall not enter into the kingdom of heaven.

Mt 18.4 /b Awrnh lukveqi tufrlinsetc memuntitif
/p awéˑn=č ləkhíkwi-tankeˑlənsíˑtˑe miˑməntə́tˑink,
/t If someone shall be as humble as a little child,
/k Whosoever therefore shall humble himself as this little child,

/b nulh nuni xifwrlumwqsw bv osavkamre sakemaokunif tali,
/p nál=č náni xinkweˑləmúkwsu yúh ɔˑsˑahkameˑíˑiˑsaˑkˑiˑmaˑɔ́ˑkˑanink.
/t then *he* shall be honored in this kingdom of heaven.
/k the same is greatest in the kingdom of heaven.

Mt 18.5 /b okh awrn wifrlumwksw nuni rlset wunhi ntclswakun,
/p ɔ́ˑk=č awéˑn winkeˑləmúkwsu nə́ni éˑlsiˑt wə́nči ntəlsəwáˑkˑan,
/t And someone who is like that shall be welcomed on my behalf,
/k And whoso shall receive one such little child in my name

/b okh nrpc nwifrlumukc.
/p ɔ́ˑk=č néˑpe nəwinkeˑləmə́kˑe.
/t and I, too, shall be welcomed.
/k receiveth me.

Lk 9.49 /b Nu Nhan tclan, Rvakrkifrs, nrovnap linw tcli paleliskaon mavtuntwu,
/p ná nčáˑn tólaˑn, "ehahkeˑkínkeˑs, nneˑɔ́hənaˑp lə́nu tə́li- palíˑi -lə́skaɔˑn mahtantˑóˑwa,
/t Then John said to him, "Teacher, we saw a man driving devils away,
/k And John answered and said, Master, we saw one casting out devils in thy name;

/b jwq fwetulawunu rli mutu naolwkwrf.
/p šúkw nkwiˑtəláˑwəna, éˑli- máta -naˑɔlukˑóˑwenk."
/t but we told him not to, because he did not follow us (exc.)."
/k and we forbad him, because he followeth not with us.

Lk 9.50 /b Nhesus tclao, Kahi qvetulavrq,
/p nčí·sas təlá·ɔ, "káči khwitəláhe·kw,
/t Jesus said to him, " Don't tell him not to,
/k And Jesus said unto him, Forbid him not:

/b rli mutu luxyevetc awrn nul nu nwehumwq.
/p é·li máta laxai·hí·t·e awé·n, nál=ná nəwí·č·əmukw.
/t for if someone does not hinder me, he is one who helps me."
/k for he that is not against us is for us.

Mk 9.39 /b Rli mutu avpet awrn krski a kunjyvoset wunhi ntclswakun mrthemet.
/p é·li- máta -ahpí·t awé·n ké·ski-=á· -kanšaehó·s·i·t wə́nči ntəlsəwá·k·an me·čí·mi·t.
/t For there is no one who maligns me who can do a miracle acting for me.
/k ... for there is no man which shall do a miracle in my name, that can lightly speak evil of me.

Mk 9.41 /b Awrnh muncvkonc eli jwq mpi, wunhi ntclswakun rli Klysteu,
/p awé·n=č mənihkóne ílli šúkw mpí wə́nči ntəlsəwá·k·an é·li-kəlaístia,
/t If anyone shall merely give you water to drink because of my deeds as Christ,
/k For whosoever shall give you a cup of water to drink in my name, because ye belong to Christ,

/b kvehe ktclwvmw, ta kuski mutu rnvawun.   [⟨aw⟩ for /aɔ́·w/]
/p khičí·i ktəllúhəmɔ, tá=á· káski- máta -e·nhaɔ́·wən.
/t truly I say to you, it will not be possible for him not to be rewarded for it.
/k verily I say unto you, he shall not lose his reward.

Mk 9.42 /b Ok tuktu awrn hanelyrmatc mawselw bl tcfrlinselethi,
/p ɔ́·k tákta awé·n čani·lae·má·t·e ma·wsí·lu yó·l tenke·lənsi·lí·č·i,
/t And if anyone causes one of these humble ones to do wrong,
/k And whosoever shall offend one of these little ones [that believe in me],
                                                            [RSV "cause .. to sin"]

/b alwe a ma wli lrp xifwi avsin wxqrkufunif wuntaptwfpanc
/p aləwí·i=á·=máh wə́li-lé·p, xínkwi-ahsə́n uxkwe·k·ánkanink wənta·ptunkpáne,
/t it would have been better if a large stone had been tied from his neck,
/k it is better for him that a millstone were hanged about his neck,

/b nali munwprkwf cntu xetqrk lanivifpanc.   [presumably ⟨nali⟩ for ⟨nrli⟩ /né·li/]
/p né·li mənəp·é·k·unk énta-xí·tkwe·k lanihinkpáne.
/t and he had then been thrown out into the deep part of the sea.
/k and he were cast into the sea.

Mt 18.7 /b Avot bni cntu lawsif wunhi hanawswakun!
/p áhɔt yó·ni entalá·wsink wə́nči čana·wsəwá·k·an,

| | /t | This world is trouble, because of wrong-doing, [misunderstood] |
| | /k | Woe unto the world because of offences! |

	/b	rli qelalr ‖ hihanawswuk.
	/p	é·li kwí·la-lé· čəčana·wsúwak.
	/t	as there is no avoiding that they do wrong.
	/k	for it must needs be that offences come;

(p. 109) /b Jwqh ave lenum awrn cntxi hanelarfrt.
/p šúkw=č áhi-lí·nam awé·n éntxi-čani·laénke·t.
/t But something bad will happen to all who tempt people to sin.
/k but woe to that man by whom the offence cometh! [RSV "for temptations to sin"]

Mt 18.8 /b Nuni a wunhi hanelyvkonc kset ji tu knaxk, tumusjasek ok puvketwf
/p nə́ni=á· wə́nči-, čani·laehkó́ne ksí·t ší=tá kənáxk, -təməš·á·s·i·k ó·k -pahki·t·unk.
/t That's why, if your foot or your hand causes you sin, it should be cut off and thrown away.
/k Wherefore if thy hand or thy foot offend thee, cut them off, and cast them from thee: [RSV "causes you to sin"]

/b rli alwe wlexun amunhe eku li tumekrn pumuwswakunif [⟨muws⟩ for ⟨maws⟩]
/p é·li aləwí·i wəlí·x·ən amənčí·i íkali təmí·k·e·n pəma·wsəwá·k·anink,
/t For, it is better to enter [eternal] life anyway,
/k is better for thee to enter into life

/b taoni a kwti kset ok knaxk mutu vatri,
/p tá·ɔni=á· kwə́t·i ksí·t ó·k kənáxk máta hat·é·i,
/t even though you would not have one foot or hand,
/k halt or maimed,

/b rli a rle vatrkc ksetu, ok knaxku eku lancmalkrun rvalumakumek tuntrbf.
/p é·li-=á·, ellí·i hat·é·k·e ksí·t·a ó·k kənáxka, íka -lanehəma·lké·an ehaləmá·kami·k tənté·yunk,
/t as, if you had both your feet or hands, you would be cast into eternal fire,
/k rather than having two hands or two feet to be cast into everlasting fire.

Mk 9.44 /b Cntuh mutu eufululeq mwxwrswmwao ok nc tunty mutu a eatri.
/p énta-=č máta -i·ankəló́li·kw mmo·x·we·s·əməwá·ɔ, ó·k nə́ tə́ntay máta=á· i·a·té·i.
/t where their worms will never die, and that fire would never go out.
/k Where their worm dieth not, and the fire is not quenched.

Mt 18.9 /b Hanelyvkonc kijkifq, kutanivenh, kpuketwnh,
/p čani·laehkó́ne kə́škinkw, kkət·aníhi·n=č, kpak·í·t·o·n=č.
/t If your eye offends you, you must pluck it out and throw it away.
/k And if thine eye offend thee, pluck it out, and cast it from thee:

/b   rli alwe wlexun amunhe eku li tumekn pumawswakunif, taoni a maot jwq kijkifq,
                                                                         [⟨tumekn⟩ for /ktəmí·k·e·n/]

/p   é·li aləwí·i wəlí·x·ən, amənčí·i íkali ktəmí·k·e·n pəma·wsəwá·k·anink, tá·ɔni=á·
     má·ɔt šúkw kə́škinkw,

/t   For, it is better [for you] to enter [eternal] life anyway, even having only one eye,

/k   it is better for thee to enter into life with one eye,

/b   rli a rlei vatrkc kijkifo tuntrewf lancmalkrun.

/p   é·li-=á·, ellí·i hat·é·k·e kəškínkɔ, tənté·yunk -lanehəma·lké·an,

/t   as, if you had both your eyes, you would be cast into the fire,

/k   rather than having two eyes to be cast into hell fire.

Mk 9.48 /b   Cntuh mutu eufululeq mwxwrsumwao, ok nc tunty mutu a eatri.

/p   énta-=č máta -i·ankələ́li·kw mmo·x·we·s·əməwá·ɔ, ɔ́·k nə́ tə́ntay máta=á· i·a·té·i.

/t   where their worms will never die, and the fire never would never go out.

/k   Where their worm dieth not, and the fire is not quenched.

Mk 9.49 /b   Rli wrmi cntxethek vwsekrvosenroh tunty, wevwfrokun rvlukveqi sekrvosek.

/p   é·li wémi entxí·č·i·k wsi·khe·hɔ·s·i·né·ɔ=č tə́ntay,
     wi·hunke·ɔ́·k·an ehələkhíkwi-si·khe·hɔ́·s·i·k.

/t   For, everyone shall be salted with fire, whenever a sacrifice is salted.

/k   For every one shall be salted with fire, and every sacrifice shall be salted with salt.

Mk 9.50 /b   Laprmkot nc sekvy,

/p   la·p·é·mkɔt nə́ sí·khay.

/t   Salt is useful.

/k   Salt is good:

/b   jwq a taofifc nc sekvrokun, ta vuh a wunhi sekvrbw?

/p   šúkw=á· taɔnkínke nə́ si·khe·ɔ́·k·an, tá=háč=á· wə́nči-si·khe·yó·u?

/t   But if the saltiness is lost, what would make it be salty?

/k   but if the salt have lost his saltness, wherewith will ye season it?

/b   Sekvrbekch kvakybu, ok wlufwnteq.

/p   si·khe·yo·wí·k·eč khak·ayúwa, ɔ́·k wəlankúnti·kw.

/t   Let yourselves be salty, and be at peace with each other.

/k   Have salt in yourselves, and have peace one with another.

Mt 18.10 /b   Trku tu kahi mavtrlumerkrq mawsw nrk tcfrlinsethek, rli ktclwvmw,

/p   "té·ka=tá, káči mahte·ləmié·k·e·kw má·wsu né·k tenke·lənsí·č·i·k, é·li ktəllúhəmɔ,

/t   "Watch out, and don't scorn one of those meek ones, for I tell you,

/k   Take heed that ye despise not one of these little ones; for I say unto you,

/b   Krnavkevqevtethi osavkamc tali fumri nrovtet Nwxo wijkifwelet osavkamc rpet.

/p   ke·nahkihkwihtí·č·i, ɔ·s·áhkame táli nkəmé·i ne·ɔ́hti·t nó·x·ɔ wəškinkwí·li·t
     ɔ·s·áhkame é·p·i·t.

Text, Transcription, and Translation

/t   regarding those who look after them, in heaven who they always see is the face of my father who is in heaven.

/k   That in heaven their angels do always behold the face of my Father which is in heaven.

Mt 18.11
- /b   Rli linw Wrqesif pchi my lclrxrmvalat trofulilethi.
- /p   é·li- lə́nu we·k·wí·s·ink -péči-mái-lehele·x·e·mhá·la·t te·ɔnkələlí·č·i.
- /t   For the man who is the Son came to save the ones that are lost.
- /k   For the Son of man is come to save that which was lost.

Mt 18.12
- /b   Krkw vuh a ktervavmw?   [⟨ktervavmw⟩ for ⟨ktetrvavmw⟩]
- /p   kéku=háč=á· kti·t·e·háhəmɔ?
- /t   What would you think?
- /k   How think ye?

- /b   Linw tolwmwnsetc kwtapxki mrkesu mawselw alumi pwlkwkc,
- /p   lə́nu tɔləmunsí·t·e kwət·á·pxki mekí·s·a, ma·wsí·lu áləmi-po·lkúk·e,
- /t   If a man has a hundred sheep, and if one goes and escapes from him,
- /k   if a man have an hundred sheep, and one of them be gone astray,

- /b   mutu vuh a wnukalaeo nrl prjkwf txenxkc ok prjkwf,
- /p   máta=háč=á· wənək·ala·í·ɔ né·l pé·škunk txí·nxke ɔ́·k pé·škunk,
- /t   would he not leave the ninety-nine
- /k   doth he not leave the ninety and nine,

- /b   li ovhwekri moi ntwnaoeo nrl pwlkwki?
- /p   lí ɔhčuwi·ké·i mɔ́i-ntɔnaɔ·í·ɔ né·l po·lkúk·i?
- /t   and go into the mountains to search for the one that escaped from him?
- /k   and goeth into the mountains, and seeketh that which is gone astray?

Mt 18.13
- /b   Muxkaotc a, kvehe ktclwvmw rlwe wlrlintam nanc wunhi,
- /p   maxkaɔ́·t·e=á·, khičí·i ktəllúhəmɔ, aləwí·i wəle·lə́ntam ná=nə wə́nči,
- /t   If he finds it, I tell you truly, he would be happier over that one
- /k   And if so be that he find it, verily I say unto you, he rejoiceth more of that sheep,

- /b   rlkeqi wlrlintuf wunhi nrl prjkwf txentxkc ok prjwf mutu pwlkwqc.
       [⟨prjwf⟩ for ⟨prjkwf⟩; ⟨txentxkc⟩ for ⟨txenxkc⟩; ⟨-kwqc⟩ for /-kó·k·wi/]
- /p   e·lkí·kwi-wəle·lə́ntank wə́nči né·l pé·škunk txí·nxke ɔ́·k pé·škunk máta po·lkó·k·wi.
- /t   than he would be over the ninety-nine that did not escape from him.
- /k   than of the ninety and nine which went not astray.

Mt 18.14
- /b   Nu ok nc tpusqi nu Kwxwa osavkamc rpet takw letrvri,
- /p   ná ɔ́·k nə́ tpə́skwi, ná kó·x·əwa ɔ·s·áhkame é·p·i·t takó· li·t·e·hé·i,
- /t   Likewise, your father who is in heaven does not intend it,
- /k   Even so it is not the will of your Father which is in heaven,

	/b	mawsw bk tufrlinsethek heme a taofulukc.
	/p	má·wsu yó·k tanke·lənsí·č·i·k, či·mí·i=á· taɔnkələk·e.
	/t	if one of these meek ones is permanently lost.
	/k	that one of these little ones should perish.

Mt 18.15
- /b Hani lisetc kemavtis, my lwmc rli hani liset ‖ xwvu tutu tali.
- /p "čáni-ləs·í·t·e kí·mahtəs, mái-ló·me é·li-čáni-ləs·i·t xó·ha tə́ta táli.
- /t "If your brother does wrong, go and tell him how he did wrong alone someplace.
- /k Moreover if thy brother shall trespass against thee, go and tell him his fault between thee and him alone:

(p. 110)
- /b Klistakonc a, nu mrhi kwlevan keavtis.   [⟨keavtis⟩ for ⟨kemavtis⟩]
- /p kələstá·k·ɔne=á·, ná mé·či ko·lí·ha·n kí·mahtəs.
- /t If he listens to you, then you will have done well by your brother.
- /k if he shall hear thee, thou hast gained thy brother.

Mt 18.16
- /b Jwq mutu klistakwunc, nu lupi kwti jitu neju ekali wehrwmc,
- /p šúkw máta kələsta·k·ó·wane, ná lápi kwə́t·i ší=tá ní·š·a íkali wi·č·e·yó·me,
- /t But if he doesn't listen to you, go back to him taking one or two others with you,
- /k But if he will not hear thee, then take with thee one or two more,

- /b wunhih neju jitu nuxa awrnek wrmi aptwnakunu wlamwrenako.
- /p wə́nči-=č, ní·š·a ší=tá naxá awé·ni·k, wé·mi a·pto·ná·k·ana -wəla·məwe·i·ná·k·ɔ.
- /t so that, with two or three people, every word shall be seen to be true.
- /k that in the mouth of two or three witnesses every word may be established.

Mt 18.17
- /b Jifih klistaqrqc, nuh ktclahemwenro myrxwrrqc.
- /p šínki-=č -kələsta·k·wé·k·we, ná=č ktəla·č·i·mwi·né·ɔ ma·e·x·we·é·k·we,
- /t If he refuses to listen to all of you, then you must report it when you all gather (in church).
- /k And if he shall neglect to hear them, tell it unto the church:

- /b Jwq jifi klistaqrqc myrxwrrqc,
- /p šúkw šínki-kələsta·k·wé·k·we ma·e·x·we·é·k·we,
- /t But if he refuses to listen to you when you gather (in church),
- /k but if he neglect to hear the church,

- /b nuh konu ktclenaonro nolwawsen ok motawsen.
- /p ná=č kóna ktəli·naɔ·né·ɔ nɔlo·wá·wsi·n ɔ́·k mɔt·á·wsi·n.
- /t then you must leave him to be a heathen and a sinner.
- /k let him be unto thee as an heathen man and a publican.

Mt 18.18
- /b Kvehe ktclwvmw, Krkwh kelwu rlextarq b tali vakif,
- /p khičí·i ktəllúhəmɔ, kéku=č ki·ló·wa e·li·xtáe·kw yú táli hák·ink,
- /t I say to you truly, anything you shall lay down as law here on earth
- /k Verily I say unto you, Whatsoever ye shall bind on earth

```
         /b   nuh nc li wlrlintasw tali osavkamc;
         /p   ná=č nə́ lí-wəle·ləntá·s·u táli ɔ·s·áhkame.
         /t   shall be acceptable that way in heaven.
         /k   shall be bound in heaven:

         /b   okh krkw mutu qvetvekrrqc b tali vakif,
         /p   ó·k=č kéku máta khwithike·é·k·we yú táli hák·ink,
         /t   And if you do not forbid something here on earth,
         /k   and whatsoever ye shall loose on earth

         /b   nuh nc li wlrlintasw tali osavkamc.
         /p   ná=č nə́ lí-wəle·ləntá·s·u táli ɔ·s·áhkame.
         /t   that shall be acceptable that way in heaven.
         /k   shall be loosed in heaven.

Mt 18.19 /b   Lupi ktclwvmw, Elih neju kelwu li wlrlintamrqc krkw wenwrrqc
         /p   lápi ktəllúhəmɔ, ílli=č ní·š·a ki·ló·wa lí-wəle·ləntamé·k·we kéku wi·nəwe·é·k·we,
         /t   Again I say to you, if even two of you agree for something to be when you pray,
         /k   Again I say unto you, That if two of you shall agree on earth as touching any thing
              that they shall ask,

         /b   Nwx tu osavkamc rpet nuh nc ktclevkwnro.
         /p   nó·x=tá ɔ·s·áhkame é·p·i·t ná=č nə́ ktəlihko·né·ɔ.
         /t   that will be how my father who is in heaven will treat you.
         /k   it shall be done for them of my Father which is in heaven.

Mt 18.20 /b   Rli cntu neju jitu nuxu marevtetc wunhi ntclswakun
         /p   é·li énta- ní·š·a ší=tá naxá -ma·e·ihtí·t·e wə́nči ntəlsəwá·k·an,
         /t   For, when two or three gather together acting for me,
         /k   For where two or three are gathered together in my name,

         /b   nrpch nwehi eku avpi.
         /p   né·pe=č nəwíči- íka -ahpí.
         /t   I shall also be present, too.
         /k   there am I in the midst of them.

Mt 18.21 /b   Nu Petul eku tclekapyen, tclao,
         /p   ná †pí·təl íka təli·k·á·p·ai·n, təlá·ɔ,
         /t   Then Peter came up to him and said to him,
         /k   Then came Peter to him, and said,

         /b   Tuh vuh txun mpuketatumaon nematis hanelyvetc?
         /p   "tá=č=háč txə́n mpak·i·t·a·t·amáɔ·n ní·mahtəs čani·lae·hí·t·e?
         /t   "How many times shall I forgive my brother if he mistreats me?
         /k   Lord, how oft shall my brother sin against me, and I forgive him?
```

	/b	nejvajh vuh txun?
	/p	ní·š·a·š=č=háč txə́n?"
	/t	Seven times?"
	/k	till seven times?

Mt 18.22 /b Nhesus tclao, Takw ktclwri nejvajh, txun,   [⟨ktclwri⟩: s.b. ⟨ntclwri⟩]
        /p nčí·sas təlá·ɔ, "takó· ntələwé·i, 'ní·š·a·š=č txə́n.'   [nt- emended from ⟨kt-⟩]
        /t Jesus said to him, "I don't say, 'Seven times.'
        /k Jesus saith unto him, I say not unto thee, Until seven times:

        /b ntclwc nejvajh txenk, txun nejvaj.   [⟨txenk⟩ for /txí·nxke/]
        /p ntə́ləwe 'ní·š·a·š=č txí·nxke txə́n ní·š·a·š.'
        /t I say, 'Seventy times seven.'
        /k but, Until seventy times seven.

Mt 18.23 /b Nc wunhi osavkamce sakemaokun mulaji sakema
        /p nə́ wə́nči, ɔ·s·ahkame·í·i-sa·k·i·ma·ó·k·an málahši sa·k·í·ma.
        /t Therefore, the kingdom of heaven is like a king,
        /k Therefore is the kingdom of heaven likened unto a certain king,

        /b kavtu avkintufc cntxrkvamakwk tolwkakunu.
        /p káhta-ahkəntánke entxe·khamá·k·uk tɔlo·ká·k·ana.
        /t when he wanted to count up how much he was owed by his servants.
        /k which would take account of his servants.

Mt 18.24 /b Mrhi rlumi avkintufc,
        /p mé·či é·ləmi-ahkəntánke,
        /t After he had begun counting it,
        /k And when he had begun to reckon,

        /b nu prjwalifc tclin txun tclin txapxki rlaotek rlrkvamakwk.   [⟨-lifc⟩ for /-línki/]
        /p ná pe·š·əwa·línki télən txə́n télən txá·pxki e·lá·ɔhti·k e·le·khamá·k·uk.
        /t then what one who was brought owed him was ten thousand dollars.
        /k one was brought unto him, which owed him ten thousand talents.

Mt 18.25 /b Jwq rli mutu wlataq krkw a rnvrt nu nrvlalkwki tclwrlen
        /p šúkw é·li- máta -wəlá·ta·kw kéku=á· é·nhe·t, ná nehəla·lkúk·i tələwé·li·n,
        /t But since he did not have anything he could pay, his master then said,
        /k But forasmuch as he had not to pay, his lord commanded

        /b my mvalumakrq, ok wehrohi, ok wnehanu ok wrmi krkw wrlvataq,
        /p 'mái-mhalamá·k·e·kw, ó·k wi·č·e·ó·č·i, ó·k wəni·č·á·na, ó·k wé·mi kéku we·lháta·kw,
        /t 'Go and sell him, and his wife and his children and everything he has,
        /k him to be sold, and his wife, and children, and all that he had,

	/b	wunhih kejrnvrt.
	/p	wə́nči-=č -ki·š·é·nhe·t.'
	/t	so that he shall be able to pay.'
	/k	and payment to be made.

Mt 18.26 /b Nu wunhi vakif laneven vokyu nu alwkakun, wenwumao, tclao,
/p nə́ wwə́nči- hákink -laníhi·n hókaya ná alo·ká·k·an, wwi·nəwamá·ɔ, təlá·ɔ,
/t Because of that, the servant threw himself down and begged him, saying to him,
/k The servant therefore fell down, and worshipped him, saying,

/b Ktumakrlumel prvel wrmih ktrnvwlun.
/p 'ktəma·k·é·ləmi·l; pé·hi·l; wé·mi=č kte·nhó·lən.'
/t 'Take pity on me; be patient with me (*lit.*, wait for me); I'll pay you everything.'
/k Lord, have patience with me, and I will pay thee all.

Mt 18.27 /b Nu wrtalwkakunumkwki qutumakrlumwkwn,
/p ná we·t·alo·ka·k·anəmkúk·i kwət·əma·k·e·ləmúk·o·n,
/t Then the one whose servant he was took pity on him,
/k Then the lord of that servant was moved with compassion,

/b ok pwnunwkw ok pwnrlintamakwn cntxrkvamat.
/p ó·k ppo·nənúk·u, ó·k ppo·ne·ləntamá·k·o·n entxe·kháma·t.   [*lit.*, 'forgot about it']
/t and released him, and forgave him what he owed.
/k and loosed him, and forgave him the debt.

Mt 18.28 /b Jwq nunul nu alwkakun krhetc
/p šúkw nánal ná alo·ká·k·an ke·č·í·t·e,
/t But when that same servant went out,
/k But the same servant went out,

/b nanc tuntu nron kwti wehi alwkakunu
/p ná=nə tə́nta-né·ɔ·n kwə́t·i wíči-alo·ká·k·ana,
/t he saw one of his fellow servants there,
/k and found one of his fellowservants,

/b tclrkvamakw avpami ct tclin ok nrwu rlaotck,
/p təle·khamá·k·u ahpá·mi=ét télən ó·k né·wa e·lá·ɔhti·k.
/t and (that one) owed him about fourteen dollars.
/k which owed him an hundred pence (*i.e.*, Roman denarii):

/b nu tolumi kpexqrnan, tclao ‖ Rnvael krkw rlrkvamaeun.
/p ná tólǝmi-kpi·xkwé·na·n, təlá·ɔ, 'e·nhái·l kéku e·le·khamaían.'
/t Then he began choking him, saying to him, 'Pay me what you owe me.'
/k and he laid hands on him, and took him by the throat, saying, Pay me that thou owest.

Mt 18.29 /b Nu nrl wehi alwkakunu vakif tclaneven vokyu, ok wenwumkw, tclkw,

[alwkakunu: ⟨alw |kakunu⟩]

(p. 111) /p ná né·l wíči-alo·ká·k·ana hákink təlaníhi·n hókaya, ó·k wwi·nəwámku, tə́lku,
/t Then his fellow servant threw himself down and begged him, saying to him,
/k And his fellowservant fell down at his feet, and besought him, saying,

/b Ktamakrlumel prvel, wrmih ktrnvwlun.
/p 'ktəma·k·é·ləmi·l; pé·hi·l; wé·mi=č kte·nhó·lən.'
/t 'Take pity on me; be patient with me (*lit.*, wait for me); I'll pay you everything.'
/k Have patience with me, and I will pay thee all.

Mt 18.30 /b Jwq mutu noxkwmaeo,
/p šúkw máta nɔxko·ma·í·ɔ.
/t But he did not assent to what the other asked.
/k And he would not:

/b nu moi puntaneven cvcntu kpavwtif tclih rnvrn tclrkvamwrokun.
/p ná mói-pəntaníhi·n ehə́nta-kpahó·t·ink, tə́li-=č -é·nhe·n təle·khamwe·ó·k·an.
/t Then he went and threw him into prison, so that he would pay his debt.
/k but went and cast him into prison, till he should pay the debt.

Mt 18.31 /b Nu wehi alwkakunwao nrvqevtetc rlsevtet jerlintamwk,
/p ná wiči-alo·ka·k·anəwá·ɔ ne·ykwihtí·t·e e·lsíhti·t, ši·e·lə́ntamo·k.
/t Then when their fellow servants saw what they did, they felt sorry.
/k So when his fellowservants saw what was done, they were very sorry,

/b ok moi lanro nrvlalqevtethi wrmi rlrk.
/p ó·k mói-la·né·ɔ nehəla·lkwihtí·č·i wé·mi é·le·k.
/t And they went and told their master everything that had been done.
/k and came and told unto their lord all that was done.

Mt 18.32 /b Nu nrvlalkwki mrhi wcnhemkwkc, tclkw, O mrtapret alwkukun,
/p ná nehəla·lkúk·i mé·či wenči·mkúk·e, tə́lku, 'ó·, me·t·a·p·é·i·t alo·ká·k·an.
/t Then his master, after he had summoned him, said to him, 'Oh, you wicked servant!
/k Then his lord, after that he had called him, said unto him, O thou wicked servant,

/b kpuketatamwlinrp wrmi nc ktclrkvamwrokun rli kavtatamun nc ntclsen.
/p kpak·i·t·a·t·amó·lənep wé·mi nə́ ktəle·khamwe·ó·k·an é·li-kahtá·t·aman nə́ ntə́lsi·n.
/t I forgave you all of your debt, because you desired that I do so.
/k I forgave thee all that debt, because thou desiredst me:

Mt 18.33 /b Mutu vuh a ma kutumakrlumaep kihi-alwkakun
/p máta=háč=á·=máh kkət·əma·k·e·ləmá·i·p kíči-alo·ká·k·an,
/t Shouldn't you have taken pity on your fellow servant
/k Shouldest not thou also have had compassion on thy fellowservant,

Text, Transcription, and Translation

/b   rli ne ktumakrlumilun.
/p   é·li- ní· -ktəma·k·e·ləmə́lan?'
/t   as *I* took pity on *you*?'
/k   even as I had pity on thee?

Mt 18.34 /b   Nu nrvlalkwki monwfselen,
/p   ná nehəla·lkúk·i mɔnunksí·li·n,
/t   Then his master was angry
/k   And his lord was wroth,

/b   qwlintvekrlen voky li cvcntu kpavwtif svaki pavkuntrnvrtc.
/p   kwələnthiké·li·n hɔ́k·ay lí ehə́nta-kpahó·t·ink sháki pahkante·nhé·t·e.
/t   and turned him over to the prison until he completely paid off his debt.
/k   and delivered him to the tormentors, till he should pay all that was due unto him.

Mt 18.35 /b   Nu ok nc ktclevkwnro osavkamre nu Nwx,
/p   ná ɔ́·k nə́ ktəlihko·né·ɔ ɔ·s·ahkame·í·i ná nó·x,
/t   That is also how my heavenly father treats you,
/k   So likewise shall my heavenly Father do also unto you,

/b   mutuh puvketatamarqc ktrvwaif wunhi kemavtwaok honawswakunwu.
/p   máta=č pahki·t·a·t·amaé·k·we ktehəwá·ink wə́nči ki·mahtəwá·ɔk čɔna·wsəwa·k·anúwa."
/t   if you will not forgive your brothers' misdeeds from your hearts."
/k   if ye from your hearts forgive not every one his brother their trespasses.

Chapter 61 (pp. 111-112). [L. section 61.] (Luke 9.51-57, 61-62.)
[Blanchard chapters numbered the same as Lieberkühn sections, 61-80.]

Lk 9.51 /b   Mrhi alumi tpisqevlrp lih vwqrbf wunhi wrttunan,   [⟨wrt-|tunan⟩]
/p   mé·či áləmi-tpəskwíhəle·p, lí·=č hukwé·yunk wə́nči -wé·t·əna·n.
/t   It had begun to be the time for him to be taken up to heaven.
/k   And it came to pass, when the time was come that he should be received up,

/b   nu amunhe Nhelwsulumif kavtu rp.
/p   ná amənčí·i †nči·lo·sələ́mink káhta-é·p.
/t   Then nevertheless he wanted to go to Jerusalem.
/k   he stedfastly set his face to go to Jerusalem,

Lk 9.52 /b   Linwu nekane lalwkalrp. Nu tolumskanro
/p   lə́nəwa ni·k·a·ní·i lalo·ká·le·p; ná tɔləmska·né·ɔ.
/t   He sent men ahead as messengers, and they departed.
/k   And sent messengers before his face: and they went,

	/b	eku pravtetc Sumrlei wtrnrtitif kotu wlyekaowao,
	/p	íka pe·ahtí·t·e †same·líɾ·i-o·t·e·ne·t·ə́t·ink, kɔ́t·a-wəlai·k·aɔwwá·ɔ.
	/t	When they arrived at a village of Samaria, they intended to arrange a place for him to stay.
	/k	and entered into a village of the Samaritans, to make ready for him.

Lk 9.53
	/b	jwq nrk wrtwtrnyethek mutu wifrlumaewao,
	/p	šúkw né·k we·t·o·t·e·naí·č·i·k máta wwinke·ləma·iwwá·ɔ,
	/t	But the villagers did not welcome him,
	/k	And they did not receive him,

	/b	rli nrovtet tcli Nhelwsulumif alen.
	/p	é·li-ne·ɔ́hti·t tə́li- †nči·lo·sələmink -á·li·n.
	/t	because they saw him to be going to Jerusalem.
	/k	because his face was as though he would go to Jerusalem.

Lk 9.54
	/b	Mrhi nc rlenamevtetc rkrkemathi, Nhimu ok Nhanu tclkw,
	/p	mé·či nə́ e·li·namihtí·t·e e·k·e·ki·má·č·i nčíma ɔ́·k nčá·na, tə́lku,
	/t	After his disciples Jim and John saw that, they said to him,
	/k	And when his disciples James and John saw this, they said,

	/b	Nrvlalerf mutu vuh a, nwcnhwtumwvwmnu tunty li osavkamc
	/p	"nehəlá·lienk, máta=háč=á· nəwenčo·t·əmo·húmənа tə́ntay lí ɔ·s·áhkame
	/t	"Master, should we not summon fire from heaven, [*lit.*, 'call to heaven for fire']
	/k	Lord, wilt thou that we command fire to come down from heaven,

	/b	wunhi a wrqviksevtet mulaji Elyusu rnifup?
	/p	wə́nči-=á· -we·khwiksíhti·t, málahši †i·layás·a ennínkəp?"
	/t	so that they would be burned up, like what Elias did?"
	/k	and consume them, even as Elias did?

Lk 9.55
	/b	Jwq ekali qwlwpe qetulao tclao;
	/p	šúkw íkali kwələp·i·, kkwi·təlá·ɔ, təlá·ɔ,
	/t	But he turned to them and admonished them, saying to them,
	/k	But he turned, and rebuked them, and said,

	/b	Takw kwavaewu tutu rlenaqset nc wcnheyek.
	/p	"takó· ko·wa·ha·íwwa tətá e·li·ná·kwsi·t nə́ wenčí·ai·k.
	/t	"You do not know what kind he that it comes from may be. [misunderstood?]
	/k	Ye know not what manner of spirit ye are of.

Lk 9.56
	/b	Rli linw Wrqesif mutu wunhi pat tcli a palevan rwrni, [⟨rwrni⟩ for ⟨awrni⟩]
	/p	é·li- lə́nu we·k·wí·s·ink máta -wə́nči-pá·t tə́li-=á· -palí·ha·n awé·ni,
	/t	For the man who is the Son did not come in order to destroy people,
	/k	For the Son of man is not come to destroy men's lives,

/b jwq tcli a lclrxrmvrn.
/p šúkw tə́li-=á· -lehəle·x·é·mhe·n."
/t but to save lives."
/k but to save them.

/b Nu pale wtrnif ton. ‖
/p ná palí·i o·t·é·nink tɔ́·n.
/t Then he went to another town. [*lit.*, went away to a town]
/k And they went to another village.

Lk 9.57 /b Nrlwxwctet kwti linw tclao, Nrvlaliun kwtrkwlin,
(p. 112) /p ne·lo·x·wéhti·t, kwə́t·i lə́nu təlá·ɔ, "nehəlá·lian, ko·t·e·kó·lən.
/t As they walked, a certain man said to him, "My lord, I'm going to follow you.
/k And it came to pass, that, as they went in the way, a certain man said unto him, Lord, I will follow thee [whithersoever thou goest.]

Lk 9.61 /b jwq vetami lrlumel nmai ofwman wekeu rpethek. [wekeu: ⟨wekəu⟩]
/p šúkw hítami lé·ləmi·l nəmái-ɔnkó·ma·n wí·k·ia e·p·í·č·i·k.
/t But first allow me to go and bid farewell to those living in my house.
/k [And another also said, Lord, I will follow thee;] but let me first go bid them farewell, which are at home at my house.

Lk 9.62 /b Nhesus tclao awrn a nrli talaxakeakun eku alinif qtukifwrxifc
/p nčí·sas təlá·ɔ, "awé·n=á·, né·li- talaxhakiá·k·an íka -alə́nink, kwtək·inkwe·x·ínke,
/t Jesus said to him, "If someone, with his hand on the plow, looks back,
/k And Jesus said unto him, No man, having put his hand to the plough, and looking back,

/b ta, vwtcpiavpewun Krtanitwet sokemaokunif.
/p tá=á· wtépi-ahpí·wən ke·tanət·ó·wi·t sɔ·k·i·ma·ɔ́·k·anink."
/t he would not be fit to be in the kingdom of God."
/k is fit for the kingdom of God.

Chapter 62 (pp. 112-114). (Luke 10.1-13, 15-24.)

Lk 10.1 /b Nu kcnh Nrvlalwrt qejeman linwu nejaj txenkc txwuk, [⟨nk⟩ for /nxk/]
/p ná kə́nč nehəlá·ləwe·t kwi·š·í·ma·n lə́nəwa, ní·š·a·š txí·nxke txúwak,
/t After that the Lord appointed men, seventy in number,
/k After these things the Lord appointed other seventy also,

/b nekane tclalwkalao wrmi nivneju li cntxif wtrnyu nrkuh prat.
/p ni·k·a·ní·i təlalo·ka·lá·ɔ wé·mi, nihəní·š·a lí éntxink o·t·é·naya né·k·a=č pé·a·t.
/t sending them all on ahead, two each to every town *he* was going to come to.
/k and sent them two and two before his face into every city and place, whither he himself would come.

Lk 10.2 /b Nunc wunhi lan, Xifwi mwnjskosek, jwq tatxetwuk mekumosthek.
            [⟨mekumosthek⟩ for ⟨mekumosethek⟩]
/p ná=nə wwə́nči-la·n, "xínkwi munšskhɔ́·s·i·k, šúkw ta·txí·t·əwak mi·kəmɔ·s·í·č·i·k.
/t Because of that he said to them, "Great is the harvest, but the workers are few.
/k Therefore said he unto them, The harvest truly is great, but the labourers are few:

/b Nanc wunhi patamw nu nrvlatuf mwnjskosek
/p ná=nə wə́nči-pá·tamo· ná nehəlá·t·ank munšskhɔ́·s·i·k,
/t Therefore pray to the manager of the harvest,
/k pray ye therefore the Lord of the harvest,

/b tcli a qeaqi peli eku lalwkalan cntu mwnjsqcf.
/p tə́li-=á· kwiá·kwi pí·li íka -lalo·ká·la·n énta-múnšskwenk.
/t that he should send still more (*lit.*, others) to where they are harvesting.
/k that he would send forth labourers into his harvest.

Lk 10.3 /b "Eku tu aq;
/p "íka=tá á·kw.
/t "Go there.
/k Go your ways:

/b punu ktclalwkalinro, mulaji mrketituk tumrekri.
/p pənáh, ktəlalo·kalləné·ɔ málahši meki·t·ə́t·ak təme·i·ké·i.
/t Look, I send you like lambs among wolves.
/k behold, I send you forth as lambs among wolves.

Lk 10.4 /b Kahi nuxpunc moni cvatrk kulinifvrq, jitu puntasunakun jitu, hepavko;
/p káči náxpəne móni ehháte·k kələnínkhe·kw, ší=tá pəntahsəná·k·an, ší=tá čípahkɔ.
/t Don't carry even a purse, or a tobacco bag, or shoes.
/k Carry neither purse, nor scrip, nor shoes:

/b ok kahi awrn ofwmerkrq nrlwxwrrq.
/p ɔ́·k káči awé·n ɔnko·mié·k·c·kw nc·lo·x·wć·c·kw.
/t And greet no one as you walk.
/k and salute no man by the way.

Lk 10.5 /b Wekwavmifh parqc, vetamih ktclwcvmw, Wlufwntwakunekch b wekwavmif.
/p wi·k·əwáhəmink=č pa·é·k·we, hítami=č ktələwéhəmɔ, "wəlankuntəwa·k·aní·k·eč yú wi·k·əwáhəmink.'
/t When you come to a house, you must first say, 'Let there be peace in this house.'
/k And into whatsoever house ye enter, first say, Peace be to this house.

Lk 10.6 /b Owlufwnsetetch kwlufwnswakunwuh topetakwnro;
/p ɔ·wəlankunsihtí·t·e=č, ko·lankunsəwa·k·anúwa=č tɔp·i·ta·k·o·né·ɔ.
/t If they are friendly, your friendliness shall be with them.
/k And if the son of peace be there, your peace shall rest upon it:

Text, Transcription, and Translation

/b kahih mutu, kwlufwnswakunwu lupih kwtxwkwnro,
/p káč·i=č máta, ko·lankunsəwa·k·anúwa lápi=č ko·txuk·o·né·ɔ.
/t But if not, your friendship will come back to you.
/k if not, it shall turn to you again.

Lk 10.7
/b Nunu nc wekwavmif myekrrqc
/p nána nə́ wi·k·əwáhəmink mai·k·e·é·k·we,
/t When you remain staying in the same house,
/k And in the same house remain,

/b mehemoc minrmoc tuktu krkw rxamwqrq;
/p mi·č·i·mɔ́·e, məne·mɔ́·e tákta kéku e·x·amúk·we·kw,
/t eat and drink whatever they give you.
/k eating and drinking such things as they give:

/b rli mcmekumoset tevtcpi wunhi rnvwnt.
/p é·li- mehəmi·kəmɔ́·s·i·t tihtépi -wə́nči-é·nhunt.
/t For a worker is compensated with the appropriate amount each time.
/k for the labourer is worthy of his hire.

/b Kahi peli wekwavmif li nuxkyelevrq.   [⟨ele⟩ for ⟨ela⟩, for /-ihəlá·-/(?)]
/p káči pí·li wi·k·əwáhəmink †lí-nahkɔ·ihəlá·he·kw.   [word conjectured]
/t Do not [go aimlessly(?)] to different houses.   [meaning conjectured]
/k Go not from house to house.

Lk 10.8
/b Ok a wtrnif parqc, wifrlumukrrqc,
/p ɔ́·k=á· o·t·é·nink pa·é·k·we, winke·ləmək·e·é·k·we,
/t And if you come to a town and you are welcomed,
/k And into whatsoever city ye enter, and they receive you,

/b kmehenroh krkw rlifwrxenrq vatakrrqc.
/p kəmi·č·i·né·ɔ=č kéku e·linkwe·x·í·ne·kw hata·k·e·é·k·we.
/t you must eat things when they are set before you.
/k eat such things as are set before you:

Lk 10.9
/b Kekrvwmroc cntxi nc tali palsehek,   [⟨-mroc⟩ for ⟨-moc⟩]
/p ki·k·e·ho·mɔ́·e éntxi- nə́ -táli-pa·lsí·č·i·k.
/t Heal as many of the sick as are there.
/k And heal the sick that are therein,

/b ktclawaokh, Krtanitwet sokemaokun kprxwsvekakwnro.
/p ktəlawwá·ok=č, 'ke·tanət·ó·wi·t sɔ·k·i·ma·ɔ́·k·an kpe·x·o·shika·k·o·né·ɔ.
/t You must say to them, 'The kingdom of God comes near you.'
/k and say unto them, The kingdom of God is come nigh unto you.

Lk 10.10 /b   Jwq a wtrnif parqc, mutu wfrlumukrrqc   [⟨wf-⟩ for ⟨wif-⟩]
/p   šúkw=á· o·t·é·nink pa·é·k·we, máta winke·lǝmǝk·e·é·k·we,
/t   But if you come to a town and you are not welcomed,
/k   But into whatsoever city ye enter, and they receive you not,

/b   eku amoc mwtumakunwaif, ktclawaokh;
/p   íka a·mɔ́·e mwǝt·ǝma·k·anǝwá·ink. ktǝlawwá·ɔk=č,
/t   go into their streets. You must say to them,
/k   go your ways out into the streets of the same, and say,

Lk 10.11 /b   Pwfq ktwtrnywaif eli wrmi prsavqevlaknvakynanif mpaovetrmunrn;
                                                                           [⟨-kn-⟩ for ⟨-k n-⟩]
/p   'púnkw kto·t·e·nayǝwá·ink ílli wé·mi pesahkwíhǝla·k nhak·ayǝná·nink mpawhitehǝmáne·n.
/t   'Even all the dust in your town that sticks to us we shake off.
/k   Even the very dust of your city, which cleaveth on us, we do wipe off against you:

/b   jwq kvehe ncni lrw, Krtanitwet sokemokun kpcxwsekakwnro. ‖
                                                               [⟨sokemokun⟩ for ⟨sokemaokun⟩]
/p   šúkw khičí·i nɔ́ni lé·w: ke·tanǝt·ó·wi·t sɔ·k·i·ma·ɔ́·k·an kpe·x·o·shika·k·o·né·ɔ.'
/t   But that is truly so: The kingdom of God comes near you.'
/k   notwithstanding be ye sure of this, that the kingdom of God is come nigh unto you.

Lk 10.12 /b   Ktclwvmw, Mifasrih lenamwk Satumebfu mukuni-kejqekc
(p. 113) /p   "ktǝllúhǝmɔ, minkahsé·i=č lí·namo·k †sa·tami·yúnka mǝkáni-ki·škwí·k·e
/t   "I tell you, it will go better for the people of Sodom on the last day
/k   But I say unto you, that it shall be more tolerable in that day for Sodom,

/b   rlenameteth nrk wrtwtrnyethek.
/p   e·li·namíhti·t=č né·k we·t·o·t·e·naí·č·i·k.
/t   than it will for those townspeople.
/k   than for that city.

Lk 10.13 /b   Avotukh ke, Kolrsin, ok ke Mpctsartc,
/p   áhɔhtǝk=č kí·, †kɔlé·sǝn, ɔ́·k kí·, †mpetsaé·te.
/t   It will be trouble for *you*, Chorazin, and for *you*, Bethsaida!
/k   Woe unto thee, Chorazin! woe unto thee, Bethsaida!

/b   rli kanjyvoswakun lenamrkup
/p   é·li- kanšaehɔ·s·ǝwá·k·an -li·namé·k·ǝp,
/t   For you have seen miracles,
/k   for [if the] mighty works [had been done in Tyre and Sidon, which] have been done in you,

	/b	Tyulifu a ok Sytunifu nc lenamevtetpanc,
	/p	†tayalínka=á· ɔ́·k †saitanínka nɔ́ li·namihti·tpáne,
	/t	(that) if the people of Tyre and Sidon had seen them,
	/k	[for] if the [mighty works] had been done in Tyre and Sidon, [which have been done in you,]

/b qulwpepanek a lelomwc
/p kwələp·í·p·ani·k=á· li·lɔ́·məwe,
/t they would long ago have repented,
/k they had a great while ago repented,

/b kuktumkavkwpanek a ok a pwfwf lumuvtapwpanek;   [⟨-mk-⟩ for ⟨-mak-⟩ or ⟨-muk-⟩; ⟨lumuvtap-⟩ 1x for ⟨lumutavp-⟩ 15x]
/p kəktəmakahkó·p·ani·k=á·, ɔ́·k=á· púnkunk ləmatahpó·p·ani·k.
/t and would have put on pitiful clothing and sat in ashes.
/k sitting in sackcloth and ashes.

Lk 10.15 /b ok ke Kpunium, qen kpunwntulilinrp,   [⟨Kp-⟩ for ⟨Kup-⟩]
/p ɔ́·k kí·, †kapɔ́niam, kwí·n kpənuntələláne·p,
/t And *you*, Capernaum, long have I shown them to you;
/k And thou, Capernaum, which art exalted to heaven,

/b homvakech ktclanrvmalkc.
/p †čɔ·mhákie=č ktəlanehəmá·lke.
/t You shall be thrown into the ground.
/k shalt be thrust down to hell.

Lk 10.16 /b Awrnh klistaqrqc ne fulsitaq,
/p "awé·n=č kələsta·k·wé·k·we, nkəlsət·a·kw.
/t "If anyone listens to you, they will listen to me.
/k He that heareth you heareth me;

/b okh awrn muvtrlumwqrqc, numutrlumwq ok prtalwkalelethi.
/p ɔ́·k=č awé·n mahte·ləmuk·wé·k·we, nəmat·é·ləmukw ɔ́·k pe·t·alo·ka·li·lí·č·i.
/t And if anyone scorns you, he shall scorn me and the one who sent me.
/k and he that despiseth you despiseth me; and [he that despiseth me despiseth] him that sent me.

Lk 10.17 /b Mrhi apavhevtetc nrk nejaj txenxkc, wlrlintamwwxwrok, tclawao   [⟨vh⟩ for ⟨h⟩]
/p mé·či a·p·a·č·ihtí·t·e né·k ní·š·a·š txí·nxke, wəle·ləntaməwo·x·wé·ɔk, təlawwá·ɔ,
/t After the seventy had returned, they walked joyfully and said to him,
/k And the seventy returned again with joy, saying,

	/b	Nrvlalirf, Mavtuntwuk ntalwvekaonanuk wunhi ktclswakun.
	/p	"nehəlá·lienk, mahtant·ó·wak ntaluhikaɔ·wəná·nak wə́nči ktəlsəwá·k·an."
	/t	"Master, we overpowered the devils by your power."
	/k	Lord, even the devils are subject unto us through thy name.

Lk 10.18	/b	Tclao, Nrop nuni mavtuntw tcli punevlan wunhi vwqrewf
	/p	təlá·ɔ, "nné·ɔ·p náni mahtánt·u tə́li-pəníhəla·n wə́nči hukwé·yunk,
	/t	He said to them, "I saw the devil fall from above,
	/k	And he said unto them, I beheld Satan [as lightning] fall from heaven.

	/b	mulaji sasapulrvlr tclkeqi kjevlan.
	/p	málahši sa·sa·p·əléhəle· təlkí·kwi-kšíhəla·n.
	/t	falling as fast as if there were lightning.
	/k	as lightning fall [from heaven].

Lk 10.19	/b	Punu kmelwvmw alwe liswakun, ktclih vupvekaonro xkwkuk,
	/p	pənáh, kəmillúhəmɔ aləwí·i-ləs·əwá·k·an, ktə́li-=č -haphikaɔ·né·ɔ xkó·k·ak,
	/t	Look, I give you power to step on snakes,
	/k	Behold, I give unto you power to tread on serpents

	/b	ok kanjiliset kenalwat mwxwrs ok wrmi tolwe liswakunwu jifalqrqek,
	/p	ɔ·k kánši-lə́s·i·t ki·ná·ləwa·t mó·x·we·s, ɔ·k wé·mi tɔləwí·i-ləs·əwa·k·anúwa šinka·lkwé·k·wi·k.
	/t	and on the powerful sharp-tailed bug, and on all the power of your enemies.
	/k	and scorpions, and over all the power of the enemy:

	/b	ok ta tcxi krkw kpalevkwvwmw.
	/p	ɔ·k tá=á· téxi kéku kpalihko·húmɔ.
	/t	And nothing at all will destroy you.
	/k	and nothing shall by any means hurt you.

Lk 10.20	/b	Kahi wlrlintamwvrq rli manutwuk alwvekarq,
	/p	káči wəlc·ləntamó·hc·kw ć·li- manət ó wak -aluɯíkae·kw.
	/t	Don't rejoice because you are greater than spirits.
	/k	Notwithstanding in this rejoice not, that the spirits are subject unto you;

	/b	jwq wunhi wlrlintamwq rli ktclwcnswakunwu lrkvasek tali osavkamc.
	/p	šúkw wə́nči-wəle·ló́ntamo·kw é·li- ktələwensəwa·k·anúwa -le·khá·s·i·k táli ɔ·s·áhkame."
	/t	But rejoice because your names are written in heaven."
	/k	but rather rejoice, because your names are written in heaven.

Lk 10.21	/b	Nu ncki Nhesus wlrlintumun wunhi vwtrvif, lwr,
	/p	ná-néke nčí·sas o·le·lə́ntamən wə́nči wté·hink, lúwe·,
	/t	At that time Jesus rejoiced from his heart and said,
	/k	In that hour Jesus rejoiced in spirit, and said,

/b Krnamul Nwxa Nrvlatamun osavkamc ok prmvakamekrk,
/p "kke·ná·məl, núxa·, nehəlá·t·aman ɔ·s·áhkame ɔ́·k pe·mhakamí·k·e·k,
/t "I thank you, father, lord of heaven and earth,
/k I thank thee, O Father, Lord of heaven and earth,

/b rli kuntvataot bl lrpohek, ok punwntulut memintitu.
/p é·li-kanthátaɔt yó·l le·p·ɔ́·č·i·k ɔ́·k -pənúntəlat mi·məntə́t·a.   [Why /-a/ obv.?]
/t as you concealed these things from the wise and showed them to children.
/k that thou hast hid these things from the wise and prudent, and hast revealed them unto babes:

/b Nanc lrw Nwxa, rli nunc ktetrvan.
/p ná=nə lé·w, núxa·, é·li ná=nə kti·t·é·ha·n.
/t That is so, father, as that is what you wished.
/k even so, Father; for so it seemed good in thy sight.

Lk 10.22 /b Wrmi krkw nvakrf ntatakwn Nwx,
/p wé·mi kéku nhák·enk nta·tá·k·o·n nó·x.
/t All things were placed in me by my father.
/k All things are delivered to me of my Father:

/b takw awrn wavaeo Wrqesifi jwq Wrtwxumunt,
/p takó· awé·n o·wa·ha·í·ɔ we·k·wi·s·ínki, šúkw we·t·ó·x·əmənt.
/t No one knows the Son but the Father.
/k and no man knoweth who the Son is, but the Father;

/b ok mutu awrn wavaeo Wrtwxifi, jwq Wrqesif,
/p ɔ́·k máta awé·n o·wa·ha·í·ɔ we·t·o·x·ínki, šúkw we·k·wí·s·ink,
/t And no one knows the Father but the Son,
/k and who the Father is, but the Son,

/b ok awrni kotu watulan Wrqesif.
/p ɔ́·k awé·ni kɔ́t·a-wwá·təla·n we·k·wí·s·ink."
/t and the son desires to reveal him to people."
/k and he to whom the Son will reveal him.

Lk 10.23 /b Nu eku tcli qulwpen rkrkemahi, keme tclao,
/p ná íka tə́li-kwələ́p·i·n e·k·e·ki·má·č·i, ki·mí·i təlá·ɔ,
/t Then he turned to his disciples and said to them secretly,
/k And he turned him unto his disciples, and said privately,

/b Wlapcnswbu wijkifwao cntxi nrmvetet krkw kelwu nrmrq;   [⟨kel-‖wu⟩]
/p "wəla·p·ensó·yəwa wəškinkəwá·ɔ éntxi-ne·mhíti·t kéku ki·ló·wa né·me·kw.
/t "Blessed are the eyes of as many as see the things *you* see.
/k Blessed are the eyes which see the things that ye see:

Lk 10.24 /b rli ktclwvmw, Xrli nrnekanewrwsetpunifu ok sakemawfu
(p. 114) /p é·li ktəllúhəmɔ, xé·li nehəni·k·a·ní·i-we·wsi·tpanínka ɔ́·k sa·k·i·ma·únka
          /t For, I tell you, many ancient prophets and kings
          /k For I tell you, that many prophets and kings

          /b kotu nrmunrop krkw kelwu nrmrq, jwq mutu wnrmwnro,
          /p kɔ́t·a-ne·məné·ɔ·p kéku ki·ló·wa né·me·kw, šúkw máta wəne·mo·wəné·ɔ,
          /t desired to see the things *you* have seen but did not see them,
          /k have desired to see those things which ye see, and have not seen them;

          /b ok kotu puntamunrop, kelwu puntamrq, jwq mutu pwntamwnro.
          /p ɔ́·k kɔ́t·a-pəntaməné·ɔ·p ki·ló·wa péntame·kw, šúkw máta pwəntamo·wəné·ɔ."
          /t and desired to hear what *you* have heard but did not hear it."
          /k and to hear those things which ye hear, and have not heard them.

Chapter 63 (pp. 114-115). (Luke 10.25-37.)

Lk 10.25 /b Nu posqen mawsw wrovat lrkvekanu koqrhevao tclao
          /p ná póskwi·n má·wsu we·ɔ́·ha·t le·khí·k·ana, kɔk·we·č·i·há·ɔ, təlá·ɔ,
          /t Then one who knew books stood up and tested (or tempted) him, saying to him,
          /k And, behold, a certain lawyer stood up, and tempted him, saying,

          /b Nrvlaleun, Ta vuh a ntclsen wunhi a nevlatamu rvulumakumek pumawswakun?
          /p "nehəlá·lian, tá=háč=á· ntɔ́lsi·n wənči·=á· -nihəlá·t·ama ehaləmá·kami·k pəma·wsəwá·k·an?"
          /t "My Lord, what should I do to in order to have (*lit.* own) eternal life?"
          /k Master, what shall I do to inherit eternal life?

Lk 10.26 /b Tclao, krkw ksi lrkvasw lrkvekunif?
          /p təlá·ɔ, "kéku=ksí le·khá·s·u le·khí·k·anink?"
          /t He said to him, "Well, what is written in the law?"
          /k He said unto him, What is written in the law? [how readest thou?]

Lk 10.27 /b Tclao Ktavoluh Nrvlalkon Krtanetwet wunhi msithri ktrvif,   [⟨-net-⟩ for ⟨-nit-⟩]
          /p təlá·ɔ, "ktahɔ́·la=č nehəlá·lkɔn ke·tanət·ó·wi·t wənči məsəč·é·i kté·hink,
          /t He said to him, "You must love your Lord God with all your heart,
          /k And he answering said, Thou shalt love the Lord thy God with all thy heart,

          /b ok msithri wunhi ktunaprokunif, ok wunhi msithri khetaniswakunif, ok msithri wunhi kpunyrlintumwakunif,
          /p ɔ́·k məsəč·é·i wənči ktənna·p·e·ɔ́·k·anink, ɔ́·k wənči məsəč·é·i kči·t·anəs·əwá·k·anink, ɔ́·k məsəč·é·i wənči kpəna·eləntaməwá·k·anink,
          /t and with all your soul, and with all your strength, and with all your understanding,
          /k and with all thy soul, and with all thy strength, and with all thy mind;

Lk 10.28

/b okh ktavolu rlafwmut rlkeqi avolat kvaky.
/p ó·k=č ktahó·la e·lankó·mat e·lkí·kwi-ahó·lat khák·ay."
/t and you must love your kinsman as much as you love yourself."
/k and thy neighbour as thyself.

Lk 10.28
/b Tclao, Kwli nuxkwmul; ncni a liseunc klclrxr.
/p təlá·ɔ, "kó·li-naxkó·məl; nə́ni=á· ləs·iáne, kəlehəlé·x·e."
/t He said to him, "I answered you right[!; error for 'you answered me right']; if you do that, you will live."
/k And he said unto him, Thou hast answered right: this do, and thou shalt live.

Lk 10.29
/b Jwq rli wlrlinset, tclao, Awrn vuh ntclafwmu?
/p šúkw é·li-wəle·lə́nsi·t təlá·ɔ, "awé·n=háč ntəlankó·ma?"
/t But as he thought well of himself he said to him, "Who is my kinsman?"
/k But he, willing to justify himself, said unto Jesus, And who is my neighbour?

Lk 10.30
/b Nhesus noxkwmao tclao,
/p nčí·sas nɔxko·má·ɔ, təlá·ɔ,
/t Jesus answered him, saying to him,
/k And Jesus answering said,

/b Awrn Nhelwsulumif wcnhi alumskatup ratup Hclikwuf
/p "awé·n †nči·lo·sələmink wénči-aləmská·t·əp, e·á·t·əp †čelikó·wunk,
/t "There was someone who set out from Jerusalem and was going to Jericho,
/k A certain man went down from Jerusalem to Jericho,

/b jwq muvtalrp krvkumwtkrsu
/p šúkw mahtále·p kehkəmo·tké·s·a.
/t but he came upon (*lit.*, caught up to) some thieves.
/k and fell among thieves,

/b nu nrk wvhekunanro rqelwt, ok pwpavkumawao,
/p ná né·k wči·k·əna·né·ɔ e·k·wí·li·t, ó·k pupahkamawwá·ɔ.
/t And they then robbed him of his clothing and beat him.
/k which stripped him of his raiment, and wounded him,

/b nu kunh pwnunanro
/p ná kə́nč ppo·nəna·né·ɔ.
/t And *then* they let him go
/k and departed,

/b nanc wvjcfexenun kavti uful.
/p ná=nə wšenki·x·í·nən, káhti-ánkəl.
/t And he lay there, almost dead.
/k leaving him half dead.

Lk 10.31 /b   Tamsc nu eku pon wrvevwfrt, nrotc wokaxwrnu.
/p   támse ná íka pón wehi·húnke·t, ne·ó·t·e, wo·ka·x·wé·na.
/t   Then at some point a priest came there and, when he saw him, walked around him.
/k   And by chance there came down a certain priest that way: and when he saw him, he passed by on the other side.

Lk 10.32 /b   Nu ok tamsc Lepae linw eku pwmskan
/p   ná ó·k tá·mse †li·paí·i-lənu íka pwə́mska·n,
/t   Then another time a Levite man went by there;
/k   And likewise a Levite, when he was at the place,

/b   pwnao jwq, nu tcli lwen.
/p   pwənaó·ɔ šúkw, ná təli-ló·wi·n.
/t   he only looked at him and proceeded to pass by.
/k   came and looked on him, and passed by on the other side.

Lk 10.33 /b   Jwq Sumrlie linw ovlumi wunheyet nrlwxrt wnro jcfexif
/p   šúkw †same·líí·i-lənu, óhələmi wənčí·ai·t, ne·ló·x·we·t wəne·ó·ɔ šenkí·x·ink.
/t   But a man of Samaria, from far away, as he was walking, saw the one lying there.
/k   But a certain Samaritan, as he journeyed, came where he was: and when he saw him,

/b   nu eku ton qwtumakrlumao,
/p   ná íka tó·n, kwət·əma·k·e·ləmá·ɔ.
/t   Then he went to him, and he had pity on him.
/k   he had compassion on him, [Lk 10.34] And went to him, ...

Lk 10.34 /b   nu wexqrptaon rvalvetrvolif, toxepelao pumi ok mrxprku   [⟨xp⟩ for ⟨xkp⟩]
/p   ná wwi·xkwe·ptáɔ·n ehalhitehó·link, tɔx·i·pi·lá·ɔ pəmí ó·k me·xkpé·k·a.
/t   Then he bound up his wounds, treating him with oil and wine.
/k   ... and bound up his wounds, pouring in oil and wine,

/b   nevlahi tolwmwnsif tovlao eku tclwxolao myekre kaonif,   [⟨-re ka-⟩ for ⟨-reka-⟩]
/p   nihəláči tɔləmúnsink tɔhəlá·ɔ, íka təlo·x·ɔlá·ɔ mai·k·e·i·k·á·ɔnink.
/t   He set him on his own animal and took him to an inn.
/k   and set him on his own beast, and brought him to an inn,

/b   nu tuntu krnavkevan.
/p   nə́ tə́nta-ke·nahkí·ha·n.
/t   And there he took care of him.
/k   and took care of him.

Lk 10.35 /b   Nu rluvparkc rlumi alumskatc,
/p   ná e·lahpa·é·k·e é·ləmi-aləmskát·e,

| | /t | Then the next morning, when he was going to depart, |
| | /k | And on the morrow when he departed, |

	/b	neju monetitu ktunum mwelan wrekelehi, tclao,
	/p	ní·š·a mɔni·t·ə́t·a ktə́nəm, mwí·la·n we·i·k·i·lí·č·i, təlá·ɔ.
	/t	he took out two coins and gave them to the one who had the house, saying to him,
	/k	he took out two pence, and gave them to the host, and said unto him,

	/b	Krnavke tutuh cntxi alwe txi afvetaon apaheanch, ktrnvwlun. [⟨ktrnv-‖wlun⟩]
	/p	'ké·nahki·; tətá=č éntxi- aləwí·i txí -ankhítaɔn, a·p·a·č·iá·ne=č kte·nhó·lən.'
	/t	'Take care of him; whatever amount more it costs you (*lit.*, you lose) I shall pay you when I return.'
	/k	Take care of him; and whatsoever thou spendest more, when I come again, I will repay thee.

Lk 10.36 /b Bqc ta vuh rlenaqselehi tclafwmao nrl nuxa linwu nu mrtalatup krvkumwtkrsu?
(p. 115) /p yúkwe, tá=háč e·li·na·kwsi·lí·č·i təlanko·má·ɔ né·l naxá lə́nəwa ná me·t·alá·t·əp kehkəmo·tké·s·a?
 /t Now, which one of those three men was a kinsman of the one who had come upon the thieves?"
 /k Which now of these three, thinkest thou, was neighbour unto him that fell among the thieves?

Lk 10.37 /b Tclao, Nunulik nrl krtumakrlumwqki,
 /p təlá·ɔ, "nanáli=k né·l ke·t·əma·k·e·ləmúkwki."   [obv. continued from Lk 10.36]
 /t He said to him, "Well, he was the one who took pity on him."
 /k And he said, He that shewed mercy on him.

 /b Nhesus tclao, My krpc nanc lisel.
 /p nčí·sas təlá·ɔ, "mái- ké·pe ná=nə -lə́s·i·l."
 /t Jesus said to him, "Go and also do like that yourself."
 /k Then said Jesus unto him, Go, and do thou likewise.

Chapter 64 (p. 115). (Luke 10.38-42.)

Lk 10.38 /b Mrhi rlumskavtetc nc wunhi, eku prpanek peli wtrnif,
 /p mé·či e·ləmskahtí·t·e nə́ wə́nči, íka pé·p·ani·k pí·li o·t·é·nink.
 /t After they went on from there, they came to another village.
 /k Now it came to pass, as they went, that he entered into a certain village:

 /b avpwp nc tali xqr lwcnswp Masi,
 /p ahpó·p nə́ táli xkwé·, luwénso·p má·si;
 /t And there lived there a woman named Martha.
 /k and a certain woman named Martha

	/b	nul nu tcli wlrlintumun moekrtakwn.
	/p	nál=ná tə́li-wəle·lə́ntamən mɔi·k·e·tá·k·o·n.
	/t	She it was who was glad for him to stay with her.
	/k	received him into her house.

Lk 10.39
	/b	Mwesu lwcnswp Mrles,
	/p	mwí·s·a luwénso·p mé·li·s,
	/t	And she had an older sister named Mary,
	/k	And she had a sister called Mary,

	/b	ok nul nu Nhesus rlsetrxif wlumutupen
	/p	ó·k nál=ná nčí·sas e·lsi·t·é·x·ink wələmahtáp·i·n,
	/t	and she it was that sat at Jesus's feet
	/k	which also sat at Jesus' feet,

	/b	ave qwlsitumulen toptwnakun.
	/p	áhi kwəlsət·améli·n tɔ·pto·ná·k·an.
	/t	and listened intently to his talk.
	/k	and heard his word.

Lk 10.40
	/b	Masi eanri xrlrnaoki li mekwmoswp;
	/p	má·si ya·né·i xe·lennáɔhki lí-mi·kəmɔ́·s·o·p.
	/t	Martha was always performing many different tasks.
	/k	But Martha was cumbered about much serving,

	/b	tamsc nu Masi eku ton, tclao,
	/p	tá·mse ná má·si íka tó·n, təlá·ɔ,
	/t	At some point then Martha went over and said to him,
	/k	and came to him, and said,

	/b	Nrvlaleun mutu vuh krkw ktetrvai, rli numes mutu kavtu wehumet?
	/p	"nehəlá·lian, máta=háč kéku kti·t·e·há·i, é·li- nəmí·s máta -káhta-wí·č·əmi·t?
	/t	"My lord, don't you care about how my older sister does not want to help me?
	/k	Lord, dost thou not care that my sister hath left me to serve alone?

	/b	lul wehumetch.
	/p	lə́l, wi·č·əmí·t·eč."
	/t	Tell her, she should help me."
	/k	bid her therefore that she help me.

Lk 10.41
	/b	Jwq Nhesus tclao, Masi Masi, krvlu krxrnaoki kwejiki lumekumosi;
	/p	šúkw nčí·sas təlá·ɔ, "má·si, má·si, kéhəla ke·x·ennáɔhki kəwi·šíki-lami·kəmɔ́·s·i.
	/t	But Jesus said to her, "Martha, Martha, you work hard at quite a few things.
	/k	And Jesus answered and said unto her, Martha, Martha, thou art careful and troubled about many things:

Lk 10.42 /b jwq a kwtrnaoki kwrtinum.
/p šúkw=á· kwət·ennáɔhki kəwé·t·ənəm.
/t But you should take one thing.
/k But one thing is needful:

/b Mrles mrhi nuni tclsen ok ta vuji awrn koski hekunawun.
/p mé·li·s mé·či nə́ni tə́lsi·n, ɔ́·k tá=á· háši awé·n kɔ́ski-či·k·əná·wən."
/t Mary has done that, and no one will ever be able to take it away from her."
/k and Mary hath chosen that good part, which shall not be taken away from her.

Chapter 65 (pp. 115-116). (Luke 11.1-13.)

Lk 11.1 /b Tamsc nu potuman, alu patumatc, nu mawsw rkrkemunt tclan,
/p tá·mse ná pɔ́·tama·n; ála-pa·tamá·t·e, ná má·wsu e·k·e·kí·mənt tə́la·n,
/t Then one time he prayed, and when he stopped praying, one disciple said to him,
/k And it came to pass, that, as he was praying in a certain place, when he ceased, one of his disciples said unto him,

/b Navlaliun wuntumaenrn rlih patumarf,   [⟨Navl-⟩ for ⟨Nrvl-⟩]
/p "nehəlá·lian, wəntamaí·ne·n é·li-=č -pa·tamá·enk,
/t "My lord, tell us how we shall pray,
/k Lord, teach us to pray,

/b mulaji Nhanu rli wuntumaotup rkrkemahi.
/p málahši nčá·na é·li-wəntamaɔ́·t·əp e·k·e·ki·má·č·i."
/t like how John told his disciples."
/k as John also taught his disciples.

Lk 11.2 /b Tclao patamrqch ktvlwcvmw,   [⟨ktvl-⟩ for ⟨ktcl-⟩]
/p təlá·ɔ, "pa·tamé·k·we=č ktələwéhəmɔ:
/t He said to them, "When you pray you must say:
/k And he said unto them, When ye pray, say,

/b Wrtwxomulrf rpeun osavkamc, xifovkunemvkotkch ktclwcnswakun.
/p 'we·t·o·x·əmɔ́lenk, é·p·ian ɔ·s·áhkame, xinkɔhkəni·mkɔ́tkeč ktələwensəwá·k·an.
/t 'You who are our father, who are in heaven, may your name be praised.
/k Our Father which art in heaven, Hallowed be thy name.

/b Prrekch ksakemaokun.
/p pe·e·í·k·eč ksa·k·i·ma·ɔ́·k·an.
/t May your kingdom come.
/k Thy kingdom come.

	/b	Ktetvrokun lrkch xqetvameqc rlkeqi lrk tali osavkamc.
		[⟨-tvr-⟩ for ⟨-trvr-⟩; ⟨-tvam-⟩ for ⟨-tvakam-⟩]
	/p	kti·t·e·he·ɔ́·k·an lé·k·eč xkwi·thakamí·k·we e·lkí·kwi·lé·k táli ɔ·s·áhkame.
	/t	May your will be done on earth, to the same degree that it is done in heaven.
	/k	Thy will be done, as in heaven, so in earth.

Lk 11.3
- /b Melenrn cntxun kejqek tcpi meherf,
- /p mi·lí·ne·n yúkwe kí·škwi·k tépi mí·č·ienk.
- /t Give us today enough for us to eat.
- /k Give us day by day our daily bread.

Lk 11.4
- /b pavketrlintumaenrn nhanawswakuninu; rli nelwnu puvketatumarf cntxi hihanelacqrfek;
- /p ɔ́·k pahki·t·e·ləntamaí·ne·n nčana·wsəwa·k·anəna, é·li- ni·ló·na -pahki·t·a·t·amáenk éntxi-čəčani·laehkwénki·k,
- /t And forgive our misdeeds for us, as we forgive all those that mistreat us.
- /kl And forgive us our sins; for we also forgive every one that is indebted to us.
- /cp And forgive us our trespasses, as we forgive them that trespass against us.

- /b ok kahi paevrf avqrhevtwakunif, jwq pale linenrn wunhi mrtvikif. ‖
- /p ɔ́·k káči pa·í·henk ahkwe·č·ihtəwá·k·anink, šúkw palí·i laní·ne·n wənči me·thíkink.'"
- /t And may we not come into temptation; but remove us from evil.'"
- /k And lead us not into temptation; but deliver us from evil.

Lk 11.5 (p. 116)
- /b Tclao, tamsc a kelwu, awrn wetesetc, lai tpwqekc eku atc;
- /p təlá·ɔ, "tá·mse=á· ki·ló·wa awé·n wwi·t·i·s·í·t·e, lá·i-tpo·kwí·k·e íka á·t·e,
- /t He said to them, "If one of you has a friend, and maybe goes to him at midnight
- /k And he said unto them, Which of you shall have a friend, and shall go unto him at midnight,

- /b my latc, nhw, Kekaevi nuxu avponu,
- /p mái lá·t·e, 'nčú, ki·kaí·hi naxá ahpɔ́·na,
- /t and says to him, 'Friend, lend me three loaves of bread,
- /k and say unto him, Friend, lend me three loaves;

Lk 11.6
- /b rli netes nwtxwq, ovlumi wcnheaet, fwelu krkw xamu.
- /p é·li ní·t·i·s nó·txukw, ɔ́həlami wenčí·ai·t, nkwí·la- kéku -xáma,'
- /t as a friend of mine from far away has come to me and I have nothing to feed him,'
- /k For a friend of mine in his journey is come to me, and I have nothing to set before him?

Lk 11.7
- /b Nu lamekwavmc wunhi lwqkc, kahi sukwevevun; rli kpavasek,
- /p ná la·mi·k·əwáhəme wənči lúkwke, 'káči sak·wi·hí·han, é·li-kpahá·s·i·k,

Text, Transcription, and Translation 385

/t and then if he says to him from inside the house, 'Don't bother me, as the door is shut, ['if he says to him': should be 'would he say to you']
/k And he from within shall answer and say, Trouble me not: the door is now shut,

/b ok ntameminsumuk nweprmkwk,
/p ó·k ntami·mə́nsəmak nəwi·pé·mko·k;
/t and my children are in bed with me;
/k and my children are with me in bed;

/b ta fuski amwei, ok melulwi.
/p tá=á· nkáski-a·mwí·i ó·k -milló·wi.' [or /-mi·ləló·wi/]
/t I won't be able to get up and give you any.'
/k I cannot rise and give thee.

Lk 11.8 /b Ktclwvmw, taa wunhi amwewun rli weteset,
/p ktəllúhəmɔ, tá=á· wwə́nči-a·mwí·wən é·li-wwi·t·í·s·i·t,
/t I say to you, he would not get up because he is his friend,
/k I say unto you, Though he will not rise and give him, because he is his friend,

/b jwk rli wenwumvkwk wunhi a amwen, ok melan cntxi kavtatumulet.
/p šúkw é·li-wi·nəwámkuk wwə́nči-=á· -á·mwi·n, ó·k -mí·la·n éntxi-kahta·t·améli·t.
/t but because he asked him he would get up and give him as many as he wants.
/k yet because of his importunity he will rise and give him as many as he needeth.

Lk 11.9 /b Ok ktclwvmw, Wenwrq, kmelkrnroh; ntwnamwq, kmuxkamunroh,
/p ó·k ktəllúhəmɔ, wí·nəwe·kw, kəmi·lke·né·ɔ=č; ntó·namo·kw, kəmaxkaməné·ɔ=č;
/t And I say to you, ask and it shall be given to you; seek it and you shall find it;
/k And I say unto you, Ask, and it shall be given you; seek, and ye shall find;

/b pwpwvetcmwq, ktwfjrnumakrnroh.
/p pəp·uhhitéhəmo·kw, ktunkše·nəma·k·e·né·ɔ=č.
/t knock on the door, and it shall be opened for you.
/k knock, and it shall be opened unto you.

Lk 11.10 /b Rli wrmi cntxi wenwrhek melanro, ok cntxi ntwnufek moxkamunro,
/p é·li wé·mi éntxi-wi·nəwé·č·i·k mi·la·né·ɔ, ó·k éntxi-nto·nánki·k mɔxkaməné·ɔ,
/t For, to all who ask it is given; and all who seek, find;
/k For every one that asketh receiveth; and he that seeketh findeth;

/b ok cntxi pwpwvetrvufek twfjrnamaonro. [⟨-maonro⟩: 1st ⟨o⟩ incomplete, like ⟨c⟩]
/p ó·k éntxi-pəp·uhhitehánki·k tunkše·nəmaɔ·né·ɔ.
/t and to all who knock on the door, it is opened.
/k and to him that knocketh it shall be opened.

Lk 11.11 /b   Mrawset kelwu qesetc, wenwumvkwkc avpon qesu,
/p   me·á·wsi·t ki·ló·wa kkwi·s·í·t·e, wi·nəwamkúk·e ahpɔ́·n kkwí·s·a,
/t   If one of you has a son, and if his son asks him for bread,
/k   If a son shall ask bread of any of you that is a father,

/b   mwelao vuh a asun?
/p   mwi·lá·ɔ=háč=á· ahsə́n?
/t   will he give him a stone?
/k   will he give him a stone?

/b   Jitu ntwxtaqc namrsu, mwelao vuh a xkwku?
/p   ší=tá nto·xtá·k·we namé·s·a, mwi·lá·ɔ=háč=á· xkó·k·a?
/t   Or if he asks for a fish, will he give him a snake?
/k   or if he ask a fish, will he for a fish give him a serpent?

Lk 11.12 /b   Jitu ntwxtaqc ool, mwelao vuh a kanji luselehi mwxwrsu?
/p   ší=tá nto·xtá·k·we ɔ́·ɔl, mwi·lá·ɔ=háč=á· kánši-ləs·i·lí·č·i mo·x·wé·s·a?
/t   Or if he asks for an egg, will he give him a powerful bug.
/k   Or if he shall ask an egg, will he offer him a scorpion?

Lk 11.13 /b   Taoni kmuhi lclrxrvmw, jwq kneta tavpalawaok knehanwaok;
/p   tá·oni kəmáči-lehəle·x·éhəmɔ, šúkw kəní·ta·-tahpa·lawwá·ɔk kəni·č·a·nəwá·ɔk,
/t   You live evilly, but even so you're good at taking care of your children.
/k   If ye then, being evil, know how to give good gifts unto your children:

/b   Krvlu nu, Kwxwu osavkamc rpet alwei
/p   kéhəla ná kó·x·əwa ɔ·s·áhkame é·p·i·t aləwí·i
/t   Surely your father who is in heaven even more
/k   how much more shall your heavenly Father

/b   wifi melao pelselehi manutwu, awrni wenwumkwkc.
/p   wwínki-mi·lá·ɔ pi·lsi·lí·č·i manət·ó·wa awé·ni wi·nəwamkúk·e."
/t   willingly gives the holy spirit to anyone if he asks him."
/k   give the Holy Spirit to them that ask him?

Chapter 66 (pp. 116-118). (Luke 11.37-54.)

Lk 11.37 /b   Nrli krkw lwrt, mawsw Paluse tclao, My wepwmi.
/p   né·li- kéku -lúwe·t, má·wsu †pá·lasi təlá·ɔ, "mái-wi·pó·mi."
/t   As he was speaking, a certain Pharisee said to him, "Come and eat with me."
/k   And as he spake, a certain Pharisee besought him to dine with him:

/b   Eku rli tumekrtc mijakr, nu tcli metsen.
/p   íka é·li-təmi·k·é·t·e, məšá·ke·, ná tɔ́li-mí·tsi·n.

Text, Transcription, and Translation

/t   When he entered there, he sat down and proceeded to eat.
/k   and he went in, and sat down to meat.

Lk 11.38 /b Mrhi nu Palase nrotc, kanjrluntum rli mutu kjelunhrlet nrsko metselet.
          /p mé·či na †pá·lasi ne·ó·t·e, kanše·ləntam é·li- máta -kši·lənčé·li·t né·skɔ mi·tsí·li·t.
          /t When the Pharisee saw him, he was astonished that he did not wash his hands before he ate.
          /k And when the Pharisee saw it, he marvelled that he had not first washed before dinner.

Lk 11.39 /b Nu Nrvlalwrt tclan; Kelwu Paluscok, ktclsenro,
          /p ná nehəlá·ləwe·t tə́la·n, "ki·ló·wa †pa·ləsi·í·ɔk ktəlsi·né·ɔ,
          /t Then the Lord said to him, "You Pharisees do it.
          /k And the Lord said unto him, Now do ye Pharisees

          /b kpeletwnro, jwq kpaintumwao, ok kwlakcnswao, xqihi wunhi;
          /p kpi·li·to·né·ɔ šúkw kpaintəməwá·ɔ ɔ́·k ko·la·k·ensəwá·ɔ xkwíči wə́nči.
          /t You only clean your cups and your dishes on the outside.
          /k make clean the outside of the cup and the platter;

          /b jwq ave neske krkw eku vatr lamwfwc,
          /p šúkw áhi-ní·ski-kéku íka hát·e· la·múnkwe,
          /t But a very foul thing is inside,
          /k but your inward part is full

          /b kmwthrokunif, ok mrtvikif wcnheyek.   [⟨kmwthr-⟩ for ⟨kmwtkr-⟩]
          /p kəmo·tke·ɔ́·k·anink ɔ́·k me·thíkink wenčí·ai·k.
          /t which comes from thieving and evil.
          /k of ravening and wickedness.

Lk 11.40 /b Kwphavmw,
          /p kkəpčáhəmɔ.
          /t You are foolish.
          /k Ye fools,

          /b mutu vuh nul nu kwti awrn toletwun nc ‖ xqihi ok nc lamwfwc?
          /p máta=háč nál=ná kwə́t·i awé·n təli·tó·wən nə́ xkwíči ɔ́·k nə́ la·múnkwe?
          /t Wasn't it the same being who made the outside and the inside?
          /k did not he that made that which is without make that which is within also?

Lk 11.41 /b alwe wlit kutumakrluman krtumakset;
(p. 117) /p aləwí·i-wəlát kkət·əma·k·é·ləma·n ke·t·əmá·ksi·t.
          /t It is better for you to take pity on one who is poor.
          /k But rather give alms of such things as ye have;

/b   punu va pelit wrmi krkw wrlvataon.
/p   pənáh=á· pí·lət wé·mi kéku we·lhátaɔn.
/t   And, see, everything you have would be clean.
/k   and, behold, all things are clean unto you.

Lk 11.42 /b   Kutumakawsevmw kelwu Paluseok,
/p   kkət·əma·k·a·wsíhəmɔ ki·ló·wa †pa·ləsi·í·ɔk.
/t   You Pharisees are miserable wretches.
/k   But woe unto you, Pharisees!

/b   rli awrn wrlvataqc tclin pwntif eli wifemakvoki jitu wifufi skeko wrtunumarq aphi kwti pwntif,
/p   é·li-, awé·n we·lhatá·k·we télən púntink ílli winki·ma·khóki ší=tá winkánki skí·kɔ, -we·t·ənəmáe·kw á·pči kwət·i púntink.
/t   For when anyone has ten pounds even of sweet-smelling or sweet-tasting herbs you always take from them one pound.
/k   for ye tithe mint and rue and all manner of herbs,

/b   takw kpunarluntamwnro, jaxakawswakun, ok tovoltwakun Krtanitwet;
/p   takó· kpəna·eləntamo·wəné·ɔ šaxahka·wsəwá·k·an ó·k tɔhɔ·ltəwá·k·an ke·tanət·ó·wi·t.
/t   You do not think about righteousness or God's love.
/k   and pass over judgment and the love of God:

/b   nuni a ma liserkpanc, lupi a ma nc peli krkw kpunarluntumunrop.
/p   nəni=á·=mah ləs·ie·kpáne, lápi=á·=máh nə pí·li kéku kpəna·eləntaməné·ɔ·p.
/t   If you had done that, you would again have thought about that other thing.
/k   these ought ye to have done, and not to leave the other undone.
                    [RSV "..., without neglecting the others."]

Lk 11.43 /b   Kutumakawsevmw kelwu Paluseok;
/p   "kkət·əma·k·a·wsíhəmɔ ki·ló·wa †pa·ləsi·í·ɔk.
/t   "You Pharisees are miserable wretches.
/k   Woe unto you, Pharisees!

/b   rli wifatumrq ktapavpenro qrnaku lclumutavpif [..] tali cvcntu mvalumaotif.
/p   é·li-winká·t·ame·kw kta·pahpi·né·ɔ kwe·ná·k·a lehələmátahpink [.. omission ..] táli ehənta-mhalamá·ɔhtink.
/t   For you like to sit on the highest seat [..] in the market.
/k   for ye love the uppermost seats in the synagogues, and greetings in the markets.

Lk 11.44 /b   Kutumakawsevmw kelwu lrporq Paluseok, kevakevokcvmw!
/p   kkət·əma·k·a·wsíhəmɔ ki·ló·wa le·p·ó·e·kw †pa·ləsi·í·ɔk, †kkihahki·hɔkéhəmɔ.
/t   You learned Pharisees are miserable wretches, and you are hypocrites
/k   Woe unto you, scribes and Pharisees, hypocrites!

	/b	Mulaji mavhekameq mutu nrvkotwq ktclsenro;
	/p	málahši mahčí·k·ami·kw máta ne·ykót·o·kw ktəlsi·né·ɔ.
	/t	You are like a grave that is not visible.
	/k	for ye are as graves which appear not,

	/b	rli a awrn pumiskatc xqihi nc mavhekumekwf,
	/p	é·li=á· awé·n pəməská·t·e xkwíči nə́ mahči·k·amí·k·unk,
	/t	For when someone walks over the top of the grave,
	/k	and the men that walk over them

	/b	taa letrvri mavhekameq ct b.
	/p	tá=á· li·t·e·hé·i, 'mahčí·k·ami·kw=ét yú.'"
	/t	he would not think it was a grave." [*lit.*, "This is (must be) a grave."]
	/k	are not aware of them.

Lk 11.45 /b Nu mawsw lupwrenw tclan, Nrvlaleun, nuni rlwrun, kmuhemivnu.
/p ná má·wsu ləpwe·ínnu tə́la·n, "nehəlá·lian, nə́ni e·ləwé·an, kəmač·i·míhəna."
/t Then one of the learned men said to him, "My lord, when you say that you malign us."
/k Then answered one of the lawyers, and said unto him, Master, thus saying thou reproachest us also.

Lk 11.46 /b Nu tclan lupwrenwuk; Krvlu kutumakawsevmw;   [⟨lupwrenwuk⟩ as in Lk 11.52]
/p ná tə́la·n, "ləpwe·innúwak, kéhəla kkət·əma·k·a·wsíhəmɔ.
/t Then he said to them, "You learned men, you are really miserable wretches.
/k And he said, Woe unto you also, ye lawyers!

	/b	rli poolrok rlufwmrqek, avhifi mutu kaetcvwkweok,
	/p	é·li pɔ·ɔlé·ɔk e·lanko·mé·k·wi·k, ahčínki máta kai·teho·k·o·wí·ɔk.
	/t	For your kinsmen struggle with burdens, having difficulty not being made to fall.
	/k	for ye lade men with burdens grievous to be borne,

	/b	jwk kelwu mutu tufeti katu wetavrmaewaok.
	/p	šúkw ki·ló·wa máta tankíti kkát·a·wi·t·a·he·ma·iwwá·ɔk.
	/t	But *you* do not wish to help them even a little.
	/k	and ye yourselves touch not the burdens with one of your fingers.

Lk 11.47 /b Kvehei kutumakawsevmw,
/p khičí·i kkət·əma·k·a·wsíhəmɔ,
/t You are truly miserable wretches,
/k Woe unto you!

/b rli wletarq mavhekameko nrvnekane wrwsetpanifu pwrkvakcvasevtet,   [⟨n e w⟩]
/p é·li-wəlí·tae·kw mahči·k·amí·k·ɔ nehəni·k·a·ní·i-we·wsi·tpanínka
    pwe·khakeha·s·íhti·t,
/t as you make the graves where the prophets of old are buried,
/k for ye build the sepulchres of the prophets,

/b kwxwawfu rli nvelavtetup.
/p ko·x·əwa·únka é·li-nhilahtí·t·əp.
/t and it was your forefathers that killed them.
/k and your fathers killed them.

Lk 11.48
/b Kvehei nrvkot ktcli wifatamunro rlsevtetup kwxwafu;
/p khičí·i né·ykɔt ktə́li-winka·t·aməné·ɔ e·lsihtí·t·əp ko·x·əwa·únka,
/t Truly it is evident that you approve of what your forefathers did,
/k Truly ye bear witness that ye allow the deeds of your fathers:

/b rli nrvlwctetc kelwu wletarq mavhekamekov.
/p é·li-, nehələwehtí·t·e, ki·ló·wa -wəlí·tae·kw mahči·k·amí·k·ɔ.
/t for, after they did the killing, *you* made the graves.
/k for they indeed killed them, and ye build their sepulchres.

Lk 11.49
/b Nc wunhi watamwrokun Krtanitwet lwrt,
/p nə́ wə́nči- o·wa·t·amwe·ɔ́·k·an ke·tanət·ó·wi·t -lúwe·t,
/t That is the reason why the wisdom of God says,
/k Therefore also said the wisdom of God,

/b Ntalwkalaokh nrvnekanewrwsehek, ok rvalwkalunhek,
/p 'ntalo·ka·lá·ɔk=č nehəni·k·a·ní·i-we·wsí·č·i·k ɔ́·k ehalo·ka·lə́nči·k.
/t 'I shall send prophets and apostles.
/k I will send them prophets and apostles,

/b alintch nvelaok, okh alintc suqelarvaok;
/p a·lə́nte=č nhilá··ɔk, ɔ́·k=č a·lə́nte sak·wi·lae·há·ɔk."
/t Some will be killed, and some will be tormented."
/k and some of them they shall slay and persecute:

Lk 11.50
/b wrmi cntxi nvelunt nrvnekanewrwsetpanifu weintvakameq
/p wé·mi éntxi-nhílənt nehəni·k·a·ní·i-we·wsi·tpanínka wi·wənthákami·kw,
/t All the ancient prophets that were killed since the world began,
/k That the blood of all the prophets, which was shed from the foundation of the
    world,

/b lih ntwtumaonro bqc lclrxrhek.
/p lí-=č -nto·t·əmaɔ·né·ɔ yúkwe lehəle·x·é·č·i·k.
/t that is what those now living will be asked about.
/k may be required of this generation;

Lk 11.51 /b Vetami puna Rpulu mwkavlrp
/p hítami pənáh †é·pəla mmó·kəm so·k·áhəle·p.
/t First even Abel's blood was spilt.
/k From the blood of Abel

/b kxunki Sakulyusu knevlawap
/p kxántki †sa·kalayás·a kənihəláwwa·p
/t In the end you killed Zacharias
/k unto the blood of Zacharias, which perished

/b tali cvctu wifemaqviksumatup ok patamwrekaonif trtae; [⟨cvctu⟩ for ⟨cvcntu⟩]
/p táli ehə́nta-winki·ma·khwiksəmát·əp ɔ́·k pa·tamwe·i·k·á·ɔnink te·t·aí·i.
/t between his incense altar and the temple.
/k between the altar and the temple:

/b kvehei ktclwvmw, ntwtumaonro ‖ bqc lclrxrhek.
/p khičí·i ktəllúhəmɔ, nto·t·əmaɔ·né·ɔ yúkwe lehəle·x·é·č·i·k.   (Cf. Lk 11.50.)
/t Truly I say to you, those living today will be asked about it. [lit., 'are asked']
/k verily I say unto you, It shall be required of this generation.

Lk 11.52 /b Krvlu kutumakawsevmw kelwu lupwrenwuk!
(p. 118) /p kéhəla kkət·əma·k·a·wsíhəmɔ, ki·ló·wa ləpwe·innúwak.
/t You are really miserable wretches, you learned men.
/k Woe unto you, lawyers!

/b rli kuntvalrq lupwrokun e twfjrkokun,
/p é·li-kanthále·kw ləpwe·ɔ·k·aní·i-tunkše·kɔ́·k·an.
/t For you have hidden the key of wisdom.
/k for ye have taken away the key of knowledge:

/b takw eku ktcli tumekrvwmw, ok awrn krtu tumekrtc qetulanro.
/p takó· íka ktɔ́li-təmi·k·e·húmɔ, ɔ́·k awén ké·t·a-təmi·k·é·t·e kkwi·təla·né·ɔ."
/t You did not enter in, and you forbade anyone when they wanted to enter."
/k ye entered not in yourselves, and them that were entering in ye hindered.

Lk 11.53 /b Mrhi nc keji lwrtc,
/p mé·či nɔ́ kíši-luwé·t·e,
/t After he finished saying that,
/k And as he said these things unto them,

/b nu lwpwrenwuk, ok Paluseok, tolumi kavtu hanelarmanro
/p ná ləpwe·innúwak ɔ́·k †pa·ləsi·í·ɔk tɔ́ləmi-káhta-čani·lae·ma·né·ɔ,
/t the learned men and the Pharisees began to seek to provoke him
/k the scribes and the Pharisees began to urge him vehemently,   [RSV "provoke"]

/b tove ntwtumaonro msi krkw avkrxkami.
/p tóhi-nto·t·əmaɔ·né·ɔ mə́si kéku ahké·xkami.
/t and immediately asked him sharply about all different things.
/k and to provoke him to speak of many things:

Lk 11.54 /b Tove klistaowao,
/p tóhi-kələstaɔwwá·ɔ
/t They listened closely to him,
/k Laying wait for him,

/b rli kavtu muxkumevtit wcnhi a muvtukunemavtet.
/p é·li-káhta-maxkamíhti·t wénči-=á· -mahtak·əni·máhti·t.
/t as they wanted to find something by which they could accuse him.
/k and seeking to catch something out of his mouth, that they might accuse him.

Chapter 67 (pp. 118-122). (Luke 12.1-59.)

Lk 12.1 /b Nu wexkaohi avi xrli awrnek eku moclanro
/p ná wi·xkaóči áhi-xé·li awé·ni·k íka mɔ·ehəla·né·ɔ.
/t Then at some point a great multitude of people gathered there.
/k In the mean time, when there were gathered together an innumerable multitude of people,

/b Kxunki avapvekaotwuk;
/p kxántki ahhaphika·ɔhtúwak.
/t Eventually, they were stepping on each other.
/k insomuch that they trode one upon another,

/b nu tolumi lanrp rkrkematpani;
/p ná tólǝmi-lá·ne·p e·k·e·ki·ma·tpáni,
/t Then he began saying to his disciples,
/k he began to say unto his disciples first of all,

/b nuxatamwq Palusei pastrk,
/p "naxá·t·amo·kw †pa·ləsi·í·i-pá·ste·k.
/t "Beware of the yeast of the Pharisees.
/k Beware ye of the leaven of the Pharisees,

/b nul nuni kokevokrokunwu;
/p nál=nə́ni kɔk·i·hɔke·ɔ·k·anúwa.
/t That is their hypocrisy.
/k which is hypocrisy.

Lk 12.2 /b rli wrmi krkw nrvkot, taoni bqc mrtukvosek,
/p é·li wé·mi kéku né·ykot, tá·ɔni yúkwe me·t·akhɔ́·s·i·k. [=č fut. missing?]

/t For everything is visible, even though now covered.
/k For there is nothing covered, that shall not be revealed;

/b okh wrmi krkw wavkot taoni bqc mutu wrovkotwq.
/p ɔ·k=č wé·mi kéku wwáhkɔt, tá·ɔni yúkwe máta we·ɔhkɔ́t·o·kw.
/t And everything shall be known, even though now unknown.
/k neither hid, that shall not be known.

Lk 12.3 /b Nuni wunhi tuktu krkw rkunwtasek tali cntu peskrk,
/p nə́ni wə́nči, tákta kéku e·k·əno·t·á·s·i·k táli énta-pí·ske·k,
/t Therefore, whatever is spoken of in darkness,
/k Therefore whatsoever ye have spoken in darkness

/b cntuh oxrrk tali puntakot;
/p énta-=č -ɔ·x·é·e·k táli-pəntá·k·ɔt.
/t shall be heard in the light.
/k shall be heard in the light;

/b ok krkw keme rlterq, xqetakch tali ahemwen.
/p ɔ·k kéku ki·mí·i e·ltíe·kw, xkwi·t·á·k·e=č táli-a·č·í·mwi·n.
/t And something you said to each other secretly shall be announced on the rooftops.
/k and that which ye have spoken in the ear in closets shall be proclaimed upon the housetops.

Lk 12.4 /b Ktclwvmw ntclafwmawtwq;
/p ktəllúhəmɔ, ntəlanko·má·wto·kw:
/t I say to you, my kinsmen:
/k And I say unto you my friends,

/b Kahi qxerkrq krski a jwq nvetaq kvakybu.   [⟨qx-⟩ for /kxw-/ (or /kwx-/?)]
/p káči kxwié·k·e·kw ké·ski-=á· šúkw -nhíta·kw khak·ayúwa.
/t Do not fear one who would only be able to kill your body.
/k Be not afraid of them that kill the body, ...

Lk 12.5 /b Jwq knekane watululunro awrn a qrxrq;
/p šúkw kəni·k·a·ní·i-wwa·tələləné·ɔ awé·n-=á· kwé·x·e·kw.
/t But I let you know ahead of time who you should fear.
/k But I will forewarn you whom ye shall fear:

/b Kxw nrku, keji nvelatc awrni trpi liset eku tclaneven mavtuntwf,
/p kxó· né·k·a, kíši-nhilá·t·e awé·ni, tépi-lə́s·i·t təlaníhi·n mahtánt·unk.
/t Fear him who, after he has killed someone, has the ability to throw them to the devil.
/k Fear him, which after he hath killed hath power to cast into hell;

/b kovun ktclwvmw, nunul nu kxw.
/p kɔhán, ktəllúhəmɔ, nánal ná kxó·.
/t Yes, I say to you, fear this one.
/k yea, I say unto you, Fear him.

Lk 12.6 /b Mutu vuh palrnuxk hwluntituk neju scns laoteeok?
/p máta=háč palé·naxk čo·ləntət·ak ní·š·a séns la·ɔhti·í·ɔk?
/t Aren't five little birds priced at two cents?
/k Are not five sparrows sold for two farthings,

/b eli nrl taa mawselw wunewunu Krtanitwet.
/p ílli né·l tá=á· ma·wsí·lu wwaní·wəna ketanət·ó·wi·t.
/t And not even one of those would God forget.
/k and not one of them is forgotten before God?

Lk 12.7 /b Jwq eli wrmi cntxako meluxk kelwaif avkcntasw.
/p šúkw ílli wé·mi entxá·kɔ mí·laxk ki·ləwá·ink ahkəntá·s·u.
/t But even all the number of hairs on your heads are counted.
/k But even the very hairs of your head are all numbered.

/b Nuni wcnhi kahi wejasevrq;   [⟨wcnhi⟩ for /wə́nči/]
/p nə́ni wə́nči káči wi·š·a·s·í·he·kw.
/t Therefore do not be afraid.
/k Fear not therefore:

/b alwei ktclaotenroek xavrli hwlintituk.
/p aləwí·i ktəla·ɔhti·ne·ó·i·k čo·ləntət·ak.
/t You are worth more than the little birds.
/k ye are of more value than many sparrows.

Lk 12.8 /b Ok ktclwvmw,
/p ó·k ktəllúhəmɔ,
/t And I also say to you,
/k Also I say unto you,

/b awrn wlufwmetc b tali cntu lawsif,
/p awé·n wəlanko·mí·t·e yú táli entalá·wsink,
/t If anyone acknowledges me in this world,
/k Whosoever shall confess me before men,   [RSV: "who acknowledges me"]

/b nrpch nwlufwmu eku tali rlifwrxenvetet, Krtanitwet rvalwkalahi.
/p né·pe=č no·lankó·ma íka táli e·linkwe·x·i·nhíti·t ketanət·ó·wi·t ehalo·ka·lá·č·i.
/t I, too, will acknowledge *him* before God's angels.
/k him shall the Son of man also confess before the angels of God:

Text, Transcription, and Translation

Lk 12.9
/b Jwq awrn muvtufwmetc b tali cntu lawsif,
/p šúkw awé·n mahtanko·mí·t·e yú táli entalá·wsink,
/t But if someone rejects me in this world,
/k But he that denieth me before men

/b nrpch nmutafwmu eku tali rlifwrxenvetet Krtanitwet rvalwkalahi.
                                                                                                 [⟨nmutafw-‖mu⟩]
/p né·pe=č nəmat·ankó·ma íka táli e·linkwe·x·i·nhíti·t ke·tanət·ó·wi·t ehalo·ka·lá·č·i.
/t I, too, will reject him before God's angels.
/k shall be denied before the angels of God.

Lk 12.10
(p. 119)
/b Awrn muvtaptwnalatc Wrqesifi linwu,
/p awé·n mahta·pto·na·lá·t·e we·k·wi·s·ínki lə́nəwa,
/t If someone speaks evilly about the man who is the Son,
/k And whosoever shall speak a word against the Son of man,

/b kuskih puvketatamaon.
/p káski-=č -pahki·t·a·t·amáɔ·n.
/t it will be possible for him to be forgiven for it.
/k it shall be forgiven him:

/b Jwq awrn muvtaptwnalatc pelselehi manitwu,
/p šúkw awé·n mahta·pto·na·lá·t·e pi·lsi·lí·č·i manət·ó·wa,
/t But if someone speaks evilly about the Holy Spirit,
/k but unto him that blasphemeth against the Holy Ghost

/b taa vuji puvketatumaowun.
/p tá=á· háši pahki·t·a·t·amaɔ́·wən.
/t he would never be forgiven for it.
/k it shall not be forgiven.

Lk 12.11
/b Tamsc lwxolukrrqc, cntu macluf,
/p "tá·mse lo·x·ɔlək·e·é·k·we énta·ma·éhəlank,
/t "When you are maybe brought to the synagogue,
/k And when they bring you unto the synagogues,

/b jitu tctvwnwrsif, jitu lenwavkusetif;
/p ší=tá tethwənəwé·s·ink, ší=tá linnuwahkəs·í·t·ink,
/t or to the police or authorities,
/k and unto magistrates, and powers,

/b kahi nekane punarluntufvrq krkwh rlwrrq,
/p káči ni·k·a·ní·i-pəna·eləntánkhe·kw kéku=č e·ləwé·e·kw.
/t don't think ahead of time about what you shall say.
/k take ye no thought how or what thing ye shall answer, or what ye shall say:

Lk 12.12 /b rlih eku prjwkrrqc jac nu pelset manitw watulwqrq rlwrrqh.
/p é·li-=č íka pe·š·o·k·e·é·k·we šá·e ná pí·lsi·t manət·u -wwa·təlúk·we·kw e·ləwé·e·kw=č."
/t For when you are brought there the Holy Spirit will immediately let you know what to say."
/k For the Holy Ghost shall teach you in the same hour what ye ought to say.

Lk 12.13 /b Nu mawsw nrk marvlahek, tclan
/p ná má·wsu né·k ma·ehəlá·č·i·k tə́la·n,
/t Then one of those assembled said to him,
/k And one of the company said unto him,

/b Nrvlaleun, Lul wu nuxuns, pavse a meletc jeqenrbwek.
/p "nehəlá·lian, lə́l wá naxáns, pahsí·i=á· mi·lí·t·e ši·k·wi·ne·yó·wi·k."
/t "My lord, tell my older brother that he should give me half of the inheritance."
/k Master, speak to my brother, that he divide the inheritance with me.

Lk 12.14 /b Nu Nhesus tclan, Linw, awrn vuh ntcli kejemkwn ntcli a pasinamun?
/p ná nčí·sas tə́la·n, "lə́nu, awé·n=háč ntə́li-ki·š·í·mko·n ntə́li-=á· -pahsə́nəmən?"
/t Then Jesus said to him, "Man, who is it that appointed me to divide it?"
/k And he said unto him, Man, who made me a judge or a divider over you?

Lk 12.15 /b Nu tolumi lan, Trku tu nuxatumwq, kuvtaohrswrokun;
/p ná tə́ləmi-lá·n, "té·ka=tá, naxá·t·amo·kw kahtaɔhče·s·əwe·ɔ́·k·an.
/t Then he continued, saying to them, "Watch out, beware of covetousness.
/k And he said unto them, Take heed, and beware of covetousness:

/b rli taa, awrn wunhi pumawsewun, xrltukc tulavhrswakun.
/p é·li tá=á· awé·n wwə́nči-pəma·wsí·wən xe·ltə́k·e təlahče·s·əwá·k·an."
/t For a person will not live from his possessions being many."
/k for a man's life consisteth not in the abundance of the things which he possesseth.

Lk 12.16 /b Nu rnwnvakrokun tclan; lwr,
/p ná e·nunthake·ɔ́·k·an tə́la·n, lúwe·,
/t Then he told them a parable, saying,
/k And he spake a parable unto them, saying,

/b Rvopret linw tokif xrli krkw tali kejekun;
/p "ehɔ·p·é·i·t lə́nu tə́·kink xé·li kéku táli-ki·š·í·k·ən.
/t "On a rich man's land many things grew.
/k The ground of a certain rich man brought forth plentifully:

Lk 12.17 /b nu nevlahi pwunarluntumun, letrvr,
/p ná nihəláči pwəna·elə́ntamən, li·t·é·he·,
/t Then he thought to himself, thinking,
/k And he thought within himself, saying,

www.ingramcontent.com/pod-product-compliance
Lightning Source LLC
Chambersburg PA
CBHW060417010526
44118CB00017B/2256